FIGHTING POVERTY WITH VIRTUE
MORAL REFORM AND AMERICA'S URBAN POOR, 1825–2000

JOEL SCHWARTZ

INDIANA UNIVERSITY PRESS
Bloomington and Indianapolis

This book is a publication of

Indiana University Press
601 North Morton Street
Bloomington, Indiana 47404-3797 USA

www.indiana.edu/~iupress

Telephone orders   800-842-6796
Fax orders   812-855-7931
Orders by email   iuporder@indiana.edu

©2000 by Joel Schwartz

The paper used in this publication meets the minimum requirements
of American National Standard for Information Sciences—
Permanence of Paper for Printed Library Materials,
ANSI Z39.48-1984.

Manufactured in the United States of America

Library of Congress Cataloging-in-Publication Data

Schwartz, Joel, date
    Fighting poverty with virtue : moral reform and America's urban
poor, 1825–2000 / Joel Schwartz.
        p.   cm.
    Includes bibliographical references and index.
    ISBN 0-253-33771-2 (cl : alk. paper)
    1. Urban poor—United States—History. 2. Poverty—Moral and
ethical aspects—United States.   I. Title.

    HV4044 .S33   2000
    362.5'8'0973091732—dc21   00-027603

1   2   3   4   5   05   04   03   02   01   00

To my mother, ANNA J. SCHWARTZ;

My wife, ANNE HIMMELFARB;

My children, EZRA, NATHANIEL, and LEAH SCHWARTZ;

And to the memory of my father, ISAAC SCHWARTZ

It was in his second and last year at Mount Diablo [Community College] . . .
that he first learned what "bourgeois" meant in its full historical context. Mr.
Wildrotsky, a contemporary of his mom and dad, was sardonic about the
concept, but that didn't diminish it for a moment in Conrad's eyes. To live the
bourgeois life was to be obsessed with order, moral rectitude, courtesy,
cooperation, education, financial success, comfort, respectability, pride in
one's offspring, and, above all, domestic tranquillity. To Conrad it sounded
like heaven.

—TOM WOLFE, *A MAN IN FULL*
(NEW YORK: FARRAR STRAUS GIROUX, 1998), PP. 170–171

CONTENTS

Acknowledgments   xi

Introduction: What Moral Reform Is and Why It's Important   xiv

PART ONE: MORAL REFORM IN THE PAST

1. Principles and Intentions: Why Moral Reform Was Undertaken   3

2. The Virtues Taught by the Moral Reformers   15

   A. Diligence and Its Difficulties   15

   B. Sobriety and Success   28

   C. Salvation through Saving?   43

   D. Family Values: More Than Just a Footnote   58

   E. Knowledge as Virtue: Why Moral Reform Could Be Implemented 67

3. Why Moral Reform Was Hard to Achieve   76

PART TWO: THE CRITIQUE AND REJECTION OF MORAL REFORM

4. The Decline of Laissez-Faire and the Critique of Moral Reform   97

   A. Introduction   97

   B. Jane Addams: The Compassionate Critique of the Industrial Virtues 109

   C. Walter Rauschenbusch: The Christian Critique of Prudence   121

5. The Rejection of Moral Reform   131

PART THREE: THE CONTEMPORARY PROSPECTS FOR MORAL REFORM

6. African Americans, Irish Americans, and Moral Reform: 161
   Historical Considerations

7. The Contemporary Climate for Moral Reform   189

8. The Contemporary Practice of Moral Reform: 211
   Urban Ministries, Public Policy, and the Promotion of Virtue

     Biographical Appendix   239
     Notes   247
     Bibliography   325
     Index   343

Illustrations appear in an insert following p. 130.

ACKNOWLEDGMENTS

I first contemplated writing this book in anticipation of a period of unemployment — not to be confused with a period of poverty. In 1995 I was employed by the federal government; but I knew that I would lose my job that December, because the agency's budget had been cut severely by the Republican Congress elected in 1994. (In October 1998 I returned to work at the same agency, having completed an all-but-final draft of this manuscript in the interim.)

Back in 1995 my impending job loss (orchestrated as it was by congressional action) was somewhat ironic, since in many ways I sympathized with the aims of the Republican Congress. The resultant experience — of a desired political victory culminating in my unemployment — furnished a useful reminder of the ways in which the policies one favors can nevertheless have painful side effects. I would like to think that this particular hard-won bit of knowledge is occasionally reflected in the pages that follow.

Unlike most people who are about to be unemployed, I had the good fortune to have a friend who worked at a foundation: Hillel Fradkin, who was then a vice president at the Bradley Foundation. Hillel, who was one of dozens of people with whom I networked in the effort to find another job, asked me if there was anything that I wanted to write.

Not having given that question any previous consideration, I quickly realized that I did want to address a particular topic. In 1991 I had published an article about Jacob Riis, a New York reformer in the late nineteenth and early twentieth centuries, who is discussed in this book from time to time. Riis embodied a constellation of attitudes toward the poor — upon whom he made serious moral demands while simultaneously acknowledging and working to alleviate the structural problems they faced — that I found attractive. I told Hillel that I would like to explore other nineteenth-century figures who embodied the same sorts of attitudes, both to understand their position and to see what lessons it could still offer us today. He suggested that I apply to Bradley for a grant. I wrote the application, Bradley awarded funds to support the project, and I began working on this book in January 1997.

I am accordingly grateful to the Bradley Foundation, and to my other funders, the Earhart Foundation and the Smith Richardson Foundation. This book could not have been written without their generous support. I owe a particular debt to Phoebe Cottingham, who expedited Smith Richardson's review of my grant application in December 1997: her efforts enabled me to continue research and writing without interruption in 1998.

Virtually all of the work on this book was done at the Hudson Institute's Washington office. Hudson graciously offered all of the facilities that a researcher-writer needs, without imposing any obligations that would have slowed my pace. I am grateful to Les Lenkowsky (Hudson's president when I began this project), Herb London (its president when I concluded it), and Tom Duesterberg (the director of the Washington office during my tenure) for their support and encouragement.

Research was greatly facilitated by the collections of a great many libraries: the Library of Congress; the New York Public Library; Columbia University's Rare Book and Manuscript Library; the library of the United States Department of Labor; the library of the National Association of Social Workers; the public libraries of the District of Columbia and Montgomery County, Maryland; and the libraries of American University, the Catholic University of America, and George Washington University. My ability to secure materials from these university libraries was greatly enhanced by the assistance of Professors Alan Levine of American University, Jerry Z. Muller of Catholic University, and Philip Hamburger of George Washington University. My research was also assisted by employees of the National Institute on Alcohol Abuse and Alcoholism and the Department of Labor's Bureau of Labor Statistics, who helped me find and interpret data incorporated in these pages.

A number of people read all or parts of the manuscript at various stages in its gestation. I would like to thank them for their comments and suggestions, which have improved it in many ways. Milton Himmelfarb, Lawrence M. Mead, and John Weicher were exceptionally careful readers, and I am particularly grateful to them. I also benefited from the thoughtful reactions of many other readers: John Barry, Bill Galston, Nathan Glazer, Philip Hamburger, David Hammack, Anne Himmelfarb, Gertrude Himmelfarb, Howard Husock, Bill Kristol, Les Lenkowsky, Herb London, Phil Lyons, Jerry Muller, James O'Gara, Naomi Pasachoff, Ed Rubenstein, Anna J. Schwartz, Rachel Schwartz, Amram Shapiro, John Walters, Joan Waugh, Richard Wolf, Alan Wolfe, and Adam Wolfson.

Several publications and institutions kindly allowed me to refine my arguments by trying them out on assorted readers and auditors. Early versions of portions of this manuscript appeared in *The American Outlook, Philanthropy,* and *The Public Interest.* I also delivered two talks that were spun off this manuscript: at a graduate seminar conducted by Francis Fukuyama and Seymour Martin Lipset at George Mason University in 1997, and at a panel at the 1999 Communitarian Summit in Crystal City, Virginia.

Everyone with whom I worked at Indiana University Press was unfailingly helpful in response to my questions. In particular I have benefited from the counsel of Bob Sloan, Marilyn Grobschmidt, and my copy editor, Kate Babbitt.

I have dedicated this book to my mother, my wife, my children, and the memory of my father, who died in the midst of its preparation. Since familial responsibility is one of the virtues that the book recommends, I would like to think that an author's predictable obsessiveness posed no more than the customary obstacles in the face of my efforts to continue to be a good son, husband, and father.

The living dedicatees of this volume can make that judgment for themselves. Whatever their view, I can honestly say that the example provided by my mother and my wife—and the inspiration offered by my children—has done far more to instruct me in the meaning of familial responsibility than the writings of the moral reformers that I expound below.

In closing, let me turn to the dedicatee who is no longer alive. Shortly before he died, I discovered that my father was unconsciously present in the manuscript. A reader who offered comments contended that my assessment of the figure whom I call the *Luftmensch* (discussed in the chapter on Jane Addams) was excessively harsh: If his family stayed together despite his poverty, what was so bad about a father who chose primarily to develop his intellectual faculties (by reading in libraries) rather than doing more to provide an income for his family?

The reaction may be a reasonable one, but I have let the passage stand more or less as it was when my reader offered it. I now realize that my criticism of the *Luftmensch* was so harsh because I was unconsciously judging him by the standard of my father: a man of enormous intellectual gifts who had the misfortune to leave the university world (having acquired a master's degree in classics) in the midst of the Depression. For the next forty years and more my father worked in a job that must have offered him little or no intellectual stimulation—precisely so as to do more rather than less to support his family. The temptation to refrain from doing remunerative work—so as to have more time available for more enjoyable though uncompensated intellectual work—must have been great for my father; but he never succumbed to it.

In short, my father was strong enough and disciplined enough to refrain from leading the life of a *Luftmensch*, tempting though it must have been to him at times. He is the principal dedicatee of this book because he so nobly incarnated the virtues that are discussed in it.

INTRODUCTION
WHAT MORAL REFORM IS AND WHY IT'S IMPORTANT

America's understanding of poverty has changed significantly in the last generation; more Americans now believe that the poor themselves must fight important battles in any war on poverty and that they need to act in ways that are self-advancing rather than self-defeating. That altered understanding—a shift away from the belief that the poor are primarily helpless victims of a society that is chiefly responsible for their poverty—returns us in crucial respects to the antipoverty strategy of those whom I call the moral reformers of the nineteenth century.

These prominent nineteenth-century Americans believed that the poor could conquer or at least alleviate their poverty by exercising virtues like diligence, sobriety, and thrift. Subsequently, prominent twentieth-century Americans came to reject that view as a mean-spirited attack upon the poor. But as we approach the twenty-first century, the nineteenth-century view again begins to seem quite plausible. The American history of moral reform of the poor takes the form of a three-act play: in Act One, we practiced moral reform; in Act Two, we stopped doing so; in Act Three (whose lines are just now being written), we are returning to that once-rejected practice.

My goal in this book (divided into three parts that parallel the play's three acts) is to explain what moral reform was and what it did and did not accomplish; why it was rejected and whether it should have been; and what it now is, how it is now being practiced, and what its prospects for success are. This focus on moral reform (spanning as it does past, present, and future) offers a window on broad historical questions of great importance: How have American poverty and its causes changed over time? How have America's favored remedies for it changed over time? What do those various remedies tell us about America's moral convictions, both today and in the past?

A look at the titles of two major pieces of antipoverty legislation helps us understand our return to moral reform and the change in our approach to poverty. A seismic shift in our efforts to reduce poverty becomes clear when we note that the War on Poverty was ushered in by the Economic Opportunity Act of 1964, whereas welfare reform was more recently enacted in the Personal Responsibility and Work Opportunity Reconciliation Act of 1996. The contrast between the names (not to speak of the substance) of these two acts points to the growing recognition that economic opportunity can be seized by the poor only to the extent that they accept personal responsibility.

But the focus on personal responsibility marks more than a turn away from the

War on Poverty. It also marks a return to the antipoverty strategy of the moral reformers of the nineteenth century, who attempted — putting it baldly — to make the poor less poor by making them more virtuous. The moral reformers argued that the poor were most effectively aided when armed with the power to help themselves, and they contended that the poor could best help themselves by practicing humble virtues like diligence, sobriety, and thrift.

My purpose here is to examine this antipoverty strategy of the moral reformers, looking at both its strengths and its weaknesses. Such a reconsideration is particularly timely today, because in an important sense our newfound method of attempting to reduce poverty — by grappling with the behaviors that lead to dependency and attempting to inculcate personal responsibility — is little more than a return to their old-fashioned method.

Some recent statements by policy analysts illuminate our return to the standpoint of the past, which was heatedly rejected only a generation ago. Susan Mayer of the University of Chicago notes that "for a brief period [beginning in the 1960s] America's welfare policies were almost exclusively aimed at meeting the material needs of the poor"; but the result of the 1996 welfare reform, she argues, is to make "welfare policies at the close of the twentieth century resemble those at the beginning of the century," to return us to an era when "states tried to break the cycle of pauperism by improving the moral character of poor families."[1]

Similarly, New York University political scientist Lawrence Mead points to the resemblances between today's social policy debates and those of a century ago: both, he suggests, focus on the theme of the "personal responsibility and competence" of the poor.[2] In important respects policy as well as rhetoric is returning to the concerns of the past. Mead speaks of a "new paternalism . . . that seeks openly to manage [the] behavior" of the poor, by "guid[ing] the lives of the dependent in many respects as well as helping them."[3] But the very term "new paternalism" reminds us of the prior existence (and continued relevance) of what might be called the old paternalism — the paternalism of earlier moral reformers who also strove to guide the lives of the dependent as well as help them (or, more accurately, to help them help themselves by guiding them).

To see the shift that has taken place, it is useful to compare Mayer and Mead's perspective with that proclaimed only a generation ago (near the onset of the War on Poverty) by the eminent historian Oscar Handlin, who began a 1966 analysis of the history of American poverty with this observation: "Since the end of World War II, the conceptions of poverty and of social responsibility for it have changed so radically that the situation of the past has become almost irrelevant. Earlier eras are so remote from our own that they scarcely offer a model against which present action can be appraised, or even an analogy that will throw light on current problems."[4]

Handlin wrote in an era in which it was widely believed that the problem of poverty could be solved simply by expanding economic opportunities and/or by providing the poor with a guaranteed income. The dysfunctional behavior of some among the poor was often considered a problem that did not need to be addressed directly, if at all: the simple expansion of opportunity or provision of income would solve it. For example, sociologist Herbert Gans argued in a 1969 essay: "If the poor are expected to live up to the moral and legal standards of the affluent society, . . . the only justifiable antipoverty strategy is to give them the same access to resources now held by the affluent and to let them use and spend these resources with the same freedom of choice that is now reserved to the affluent."[5] Many poverty analysts still maintain this view (including Gans himself); still, both lay and expert opinion have clearly shifted toward believing that poverty cannot be meaningfully reduced unless problems of culture, morality, and morale are addressed more directly and effectively.

I propose to shed some light on our contemporary efforts to remoralize the poor by looking at the rhetoric and actions of some of the nineteenth-century moral reformers who were our predecessors. I will focus in particular on four largely forgotten figures from the past: the Reverend Joseph Tuckerman (1778–1840), a Unitarian who served as minister-at-large to the poor of Boston in the 1820s and 1830s; Robert M. Hartley (1796–1881), who founded New York's Association for Improving the Condition of the Poor (AICP) in 1843 and was its guiding spirit for over thirty years; Charles Loring Brace (1826–1890), who in 1854 established New York's Children's Aid Society—an organization dedicated to assisting the vagrant children who lived on the city's streets—and headed it until his death; and Josephine Shaw Lowell (1843–1905), the Civil War widow of one of the Boston Lowells, who settled in New York and was the leading theoretician of New York's Charity Organization Society (COS), which she helped found in 1882.[6]

These four moral reformers did not always see eye to eye, and occasionally I will address some of their tactical and strategic disagreements. Many of these disagreements are explained by the fact that they lived in different eras. Tuckerman's Boston, which had yet to experience either industrialization or the mass influx of European immigrants, was unlike Lowell's New York in important ways. The differences between Boston in 1830 and New York in 1900 do much to explain, for example, why Lowell was far more sympathetic to departures from laissez-faire economics than Tuckerman had been.

Other disagreements can perhaps be explained by the differing personalities of the moral reformers. To judge from their writings, Brace seems to have had a cheerful disposition, Hartley a dour one. This difference is reflected in their respective assessments of the character of the poor; there is reason to suppose that Brace's interactions with the poor, which reflected his genuine affection for them, were accordingly better received—and more effective—than Hartley's.

But despite the ways in which Tuckerman, Hartley, Brace, and Lowell differed from (and with) one another, it is nevertheless fair to speak of them all as advocates of a unified tradition of moral reform.[7] All four opposed unconditional doles to the poor, which they feared would pauperize the poor or encourage and confirm their dependency. All four instead emphasized the need to help the poor by enabling them to help themselves, specifically by inculcating and encouraging the poor to practice the virtues of diligence, sobriety, and thrift (alternatively, by pressing them to avoid what can be thought of as the three "I's"—indolence, intemperance, and improvidence). To mitigate poverty, then, the poor needed to work and earn, to avoid drinking (which both made workers less employable and cost them money that could have been spent on more essential goods), and to spend within their means and if possible to save. Finally, all four reformers attempted to teach these virtues through personal contact with the poor, who were visited by wealthier individuals offering counsel and guidance.

None of the reformers believed that poverty was invariably a proof of moral failing (and still less that wealth was invariably a sign of moral excellence). Nevertheless, all of them emphasized character training as a necessary (if not sufficient) weapon in the arsenal of those seeking to escape poverty. Brief samples of their rhetoric should help in giving a provisional sense of their views. Tuckerman advocated a "solicitude for [the] highest improvement and well-being [of the poor]," believing that "their happiness [could be attained] through their . . . virtue."[8] Hartley argued that "in most cases, [the] destitution and misery [of the poor] are owing to moral causes, and will admit only of moral remedies. Condition must consequently be improved, by improving character."[9] Brace regarded all assistance to the poor as "superficial and comparatively useless," unless it "touch[ed] habits of life and the inner forces which form character."[10] Finally, Lowell insisted on "the fundamental principle . . . that all charity must tend to raise the character and elevate the moral nature, and so improve the condition of those toward whom it is exercised."[11]

But for all their emphasis on character, the moral reformers cannot fairly be understood simply as preachers content to compose paeans to the virtues for the benefit of the poor. They, and their organizations, also attempted to provide more material assistance. Tuckerman strove to find work for the unemployed and to improve the housing and schooling of the poor; Hartley's AICP built a model tenement to house the poor, ran a public bath and laundry, and supplied medical assistance to the poor; Brace's Children's Aid Society established lodging houses and industrial schools to assist New York's vagrant youths; and Lowell's COS attempted to find employment for clients in need of work, offered child care, ran a homeless shelter (in which the homeless were required to work in exchange for room and board), and created a bank (to encourage the poor to save). Still, it is evident that most if not all of these practical methods of assisting the poor were themselves intended to help them exercise the virtues that would promote self-reliance.

Learning from the Moral Reformers

A study of nineteenth-century moral reformers is helpful to us today, because it suggests a way out of what until recently has been a rigidly polarized debate between left and right about poverty. The moral reformers were "conservative" in a sense: unlike some on today's left, they believed that the poor could and should be expected to help themselves by practicing the traditional virtues of diligence, sobriety, thrift (and familial responsibility). They did not believe that placing a moral obligation on the poor—the not particularly onerous obligation to act prudently as a means of self-advancement—was a form of "blaming the victim"; instead they thought that fulfilling that moral obligation offered a route out of victimhood.

But there was also a sense in which the moral reformers were "liberal": unlike some on today's right, they were often sympathetic to governmental efforts to regulate the market for the benefit of the poor. They were undeniably supporters of market capitalism, and they were certainly opposed to government (or, for that matter, private) efforts to bestow an income upon those who did not work. Nevertheless, they were not dogmatic proponents of economic laissez-faire (any more than they were dogmatic proponents of moral laissez-faire). The moral reformers were led by the logic of their moral position to support such structural reforms as the construction of housing projects for the poor as a response to the perceived failures of the housing market (Hartley), the enactment of old-age pensions and workers' compensation (Brace), and the unionization of labor (Lowell).

A serious reconsideration of nineteenth-century moral reformers is therefore timely, because they offer complementary messages to both the contemporary left and the contemporary right. They suggest to the left that promotion of the self-advancing behavior entailed by the reformers' virtues is not an attack upon the poor in the name of "middle-class morality" or "bourgeois values," but sensible and commonsensical advice that really does benefit the poor. It is absurd to suppose that recommending the virtues of diligence, sobriety, thrift, and familial responsibility to the poor is somehow an attack upon them; it is a measure of the ideological character of much recent discussion of poverty that this truism should ever have been disputed.

The complementary advice of these four reformers to the right is that preaching virtue to the poor does not preclude bestowing any form of material assistance upon them. The moral reformers certainly believed that it was necessary for the poor to help themselves by acting virtuously; but they also believed that in some cases it was proper and desirable for government to help them to help themselves, for example by underwriting pension plans, regulating maximum work hours, or mandating collective bargaining. There has been much interest of late in the search for a "third way," some sort of mean between the extremes of unbridled capitalism, which perhaps excessively penalizes those who lose in this economy, and heavy-handed bureaucratic regulation (or, still worse, elimination) of the market, which tends to stifle individual initiative. It is fair to say that more than a century ago, many moral reformers were already articulating the desirability and feasibility of a third way of this sort.

The perspective of the moral reformers offers some guidance for the contemporary policy debate. The recent debate about poverty has too often been sterile and counterproductive because of a shrill insistence that only *one* factor—whether moral or structural-environmental—can legitimately and properly be addressed. By contrast, the moral reformers were admirably willing to consider both moral and structural-environmental factors in their explanations of—and remedies for—poverty.

Their example suggests that we need not choose between two mutually exclusive alternatives, with the poor being either wholly responsible for their condition (hence in need of nothing but moral reformation) or wholly unable to remedy it (hence in need of nothing but material assistance). There is no reason to believe that the poor are prevented by social and environmental forces from doing anything to improve their condition, or that they are completely able to improve it on their own. Instead it makes more sense to suggest, with the moral reformers of the past, that different factors can and do interact: structures and environment do constrain the poor, who nevertheless can and should still take steps on their own to improve their condition.

Fortunately, that reasonable middle ground seems increasingly to characterize contemporary efforts to fight poverty. Even as disputes between intellectuals of right and left continue to rage, on a practical level public policy no longer treats the poor as helpless victims of social injustice—or as self-reliant individuals who are able to take all necessary steps to better their condition on their own. We are less embarrassed to proclaim the need for self-advancing, virtuous behavior to the poor; but we are also implementing policies (for example, state subsidization of transportation and child-care costs) that are designed to facilitate the diligence of the poor.

In short, after a long historical detour, we are returning to an antipoverty approach in many respects reminiscent of that of the moral reformers. Since we are beginning once again to do what they did, we need to know more about what they did in order to understand the reasons for their successes (and for their failures). My goal here is to offer that information; to look backward in an effort to offer us guidance as we move forward.

What This Book Is—and What It Is Not

So as not to mislead the reader, it may be helpful at the outset to explain what this book is not: among other things, it is not a chronological history of moral reform (and still less of its rejection and current resuscitation), nor is it a detailed study of public policy and philanthropic practice today. Let me now elaborate on why it is not those things, while also saying more about what the book is intended to be, by briefly introducing some of its central themes.

Part One attempts to explain what moral reform—the effort to promote the self-reliance of the poor—actually meant in the past. To speak of diligence, sobriety, and thrift as virtues may seem unobjectionable but also abstract and insubstantial, if not platitudinous. I therefore attempt to make these abstractions come to life: to explain concretely what the reformers meant by diligence, sobriety, and thrift, and how they sought to promote these virtues (through deeds as well as speech).

More broadly, I also attempt to explain the reformers' own understanding of the possibilities and limits of moral reform. Did the reformers hope and expect that moral reform would transform the indolent into the diligent, the intemperate into the sober, the improvident into the thrifty? They obviously hoped to do so, but they were realistic enough not to expect to succeed in such efforts very often. Instead they seem to have aimed chiefly to educate those who were already predisposed to practice the virtues, to explain how to be (successfully) diligent, rather than why one ought to be diligent. They rightly believed that facilitating the practice of virtues on the part of people predisposed in their favor is itself a significant accomplishment.

As the title indicates, the focus is on American urban poverty, 1825–2000. The adjective "urban" is an important limitation: all four of the moral reformers lived in cities, and their advice was directed at city dwellers. Their advice may well be transferable to the rural poor in areas like the Appalachians or the Mississippi Delta; still, the book does not attempt in any way to address the very serious problems of the rural poor, past or present.

The book surveys work with the American urban poor, beginning in 1825 (the round date just before 1826, when Tuckerman began his ministry to the Boston poor). The approach is not chronological, though; instead it is topical, examining the common goals that united moral reformers whose work spanned almost a century (as well as the divergent means that they sometimes chose to reach those goals).

To make sense of the critique and rejection of moral reform, Part Two principally examines two pivotal figures from the late nineteenth and early twentieth centuries, the settlement house leader Jane Addams and the social gospel advocate Walter Rauschenbusch. Addams and Rauschenbusch contended that bourgeois standards are largely inapplicable to the life of the poor, and that it is unfair to demand individual effort by the poor to rectify poverty for which society is collectively responsible. Views like these grounded an understanding of poverty—a view that was antithetical to that of the moral reformers—that was widely accepted until recently.

Part Two pays close attention to the critique of bourgeois morality—and the accompanying suggestion that the poor are somehow superior to the middle class insofar as they reject bourgeois morality. In effect, the moral reformers preached what can be called bourgeois virtue to the poor: they contended that poor people who manifested virtues—diligence, sobriety, thrift, and familial responsibility—that were thought to characterize the middle class increased their likelihood of attaining the prosperity of the middle class.

But their argument held only as long as it was believed that bourgeois morality was intrinsically admirable and applicable to the poor as well as the middle class.

These premises were called into question a century ago by Addams, who criticized "the middle-class moralist" for urging "upon the workman the specialized virtues of thrift, industry, and sobriety."[12] Such virtues were less relevant to the poor, she contended, because they did not fit their "bigger, more emotional, and freer lives" and were not applicable to such "primitive, emotional [men]."[13]

In later years critiques like hers achieved great influence. Bourgeois virtues were seldom preached to the poor any longer, in some measure because (as Daniel Bell argued in *The Cultural Contradictions of Capitalism*) they were no longer held in high esteem by prominent members of the bourgeoisie itself. The critique of bourgeois morality was eventually to take such great hold, Daniel Patrick Moynihan once suggested, that the "family patterns of the poor"—characterized as they too often are by "illegitimacy, desertion, and failure to provide"—came to be seen by many as "an admirable, even enviable, rejection of bourgeois repression."[14] In short, the poor were not urged to emulate the middle-class virtues; instead, the middle class was urged to emulate the poor by rejecting spurious virtues.

A central aim of this book is to trace the rise, decline, and restoration of the "bourgeois" virtues as an appropriate remedy for poverty. With good reason, we are currently much more respectful of the virtues espoused by moral reformers as weapons against poverty than we were a generation ago. I seek to explain what recommending those virtues once meant concretely (Part One), why their utility was called into question (Part Two), and how we are once again attempting to promote them (Part Three). In the book's epigraph, Tom Wolfe suggests—I believe with little irony—that "to live the bourgeois life . . . sound[s] like heaven" to poor people aspiring toward upward mobility.[15] Perhaps few of us would agree to the heavenliness of bourgeois life; but certainly fewer of us assert its damnability than was the case not that many years ago.[16]

We are currently more sympathetic to the moral reformers' perspective than we have been. Part Three examines the practical impact of that sympathy, evident in the great respect currently accorded faith-based charities for their efforts to improve the lot of the poor and in several public policies that have been adopted or are being contemplated as responses to poverty. Part Three does not, however, systematically address attempts by contemporary charities and public policy to promote middle-class virtues—an appropriate topic for another, equally lengthy tome. Drawing from the historical study of the moral reformers, instead I seek more to offer a useful perspective on current policies and philanthropic practices than to assess those policies and practices comprehensively.

Finally, a guiding premise of the book is that the approach of the moral reformers continues to provide useful guidance to us in formulating antipoverty strategy today. To say this, however, is obviously not to say that the conditions facing us today are identical to those that the reformers confronted in the nineteenth century. The crucial difference is not the differing ethnic composition of the urban poor (in the nineteenth century the urban poor consisted disproportionately of immigrants from Europe; today the urban poor consist disproportionately of African Americans). I address that contrast in Chapters 6 and 7, arguing that the experience with poverty of at least one European immigrant group (Irish Americans) does in fact offer a relevant example for the contemporary African American experience—and, in addition, that the remedies for poverty suggested by the moral reformers are in many ways strikingly reminiscent of the remedies advanced by notable African American leaders such as Booker T. Washington, W. E. B. DuBois, and (most recently and strikingly) Malcolm X.

Nevertheless, our situation does differ notably in one respect from the situation confronting the moral reformers of the nineteenth century: to a much greater extent, contemporary poverty is characterized and explained by family decomposition. The three cardinal virtues emphasized by the moral reformers were diligence, sobriety, and thrift. For them, familial responsibility was simply an important secondary virtue that could mostly be taken for granted.[17] They certainly understood the relevance and desirability of familial responsibility, and they had interesting things to say about it; but promoting that virtue was nonetheless a tangential enterprise of theirs, not the central one. Single-parent families were comparatively rare among the nineteenth-century poor, so the decline of the two-parent family was not a prominent concern of theirs.

Today, by contrast, family decomposition is probably—and deservedly—the major concern of those seeking to fight poverty with virtue. And solutions for that problem are not to be found in the corpus of the moral reformers. As I will try to show, their advice continues to be valuable in many respects. But the rise of the single-parent family poses grave difficulties for the proper socialization of a great many of the children of the poor—and the writings of the moral reformers do not offer relevant insights. We would do well to try to emulate the antipoverty approach of the moral reformers in many respects; but in doing so we must realize that family decline—for which they provide no solution, and for which we have no solution—may greatly hamper the success of our efforts.

As I hope the foregoing will indicate, I have tried to write not as a cheerleader for moral reform, or as a prosecutor of its critics, but as a dispassionate analyst. I am less concerned to argue the case for moral reform than to understand moral reform in its full ramifications, acknowledging both its strengths and its limitations. To deny the promise of moral reform would be to reject an important component of the reformers' fundamentally optimistic legacy; but to ignore the genuine difficulties—past and present—in implementing it would be to reject an equally important component of their fundamentally realistic legacy.

PART ONE
MORAL REFORM IN THE PAST

1 PRINCIPLES AND INTENTIONS
WHY MORAL REFORM WAS UNDERTAKEN

Moral reform was guided by two principles. The virtues of diligence, sobriety, and thrift were inculcated with the intention first of reducing poverty and second of reducing avoidable dependency—that is, the dependency of able-bodied, mentally healthy people who were capable of self-support. In many ways, of course, these two principles went together: able-bodied individuals supported by charity could increase their income by getting jobs; they would thereby attain self-reliance, forswearing their dependence on alms to meet their material needs.

To some extent, however, the two principles were also at odds with one another, because theoretically at least it might have been possible to reduce poverty by increasing dependency. The generous provision of alms for all, regardless of their capacity to support themselves, could arguably have reduced poverty while also increasing dependency. But the hallmark of moral reform was strenuous opposition to such a policy. Reducing poverty was desirable, but the reduction could not come at the expense of the self-reliance of the poor. Instead, any reduction in poverty had to result from the exertions of the poor themselves; the route out of poverty (or at least into diminished poverty) lay in the practice of the virtues.

In short, the poor were expected to take active steps to get increased resources by and for themselves; the poor were not to be passive recipients, to whom increased resources would simply be given. The priority between the two aims of moral reform was always clear: it was more important to oppose avoidable dependency than to reduce material poverty.

To contemporary opponents of moral reform, such as University of Pennsylvania historian Michael B. Katz, that priority was at best misguided, at worst cynical or even cruel: evidence of callous indifference to the sufferings of the poor. The moral reformers, their critics today charge, stubbornly relied on ineffectual strategies aimed at moral regeneration—such as "educational reform, the regulation of drinking and sexuality, evangelical religion, reinvigorated personal contacts between rich and poor, and institutionally based programs directed at personal transformation." At the same time, it is charged, because the moral reformers made a fetish of self-reliance, they opposed the structural reforms that would have reduced poverty far more effectively:

> They did not intervene in market relations. They did not attempt to relieve poverty by redistributing power or resources, by . . . raising wages, or by using public authority to control the cost of housing or the price and use of land. Instead, they translated the conditions and activities that alarmed or disturbed them into questions of behavior, character, and personality.[1]

This is a serious criticism that deserves a serious response. Was the belief of the moral reformers that the virtues help reduce poverty a reasonable one? What about their additional belief that avoidable dependency is a fate worse than material deprivation? Although questions like these obviously cannot be answered definitively, one can plausibly argue that the reformers' position was defensible on both empirical and moral grounds.

The Efficacy of the Virtues

Prima facie there is certainly reason to suppose that the virtues of diligence, sobriety, and thrift would indeed be helpful to poor people seeking to get out of poverty. Interestingly, there is also suggestive historical evidence that supports this prima facie expectation by pointing toward their utility. One source of such evidence is found in the contrasting experiences of various immigrant groups in the United States. Thomas Sowell's *Ethnic America* offers a compelling rendition of their respective stories. Consider his summary:

> Groups that arrived in America financially destitute have rapidly risen to affluence, *when their cultures stressed the values and behavior required in an industrial and commercial economy.* Even when color and racial prejudices confronted them—as in the case of the Chinese and Japanese—this proved to be an impediment but was ultimately unable to stop them. Nor was their human capital even a matter of bringing specific skills with them. . . . The Chinese and Japanese came as unskilled young men working in the fields tending crops—but *working harder and more relentlessly than anyone else.* Later, the ubiquitous Chinese hand laundry did not require any technical skill not already possessed by the Irish or the black washerwoman of the same era. But the Irish and the blacks never set up laundries, or any other businesses, with the frequency of the Chinese or Japanese, although the two Asian groups were initially hampered by lack of money and lack of English, as well as by a lack of technical skills. Japanese gardeners did not have to master any equipment more technical than a lawnmower. *What made these humble occupations avenues to affluence was the effort, thrift, dependability, and foresight that built businesses out of "menial" tasks and turned sweat into capital.* In the same way, many Jewish pushcart peddlers eventually became storeowners, and sometimes owners of whole chains of stores.[2]

In attempting to inculcate the virtues, the reformers in effect were striving to make the poor with whom they worked more like the Chinese and Japanese workers Sowell describes. (That formulation would no doubt have struck the moral reformers as odd, since they presumably thought that they were trying to make the immigrant poor more like white Anglo-Saxon Protestants. To make the same point less facetiously, the moral reformers were trying to inculcate universal virtues that were commonly practiced, they believed, by white Anglo-Saxon Protestants.)

As we learn from Sowell, the virtues stressed by the reformers were ones that enabled ethnic groups to escape from poverty more rapidly;[3] if the virtues were collectively helpful to groups of poor people, there is every reason to suppose that they were equally helpful to individual poor people. To say this is not, of course, to say that the virtues can easily be taught—or that they were effectively taught by the reformers. (Sowell himself, for what it is worth, seems dubious about the teachability of the virtues.)[4] But it is to say emphatically that the virtues are indeed worth learning and practicing, because they do indeed facilitate the exit from poverty.

Social historians who study the lives of mid-nineteenth-century workers in northeastern cities offer further evidence pointing toward the efficacy of the virtues. Bruce Laurie, a historian of working-class Philadelphia, has noted that in 1840 an evangelical minister credited his colleagues with inspiring "habits of sobriety, industry, [and] economy" among their working-class congregants; as a result, the minister contended, the workers were often able to acquire a "competency," and to enjoy "domestic comforts to which they had [previously] been strangers."[5]

Was this claim plausible? Laurie found evidence "tend[ing] to support the relationship that ministers perceived between evangelicalism and modest property accumulation." About one-third of the 151 members of two working-class churches (one Methodist and one Presbyterian) owned real estate by 1850, with an average holding of about $4,000, or "more than enough for a well-furnished house on a good-sized lot." By contrast, only 10 percent of Philadelphia's adult male population owned any property at all in 1850.[6] Furthermore, well over half of the members of both churches had been journeymen in the late 1820s; but by 1850 more than half of these evangelical journeymen rose to become master craftsmen or small retailers.[7] Laurie then summarizes the evidence:

> For these workers, at least, the promise of social mobility that was rapidly becoming a national faith, thanks in large part to the efforts of their own ministry, was no pipedream. Highly mobile men, they had careers that coincided with, and might have hinged on, the Protestant work ethic. . . . Worldly success and evangelical morality reinforced one another, and the mobile journeyman became a model to emulate, living proof of the promise inherent in evangelicalism.[8]

Jill Siegel Dodd, a historian of antebellum Boston, has found similar evidence. She compared a 72-member group—made up primarily of shopkeepers and skilled manual workers—that supported the enforcement of temperance legislation with a 43-member group—also composed primarily of shopkeepers and skilled manual workers—that formed a mob to oppose such legislation. Her research shows that the temperance proponents were three times as likely to own property: 27 percent of the proponents had property, compared with only 9 percent of the opponents.[9] Dodd also presents evidence indicating that 44 percent of the temperance supporters were upwardly mobile between 1839 and 1859, compared with only 8 percent of the anti-temperance mob in the same years.[10]

While conceding that "these are rough calculations based on a very small sample," Dodd nevertheless observes that "being temperate was associated with . . . economic success." She does not assert that temperance *caused* the Boston workers' upward mobility; they might instead have adopted temperance as part of "a complex of behavior patterns" appropriate to the upward mobility that they were experiencing.[11] Still, even the more limited claim of association rather than causation is significant; workers as well as moral reformers in Boston would at the least have had some reason to believe that temperance (accompanied, as Dodd remarks, by "frugality, industry, and especially an ethos of self-help and respectability")[12] went along with improved economic circumstances.

In short, the virtues expounded by the reformers could plausibly be linked to decreased destitution in the past. Furthermore, evidence for this link can also be found in the late twentieth century. For example, a 1970 study done for the U.S. Department of Labor compared two groups of men, aged 21–30, all of whom were black or Mexican American, had grown up in a large urban ghetto, and had grown up in families who were on welfare or lived in public housing. Thirty-two of the men had "made it" (had worked steadily for the last two years, had not received welfare, and had not been in trouble with the law). The other 38, who had not made it, experienced widespread unemployment.

Not surprisingly, the successes were "characterized by a work and achievement ethic"; they also valued "close family ties and loyalty, avoidance of trouble with the law, stability on the job, [and] taking responsibility for one's own destiny." By contrast, the unsuccessful were "characterized by an ethic of toughness, shrewdness, hustling, violence, . . . less concern with family ties than with ties to peers, . . . [and] a disposition in favor of immediate gratification."[13]

The link between virtue and increased success is also apparent in a passage in which Katz in effect makes the prima facie case for the utility of the virtues. He does so by summarizing the characteristics that nineteenth-century charity workers imputed to those whom they saw as the deserving poor:

> Most deserving were widows who kept their children clean, taught them manners, sent them to school, managed their meager incomes effectively, and spent hours every day sewing or scrubbing for tiny wages. The other able-bodied poor [thought to be deserving] were family men out of work, sober and responsible, willing to chop wood or break stone.[14]

Is it not likely that poor people really were aided by characteristics like these in their quest to escape poverty? Can anyone seriously doubt that the poor people described here by Katz were—other things being equal, obviously—more likely to emerge from poverty than poor people who were slovenly, ill-mannered, scornful of education, extravagant, and reluctant to work?

In other words, Katz's discussion suggests that the reformers' concept of deservingness was not the product of some bizarre or arbitrary moral code; instead it reflected a wholly reasonable understanding that some behaviors should be encouraged because they help poor people escape poverty (whereas others should be discouraged because they worsen poverty). To say this is not, of course, to show that good behavior is easily promoted; we have yet to consider how (and whether) the virtues can be taught, how (and whether) people can learn to change their behavior. But it is to say that good behavior is eminently desirable for the poor.

Fighting Pauperism as a Priority

Good behavior as the reformers understood it was largely synonymous with behavior furthering self-reliance. The reformers strove to encourage attitudes and behavior thought likely to promote the independence of the able-bodied poor; they wanted to reduce their dependence on either charity or government relief. The vices decried by the moral reformers—indolence, intemperance, improvidence—were attacked because of their role in fostering or exacerbating dependence.

As I have already indicated, the reformers were more concerned to reduce pauperism—avoidable dependency, dependency accompanied by vice—than poverty. Their focus on pauperism is, in fact, central to the critique of their efforts. Katz finds fault with the moral reformers for not trying "to eliminate poverty" or even to advocate "redistributing wealth"; instead they strove only "to keep the genuinely needy from starving without breeding a class of paupers who chose to live off public and private bounty rather than to work."[15] Criticisms like this have been voiced by many others as well; Robert Bremner, the dean of historians of American poverty, has noted that "nineteenth[-]century reformers were so obsessed with pauperism that they seldom paid much attention to the underlying problem of poverty."[16]

That characterization is accurate, but it is also somewhat ahistorical: there was simply too little wealth to go around in the nineteenth century for poverty to be seen as a soluble problem. Elsewhere Katz himself admits as much: "Before the twentieth century, it would have seemed preposterous to imagine the abolition of poverty. Resources were finite; life was harsh. Most people would be born, live, and die in poverty."[17]

For that reason, the reformers' focus on pauperism rather than poverty was in one sense more an inevitability than either an ill-considered or a defensible choice. It made sense to tackle pauperism rather than poverty, if only because pauperism was more soluble: it was easier to reduce dependency than to bestow nonexistent material abundance upon the poor. That would have been true even if massive redistribution had been politically feasible (which of course it was not). Historian Oscar Handlin points to the constraints faced by the moral reformers:

> Within a social order the dominant characteristic of which was scarcity, there seemed no alternative to measures which encouraged the ablest to shed their poverty, for there was no way of distributing an income—the totality of which was insufficient—that would avoid the deprivation from which some suffered.[18]

But in another sense, the reformers' attempt to discourage unnecessary dependency conjoined with vice was a choice—and a defensible one. When it is attainable, self-reliance is clearly preferable to dependency—preferable for society, but preferable for the poor as well. And to the extent that vice exacerbated dependency (and virtue reduced it), it made obvious sense to oppose vice and to encourage virtue.

To summarize the reformers' position, we can say that they were more distressed by the dependency occasioned by vice than by the simple fact of material hardship. That formulation accounts for their program, as characterized by Handlin:

> The vigorous reform movements that agitated much of the nineteenth century had not, until the 1890s, addressed themselves squarely to the problems of poverty. . . . There was, paradoxically, a keen sense of communal responsibility for such social disorders as criminality, prostitution, poor housing, and intemperance, which were often linked to poverty. But the thrust of remedial efforts, whether by reformers or conservatives, stressed the capacity of the individual to improve himself by acts of his own will while accepting the persistence of poverty as a given and unalterable fact of life.[19]

Was dependency always a sign of moral failing? By no means. Joseph Tuckerman, for example, understood that poverty (which he equated with dependency)[20] *"may consist, and is to be found in connection with, the highest religious and moral excellence to be attained in this world."* He worried less about this poverty than the *"poverty . . . connected with filth, and ignorance, and recklessness, and sin, [which] . . . is a condition from which it is a most plainly expressed intention of Christianity to redeem every individual who has fallen into it."*[21]

Tuckerman believed that "recklessness and sin" were chiefly responsible for the misery in which some of the poor lived. But at the same time, he also understood material deprivation as a serious problem for many who worked to support themselves (and thus were not "poor" by his definition). Tuckerman was very well aware that many people lived at best a hand-to-mouth existence even when they were employed;[22] unfortunately, he saw no obvious means of raising their wages.[23] Poverty in the sense of material hardship could not be ended, or perhaps even seriously mitigated; but that only made it all the more important to combat the dependency connected to vice.

All dependency, however, was not connected to vice. Many of the dependent were virtuous but not able-bodied; they were dependent because they were unable to work as a result of age, disability, or disease. But even able-bodied dependents were often virtuous: for example, workers of exemplary moral character who nevertheless lost their jobs through no fault of their own. This category was made up of people who "have been industrious, temperate, and upright, as well as frugal," who "never wanted [i.e., lacked] work while there was any active demand for service in the department of labor in which they were educated"; still, they could be "thrown out of employment" during economic downturns.[24] Tuckerman's solution was to provide them with "temporary assistance,"[25] and to help them find other employment.

Still, Tuckerman was most concerned about those who, while able-bodied, were unwilling or unable to work because of their vices. He worried about the able-bodied, virtuous poor, in fact, in large part because he feared that their "moral dangers [were] . . . very great in the time of any considerable and continued distress, arising from the difficulty of providing for their daily wants." In other words, he feared that dependency and its accompanying vices might ultimately become attractive to them.[26]

At bottom, then, Tuckerman believed that moral depravity was a greater problem than material insufficiency—in part, but only in part, because material insufficiency was in his time a problem without a solution. But he also worried more about moral depravity because it posed a greater threat to human happiness (of the depraved themselves, but also of those who lived in their families and communities)—and because it dehumanized people by depriving them of the rationality and self-control that are among the hallmarks of human excellence.

William Ellery Channing, Tuckerman's friend and fellow Unitarian minister, was the theoretician of Boston's ministry for the poor (whereas Tuckerman was the practitioner). Channing clearly articulated their joint understanding that vice rather than material hardship was the great danger facing the poor:

> [The] physical sufferings [of the poor] are not their chief evils. The great calamity of the poor is not their poverty, understanding this word in the usual sense, but the tendency of their privations, and of their social rank, to degradation of mind. . . . Remove from them the misery which they bring on themselves by evil-doing, and separate from their inevitable sufferings the aggravations which come from crime, and their burden would be light compared with what now oppresses them.[27]

Can Channing's supposition that vice is more harmful and dangerous than material hardship be taken seriously today? Yes. Consider, for example, this fascinating thought experiment proposed by Charles Murray:

> Imagine that you are the parent of a small child, living in contemporary America, and in some way you are able to know that tomorrow you and your spouse will die and your child will be made an orphan. You do not have the option of sending the child to live with a friend or relative. You must choose among other and far-from-perfect choices.

> Suppose first this choice: You may put your child with an extremely poor couple according to the official definition of "poor"—which is to say, poverty that is measured exclusively in money. This couple has so little money that your child's clothes will often be secondhand and there will be not even small luxuries to brighten his life. Life will be a struggle, often a painful one. But you also know that the parents work hard, will make sure your child goes to school and studies, and will teach your child that integrity and responsibility are primary values. Or you may put your child with parents who will be as affectionate to your child as the first couple but who have never worked, are indifferent to your child's education, who think that integrity and responsibility (when they think of them at all) are meaningless words—but who have and will always have plenty of food and good clothes and amenities, provided by others.

Murray concludes, I think correctly, that "a great many parents on all sides of political fences will knowingly choose hunger and rags for their child rather than wealth."[28] Why? The answer seems clear: because to a surprising extent many of us—like the moral reformers of yesteryear—really do continue to believe, in spite of modern affectations of cynicism, that virtue is more important than wealth for our happiness.

In short, there are plausible reasons for supposing—as the moral reformers did—that vice causes more unhappiness than material deprivation. That is true today, in conditions of abundance that have drastically reduced the material deprivation of the poor; it was arguably just as true in an era of scarcity, when much less could be done to lessen material deprivation.

Tuckerman and the other moral reformers strove to reduce pauperism because they associated it with vices that were harmful to the poor. If avoidable dependency was the problem, then by definition the provision of material aid to the potentially self-reliant poor could not be the solution: material aid simply made dependency more attractive, made it easier for the poor to get by without exercising the virtues that increased self-reliance.

It is important to understand, though, that one can oppose avoidable dependency and associate it with vice while denying that the able-bodied poor are dependent because they are inherently attracted to vice. We have already seen Tuckerman's concern that even the virtuous might suffer degradation if protracted unemployment were to make them dependent. In short, avoidable dependency can be opposed not just because it results from vice, but also because it causes it.

Thus one can legitimately fear that vice is contagious without believing that the mass of poor people have been contaminated by it. This was, as it happens, the position of most of the reformers most of the time (though Hartley's rhetoric, as we will see, at times suggests otherwise).

Tuckerman, for example, understood that "there is . . . a very great amount of want and of distress which is not to be ascribed to vice."[29] Similarly, Charles Loring Brace believed that "the natural drift among the poor is towards virtue."[30] And Josephine Shaw Lowell approvingly echoed the judgment of an editor of the British *Charity Organisation Review*, who denied that "the percentage of those who are willfully idle and dissolute is a large one," asserting to the contrary that "it is small."[31]

These reformers obviously believed that the poor could learn lessons from the middle class about how to practice the virtues—and that these lessons would help reduce their poverty. But the need to learn is consistent with the desire and the ability to learn, and reformers generally did not attribute much if any recalcitrance to the poor, who were assumed for the most part to be willing learners. Poor people were thought to be deficient more in knowledge than in morality; they were not dependent because they were more vicious than people who were not poor. On the contrary, reformers feared that dependency might encourage vice among the poor, who might cease exerting their own efforts to support themselves unless dependency was discouraged. Lowell made this argument most explicitly:

> We relieve men and women of the necessity of working, we reward them for idleness, we encourage them in vice. . . . We tempt our poor weak brothers and sisters to give up the struggle which has been appointed to make them strong and brave.[32]

In other words, Lowell did not believe that the dependent poor were innately any more vicious or "unworthy" than anyone else:

> Public relief does not have an enervating effect upon the character of those who receive it because they are different from other human beings, but because they are human beings, and are actuated by exactly the same motives as the rest of the race. It is not because paupers are primarily more lazy than other people that they will not work for a living if they can be supported without working. . . . The whole difference between a pauper and any of the rest of us . . . is that he wants and gets very little, while we want and get a great deal, and that our views of what are honorable and dishonorable conditions differ materially from his.[33]

Because Lowell believed that dependency could easily attract people, she thought that people had to be dissuaded from choosing it: "There are two means of reducing pauperism: 1st, by preventing accessions to the ranks of paupers from without, which can be accomplished by rendering pauperism unattractive and by the general enlightenment of the people, and 2nd, by restoring individual paupers to manhood and independence."[34]

The order here is significant: as we will see in Chapter 3, Lowell was not particularly confident that paupers could be rehabilitated. For this reason she thought it more important both "to make the life of wage-earners less hard"[35] (so as to make self-reliance more easily attainable for the diligent) and to make dependency or pauperism comparatively unattractive. Lowell regarded the life of the laboring poor as a struggle; she wanted to make it easier for them to continue it, and she wanted at all costs to dissuade them from throwing in the towel by reconciling themselves to a life of dependency.

For these reasons Lowell's strategy involved both a carrot and a stick: labor was to be made more attractive to the employable poor (as we will see in the next chapter, she was a union supporter who also organized consumers with the aim of raising wages and shortening work hours), and dependency was to be made less attractive. If one associates self-reliance with virtue and avoidable dependency with vice, both courses of action make obvious sense. Much of the charity work that Lowell oversaw had as its aim (in the formulation of Amos Warner, a late-nineteenth-century analyst of American philanthropy) "the saving of individuals and families from crossing the pauper line."[36] That purpose was evident in Lowell's support for labor but also in her opposition to relief for the nonworking but employable poor: both reflected her determination to keep people from crossing the line into pauperism.

The emphasis Lowell and others placed on the need to make avoidable dependency less attractive *pour encourager les autres*—those who had not yet succumbed to pauperism—is seen by critics of moral reform as the dirty little secret of nine-teenth-century welfare policy:

> Opponents [of outdoor relief—that is, cash relief that did not require entry into a poorhouse] feared not just the people on relief but those who might be. Outdoor relief was dangerous not because of whom it helped but because of the lesson it taught by example. Its very existence was a threat to productivity, morality, and the tax rate, because the respectable working class might learn the possibility of life without labor.[37]

It cannot be denied that restrictions on outdoor relief caused considerable suffer-ing.[38] Still, opposition to outdoor relief can be placed beyond the moral pale only by those who ignore the likelihood that a "life without labor" really will degrade and demoralize most people who are capable of self-support.

The Importance of Self-Help

Above we took note of Oscar Handlin's observation that the reformers "stressed the capacity of the individual to improve himself by acts of his own will." To para-phrase John F. Kennedy, the reformers principally asked not what others had done to impoverish the poor; instead they asked the poor what they could do themselves to reduce their poverty.

Why did the reformers emphasize self-help? As was the case in our discussion of pauperism and poverty, two reasons—one practical, the other moral—emerge. The practical reason is evident in a statement by Tuckerman, who noted that "many of the poor suffer greatly . . . from ignorance, or a disregard of the means of comfort which are within their reach."[39] As we saw above, material insufficien-cy could not be greatly reduced by any actions that either the reformers or the poor themselves could undertake: both were effectively powerless to increase abun-dance or to alter the distribution of goods.

But precisely because changes on a macroeconomic level were beyond the reach of the reformers and the poor, it made sense for the reformers to urge changes on the microeconomic level that arguably were within the reach of the poor. Hence they urged the poor to do what they could to increase their incomes and decrease their unnecessary expenditures. To do so was not to blame the victims of poverty; it was instead to urge the poor to do what they could to avoid further victimization.

In this respect the reformers paid the poor a compliment by presupposing their capacity to act rationally to better their situation. To deny the poor any capacity for self-improvement would have been demeaning to them. That point was powerfully argued by Charles Stewart Loch, who oversaw the operations of the British Charity Organisation Society:

> We must not get into the habit of saying, "Poor things; they can do nothing." We should rid ourselves of the habit of treating them, not as men and women, people who can look after themselves with strength in their muscles and brain-power in their heads, but as animals whom we allow to live in society along with ourselves, taking for granted that they are deprived of, or cannot exert, those faculties which

go to make up the strength and fibre of men and women. I assure you, those who are inclined to take a sentimental turn have great temptations put before them to treat the poor as if they were dependent animals.[40]

The moral reformers refused to see the poor as dependent animals. Their refusal points to their moral ground for advocating self-help: the human dignity of the poor is affirmed when they are able themselves to take steps to improve their condition through the exercise of their virtues. Thus self-help was not only the most practical, most attainable help for the poor; it was also the help that did most to elevate them morally.

That moral argument is evident in a second statement by Tuckerman:

We are instruments of the most important good to our suffering fellow creatures, when we aid them, as far as shall be possible, to obtain [the] good from resources within themselves;—by assisting them to understand the true causes of their sufferings, when these sufferings are the results of imprudence, or extravagance, or idleness, or intemperance, or of other moral causes which are within their own control; and by doing what we may to call forth, to direct, and to strengthen their capacities of self-support, of usefulness, and happiness.[41]

All of the sufferings of the poor were not by any means occasioned by moral failings; but when the poor were able to improve their condition by exerting "their own control" over their moral destiny, they became more self-reliant, more useful to society, and happier.

Self-reliance was also a major theme of Robert M. Hartley. He emphasized it even in passages that at first glance might seem to argue for environmental determinism. In Chapter 3 we will examine Hartley's belief that the poor needed better housing if they were to make the moral and material improvements that he desired. But Hartley did not assert that better housing should or could simply be given to the poor; instead he contended in part that the poor needed to take steps themselves to improve their housing, by implementing "some remedies which are in the power of the laboring classes to apply," such as "domiciliary and personal cleanliness; the prompt removal of all slops and refuse matter; ventilation at all seasons; . . . avoiding underground tenements, and those in close courts and alleys; and when there are many in a family, making any sacrifice to secure two or more apartments."[42]

One can reasonably question whether all of these improvements were within the power of all impoverished workers: if they lived underground or in extremely overcrowded conditions, in most if not all cases that must surely have been because they were too poor to afford anything better. (Here, and in other cases as well, the prospects for moral reform were complicated by material insufficiency: a condition that is thought to exacerbate poverty proves hard to alter because of the very poverty that the change is intended to alleviate.) Still, in principle Hartley was right to propose that the poor themselves should take steps to improve their condition in tandem with the steps to be taken by others on their behalf.

Not surprisingly, the theme of self-help also echoes in the writings of Brace and Lowell. Brace asserted that the Children's Aid Society "has always sought to encourage the principle of Self-help in its beneficiaries, and has aimed much more at promoting this than merely relieving suffering. All its branches . . . aim to make the children of the poor better able to take care of themselves; to give them such a training that they shall be ashamed of begging, and of idle, dependent habits, and to place them where their associates are self-respecting and industrious."[43] And Lowell, too, agreed that "the best help of all is to help people to help themselves. . . . Instead of receiving the means of living, men should receive from the benevolent the means of earning a living— . . . their brains should be released from ignorance, their hands freed from the shackles of incompetence, their bodies saved from the pains of sickness, and their souls delivered from the bonds of sin."[44]

Clearly the moral reformers advocated teaching the virtues to promote self-help. But their strategy raises a broad theoretical question to which we have already alluded: How precisely does one teach virtue? It is at least conceivable (as Plato, among other philosophers, urged us to consider) that the virtues cannot be taught. A narrower but nonetheless important pedagogical question also suggests itself: Even if the virtues are genuine and in principle teachable, how could the moral reformers possibly have inculcated them across the vast divides—of class, culture, ethnic origin, and religion—that separated them from the poor?

I will address these momentous questions of educational procedure at the end of Chapter 2. First, however, we must turn to an equally pressing substantive question. What, specifically, were the reformers trying to teach the poor to enable and encourage them to help themselves? To answer it we will examine the reformers' advocacy of their three cardinal virtues—diligence, sobriety, and thrift (as well as the important secondary virtue of familial responsibility). Again we will focus on both the moral and practical aspects of their work, examining both the moral arguments made by the reformers and the concrete actions that they took.

2 THE VIRTUES TAUGHT
BY THE MORAL REFORMERS

SECTION A. DILIGENCE AND ITS DIFFICULTIES

In principle perhaps all of us can agree with the moral reformers that diligence is a virtue to be commended to the poor. But in practice two objections can obviously be raised: first, work was often difficult if not impossible for the poor to obtain; second, the jobs available to the poor all too often demanded that they work excessively long hours for excessively low pay.

In fact, the reformers were very well aware of both of these objections. Still, they preached diligence to the poor. Work was often difficult to find and often hard to do, but in spite of all the problems, work was still essential for the able-bodied poor.

The moral reformers urged employment upon the poor in large measure for moral reasons: they believed that it was good for people to work. The poor were better off—morally as well as materially—when they could rely on their own efforts, as opposed to charity or government relief, to support themselves. Hartley proclaimed that labor was "not only essential to happiness, but the parent and guardian of virtue."[1] "The moral results of labor," he also contended, "are the objects mainly sought," because they "are incomparably more important than mere pecuniary gain."[2]

Tuckerman's colleague Channing elaborated on these abstractions, praising work for its effect upon human character: labor's function, he argued, "is to give force to the will, efficiency, courage, the capacity of endurance, and of persevering devotion to far-reaching plans. Alas for the man who has not learned to work! He is a poor creature. He does not know himself. He depends on others, with no capacity of making returns for the support they give."

But at the same time, Channing (if not Hartley) acknowledged that work—in this respect, ironically, just like idleness—could also demoralize. Echoing a concern that Adam Smith had famously voiced, Channing observed that "the division of labor . . . tends to dwarf the intellectual powers, by confining the activity of the individual to a narrow range, to a few details, perhaps to the heading of pins, the pointing of nails, or the tying together of broken strings."[3]

Thus Channing was an enthusiast for work in principle; but in practice, he recognized that onerous labor could dehumanize workers. Daniel Rodgers, an historian critical of the American work ethic, acknowledges that in this respect proponents like Channing tended not to make unreasonable demands upon workers: "For all their intense fears of the idle life, mid-nineteenth-century moralists did not demand that men work with the ceaseless regularity of machines, but merely asked that they keep soberly and steadily to what tasks lay before them."[4]

Lowell acknowledged that work could, under certain conditions, degrade the poor as well as elevate them. Still, in principle she sang its praises, arguing that "to be an idler is a very bad thing—bad for the man himself, whether he be rich or poor, because . . . he loses energy, intelligence, and perseverance, and finally the power of work, and becomes, by the disuse of these faculties, a distinctly lower creature than he was before, or than he might have been had they been developed by exercise."[5] For Lowell, labor was a means to both material and moral ends: "Efficient labor makes high wages possible, while it also develops and fosters the moral qualities without which high wages will be of but very little use."[6]

Mary Richmond (an important disciple of Lowell and a founder of the discipline of social work) made similar arguments: she contended that work "is a man's best protection from bad habits, from disease, selfishness, and vice. . . . If a man pays all his family and personal expenses, including his own drink bill, from the earnings of his own hard work, he is more likely than not to be a fairly sober, honest citizen."[7]

It is noteworthy that Richmond's argument in particular is not undercut in any way by the impact of industrialization upon work. To be sure, industrialization cast doubt upon some of the moral arguments that had traditionally been advanced to support the work ethic. As Rodgers has shown, the defenses of work as an outlet for creativity and as a means of mobility into the entrepreneurial class (with apprentices becoming journeymen and ultimately masters) came to be distinctly less plausible in the era of industrial factory work than they had been in a preindustrial artisan economy.[8] Nevertheless, the bedrock argument in support of work as a guarantor of stability and self-reliance remained (and remains) fully valid during and after industrialization.

Moral arguments on behalf of work continue to be echoed today, of course. Eugene Bardach notes that the contemporary impetus to get welfare recipients into the workforce reflects the belief that "a job improves self-respect even if it does not pay enough to make one economically self-sufficient." Employment, he contends, represents "liberation from a life of passivity and disorganization."[9]

William Julius Wilson has recently issued a comparable paean to the moral benefits of work: "Work is not simply a way to make a living and support one's family. It also constitutes a framework for daily behavior and patterns of interaction because it imposes disciplines and regularities. . . . In the absence of regular employment, life, including family life, becomes less coherent. Persistent unemployment and irregular employment hinder rational planning in daily life."[10] In effect, Bardach and Wilson revive the arguments of Hartley, Channing, Lowell, and Richmond.

But as Wilson would be the first to note, simply composing homilies to the merits of work does little good for the poor: the important questions—then as now—are whether jobs exist for the poor and what is done to help them find work. Just as it takes two to tango, to be diligent is not something that most people (the self-employed obviously excepted) can always practice on their own; ordinarily, prospective workers who would be diligent need employers to hire them to provide situations in which they can be diligent.

Acknowledging Unemployment and Coping With It

The reformers did not blithely proclaim that anyone who wanted a job could find one—at least in the cities in which they did their own work. For example, in 1892 the noted photojournalist (and proponent of moral reform) Jacob Riis argued as follows: "I have heard it said a thousand times that in this busy city of ours no one who really wants work need go idle long; but in the best season, when work and wages are most plentiful, that is only half-true. The work may be there, and at the same time thousands may be going around looking very hard for it, yet fail to find it."[11]

On the face of it, Mary Richmond sounded a more optimistic note seven years later, contending that "there is still work somewhere for those who have the will and the skill to do it." But she qualified that statement by conceding that this was true only "in ordinary times," not during depressions; furthermore, her focus on "skill" amounted to a second qualification, because it meant that unskilled workers—"porters, day-laborers, stevedores, etc."—were often without employment.[12]

Earlier reformers like Tuckerman and Hartley also emphasized employment problems; they stressed that the law of supply and demand made it hard to find work—in particular, work that paid adequately. Wages were low, Tuckerman explained in 1830, because "the number of labourers [was] essentially greater than the demand for them."[13]

Similarly, Hartley acknowledged in 1852 that "the laboring population . . . appear not to obtain a proportionate share of the growing prosperity around them," as a "result of those irresistible laws of supply and demand."[14] As one might expect, the problem was most severe for those who lacked training in any "trade or regular employment" and had "little skill." These unskilled laborers were concentrated in occupations that were "at best, irregular and precarious"; it was "not surprising that they ha[d] but little work and small wages." But Hartley's pessimism extended even to the ranks of skilled laborers: "In this city, where there is so large a redundance of labor, even the possession of industrial skill affords no guaranty either for employment or good wages."[15] In 1855 Hartley again emphasized the problem of unemployment, declaring that "at all times" in New York there were "thousands and thousands of persons, both male and female, beyond the actual industrial demands, who, while they remain, are necessarily doomed to idleness and dependence."[16]

Hartley ascribed the problem to the constant influx of immigrants into New York:

> The increased emigration from Europe in late years, has operated adversely to the interests of the native laboring and mechanic classes in this city, both by crowding them out of employment, and diminishing the rewards of industry. Needy foreigners accustomed to live upon less than our own countrymen, are enabled to produce articles cheaper, and to work for lower wages.[17]

In short, the three moral "I's" thought to immiserate the poor (indolence, intemperance, and improvidence) were supplemented by a fourth, structural "I": immigration.

Reformers like Tuckerman and Hartley were anything but blind to the structural difficulties now emphasized by historians critical of moral reform. The supposition that reformers recommended diligence to the poor because jobs were readily available (or because they thought they were) is at best half true. Instead, diligence was quite sensibly recommended for precisely the opposite reason: because jobs were often somewhat hard to find. In a buyer's market for labor (which is what the eastern cities generally were because of the constant influx of immigrants), it was in the best self-interest of workers to make themselves attractive to employers by being willing to work hard and efficiently.[18]

To judge from the historical evidence, unemployment was indeed a danger that all-too-frequently confronted urban workers—and not only (though of course primarily) during the business depressions that littered the nineteenth century.[19] Although we lack reliable estimates of unemployment before the 1870s,[20] the unemployment figures for later in the nineteenth century are remarkably unsettling.[21] In the summary of historian Alexander Keyssar, "Involuntary idleness was a persistent and pervasive feature of working-class life" in the late nineteenth century. "Despite the traditional and hallowed image of the United States as a vast, thinly populated continent eagerly welcoming the brawn of millions of immigrants, the nation . . . was not a labor-scarce society during these years, not if the concept of labor scarcity implies that jobs were plentiful and easy to keep."[22]

The most reliable early figures are from Massachusetts, whose Bureau of Statistics of Labor launched path-breaking surveys to measure unemployment. The Massachusetts compilations show, for example, that at some point in each of the two depression years of 1885 and 1895 almost 30 percent of workers were unemployed for an average spell of three to four months.[23] Even in the relatively prosperous years of 1890 and 1900, roughly 20 percent of the Massachusetts labor force experienced some unemployment for an average duration of over three months.[24] And the charity reformers of the late nineteenth century were familiar with statistics like these. Amos Warner, for example, cited the Massachusetts figures for 1885: he noted that over 29 percent of workers there "were unemployed during part of the year" for an average unemployment spell approaching four months.[25]

The question facing the reformers, of course, was what to do about the threat posed by unemployment. Although they were well aware that the labor market could be altered (most obviously by creating public works programs), they had plausible reasons for opposing such alterations. For example, the reformers generally rejected artificial measures to create employment, which they thought would be counterproductive: increasing the supply of urban jobs would also augment the supply of urban job-seekers. Tuckerman contended that the artificial creation of jobs in the city would "offer a most effectual encouragement to the poor of the country to come here for the labor with which we thus offer to supply them. And having thus kept those among us who might otherwise have left us, and even increased the number, it will be found, after all, that we have relieved but a very few in comparison with the whole."[26]

Hartley also observed that artificial employment in the city would be self-defeating, because "the knowledge of this fact would attract other thousands, equally needy and deserving; these supplied, others would press in, and so onward *ad infinitum*, always leaving the demand unsatisfied."[27] More fundamentally, he pointed out that such a program, even if desirable, was impracticable. The AICP itself clearly lacked the resources to create artificial employment:

> Evidently no association of citizens is competent to change this state of things [the oversupply of labor], by creating permanent employment beyond the actual demand. For such a result presupposes a sudden increase of capital, enterprise, commerce, manufactures, and indeed, of all the elements essential to a state of unwonted prosperity, to an extent which shall put in requisition the labor of all the unemployed.[28]

It made sense to emphasize things that were "within the control" of job-seekers anxious to find work—not because job-seekers were victims who were blamed, but because the job-seekers themselves had the most incentive and at least some capacity to improve their situation.

If there were too few jobs in the cities, one thing that job-seekers could do was to leave them and move west, where opportunities were more plentiful. Tuckerman advanced this argument: "The inhabitants of a city are acting for the best good of that part of the very poor among them who belong to the country by using all fair and Christian means of inducing them to return, or of sending them to the places from which they came, where they will be far less exposed to vice, and where their wants will be at least equally well supplied."[29] Hartley advocated emigration even more strongly, advising the poor that "a few dollars will take you hundreds of miles, where, with God's blessing on willing hearts and strong hands, you will find health, competence, and prosperity."[30]

How should we evaluate this suggestion? Robert Bremner effectively dismisses it: "Reduced to its essence, Hartley's advice to the poor amounted to little more than this: Go somewhere else."[31] But this dismissal is itself unjust. To begin with, Hartley's advice cannot fairly be seen as a reflection of his disdain for the immigrant unemployed (discussed below in Chapter 3), because it was also given by others who were better disposed to them. Unlike Hartley, newspaper editor Horace Greeley believed that unemployed men had a right to be supplied with jobs;[32] in fact, the AICP's critique of artificial employment schemes appears to have been directed against a job-creation proposal that Greeley espoused.[33] Yet Greeley's advice to the unemployed of New York was identical to Hartley's: "Fly, scatter through the country, go to the Great West, anything rather than remain here."[34] That advice was also given by "every immigrant aid association" in New York to its clientele.[35]

Everyone gave this advice because it was obviously a helpful thing to suggest: going somewhere else really can be an effective antipoverty strategy for the jobless. In 1859, for example, Hartley saluted the workers who had responded to the ongoing depression by migrating in search of work: "Of the thousands of [New York City mechanics and laborers] thrown out of employment, many removed with their families to places where living was cheaper and work more abundant."[36] Immigrants to the United States were (and are) pursuing this strategy all the time; it is also pursued by internal migrants, like the midwestern auto workers who moved south in droves in the early 1980s in search of better job opportunities.

The mobility of labor should therefore not be denigrated as a means of individual advancement. Recognizing its importance, Adam Smith opposed the impact of the Elizabethan law of settlement on the poor of England, because it impeded the mobility of labor, obstructing "a poor man who would carry his industry from one parish to another. The scarcity of hands in one parish, therefore, cannot always be relieved by their superabundance in another."[37] That redundant workers in New York or Boston could freely move west to find work was surely a good thing, not a bad one.

At the same time, it is likely that many impoverished immigrants actually lacked the "few dollars" of which Hartley spoke to pay for transporting themselves westward. Historian Robert Ernst suggests as much: "In the forties and fifties [New York's] Irish community was considerably enlarged by extremely poor immigrants who possessed neither the fare for leaving town nor the funds to rent or buy land, had they so desired."[38] (This is another case where poverty itself—material insufficiency—frustrates, if it does not prevent, the adoption of a course of action that is meant to relieve poverty.) Still, emigration must have helped some of the urban poor—though it clearly could not and did not help all of them.

In view of the widespread prevalence of urban unemployment, the reformers' reluctance to offer financial relief to those out of work can, of course, seem questionable. But in the reformers' view, the very fact that unemployment was a relatively commonplace occurrence meant that the urban poor themselves had evolved methods of coping with it. Our initial assumption today—that the alternatives used to consist of holding a job, receiving relief, or starving—is false; other options were also available to the urban poor.

In a 1921 memorandum Richmond discussed the courses of action open to the unemployed. While not at all belittling the problem of unemployment ("homes will be lost . . . ; dwellers in decent neighborhoods will be driven into meaner streets; . . . large families will be insufficiently fed"),[39] Richmond also emphasized that options (she called them "exits") were available to those out of work apart from going on relief:

> The best exits . . . are those that the unemployed, left to themselves, instinctively seek. Usually they are emigration, migration, change of occupation, part-time work, savings, credit, help of relatives, neighbors, and friends. One examining this list may feel that it is a great cruelty to expect the unemployed man or woman to seek any such adjustments as the foregoing. The only reply is that it would be a far greater cruelty to encourage him or her to believe that any better ones are possible, given the situation as we find it.[40]

Keyssar's study of past Massachusetts unemployment shows that those without work coped by precisely such mechanisms. "Virtually all of the unemployed" were extremely reluctant to ask for relief from charity organizations, calling on it only as "a last resort."[41] Instead they relied on savings; the existence of multiple breadwinners in the family; odd jobs; the reduction of expenditures; credit from local grocers and shopkeepers; and help from relatives, neighbors, and friends.[42]

The availability of these options provides a needed context for the reformist opposition to relief for the jobless, which can otherwise seem too inflexible and dogmatic: in moral reform rhetoric, accepting a single unearned dollar was sometimes said to lead directly and ineluctably to pauperism.[43] Opposition to relief becomes rather more plausible when one recalls the "exits" apart from relief that the unemployed would "instinctively seek" themselves.

Promoting Diligence

How did the reformers attempt to aid the poor who sought work? In part, they strove to make them more employable. Brace's efforts along these lines are particularly noteworthy. His Children's Aid Society created over twenty industrial schools to train its youthful beneficiaries—both boys and girls—to help them find employment; youths residing in the society's lodging houses were also aided in finding jobs or in going into business for themselves in street trades like bootblacking.

Brace more or less took for granted the existence of a work ethic in his young charges, who had not been pauperized. In his view, "the best characteristic of the class" of children whom he tried to help was "their power of self-help," evident in the fact that each individual inhabitant of the lodging houses went forth daily "to earn his own living."[44]

In view of the work ethic of his charges, Brace simply attempted to channel their energies more productively. He did so, notably, by emphasizing moral education more than narrow vocational training: his principal goal was to promote morality, to "train the children of the streets to habits of industry and self-control,"[45] not to teach plumbing or carpentry. He thought it more important to inculcate the sorts of attitudes that attracted employers rather than particular industrial skills.

Because of his emphasis on character, it is interesting to note, Brace also discouraged boys from remaining too long in the street trades, which he regarded as what we would call "dead-end jobs." (To be sure, Brace preferred steady employment to working in street trades; he did not prefer unemployment or living on relief to working in street trades.)

And if Brace doubted the value of dead-end jobs (like many on the left), he did so largely because he thought that they had a bad effect on character (much like those on today's right who criticize ghetto youth who prefer "hustling" to work in the formal economy). Street trades were bad because they promoted idleness and irresponsibility among those who remained in them: "I am sorry to see so many lads . . . who will hold on to blackening boots and sweeping side-walks for years. They ought to get ahead in the world. They should take trades, or enter factories, or become office-boys, and, above all, they should accept the splendid chance opened to them in the great and fertile West. Boot-blackening is a kind of idle, vagrant business."[46]

To make themselves more employable, the poor were urged by the reformers to make themselves more presentable. Hartley explained some unemployment in these terms: "Because of your disgustingly filthy and ragged appearance, respectable people will not employ you. The cleanly, the industrious, and the sober, readily find work where persons of your description would not be endured."[47] The implicit advice here (in part, dress for success) was not only harshly but also counterproductively put. Yet for all that, it was (and still is) good advice.

Finally, the reformers strove to help find jobs for the poor. In theory, home visitations of the poor by the nonpoor—a strategy employed by all of the reformers in their efforts to inculcate virtue—were supposed to provide the jobless with leads about possible openings; but in practice, some reformers seem to have emphasized finding employment more than others.

Tuckerman apparently put much effort into helping the poor find work. He described the minister-at-large as "not a man . . . who is engaged in trade or merchandise; but one who will know how to avail himself of the facilities which men in business can give him of obtaining employment for the poor."[48] In his eulogy for Tuckerman, Channing observed that "at the very moment when he passed with some for an enthusiast, he was . . . contriving employment for [a man], or finding a place for [his] child."[49]

Employment searches seem to have been emphasized less by the AICP, however. Article VI of the AICP Visitor's Manual did enjoin the visitors to "show [the poor] the absolute necessity of employment, and, as far as in your power, aid them in obtaining it."[50] But it is striking how seldom Hartley's AICP reports discussed aid in finding employment. Hartley prepared over thirty annual reports for the AICP;

to the best of my knowledge, the subject was raised only twice. In 1847 Hartley quoted one visitor's accounts of helping various poor people find work ("In a few weeks I succeeded in obtaining permanent employment for the father and one of the sons, who were blacksmiths, at Mr. W's factory"; "through my solicitations, the gentleman who had previously employed [a widow's] children, again gave them work").[51] In 1868 he quoted a visitor's account of "special efforts" through which he "procured work for many I have helped."[52] In general, though, it is fair to say that Hartley spoke much more of compelling the poor to work than of any concrete measures that the AICP actually took to help them find work.[53]

This comparative de-emphasis presumably stemmed from Hartley's fatalistic belief that jobs were often nowhere to be found because of the excess supply of labor. Still, even if one grants that Hartley accurately portrayed the New York labor market, it is one thing artificially to create employment and another to apprise potential applicants of such job openings as exist; to judge from the annual reports, the AICP certainly did less of the latter than it might have. Other organizations—both public and private, some led by native-born Americans, others by recent arrivals—apparently did more than the AICP in attempting to match workers with available jobs.[54]

Lowell's organization, on the other hand, did more to help the poor find employment: one of the six "objects" enshrined in the constitution of New York's Charity Organization Society was "to procure work for poor persons who are capable of being wholly or partially self-supporting."[55] Lowell believed that a crucial aspect of visiting the poor was helping them find employment. The employment in question might only be temporary, an odd job to help an unemployed person make ends meet: "A visitor can usually, if he or she will only take trouble enough, find some sort of means of letting the head or some member of the suffering family earn a dollar to provide for their immediate necessities."[56] Conceivably, however, it could be permanent: "In regard to seeking for work, a visitor can often help with suggestions and letters of introduction." But Lowell sensibly emphasized that visitors' assistance could only supplement a job-seeker's efforts, not replace them: "As a rule, no one has so much time to look for work as the [unemployed] man himself."[57]

One of the many functions of charity organization societies was to help job-seekers find employment: Lowell's New York COS was not unusual in that respect. Amos Warner described the practice, frankly noting both its possibilities and its limitations:

> Each Charity Organization Society is . . . an employment agency, dealing for the most part and in ordinary times [that is, not during industrial depressions] with the semi-capable, with those who from some perversion of character or defect of mind or body cannot fit themselves into the industries of the time, but may be able to do certain things if those things are sought out and brought to their attention. Many of those with whom the society deals are able-bodied, but not whole-

minded; or they may be both strong and intelligent, but not reliable. There are comparatively few cases where there is not some limitation of capacity more than that belonging to the average person.

Warner praised the Brooklyn COS in particular for being "peculiarly success-ful in finding suitable work for everybody that was willing to work. It was said that if a woman without character and without skill could pick black rags from white ones, and was willing to do it, she could be given work; and if she was improvable, different grades of work would be found for her until finally she was taught some-thing that would make her self-supporting. The same was true, though not in so complete a way, of the agencies for giving work to men."[58]

As Warner's commentary makes clear, the reformers understood perfectly well that failure to find work did not necessarily indicate (though it could indicate) moral deficiency, or "perversion of character." But while Warner did not demonize the unemployed, he also did not romanticize them: he commonsensically resisted any sort of stark dichotomy, refusing to see those without work either as good-for-nothing laggards or noble and capable unfortunates victimized by society. Instead, the unemployed in ordinary—that is, nondepressed—times tended simply to be the least capable workers:

> No one well acquainted with the cases with which the Charity Organization So-cieties deal can at all doubt that most of those whose poverty is said to result from lack of employment are somehow and to some extent incapable or unreliable. . . . They may lack one thing or another, but they almost always lack something; it may be skill, or strength, or judgment, or reliability, or even temper. For the faith-ful and efficient there is work in all ordinary times.[59]

Warner's focus on skill is of particular interest, because his 1894 analysis of the labor market should sound eerily contemporary to us: "Man as a source of me-chanical energy at the present time is . . . a cumbrous and uneconomical tool, . . . not nearly so adaptable in many lines as machinery. . . . The strength and sinews of a man are at discount in the modern labor market, and there is wanted the skill, intelligence, and adaptability of a man in order that he may be useful."[60] The de-creasing demand for brute physical strength is presumably more of a problem to-day than it was a century ago: but it is striking that the problem was already ac-knowledged over a century ago by observers who nonetheless expected the poor to support themselves by working.

It would be wrong to exaggerate the assistance that charitable organizations were able to offer the jobless, because it was necessarily limited. It is estimated that they could find work for only "a minute proportion of the unemployed."[61] To begin with, charity workers were not (and could not reasonably have been expected to be) experts on the local (let alone the long-distance) labor market. As an AICP worker noted early in the twentieth century, "Practically every visitor with whom I have talked admits frankly and without hesitation that she does not know where to look for work for an unemployed applicant and how to advise him to seek work except to give him a card to an unemployment agency."[62] Furthermore, businesses tended (with some reason, as we have seen) to doubt the quality of job applicants from charitable organizations, so they seldom informed the organizations of openings that existed.[63] Finally, charity organizations could only inform prospective workers of such openings as existed; they could not, of course, create jobs themselves. For all of these reasons, it is fair to say, finding work for the unemployed—especially during depressions—was generally the weak suit of moral reform.

Because they understood the constraints of the labor market, moral reformers were sympathetic to attempts to match employers with workers through employment bureaus. As early as 1884 a New York COS committee (of which Lowell was one of four members) advocated establishing an employment bureau in New York, because the able-bodied unemployed were judged to "have no means, or comparatively inefficient means, of procuring [employment] for themselves."[64] A quarter of a century would pass before the New York COS—recognizing the failings of commercial employment agencies—spearheaded the creation of a sort of philanthropic employment bureau, to be run on businesslike principles.[65] Edward T. Devine, the COS general secretary, insisted that such an agency would not undermine the personal responsibility of workers in search of employment:

> If . . . the workers themselves pay a fee, which I believe on the whole to be advisable, and if they learn to insist upon getting a return worth the fee which they pay, they have not only avoided the danger [of shirking responsibility] but may easily in the process have developed a higher degree of personal responsibility. What is proposed is not a paternalistic assumption of responsibility for employees, but the rendering of definite economic service in return for suitable compensation.[66]

Employment bureaus also failed to provide any sort of panacea. They could only apprise applicants of existing positions, not create them.[67] Still, the reformist support for employment bureaus (Jacob Riis, for example, was a great proponent)[68] underscores how the reformers not only preached diligence to the poor but also strove to enable the poor to practice it. If it was never questioned that the able-bodied poor needed to support themselves through work, it was also understood that work was often hard to obtain and that helping the poor secure it was always legitimate.

The reformers were unable to revolutionize the social order (and had no desire to do so). But they did what little they could to help the poor find work, staunchly insisting that the poor were better off—morally as well as materially—when employed. As the reformers recognized, it was not always possible for the able-bodied poor to exercise diligence as job-holders; but if nothing else, they could exercise it as job-seekers.

Creating Work and Defending the Rights of Labor

Lowell was more radical on economic issues than the other moral reformers. She supported a socialist candidate for Congress and the presidential candidacy of

William Jennings Bryan.[69] (By contrast, Jane Addams, who would generally be considered far to the left of Lowell, voted for Herbert Hoover for president in 1932 as well as 1928.)[70] For that reason we can get a better sense of the range of moral reform opinions regarding diligence by briefly considering her views.

During the industrial depression of 1893–1894 in New York, Lowell served on a committee that provided emergency work relief to the unemployed—in effect, the artificial employment criticized by Tuckerman and Hartley. Roughly 4,500 people were given work for a few weeks at a time as street-sweepers, tailors, and whitewashers of tenement houses.[71]

Lowell was aware of the sorts of criticisms voiced by Tuckerman and Hartley, and she attempted to organize the relief work to meet them. The work was not advertised in order to avoid drawing applicants from outside the city; instead work tickets were distributed to unions and churches, whose officials "were requested to give them to persons known to them to be heads of families in need of relief. By this means the attracting of crowds of those needing work and the exciting of false hopes were reduced to a minimum."[72] The work was also organized not to "interfere with any regular or existing industry": the street-sweepers supplemented but did not replace the regular street-cleaning force; the clothes produced by the tailors were not sold but donated to the Red Cross to benefit victims of a cyclone in South Carolina; whitewashing was done only in tenements that would not otherwise have been cleaned (subject, of course, to the landlords' approval).[73] All of the work was intended to supply genuine needs that would otherwise have gone unmet.[74]

The committee's goals were "to reach and to help men and women who would rather starve and see their children starve than accept ordinary 'charitable relief,' . . . to sustain them in self-respecting independence, . . . and to enable them at least to keep their families together during the bitter winter they were entering upon."[75] Work relief was preferable to relief without work in large part because of its moral impact upon the beneficiaries:

> The demoralizing physical and moral results of long continued idleness have been prevented in the case of the five thousand men and women to whom work has been given for weeks at a time during the past four months. The same amount of direct relief would have left the recipients weaker in body and poorer in their only real capital, the power to work, than they are now, and also with habits of idleness, which, in many cases, it would have been difficult for them to overcome when the opportunity for real work returned.[76]

Lowell also thought it important to make moral demands on the beneficiaries. For that reason she regretted the failure to prevent those discharged for cause from one branch of the relief work from applying to others; instead, "there should have been a system of exchange of names of men found incompetent, indolent, or vicious, and a discharge for cause by one Sub-Committee should have been a bar to re-employment by all."[77]

Finally, Lowell insisted that work relief was appropriate only during an industrial emergency, not as a general course of action. In principle she accepted Tuckerman and Hartley's rule, but she was willing to make an occasional exception to it:

> The present acute distress may be said, broadly speaking, to be among men and women who have always supported themselves, and who have done their best to provide for the future of themselves and their families; and the want in which they now find themselves is not due usually to moral or intellectual defects on their own part, but to economic causes over which they could have had no control, and which were as much beyond their power to avert as if they had been natural calamities of fire, flood, or storm.[78]

In the view of the committee on which Lowell served, "efforts of philanthropists to compensate, by artificial means, for irregularity of work or low wages can only result in mischief." The committee's "efforts [were] undertaken at a time when for thousands there was no work either in this city or elsewhere," and thus did not constitute "an argument in favor of the same methods of relief in normal times, when there is work to be done, and what is needed is individual effort to find it, or concerted effort to make it worth doing."[79]

Lowell did not regard work relief as anything more than an emergency stopgap. She would not have been particularly surprised by the judgment of later historians that work relief was problematic, largely because "it was exceedingly difficult to create productive jobs that did not compete either with ongoing municipal projects or with private enterprise."[80] Yet whatever its shortcomings, relief with work was still preferable to relief without it.

Lowell's belief in the redeeming power of work made her a strong supporter of the rights of labor. Even a critic of moral reform like Michael Katz cannot help admiring her: "Tough, sharp, and perceptive, [she] dedicated her adult life to social reform. Her overriding commitment to improving the condition of the poor led her through scientific charity to the left wing of respectable reform." As Katz notes, Lowell helped organize the Consumers' League, which tried to organize boycotts of retail stores that underpaid their workers, and strongly supported unionization.[81]

Lowell supported unions, characteristically, for both moral and material reasons. She thought that "combinations of wage-earners" were "naturally . . . beneficent, . . . both a sign and a cause of moral and intellectual progress."[82] In addition, she believed that "the natural remedy for low wages is the formation of the various trades into Unions."[83]

Lowell came to her support for labor from her belief that prevention was easier than rehabilitation. She believed that the harshness of industrial conditions led too many workers to give up their "struggle" and become paupers. She wanted to improve those conditions: "If the working people had all they ought to have, we should not have the paupers and criminals. It is better to save them before they go under, than to spend your life fishing them out when they're half drowned and taking care of them afterwards."[84]

Lowell wanted to raise wages because she thought that better conditions would morally uplift workers: a living wage that was sufficiently high would enable workers "really to live, . . . so that their bodies, their minds, and their souls may reach the highest development."[85] Far from being an inflexible proponent of laissez-faire economics, Lowell also advocated government regulation to improve working conditions in some circumstances: she believed in placing vulnerable "young women and children under the protection of the Government, in order that their health may not suffer by excessive hours of labor and other unfavorable conditions."[86]

The normal factory work week shrank notably after the mid-nineteenth century, falling from about 66 hours in 1850 to about 55 in 1914 (and about 48 by 1920).[87] Simultaneously, wages also seem to have increased greatly. Although statistics on income (like those on unemployment) are "unreliable and controversial," historians generally agree that working-class wages rose sharply after 1850. According to one estimate, "Both daily and annual earnings increased about 50 percent between 1860 and 1890."[88]

Welcoming both shorter hours and higher wages, Lowell contended that shorter hours were more likely than higher wages to promote moral improvement (and ultimately greater material gains as well): "Securing leisure affords the opportunity for improvement in intelligence and in character, and, as the natural consequence, improvement also in work and in wages."[89] (Hartley, in contrast, was unsympathetic to the cause of shorter hours, believing that "idleness and profligacy too often go hand in hand together." In 1872 he predicted that the likely result of a shorter workday would be an increased amount of "lounging about street corners, gossiping and drinking at liquor-shops.")[90]

No one ever made a more compelling case for the virtue of diligence than Lowell. But Lowell also had the courage and intelligence to recognize that diligence, like all other virtues, is a mean between extremes. Her recognition of the moral benefits of work was compatible with the acknowledgment that overwork can cause both moral and physical harm, that "the relentless machine of daily toil [was] all too often grinding and crushing those who labor[ed]"[91] in her lifetime.

SECTION B. SOBRIETY AND SUCCESS

The reformers' promotion of temperance among the poor is often regarded today as an odd moralistic fixation of theirs, of little relevance to the genuine problems of the poor. Michael Katz argues that the reformers were wrong to try "to improve the character of poor people"—in part by promoting "temperance legislation"—instead of "attack[ing] the material sources of their misery."[92] Even those who today might approve of attempts to reduce drinking are likely to criticize the temperance advocates of the past for exaggerating the importance of drinking as a social problem and abstinence as a solution[93]—and for moralizing about what is at bottom a medical condition (uncontrollable addiction).[94]

But all of these criticisms are misplaced. To address the medical critique briefly, we will see that at least one of the moral reformers (Tuckerman) did in fact understand heavy drinking as a medical problem that required medical (as well as moral) attention. The more fundamental consideration, though, is this: drinking in the past was far heavier than it is today. There is good reason to suppose that it really did pose an enormous problem in mid-nineteenth-century America, particularly among the urban immigrant poor. In short, drinking to excess genuinely was a "material source" of much poverty.

Thus the moral reformers were right to take intemperance seriously as a social problem. But at the same time, they never believed that it was the only social problem or the unique cause of all other social problems. Moral reformers realized very well that excessive drinking was an effect as well as a cause of social problems that existed in their own right.

Finally, and most surprisingly, moderation generally characterized the reformers' proposed solutions to the problem of intemperance. Both moral and prudential considerations led them—for the most part—to oppose stringent prohibitionist legislation as a means of reducing intemperance. On balance, it is fair to say, the moral reformers were notably temperate in their defense of temperance.

Alcohol Consumption and Social Problems

How heavily did alcohol abuse correlate with poverty and other social problems in the past? Tuckerman thought that they were closely intertwined, asserting that "three-fourths of the inmates of alms-houses were brought to the abjectness and degradation in which they are seen there by intemperance,"[95] and that the principal immediate cause of "three-fourths of the profligacy, as well as other vices of cities, and of the desperation which leads to crime, is the free use of intoxicating liquors. . . . No one who has had any very extensive acquaintance with the poor will dispute this position."[96]

Later reformers, though, tended to ascribe less blame to excess drinking. More than half a century after Tuckerman wrote, a group of progressive advocates of temperance, the Committee of Fifty, surveyed almost 30,000 individuals in distress to which some thirty-three charitable organizations ministered between 1896 and 1898:[97] using cautious assumptions (i.e., attributing drink as a cause of poverty only when "the connection was direct and immediate," e.g., when "drink led to loss of employment, or prevented the person from getting a situation"),[98] the Committee blamed little more than one-fourth of all poverty (the overly precise figure was 25.06 percent) on drink.[99] Similarly, Amos Warner contended that intemperance was "the chief cause [of pauperism] in only from one-fifteenth to one-fifth of the cases, and . . . had a contributory influence" in less than 30 percent of cases.[100]

Because ascribing causes to the poverty of large numbers of individuals is inevitably a subjective venture at best, statistics like these are not particularly conclusive. Their reliability as proof of the need to reduce alcohol consumption was, in fact, called into question even by some supporters of temperance. For example, Lilian Brandt, a New York COS researcher, believed that "the relation of alcohol to . . . poverty . . . and no doubt to many other social problems . . . seems self-evident"; yet she also asserted that there was "little scientific basis" for "percentages (worked out to two decimal points!) which tell exactly how much of the poverty. . . in the United States is 'due to' intemperance."[101] Furthermore, there is reason to believe that even the promulgators of the statistics occasionally doubted their value. More than likely a certain skepticism accounted for the deadpan humor evident in the Committee of Fifty's discussion of its finding that poverty stemming from intemperance was more common among naturalized than unnaturalized immigrants:

> While among aliens only 14 per cent. have become destitute through the personal use of liquor, . . . the [figure for] naturalized citizens [is] 25 per cent. The figures . . . seem to indicate one or both of two things: either that those nationalities which are most addicted to liquor are those which are most apt to become naturalized, or that the effect of naturalization is to encourage drinking.[102]

Still, to the extent that we might take statistics like these seriously today, we would naturally tend to assume that the decreasing share of blame placed on alcohol points to the greater sophistication of social analysts in the 1890s as opposed to the 1830s. And that assumption may in fact be partially correct. But statistics that are far more reliable because they are less subjective (on the consumption of alcohol, as opposed to its social impact) should cause us to rethink it. It is important to realize that consumption of alcohol was incredibly high in the 1830s, but substantially lower in the 1890s: per capita consumption of alcohol in the United States is estimated to have stood at 3.9 gallons per year in 1830 and to have dropped to 1.4 gallons per year in 1895.[103] If almost three times as much alcohol was consumed per person in 1830 as in 1895, it is plausible that drinking actually was responsible for a significantly greater share of social problems in the earlier year. In other words, the shift in views between Tuckerman and the Committee of Fifty in all likelihood reflects an objective change in reality, not just a subjective change in its interpretation.

The Success of the Temperance Movement

Why was consumption so heavy in 1830? As one might expect, it is too simple just to denounce the Americans of that era as a bunch of drunkards. Instead, several reasons account for the pervasiveness of drinking then. On the demand side, there was little else affordable to drink. Potable water, for example, was hard to find. It became generally available in New York City only when water from the Croton River was first transported there in 1842; New York's liquor consumption began to decline shortly thereafter.[104] Furthermore, in 1830 coffee, tea, and milk were all more expensive than whiskey.[105]

The low cost of liquor obviously suggests that the supply was great, which was indeed the case. Then as now, American farmers produced a substantial grain surplus; but their most efficient means of disposing of it then was to distill it themselves or to sell it to distillers, because whiskey was much easier to transport than grain.[106]

Finally, drinking—even to excess—was not considered particularly problematic. Great amounts were consumed in social situations and on the job, not only by laborers but by merchants and professionals as well: liquor was regarded as a stimulant to physical labor, a means of relieving fatigue and bolstering energy.[107]

Drinking began to decrease as circumstances and attitudes changed. The alternative beverages came to be cheaper and more readily available. Economic conditions were altered, as the rise of a national grain market—made possible by improved transportation—offered farmers an outlet for their produce apart from selling it to distillers.[108] Furthermore, industrialization and the mechanization of agriculture increased the demand for workers who were efficient and reliable—in other words, sober.[109]

The foregoing considerations help explain the prevalence of drinking as of 1830 and its decline thereafter. But the decline was also spurred by a revolution in moral attitudes: drinking began to be considered shameful by many. Previously, communal drinking to excess had been thought to signify not just good fellowship but also equality and liberty.[110] But with the temperance revolution, freedom and equality were to be attained not by succumbing to indulgences but by rising above them.[111]

This moral revolution was spurred in turn by practical motives, as it became clear that alcohol consumption was imposing huge social costs. In 1830, for example, three-fourths of the nation's workers were estimated to drink at least four ounces of distilled spirits a day.[112] During the period of peak consumption, historians today agree, drinking brought about increases in wife-beating, family desertion, and assaults, as well as heightened government expenditures to support drunkards and their families.[113]

The temperance movement, with which Tuckerman, Hartley, Brace, and Lowell all sympathized, had great success in reducing drinking in the United States: by 1850, twenty years after annual consumption reached 3.9 gallons per capita, it fell to 1.0 gallon per capita.[114] Cutting consumption by almost 75 percent in less than a generation is nothing short of remarkable.

Noteworthy as they are, though, the statistics on per capita consumption do not tell the whole story by themselves. Consumption bottomed out in 1850 and rose slightly thereafter, to 1.4 gallons per capita in 1895. But at the same time, a radical shift took place in the beverages that were consumed: consumption of spirits fell from 2.1 gallons per capita in 1850 (nine-tenths of a gallon of absolute alcohol) to 1.2 gallons in 1895 (half a gallon of absolute alcohol). Meanwhile, consumption of beer rose sharply, from 1.6 gallons per capita in 1850 (one-tenth of a gallon of absolute alcohol) to 15.2 gallons in 1895 (eight-tenths of a gallon of absolute alcohol).[115]

This shift from whiskey to beer is significant, sociologist Joseph Gusfield has noted, because it points to "a change from a pattern of extremes to one of moderation. A heavy consumption of distilled spirits and a low consumption of beer suggests there are few drinkers but that those who are drink heavily. A high consumption of beer indicates many users of alcohol but relatively few heavy drinkers." Although Gusfield is a severe critic of the American temperance movement, he agrees that the prevalence of heavy drinkers in earlier years lends credence to one of its central claims, which does much to explain the great hostility that drinking evoked: three out of every ten drinkers became chronic alcoholics then (as opposed to only three out of 200 today).[116] Thus, even if the temperance movement did not reduce alcohol consumption below the 1850 level (in other words, did not bring about abstinence), drinking in its aftermath was less likely to harm individuals and society. The temperance movement was arguably effective in bringing about drinking that for the most part was, in fact, temperate.

Both the rapid drop and the subsequent shift in consumption strongly suggest that moral reform did much to alter drink habits: James Q. Wilson plausibly describes the temperance movement as "the single most effective effort in American history to change human behavior by plan."[117] Yet critics of moral reform are oblivious to the success of the American temperance movement, decrying moral reform's failure "to eradicate . . . intemperance or to reduce crime."[118] Intemperance was not, of course, eradicated by Tuckerman and the other moral reformers, but in view of the statistics on alcohol consumption, it must surely have declined significantly in the years of their efforts to combat it. (It is also worth pointing out that crime rates appear to have fallen as well in this era—a result that Wilson ascribes to the impact of the moral reform movement.)[119]

Reducing Poverty, Elevating Character

Moral reformers regarded temperance as an antipoverty program for reasons that are self-evident: buying liquor is an unnecessary expenditure, and drinking it to excess makes workers less attractive to prospective employers. Channing observed that "the working class, above all men, have an interest in the cause of temperance": if workers were sober, "their labors would exhaust them less, and less labor would be needed for their support."[120] Hartley made a less abstract argument, advising the poor that "the money you spend for this useless and pernicious drug, would buy your bread. Sixpence a day is $22.81 in a year, a sum, if saved, that would carry you comfortably through the winter. . . . Who that drinks at all, does not, if he can get it, often spend three or four times this amount?"[121]

But the deeper arguments on behalf of temperance related to human character: the reformers hoped to facilitate human excellence, or at least to keep men and women from a dependence that is in some way dehumanizing. Wilson voices an argument like this today, sympathetically restating the popular view that "the more debilitating addictions [constitute] . . . a moral problem," insofar as they "degrade the spirit."[122]

That sort of moral evaluation was central to the reformers' critique of intemperance. Channing, for example, excoriated it as "the *voluntary extinction of reason.*" He conceded that "much importance is given to the poverty of which [intemperance] is the cause," but he thought it comparatively insignificant, arguing that "we look too much at the consequences of vice, too little at the vice itself. It is vice which is the chief weight of what we call its consequence—vice which is the bitterness in the cup of human woe."

Channing provided a concrete illustration to support his claim, persuasively arguing that it was not the drunkard's resultant poverty but his drunkenness itself that was truly lamentable:

> The poverty of the intemperate man owes its great misery to its cause. He who makes himself a beggar by having made himself a brute, is miserable indeed. . . . Intemperance is to be pitied and abhorred for its own sake much more than for its outward consequences. These consequences owe their chief bitterness to their criminal source. . . . Suppose the drunkard to have been a virtuous husband and an affectionate father, and that sickness, not vice, has brought his family thus low. Suppose his wife and children bound to him by a strong love, which a life of labor for their support and of unwearied kindness has awakened. . . . Suppose this, and how changed these rags! How changed the cold, naked room! . . . . What breaks the heart of the drunkard's wife? It is not that he is poor, but that he is a drunkard.[123]

Similarly, Hartley's critique of intemperance was clearly actuated at least as much by moral as by material concerns:

> Intemperance is peculiar in this. It is both a moral and physical malady, whose necessary and inseparable effects are to impoverish and debase. Most other causes of indigence are incidental and outward, and leave energy and integrity unimpaired; nay, their very pressure may nerve the oppressed to successful resistance. But intemperance, itself a vice, is the grand instigator and ally of other vices, and enervates while it pollutes. Producing, moreover, idleness, recklessness and improvidence, what hope is there for its infatuated victims, who not only dig for themselves the pit which ingulfs [sic] them, but fearfully multiply want and wretchedness, by dragging down their families into like ruin?[124]

In short, the moral reformers opposed intemperance as an evil in itself—not just because it was linked to poverty. As historian Norman Clark has noted, precisely the same attitude was adopted by Sweden's social democrats in this century. Whereas many progressive American reformers shied away from a direct moral critique of intemperance, hoping instead to "cure crime and drunkenness" by "concentrating a scientific attack upon poverty and social inequity" (and thereby to avoid "having to contaminate themselves in the moralism of the older generation"), in the 1930s Swedish social democrats took a different approach. They recognized that the welfare state, successful as it was in reducing crime and poverty, "did not diminish public drunkenness, the persistence and the extent of which seemed to threaten every other reform achievement. Rather than live in a nation of fully-employed, well-housed, well-educated, and well-fed drunks, the reformers accepted the older moralism that drunkenness is a social evil which must be attacked directly. They then began the exceedingly strict regulation of the sale and public consumption of all alcoholic beverages."[125]

Cause and Effect

But opposing intemperance as an evil in itself is compatible with a recognition that intemperance is also in part a product of other evils. The moral reformers accordingly understood very well that intemperance was an effect of poverty as well as its cause. In fact, the moral reformers regarded poverty as a serious social problem in large part because they believed that it encouraged the vice of intemperance. Tuckerman understood that an unemployed "journeyman mechanic, or . . . handcartman, or . . . day-labourer, . . . who would have revolted at the thought that he would ever have become a drunkard, [is] most alarmingly exposed to the sin and misery of living, and dying a drunkard."[126] Hartley saw heavy drinking in part as the result of the "absence of domestic comfort, . . . hard living and harder labor":[127] he believed that many poor men were driven to drink because they were housed in intolerable tenements.[128] Similarly, Brace argued that "poverty and want of employment sow bad habits. Thoughts of wretchedness are drowned in drink. [The poor] have no amusements or books, and the grog-shop becomes the club and the reading-room; liquor-shops, and porter-houses soon abound in the quarter."[129]

The reformers took concrete measures that they hoped would lessen poor people's self-destructive dependence on alcohol. In Chapter 3 we will see that Hartley constructed a model tenement, and tried to spur others to build similar dwellings, in the hope that improved housing would make alcohol less tempting to desperately poor people eager to blot out their misery. Similarly, Brace supported the creation of Central Park and the construction of free reading rooms in New York, regarding them as "temperance-societies of the best kind." Brace believed that the laborer would be guarded from "habits of intoxication" by anything that "elevate[d] his] . . . taste . . . , or expand[ed] his mind, or innocently amuse[d] him, or passe[d] his time pleasantly without indulgence, or agreeably instruct[ed], or provide[d] him with virtuous associations."[130]

Tuckerman attempted to attack the problem of alcohol dependence more directly, by employing medical means: he cited numerous cases in which he succeeded in weaning inveterate drinkers away from their addiction by plying them with medicated rum—perhaps an early-nineteenth-century equivalent of treating heroin addiction by means of methadone. But in Tuckerman's understanding, medicated rum did not provide a physiological fix to what was at bottom a moral problem. Instead, in the words of Tuckerman's biographer, "This treatment in no way involved a minimizing of the importance of moral factors, but rather was employed to provide a free period in which the moral sense of self control might recover its strength."[131]

The environmental improvements advocated by Hartley and Brace can be understood in precisely the same way: it was important to create a better environment for the poor, to make it easier for them to exert "the moral sense of self control" that could help ease their plight by reducing alcohol dependence among them.

Advocates of temperance are often faulted today for ignoring the true causes of social problems, and hence for indifference if not downright opposition to needed social reforms. Consider an assertion by Harry Gene Levine: "In temperance thought, poverty, crime, slums, abandoned wives and children, business failure and personal ruin were not produced by any major flaws in the structure or organization of the society and economy, but by alcohol."[132] But because intemperance was understood as an effect of poverty (not just a cause), the exact opposite is probably closer to the truth: many important social reforms were supported precisely in the hope of promoting temperance. In the words of Edward Everett Hale (the author of *The Man Without a Country*, a Boston charity organizer of the late nineteenth century, and the editor of a posthumous collection of Tuckerman's writings), "Almost every effort in the direction of better food, better ventilation, more country exercise, better physical conditions for toilers, has, for its avowed or unavowed object, the holding of men and women back from the temptation of the saloon."[133]

At the same time, the recognition that drinking to excess is not the only social problem does not mean that drinking to excess is not itself a social problem. Moral reformers were quite consistent in being able both to recognize a range of other social problems (some of which encouraged intemperance) and to attack drinking to excess in its own right. Poverty, crime, and disease were obviously not brought about by drinking alone; other causes (those that liberals today sometimes call "root causes") do indeed exist. Nevertheless, a reduction in drinking was desirable, because it could plausibly be expected to help reduce poverty, crime, and disease. It made no sense to delay the attack on drinking until the utopian era when the root causes had at last been fully addressed.

The reformers' position was nicely articulated in 1944—long after the heyday of moral reform—by Joseph T. Zottoli, a municipal judge in Boston:

> It will serve no useful purpose to talk about non-removable causes [of social problems]; these will have to wait the action of a more enlightened era. Society should concentrate attention on those causes and means that are removable, for many such have been attacked and treated. But here I can deal only with what I firmly believe to be the greatest removable blot on our social fabric—intemperance due to alcohol.[134]

Workers and Temperance

It should not have to be said that the reformers' opposition to alcohol dependence did not represent an attack on the true interests of workers, or even a diversion from their true interests. Instead, workers who did not drink to excess were better off because they were more reliable and responsible (hence more desirable as employees) and because more of their income was available to purchase more pressing necessities.

Upper-class reformers were probably not the emissaries best qualified to convey the message of temperance to the poor. That difficulty was well understood by the most famous nineteenth-century reformer of them all, Abraham Lincoln. Because he wanted the message of temperance to be conveyed as effectively as possible, Lincoln bemoaned the fact that it was too often transmitted by "Preachers, Lawyers, and hired agents," between whom and ordinary people "there is a want of *approachability*."[135]

Historians today substantiate Lincoln's concern. A historian of Philadelphia has found that upper-class moral reformers were generally ineffective in promoting temperance among workers, who resented the reformers' insistence on total abstinence and their "upper-class pretentiousness."[136] But at the same time, the defects of these messengers should not lead us to suppose the deficiency of their message: the Philadelphia evidence suggests that the temperance message was persuasively conveyed to workers by humble clergymen, who "related to [wage earners] more effectively than did the prominent divines."[137]

Nor was the Philadelphia case by any means unique in pointing to the potential attractiveness of moral reform to a working-class clientele. In Paul Boyer's formulation, moral reform efforts that strove to reduce intemperance and other social disorders were not "confined to the well-to-do" and were not invariably greeted "with hostility" by the urban poor. "To the poor . . . prostitution, drunkenness, and family disintegration were not abstract symptoms of urban disruption but the stuff of day-to-day existence. It should hardly surprise us that they sometimes gave at least cautious support to organized efforts to erect a shield against these threatening features of city life, or at least to inoculate the young against their ravages."[138]

Temperance should not be seen as an irrelevant ideology that was somehow foisted on workers by their social superiors. Many workers adopted it for and by themselves. As historian Ian Tyrrell summarizes the evidence, "The very same people whom temperance entrepreneurs sought to reform in the 1830s, their workers, were among those reforming themselves in the . . . early 1840s."[139] Temperance came to be espoused by Philadelphia artisans, for example, because "it enabled them to assert their dignity and sense of self-worth. It held out the prospect of prosperity and worldly success to those who would shun drink, the gaming room, and moral laxity in favor of sobriety and self-discipline."[140] In particular, temperance proved attractive to workers because it offered a means for them to take steps on their own to better their condition. Other proposed solutions to their economic problems (e.g., legislation to curtail the supposed depredations of bankers) were of lesser interest because they "left workers relatively powerless to effect much change" and did not leave room "for individual effort."[141]

Working-class temperance organizations arose and had considerable success in nineteenth-century America, because the temperance message appealed to many workers—and for very good reasons. In the words of one historian, "In the new commercial world fostered by expansion of the market economy, self-discipline did matter for those who lacked a cushion of inherited wealth. The workers who listened to [temperance advocate] Neal Dow's equation of industry, thrift, and sobriety with material success had cause to feel that it made sense. . . . In the stormy seas of a market economy the bourgeois virtues could not guarantee an individual's safe arrival, but they could at least help him steer a steady course."[142]

The most prominent working-class temperance organization in the 1840s was the Washington Temperance Society. (Lincoln delivered his remarks about temperance during an 1842 Washington's birthday oration to the Springfield, Illinois, chapter.) Interestingly, Hartley played a key role in originating the Washingtonian movement in New York in 1841.

The first Washington society was founded in Baltimore in 1840; the next year, Hartley, then active in the New-York City Temperance Society, invited the Baltimore group to send five of its members to help form a New York chapter. The organization achieved great success in New York, which soon became known as the "banner city" of Washingtonianism; by 1843 New York chapters had enrolled over 60,000 members.[143]

The Washingtonians differed in several respects from the upper-class temperance movement with which Hartley was affiliated. Unlike more aristocratic temperance advocates, they emphasized economic assistance as a complement to temperance preaching. Many Washington societies offered mutual aid assistance—in effect, insurance benefits—to their members; reformed alcoholics were also given help with housing and employment.[144] The Washington societies were also more populist in their orientation, attempting to supply the good fellowship and camaraderie of the grog shop without its alcoholic stimulants; they were the first temperance organizations to strive to create what a later generation of reformers would call "substitutes for the saloon."[145] (Upper-class temperance reformers responded by criticizing the "vulgar tone" of Washingtonian proceedings.)[146] In addition, the Washingtonians appear to have been more secular and less evangelical in their orientation than the upper-class reformers.[147] Finally, they distrusted upper-class temperance advocates who attempted to reform working-class drunkards while having no experience either as workers or as drinkers.[148]

In view of these various disagreements, it is not surprising that Hartley soon became a critic of the Washingtonians; he complained in particular that they wrongly emphasized the reformation of drunkards more than the prevention of intemperance.[149] But at the same time, it is likely that Hartley was learning from the Washingtonians even as he was denouncing them. The Washingtonian insistence that excessive drinking was only one problem (albeit a crucial one) out of many facing workers foreshadowed Hartley's dawning recognition that intemperance could be fought most effectively only through a broader attack on poverty. That recognition, in turn, led him to give up his position at the New-York City Temperance Society in order to found the AICP.[150]

Because the Washingtonians criticized intemperance while also attempting to mitigate some of the economic causes of poverty, they were able to appeal not only to evangelical workers who emphasized submission to their employers but also to radical freethinkers who disliked capitalism. Radicals could and did unite with other workers on the temperance issue: all agreed that drinking made hard times worse and that self-restraint was needed to ensure survival.[151]

Radical support for temperance has in fact led one historian to conclude that "the connection between working-class radicalism and a code of morality that was later termed 'middle-class,' is the reverse of what some interpreters have argued." That is to say, radical workers did not spurn the morality of self-restraint as some sort of attack on working-class spontaneity. Instead, "the most vigorous opponents of capitalist exploitation were those wage earners who had accepted a code of morality which they shared with their employers but used in their own class interest." The stringent moral code enabled the radical worker to proclaim his "independence from those external forces that governed him—whether employer or liquor."[152]

Radical support for temperance continued into the late nineteenth and early twentieth centuries. Many labor union organizers were temperance advocates, arguing that abstinent workers could more effectively combine to stand up to their employers. Union temperance advocates believed that temperance promoted self-respect and self-discipline, essential components of a workers' community and a movement to confront the bosses. Their understanding was nicely conveyed in these words of a railway brakeman: "As soon as a man has spent all his money for drink he becomes a slave to the corporation."[153]

Labor unions supported temperance because they feared that workers sought to escape from their miseries by drinking rather than organizing. Unions argued (in terms that Lowell would have applauded) that they themselves were the best temperance agencies for workers because they "introduced the wage earner to a higher order of corporate life, educated him, enhanced his self-respect and dignity, awakened in him a greater sense of social responsibility, and inspired him with higher ideals. As a result, he was less inclined to waste his time and money on liquor."[154]

Unions took concrete measures to promote temperance. Local chapters were generally discouraged from meeting in halls adjacent to saloons. Remarkably, many unions offering benefits did not bestow them on members whose sicknesses, injuries, or deaths were caused by intoxication.[155] In 1900, a survey showed that thirty-three of the thirty-nine constituent unions in the American Federation of Labor (AFL) attempted to promote the sobriety of their members: perhaps not surprisingly, one of the six holdouts was the Brewery Workers.[156] It is true that the AFL opposed Prohibition (in part because of the fear that it would cost union men working as brewers, bartenders, waiters, and musicians their jobs).[157] But then the example of the moral reformers themselves demonstrates that one could advocate temperance while opposing Prohibition.

The Pros and Cons of Prohibition

For all that the moral reformers saw drinking as a cause of great harm to the urban poor, they were surprisingly and commendably cautious in their proposed remedies: although they wanted to reduce alcohol consumption greatly, for a variety of reasons they tended to oppose state efforts to mandate prohibition.

Tuckerman opposed prohibition legislation on moral grounds. He did not want to coerce drinkers into abstaining, only to make it easier for them freely to choose abstinence. As we saw above, he administered medicated rum to drinkers in the hope of expanding their powers of moral choice; so, too, did he support temperance legislation only insofar as it increased—and did not dictate—moral choice:

> It certainly would be a wise principle in legislation never to attempt the attainment of moral objects by law, till it shall have been proved that moral means are insufficient for their attainment; and, even then, that such objects should be made the aim of law, not by assuming the power of enforcing moral obligation, but by removing, as far as they are within the fair scope of law, the impediments which are in the way of a free moral action in society—the outward and visible facilities and excitements to evil. In this way legislatures, for example, may do much for the cause of temperance. They may impose heavy excise duties, and require heavy costs for licenses to sell ardent spirits. They may also not only imprison the drunkard, making no distinction between the rich and the poor, but may give his property, if he have any, to trustees or to guardians, for his own support and that of his family. But, even while thousands are dying the victims of lawless appetites, it is not the province of law *to command temperance*, or to prescribe to men what, or when, or how much they shall eat or drink.[158]

Early in his career Hartley, by contrast, made a prudential argument against legislative prohibition: he believed that laws should not be enacted if the community would not tolerate their enforcement. In 1839 Hartley opposed a measure to prohibit alcohol sales throughout the state of New York:

> Desirable as may appear high moral legislation, in a matter on which the minds of the people are so sensitive as the license law, it is worse than idle to adopt such harsh or impracticable measures; or to urge, as many do, that the country must rule the towns. One-third of the population and two-thirds of the wealth of the state are in our cities and large towns, where doubtless will exist the strongest opposition; and there is ground for the apprehension, that coercion, in the execu-

tion of laws directly hostile to the wishes and to the real or supposed interests of so large a body of citizens, would produce open resistance.[159]

But as Hartley's biographer (and son) observed, he opposed the legislation because of "the absence of precedents in other States, where less exclusive enactments had with difficulty carried."[160] After Maine established a precedent by enacting the first statewide prohibition law in 1851, Hartley reversed himself, becoming one of the "most insistent advocates" in New York of comparable legislation. He did so, however, in his private capacity: the AICP itself took no official stand on the merits of prohibitionist legislation.[161]

Hartley's ultimate endorsement of prohibition becomes more comprehensible if two considerations are kept in mind. First, we have already seen that Hartley criticized Washingtonian efforts at temperance for wrongly emphasizing reformation rather than prevention. Once one concedes that reformative efforts are likely to fail (and as we will see in Chapter 3, all of the moral reformers did), it obviously makes sense to endorse preventive measures: since drinking is habit-forming, a good way of preventing people from getting the habit is to prevent them from buying liquor. And just as the failures of reformation led Lowell to endorse preventive measures to improve the conditions and remuneration of labor, so did they lead Hartley to endorse another preventive measure—prohibition—that was also designed to improve the living conditions of the poor. Whether in the 1850s or the 1920s, prohibition must be understood (for better and worse) as a progressive reform: an admittedly coercive measure (but so was the prohibition against child labor) that was plausibly advocated with generally good intentions.[162]

Second, surprising as it may seem, in many respects prohibition arguably worked as a social welfare measure. Social workers in the 1920s (among them Jane Addams) were generally at least cautious believers in the success of Prohibition. Not only did they think that drinking had previously been responsible for a significant measure of destitution; they also judged that Prohibition was notably lessening working-class drinking, cutting it in half—and that it was helping generate the prosperity that workers experienced for the most part in the 1920s.[163] Hartley had reason to believe that nothing would do as much as prohibition to eradicate the misery that alcohol visited upon the poor. There is reason to believe that the enactment of Prohibition actually did help eradicate it.

Nevertheless, it was clearly possible to endorse temperance while rejecting prohibition, as Brace did. Brace opposed prohibition on prudential grounds, as Hartley initially had. Because he insisted on acting prudently, Brace was a remarkably temperate advocate of temperance. Although sympathetic to teetotalism as an ideal, Brace went so far as to doubt its long-term practicality; he saw total abstinence as "a kind of noble asceticism" that "could not continue as a permanent condition."[164]

In practice Brace had qualms about coercive legislation that sought to achieve far less than prohibition. For example, he opposed a New York licensing law that banned the sale of all alcoholic beverages on Sundays, criticizing reformers who "are exceedingly averse to concessions; they look at questions of habits as absolute questions of right and wrong, and they will permit no half-way or medium ground." Arguing instead that "legislation is always a matter of concession," because "we cannot make laws for human nature as it ought to be, but as it is," Brace would have banned the sale only of hard liquor while permitting the continued traffic in beer and wine.[165]

This search for a "half-way or medium ground" also characterized the approach of charity organization societies to drinking. On one hand, Lowell inveighed against intemperance, describing "the liquor business" as the "most potent of all the causes of crime."[166] On the other hand, like Brace she was critical of anti-vice campaigns that sought to close down beer halls and saloons on Sundays; she feared that their strident moralism would only alienate immigrants from the cause of moral reform.[167]

Similarly, Mary Richmond, who wrote the most thoughtful and comprehensive COS guide for friendly visitors to the poor, was anything but an apologist for alcohol: she spoke forthrightly of the "drink evil," which she ascribed chiefly to the "selfishness of the human heart."[168] But Richmond also understood that not all drinking was destructive. She insisted on the need "to make allowance for national, neighborhood, and family traditions" in judging drinking habits. She believed that "only the benighted social reformer . . . thinks of all who drink as drunkards, and of all places where liquor is sold as dens of vice. The saloon is still the workingman's club."[169]

Richmond's sensible advice, urging discrimination between destructive and comparatively harmless drinking, seems to have been heeded by COS workers generally. Michael Katz summarizes their attitude (based on a study of case records of the New York COS) in this way: he concludes that they accepted "that most people drank a little. Only when drinking translated into incapacity for work, domestic violence, or an excessive financial drain did COS workers assert their authority."[170] That strikes me as an altogether sensible approach.

Temperance, Not Abstinence

The contrast between destructive and comparatively harmless drinking offers an important clue for any assessment of the overall impact of moral reform temperance upon the class that it was most intent on reaching—urban immigrant workers. If we judge its impact by the strict standard of abstinence, it was clearly a colossal failure; there were very few dry immigrant workers in cities like New York or Chicago. We have some evidence on this score from budget studies of workers' families that were undertaken in the late nineteenth and early twentieth centuries with the goal of determining whether their standard of living was adequate. One of the most important of these studies was undertaken in New York City in 1907, surveying 318 families with incomes between $600 and $1,100. Of these 318 families, 91 families (67 white and 24 black) had American-born fathers. Apart from the families with American-born white fathers (46 percent of whom reported expenditures for drinks), at least two-thirds of the families in every other group (Teutonic, Irish, black, Bohemian, Russian, Austrian, and Italian) reported expenditures for alcohol.[171]

If anything, these results may understate the prevalence of immigrant, working-class drinking, since some families might have told the investigators what they thought they wanted to hear.[172] Still, with (for example) 56 of 57 Italian families reporting expenditures for drinks, there is a distinct limit to how much the report can have understated the reality.

But if drinking was commonplace among immigrant families, the survey found very little evidence of drinking to excess.[173] Robert Chapin, who compiled the study, did not deny that self-destructive alcoholic binges occasionally occurred. In fact, he cited a set of "illustrations for the temperance lecturer": one woman bought heavy cups so that her drunken husband would not break them and reported that the only time her children had been given toys was when the father got drunk and bought a five-cent toy for each of them.[174]

Nevertheless, that family's experience was the exception to the rule. Of fifty immigrant families with incomes below $700, only six reported expenditures for alcohol exceeding $50—less than the number (nine) reporting no expenditures for alcohol at all.[175] Underfed families were far more likely to be characterized by many children, the desire to save at any cost, and low income than by excessive indulgence in alcohol.[176] Chapin concluded that the number of cases in which overindulgence in alcohol could be said to have caused a standard of living below normal was "not large enough to warrant us in making this a comprehensive explanation."[177]

In fact, the study showed that proportionately less was spent on drinking by the poorer families than by the more successful: not surprisingly, increased income tended to promote greater expenditures for alcohol, as a surplus existed for what we now call discretionary spending. Chapin found that 4.2 percent of the income of those earning between $600 and $700 was spent on alcoholic drinks—compared with 4.9 percent of the income of those with incomes between $1,000 and $1,100. In other words, "a rise in the standard of living to certain families means, among other things, an increased indulgence in intoxicants."[178] Drawing on comparable data from an 1889 survey by the U.S. Bureau of Labor, historian Roy Rosenzweig concludes that "increased public consumption of alcohol might indicate the growing prosperity of the working class rather than its pathological degeneration."[179]

In short, it seems likely that much of the drinking was done by relatively prosperous solid citizens—immigrants who could afford to drink in moderation because they held steady jobs, and who were able to hold steady jobs because they drank only in moderation. Further evidence of that moderation appears in comparisons between American and European budget studies, which show that American families of European origin spent less for liquor than did similar families in Europe. Summarizing these findings, one historian concludes that "the American environment appears to have modified immigrant drinking patterns in the direction of temperance."[180]

Drinking behavior, then, was far more moderate in the America of 1895 than it had been in the America of 1830, despite an enormous influx of European immigrants who were strongly opposed to abstinence. And as drinking behavior came to be more moderate, social analysts late in the century ascribed to intemperance much less of the poverty that they witnessed than their earlier counterparts had. One can quite plausibly argue that these two developments point not to the irrelevance but instead to the success of moral reform as an antipoverty strategy. The moral reformers were right to believe that intemperance worsened the plight of the poor, and they were right to wage a serious antipoverty campaign that fought hard against it.

SECTION C. SALVATION THROUGH SAVING?

Of all the virtues that moral reformers preached to the poor, thrift can seem the most questionable. Few would deny that able-bodied people who can support themselves and their families ought to do so; apart from the occasional acolyte of Timothy Leary, fewer still would recommend inebriation over sobriety to either rich or poor. Thrift, however, may strike us at first glance as more problematic. It is not always clear, after all, where "thriftiness" ends and "miserliness" begins. Thrift can seem unattractive, to the extent that it embodies the mean-spirited, penny-pinching attitude of a Scrooge. In addition, preaching thrift to the poor in particular can seem heartless and uncomprehending. How, one might ask, can anyone extol self-denial and belt-tightening to those who already consume far too little?

Some moral reformers were aware of objections of this sort, which were voiced by advocates for the poor like Jane Addams. Addams contended that the poor simply could not afford to save: whatever money they possessed was needed to increase their consumption. She granted that saving might seem "quite commendable in a comfortable part of town," but contended that it "appears almost criminal in a poorer quarter where the next-door neighbor needs food, even if the children of the family do not." She approvingly quoted a socialist tailor, who "always speaks of saving as a bourgeois virtue, one quite impossible to the genuine workingman. . . . He insists it would be criminal not to expend every penny [that he earns] upon food and shelter."[181]

Mary Willcox Brown, a Baltimore charity worker who defended preaching thrift to the poor, nevertheless pointed to other arguments against it. She acknowledged that many workers suspected that "the practice of thrift [on their part] tend[ed] to lower wages": when employers discovered that their workers earned enough to put something by, they concluded that they had been overpaying them.[182] Brown also took note of the more general critique of thrift, quoting an unnamed settlement worker who regarded it as "rather demoralizing, because it is so absorbing, so limiting, so selfish."[183]

Perhaps because the critique of thrift emerged at the end of the nineteenth century, its defense was mounted most extensively not by Tuckerman, Hartley, Brace, or Lowell, but by two workers in the charity organization movement that Lowell helped create: Brown and Mary Richmond, who set out both moral and practical reasons for encouraging thrift among the poor. Richmond, like Brown, acknowledged the case against thrift, admitting that, like other virtues, it had "an unlovely side." Still, she also insisted that "the thriftless and the extravagant, whether rich or poor, are often mean and self-indulgent." The thriftless were characterized by "lack of self-control, the lack of power to defer their pleasures." The self-mastery that thrift exemplified meant that it was not a narrowly "economic virtue," but an "element out of which not only character but all the social virtues are built."[184] And Brown regarded thrift as the "symbol and the instrument" of a person's independence; the self-discipline to which thrift testified was an indication of one's freedom.[185]

The argument that saving relates to all the social virtues continues to resonate today, in particular in the work of Michael Sherraden, a policy analyst at Washington University. Sherraden contends that we can more effectively fight poverty if we do more to encourage the poor to save, for example through government matching of contributions made by poor people to special savings accounts known as Individual Development Accounts.[186] Saving should be encouraged, in his view, because it promotes better behavior. "People think and behave differently when they are accumulating assets": specifically, asset-holding makes for more stable households (by providing a cushion when income drops), encourages people to care about and plan for the future, and enables them to overcome "learned helplessness and vulnerability" by increasing control over their lives.[187]

Sherraden questions an assumption of neoclassical economics, which holds that saving and consumption are morally equivalent (in that saving simply represents consumption that is deferred until later).[188] To the contrary, he argues: in a variety of ways savers improve themselves morally as well as materially, by acting more responsibly and thinking more about the future. As Sherraden unapologetically declares, encouraging the poor to save is desirable in that it attempts to make them "middle class," by promoting "accumulation of wealth, long-term thinking, active citizenship, and so forth."[189]

The Practicality of Saving

Sherraden's case for thrift is, of course, motivated by practical as well as moral considerations: saving is good for the poor in particular, for example, because it decreases the risk that, say, a sudden spell of unemployment will be calamitous.[190] Not surprisingly, that note of practicality was also evident in the moral reform argument for thrift. Brown believed that the poor had greater need of thrift than the wealthy: "The rich man does not feel the effect of his extravagance as does the poor man, because his purse yields him a margin for imprudent spending."[191] Richmond contended that workers' thrift helped strengthen their position in conflicts with their employers: "No one is more helpless against the encroachments of employers than the man who lives from hand to mouth, whose necessities press ever hard upon him, crippling him and crippling those with whom he competes in the open market."[192]

Richmond and Brown did not understand thrift as a manifestation of asceticism, an exercise in self-denial for its own sake. Instead, saving was in part a means to the end of later consumption. In Brown's view, "The whole secret of right thrift lies in the formula: *Save wisely, so as to be able to spend judiciously in a time of need which will probably be greater than that of the present.*"[193] And Richmond emphasized saving "for some definite and immediate object, because [a poor man] cannot spend in any effective way until he has saved."[194]

Richmond and Brown were realists who understood that saving could not be recommended to the poor in all cases. In one sense, of course, thrift was always possible and desirable: one could and should always spend frugally and wisely rather than extravagantly and foolishly.[195] But saving money for future as opposed to current consumption could not always be recommended, because poor people's income was often so low that all of it had to be spent on immediately pressing necessities.

To their credit, moral reformers were well aware of this issue of practicality. Brown wrote that a friendly visitor should not urge a poor family to save "until she has carefully considered whether there is a surplus that can be safely withdrawn from the sum that goes to meet the daily needs."[196] Brown recognized that "in many cases, it would be a farce" for a visitor to urge her family to spend less than it earned.[197] Similarly, Richmond advocated saving as a strategy only when "acute distress is past, . . . when improved material conditions" meant that there was actually something to save.[198]

It is fair to say, then, that Brown and Richmond regarded saving as a situational virtue that could not always be practiced. This sensible appreciation that saving was not always practicable is also evident in the views of the earlier reformers. They encouraged the poor to save for a rainy day, but they were also perceptive enough to realize that poor families regularly had to wade through monsoons.

Hartley, for example, urged workers "to improve the season when expenses are diminished and labor most abounds, so as to save a small sum each week for deposit in the Savings' Bank." He thought that saving would benefit the poor not only materially (the money laid aside would enable many of them subsequently "to subsist without alms"), but also morally (it would promote "a sense of self-respect and praiseworthy independence").[199] Still, he understood saving to be practical only "when expenses are diminished and labor most abounds."

Lowell also thought it possible to recommend thrift only in comparatively good times: "After the slack time is past and the man is again at work, the opportunity comes for the visitor to make special efforts to persuade the family to prepare for the future and to lay by for the idle time of the next year; he can *then* inculcate lessons in economy and in saving which may be the means of lifting the family permanently on to a higher level than they would ever have attained without his friendly encouragement."[200]

Saving as Philanthropy

The moral reformers venerated savings banks in ways that may seem odd to us today, because banks were thought to facilitate the exercise of prudence and forethought among the poor. Tuckerman, for example, spoke of the savings bank as "an instrument of great moral power."[201] Lowell regarded savings banks as among "the best manifestations of true charity" because of their influence in "encouraging thrift" and "teaching providence and self-control."

Lowell noted that savings banks were actually created as a sort of philanthropic venture: "The great scheme of Savings Banks was originally conceived and put into operation as a means of helping the poor," beginning in Hamburg in 1778 and in Berne in 1787. "Savings banks have grown to be such immense business enterprises, and are so necessary a part of the life of every nation, that they are never thought of as a 'charity'—but they should be constantly pointed to as an example of what true charity can do."[202]

Remarkable as it may seem, American savings banks were indeed created as charitable ventures. The savings bank movement was dominated by philanthropists at its inception; in the words of one nineteenth-century observer, savings banks were "intended to elevate the character and improve the condition of . . . people of small means."[203] The banks hoped to achieve these goals by promoting self-reliance, enabling workers to rely on their own savings (rather than charitable relief) to see them through hard times. In addition, workers who could safely deposit their wages (and earn interest on the deposits) would be less likely to spend them recklessly.[204] Workers with savings were also expected to lead lives that were more stable: the ownership of property would tend to discourage excesses in either morality (intemperance and crime) or politics (riot and revolution).[205]

Not surprisingly, the alterations in the behavior of workers that savings banks were expected to facilitate were regarded as important means of lessening urban poverty. The nineteenth-century economist Willard Philips considered the establishment of the banks as "a great event in the world," comparable to "the introduction of the compass, or the invention of printing."[206]

The founders of the earliest banks certainly understood themselves as philanthropists. One of the first American savings banks—the Philadelphia Saving Fund Society, begun in 1816—declared that its aim was to promote economy and the practice of saving amongst the poor and laboring classes of the community—to assist them in the accumulation of property that they may possess the means of support during old age or sickness—and to render them in a great degree independent of the bounty of others.

Somewhat immodestly, Philadelphia's benevolent bankers even argued that "of the charitable Institutions that have had for their object the amelioration of the human condition, none perhaps deserve higher commendation than those which, under the title of *Provident Societies* or *Savings Banks*, have lately been established."[207]

New York's first savings bank, the Bank for Savings, was founded in 1819 by citizens who were active in the Society for the Prevention of Pauperism, an important precursor to the AICP. The leading savings bank advocate, John Pintard, predicted at the time that three-fourths of the deposits would otherwise have been squandered in "dram shops" and on "frippery." A decade later he boasted that the bank was "working wonders" among the city's Irish population, notably by encouraging their temperance.[208]

The origin of savings banks was in fact linked historically to the growth of the temperance movement: not surprisingly, sobriety and thrift, each a manifestation of self-control, were thought to reinforce one another. Historian W. J. Rorabaugh elaborates on Pintard's rationale, explaining that savings banks were established to encourage the poor to avoid spending their "modest savings of 25¢ to $1 for refreshment in a tavern or grocery." Thus "interest-bearing funds" were intended to give "the poor an alternative to spending their money on liquor." One temperance society (in Newton, Massachusetts) even opened its own bank.[209]

Encouraging Saving

Moral reformers did more than sing the praises of thrift as a virtue and savings banks as institutions. They also took practical steps to promote saving by the poor, establishing and encouraging institutions designed to make it easier for the poor to put away rather than spend whatever small amounts of cash were available to them. For example, Brace created savings institutions as a charitable undertaking, attached to Children's Aid Society lodging houses. A great advocate of saving, Brace was fond of a remark by a British charity worker, who declared that "we never give [to the poor] now; we take!" This worker's "great object was . . . to induce the poor to save"; thus he constantly strove "to get money from these people, when they had a little," rather than to give it to them.[210] Brace applied this policy in his own charitable institutions; the poor boys who lived in the lodging houses were not given clothes ("unless under some peculiar and unfortunate circumstances"), but were instead "induced to save some pennies every day" until they could afford to buy their own clothing.[211]

To encourage saving, the first superintendent of the newsboys' lodging house set up a bank, in part to promote self-advancement by encouraging stricter morals among its residents: the idea was to dissuade the boys from wasting their money on "follies—theatres, cards, dice, policy-tickets, and games with pennies, while the lads themselves remained ragged and poor." Brace described the bank as a great success: "This simple contrivance has done more to break up the gambling and extravagant habits of the class, than any other one influence. The superintendent now pays a large interest on deposits, and our Trustees have offered prizes to the lads who save the most."[212]

Lowell was also instrumental in encouraging the poor to save. Among the six goals listed in the constitution of the Charity Organization Society of the City of New York was the promotion of "the general welfare of the poor . . . by inculcation of habits of providence and self-dependence."[213] A field was open for that work because only one savings bank in the city would accept deposits of less than a dollar. As a result, many of the poor (in particular poor children) were effectively encouraged to spend rather than save whatever small amounts they possessed.

Desiring to encourage even the smallest savings imaginable, the COS established a committee (on which Lowell served) that created the Penny Provident Fund in 1888.[214] The fund aimed to prevent the "waste of small sums in unnecessary expenditures."[215] It did so by selling savings stamps (in denominations ranging from one cent to one dollar) to the poor. As soon as depositors accrued ten dollars in stamps, they were encouraged to take the proceeds and open accounts in savings banks; to give depositors an incentive to transfer their savings to banks, amounts in the fund earned depositors no interest.

In the estimation of the COS, many depositors ended up with savings accounts in banks: "Hundreds . . . have been graduated from what may be called this kindergarten of thrift into the high schools of providence, and become investors in regular savings banks." By encouraging saving the fund was thought to have awakened "the self-respect, the independence, the dignity and ambition [of] thousands of the poorest of the poor."[216] Since so many of the depositors were children, it was claimed that the fund's only opponents were the city's "cigarette and candy venders [*sic*]."[217]

The fund was able to facilitate savings by the poor by making its stamps readily available for purchase in a great many venues. In addition to selling its stamps in over 300 locations (including savings banks, churches, boys' and girls' clubs, settlement houses, libraries, retail stores, charity offices, and public schools), the Penny Provident Fund also employed paid collectors who would go from tenement to tenement soliciting deposits. As Brown observed, the fund was notable for its "aggressiveness," its zeal in "find[ing] the mites that in [its] keeping accumulate[d] until they ma[d]e an imposing total."[218]

At its peak (in 1903), just under 100,000 depositors held accounts with the fund. That is an impressive total, since the turnover among depositors must have been substantial; as we have seen, once accounts grew large enough to be accepted by savings banks, depositors were expected and encouraged to close and transfer them. The fund finally met its demise in 1915, after the introduction of the postal savings system (which Lowell had advocated as far back as the 1880s)[219] had made it redundant.

There is obviously something hard-headed and individualistic about the moral reformers' advocacy of saving; clearly they wanted individuals to stand on their own two feet whenever possible. At the same time, it is important to realize that the case for saving had a sentimental component as well. If detractors of saving (e.g., Jane Addams's socialist tailor) believed that familial responsibility made saving impossible for the poor, its advocates countered by contending that the desire to support one's family was the great emotional factor providing an impetus for saving. Familial love offered a powerful inducement to save; thrift, after all, was practiced not only by Ebenezer Scrooge but also by Bob Cratchit.

Love of family was what enabled impoverished workers to deny themselves so that their dependents might live better. The COS unabashedly sounded this sentimental note, as when it told of "a little daughter who meets her father every pay day before he can reach his saloon, and relieves him of part of his wages to invest in stamps of the Penny Provident Fund."[220] A more sophisticated variation on this theme was put forth by Channing, who beautifully articulated the emotional (as opposed to narrowly practical) rationale for thrift:

> It is the common doctrine of the day, that the poor are to be raised by being taught to save, to hoard, to economize their scanty earnings. By all means teach prudence, but do not make the poor anxious, selfish, sordid. Teach prudence; but still more teach love; and so doing you will teach economy. Inspire the poor with strong and tender affections towards their families and fellow-creatures and they will deny themselves, and practise thrift with a cheerfulness and fidelity, not often learned from the maxims of worldly wisdom.[221]

Not only is Channing's declaration beautifully worded; remarkably, there is even some reason to suspect that it may be true. RAND economist James P. Smith observes that married couples have far more wealth than do unmarried people. If the pooling of assets when marriage occurs were the only thing at issue, we would expect the assets of married couples to be twice as large as those of people who are separated, divorced, widowed, or have never married; but the gap is much greater than that. Smith concludes that "marriage strongly encourages savings behavior."[222] Perhaps, as Channing believed, it does so in part by giving individuals a reason to save, in the form of dependents whose welfare they care about.

Working-Class Savings

Ultimately, of course, the crucial question is less what the moral reformers believed than what workers actually did. Clearly the reformers thought that workers should and, for the most part, could save. It remains to be seen, though, whether workers were really able to follow the reformers' advice.

In putting together the AICP annual reports, Hartley occasionally included statistics on saving; he evidently thought that they offered a measure of the moral and economic health of the city's workers. In 1855, which was not a prosperous year, he noted that deposits of more than $2,348,000 had been made, compared to withdrawals exceeding $3,323,000 — proof of the "pressure on labor," but also of "its ability, by forecast, to care for itself." Workers had prudently saved in prosperous times; funds were therefore at their disposal to draw upon during the economic contraction of 1855. In Hartley's view, these figures showed that "the majority of the working classes are intelligent, industrious, and thrifty, and consequently seldom feel the privations of poverty."[223]

In 1861 Hartley intoned that "the Savings Bank as clearly reveals the condition of the laborer, as the banking house that of the merchant," because "the deposits in these institutions are chiefly the earnings of mechanics and laboring men." Thus the $40 million in the accounts of 40,000 families "afford[ed] very significant evidence of their thriftiness and prosperity."[224] By 1872 many more families were saving, but with so many new accounts, the average amount saved had — not surprisingly — sharply declined. There were almost 447,000 depositors in New York's 41 savings banks; the average deposit, though, stood just above $360 (down from $1,000 per account in 1861).[225]

But what Hartley's figures did not show was who, precisely, was doing the saving: he assumed but had no way of proving that the depositors were ordinary workers. Savings banks were undeniably created to encourage the working class to save; because many banks were quasi-philanthropic institutions intended to promote the welfare of the working class, they often limited the size of accounts or individual deposits to increase the likelihood that it was workers and not their employers who were the beneficiaries.[226] Nevertheless, the banks understandably published data only about the number and size of their accounts, not the incomes or occupations of their account holders.[227] Equally understandably, workers themselves were often reluctant to answer questions about their personal finances.[228] For these reasons, neither nineteenth-century observers nor twentieth-century historians have been altogether certain about the prevalence of saving among nineteenth-century workers.

The contention that nineteenth-century workers seldom saved seems to rely on the premise that they cannot have saved. In the absence of directly relevant evidence, the Massachusetts Bureau of Statistics of Labor (MBSL) concluded in the 1870s that the commonwealth's savings institutions chiefly benefited the middle class, not the working class; since the banks would not release information about their depositors, the MBSL's case essentially rested on "arbitrary assumptions as to the size of deposit a 'typical workman' might make." Ignoring the strenuous objections of bankers, the bureau's statisticians assumed that deposits exceeding fifty dollars could not have been made by workers, and must therefore have been made by their employers or other members of the middle class.[229]

The evidence recently amassed by historians and economists does much to refute this contention. It is now clear that savings accounts were indeed commonly held by nineteenth-century workers. For example, historian Stephan Thernstrom has shown that even unskilled laborers in Newburyport, Massachusetts, were often regular depositors in banks. There were 327 laboring families in Newburyport, according to the 1860 census (and 410 according to the 1870 census). Of these families, some 154—38 percent of the 410—opened savings accounts between July 1866 and July 1876 in one of Newburyport's two banks—funds which were generally used to pay off mortgages on their homes.[230]

The Newburyport evidence is unlikely to be anomalous. Thernstrom argues that Newburyport was broadly representative of the rest of the country, since social mobility there was "the result of forces which were operating in much the same way in cities throughout the entire society."[231] But in any case, comparable evidence from the large northeastern cities confirms his conclusion: although the savings banks were not the exclusive preserve of working-class depositors, a substantial proportion of depositors were indeed workers.

In antebellum New York, for example, "the majority of mutual [savings bank] customers were domestics, unskilled laborers, or semi-skilled persons of small means for whom the first mutuals were intended. Given their meager incomes, it is surprising that some of these individuals actually managed to accumulate sums in excess of $1,000. The account books of the Bank for Savings contain numerous examples of unskilled persons' accumulating substantial balances by depositing a few dollars a month over several years."[232]

Similarly, in 1850 over half the male account holders at the Philadelphia Saving Fund Society were grouped under one of two headings: either "mechanics, artisans or handycraftsmen [sic]" or "porters or labourers." On average, active account holders saved 10 to 15 percent of their income each year. It is estimated that the median bank balance of male depositors (who had accounts lasting four to five years) almost equaled the annual gross income of working-class men in that era.[233] And later in the century, most Boston workers appear to have possessed small savings accounts, which cushioned the impact of unemployment. Seasonal workers saved when they were employed to help cover their expenses during slack times; virtually all workers saved in good years and expended their savings during depressions.[234]

By 1897 there were over 5,200,000 depositors in American savings banks, with the average account approaching $373.[235] Clearly all of these depositors were not workers. But then savings banks did not offer the only vehicle enabling workers to save. In 1893 America's savings and loan associations had over 1,745,000 shareholders, who tended to be workers with steady incomes (so that they could plausibly contemplate the purchase of homes).[236]

In addition, workers routinely invested in what was known as industrial insurance, which in effect covered burial costs for all members of a worker's family—

thereby ensuring that none of them would have to endure the posthumous indignity of a pauper's burial. There were many more policyholders for industrial insurance (6,944,000 in 1895) than depositors in savings banks;[237] furthermore, it is estimated that over 80 percent of American-born white families and over 90 percent of immigrant and black families in industrial towns held such policies.[238]

Charity workers tended to disapprove of expenditures on industrial insurance: thus Brown lamented workers' inability to understand "that industrial life insurance is a very expensive form of saving, and that a man should provide against the misfortunes of sickness, slackness of work, and old age before he provides for funeral benefits."[239] Radicals were equally critical, complaining that the real beneficiaries were the undertakers, who profited from the survivors' "deplorable extravagance in funeral arrangements."[240] As the radicals noted, the small size of the typical payment ($138 in 1911) meant that it really provided "not life insurance at all, but merely funeral insurance."[241]

Still, the evidence—from savings banks, savings and loans, and industrial insurance—is clear: although working-class wages were anything but munificent, large numbers of workers were nevertheless able to put away at least small (and often substantial) amounts of money. The banks themselves deserve much of the credit for the rise in working-class saving: deposits appear to have increased in part because banks made it convenient for workers to save. Mary Brown realized that the number and accessibility of banking institutions affected the rate of savings: she contended that if the poor were to save, "a bank needs oftentimes to be brought to the very door of the small saver."[242]

Historians today agree that savings increased because and to the extent that banks made saving easier and more attractive for their prospective working-class customers. The emergence of New York's mutual banks is thought to have increased saving by offering attractive interest rates to prospective depositors.[243] Similarly, the Philadelphia Saving Fund Society appears to have encouraged working-class thrift by offering "opportunities to accumulate savings that were secure, liquid, and yielded attractive returns."[244]

But the clearest proof of the importance of banks in making savings possible is found in comparisons of savings rates in different parts of the country. As we have seen, savings banks began as a northeastern phenomenon. They remained concentrated in the northeast; remarkably, in 1897 as many as 657 out of 668 mutual savings banks were located in New England and other eastern states.[245] Not surprisingly, savings accounts were also far more common in the northeast (where half the population had them) than elsewhere (only one out of every 57 Americans held an account in other parts of the country). This striking discrepancy was understandably attributed to the absence of secure banking facilities outside of the northeast, which the postal savings system was introduced to remedy. In the words of a postmaster general who advocated postal savings, "The widespread extravagance and improvidence among our people is not so much a defect of character as it is a defect of conditions that surround our people."[246]

The declaration that "a defect of character" was generally not at issue is worth developing. Contrary to the more implausible beliefs of some of their advocates, it is unlikely that the introduction of savings banks somehow revolutionized the moral character of the poor, suddenly turning improvident wastrels into prudent accumulators. What is more likely (and of great importance) is that savings banks must in many cases have altered behavior by making it easier for those workers who wanted to save to reach their goal. In that sense, it is fair to say that banking institutions (and the lack thereof) did indeed shape and alter the behavior of workers. Just as the moral reformers believed, prudent, self-advancing, thrifty behavior really was facilitated by the introduction of banks (and hindered by their absence).[247]

The Limits of Savings

Saving was by no means a panacea for all of the problems of the poor. To begin with, clearly not everyone saved. As I have just suggested, saving was of use to those who were already predisposed to be prudent accumulators; it was not much use to (and did not much affect the lives of) those without that predisposition—or to those who simply earned too little to be able to save anything. That shortcoming was acknowledged even by the partisans of savings banks. Emerson Keyes, who wrote a history of American savings banks in 1876, believed that they were of use to the frugal majority of workers, who banked their surplus earnings in prosperous years in preparation for hard times. Nevertheless, he also recognized the limitations of savings banks, admitting that they would never "make the slothful vigilant; the wasteful frugal; the vicious virtuous."[248] Similarly, in 1897 New York's COS lamented the fact that savings banks, life insurance, and the Penny Provident Fund, valuable as they all were, "d[id] not yet insure saving with sufficient regularity and d[id] not reach the poorest families with sufficiently strong arguments for thrift."[249]

A second limitation related to the amount that workers could save. Even if they did save, were workers really able to save enough to prepare themselves for the bad times that were brought on by unemployment, illness, accident, and old age? The recognition that savings were in many cases too small to make it possible to cope with these eventualities led some to advocate a compulsory system of social insurance (incorporating programs like workers' compensation, unemployment insurance, health insurance, and old-age pensions): if the individualistic remedy of personal savings did not (and could not reasonably be expected to) suffice, then it should be supplemented by a more collectivist system that could cope with them more effectively.

In 1913 that argument was forcefully made by I. M. Rubinow, a fervent advocate of social insurance. Rubinow did not deny that many workers were able to save: in fact, he cited a U.S. Bureau of Labor survey showing that more than half of all workers had income exceeding their expenditures. But he discounted the significance of these savings, noting that surpluses were substantial only when families had more than one breadwinner and only when they had two or fewer children.[250] He also discounted the significance of workers' personal savings by asserting that they almost never exceeded $1,000.[251] (He could only assert this because, as we have seen, banks did not release information about the economic status of their depositors.)

Disparagements of savings along these lines, joined to support for social insurance, were voiced not by moral reformers but by radicals, who denied that individuals could take meaningful steps on their own to mitigate their poverty. On the other hand, it is striking that advocates of thrift and individual saving were often surprisingly receptive to arguments for social insurance. Mary Brown, for example, was quite open to the principle underlying social insurance. She declared that unemployment insurance would be "valuable . . . if it were practicable."[252] Brown also restated an argument advanced by Charles Booth, the great British analyst of poverty, who supported old-age pensions, believing that they would reduce poverty without undermining individual self-reliance: "The small pension received by a man at sixty-five years of age will encourage thrift (since he that has wants more)." Like Booth, Brown seems to have been skeptical of social insurance only to the extent that it "undermined . . . self-respect or the forces of individuality, upon which morality as well as industry depends."[253]

The compatibility of moral reform with social insurance is far more evident, though, in Brace's work. Brace was actually among the earliest proponents of social insurance (a fact that has gone unrecognized, to my knowledge, in the literature on either Brace or social insurance).[254] He advocated social insurance in his next-to-last book, originally published in 1882, a full generation before it was seriously considered in the U.S.,[255] in fact a year before its first implementation in any form anywhere in the world. (Germany enacted national health insurance in 1883.)[256]

Brace made the following case for social insurance:

> In a distant future all men and women can be guarded against the inevitable calamities and losses of life, and thus preserved from sinking into the lowest depths of misery, by a wise system of insurance by society or government—the insured contributing a fixed annual payment during health and strength (itself a preservative from pauperism), and the State taking charge of the funds, and appropriating from taxation enough to fill out the necessary annuity.

Such "provisions against accident, sickness, calamity and old age" would constitute "one of the greatest blessings of modern society," because they would reduce poverty without creating pauperism. Brace claimed that his plan would not "produce dependence, because the ultimate enjoyment of the insurance would depend on savings made during health and prosperity."[257] But those savings would be supplemented by tax revenues: Brace evidently did not believe that the poor could or should reasonably be expected to be altogether self-reliant, to be able to save enough on their own to secure themselves against accident, illness, and old age. Thus Brace was not an inflexible proponent of laissez-faire and did not rule out governmental efforts to assist the working poor in their quest for self-reliance.

The examples of Brown and especially Brace suggest that moral reformers could and did encourage individual saving without dogmatically asserting that it solved or ever could solve all of the worker's financial problems. Brace's joint emphasis on the need for both social insurance and individual providence also characterized other advocates of social insurance. Its proponents thought it significant that workers enjoying coverage would have to defray at least some of its costs: in virtually all proposals (and in the legislation that was finally enacted), coverage for social insurance was financed at least in part by deductions from workers' paychecks (which were then supplemented by payments from employers).

In important respects, then, the individualism espoused by advocates of saving proved compatible with social insurance. Individualism could, and for many did, mandate only that workers help themselves by making contributions for the insurance that protected them. But because much unemployment and many industrial accidents were rightly believed to have social rather than exclusively individual causes, individualism did not necessarily mandate that the whole cost of insurance be borne by the workers alone.[258]

The debate over social insurance erupted when it was realized that workers could not easily save enough by themselves to withstand the ravages of predictable dangers like unemployment, old age, illness, and industrial accidents. In that sense, it pointed to one of the limits of saving—that too little was or likely could be saved. Ironically, another limit pointed to precisely the opposite problem—that too much was being saved. Here the issue was not what workers' savings often could not comfortably buy—protection against age, illness, and unemployment—but what the workers themselves did not buy in order to put aside such savings as they could manage.

The Danger of Underconsumption

Thernstrom's analysis of Newburyport savers points to the problem. Thernstrom does not romanticize working-class thrift; as he points out, it was made possible only by the early entrance of children into the workforce (which prevented them from receiving an education that might have enabled them to rise on the occupational ladder) and by "ruthless underconsumption." Saving was possible despite the fact that few Newburyport working-class families had incomes much above the minimum subsistence figure calculated by the Massachusetts Bureau of Statistics of Labor. Obviously, then, families with savings were consuming far less than this minimum.[259]

In some respects moral reformers could applaud ruthless underconsumption. For example, the desire to reduce expenditures often seems to have motivated aspiring savers to practice total abstinence. As Thernstrom notes, "The workman who wished to accumulate and maintain a property stake in the community had compelling reasons for sobriety; it was no coincidence that a Roman Catholic Temperance Society was formed in Newburyport at just the time that the Irish immigrants began their climb upward into the propertied sector of the working class."[260]

But in other respects the immigrant zeal for saving clearly troubled reformers. As I noted above, the moral reformers understood thrift as a situational virtue: it was inappropriate to save by forgoing expenditures on necessities. Thus Brown did not advocate savings that were made possible by families' depriving themselves of "hygienic or educational" advantages, or forcing their children "prematurely to enter the labor market" (a "very real" danger).[261]

Unfortunately, given the exigencies imposed by working-class incomes, too often those were the only strategies that could be employed by those eager to save. In his 1907 New York City budget study, Robert Chapin found that half of all the underfed families (as compared with less than 37 percent of all families) reported a budget surplus; he lamented the "desire to save money even at [the] cost of inadequate nutrition."[262]

In his classic account of late-nineteenth-century urban poverty, *How the Other Half Lives*, Jacob Riis voiced the ambivalence (at best) of moral reformers about the immigrant thrift that was made possible by a below-normal standard of living:

> Thrift is the watchword of [New York's] Jewtown, as of its people the world over. It is at once its strength and its fatal weakness, its cardinal virtue and its foul disgrace. Become an overmastering passion with these people who come here in droves from Eastern Europe to escape persecution, from which freedom could be bought only with gold, it has enslaved them in bondage worse than that from which they fled. Money is their God. Life itself is of little value compared with even the leanest bank account. . . . Over and over again I have met with instances of these Polish or Russian Jews deliberately starving themselves to the point of physical exhaustion, while working night and day at a tremendous pressure to save a little money.[263]

If we can ignore the anti-Semitic overtones of this passage,[264] how should we evaluate its substance? Since Riis elsewhere lauded the development of "habits of thrift and ambitious industry" (around the "sound core of self-help"),[265] it is tempting to attack the hypocrisy of moral reformers who advocated thrift but then criticized the immigrant practitioners of the very virtue that had been preached to them.[266]

On the other hand, a more sympathetic assessment of the reformers is possible. It is to the reformers' credit—not their shame—that they understood thrift as a situational virtue, more valid in some circumstances than others. To have done otherwise, to have suggested that additional belt-tightening was always appropriate for the poor, would surely have been still more unfair to them. Although Riis might (and should) have shown more sympathy for the plight of the self-denying residents of "Jewtown," he was not wrong to warn against underconsumption as a genuine danger. Nor was Brown wrong to see child labor as a strategy that had costs for the poor as well as the obvious benefit—increased income—that made greater savings possible.

In effect, Riis's critique constitutes an acknowledgment that material poverty itself frustrated many of the moral strategies that were meant to reduce it (e.g., migrating westward in search of employment or renting larger and cleaner apartments). For that reason, the "morals" strategy of the reformers was not and could not be altogether effective on its own, but instead needed to be supplemented by an "income" strategy. Greater virtue was surely desirable in the poor (as it would have been in the nonpoor as well). Ultimately, though, the poor needed to earn more money as well as to improve their morals. In some ways, earning more would actually facilitate moral improvement, for example by making it possible to migrate in quest of jobs or to occupy housing that was less demoralizing and also conducive to better health.

Riis himself explained that material privation and not moral failure was at issue only two paragraphs after his critique of Jewish miserliness. There he approvingly quoted this statement from doctors who ministered to charity cases on the Lower East Side: "The diseases these people suffer from are not due to intemperance or immorality, but to ignorance, want of suitable food, and the foul air in which they live and work."[267] Clearly Riis understood that the poor could benefit from using their income wisely (by spending it wisely as well as saving it wisely), but he also realized that simply increasing their income (so that they could eat more and work less) would also benefit them greatly.

Riis (like Brown) recognized that thrift was desirable in some circumstances but not all, that it could solve some problems but not all. His discussion of thrift amounted to an implicit critique of those who saw working-class thrift as a panacea. Significantly, the qualified defense of thrift that Riis and Brown espoused is supported by Thernstrom's assessment of the historical evidence. Thernstrom criticizes those who regarded savings banks as a remedy for all the ills of the poor: their position could be sustained only by adopting the untenable "premise that the problem of working class poverty was not essentially a deficiency of total income, but only a failure to use income rationally."[268]

But this is to say only that the unequivocal supporters of saving (like its unequivocal critics) employ a false dichotomy of a sort that is all too frequently found in discussions of poverty: poverty need not be caused *exclusively* by either insufficient income or unwise expenditures. Let us grant that some enthusiasts for savings were wrong to deny that workers' income was too low to enable them to escape poverty; but precisely for that reason, the enthusiasts were nevertheless right to encourage the rational use of income, in that the workers had every incentive to use what little income they had wisely. The case for spending wisely is obviously strengthened (not weakened) if existing income is insufficient. Thus one can acknowledge that workers were often paid too little to live adequately and at the same time recognize that it was in their own best interest to stretch their earnings as far as possible by spending thriftily (and saving whenever possible).

As it happens, that is Thernstrom's own conclusion. Contrary to the claims of savings bank enthusiasts, he notes that very few laborers managed to save enough to go into business for themselves. But they still accrued savings, which markedly improved their lives: "The savings banks played an important role in the process of homeownership, and they made it easier to set aside small amounts for emergency use. The thrifty and temperate laborer might reasonably hope, with luck, to accumulate a few hundred dollars on which to survive old age at a time when pension plans and social security were unknown."[269]

Thernstrom offers a defense of working-class saving that is marked by sobriety and realism. He concludes that laborers in Newburyport were able to establish themselves "as decent, respectable, hard-working, churchgoing members of the community," without being able to set foot on an escalator that would elevate them to the status of "merchants, professionals, and entrepreneurs." Just as the moral reformers would have predicted, "hard work and incessant economy did bring tangible rewards—money in the bank, a house to call [one's] own, a new sense of security and dignity."[270]

Clearly saving was not always possible for all workers; just as clearly, it was not even always advisable for all workers. Nevertheless, the historical evidence strongly suggests that spending prudently and saving did offer many working-class families a means of mitigating and in some cases even exiting from poverty. The moral reformers correctly understood that saving was not always a virtue appropriate for the poor, but they also correctly understood that it was often highly appropriate for them.

SECTION D. FAMILY VALUES: MORE THAN JUST A FOOTNOTE

The advice given by the moral reformers to the nineteenth-century poor still seems pertinent in many respects. What may strike us more today, however, is the advice that they did *not* give, or at least saw comparatively little need to give. Because of the alarming concentration of poverty among single-parent families today, any contemporary of ours who wanted to remoralize the poor would surely emphasize the importance of marriage and the two-parent family above all else.

But the sanctity or even the advisability of marriage was never a prominent theme of the moral reformers; for the most part they could simply take for granted the predominance of two-parent families among the poor. To be sure, there were many exceptions to the rule of family stability among yesterday's poor, and poverty was often caused or exacerbated when parents died or left their families. Still, the family instability that we face today is far more severe than that confronted by the moral reformers.

The one reformer who discussed family breakup extensively was Brace—not surprisingly, since the youths whom he tried to help were so often the products of broken homes. Brace can in fact sound remarkably prophetic in his analyses. He regretted the "weakness of the marriage-tie" that characterized many of the Irish immigrants in New York (but not in Ireland, where their "religion ha[d] especially guarded female purity and the fidelity of husband and wife," so that they were "peculiarly faithful to the marriage-tie").[271] Brace regarded broken homes as an important cause of juvenile crime: "It is extraordinary, among the lowest classes, in how large a number of cases a second marriage, or the breaking of marriage, is the immediate cause of crime or vagrancy among the children."[272] Even in this discussion, though, Brace emphasized conflict between stepparents and stepchildren—the problems posed by a "second marriage"—more than desertion or illegitimacy; he thereby implicitly acknowledged that the two-parent family remained the norm among the poor.

In other passages, however, Brace might almost be describing New York today instead of New York in the 1850s. He lamented the fact that too many poor people were "continually making a practical test of 'Free-Love' doctrines"; that was regrettable, he argued, because mothers unassisted by fathers could seldom discipline their sons adequately. When a mother tried to raise her sons by herself (after her husband abandoned the family), "the boys gradually get beyond her control; . . . they become wild and vagrant, and soon end with being street-rovers, or petty thieves, or young criminals." The fruits of "'Free Love' or a weak marriage-bond" could often be traced, he declared, in "the histories of great numbers of the young thieves and outcasts . . . in this city."[273]

It is noteworthy that a very similar chain of causation was discerned some ninety years later by another analyst who feared the harm done to society by family dissolution—Daniel Patrick Moynihan:[274]

> From the wild Irish slums of the 19th-century Eastern seaboard, to the riot-torn suburbs of Los Angeles, there is one unmistakable lesson in American history: a community that allows a large number of young men to grow up in broken families, dominated by women, never acquiring any stable relationship to male authority, never acquiring any set of rational expectations about the future—that community asks for and gets chaos. Crime, violence, unrest, disorder—most particularly the furious, unrestrained lashing out at the whole social structure—that is not only to be expected; it is very near to inevitable. And it is richly deserved.[275]

In short, almost a century beforehand Brace articulated some of the wisdom incarnated in the 1965 Moynihan report: the family dissolution that Brace observed in "the wild Irish slums of the 19th-century Eastern seaboard" would recur generations later, as Moynihan showed, in black slums in the same cities. Remarkably, Brace pointed to the problem even though—at least as measured by illegitimacy—it was minuscule by our standards: he estimated that only 4 percent of all births in New York City were illegitimate.[276] Or as we would say today, the illegitimacy ratio then equaled 4 percent. By contrast, the illegitimacy ratio among blacks that so alarmed Moynihan stood at 23.6 percent in 1963;[277] the illegitimacy ratio among black New Yorkers exceeded 67 percent in 1992;[278] and the illegitimacy ratio for all New Yorkers in that year was no less than 46 percent.[279]

Family Ties

If the reformers did not for the most part call attention to problems posed by the weakness of family ties among the poor, they did recognize that their strength benefited the poor. Channing in particular emphasized this theme, which we have seen him explore earlier in discussing intemperance and thrift. The ties of familial affection could serve to make poverty far more bearable:

> The domestic affections may and do grow up among the poor, and these are to all of us the chief springs of earthly happiness. And it deserves consideration that the poor have their advantages as well as disadvantages in respect to domestic ties. Their narrow condition obliges them to do more for one another than is done among the rich; and this necessity, as is well known, sometimes gives a vigor and tenderness to the love of parents and children, brothers and sisters, not always found in the luxurious classes, where wealth destroys this mutual dependence, this need of mutual help.[280]

One need not be a devout Unitarian moralist to voice this sort of argument; hard-headed social scientists can do so as well. For example, Herbert Gans has argued that the immigrant poverty of the past was endurable largely because of the strength of the immigrant family: "Most families were sufficiently intact most of the time to enable most parents to find satisfactions in family life that compensated for the bad jobs they had to take, and the hard work they had to endure."[281]

Gans's judgment about the stability of immigrant family life appears to be borne out by the empirical evidence. In studies of family composition among immigrants in Paterson, New Jersey, in 1880 (and in lower Manhattan in 1905), labor historian Herbert Gutman found very few broken homes. Instead, husband-wife and two-parent families were exceedingly common: in Paterson, nine out of ten households of German and British immigrants (and four out of five Irish immigrant households) consisted of either a husband and wife or two parents and their children; in Manhattan, 93 percent of both Jewish and Italian immigrant households fit into one or the other of these categories.[282]

But stable families did more than make poverty more bearable; they also offered the poor an emotional incentive to undertake the actions and exercise the virtues that would make their poverty less burdensome. Lowell generally opposed institutionalizing children who had living parents (even children subject "to occasional sufferings, neglect, or evil example"), because the result would be to deprive the parent "of the strongest incentive he can possibly have to exertion and right living."[283]

Similarly, Mary Richmond approvingly quoted Charles Booth's observation that "the two conditions of human happiness are work and affection. And these conditions are best fulfilled when a man works hard for those he loves."[284] Like Booth, Richmond valued family life not only because it brought consolation to the poor but also because it motivated the behavior that could mitigate poverty. Channing, Lowell, and Richmond all believed that family ties could and did motivate the diligence, sobriety, and thrift that the reformers commended to the poor.

Historians today clearly agree that the intact family was an important bulwark against poverty in the past—though their explanations ignore the emotional and motivational issues stressed by Channing, Lowell, and Richmond, focusing on material concerns instead. The presence of multiple breadwinners in families lessened the sting of the primary worker's unemployment in bad times and provided the extra income that made saving possible in better times. For these reasons, Stephan Thernstrom emphasizes that "kids were an economic asset" in the past. Families with several earners reaped the benefit of "a kind of primitive unemployment compensation scheme," since it was unlikely that all of the providers would lose their jobs at the same time.[285]

In criticizing nineteenth-century analysts who ascribed dependency to moral failings, Michael Katz also points to the centrality of the intact family as a weapon against poverty. He argues that "the single most important characteristic" of the dependent poor was "their lack of spouses or children to whom they could turn for support."[286]

That is an important statement, whose full implications deserve to be considered. If family ties are truly central to escaping poverty, one should endorse the ethic—stressed by some of the moral reformers (and taken for granted by others)—that urged male breadwinners to look after their families. As we will see, Richmond in particular heavily emphasized the need to accept familial responsibilities if poverty was to be reduced. In her thought, at least, the revitalization of the family was more than a footnote.

In many cases, obviously, no one is to blame for lacking a family: being single or childless, or outliving other family members, is not ordinarily a sign of a moral failing. But to the considerable extent that desertion (and, more broadly, nonsupport) by male breadwinners impoverished the remaining family members, moral issues really do emerge.

Desertion and Poverty

As we have seen, moral reformers did not for the most part emphasize desertion as an important cause of poverty. Late in his life, though (perhaps influenced by Brace's observations), Hartley raised the issue in one of his few discussions of the family. In 1872 he pointed to "the sundering of the marriage relation, through the desertion of wives by their husbands," as "a frequent cause of poverty, wretchedness, and often of demoralization among the poor in this city." But he provided no statistics to demonstrate its importance—though he did observe that "this flagrant crime against social order is most frequent among our immigrant population."[287]

A generation later, Lilian Brandt, a researcher at the New York COS, attempted to estimate the severity of the problem—and to assess its causes—through a statistical study. She examined 574 cases, drawn from the files of twenty-six charitable
organizations, in which husbands had deserted wives in 1903 and 1904: over 56
percent of the incidents occurred in three large northeastern cities, New York,
Philadelphia, and Boston. The charities judged that between 7 and 13 percent of
all cases of poverty with which they dealt were occasioned by a husband's desertion.[288]

As one might expect, the deserters came in for harsh moral criticism. Brandt
noted that they had abandoned a total of 574 wives and 1,665 children, including
102 born just before or not long after the desertion.[289] More than half of the men—
325—were said to be intemperate.[290] Most damning of all, though, was Brandt's
judgment that the search for work could account for only a small fraction of the
desertions. Only seventeen of the deserters "left in discouragement about work
or with the avowed purpose of looking for work" (compared with forty-eight who
"went just after a spree or while drunk").[291] The records pointed to only three men
who were unable to support their families because they were incapacitated (two
had taken seriously ill, and one had lost his sight). In Brandt's summation, these
three were the

> only clear examples, among the five hundred and seventy-four cases, of the "hun-
> dreds and hundreds" of men who are popularly supposed to be driven to the des-
> perate measure of relieving their wives and children of the disadvantage of their
> presence in order that the public shall see to it that they do not suffer.[292]

Brandt denied that the men's inability to support their families motivated—
much less excused—many of the desertions. (To be sure, a much higher proportion of deserters might have been unable to find work during a depression; but
1903 and 1904 were prosperous years.) Only 10 percent of the deserters were unskilled laborers; only 36 percent were "comparatively unskilled"; 51 percent "had
definite trades or occupations in which training was required, many of them im-
plying a high degree of skill."[293]

Brandt concluded that "a large proportion of these men were quite able to
support their families"; unfortunately, "the large amount of intemperance and laziness among them . . . much reduced their earning capacity." Although only 175
were said to be in the habit of working regularly, 270—almost exactly half—were
working just before they deserted, and "several had savings which, providently,
they took with them." In one case the savings amounted to $800.[294]

Personal irresponsibility, then, lay at the root of the poverty occasioned by desertions: "The most constant element in the situation is the irresponsible, ease-
loving man who acts on the theory that when hard times of any sort come he is
justified in making arrangements for his own comfort which do not include his
wife and children."[295] Even the deserters' economic problems were at bottom at-

tributable to their moral failings: "When lack of employment is the apparent cause of desertions, it is probably only the occasion for it," because "the same characteristics which make a man desert when he is out of work are responsible for his not being steadily employed."[296]

What could be done to discourage desertion? Brandt discussed the efforts to rehabilitate deserters that were made by charitable organizations, noting their occasional successes in "restoring to the natural head of the family a sense of his obligations." Still, rehabilitation was seldom effective: overall, in only 49 of the 574 cases was the deserter "persuaded or compelled to resume complete or partial support of [his] family."[297]

A more promising strategy was to help the family become self-supporting, as happened in more than half—292—of the cases.[298] Ultimately, however, Brandt pinned her hopes for the future on continued adherence to strict moral standards, coupled with an improved material environment for the poor:

> The deserting husband must not be permitted to succeed in evading his responsibilities[,] and opportunities must not be neglected for reclaiming the individual deserter of whatever type and improving the standard of the deserted home. The main hope, however, for the solution of the problem, lies in the providing of decent living conditions, and fair opportunities for work, and in the education of this generation of children, and the next, and the next, and the next, in whatever makes for stability of character, for economic efficiency, for a realization of responsibility, and for a wholesome family life.[299]

On one level, Brandt's proposed moral remedies were obviously so vague as to be useless: she herself presumably realized that "whatever makes for stability of character" is not a very precise prescription. Nevertheless, and to her credit, Brandt understood that desertion poses a problem that is moral as well as material. The problem is not restricted to the loss of income suffered by wives and children and cannot be solved simply by replacing that income. Unfortunately, fathers who reject their moral responsibilities also create a moral vacuum in the home that the mere provision of material aid cannot begin to fill.

That realization is still more evident in Richmond's thought. Richmond harshly criticized "married vagabonds"—that is, husbands and fathers who shirked their familial responsibilities.[300] The specific responsibility of married men was to do their utmost "to secure for the other members of the family the means of subsistence."[301] When they failed to do so, they brought into being homes in name only, in which "all sense of responsibility seems lacking"; such homes, Richmond argued, became "breeding places of vice, of disease, and of moral death."[302] By contrast, when responsibility was accepted (that is, when the husband "struggl[ed] to provide for his family" and the wife "[strove] to make the little shelter homelike"), charity workers were confronted with true homes, those in which "home life work[ed] *with* the visitor to win back independence."[303]

Richmond insisted that simply providing material relief to families without responsible fathers was not a satisfactory response. Providing relief—on the grounds that one "cannot let the children suffer"—was insufficient. "No matter how lavish . . . our material assistance, we *do* let the children suffer, and suffer very terribly, so long as we leave them in the clutches of a man who will make no effort to care for them, who is often diseased or depraved. . . . What idea of a home, of industry, of decency, can children get in such surroundings?"[304]

In a remarkably prescient passage, Richmond elaborated on her reasoning:

> What folly . . . to make it possible for a man voluntarily to live without work! What more than folly to make it possible for the head of a family to do so! His children are born into a world where the father is inconsiderate and abusive of the mother; . . . where all the economic laws of the civilized world seem topsy-turvy; where things sometimes come miraculously, without any return for them in labor, and where they sometimes do not come at all. . . . How can we say that we "do not let children suffer," so long as alms keep together thousands of these so-called homes in our large cities, and worst of all, so long as into these homes thousands of helpless unfortunate babies are born every year?

To illustrate her point, Richmond imagined how an infant born into such a home would react to the material relief meant to sustain it:

> Ladies and gentlemen, you have supplied the doctor, and the nurse, and the fuel, and the sick diet. Doubtless you mean it kindly; but I have been assisted into a world where you don't intend to give me a fair chance. You know that my father won't work for me, that my mother has no time to care for me, and that my brothers and sisters must fare worse than ever, now that there's one more mouth to feed. . . . Unless you intend to do a great deal more for me, I'm sorry you didn't do less. Frankly, I don't thank you.[305]

What was the "great deal more" that needed to be done? Husbands and fathers who failed to provide had to be urged to change their ways—and, if need be, co-erced to do so. "Moral suasion" (fortified by "the cutting off of supplies from every available source, the frequently renewed offer of work, and, last of all, the law") had to be exerted by charity workers.[306]

Sometimes this policy was successful: charity workers could "offer . . . work accompanied by the withdrawal of all other aid," or at least make their expectations clear: "One vagabond said to a friendly visitor, 'If charitable people hadn't come in and clothed my children every year, I would.' After that, he did."[307] Ideally, one could turn a "sham home into a real one," by "helping a man who has lost his sense of responsibility toward wife and children to regain it."[308]

In many cases, of course, the policy failed. In these circumstances Richmond preferred family breakup to subsidizing husbands and fathers guilty of nonsupport: the married vagabond's "wife should consider her duty to her children, born and unborn, as higher even than her duty to her husband; and, every effort to transform the sham home into a real home having failed, it should either get rid of its lazy head or be broken up altogether."[309] With this recommendation as her last resort, one is tempted to say that Richmond was ultimately willing to destroy the family in order to save it. But she would have said that it was the nonproviding husband who had truly destroyed it; she simply had the honesty and courage to conclude that in reality his family could not be saved.

The issue of male nonsupport that Brandt and Richmond highlighted comes to the fore in an important historical essay by Kathryn Neckerman on family patterns and poverty. Neckerman emphasizes the economic interdependence that characterized families at the turn of the century, when wages were pooled and married women combined housework with cooking and cleaning for others (boarders) to supplement family income: "Only through cooperation could the family keep itself from the brink of destitution. . . . In the recollections of working-class children, the values of unity, loyalty, and hard work were paramount in their family lives."[310] Her analysis suggests that Channing was right: close familial ties did make poverty bearable and did help offer a route out.

As Neckerman tells the story, this interdependence waned for structural reasons: the demand for boarding decreased as housework became less difficult and children had fewer opportunities to earn money. Most crucial, though, was the male flight from the family: "Resentful of the conditions of industrial work, and of the family needs that tied them to their jobs, some men rebelled against both work and family by drinking, deserting, or refusing to work. . . . At the extreme, some men found no other way to regain lost autonomy or escape oppressive working conditions than to deny or dissolve ties to their families."[311]

Neckerman's chronicle of these developments is meant to be value-free: she appears to be more interested in criticizing the oppressive working conditions that sometimes led to desertion and nonsupport than the desertion and nonsupport themselves. Still, it is remarkable how closely Neckerman's account accords with the judgments expressed by Brandt and Richmond: however much one might stress the oppressiveness of industrial conditions (and as we have seen, Lowell for one was very well aware of their occasional horrors), those conditions cannot altogether excuse the self-indulgence that led some men to reject their responsibility to their families.

Neckerman notes that "heavy drinking . . . diverted funds from the family budget, often leading to a deterioration of material and emotional conditions at home"; she speaks of deserters who "often left when their families were most dependent upon them: right before childbirth . . . or in the early years of marriage." Such men were homeless "in the sense that they had left behind whatever family connections they had had."[312] She also notes (approvingly) that women "sought the support of others who might exert social pressure on their husbands to drink less and be better providers."[313]

In Neckerman's reading the efforts of moral reformers like Richmond to promote responsibility, diligence, and sobriety appear laudable. Obviously it is unfair when the wife and children of a deserting male are impoverished; at the same time, presumably it is a good thing when moral pressure is exerted on males to encourage them to support their families.

Promoting Women's Self-Reliance

As we saw above, in Brandt's analysis the economic problems caused by desertion were far more often resolved by enabling fatherless families to support themselves than by getting erstwhile deserters to resume supporting their families. Charitable societies did much to enable deserted wives and mothers to earn income; they offered advice, of course, but material assistance as well: assistance in "placing children in the day nursery, as well as financial aid at critical moments."[314]

Clearly it made sense for women to be able to support themselves not only as a remedial measure but also as a preventive one. Women who were dependent on unreliable men benefited from being able to provide for themselves when necessary: dependence on male breadwinners can have dangers of its own, just like dependence on government or charitable relief.[315] In her essay Neckerman shows that workers' wives drew precisely this conclusion: "More married women sought employment to supplement family incomes and guard against the vulnerability of complete dependence. But having their own wages gave women a new kind of independence, the possibility of living apart from their husbands."[316]

Surprisingly, women's need to be able to support themselves was stressed by at least one of the moral reformers—Hartley. He wrote that it was unwise for women of the middle and upper classes to "look directly to the marriage relation, as their aim and resource."[317] It was foolish to do so because not all women married, and not all marriages were happy:

> The option of marriage, to which so many look with strong confidence as a future dependence for their daughters, is not presented to every woman who deserves it. Should that condition, however, be realized, the expectations therefrom are certain in an indefinite number of cases to be blighted by bereavement and misfortune.[318]

In many cases, women who were raised in comfortable circumstances were disappointed in their hopes that their husbands would provide for them; when the husbands failed to do so, such women were often condemned to a life of (at best) genteel poverty. Hartley called for the overthrow of "the present false and mischievous theory of female education," which held that middle- and upper-class women should not be trained to support themselves.[319] He hoped that more women workers would enter fields that had customarily been reserved to men:

> When the eligibility of the employees are [sic] equal, and the preference for males has no better claims than mere usage, such preference is unjust to female workers, and like every other injustice, is partial and injurious. Many occupations, which from their nature are peculiarly appropriate to females, are now exclu-

sively monopolized by males. An impartial redivision of labor should remedy this injustice, and it probably would soon remedy itself provided female operatives were qualified by training to assert their rights. Skill, competency, fitness, and not sex, should be the test of preference.[320]

Hartley obviously in no way opposed marriage and family ties; instead he believed that "the marriage relation . . . [gives] rise to the primary elements of social order and civilization."[321] But he did take the ideals of self-reliance and self-help with the utmost seriousness, sufficiently enough that he emerges as a sort of protofeminist: to the extent possible, women—just like men—had to be prepared and hence trained to support themselves. No less than Katz, Hartley recognized that family ties could not prevent poverty and dependency for those without them.

The potential dangers posed by women's economic dependence on men emerge most clearly, of course, among women who were deserted by their husbands. One obvious remedy for their plight would have been to provide such women with relief. But moral reformers like Lowell and Richmond were reluctant to do so, because they did not want to encourage desertion. In Lowell's formulation, "Deserted wives with children must not be treated as widows [that is, given "long continued relief" if they have young children], for it has been found that to deal as tenderly with them as sympathy would dictate, leads other men to desert their families, trusting them to charitable care."[322]

One can concede that this policy must have caused great suffering in many individual cases; Lowell herself was honest enough to acknowledge that cases in which "the cause of suffering is moral," and "the innocent suffer with the guilty," are "the most painful," because "there seems almost nothing to be done"[323]—one either ensured the suffering of the innocent or implicitly encouraged the desertions that led to even more suffering. But leaving aside this insoluble dilemma, one can at least say that a moral reformer like Richmond was right to emphasize the acceptance of personal and familial responsibility as a weapon against poverty, right to denounce the abandonment of personal and familial responsibility as a factor that exacerbated it. As all the reformers knew, there are obvious difficulties in attempting to teach people to act responsibly; but then in our time we have discovered that there are also great dangers in refraining from doing so.

SECTION E. KNOWLEDGE AS VIRTUE: WHY MORAL REFORM COULD BE IMPLEMENTED

Preaching the virtues of diligence, sobriety, and thrift, as moral reformers did, can seem to be nothing more than "delivering banal homilies" (in James Q. Wilson's phrase).[324] In fact, as we have seen, reformers preached virtue concretely as well as abstractly: that is to say, they not only explained that diligence, sobriety, and thrift were good for the poor (and why they were good); they also showed how to exercise these virtues—how to increase one's likelihood of finding work, how to motivate oneself to stop drinking or drink less, how to save. Moral reformers were no less eager to convey information to the poor than to preach moral virtue to them.

A classic theme of moral philosophy, dating back to Plato, is that knowledge is virtue. In an important sense, that was the moral reformers' view. Knowledge—about making oneself presentable to an employer; about the cost, taste, and nutritional value of beverages other than liquor; about the wonders of compound interest—was what facilitated and in fact made possible the exercise of the virtues.

It is important to dwell on this point, because these reformers are badly misunderstood if they are seen primarily as stern moralists who despised the poor for dooming themselves to a life of impoverishment by failing to comply with obvious moral truths. Instead, far more often the emphasis was on the ignorance of the poor: by and large, the reformers held, the poor wanted to do what was right; unfortunately, too often they did not know how.

A similar understanding, it is worth pointing out, underlies the "new paternalism" advocated by Lawrence Mead today. Mead explicitly argues that the poor can and should be compelled to obey societal norms—for example, to work in exchange for welfare payments. But the chief reason for expecting that the poor will do what they are told to do is that they "do not question conventional values in principle."[325] If the poor were for the most part truly recalcitrant, truly opposed to working, the compulsory enforcement of the work norm could not succeed; in Mead's view, it can succeed only because in principle the poor want to do what is right.

To be sure, Mead is less concerned to convey items of specific information to the poor than were yesterday's moral reformers: of greater importance for him is the need to alter the psychology of the poor by promoting nondefeatist attitudes.[326] Nevertheless, the moral reformers' efforts to convey information must also have included a psychological component: in effect, the reformers were exhorting the poor to believe that they were competent to master the knowledge needed to reduce their dependency and increase their income.

The reformers' belief that the poor suffered from ignorance more than immorality, however less harsh it may be, can still strike us today as insufferably condescending. But in fact, the attitude must surely have been more or less objectively correct in numerous instances: it would have been astounding if masses of immigrants—many of whom could not speak English—from European peasant societies had arrived in the United States magically equipped with the abilities and attitudes needed to extricate themselves from poverty in urban industrializing America. In reality, of course, the immigrants often did lack the needed abilities and attitudes on arrival, which had to be learned instead on our shores.

The reformers spent a great deal of effort offering practical advice to the poor, who were assumed not to know—but to want to know—essential information. Thus Tuckerman argued that "many of the poor suffer greatly . . . from ignorance, or a disregard of the means of comfort which are within their reach."[327] Channing's eulogy for Tuckerman gives a good sense of the practical advice that he conveyed:

> He was not merely a spiritual guide. He had much skill in the details of common life, was a good economist, understood much about the trades and labors in which the poor are most occupied, could suggest expedients for diminishing expense and multiplying comforts, and by these homely gifts won the confidence of the poor. . . . At the very moment when he passed with some for an enthusiast, he was teaching household management to a poor woman.[328]

Home visitation of the poor, and advising them, figured less prominently in Brace's efforts (since his primary clientele consisted of the children—not the parents—of the poor). But Brace also used visitors:

> Our first effort for any poor district, is to engage a "Visitor," who shall make it his especial duty to find out the deserted and vagrant children of the quarter. He visits regularly from house to house; he searches the docks and lumber-yards, and low lodging-houses, where these children congregate. His first object is rather to gain an influence, to remove prejudices and suspicions, than to effect any immediate result. He advises with the parents, gives clothes and food to the poorest of the children, and tries to become known in the ward as the Friend of the poor—not technically, as a Missionary or Minister, but as a helper.[329]

Hartley, like Tuckerman, believed that many among the poor were ignorant rather than willfully improvident: "Many would be prudent and saving, *if they knew how to be.*"[330] Hartley also realized that the inability of many among the poor to save was seldom a sign of their improvidence: "What opportunity, as a general fact, has a laborer to be extravagant, when the price of his day's work would hardly pay that day's living and lodging in a comfortable tenement in our cities?"[331]

An obvious response to this predicament was not moral reformation of the underpaid, but advice to enable them to stretch their meager wages as far as possible. To convey some of this needed information to the poor, at Hartley's instigation the AICP published a twelve-page pamphlet—"The Economist: Or, Plain Directions About Food and Drink with the Best Modes of Preparation"—of which it distributed 10,000 copies to the poor annually.[332]

Practical Advice

What sort of advice did "The Economist" convey? To buy (or, preferably, bake one's own) bread made out of Indian meal, since it is "almost as nourishing as wheat, and costs not more than half as much"; in general, to buy "such articles as afford the most nourishment for the least money" (including meat, to be eaten by "persons with active out-door employment or other severe bodily labor . . . once a day"); to buy provisions "fresh, and of good quality, from the boats" in the fall, "at a saving of from one third to one half the price you would have to pay the grocer, for poorer articles, at retail"; to "be economical in cooking as well as in buying," by boiling and stewing in covered vessels, without overheating the water (and thereby wasting fuel); and, of course, to drink milk, coffee, tea, or water—anything but liquor (three cents a day spent on liquor "would supply a small family with fuel through the winter"). The pamphlet also offered recipes for cooking items ranging from hasty pudding to beef soup to codfish and potatoes.[333]

Some of these recommendations would presumably have been more applicable than others: one doubts that many tenement residents baked their own bread.[334] Hartley himself tacitly conceded that buying produce in bulk directly from the boats would often have been made difficult if not impossible by the very poverty it was designed to ease. ("Most persons, I believe, by industry and good management, might contrive to save something beforehand, with which to lay in their winter store. To do this may require close living for a while.")[335]

It is true that advice like this, even when most applicable, can seem rather homely when contrasted with the great structural causes of mid-nineteenth-century urban poverty on which historians today focus. Still, given that it was comparatively easy for the poor of New York to learn, say, how to salt pork (and comparatively impossible for them to alter the structural conditions that they confronted), one can reasonably suppose that mundane advice of this sort actually did much good to thousands of poor families.

Reviewing other examples of what he calls "mobility writing" from the same period, Stephan Thernstrom draws a similar conclusion: "A substantial amount of practical information on household management and budgeting was conveyed. . . . The advice . . . offered about economical living was, on the whole, sensible and educational."[336] The humble advice of the AICP and other moral reform organizations—coupled with their advice on practicing the virtues of diligence, thrift, and sobriety—can plausibly be understood (in the words of one welfare historian) as "a liberating creed—there were rules of success and the poor could learn them."[337]

The practical advice conveyed by charity workers in the past can, admittedly, be criticized in the name of a loftier conception of social work. Historian Kathleen Woodroofe dismisses those who "deliver[ed] homilies on the cheapest kinds of food and the mending of clothes," contrasting them unfavorably with the "determined few who preached the worth and dignity of the individual, and believed passionately in the social worker's trained skill to use individual, group, and community resources to help men and women to lead happier lives."[338] Similarly, she hailed the changes in social work that occurred between 1883 (when a typical client was encouraged to mend "a hole in his pocket") and 1948 (when he was encouraged "to know himself").[339]

But this criticism is misdirected. The dichotomy between belief in "the worth and dignity of the individual" and advice about food and clothing is simply false: helping people to live better on small means does not diminish their worth and dignity, but at least potentially enhances them. One may also reasonably suspect that practical advice was far more helpful to most of the poor than Socratic directives to know themselves.

As the example of "The Economist" indicates, the moral reformers understood that a virtue like thrift could effectively be exercised only by those with some knowledge of home economics. Nor was this the only sort of technical information that visitors to the poor attempted to convey. In Mary Richmond's words, the friendly visitor "could do her work better . . . if she were in her own person a lawyer, a sanitary engineer, a trained cook, a kindergartner, and an expert financier."[340] To give an example of the level of expertise that was desired, Richmond went on to note that an observant visitor

> will learn the condition of the cellar, walls, yard, plumbing, and outhouses; will learn to take the cubic contents of a room in order to find out the air space for each sleeper; will learn the family method of garbage disposal; will see how the rooms are ventilated; and will learn all these things without asking many questions.[341]

A crucial component of friendly visiting, then, was the development of expertise in the visitors that could then be passed on to the poor who were visited. In the words of a historian of the practice, "Lady Bountiful brought food baskets to the poor; the friendly visitor hoped to bring scientific knowledge about nutritious diet."[342]

Crossing Class and Ethnic Lines

In theory, of course, conveying helpful information to the poor is unquestionably desirable. In practice, though, one can wonder how often the middle- and upper-class visitors were able to acquire enough expertise truly to provide useful information. To be kind, some of the schemes that were designed to ease the lot of the poor do not inspire confidence: one group of charity workers hoped to supplement the income of a disabled widow "by appealing to ladies leaving town for the summer to board their canaries with the widow for the summer months at the rate of $1 per month."[343] It must also be admitted that, whatever their quality,[344] the quantity of friendly visitors was insufficient: there were rarely enough to go around.[345] In 1887, for example, the New York COS reported a total of only 130 friendly visitors, as compared with Boston's 870.[346] In 1890 the New York COS declared that "we experience our chief failure and discouragement" in friendly visiting.[347]

Finally, it must be admitted that the process of conveying information to the poor was somewhat convoluted: it involved comparatively wealthy people learning about the conditions of the poor in order to offer the poor advice. Would it not have made more sense for the visitors themselves to be poor, since the poor already knew about the conditions in which they lived?

In one sense, the answer to this question is clearly yes, and Richmond for one was obviously aware of the anomaly. She understood that "not every visitor is skilled in buying and preparing food, or in arranging a household budget, and the visitor that is skillful in doing this on one scale of expenditure may be quite ignorant and helpless in dealing with another and much smaller scale."

She contended that "the visitor's best teachers are . . . the poor themselves. One can learn a great deal from the more frugal and industrious of the very poor, and these are proud to explain their small economies, when our reasons for wishing to learn are made clear to them."[348] Similarly, "In teaching thrift in a careless and shiftless home, we can get many valuable suggestions from more thrifty families in the same neighborhood, or with the same income."[349]

At the same time, Richmond recognized that there were practical reasons why the visitors were rich rather than poor. The poor simply lacked the time to do volunteer work: "The visitor may not know [about homemaking], but as compared with the homemaker in a poor family, has far more time and a greater facility, perhaps, in learning."[350] (It is worth mentioning that Richmond herself had personal experience with poverty that differentiated her from almost all of the other figures in the moral reform tradition: she was orphaned at two, brought up by working-class relatives, and "worked for two years at starvation wages" before going to work for the Baltimore COS.)[351]

Many charity workers lamented the fact that visiting was not done by the poor themselves. One, who noted that "an experienced visitor should be able to bring to any work for the material, moral, or legal improvement of the condition of the lowest classes the kind of knowledge of their lives that is possessed by one of themselves," concluded that it would be highly advantageous "if a day laborer of intelligence and character, whose life had brought him very near to his shiftless, destitute neighbors, would become a member of a relief or tenement-house committee."[352] A second observed that "when the friendly visitor coming from a higher grade in society comes into the [poor] family, . . . you meet suspicion and distrust that it takes you a long, long time to overcome," because "the visitors ordinarily know absolutely nothing about the people whom they are called upon to visit," since they have not been "compelled to exercise the small economies, nor undergo the disagreeable things of the life of the working man with all the accompaniments, which are disagreeable." He advocated paying social workers (as opposed to using volunteers), who would have the advantage of "knowing how to make garments, . . . how to purchase food, . . . how to secure a cheap tenement, and all those things which are absolutely necessary to the working man."[353] In practice, however, notes a social welfare historian, "There was no serious effort to recruit visitors from the low-income groups."[354]

The problem posed by visiting across class lines was, of course, exacerbated by the fact that the poor were often of different nationalities than the visitors. An 1892 conference of the Boston Associated Charities pointed to the difficulty of visiting Italian immigrant families:

> Until the Italians became numerous, we had at least intelligent means of communication with most of the families we knew. We not only spoke the same language, but they knew what we were talking about when we urged the advantages

of temperance, industry or economical living. Though their acquiescence in our standards might be feigned and though they might never live up to them, we seldom failed to agree in theory. . . . [But the Italians] are truly foreigners to us. We do not speak a common language; our standards have no meaning to them, and we may well doubt whether they have any applicability.[355]

But this statement almost certainly exaggerated the gulf between the standards of the upper-class reformers and those of the Italian immigrants, to many of whom "the advantages of temperance [if not abstinence], industry [and] economical living" were quite clear. That Italian immigrants were receptive to the virtues extolled by upper-class reformers soon became evident to the reformers themselves. It is significant, for example, that a second Boston charity could declare only seventeen years later that "Italians rank with the most frugal people of the world."[356] Similarly, by 1899 Progressive Era advocates of temperance understood that "the Italians are a temperate people."[357]

More recently, historians have also praised Italian immigrants for their "pattern of hard work" (and concomitant reluctance to accept charity), "frugality," and "low rates of alcoholism."[358] Paradoxically, it was the Italians' "sense of self-reliance" (the very virtue that the visitors hoped to inculcate) that caused them to keep their distance from charity organizations.[359] Italian immigrants may thus have seemed uninterested in the visitors' message precisely because they had already absorbed and accepted much of it.

Still, even if Italian immigrants had more in common with the charity workers than the charity workers (or, one presumes, the immigrants) realized, the fact remains that cross-cultural visiting must have been fraught with difficulties. To be sure, in principle it is obviously the case that knowledge of, say, how to practice household economies can only be beneficial to the poor. But as a practical matter, there is little point in denying that people are more likely—everything else being equal—to accept such advice from people who are like them than from those who are radically different. As we will see in Chapter 3, the contrasting reception apparently given by New York's Irish to the remarkably similar moral messages promulgated by Robert Hartley and Archbishop John Hughes suggests that this was no less true in the nineteenth century than today.

Why the Virtues Were Teachable

The ethnic and religious differences between the reformers and those who were to be reformed point, then, to a difficulty that confronted and still confronts proponents of moral reform. Nevertheless, our discussion of the similarity in outlook between many Italian immigrants and the mostly Protestant reformers who strove to "improve" them (and, more broadly, our focus on virtue as knowledge—facts and techniques needed to facilitate practicing the virtues) may also help answer crucial pedagogical questions about the teachability of virtue. One can plausibly contend (though one certainly cannot prove) that moral reform enjoyed such successes as it did precisely because it was *not* for the most part an exercise in radically transforming the moral outlook of the immoral or amoral.

In other words, one can hypothesize that the reformers could teach the virtues because their "pupils" were to a large extent interested in learning them: the reformers' teaching, that is to say, consisted more of answering "how" questions ("How can I be more thrifty?") than "why" questions ("Why should I try to find work?").[360] If that hypothesis is valid, for the most part the reformers were not trying (and, we will see in Chapter 3, were by their own admission not very successful in trying) to convert nonbelievers, so to speak—to transform the indolent, intemperate, and improvident into the diligent, sober, and thrifty. Instead, moral reform largely presupposed that the poor generally believed something that was surely credible— that virtues like diligence, sobriety, and thrift really would assist them in escaping or at least ameliorating poverty.

But if virtue was understood to be knowledge, the converse was also true. The knowledge that was imparted presupposed the importance of the virtues, and to a large extent consisted of explaining how they could be practiced. Clearly the reformers did not mean to be passing along "value-free" bits of knowledge that the poor could use for any purpose whatsoever.[361] The reformers' message to the poor was not something like this: "You can decide for yourself whether you want to be diligent, but in either case this is what diligence means." Instead, of course, the moral end of diligence (and sobriety, and thrift) was taken for granted: "Obviously, you want to succeed, and obviously, diligence is a virtue that will increase your likelihood of success. Here, then, is what you must do in order to be successfully diligent."

Interestingly, this same focus on the practical application of the virtues—as opposed to theoretical assessment of their merits—is also a hallmark of the new paternalism in welfare policy today. The moral or prudential end is taken for granted; the only question is how to achieve it. Home visitation programs in which nurses counsel low-income expectant mothers about avoiding subsequent pregnancies have shown impressive success. The *Washington Post* accounted for that success in these terms: "The old strategy has been to say, 'If you want to avoid a second baby, here's a condom and how to use it.' The directive approach says, 'You shouldn't have another baby, and here are ways to prevent it.'"[362]

Because they prized knowledge so heavily, the moral reformers thought it more important and more effective to teach the poor than to provide them with material assistance. Lowell, for example, argued as follows:

> To teach some one something—that is a charity in which there is no danger; it is a charity where there can be no overlapping; it is a charity of which there cannot be too much, and the good results of which will never end. No matter who it is, no matter what you teach, whether it be sewing to a little girl, cooking to a big girl, honesty and purity to a youth, neatness and thrift to a woman, industry and

self-control to a man, temperance, morality, or religion, you have done a service, and a service which will never end.[363]

Similarly, Amos Warner contended that "there are dangers inherent in the gifts of free food which do not inhere in the gift of free education. Benevolence may set aside the rule that if a man will not work neither shall he eat, but not the rule that if a man will not study neither shall he learn."[364]

Perhaps the moral reformers were too vehement at times in their opposition to material relief; it is easy to sympathize with the view of C. L. Sulzberger, a former president of New York's United Hebrew Charities, who observed in 1914 that "a hungry widow cannot eat a friendly visitor."[365] But at the same time, it is also unfair to criticize the moral reformers (as historian Robert H. Bremner does), because "the only commodity [that] they dared offer [the poor] was advice."[366] Advice was and still is a commodity of potentially great use to the poor, who are better off insofar as they can improve their condition by actively taking steps on their own to do so (instead of passively receiving alms).

The poor were receptive to the education that they were offered, I suggest, in large measure because and to the extent that the reformers were in effect preaching to the converted, or at least teaching moral and practical lessons that poor people already wanted to learn. And their receptivity had moral as well as material advantages for the poor, the reformers believed; the poor had to exert themselves to acquire their education, by practicing the lessons that were taught, and the poor benefited from doing so.

We now have a sense of what the reformers meant in striving to fight poverty with virtue: how they understood the different virtues, why and how they attempted to teach them. As I hope I have shown, moral reformers had reason to be at least cautiously hopeful about the impact of their work.

It is important to realize, though, that moral reformers were also at most cautiously hopeful about its impact. They were very well aware of many of the difficulties confronting their enterprise, because they understood that the attempt to teach virtue was problematic. It was problematic because of the pedagogical failures of some of the reformers themselves, because of the incorrigibility of some of those most in need of reformation, and because of the gaps—material as well as cultural—that separated almost all of the poor from the proponents of moral reform.

As we have already seen and will see repeatedly in Part Two, the enterprise of moral reform has aroused a great deal of criticism. In some respects, though, the moral reformers were themselves perceptive analysts of its shortcomings. Before turning in Part Two to the external critique of moral reform, we must next consider the reformers' own internal critique, their conception of the obstacles and difficulties confronting moral reform. Doing so will give us a better sense of what moral reform could and could not accomplish in the past—and of what it can and cannot accomplish today.

3 WHY MORAL REFORM WAS HARD TO ACHIEVE

I argued in the introduction that we have returned today by a somewhat circuitous route to the central insight of the nineteenth-century moral reformers: increasingly we recognize that poverty can be fought most effectively to the extent that the poor themselves take personal responsibility for their lives.

But once one agrees about the importance of aiming at moral improvement, the crucial issue, of course, becomes how (not whether) to effect it. And when one thinks through the legacy of the nineteenth century's moral reformers, an important but perhaps unwelcome lesson emerges. According to the reformers' own testimony, assorted obstacles ensured that moral reformation was hard to achieve.

The reformers point to several difficulties that often frustrated their task. The first obstacle was generated by some reformers themselves, who delivered their message ineffectively, insofar as they seemed to attack those whom they wished to improve. A second obstacle was produced, ironically, by the very force providing a basis and motivation for much, if not all, moral reform—the power of religion dramatically to transform people's lives. The religious and cultural heterogeneity of the poor often made it hard for reformers to appeal to the poor in God's name: religious appeals were easily (and appropriately) resisted when they seemed to aim at proselytization, conversion of the poor from their own faith to that of the reformer. And the third obstacle was (and is) intrinsic to the reformist enterprise itself: in the nature of things, transforming seriously misbehaving adults into paragons of virtue (or even average citizens) is an outcome that is devoutly to be wished, but seldom achieved.

Finally, nineteenth-century moral reformers believed that material preconditions greatly affected the likelihood of the success of moral reform; for that reason, they did not regard moral reform as a wholly autonomous enterprise. The reformers held that moral teaching by itself could seldom generate moral improvement; instead, moral improvement often hinged on the prior or at least simultaneous introduction of material improvements in the life of the poor.

Even according to its exponents moral reform was hard to achieve in the past. If their experience is any guide, utopian expectations of the potential impact of moral reform today are unwarranted. In that sense, one important lesson to be learned from our predecessors is not to exaggerate what we can hope to accomplish.

Messages and Messengers

How ought reformers to approach those among the poor whom they seek to improve morally? The obvious answer is with an attitude embodying "tough love":

reformers must make legitimate moral demands upon the poor without despising or degrading them. Tough love, of course, represents a virtuous mean between the extremes of excessive harshness (too tough) and excessive softness (too loving, in a sentimental, undemanding, undiscriminating way). In practice, it is reasonable to ask, how well did the reformers live up to the "tough love" standard? A fair reading of the historical evidence suggests that the record was unfortunately somewhat mixed.

So far as we can tell, Tuckerman beautifully embodied "tough love" in his interactions with the poor. Such, at any rate, was Tocqueville's judgment, based upon his meetings with Tuckerman during his visit to the United States in 1831. Tocqueville praised Tuckerman for being both loving and tough: "If his kindness for [the poor] is extreme, it must not be believed that his severity, whenever just or necessary, is less manifested: the poor love him, because he is their benefactor, and they respect and fear him, because they know the austerity of his virtue."[1] A contemporary historian, wholly unsympathetic to the idea of morally reforming the poor, echoes the conclusion that Tuckerman was loving as well as tough: he observes that Tuckerman "presents antebellum moral reform's most humane face" and grants that "his views helped gain him an audience among the poor."[2]

Tuckerman appears to have manifested genuine respect for the poor in interacting with them. Tuckerman believed that "the minister of the poor can never be authoritative, harsh, severe, or reproachful in manners or in language,"[3] and he strove to live up to this injunction. In one instance, when visiting a married couple (the husband "a journeyman mechanic and abundantly able to provide for his family if he would but give up the use of strong drink"), he saw the husband "lying upon the bed in the deep sleep of thorough intoxication." Returning on another occasion, Tuckerman did not accuse the man, "did not say to [him], 'I saw you drunk upon your bed.'" Instead, he "addressed him with the respect due to a man, and the interest due to a brother." The man subsequently assured Tuckerman that "he would not taste any intoxicating drink till he should see me on the next Sunday."

Tuckerman's story had a happy outcome: the man ceased drinking and the family emerged from poverty. The wife told Tuckerman that "I have now been married twenty years; and in all those years I have not been so happy as I have been during the last three months." Tuckerman ended his account with the following rhetorical question: "Had I treated this man otherwise than with respect, and sympathy, how would he have received me, and how would he have treated my endeavors to reclaim him from intemperance?"[4]

As the preceding quotation suggests, Tuckerman believed that the success of moral reform largely depends on how it is undertaken. One sort of approach, he suggested, is sure to fail—even if its proponent is "by no means deficient in general knowledge, or in earnestness for the cause and kingdom of Christ, or in the qualities of character which command respect—of a certain kind." Nevertheless, such a man might well be unable to speak to the poor of their moral and religious condition, and prospects, except in a manner which could hardly fail to produce a shrinking in the timid; and to make the hardy in sin, through mere opposition to him, more strongly determined in wrong-doing. His views of human nature, and of unregenerated human beings, [would make] him . . . repulsive to those whom he considered sinners.

To succeed, Tuckerman concluded, a moral reformer must instead look "not only to desirable results, but to the means required by common sense, and by some knowledge of the common workings of the human heart, for acting upon human beings in the circumstances in which we are thus called to act upon them."[5]

Unfortunately, those seeking the moral reformation of the poor have not always lived up to Tuckerman's standard or heeded his advice. In fact, Tuckerman's observations on how *not* to attempt moral reform point effectively to the rhetorical shortcomings of a second important reformer—Hartley. Although Hartley's AICP enjoined its agents against "all appearance of harshness, and every manifestation of an obtrusive and censorious spirit,"[6] Hartley himself does not seem to have lived up to this instruction.[7]

The rhetoric directed by Hartley at the poor was harsh; it must sometimes have been counterproductive. He spoke so harshly of the poor in part because they were alien to him: the poor served by the AICP—whose members were mostly native-born Protestants—were predominantly foreign-born and Catholic. In 1852 Hartley noted that "most of the destitution is among foreigners. If the relieved were divided into eight parts, as near as can be estimated, four parts would be Irish, three German and miscellaneous, and but one part American. If divided according to religion, it would be found that at least three-fourths of those asking aid are Roman Catholics."[8]

America's interactions with its poor have always been complicated by the ethnic distinctions that have divided the poor—more precisely, the most visible, urban poor—from the nonpoor: that is obviously true of the black and Hispanic poor today, and it was equally true of the immigrant poor a century ago. A good illustration of the impact of these differences was offered once by Robert Woods, an early leader of the American settlement movement. Woods hypothesized why he, Jane Addams, and so many of his other colleagues were more struck by the problems of poverty during trips to England than at home: because the poor of London had English faces (rather than the faces of Irish, Italian, or Polish immigrants), their poverty made more of an impact on Americans of Anglo-Saxon stock, who "unconsciously . . . saw themselves in tatters."[9] In other words, it was all too easy for Americans of English ancestry to ignore immigrant poverty and take it for granted.

By contrast, Hartley obviously did not ignore the immigrant poverty that he observed. But Hartley was anything but sympathetic to the immigrant poor, whom he criticized harshly. Consider this sample of his rhetoric:

They love to clan together in some out-of-the-way place, are content to live in filth and disorder with a bare subsistence, provided they can drink, and smoke, and gossip, and enjoy their balls, and wakes, and frolics, without molestation.[10]

The reference to "wakes," of course, shows that Hartley had the Irish Catholic poor in mind here.[11]

In a second passage, Hartley imagined a dialogue with interlocutors who were poor. This imaginary dialogue is instructive because it gives us a sense of what Hartley would have liked to say to the poor—whether or not he actually ever said anything like it:

> "We can find no work," is the ready plea of many who ask aid. This may be so, but the plea would come with better grace from many females, after cleaning their own intolerably filthy tenements, and mending their own and children's garments, that are hanging in tatters for want of timely repair. How can we believe you desire work, when you neglect that which thrusts itself on your notice every moment, and the commonest decency requires you to do? It is unreasonable to expect others to trust you with their work, when you so shamefully neglect your own. And because of your disgustingly filthy and ragged appearance, respectable people will not employ you. The cleanly, the industrious, and the sober, readily find work where persons of your description would not be endured. Many of you, therefore, can only blame yourselves that you have no employment. And should we, knowing these things, and our fruitless efforts for your reform, encourage your vile habits by ministering to your relief?[12]

To point to Hartley's grave rhetorical shortcomings is not in any way to deny the reality of the counterproductive, self-destructive behavior that he lamented. It is all too clear from the historical record that large numbers of Irish immigrants did indeed live irregular lives that only perpetuated and worsened the poverty from which they suffered.[13] Nevertheless, Hartley's rhetoric cannot have improved matters, suggesting as it does (in a formulation by social welfare historian Walter I. Trattner) that "members of the A.I.C.P. probably loved the poor less than they feared or perhaps even hated them."[14] It is important to criticize—flatly and unapologetically—self-destructive and immoral behavior that worsens the plight of the poor; but if the criticism is to have any hope of achieving its goal of altering behavior, it must be addressed in such a way that the poor themselves are not treated contemptuously.

This injunction becomes doubly important—as was the case in Hartley's time, and as the case still is today—when religious, ethnic, or cultural divides separate reformers from the objects of their reformation. It is true that we should not stifle all criticism of self-destructive behavior for fear that such criticism amounts to "blaming the victim"; incalculable damage has been done to the poor by the refusal to address the real damage sometimes brought about by their own actions. But at the same time, there is a genuine distinction between constructive and destructive criticism that must also be kept in mind. In other words, the actions of reformers—not just the efforts of those whom they would reform—can be self-defeating.

Hectoring the poor, as Hartley did, is (to use a formulation that has been attributed to Talleyrand) worse than a crime for reformers—it is a blunder. Furthermore, the blunder is particularly serious for a reformer who can plausibly seem—

to those whom he wishes to influence—to be an oppressor; and Hartley, it must be realized, was an English-born Protestant addressing Irish Catholics who had excellent historical reasons to distrust English-born Protestants.

The virtues that Hartley preached—diligence, sobriety, and thrift—were and are genuine virtues whose adoption benefits the poor; when virtues like these were preached to the Irish Catholic poor by a co-religionist like Archbishop John Hughes (a contemporary of Hartley's), they seem to have had much impact in altering self-defeating behavior.[15] But if the message of virtue is universal, it also makes a difference who the messenger is and how he or she words it: one can certainly believe that many of Hartley's Irish Catholic auditors would have concluded that to be diligent, sober, and thrifty was to "act English" (just as self-advancing behavior—studying hard, being sexually continent—is occasionally derided in the black ghettos of today as "acting white").[16] Sociologist David Matza has argued that "pauperization implies . . . a view in which work is taken as punishment or penalty."[17] It is more than conceivable that Hartley's tone would have led some among the Irish Catholic poor to the view that Hartley was attempting to penalize them by urging them to find work.

It is insufficient to celebrate the ends at which moral reform aims, important and worthy as those ends undoubtedly are. Because the medium is an essential part of the moral message, moral reform has been and can be undertaken in ways that are guaranteed to ensure its failure: those who would improve the poor err grievously when they seem to attack them.

Difficulties of Religious Reformation

In a sense it is misleading to refer to Tuckerman and Hartley as moral reformers, because they can more accurately be understood as religious reformers. Their moral vision flowed directly from their belief in God. Religion is an omnipresent theme in the writings of Tuckerman, Hartley, and Brace. (Like Tuckerman, Brace was an ordained Protestant clergyman.)

But in what respects did the reformers' work among the poor actually aim to convey any sort of religious teaching? Here matters become more complicated: religion—more precisely, religious pluralism—posed problems for the reformers in addition to offering solutions.

A recent student of the moral reformers, Marvin Olasky, has made much of the religious component of their work. For instance, he celebrates their insight that "the most important need of the poor who were unfaithful was to learn about God and God's expectations for man," and he alludes to the AICP's emphasis on "piety" as well as "frugality and industry" as a remedy for poverty.[18] In discussing the twentieth-century rejection of the moral approach to poverty, Olasky—who is himself a Christian conservative—harshly criticizes the settlement houses for rejecting religious affiliations: "Out went the hymns and testimonies and in came political action."[19]

But these remarks gloss over genuine difficulties that the antipoverty reformers were well aware of, difficulties with which they wrestled (not altogether successfully). They reflect a notion of piety that is too abstract: it ignores the vital differences among individual religious denominations. Pascal, the great seventeenth-century French defender of religion, is renowned for arguing that the God of the philosophers differs from the God of Abraham, Isaac, and Jacob; but it is also true —and of great practical importance for moral reform—that the God of Abraham, Isaac, and Jacob tended to be understood somewhat differently by Protestants (the reformers) than by Jews and (especially) Catholics (those who were to be reformed).

This difficulty, already evident in Tuckerman's time, is chiefly responsible for the secular tone of settlement houses at the turn of the century. If Jane Addams's Hull House was determinedly nondenominational, it was not because Addams herself was irreligious (though she did become an agnostic in later years);[20] in fact, she argued at its founding that Hull House was "better" than a New York settlement house, because it was "more distinctively Christian and less Social Science."[21] Why, then, did Hull House de-emphasize religion? Because Addams was Protestant and the large majority of those she hoped to serve were Catholics and Jews: a seriously religious settlement house (that is, one devoted to espousing the spiritual views of a particular denomination) could not possibly have appealed to the immigrant clientele on the west side of Chicago.[22]

But the difficulties faced by Addams were no different from those confronted by earlier reformers, who made comparable attempts to secularize their philanthropy. Reformers like Hartley, Brace, and Lowell were acutely aware of the fact that it would be deeply counterproductive for their organizations to preach Protestant piety to the Catholic poor. In the words of historian Paul Boyer, "With the immigrant population becoming increasingly Roman Catholic, the sectarian coloration" of earlier efforts to moralize the urban poor "came to be seen as a liability, and it was played down by the new generation of urban reformers"—specifically, by Hartley and Brace.[23]

For exactly the same reasons, Boyer adds, Lowell's "charity organization movement not only arose outside the [Protestant] church but took pains to remove itself from the church's shadow."[24] In fact, when New York's COS was founded in 1882, the first two of its three "fundamental principles" highlighted its wholly secular character: the first declared that "every department of its work shall be completely severed from all questions of religious belief"; the second proclaimed that "no person representing the Society in any capacity whatsoever shall use his or her position for the purpose of proselytization or spiritual instruction."[25]

As early as Tuckerman's time, this split between Protestant reformers and a largely Catholic poor thought to be in need of moral reformation posed obvious difficulties. Most notably, it precluded any serious attempt at instilling piety in poor people of a different denomination. Although Tuckerman lived before the huge influx of Irish Catholics into Boston, some of the poor with whom he dealt were Catholic. He had the good sense to recognize that "We as christian [sic] ministers [i.e., Protestant ministers] can accomplish comparatively little good" working with the Catholic poor.[26] He worked with the Catholic bishop of Boston to set up a lay Catholic ministry for the Catholic poor.[27]

Hartley also came to the realization that Irish Catholics could not "to any considerable extent be reached and influenced by Protestants, whom they regard as schismatics and heretics." He called upon "the Romish church" to undertake the "great work" of "recover[ing] . . . these semi-barbarous masses to civilization, and to such habits of self-control as are, at least, necessary to the order and stability of society."[28] If only religion could motivate moral reform, Hartley perceived, only Catholicism could motivate the moral reform of Catholics.

Responding to the problems posed by disputes between rival denominations, Hartley explicitly de-emphasized the religious character of the AICP's work. Although he was a deeply religious man, accurately described by one historian as "intensely evangelical,"[29] Hartley also took pains to declare that the "design" of the AICP was "economical and moral, rather than religious—more preventive than remedial."[30] We can reasonably suppose that Hartley rejected religious reformation as the goal of the AICP because he correctly realized that most of the poor whom he hoped to elevate professed a religion different from his own. Moral reform had to be secular—"economical and moral, rather than religious": religious pluralism made any other course unthinkable.

The problems that religion posed for the moral reformers emerge still more clearly in Brace's work. If his rhetoric is any indication, Brace must have been a more appealing figure than Hartley. In the words of a notable critic of moral reform, he seems to have been "one of the few reformers who liked the people with whom he worked."[31] Brace's affection for the poor is, in fact, evident in his social theories. He was an optimistic social Darwinist, who believed that "in the lowest class, the more self-controlled and virtuous tend constantly to survive, and to prevail in 'the struggle for existence,' over the vicious and the ungoverned, and to transmit their progeny. The natural drift among the poor is towards virtue."[32]

Nevertheless, the Catholicism of so many of the intended beneficiaries of his organization's largesse posed great problems for Brace—much more than it did for Hartley. This was because the centerpiece of Brace's charitable efforts was not just the transformation but the transportation of his clientele: Brace hoped to benefit the street urchins of New York by placing them with farm families in upstate New York and the midwest, where their reformation (begun in institutions like the Children's Aid Society's lodging houses and industrial schools) would be confirmed by newly acquired familial ties, away from the temptations to immorality presented by the big city.

Brace referred to the family as "God's reformatory."[33] Unfortunately, by that he meant not the natural families of the street urchins whom he attempted to assist (many of whom were Catholic, and by no means all of whom were orphans)[34]—but their prospective rural adoptive families, virtually all of which were Protestant.

Not surprisingly, many Catholics opposed Brace's efforts, which they feared would culminate in the proselytization of Catholic youths. Brace, for his part, resented the Catholic suspicion of his efforts. He wrote of "the opposition . . . of the bigoted poor, . . . undoubtedly under the influence of some of the more prejudiced priests, who suppose that the poor are thus removed from ecclesiastical influences. A class of children, whom we used thus to benefit, are now sent to the Catholic Protectory."[35]

Daniel Patrick Moynihan has observed that "doing good for others can be a risky business if the others in question do not happen to share the same tastes."[36] Clearly that was part of the difficulty that Brace confronted: he was frustrated by the reluctance of Catholic parents to allow their offspring to receive his benefactions. But their reluctance was hardly perverse. As Boyer has pointed out, it was not at all unreasonable of Catholic parents to fear "an urban order in which the frayed bonds of family, community, and church could be severed with a single stroke by a charitable organization determined to release slum children from the few social strands still holding them, thus granting them the ambiguous gift of total freedom."[37]

Oblivious to the Catholic point of view, Brace criticized "the chilling formalism of the ignorant Roman Catholic," in whom "the very inner ideas of our spiritual life of free love towards God, true repentance and trust in a Divine Redeemer, seemed wanting." Brace insisted that he "never had the least ambition to be a proselytizer, and never tried to convert [Catholics], and . . . certainly had no prejudice against the Romanists." But at the same time, he also contended that certain "poor people seemed stamped with the spiritual lifelessness of Romanism."[38]

For our purposes here, though, the central issue is not Brace's low opinion of Catholicism but the impact of the Catholicism of the poor upon his philanthropy. Because so many of his potential clients were Catholic, Brace had to mute the religious instruction that he offered: the preponderance of Catholics among the poor, he observed, "compelled us to confine ourselves to the most simple and fundamental [religious] instructions, and to avoid, in any way, arousing religious bigotry."[39] Like Tuckerman and Hartley, Brace also recognized that the Catholic priesthood might remoralize the Catholic poor in a way that Protestants like him could not.[40]

The crucial point, though, is that in many respects Brace's Children's Aid Society had to act as a secular charity. Its secularism is evident first in Brace's willingness to hire charity workers of "no defined religious belief."[41] And it becomes clearer still in a comment reported by Jacob Riis (a great supporter of Brace's work). Riis quoted a Children's Aid Society worker who insisted that "No Catholic child . . . is ever brought to us. A *poor* child is brought and we care for it."[42]

This statement implies that religion is irrelevant: it could easily emerge from the lips of a staffer at an altogether secular contemporary charity like the Children's Defense Fund. But the statement also perfectly exemplifies the dilemma faced by the Protestant moral reformers. Because Catholics and Protestants worship God in different ways, charities that were—so to speak—compelled to be nonsectarian simply could not promote piety in any serious way.

Brace himself was undeniably an intensely religious man. Nevertheless, good reasons explain why Brace's confederate had to ignore religion by emphasizing the poverty rather than the Catholicism of the children whom he served. Nineteenth-century Protestant reformers had to soft-pedal religion while emphasizing what in effect was a secular (or at least an ecumenical) moral consensus in support of the virtues of diligence, sobriety, and thrift.

Skepticism about Rehabilitation

Olasky rightly notes that the moral reformers insisted that recipients of charitable aid had "an obligation to change" the behaviors thought to be responsible for their impoverishment; he celebrates "the challenge to change [self-destructive behavior], not subsidy of sordidness" that characterized their philanthropy.[43] Unfortunately, though, to say that charities strive to change their recipients' behavior is not to say that they succeed in doing so easily or often.

The moral reformers were all too well aware of this particular distinction between "ought" and "is," between what they tried to do and what they actually achieved. When one examines the reformers' evaluations of their own activities, it is striking how dubious they were about their capacity to reform the misbehaving adult poor. Indications of skepticism about the likelihood of genuine moral rehabilitation are scattered throughout the reformers' writings.

A fair generalization would be that the earlier reformers—Tuckerman and Hartley—were more confident of the possibility of rehabilitation than their successors. Still, even Tuckerman and Hartley were clearly aware that in practice rehabilitative efforts were often doomed to failure.

At times, Tuckerman expressed great optimism about moral reformation. (For that reason, Beaumont and Tocqueville gently mocked his belief that "a day will appear, when, all the wicked having been regenerated, prisons will no longer be wanted.")[44] Yet Tuckerman was remarkably cautious in his estimation of what could be accomplished, declaring only that "there may be at least an *apparently real restoration*," even in a "desperate" case.[45]

Tuckerman, a comparative optimist about the possibility of rehabilitation, thought that in dealing with the degenerate one could perhaps prove that "the principle of moral life, and the capacity of moral feeling, are not, in truth, *wholly* extinct"—not exactly a ringing endorsement of the likelihood of regeneration. "To carry out the rule that human nature is never to be given up," Tuckerman recognized that in "many" cases we must "hope against hope, and labor without making even the smallest apparent progress"; if we do, he contended only that "*some* occasion *may* be given in the providence of God, in which a way will be opened for us that we thought not of."[46] It is safe to say that the Reverend Joseph Tuckerman was not a betting man; but if he had been, he would presumably have offered long odds to anyone wishing to wager in favor of the likelihood of thoroughgoing moral reformation.

Like Tuckerman, Hartley possessed a millennial streak; he believed in the possibility of universal reformation, at least in the long run. (Conceivably it was this very hope for universal reformation that brought about the irritation with the poor evident in Hartley's writings: if poor people's recalcitrance was delaying the onset of the republic of virtue that he hoped to bring into being, it is no wonder that Hartley was angry about it—and with them.) Hartley's millennialism is most evident in his 1856 declaration that

> the masses, beginning with the individual, are improvable. They can be improved physically, morally and intellectually. And if the individual can be reclaimed, why not the masses? Who will affirm of any living man that he is irreclaimable?[47]

But in practice it was Hartley himself who affirmed that some men are irreclaimable. He believed that "little is to be hoped from any reformatory efforts" directed at "grossly immoral" adults.[48] In fact, that pessimism is apparent even in the millennial passage quoted above, which concluded with these words: "If there is less hope of adults, there is greater hope of children, who are the promise of the future."[49]

This theme of irredeemable adults and reformable children was central to Brace's outlook as well. Brace, in fact, unambiguously proclaimed the futility of attempting to rehabilitate adults. He founded the Children's Aid Society precisely because he despaired of doing so:

> I became convinced that no far-reaching and permanent work of reform could succeed among [the unfortunate and criminal population]. It was right that those who loved humanity in its lowest forms should labor for the forlorn prostitute, and the mature criminal. But on a broad scale no lasting effects could be expected to society from such efforts. The work seemed like pouring water through a sieve. The hopeful field was evidently among the young. There, crime might possibly be checked in its very beginnings, and the seed of future good character and order and virtue be widely sown.[50]

Brace's view was shared by Lowell, who proclaimed in 1898 that "the most important work to be done among the poor is for the children." She went on to add that "I am almost inclined to declare that nothing else is of any importance at all, as compared with it, for *every other branch of charitable work produces but small results* and for only short periods of time, while what is done for the children may make the difference for each child between a whole long life of virtue or of vice, and may make the difference for the community between a large or a small number of paupers for hundreds of years."[51]

At issue here is not simply the particular beliefs of Brace and Lowell. More

85

broadly, it is important to realize that American social policy's emphasis on the importance of reforming the young—an emphasis already apparent in efforts undertaken by Tuckerman to assist wayward children, and still evident in the hopes placed in a contemporary program like Head Start—amounts to a tacit concession of the likely incorrigibility of self-destructive adults. Stephan Thernstrom once expressed this view pungently, speaking of "the old American belief that the adults can go to hell so long as you do something to rescue the kids."[52]

The comparatively greater ease of forming children (as opposed to reforming adults) relates to a second important belief of the moral reformers—that prevention is easier to effect than cure. The importance of prevention—and the concomitant difficulty of cure or rehabilitation—was a theme that Lowell in particular emphasized.

In one paper Lowell went on at some length about the importance of creating institutions to reform vagrant and wayward girls and young women, "to convert them, to make them take an entirely different view of life, of themselves and of the world."[53] Abruptly, though, at the end of the paper Lowell reversed herself, discounting the likelihood (and even the importance) of the reformation that she herself had been arguing for: "But after all it is not by means of such institutions . . . that we shall finally succeed in really diminishing the number of unhappy women who need 'reformation.'" Instead, she emphasized prevention (specifically, improving the lot of female wage earners).

Lowell advocated "mak[ing] the life of wage-earners less hard" as an appropriate response to the efforts of "the loathsome beast, Sin," that lay in wait for those who fled from "the relentless machine of daily toil, grinding and crushing those who labor." It was better to strive "to diminish the killing speed, and the crushing weight" of that machine than to concentrate exclusively on "trying to rescue a few from the jaws of the beast."[54] It was more important to alter the conditions that led women to go bad than to reform them once they had gone bad.

Elsewhere Lowell was to develop this contrast, declaring that the "preventive" work of charity organizations was "by far" more "valuable and . . . encouraging" than the "curative" work. Because curative or rehabilitative work was "difficult" and "disheartening," it was important instead "to start from the beginning to *prevent* pauperism rather than to wait until it has assumed gigantic proportions, and then try to crush it."[55]

Nor was Lowell by any means unusual in believing that rehabilitation was seldom effected. Instead, that view seems to have been standard among her contemporaries in the charity organization movement.[56] Lowell's judgment was certainly shared by Amos Warner, the author of the first scholarly assessment of American philanthropic accomplishments. Surveying the work of all American charities as of 1894, Warner concluded: "Except among dependent children, the cure of dependency is the exception rather than the rule."[57]

To say that moral rehabilitation is unlikely is not, of course, to say that it is impossible. Charities that spurn moral uplift altogether still deserve criticism, because their failure to attempt it virtually assures that rehabilitation will not occur. Even the reformers who discounted rehabilitation acknowledged that it occasionally took place. While Brace declared that working for adult reformation was "like pouring water through a sieve," he also recounted the example of one Orville (nicknamed "Awful") Gardner, a prizefighter whose case, he claimed, showed "the reforming power of Christianity on the most abandoned characters."[58]

Still, it is important to realize that the reformers' hopes for moral rehabilitation of the fallen were on the whole remarkably muted. We hear much today of the wonders that might be worked (and are being worked) by faith-based charities; but a glance at the historical record suggests that caution is indicated. In an age in which elites tended to take faith far more seriously than they generally do today, reformers who were deeply religious and deeply intent on effecting moral improvements doubted that their efforts redeemed many of the dissolute.

The Interplay of Matter and Morals

The moral reformers certainly believed that the moral virtue of the poor would render their poverty less onerous; but as our discussion of Lowell has already suggested, at the same time they also thought that material improvements might have to be made before large numbers of poor people could reasonably be expected to act virtuously. The Marxist playwright Bertolt Brecht is famous for cynically asserting that *"Erst kommt das Fressen, dann kommt die Moral"* (first comes eating, and morality comes only thereafter). The moral reformers were anything but cynical. Surprisingly, though, in some respects they agreed with Brecht.

The supposed gulf between nineteenth-century reformers intent on morally uplifting the poor and their twentieth-century successors eager to better their environment can easily be exaggerated; the nineteenth-century reformers consistently advocated both moral and environmental reforms, which were thought to be complementary rather than contradictory. For that reason it is unfair to portray environmental reform (for example, the construction of better housing for the poor) as a total departure from moral reform, a reflection of the superficial belief that "the primary cause of immorality [is] not sin, but lack of housing projects."[59]

To be sure, it is unreasonable to suppose that housing projects in and of themselves will eliminate sin or somehow render sin irrelevant as a cause of human misery; and the moral reformers never made this error. But it is not at all unreasonable to suppose, as the moral reformers did, that preaching salvation to the miserably destitute will do them little good. It may well be the case that compassion should not mean "accepting wrongful activity and postponing any pressure to change until the person [is] in a good environment";[60] on the other hand, as a prudential judgment it may also make sense to believe that people must be "in a good [or at least not in a terrible] environment" before results can be expected from exerting "any pressure to change" their self-destructive behaviors.

At any rate, that was the judgment of the moral reformers. Tuckerman believed that "religious instruction . . . forms but one, though without doubt the most important," part of the service of the ministry of the poor. It formed only one part because physical wants "must not, and by a mind which has any of the benevolence of the gospel cannot, be disregarded; for how can we hope to make religious impressions, or to exert religious influences upon the soul, while the half-clad, shivering starving body asks for fuel, or for food, or for a garment as the greatest of blessings?"[61]

Moral reform, then, was impossible without relief of pressing material needs. But at the same time, satisfying physical needs was also not an end that could be addressed in and of itself. Tuckerman went on to argue that "even to meet these pressing necessities wisely and effectually, we must look beyond them"[62] — toward the development of character, specifically toward the increase of the powers of self-reliance. While he did not understand physical relief as an end in itself, he did see it as a necessary means to a higher, spiritual end.

Similarly, Lowell endorsed environmental and structural reforms — "mak[ing] the lives of wage-earners less hard" — as the most effective means to a moral end, decidedly more effective than moral rehabilitation itself. As we saw in Chapter 2, she was a great proponent of labor unions and a supporter of William Jennings Bryan's presidential candidacy.

Lowell attempted to use what might today be considered "liberal" means (improving the material environment of the poor) to achieve "conservative" ends (improving their character). We may surmise that she would have been uncomfortable with much of the contemporary debate over poverty, in which partisans of right and left too often argue as though a moral and a material focus are mutually exclusive.

Housing Reform and Moral Reform

The real question regarding the interplay of material and moral factors arose, though, with respect to housing — the very issue on which environmental reformers are sometimes taken to task for ignoring the importance of moral considerations. Tuckerman argued that if the poor were "to have the domestic virtues, they must have *homes* in which these virtues may be cultivated"[63] — as opposed to the overcrowded, pestilential slums in which too many of the poor were compelled to reside.

The theme of housing reform as the key to moral reform was amplified by Hartley. A stringent critic of the morals of the poor, Hartley nevertheless believed that moral reform could be achieved only after improvements were made in the environment in which they lived. Hartley contended that improved housing for the poor was a necessary — though obviously not sufficient — condition for their moral improvement. He argued that housing reform "lies at the basis of other reforms; and as the health and morals of thousands are injured or destroyed by the influence of circumstances around them, an improvement of the circumstances in connection with other appropriate means, afford[s] *the only rational hope of effectually elevating their character* and condition."[64]

Hartley developed these ideas in an 1853 AICP special report "on the sanitary condition of the laboring classes in the city of New-York." Here he linked all manner of moral improvements to the housing question. For example, better housing would encourage the poor to be both thrifty and clean. The poor were made "filthy, reckless and vicious, by the force of circumstances, over which, in most cases, they have no control."[65]

Better housing would also improve sexual morality: "The absence of all necessary accommodations in many dwellings, and the crowded state of the rooms, which defies all attempts at decency and modesty, breaks down the barriers of self-respect, and prepares the way for direct profligacy. How should members, often of different families and of different sex, sleep in the same room, nay, often in the same bed, without danger?"[66]

Bad housing was even held responsible for the intemperance of the poor: "In regard to the proneness of [the poor] to *intemperance*, it is said, 'That the dreadful depression consequent on ill health (the effect of crowded, filthy, badly ventilated dwellings), tempts these poor creatures with a force we cannot adequately appreciate, to have recourse to stimulating drink.'" And if bad housing promoted intemperance, better housing would reduce it. Hartley approvingly quoted an employer who contended that "if you make the workingman's home comfortable, he will give up the public house and its ruinous consequences."[67]

Hartley concluded that attempts to elevate the character of the degraded poor would be fruitless unless one "first improv[ed] their physical condition."[68] "If many are debased," he contended, "what better could be expected from the circumstances in which they are obliged to live? Physical evils produce moral evils. Degrade men to the condition of brutes, and they will have brutal propensities and passions."[69]

Hartley advocated building model tenements as a means to the moral elevation of the poor. Sin, rather than bad housing, may have been the cause of immorality for Hartley; but bad housing would have to be improved—in effect, by the creation of housing projects (to be run not by the government but by philanthropic investors satisfied with a small profit)—if sin was to be reduced among the poor:

> If those who are now crowded into filthy and uncomfortable rooms, were put in clean, well-contrived apartments, suited to their necessities, and charged less for the new accommodations than they paid for the old; if they were assured that there is a disposition to improve their condition, by giving all that in this respect is necessary for their comfort, and can be afforded for the rent, on the expressed condition of punctuality and good conduct on their part, we would not only have a strong hold upon their gratitude, but upon their selfishness. They can in no other way serve themselves so well, as in doing their duty to the landlord, by the prompt payment of rent, and the preservation of his property. It is reasonable,

therefore, to conclude, that they will make every effort to do this, and not deliberately oppose their own interests.[70]

The poor to be housed in model tenements were not to be subsidized but were to pay a fair rent; thus the poor would not be pauperized by such housing, since "self-reliance . . . would not be undermined." Instead, "the prospect of a healthful, comfortable home would stimulate exertion, while its possession would exert a most salutary influence in reforming and elevating character. . . . An increase of physical comforts will induce a higher tone of morals, and prepare the way for the success of religious influences."[71] Hartley would have amended Brecht, it appears, only by focusing on housing rather than food as the necessary precursor to moral improvement: *Erst kommen die Häuser, dann kommt die Moral—und die Religion.*

The model tenement movement inaugurated by Hartley and the AICP did not, in fact, solve either the moral or material problems of the poor. The movement has been persuasively criticized by both left and right. Critics from the left have noted that far too few model tenements were ever built to improve the housing of the poor, in large part because entrepreneurs were unwilling to accept the below-market profits that were essential if housing that was both better and more affordable was to be constructed.[72] Critics on the right agree, differing chiefly in arguing that the market (hampered as it was by well-intentioned but counterproductive government regulations) was doing much to improve the housing of the poor.[73] Both sorts of critics contend that Hartley's central premise—that better housing for the poor would uplift them morally—was faulty.[74]

Furthermore, the AICP's own pilot project for model tenements—a lower-Manhattan building that was constructed for the AICP in 1854—failed spectacularly; it degenerated into a terrible slum that the AICP itself was to denounce (after it had changed ownership several times) as unfit for human habitation.[75] (Interestingly enough, though, the tenement's failure points to the centrality of the very moral issues that Hartley highlighted in his analysis of poverty. One important reason for its deterioration was the bad character of the surrounding neighborhood and the failure to exclude criminals from the property. The vast majority of the tenants were "law abiding, industrious, and necessarily thrifty souls" who became the prey of the drunks, prostitutes, loiterers, and opium addicts who frequented the neighborhood and rented some of the rooms. A contemporary observer concluded that the tenement failed chiefly because the property was never policed and supervised by "an agent equal to the preservation of peace or the enforcement of any rules.")[76]

Hartley signally failed to improve the moral character of the poor by building a model tenement for them. But at the same time, the failure of a remedy does not prove the faultiness of a diagnosis. The slum conditions denounced by Hartley (and, a generation later, by Jacob Riis) really were intolerable. Hartley had good reason to be horrified by New York's cellar dwellings, "in some instances six feet under ground—which have to be baled [*sic*] out after every rain storm—and are so damp as to destroy health—so dark as to prevent industry—and so low that ventilation is impossible."[77] He also spoke of areas where "sewerage [was] but partly introduced," which were characterized by "accumulations of fluid, filth, and putrid mud, poisoning the atmosphere."[78] Other contemporary observers testified to tenement conditions made unbearable by overcrowding: for example, an 1853 newspaper article depicted a room twenty feet long and twelve feet wide, which housed twenty residents from some five families but contained only two beds.[79]

Descriptions like these do much to strengthen the credibility of Hartley's analysis: the filth and the overcrowding must certainly have made it difficult if not impossible for families and individuals to live healthy and virtuous lives. But his analysis was most plausible, of course, in the particular circumstances that he witnessed. By contrast, once rudimentary improvements in housing had been made, hopes that better housing would continue to promote moral regeneration became far less realistic—and critiques of housing reform as a panacea became far more pertinent.

The moral utopianism of latter-day housing reformers was effectively satirized in 1958 by *Fortune* editor Daniel Seligman, quoting an amusing if cruel observation offered by a cynic described as a "close student of New York's slums":

> Once upon a time we thought that if we could only get our problem families out of those dreadful slums, then papa would stop taking dope, mama would stop chasing around, and Junior would stop carrying a knife. Well, we got them in a nice new apartment with modern kitchens and a recreation center. And they're still the same bunch of bastards they always were.[80]

By contrast, the poor of Hartley's time were confronted not by the absence of "modern kitchens and a recreation center," but by conditions that are unimaginable today: unbelievably overcrowded dwellings with no ventilation and no plumbing. In those circumstances it made much intuitive sense to suppose that a threshold of material provisions exists—and that those living beneath it could not reasonably be expected to practice the moral virtues.

Let us return, though, from the specific question of housing to the larger issue of moral character in relation to the material environment. What role does the material environment play in affecting moral character? As we have seen, moral reformers believed that material circumstances mattered: although moral character does not simply depend on the environment, in practice it is greatly affected by it. That view was well formulated by the most important of the twentieth-century moral reformers, Mary Richmond: "There is a level [of environmental and material conditions] below which character has no opportunity to assert itself."[81]

Richmond, who was always admirably level-headed, went on to point out that "everything . . . depends upon where this minimum level is established. It is easy to place it for large groups much too high and thereby only cripple them; but it is also possible to place it too low." For our purposes here, though, what matters is that moral reform depends upon a material threshold being met. The moral reformers were not (and today's moral reformers cannot be) indifferent to the material circumstances affecting the lives of the poor.

That is particularly true because the virtues preached by moral reform—diligence, sobriety, and thrift—are themselves intended precisely to better those material circumstances. But as the reformers realized, the relation between the virtues and material circumstances is reciprocal. For that reason, if material circumstances decreased the effectiveness of the virtues, the moral reformers were perfectly willing to endorse structural reforms: the hope was that better material circumstances would increase the effectiveness of the virtues as weapons against poverty. For example, if long hours of hard work failed to reduce poverty because workers were underpaid, a moral reformer like Lowell eagerly advocated measures like the unionization of labor and the imposition of maximum-hour laws.

To summarize, we can say that the moral reformers were very well aware that it is hard to fight poverty with virtue, because it is often hard to teach and to learn the practice of the virtues. Virtue can be taught ineffectively; even when it is taught well, the lessons may nevertheless go unapplied in many cases, for a variety of psychological, cultural, and material reasons.

Significantly, though, the problems to which the moral reformers pointed raised questions of practicality rather than principle. Various circumstances might make it difficult to encourage the practice of the virtues; in principle, however, the teaching of the virtues was always desirable, because the virtues were thought to enable those armed with them to combat poverty more effectively.

But the reformers' own critique, which raised questions about the practicality of teaching the virtues in some circumstances, should not be confused with a more radical critique—launched not by the reformers but by their opponents—that questioned the desirability of teaching the virtues in principle. In a remarkable transvaluation of values, the moral reformers' preference for teaching the poor (as opposed to granting them unconditional material aid) was reversed. The reformers had argued that material assistance was pauperizing. By contrast, a contemporary critic of moral reform contends that the true agent of pauperization was the very teaching that the reformers thought essential: in attempting to "reorder [the] lives" of the poor, in purveying "advice" that they insisted be accepted, nineteenth-century charity workers undermined independence, "taught the poor to be paupers."[82] In this view, independence is not to be achieved by practicing behaviors likely to facilitate self-reliance (at least if those behaviors are taught by someone else); instead it is to be achieved by receiving subsidies that make it easier to behave however one likes.

That altered understanding points to the collapse of the moral consensus regarding the intrinsic desirability of the virtues as well as their utility as weapons against poverty. But how and why did that consensus collapse? We can begin to understand its collapse by considering the motives for rejecting laissez-faire economics and individualist ethics, as articulated by two of the towering figures of the early twentieth century: settlement house leader Jane Addams, and the influential proponent of the Social Gospel, Walter Rauschenbusch. Addams and Rauschenbusch by no means opposed moral reform in all respects; but they did level important criticisms that continue to resonate today.

PART TWO
THE CRITIQUE AND REJECTION OF MORAL REFORM

4 THE DECLINE OF LAISSEZ-FAIRE AND THE CRITIQUE OF MORAL REFORM

SECTION A. INTRODUCTION

Two themes have emerged in Part One that must now be developed as we continue to analyze the meaning and fate of moral reform. First, proponents of moral reform increasingly came to recognize the desirability of structural reform as its complement, if not its precondition. In other words, moral reformers began to favor abridgments of individualist, laissez-faire economics in order to increase the efficacy of the virtues of individuals in relieving poverty. Brace's prophetic support of social insurance (to supplement the workings of individual thrift) and Lowell's advocacy of collective bargaining and maximum-hour laws (to increase the likelihood that diligence would receive its just reward, and to maintain diligence as the virtuous mean between enervating indolence and killing overwork) exemplify this development.

Second, there is reason to suppose that the immigrant poor were for the most part receptive to the virtues espoused by the reformers. Soon we shall look at additional evidence supporting this contention. In the meantime, it is worth noting that the policies put forth by Brace and Lowell implicitly confirm it as well. Support for social insurance, collective bargaining, and maximum-hour laws involved a recognition that the poor on the whole were virtuous (diligent and thrifty), but that their virtue was insufficiently rewarded: the poor worked and strove to save, but they could not save enough to support themselves when out of work (or old, or ill), because they were underpaid and overworked.

The later moral reformers unquestionably believed that the poor were not receiving the just deserts of their diligence—and that certain restrictions on laissez-faire capitalism were justifiable. Brace contended that "the great problem of the future is the equal distribution of wealth, or of the profits of labor," because he believed that "in general, the laboring classes do not receive their fair share." Brace was sympathetic to strikes ("one of their means of getting more")[1] and to profit-sharing schemes (in which industrial society could rise "to the Christian ideal," as laborers enjoyed "a pecuniary interest in the profits of production beyond their wages").[2]

Similarly, Lowell declared that it was "more vital" to secure the interests of the "five hundred thousand wage earners" in New York, 75,000 of whom "work[ed] under dreadful conditions or for starvation wages," than to worry about the existence of "25,000 dependents, counting the children"—that is, pauper families. "If the working people had all they ought to have, we should not have the paupers and criminals."[3]

Support for laissez-faire policies decreased, even among moral reformers, as it came to be believed that the virtues of the poor were not fairly rewarded in and by the unrestricted free market: the moral virtues that precluded pauperism did not always or automatically lift people out of poverty. But once the link between virtue and prosperity began to be questioned, one can wonder about the fate of the virtues espoused by the reformers: Could those virtues consistently be promoted (and be expected to flourish) once laissez-faire capitalism began to be abridged (if not abandoned)?

After all, the reformers' virtues were individualist virtues, advocated not only as ends in themselves, but also as means to the end of success in an individualist economic order. It is certainly arguable that these virtues are most compatible with an individualist economic order and will wane in a more collectivist one: Why strive to be provident if the state will extract you from poverty despite your improvidence?[4]

As an empirical matter it is also fair to say that the virtues had been espoused in part because of America's commitment to laissez-faire—and, concomitantly, that laissez-faire had prevailed because it was believed that the virtues sufficed to get people out of poverty. Since the poor could not count on assistance from anyone else (and certainly not from the government), they were not unreasonably urged to take steps themselves to better their condition by manifesting the virtues. And since the virtues were thought to be effective in mitigating poverty, there was little justification for government to interfere in the marketplace on behalf of the poor.

The question, then, is whether and to what extent the slow movement of America's economic order toward a greater measure of collectivism necessarily implied that individualist virtues could and should no longer be preached to the poor. Did the economic evolution away from laissez-faire chiefly reflect the recognition that individualist moral virtues were not omnipotent in and of themselves (and stood in need of governmental action to become more effective)? Or did the push toward collectivism in economics also reflect a belief that the individualism characterizing the virtues promulgated by moral reformers was somehow problematic morally, not just economically? Was the economic rejection of laissez-faire joined to a moral revolution in which virtues like diligence, sobriety, and thrift fell into disrepute?

To address that issue, let us now examine the ambivalent assessment of individualist virtues offered by two enormously influential critics of laissez-faire: Jane Addams, the most important leader of the settlement house movement that took root in America in the late 1880s, and Walter Rauschenbusch, the most thoughtful and prominent exponent of the social gospel movement that radically altered American Protestantism's approach to social questions at the turn of the century.

Like Brace and Lowell, Addams and Rauschenbusch offered both an economic program to reduce poverty and a moral assessment of the virtues of diligence, sobriety, and thrift. My purpose here is to question not so much the economic program of Addams and Rauschenbusch as their moral analysis: arguably their economic disagreements with Brace and Lowell—concerning the extent of the desirable abridgment of laissez-faire—are more in degree than in kind. Instead, the true significance of Addams and Rauschenbusch rests in their moral analysis: unlike Brace and Lowell, in some respects they were critical of the traditional virtues.

Addams and Rauschenbusch were far from being consistent moral revolutionaries, and in many respects they genuinely appreciated the virtues that the reformers strove to inculcate. But in other crucial respects they launched important critiques of the desirability—not just the efficacy—of the virtues espoused in moral reform. To do justice to the complexity of their position, I will begin by briefly sketching the common moral ground between Addams and Rauschenbusch and the moral reform tradition; I will then examine the more important (because more revolutionary) component of their thought—their moral critique of the individualist virtues.

Critiques like theirs came to be increasingly influential, and the virtues began to be derided, if not discarded. To make a compelling case for a contemporary return to moral reform, we need to judge the validity of the arguments that led to its rejection. We can profitably do so by engaging Addams and Rauschenbusch, two of the most thoughtful and intelligent critics of moral reform. Their two sets of views have the additional merit of complementing one another: since moral reform was (and is) an amalgam of secular and religious elements, Rauschenbusch's position—based as it was on religious premises—can usefully be juxtaposed with the more secular assessment offered by Addams. As we will see, Rauschenbusch posed a serious religious challenge to the moral reform tradition, because he charged that the Christian piety proclaimed by many reformers was in some ways incompatible with their espousal of the individualist virtues.

The Virtues of the Poor

Addams and Rauschenbusch developed their views on poverty much as the earlier reformers had: on the basis of extensive experience working closely with the poor. Addams co-founded Chicago's Hull House in 1889, and lived there, working with the immigrant population on Chicago's West Side, until her death in 1935. Rauschenbusch began his career by ministering to a congregation of impoverished German Baptists in New York's Hell's Kitchen from 1886 until 1897. (He then followed in his father's footsteps, receiving a professorship at Rochester Theological Seminary in upstate New York, where he taught until his death in 1918.)

What conclusions did Addams and Rauschenbusch draw from their work with the poor? Among other things, they came to the realization that the poor were for the most part virtuous, as the moral reformers understood the term; nevertheless, they were poor. Rauschenbusch's biographer summarizes his experience in these words: "His flock were all immigrants, part of the vast flood of cheap labor pouring in through the gates of Ellis Island. When work was plentiful they got along, most of them being thrifty and industrious; when work was scarce they suffered[,] and industry and thrift were of no avail. When the hard times came they sank into destitution, demoralization, prostitution and crime."[5]

Rauschenbusch perceived that the virtues preached by the moral reformers tended not to have much of a reward, at least in this life. In one of his earliest writings, a story that presumably reflected his actual experiences, the narrator depicts an elderly couple who "have just toiled and toiled all their lives, . . . standing at the close of a life of work and frugality, and watching old age and helplessness creeping down on them." The couple had "$70 in the savings bank, . . . but no soul knows how they stinted to get that much." He concluded the vignette with the narrator addressing his interlocutor: "Wish you'd trot around with me for a week; you wouldn't think so highly of things as they are."[6]

Along with many others in his era (and ours), Rauschenbusch was also troubled by the frequent lack of evident connection between the great fortunes that were being amassed and the virtues that were supposed to lead to success.[7] Rauschenbusch declared categorically that "*it is not possible to get great wealth except by offending against justice.*"[8] Not only did Rauschenbusch argue that the rewards reaped by the wealthy were seldom the product of diligence or thrift; he also asserted that wealth itself tended to undermine the virtues. Owners of great wealth (especially inheritors of great wealth) tended to become less diligent,[9] sober,[10] and thrifty[11] than they had been; in addition, the family life of the rich tended to degenerate.[12]

Unlike Rauschenbusch, Addams did not draw up moral balance sheets for the rich and poor, pointing to the evident disproportions between virtues and rewards. But she clearly distinguished between the economic problem of poverty and the moral problem of pauperism: the poor were poor even though they were mostly free of the vices that exacerbated the dependency of able-bodied paupers. Like Charles Booth, the British analyst of poverty, Addams regretted the frequency with which "the problems of the working class are . . . confounded with the problems of the inefficient, the idle, and distressed."[13] Addams stressed that the clientele of Hull House consisted not primarily of charity recipients but of "working people," who "require and want" no charity, "so long as they have health and good wages."[14] The settlements were to "represent the sentiments of working people who have received no charity."[15]

But working people who rejected charity and practiced the virtues touted by moral reformers could nevertheless face lives of grinding poverty. That problem was pithily described by one of Addams's most important colleagues, Florence Kelley—an influential advocate of governmental intervention to improve working conditions—in a collection of essays by Hull House associates to which Addams also contributed. As Kelley noted, the condition of those employed in sweatshops

> is a conclusive refutation of the ubiquitous argument that poverty is the result of crime, vice, intemperance, sloth, and unthrift; for the [sweatshop employees] are probably more temperate, hard-working, and avaricious than any equally large body of wage-earners in America. Drunkenness is unknown among them. So great is their eagerness to improve the social condition of their children, that they willingly suffer the utmost privation of clothing, food, and lodging, for the sake of keeping their boys in school. Yet the reward of work at their trade is grinding poverty, ending only in death or escape to some more hopeful occupation.[16]

As I have already implied, though, Addams and Rauschenbusch in no way broke from the moral reform orthodoxy of the late nineteenth century in arguing that the poor were mostly virtuous. Thus, speaking of the poor population with whom he worked, Brace could observe that "New York . . . is superior to any great city in . . . the virtue of its laboring poor."[17]

Similarly, Lowell extolled "the mass of workers who do not break down, but who only die; who are not drunken and shiftless, but who lead lives of such heroic self-sacrifice and devotion as we cannot lead because the demand is not made on us," and "the boys and girls, who grow up brave and pure through and in the midst of circumstances which . . . seem to us fatal."[18]

Nor were these judgments in any way idiosyncratic. In his 1894 overview of American philanthropy, Amos Warner presented statistics classifying cases of poverty according to their causes, grouped under two general headings: "misconduct" and "misfortune." One can obviously question the objectivity and validity of this sort of classification, as Warner himself did.[19] For our purposes, though, the relevant fact is the conclusion necessarily drawn by advocates of this classification: the data pointed overwhelmingly to misfortune rather than misconduct as the principal cause of poverty.

Warner's statistics, drawn from twelve surveys—all but one from the late 1880s and early 1890s—conducted by charity organization societies in five American cities, showed that "misconduct" (specifically, "drink," "shiftlessness and inefficiency," "crime and dishonesty," or a "roving disposition") seldom accounted for poverty: "The percentages for all causes indicating misconduct vary only between 10 and 32."[20] By contrast, causes indicating misfortune—lack of normal support, matters of employment, and matters of personal capacity—accounted for upward of 65 percent of cases of poverty in eleven of the twelve surveys. (In the twelfth survey, causes that were unclassified accounted for 21 percent of all cases.)

Similarly, in a second compilation of surveys from four American cities, in which the poor were classified by ethnicity (Americans, Germans, "colored," Irish, English, French, Russian and Polish, Spanish, Italian, Scandinavian, and a catch-all group of those from "other countries"), Warner found that "destitution held to result from causes indicating misconduct" accounted for less than one-third of all cases for each nationality. (Interestingly, the "colored" group was the one in which misconduct accounted for the smallest percentage of poverty—less than 14 percent.)[21] Thus, as one social welfare historian points out, the evidence compiled by organizations espousing moral reform pointed to a clear division "between a relatively small group of dependents with special problems and a much larger group—indeed the more unfortunate of the healthy wage earners—in need of little or no character rehabilitation."[22]

In the view of late-nineteenth-century moral reformers, then, the poor overall were morally healthy. But their moral health did not, of course, testify to the irrelevance of the moral virtues—any more than a person's physical health makes good diet and regular exercise irrelevant as means of remaining healthy. For the reformers, moral health was displayed by practicing the virtues; they advocated structural reforms not because the virtues were irrelevant, but instead precisely to increase their relevance and efficacy as weapons against poverty.

Restricting Laissez-Faire to Promote the Virtues

Since the problems of poverty could not often be ascribed to the moral failures of the poor, Addams and Rauschenbusch advocated reforming society as opposed to reforming individuals. If much poverty was caused by factors like unemployment, overwork, old age, or industrial accidents, it made sense to mitigate them by abridging laissez-faire. Like Brace and Lowell, Addams and Rauschenbusch called on government to enact maximum-hour laws and to sponsor social insurance programs.

Hence Addams could argue that structural reforms would increase the likelihood of virtuous behavior. She wanted to restrict child labor, because "the monotony and dullness of factory work" helped bring about "the petty immoralities which are often the youth's protest against them."[23] And since "there is a distinct increase in the number of registered prostitutes during periods of financial depression and even during the dull season of leading local industries," there was a moral case for making the wages of virtue more nearly comparable to those of sin: "Out of my own experience I am ready to assert that very often all that is necessary to effectively help the girl who is on the edge of wrong-doing is to . . . find her another place at higher wages. Upon such simple economic needs does the tried virtue of a good girl sometimes depend."[24]

"Discontinuous employment and non-employment" were "factors in the breeding of discouragement and despair" that promoted vice; that fact justified "the steadily increasing function of the state by which it seeks to protect . . . workers from their own weakness and degradation," so that "the livelihood of the manual laborer shall not be beaten down below the level of efficient citizenship."[25] In a passage that could easily have been written by Lowell, Addams declared that "the labor movement is bound . . . to work for shorter hours and increased wages and regularity of work, that education and moral reform may come to the individual laborer." Although the labor movement sometimes wrongly construed means as ends in themselves, in fact shorter hours and increased wages ought to be understood as means to the end of "the quiet inculcation of moral principle."[26]

Rauschenbusch shared the conviction that virtue was threatened by the social conditions and poverty that he thought were promoted by adherence to laissez-faire.

> During the great industrial crisis in the 90's [i.e., in the course of his pastoral work in Hell's Kitchen] I saw good men go into disreputable lines of employment and respectable widows consent to live [presumably out of wedlock] with men who would support them and their children. One could hear human virtue cracking and crumbling all around. Whenever work is scarce, petty crime is plentiful. But that is only the tangible expression of the decay in the morale of the working people on which statistics can seize. . . . But industrial crises are not inevitable in nature; they are merely inevitable in capitalism.[27]

Rauschenbusch did not deny a connection between poverty and moral degradation, but he did assert that poverty was often the cause and degradation the effect: "Poverty and luxury alike enervate the will and degenerate the human material for religion. Both create the love of idleness, vagrant habits, the dislike of self-restraint, and the inclination to indulge in the passing emotions."[28] If poverty produced vice, and if laissez-faire created poverty that state action could reduce, laissez-faire could fairly be blamed for failing to promote (because it failed adequately to reward) the individualist moral virtues. Addams and Rauschenbusch would both have agreed with the following critique of laissez-faire, offered by a historian to summarize the social gospel position: "Laissez-faire competition failed to encourage industry, thrift, and purity in either the worker or the capitalist class."[29]

Moral Traditionalism

Addams and Rauschenbusch departed from individualist economics, while in certain respects retaining a commitment to the individualist virtues endorsed by moral reform. It is an oversimplification to denounce the Social Gospel of Rauschenbusch and others for supporting a "universalistic and unconditional . . . charity without challenge" that made no moral demands upon the poor,[30] or to criticize Addams for emphasizing "the material over the spiritual and the political over the personal."[31]

Rauschenbusch in particular held very closely to the tradition of moral reform in many respects. He did not believe that a bad environment deserved all the blame for poverty, recognizing instead that "there will always be slaves to passion who will waste their substance." (He did, however, insist that the "masses of poverty as our great cities possess have not been created by private fault or misfortune but by social injustice.")[32] Rauschenbusch spoke of "the parasitic habit of mind" that grows on men "when they have once learned to depend on gifts," so that "it becomes hard to wake them back to self-support."[33] He also worried that charity workers "weaken[ed] parental responsibility" by "feed[ing] and cloth[ing]" recipients' children.[34]

As we will see, Addams was more reluctant to criticize unconditional charity and to regard pauperism as an evil. Yet she too spoke of "the error of indiscriminate giving with all its disastrous results,"[35] and she attacked the "dissipated young men who pride themselves upon their ability to live without working, and who despise all the honest and sober ways of their immigrant parents."[36]

As this last comment indicates, Addams was a remarkably stern moralist in many respects; she was an economic egalitarian, but not a moral latitudinarian. She was certainly skeptical of moral reform's emphasis on the power of economic self-help that was thought to be latent in the poor; nevertheless, insofar as moral reform embodied revulsion at—and the determination to reduce—the vice and disorder that characterized urban slums, Addams was unquestionably a moral reformer.

In fact, although Addams was clearly on the redistributive economic left, by many standards her views would position her quite comfortably on today's cultural right. She was troubled (for example) by the presence of "hundreds of degenerates" in every city; having been "over-mastered and borne down" by what Addams called the "sex impulse," they now filled "the casual lodging houses."[37] One can only imagine how Addams would have characterized urban America today when one contemplates her lament for the America of 1912, in which, she worried,

> thousands of young men and women in every great city have received none of the lessons in self-control which even savage tribes imparted to their children when they taught them to master their appetites as well as their emotions. These young people are perhaps further from all community restraint and genuine social control than the youth of the community have ever been in the long history of civilization. Certainly only the modern city has offered at one and the same time every possible stimulation for the lower nature and every opportunity for secret vice.[38]

Not surprisingly, Addams concluded that American educators should "train their pupils to continence and self-direction, as they already discipline their minds with knowledge in regard to many other matters."[39] An unapologetic advocate of social control, she welcomed the "wholesome fear of public opinion" that counteracted the "specious and illegitimate theories of [sexual] freedom" that were propagated.[40]

Addams also worried greatly (and presciently) about the corrosive effects of the vulgarity of popular culture. She feared that the violent content of the media of her day (specifically, the theaters charging a nickel for admission) did moral harm to the "overworked city youth of meager education"[41] whom their offerings targeted. Citing a play in which a seven-year-old kills the five men who murdered his father, and another in which two brothers (aged nine and ten) kill a Chinese laundryman and rob him of $200 to aid their impoverished mother, Addams found it "astounding that a city allows thousands of its youth to fill their impressionable minds with these absurdities which certainly will become the foundation for their working moral code."[42] It was "by no means rare," she contended, for theatrical glorifications of violence to spur impressionable members of the audience to acts of violence in real life.[43]

Addams was equally concerned about the destructive influence of popular music upon morals. Pointing to "the trivial and obscene words" in many songs, and their "meaningless and flippant airs," she observed that "we have grown singularly careless in regard to [music's] influence upon young people." America was wrong "totally [to] ignore that ancient connection between music and morals which was so long insisted upon by philosophers as well as poets," wrong "constantly [to] permit music on the street to incite that which should be controlled, to degrade that which should be exalted, to make sensuous that which might be lifted into the realm of the higher imagination."[44]

The Noneconomic Virtues

In view of their moral traditionalism it is not altogether surprising that Addams and Rauschenbusch continued in many ways to express allegiance to the virtues praised by the moral reformers—though on the whole, Rauschenbusch was more supportive than Addams of the economic virtues of diligence and thrift, which Addams called the "industrial virtues."[45] I will argue shortly that in important respects Addams and Rauschenbusch were moral revolutionaries, that their moral critique of the reformers' virtues—far more than their economic critique of laissez-faire—was wrongheaded in important respects. But like many revolutionaries, Addams and Rauschenbusch also kept a foot in the traditionalist camp. To assess their departure from the moral reform tradition fairly, we must take account of the respects in which they continued to adhere to it.

Addams and Rauschenbusch wholeheartedly endorsed the reformers' noneconomic virtues of sobriety and familial responsibility. With regard to sobriety, Addams and Rauschenbusch can in fact be said to have stood to the right of the earlier moral reformers (Hartley excepted), since they endorsed Prohibition.

Like the reformers, Addams understood that saloons had their good points and served important social functions: she believed that "substitution is the only remedy against the evils of the saloon."[46] Recognizing that "the saloon is not altogether vicious, . . . [that] it is the most attractive thing that many people have," she described Hull House's programs as a means of "coping with that attractiveness."[47]

Hull House's meeting places were created with the explicit intention of providing alternatives to the saloons for immigrants, since formerly "the saloon halls were the only places in the neighborhood where the immigrant could hold his social gatherings, and where he could celebrate such innocent and legitimate occasions as weddings and christenings."[48] (The inevitable shortcomings of efforts to provide substitutes for the saloon, with which the earlier moral reformers were undoubtedly familiar, are apparent in a wonderful anecdote recounted by Addams about the opening of the Hull House coffee house: "I remember one man who looked about the cozy little room and said, 'This would be a nice place to eat in all day, if one could only have a beer.'")[49]

But while Addams acknowledged the attractiveness of the saloons, she was more impressed by the damage that they did: fathers who had "fallen into the evil ways of drink" brutalized their families.[50] Because "alcohol was associated intensively with . . . gross evils," because it was "hard to exaggerate what excessive drinking did in the way of disturbing domestic relations and orderly family life,"[51] Addams endorsed Prohibition. In her judgment, it was at least a qualified success,[52] largely because of its economic impact on the working class:

> Certainly since 1919 the usual family has received the envelope of wages more nearly full than was possible under the old treating system. The man coming home from work with his own crowd, would stop in a saloon and treat six or eight or even ten men, each one of whom would in turn treat him with the others. It would end in each man drinking more than he really wanted and paying much more than he could afford.[53]

True to his Protestant clerical background, Rauschenbusch was a still more implacable opponent of intemperance. A prayer that he composed gives a good sense of his position:

> O Lord, we cry to thee in the weary struggle of our people against the power of drink. Remember, Lord, the strong men who were led astray and blighted in the flower of their youth. . . . O God, bring nigh the day when all our men shall face their daily tasks with minds undrugged and with tempered passions; when the unseemly mirth of drink shall seem a shame to all who hear and see; when the trade that debauches men shall be loathed like the trade that debauches women; and when all this black remnant of savagery shall haunt the memory of the new generation but as an evil dream of the night. For this accept our vows, O Lord, and grant thine aid.[54]

Perceiving alcohol as a "cause . . . of poverty" as well as an "effect,"[55] Rauschenbusch called upon the church to "undertake a new temperance crusade with all the resources of advanced physiological and sociological science."[56]

Like Hartley in this respect (though he was like him in few other ways), Rauschenbusch was driven to support a political remedy for intemperance because of the failure of efforts at individual rehabilitation:

> Temperance reformers began by working on individuals, but experience has driven them more and more to seek social remedies first. They found that drunkards create saloons, but that saloons even more create drunkards. They have refused to go on merely curing the drunkard after he has been made. They see that the best way to cure him is to stop the making of him as far as society can.[57]

Rauschenbusch favored legislative efforts to secure temperance such as local option laws;[58] writing in 1917 (that is, shortly before Prohibition was implemented), he applauded the fact that the disappearance of "the idealization of . . . drinking customs . . . from public opinion" had made possible "the rapid progress in the expulsion of the liquor trade in America."[59] With some justice it has been said that the most "notable progress in legislating the social gospel belonged to the crusaders against liquor," as opposed to the crusaders against economic exploitation;[60] clearly Rauschenbusch played an important part in both crusades.

Addams and Rauschenbusch were also thoroughly traditional in their support for family life as a necessary bulwark for the poor (and, for that matter, everyone else). Addams (who, like many career women in her day, never married),[61] regarded the family as the "bond which holds society together" and "the fountain of morality."[62] Although she criticized charity workers for opposing early marriages by the poor,[63] she would have been appalled at the idea that the poor (and the non-poor) might routinely procreate without marrying at all.[64] Addams had nothing but contempt for the man "who deserts his family that he may cultivate an artistic sensibility, or acquire what he considers more fulness [sic] of life for himself"; she thought that he "deliberately renounce[d] a just claim and [threw] aside all obligation for the sake of his own selfish and individual development."[65]

Rauschenbusch was no less traditional in his veneration for the family, describing it as "the foundation of morality, the chief educational institution, and the source of nearly all the real contentment among men." His economic radicalism (Rauschenbusch unapologetically described himself as a socialist, although he never joined any socialist organization)[66] was accompanied by what was in many respects a thoroughgoing moral conservatism. Not surprisingly, this moral conservatism has subjected Rauschenbusch to attack from feminists today: Janet Forsythe Fishburn has noted that "given such passion concerning the role of the family in society, it becomes more clear why the socialism of Rauschenbusch was so limited. He wanted an economic revolution without a change in the family unit. . . . Family love, and social order, depended on the continued purity of both male and female."[67]

The Economic Virtues

As we will soon see, Addams was quite critical of the moral reformers' emphasis on the "industrial virtues" of diligence and thrift. Still, it would have been impossible effectively to serve the poor without in some way encouraging those virtues, and Addams clearly did encourage them. In practice Hull House — in this respect just like a Charity Organization Society — created institutions to facilitate the diligence and thrift of the poor. An 1895 description of the settlement, co-authored by Addams and its other founder, Ellen Gates Starr, spoke of efforts to supply and find jobs for neighborhood residents. Hull House ran a labor bureau designed to match applicants with available jobs; regrettably, it was "necessarily small" then (during the great depression that began in 1893) because of the "extreme difficulty of finding work for men or women." The Hull House kitchen "supplied work to unemployed women during the stress of the last winter" — that is, the winter of 1894–1895.[68] Hull House also encouraged thrift: it opened a branch of the Penny Provident Fund that Lowell's New York COS had instituted.[69] In addition, Addams (like Lowell) was an early advocate of the postal savings system that was designed to facilitate savings by the poor.[70]

We know nothing about practical steps that Rauschenbusch may have taken to encourage diligence and thrift among his immigrant German congregation. In the realm of theory, though, he clearly regarded them as virtues. One of the rare compliments that Rauschenbusch bestowed on capitalism (in effect a reworking of a passage in the *Communist Manifesto*, altered by the addition of moral sentiments) related to its encouragement of diligence:

> Capitalism is the most efficient system for the creation of material wealth which the world has ever seen. Wherever it invades an old civilization, the ancient organization of production is doomed and goes down before it. This technical efficiency proves that the system must have powerful moral forces and cohesions in it.
>
> It has put humanity under the law of work as never before. The pace of work has speeded up in all the industrial nations. Its dire compulsion has overcome the primitive laziness and intermittent working habits of undeveloped men, and forced their latent resources of physical and mental energy into use. It has done for society what parental compulsion or hunger has done for countless boys who knew how to work when they wanted to, but usually preferred to go fishing or "hang out with the other fellows."[71]

But if Rauschenbusch praised capitalism for encouraging diligence, he also condemned it for discouraging thrift. In an early statement of an argument that we will examine in Chapter 5, Rauschenbusch pointed in 1912 to what Daniel Bell in 1976 would call "the cultural contradictions of capitalism":[72]

> All serious observers agree that the generation now growing up in our country is lacking in that stern faculty of self-restraint which was ground into their fathers and mothers by their religion and education. . . . The active agent in breaking down the old frugality is profit-making business, which surrounds the young with lures and stimulates their desires. Capitalism is sapping its own foundations. It got its first start in the Calvinistic countries, because Calvinistic religion induced saving and the accumulation of reserve capital. . . . Calvinism taught sobriety of dress and made conscientious work a fundamental Christian duty. By thus increasing earnings and decreasing expenditures it helped to create the economic reserves which financed the new industry created by the power machine. So religious frugality laid the foundations for capitalism and put civilization on its legs financially. Now capitalism is disintegrating that virtue in the descendants of the Calvinists and persuading them to buy baubles that capital may make profit.[73]

The Critique of the Reformers' Virtues

The foregoing analysis should serve to indicate that both Addams and Rauschenbusch were highly intelligent and morally serious. There was considerable common ground between them and the moral reformers, and in many respects they genuinely esteemed the virtues that the moral reformers attempted to inculcate.

But to say that is to tell only half of the story, ultimately the less important half. Addams wrote a critique of moral reform (the chapter on "Charitable Effort" in *Democracy and Social Ethics*) that is occasionally wrongheaded, often perceptive, but undeniably powerful: it still stands as the most important and effective polemic against moral reform. In the chapter she argued, however equivocally, that charity workers were wrong to "stress . . . the industrial virtues," to insist that recipients "must work and be self-supporting, that the most dangerous of all situations is idleness."[74] Despite her recognition that "indiscriminate giving" was an "error" that had produced "disastrous results,"[75] Addams looked forward to an era in which "our affection becomes large enough to care for the unworthy among the poor as we would care for the unworthy among our own kin."[76]

Working from theological as opposed to secular premises, Rauschenbusch came to similar conclusions. Rauschenbusch's revolutionary departure, it must be said, is most apparent not in his published works, but in an early manuscript that he discarded, which was published posthumously after its discovery in 1968.[77] Even in the unpublished manuscript any revolution that he advocated was more in the realm of theory than of practice: as we have already seen, in practice Rauschenbusch opposed indiscriminate charity. Nevertheless, he heatedly denied the authentic Christianity of the view (common to Tuckerman, Hartley, and Brace) that "the command to give to him that asks and to lend without expectation of return must be interpreted by sanctified common sense, which tells us that indiscriminate charity is a great evil."[78] In theory it was instead incumbent to give to those in need, with no questions asked: "If another is in need and we have what he needs, of course we should give it to him."[79]

My chief concern, though, is less with support for indiscriminate charity in itself than with what accounts for that support: in different though related ways, both Addams and Rauschenbusch regarded the reformers' basic expectation—that the poor could and should be expected to take steps to improve their condition by practicing the virtues—as morally problematic. Let us turn, then, to a detailed consideration of Addams's and Rauschenbusch's respective critiques of moral reform.

SECTION B. JANE ADDAMS:
THE COMPASSIONATE CRITIQUE OF THE INDUSTRIAL VIRTUES

Addams's critique of the industrial virtues is not particularly daring at first sight; it simply consists of the claim that they do not encompass all of human excellence. When she first raised the question of their status in an 1897 address, she implied that the settlements benefited from an advantage that was denied to charitable organizations, in that the settlements could take a broader view of human charac-ter. The settlements could emphasize not only the "industrial virtues" (thrift and diligence, the keys to being a good provider), but also the "social virtues" (the quali-ties that enable one to cooperate with others, hence to be a good colleague, friend, neighbor, or family member):

> You are bound, when you are doing charitable work, to lay stress upon the indus-trial virtues. You are bound to tell a man he must be thrifty, in order to keep his family; that his first duty is to keep at work, and support them. You must tell him that he is righteous and a good citizen when he is self-supporting, that he is un-righteous and not a good citizen when he receives aid. You must continually press upon him the need of the industrial virtues, and you have very little time for going out into the broader and more social qualities of life. Now the settlement does not ignore, I hope, those virtues; but it does not lay perpetual and continual stress upon them. . . . It does not lay so much stress upon one set of virtues, but views the man in his social aspects.[80]

Addams returned to the need to recognize elements of human character apart from diligence and thrift in her essay on charity in *Democracy and Social Ethics*. In it she contended that times had changed. America had thankfully departed from an earlier era in which its citizens supposedly "accord[ed] to the money-earning capacity exclusive respect" in judging their fellows:

> We have learned to judge men by their social virtues as well as by their business capacity, by their devotion to intellectual and disinterested aims, and by their public spirit, and we naturally resent being obliged to judge poor people so solely upon the industrial side. Our democratic instinct instantly takes alarm.[81]

The "modern tendency to judge all men by one democratic standard" was appropriately leading to the rejection of "the old charitable attitude," which judged the poor—though not the nonpoor—solely by their aptitude for "the industrial virtues" that had been stressed by the moral reformers.[82]

On the face of it, then, Addams's critique of the industrial virtues amounted to a rejection of a moral double standard. Her charge that a double standard had been unfairly applied was significant, because the insistence on judging both rich and poor by a single standard was a staple of moral reform rhetoric: diligence, sobriety, and thrift were held to be universal virtues, to which all could and should aspire. Lowell argued that the poor could not be helped "if we judge ourselves by one standard and our brothers by another."[83]

It was unfair to demand more of the poor than of others. For that reason Rau-schenbusch also insisted on a single standard applying to all, to put the occasional moral failings of the poor in perspective. It was wrong for "the propertied classes" to feel "the moral turpitude of idleness when they have seen it in the working class," but to believe that "for a man who is rich, it is no disgrace to idle." Rau-schenbusch protested against our "double weights and measures for the rich and poor in ethics": God's law—"If any will not work, neither let him eat"—should in justice be applied to rich as well as poor.[84] To borrow the formulation of Charles Krauthammer, Rauschenbusch can be said to have defined deviancy up:[85] indolence characterizes the idle rich as well as the pauperized poor.

Addams's position, though, was more radical than Rauschenbusch's. To make use of Daniel Patrick Moynihan's complementary formulation, she defined deviancy down.[86] Her point was not to apply strict moral standards in judging the rich as well as poor; instead it was to question the application of such standards to the poor, because they were no longer thoroughly applied to the rich.

But did emphasizing the importance of the industrial virtues for the poor amount to a double standard? Two points must be made here. First, if the nonpoor were not judged solely by their practice of the industrial virtues (and they should not have been judged by them alone), that is because they could generally be said, almost by definition, to possess the necessary minimum of industrial virtue: apart from the few who lived on inherited wealth, they were, after all, self-supporting. It is wrong to regard the capacity to support oneself as the sum of all moral virtue; but one can quite plausibly claim that for the able-bodied it is a sine qua non for many other virtues.

Second, and more significant, it is odd to say that the poor should not be judged in their capacity as moneymakers, because—again by definition—the poor are poor because they are deficient as moneymakers. Although Addams took charity workers to task for stressing the industrial virtues, there is an obvious rationale for that emphasis: the problem of the poor was lack of money, and one could reasonably believe that the poor would likely get more money by practicing (or finding opportunities to practice) the industrial virtues of diligence and thrift. To be sure, Addams could have criticized charity workers for failing to advocate structural reforms that might more effectively have eased the lot of the poor: the point of her essay, though, was not to argue the need for structural reforms but to cast doubt upon conventional moral assessments of the poor.

There are good reasons, then, to question Addams's radical claim that it was wrong single-mindedly to insist that the poor "must work and be self-supporting, that the most dangerous of all situations is idleness, that seeking one's own pleasure, while ignoring claims and responsibilities, is the most ignoble of actions."[87] That statement goes beyond the cautious claim that the reformers exaggerated the ease with which the industrial virtues could be applied in many circumstances; instead it comes close to challenging the worth of the industrial virtues as a matter of principle.

By contrast, Addams would not have been particularly bold in saying that it may at times be unreasonable to insist that the poor "must work and be self-supporting," in view of the frequency of industrial depressions and downturns. Addams of course understood (as had the reformers) the fatuity of the unqualified claim that "any man can find work if he wants it."[88] As we saw in discussing diligence, the weak suit of moral reform had always been its relative incapacity to aid those seeking employment precisely when they were most in need of it—when depressions rendered jobs scarce.

But instead of making a modest claim about the frequent difficulty of finding work, Addams far more boldly asserted that the moral assessment of the able-bodied poor should not rest principally on their efforts to support themselves. And with this assertion, it is fair to say, Addams herself committed precisely the error against which she warned: she applied a double standard, judging the poor by a criterion that she would never have applied to the nonpoor. She contended that the poor could not reasonably be expected to manifest the same virtues as the nonpoor.

She derided the standards of the hypothetical charity worker who was insistent upon the industrial virtues as "incorrigibly bourgeois"[89]—as though the effort to work, support oneself, avoid idleness, and forgo pleasure in the name of duties and responsibilities was something that could not fairly be expected of the poor. Similarly, she held that it was wrong "ruthlessly [to] force our conventions and standards" upon the poor; again, as though self-reliance was a bourgeois aspiration that was somehow irrelevant to the lives of the poor.[90] Finally, she criticized "the middle-class moralist" who urged "upon the workingman the specialized virtues of thrift, industry, and sobriety"; those virtues, she maintained, were less applicable to workers, who were necessarily inclined toward collectivism, than to others: after all, they pertained only to "the individual" (as opposed to the larger social group).[91]

The Moral Impact of the Industrial Revolution

Addams believed that the individualistic virtues were in some sense relics of the past, whose importance had receded as historical conditions altered dramatically. Addams's argument in favor of transforming the moral standards for judging the poor rested on the conviction that the industrial revolution had (or ought to have) changed everything—including the value of the individualistic virtues.

Virginia Woolf, a contemporary of Addams, once flatly asserted that "on or about December, 1910, human character changed," as demonstrated by the fact that "all human relations . . . shifted—those between masters and servants, husbands and wives, parents and children."[92] Human relations had changed, Woolf contended, because they had been democratized.[93] Although Addams did not make a comparably stark pronouncement, she too believed that a moral revolution was occurring: she agreed with Woolf that all of these relations were shifting, and for the very same reason: they were being democratized.[94] As its title indicates, that democratic revolution in morality formed the theme of *Democracy and Social Ethics*.

The word "social" in the title was particularly important: the democratic revolution was apparent, Addams contended, in the shift from individualist to social ethics. Unlike Woolf, Addams did not baldly assert that human nature had changed; but she did boldly argue for a dramatic alteration of our moral standards. She called for placing far less emphasis on the individualist virtues previously commended by the moral reformers: "To attain individual morality in an age demand-ing social morality, to pride one's self on the results of personal effort when the time demands social adjustment, is utterly to fail to apprehend the situation."[95] Whether or not human nature had changed, Addams undeniably believed that the individualist moral virtues were rightly beginning to deserve less esteem.

In Addams's judgment what might be called the ideology of self-help had lost much of its credibility: "Nothing is more fallacious than an argument based upon a personal experience of thirty years ago," she wrote in 1903. "Since then an indus-trial revolution [has] taken place."[96] That same conviction informed her critique of the industrial virtues: "The benevolent individual of fifty years ago honestly be-lieved that industry and self-denial in youth would result in comfortable posses-sions for old age," but that belief was no longer credible.[97] Whereas "fifty years ago . . . [boys] were told that the career of the self-made man was open to every Ameri-can boy, if he worked hard and saved his money, improved his mind, and followed a steady ambition," urban youths, impressed by the stature of political bosses in the community, now had reason to believe that "the path which leads to riches and success, to civic prominence and honor, is the path of political corruption."[98]

Addams illustrated the contemporary need for social rather than individual virtues by recounting the story of the way in which the railway sleeping-car mag-nate George M. Pullman related to his workers. She told his story, oddly enough, without once mentioning his name—as though thereby to illustrate that the prob-lem was not the failure of a single individual but of the collective class of industri-alists to which he belonged.

Pullman had constructed a model town for his employees, encompassing work-shops as well as homes. He did so in the hope that a model environment—free of bad influences like "disorderly neighbors, slum landlords, saloon keepers, pawn-brokers, prostitutes, political bosses, and labor agitators"[99]—would produce model employees, who practiced the virtues of diligence, sobriety, and thrift. The model town included parks, playgrounds, meeting rooms, a library, billiard rooms, a the-ater, a kindergarten, excellent schools (for adults as well as children), a savings bank, musical groups, and clubs. All of these facilities were intended to promote the sobriety of the residents and to facilitate their efforts to help themselves.[100]

Yet despite Pullman's laudable efforts to promote the individualist virtues, Ad-dams criticized him severely, because he resisted the collective action of his em-ployees. Pullman failed to understand that "we are passing from an age of individu-alism to one of association."[101] Thus, when his employees went out on strike after he had reduced their wages (by reducing their hours) in 1894, Pullman adamantly refused arbitration.[102]

In Addams's judgment, Pullman's refusal to negotiate with his workers collec-tively showed that he "fail[ed] to catch the great moral lesson which our times offer," because he was "too absorbed in carrying out a personal plan of [individual] improvement." Pullman's "conception of goodness for his men had been [restricted to] cleanliness, decency of living, and, above all, thrift and temperance."[103] While he "believed strongly in . . . steadiness of individual effort," he "failed to apprehend the greater movement of . . . collective action." Because Pullman did not attain "a conception of social morality for his men," he wrongly "imagined that virtue for them largely meant absence of vice."[104] As a result, although he wanted his employees to "possess the individual and family virtues," he "did nothing to cherish in them the social virtues which express themselves in associated effort."[105]

Addams's praise for the collective virtue of labor solidarity is unobjectionable. She was undoubtedly right to criticize Pullman for practicing a form of benevolent despotism,[106] in that he failed to consult with the intended beneficiaries of his model town. As she noted, his failure illustrates the danger of being "good 'to' people rather than 'with' them," of "decid[ing] what is best for them instead of consulting them."[107]

Nevertheless, although her essay points principally—and appropriately—to the desirability of collective virtue, at times it also suggests the inadequacy of the individualist virtues—not just the need to supplement them with collective virtue. Addams intimated that the virtues extolled by Pullman were passé: they had "distinguished the model workmen of his youth" and "had enabled him and so many of his contemporaries to rise in life, when 'rising in life' was urged upon every promising boy as the goal of his efforts."[108] But why was the goal of "rising in life"— or upward mobility—as a result of one's own individual efforts seemingly now obsolete? Implicitly Addams believed that the industrial revolution had somehow rendered it a false or inappropriate aspiration for the poor.

Eager to extol collective virtue, Addams criticized the "exaggerated personal morality [that] is often mistaken for a social morality."[109] But while the individualist virtues cannot replace collective virtue and do not constitute it by themselves, they can be seen as a necessary precondition for it. For that reason Mary Richmond took issue with Addams's contention, rejecting the view that "industry and thrift [are] . . . merely 'economic virtues.'"[110] Noting that "the thriftless and the extravagant, whether rich or poor, are often mean and self-indulgent, lacking the first quality of the unselfish in lacking self-control," Richmond asserted that industry and thrift are "two of the elements out of which not only character but all the social virtues are built."[111]

Richmond went on to note that the individualist virtues are of particular importance to workers locked in combat with their employers:

> No one is more helpless against the encroachments of employers than the man who lives from hand to mouth, whose necessities press ever hard upon him, crippling him and crippling those with whom he competes in the open market. Then again, successful cooperation is impossible to the thriftless. The lack of self-control, the lack of power to defer their pleasures, unfits them for combined effort and makes it more difficult for them to be loyal to their fellow-workmen.[112]

The individualist virtues can plausibly be understood as necessary preconditions for the attainment of collective virtue, rather than relics of the past in an age when collective virtue was of pressing importance. In fact, Addams herself suggested as much by showing how Pullman's workers had—ironically—profited from the very moral teaching that they were led to reject:

> The morals he had advocated in selecting and training his men did not fail them in the hour of confusion [that is, during the strike]. They were self-controlled, and they themselves destroyed no property. They were sober and exhibited no drunkenness, even although [*sic*] obliged to hold their meetings in the saloon hall of a neighboring town.[113]

Industrial Revolution and Upward Mobility

Addams was skeptical of the individualistic virtues because she implicitly doubted their efficacy in promoting upward mobility in the industrial era. Rauschenbusch made this argument explicitly. Formerly, he contended, apprentices could hope "to become masters themselves when their time of education was over"; but now "the wage-earner . . . could only in rare and lessening instances hope to own a great shop with its costly machinery."[114] The change was dramatic, sharply decreasing the likelihood of self-advancement: "In the old [preindustrial] order the aim was to make a living, to give the children an education and a start in life, to lay something by for a rainy day, and to rise a step in life if possible."[115]

Rauschenbusch was right to argue that the typical instance of preindustrial upward mobility—the progress from apprentice to journeyman to master—had ceased to offer a useful model. Most, if not all, of the nineteenth-century American "rags-to-riches" literature offering advice on how to succeed (e.g., the novels of Horatio Alger or the ubiquitous claim that "any boy can grow up to be President") was obviously—though obviously understood to be—unrealistic.[116]

That literature was easy to debunk, as in this comment by Rauschenbusch's predecessor in the social gospel movement, Richard T. Ely:

> If you tell a single concrete workingman on the Baltimore and Ohio Railroad that he may yet be president of the company, it is not demonstrable that you have told him what is not true, although it is within bounds to say that he is far more likely to be killed by a stroke of lightning; but it can be mathematically proved that by no amount of diligence, thrift, and intelligence can one out of a thousand employés [*sic*] attain that position.[117]

But no serious thinker had ever asserted that limitless upward mobility was ever conceivable for all, that the poor could inhabit a sort of Lake Wobegon in which all of them could have incomes well above average. Certainly the moral reformers never did so. Ely himself cited a statement by Channing—that "only a few of the laboring class can rise," in the sense of departing from that class by becoming wealthy—to support his belief in the limits of upward mobility.[118]

But even if the typical workman on the B & O could not reasonably hope to become the railroad's president, could he not reasonably hope to rise modestly and to better the condition of his family over time? The moral reformers had pointed to limited upward mobility of that sort as a realistic aspiration that was more likely to be achieved if the virtues were practiced. Questioning the efficacy of the individualist virtues, Addams and particularly Rauschenbusch denied that even modest upward mobility was likely at the turn of the century—a much harder claim to make.

Conceivably Addams's and Rauschenbusch's pessimism exemplified what Stephan Thernstrom has called "the old American habit of judging the present against a standard supplied by a romantic view of the past."[119] Important as the industrial revolution undoubtedly was, a good case can be made that the "industrial virtues" were just as practicable—and just as likely to be rewarded—in 1890 as in, say, 1830.

To begin with, the available evidence suggests that wages continued to rise in the years in which Addams and Rauschenbusch expressed their doubts about upward mobility. Summarizing that evidence, historian James T. Kloppenberg observes that "recent studies suggest that wages did reflect the turn-of-the-century economic boom. . . . In the United States, . . . real income rose steadily throughout the late nineteenth century and into the second decade of the twentieth."[120]

Addams's and Rauschenbusch's pessimism is nevertheless understandable—and not simply as a reflection of the ravages visited upon the poor by the great economic downturn of 1893. In addition (then as now), the condition of the economically disadvantaged relative to others can easily be confused with their condition in absolute terms:

> The working-class share of national income seems not to have increased substantially [in the late nineteenth century], and it may even have declined in the course of industrial expansion. Not surprisingly, contemporaries only imperfectly understood that the general increase in prosperity among the populations of industrialized nations occurred simultaneously with the continuing immiseration of industrial workers *compared to other economic groups*. Although *the working classes improved their status in absolute terms*, their position deteriorated relative to those in the middle and upper economic strata. Observers had difficulty distinguishing real from relative deprivation.[121]

The data on wages suggest, then, that diligence continued to be rewarded in the industrial era—though perhaps (as Brace and Lowell would have agreed) not sufficiently rewarded. And with respect to thrift, it is noteworthy that even Rauschenbusch granted that "great numbers" of workers were still able to save, "as our savings banks and insurance companies can testify": "The brave, the wise, and the religious families succeed almost miraculously in educating their children and having a margin left."[122]

Did modest upward mobility, if not an advance into the ranks of capitalists and entrepreneurs, remain a realistic possibility for workers in the aftermath of the industrial revolution? Although no definitive data bear on this question, Thernstrom's conclusions about nineteenth-century workers in Newburyport, Massachusetts are certainly relevant:

> To practice the virtues exalted by the mobility creed rarely brought middle[-]class status to the laborer, or even to his children. But hard work and incessant economy did bring tangible rewards — money in the bank, a house to call his own, a new sense of security and dignity. . . .

> The ordinary workmen of Newburyport, in short, could view America as a land of opportunity despite the fact that the class realities which governed their life chances confined most of them to the working class. . . . The typical unskilled laborer who settled in Newburyport could feel proud of his achievements and optimistic about the future. Most of the social gains registered by laborers and their sons during these years [1850–1880] were decidedly modest — a move one notch up the occupational scale, the acquisition of a small amount of property. Yet *in their eyes* these accomplishments must have loomed large.[123]

The crucial question, of course, is whether this sort of modest upward mobility more or less came to a halt after 1880 (the concluding year for Thernstrom's Newburyport investigation). Fortunately, evidence on that score is available in the form of Thernstrom's follow-up investigation of social mobility in Boston after 1880.

Before conducting his Boston research, Thernstrom had hypothesized that the prospects for upward mobility in larger metropolitan areas like Boston or New York were probably slightly less good than in Newburyport.[124] But in fact he found that upward mobility turned out to be even more common in industrial Boston after 1880: "It does appear either that Newburyport was an unusually sluggish place for aspiring laborers, or that small cities in general offer fewer opportunities; rates of movement from blue-collar to white-collar posts, both in the course of a career and between generations, were much higher in Boston."[125] Between 25 and 30 percent of working-class Bostonians rose to employment in middle-class posts at some point in their careers; 40 percent of sons of working-class fathers held middle-class jobs during their careers — a figure that applied equally to sons of unskilled and semiskilled workers and to sons of skilled workers.[126]

Significantly, Thernstrom also noted that "both types of mobility — career and intergenerational — occurred at a relatively constant rate over [the] entire eighty-year period" that began in 1880.[127] With the benefit of hindsight there is reason to believe that industrialization was not — contrary to the supposition of Addams and Rauschenbusch — a major impediment to upward mobility after all. In fact, as Thernstrom concluded, the historical "evidence . . . challenge[s] the socialist critic's assumption that the dream of individual mobility was illusory and that collective advance was the only realistic hope for the worker."[128]

The industrial revolution indisputably changed much about American life and work, and not always for the good. Still, one can plausibly claim that Addams and Rauschenbusch exaggerated its impact: it is far from clear that the industrial revolution suddenly and drastically decreased the likelihood of modest upward mobility spurred by practice of the individualistic virtues.

Compassion as Condescension

As we saw above, Addams claimed that the reformers' virtues could be understood as "bourgeois" virtues of limited relevance to the poor. Addams made two different arguments in support of this contention. The first argument was cautious and often persuasive: because the circumstances confronting the poor differed greatly from those confronting the bourgeoisie, the two classes could not apply the virtues in the same way. Early marriage really was imprudent for the bourgeoisie, but not for laborers, whose earnings peaked in their youth when they were physically stronger. Saving was desirable for the bourgeoisie but not for the poor, who needed to spend their earnings to avoid underconsumption: a worker saved by spending on his children, who would then support him in his old age.[129]

But Addams also made a second argument that was less cautious and far more problematic. She suggested that the poor were almost a species apart. It was not just their circumstances that differed: the poor themselves were a very different sort of people, for whom "temperance and cleanliness and thrift" were "impossible virtues," or "ethical ideals" that could not be understood.[130]

From this perspective Addams could claim that "the conventions" of the typical charity worker who commended the industrial virtues "fail to fit the bigger, more emotional, and freer lives of working people."[131] In a second passage, intended to rebut the charge that the poor were improvident, Addams made the astonishing claim that "the sense of prudence, the necessity for saving, can never come to a primitive, emotional man with the force of a conviction."[132]

In these passages, it is fair to say, Addams's compassion for the poor lapses into romanticization and condescension. The poor, Addams here declares, really are different from you and me: in many ways they are preferable, because they are more emotional, more primitive, freer of what we now would call bourgeois hang-ups about personal responsibility. Writing in 1902, Addams seems to ascribe to the immigrant poor of her day some of the same characteristics that "liberal racists" (in the formulation of the journalist Jim Sleeper) sometimes apply to poor blacks today.[133]

Addams's condescension masquerading as compassion is also apparent in her occasional comparisons of the poor to children. In one instance, Addams tells the story of a woman who had been arrested for buying and selling books that belonged to the Chicago public schools (and were clearly marked as such). The woman appealed to a Hull House resident to end the judicial proceeding against her, which the resident of course was unable to do. After an unsatisfactory discussion with the woman, who failed to understand what she had done wrong, the resident was "utterly baffled and in the state of mind she would have been in, had she brutally insisted that a little child should lift weights too heavy for its undeveloped muscles."[134]

In a second passage, Addams compares charitable efforts "ruthlessly [to] force our conventions and standards" upon the poor with a harsh parent's attempts to deal with a timid child, afraid to sleep by himself in the dark: the parent "talks of developing his child's self-respect and good sense, and leaves him to cry himself to sleep, demanding powers of self-control and development which the child does not possess."[135] And elsewhere Addams explained that she did not share many charity workers' "fear of pauperizing people," because "we have all accepted our bread from somebody, at least until we were fourteen."[136]

These analogies cannot be dismissed as meaningless figures of speech. Common to all of them is the suggestion that the childlike poor are unable to aspire to the moral and economic independence characteristic of the middle class, whose members act like grownups by obeying the law and supporting themselves. Unlike the rest of us, it seems, the poor cannot be expected to understand the illegality of trafficking in stolen merchandise, cannot be expected to manifest the "self-control" characteristic of the nonpoor, cannot be expected to avoid dependency.

The last example is particularly revealing, because the dependency of children is considered unproblematic and inevitable: here Addams infantilizes the poor by suggesting that the dependency of the adult poor is in principle just as unproblematic and inevitable as the dependency of children. In fairness, comparisons of the poor to children can also be found in moral reform rhetoric.[137] Still, the lapses of moral reformers do not excuse Addams's comparable lapses.

The *Luftmensch* as Test Case

One of the hypothetical test cases for Addams's devaluation of the industrial virtues is a man who has been blacklisted in a strike; his reputation as an agitator, together with the fact that he is "not a very good workman," keeps him unemployed for a long spell. His situation led Addams to speak of "the fatal result of being long out of work," as he becomes "less and less eager for work, . . . [getting] a 'job' less and less frequently." His wife, who is "accustomed to . . . earn, by sewing and cleaning, most of the scanty income for the family," admires him; she does not believe that "he has grown lazy."

How is the charity worker to react? Although she realizes that the other strikers have gone back to work, and that the man is not skillful, she "cannot . . . denounce him as worthless," because of his intellectual attainments:

> She sees other workmen come to him for shrewd advice; she knows that he spends many more hours in the public library reading good books than the average workman has time to do. He has formed no bad habits and has yielded only to those subtle temptations toward a life of leisure which come to the intellectual man.[138]

The unemployed worker who is also an intellectual is what is known in Yiddish as a *Luftmensch*—a dreamy, sensitive, impractical type, who is by no means immoral but also not greatly concerned with the mundane reality of making a good living.

This story, like others recounted by Addams in her essay, has the merit of reminding us that the reformers' virtues are not all of a piece; it is possible to have some of them but not others.[139] But even if we grant that the unemployed worker has many admirable qualities, Addams's gloss on his situation is still puzzling. In particular, why are the charity worker's alternatives either to "denounce him" or say nothing? Could she not suggest to him that his wife and children would live more comfortably if he made more of an effort to provide for them, that his intellectual interests—laudable as they are—should have a lower priority than his family's economic welfare?

Addams tells this story to illustrate the comparative insignificance of the industrial virtues; but in fact exactly the opposite moral seems more appropriate. Rightly understood, the story points to the central importance of the industrial virtues as means of relieving poverty. At bottom, it is the story of a man and his family who suffer poverty in some measure because he lacks (or at least is less than eager to practice) the industrial virtues: if the charity worker is intent (as she should be) on helping them reduce their poverty, she fails them—not to speak of her own mission—by refusing to stress the importance of the industrial virtues.

Addams's theme throughout her essay on charity is the disproportion between the moral standards upheld by the bourgeoisie and the lives led by the poor. As we have seen, she often voices it effectively: the different situations of the two classes sometimes do prove the folly of judging the poor not by their own standards but by those of the bourgeoisie. But in the case of the *Luftmensch*, interestingly, by Addams's own account the charity worker knowingly flouts the standards of the poor: she rejects the view of the family's poor neighbors, who resent the man "because . . . he does not 'provide.'"[140]

Elsewhere, we have seen, Addams urges us to beware of the moral imperialism of a bourgeoisie that imposes what we would call its "middle-class values" on the poor: in her discussion of Pullman she rightly warned of the danger of being "good 'to' people rather than 'with' them," of "decid[ing] what is best for them instead of consulting them."[141] That is good advice. Still, if we are to heed it consistently, we should also condemn the moral imperialism of a bourgeois charity worker, impressed by the leisurely life of intellectuals that is more practically attainable for the rich than the poor, who discounts the importance—to which the poor themselves point—of parents sacrificing their comfort to provide a better living for their families.[142]

Different Virtues, Different Rewards

Throughout her discussion of the *Luftmensch* Addams raises questions about virtues and rewards that are dealt with more satisfactorily and profoundly by Adam Smith in *The Theory of Moral Sentiments*. Like Addams, Smith understood that the industrial virtues do not exhaust all of virtue; hence he distinguished between "industry, prudence, and circumspection," on one hand, and "truth, justice, and humanity" on the other. He insisted, though, that each set of virtues tends to meet with a different and appropriate reward. "Industry, prudence, and circumspection" —Addams's industrial virtues—tend to meet, not surprisingly, with industrial or economic "success in every sort of business." In contrast, "truth, justice, and humanity" tend to meet with an appropriately noneconomic reward, "the confidence and love of those we live with."[143] Keeping in mind Smith's classification of the virtues, we can say that Addams's error is her failure to see the connection between industrial virtues and economic success, or perhaps her wish to link noneconomic virtues to economic success.

It is no denigration of the noneconomic virtues to say, with Smith, that they are of little use in relieving poverty; their sphere is a vital one, but it happens not to include the creation of wealth. If our aim is to reduce poverty, it is of little avail to point—correctly—to the attractiveness of virtues that will not reduce it; instead it makes far more sense to promote precisely the industrial virtues that Addams devalued.

Smith would certainly have understood and in some measure even approved Addams's devaluation of the industrial virtues, because he emphatically shared her admiration for the noneconomic virtues: "Magnanimity, generosity, and justice, command so high a degree of admiration, that we desire to see them crowned with wealth, and power, and honours of every kind, the natural consequences of prudence, industry, and application; qualities with which [magnanimity, generosity, and justice] . . . are not inseparably connected." Acknowledging the force of this desire, in effect Smith anticipates Addams's argument: he notes that "man is by nature directed to correct, in some measure, that distribution of things which [nature] herself would otherwise have made"[144]—that is, to provide an economic reward for the noneconomic virtues.

Nevertheless, Smith would have said that the economic condition of poverty could more effectively be remedied by promoting economic virtues like "prudence, industry, and application." Those are the virtues of chief importance to the poor, even though they undoubtedly have the shortcomings to which Addams pointed: prudence, for example, "never is considered as one either of the most endearing or . . . the most ennobling of the virtues," commanding only "a certain cold esteem," rather than "any very ardent love or admiration."[145] But if the goal is to promote the independence of the poor by enabling them to increase their earnings, the industrial virtues are the appropriate means: hence their celebration rather than denigration is in order.

SECTION C. WALTER RAUSCHENBUSCH: THE CHRISTIAN CRITIQUE OF PRUDENCE

Rauschenbusch was still more troubled by the less endearing aspects of prudence—meaning rational calculation seeking individual self-advancement—than

Adam Smith had been. But to understand the basis of Rauschenbusch's critique of prudence as an individualist virtue, we must begin by comparing his view of Christianity in relation to moral reform with that of the two other Protestant ministers discussed extensively in this narrative: Tuckerman and Brace.

Tuckerman once commented on the apparent oddity of his mixture of free market economics and evangelical Christianity. As an exponent of laissez-faire economics, he predictably opposed various means of assisting the poor: constructing low-rent housing, creating artificial employment, and establishing soup kitchens providing free food. In each case Tuckerman raised the same practical objection: artificially increasing the supply of houses, jobs, and food for the poor would be matched by an increase in the demand for them, as poor people migrated to Boston to avail themselves of the offerings. Meanwhile, "the excitement to personal effort . . . will be . . . checked."[146]

But in a revealing discussion, Tuckerman attempted to ward off an obvious objection: "It may be said that I have learned to look upon the poor rather in the light in which they are seen by the political economist than as a Christian. But I answer, that I should esteem that to be a false and injurious principle in political economy which is not in perfect consistency with Christian morality."[147]

Tuckerman did not argue that laissez-faire economics was somehow ordained by God, or that governmental intervention was somehow un-Christian. Instead, while he acknowledged that Christianity enjoins us to supply "the wants of the destitute," he nevertheless insisted that the injunction must be understood in terms of "good common sense" and in light of the related injunction "that we are not by our charity to encourage idleness and vice, and thus to increase and perpetuate pauperism and misery."[148]

But Rauschenbusch rejected what he called the "sanctified common sense" displayed by Tuckerman in his critique of indiscriminate charity.[149] Rauschenbusch (like the Unitarian Tuckerman) was a theological liberal, but he took New Testament economics far more seriously and literally than Tuckerman. In fact, he had almost a fundamentalist faith in the accuracy and continued relevance of Jesus' economics.

To be sure, Rauschenbusch's fundamentalism did not extend to acknowledging the ascetic and eschatological elements in Christianity, which lower the priority of this-worldly relief of poverty; instead he charged that "the professional theologians of Europe, who all belong by kinship and sympathy to the bourgeois classes and are constitutionally incapacitated for understanding any revolutionary ideas, past or present, have overemphasized the ascetic and eschatological elements in the teachings of Jesus."[150] Leaving this notable exception aside, though, we can say that Rauschenbusch insisted on taking Jesus' teaching at face value. He thought that those who denied the applicability of Jesus' economic teaching were guilty of condescension to the son of God: in effect they contended that Jesus was "'a good soul, but a limited intellect,'" who "knew nothing about political economy."[151]

In contrast, Rauschenbusch wholeheartedly accepted Jesus' critique of wealth and the wealthy. As he noted, Jesus said "that it is hard for a rich man to enter the Kingdom [of God], not that it is hard for *any* man."[152] Rauschenbusch believed that "the possession of wealth is very closely bound up with injustice and selfishness";[153] he asserted that "money-getting is not well compatible with the justice and love of the Kingdom of God."[154]

One can obviously question the practicality of Rauschenbusch's (or should I say Jesus') economic ethics; one can also wonder whether these ethics were and are particularly useful to the poor—whose this-worldly need, after all, was and is to succeed better at the very money-getting that is allegedly incompatible with justice and love. Still, Rauschenbusch could rightly point to a tension between the self-abnegation and the critique of money-making espoused in the Christian Bible and the emphasis on individual economic self-advancement characteristic of moral reform: the Christian injunction to turn the other cheek obviously differs from the prudential encouragement of virtues that help people push themselves to the front of the line. In this respect Rauschenbusch could plausibly criticize the moral reformers' attempt to yoke Christian piety to the virtues needed for success in a free-market economy.

Rauschenbusch regarded the more moderate and practical Christian economics of ministers like Tuckerman and Brace as a "dulling off of Christ's teaching." It was not enough to believe (as Tuckerman and Brace presumably did) that "the rich must keep within the civil law, not acquire *too* much, give away at least a tenth of their income, and not set their heart on wealth";[155] it was not enough simply "to acknowledge the necessity and rightfulness of the scramble," while also "try[ing] to dull the roughest edge and check the worst brutality of it."[156] Instead, Rauschenbusch believed, on Christian grounds there was need for a more fundamental and radical change in the economic system.

The necessity of radical change emerges still more strongly in Rauschenbusch's treatment of Brace, the only moral reformer whose views he explicitly discussed. Rauschenbusch did not examine Brace's more practical discussion of assisting the poor (his account of the work of the Children's Aid Society in *The Dangerous Classes of New York*), but a more theoretical book, *Gesta Christi*, whose theme is well indicated by its subtitle: *A History of Humane Progress under Christianity*. As one would expect, Rauschenbusch thought that Brace's celebration of the humanitarian impact of Christianity gave the religion more credit than it deserved.

Rauschenbusch agreed with Brace that Christianity had done much "in taming selfishness and stimulating the sympathetic affections," for example by elevating the status of women and children, abolishing slavery, decreasing the horrors of war, promoting charity, providing education, and furthering civil liberty and social justice. In fact, he praised Brace for providing "a fine, popular statement of these changes."[157]

Nevertheless, Christianity had not gone far enough, because it (and, implicitly, its defenders like Brace) had been too content with piecemeal rather than systemic reforms:

> The social effects which are usually enumerated [by Christian apologists like Brace] do not constitute a reconstruction of society on a Christian basis, but were mainly a suppression of some of the most glaring evils in the social system of the time. . . . The Church is rendering some service to-day in opposing child labor and the sweat-shop system, which are among the culminating atrocities of the wages system, but its conscience has not at all awakened to the wrongfulness of the wages system as a whole, on which our industry rests. Thus, in general, the Church has often rendered valuable aid by joining the advanced public conscience of any period in its protest against some single intolerable evil, but it has accepted as inevitable the general social system under which the world was living at the time.[158]

It is fair to say that Tuckerman and Brace did indeed accept as "inevitable" the general social system of capitalism—though they obviously also believed that it produced desirable moral effects, by stimulating individuals' exertions to provide for themselves and their families. But Rauschenbusch accepted neither the inevitability nor the moral defensibility of capitalism. He rejected moral reform because he denied that simply striving to help the poor help themselves—or even advocating a few structural reforms so that they could do so more effectively—sufficed: "As long as a man sees in our present society only a few inevitable abuses and recognizes no sin and evil deep-seated in the very constitution of the present order, he is still in a state of moral blindness and without conviction of sin."[159] Rauschenbusch argued that instead it was necessary to change the system, by constructing a new, socialized economy in which production would no longer be linked to the quest for individual self-advancement.

The Critique of Prudence

For Rauschenbusch, then, promoting the individualistic virtues was insufficient because it made too few demands on society, ignoring the need for systemic rather than individual reform. That is a familiar—though not for that reason necessarily an invalid—critique. A less global version of it—in the name of governmental regulation rather than ownership—was accepted by undoubted partisans of moral reform.[160]

Rauschenbusch offered a second critique, though, that is less familiar and more interesting, because it addresses the individualistic virtues on their own moral ground. The charge here is not that the individualistic virtues ask too little of society, but that they ask too little of the individual because they are necessarily infused with selfishness.

In Rauschenbusch's view, a Social Gospel was needed because American Protestantism had traditionally preached only an individualist gospel, which restricted itself to excoriating the sins of individuals and inculcating individualist virtues. He charged that "the moral teaching of the church in the past" was defective because it dealt exclusively with "private and family life" rather than social and economic life. It had "boldly condemned drunkenness, sexual impurity, [and] profanity," while remaining "dumb" about "the most pressing questions," having "nothing to say about the justice of . . . paying wages fixed by the hunger of the laborers." The burden of Rauschenbusch's critique was that "the morality of the church is not much more than what prudence, respectability, and good breeding also demand."[161]

To be sure, business dealings in which employers unfairly get the better of comparatively powerless employees deserve condemnation, as Brace and Lowell would undoubtedly have agreed. But at the same time, one can argue that Rausch-enbusch's dichotomy between private life and economic life was too sweeping, because the conduct of private life affects people's economic performance and rewards. As Rauschenbusch himself understood, to condemn drunkenness was to criticize individual misbehavior in part because of its economic consequences. The misspending of wages could only exacerbate poverty, and there were sound economic reasons for campaigning against it in the workers' own interests.

The deeper question, though, concerns the status of prudence. Rauschenbusch rightly argued that Christian morality should do more than merely inculcate it. But in doing so, did he simply suggest that prudence is a necessary but hardly a sufficient moral guide for our lives? Or did he argue more radically that prudence is somehow morally tainted, morally suspect, because it is at bottom an aid to self-seeking and self-advancement?

Clearly Rauschenbusch believed—with good reason—that American Protestantism's traditional faith in the efficacy of the prudential or individualist virtues blinded it to the social causes of much poverty for which the moral failings of individuals could not fairly be blamed. Rauschenbusch's most important theological critic, Reinhold Niebuhr, called attention to this element in his thought: as Niebuhr observed, Rauschenbusch "ascribed all of [middle-class Protestantism's] blindness to its individualism, and he meant that kind of Calvinism which believed it exhausted the moral demand of Christianity in inculcating thrift, industry, and honesty."[162]

But Rauschenbusch's critique of the prudential virtues went beyond the claim that they did not relieve poverty on their own. The wider scope of his criticism is suggested by a historian of Protestant social thought, who observes that advocates of the Social Gospel like Rauschenbusch tended not to speak of "the productive virtues," such as "industry, thrift, calculation, the classic virtues of the later Calvinism." Instead, "they dwelt on the social virtues, not the productive virtues," because they favored "the generation of new motives" for the social order.[163] It was not enough to make better accumulators out of the poor, because accumulation itself was suffused with selfishness. The proper aim was not to achieve more effective self-seeking, but more altruism and less self-seeking.

It is Rauschenbusch's moral concern to promote new motives—not just his economic concern to reduce poverty—that explains his socialism. He distrusted and disliked an economic system based on individuals' competitive quest for self-advancement, in which self-interest rightly understood was a principal check on wrongdoing. For Rauschenbusch, capitalism was morally defective, because its "only restraint is that of prudence; the tricks of the trade must not injure sales or anger customers. Thou shalt not kill the goose that lays the golden eggs."[164]

Significantly, this critique of prudential morality also colored Rauschenbusch's understanding of the efforts of individuals to improve their lot. At least in his early unpublished manuscript it led him to criticize thrift, which in his view contradicted the spirit of Christianity:

> Christ . . . forbids us to insure ourselves against the future by the hoarding of wealth, because we are sure to fasten our heart to our treasure. He bids us not worry about the future, but to seek the establishment of the Kingdom of God on earth. . . . He commands us to share with one another as any man needs it, and this mutual help of the community will afford the stability and the insurance against cases of sickness or distress.[165]

Money saved for a rainy day was always suspect—theoretically because it implied a distrust of God's providence, practically because it could instead have been dispensed to aid the poor. (The practical argument also formed part of Addams' case against thrift: "Saving . . . appears almost criminal in a poorer quarter where the next-door neighbor needs food, even if the children of the family do not.")[166]

As we have seen, Brace supported social insurance to supplement individual efforts at thrift that were likely to be inadequate; by contrast, Rauschenbusch made a far more radical argument. In a remarkable passage, he advocated social insurance as a replacement for individual efforts at thrift that were morally suspect because self-seeking: if a man "lays by something to educate his children, if he lays by something for his wife's old age—who will condemn him until we have a society Christian enough to relieve the individual of self-insurance."[167]

In the current, not-yet-socialized order, one could not fairly "condemn" a man for being provident to secure his family's future; in a better order, though, individuals would no longer need to exercise individualist virtues to secure their future, because society would collectively "relieve the individual" of the burden of self-insurance. For Rauschenbusch (and, we just saw, for Addams as well) thrift was suffused with selfishness—if only the muted selfishness that leads parents to prefer the welfare of their family to the welfare of all others. In this remarkable passage, the individualist's nightmare vision—a collectivist society in which aspirations to self-reliance wither away—emerges as Rauschenbusch's utopia. In a truly socialized society, human affection would be extended from the family to encompass all one's fellow citizens.[168]

Elsewhere Rauschenbusch elaborated on his moral critique of prudential self-regard in this way:

The single acts of religion and morality are not supposed to earn anything, but everything is lumped together and reward expected. It is a more long-range self-ishness than that which seeks immediate gratification, but it is selfishness still. The farmer who deposits the proceeds of his market sales in the bank on Saturday instead of investing them in a store suit or mixed drinks, is a prudent man; by and by he will use his savings to buy another meadow lot. On Sunday he abstains from carrying in his hay, misses a whole working day, walks three miles in the broiling sun to the meeting-house where he succeeds in keeping awake part of the time. He is looking for "the welfare of his soul," his "eternal well-being." He is the same prudent man in the one case as in the other; it is in each case his "well-being" that he is thinking of; only one investment is to be realized in this world, and the other in the next.[169]

It would be wrong to make too much of this critique of prudence, which is directed at the church, not the poor: it focuses on what the church should teach, not what the poor should do. Rauschenbusch immediately went on to qualify the critique: "We should not condemn" the farmer's behavior, he added, because it is "natural." Rauschenbusch also conceded that "that self-control which can re-nounce immediate gratification for the sake of some larger and higher profit in the future is the necessary condition of all noble pursuits and of an established soci-ety."[170]

Nevertheless, Rauschenbusch was genuinely critical of the virtues linked to individual self-advancement. He worried that the prudential emphasis on the re-wards of virtue would only harden men "in their selfishness instead of rousing them out of it," thereby "chang[ing] the range but not the quantity of it." And this criti-cism applied to contemporary Christianity, which was defective because exces-sively individualistic. Paradoxically, even Christianity's focus on self-denial pro-moted selfishness, because it taught us only "to sacrifice ourselves to ourselves," to forgo pleasure in this world to secure it in the next: the secular counterpart of such self-sacrifice was saving, which was admittedly made possible by the deferral of gratification, but was nevertheless merely a sublimated form of selfishness. Osten-sibly Christian ethics (and, it need hardly be said, secular ethics) were defective because they failed to teach us to sacrifice ourselves for others.[171]

How should we evaluate Rauschenbusch's critique of prudence?[172] On one level, the critique is persuasive: even Adam Smith granted that there was nothing noble or inspiring about prudence, an ordinary virtue that aims to facilitate the mundane accomplishments of mundane people. Prudence is not an altruistic vir-tue; it does indeed seek only to rationalize selfishness, not to overcome it.

But the important consideration, again, is the goal at which Rauschenbusch aimed. If the goal was to reduce poverty, the propensity to seek one's own advan-tage offers benefits that Rauschenbusch consistently underestimated. For that rea-son, there is a tension between Rauschenbusch's desire to reduce poverty and his critique of "utilitarian morality" as "the morality of natural selfishness, which even bad men know well how to handle." Rejecting utilitarian morality, he argued instead for what he saw as a higher morality: "Only the morality which does good for its own sake, independently of considerations of usefulness [to the doer of good] allies us to God."[173]

But in practice, as the moral reformers understood, the "morality of natural selfishness" facilitates—though it does not ensure—the movement of poor people out of poverty. In preaching the individualistic, prudential virtues, the moral reformers assumed that the poor—like the nonpoor—were motivated by a self-interest that was not particularly problematic from a moral standpoint. Like all of us, the poor were self-interested; for the moral reformers, a key to reducing their poverty was to teach them to be more effectively self-interested. In different ways, diligence, sobriety, and thrift are all manifestations of sublimated self-interest, through which gratification can be heightened by being deferred. In practice, one can suggest, the poor did not need to learn that (and why) self-seeking was wrong; instead they needed to learn how to mobilize the virtues to be better at self-seeking.

Rauschenbusch's critique of the moral merits of deferred gratification was theoretical rather than practical: it was obviously not delivered to guide or even to affect the action of the poor.[174] One can legitimately question the fairness of expectations that the poor, who receive few enough gratifications in any case, should defer them as a matter of course. Nevertheless, it remains the case that prudent self-regard—Tocqueville's self-interest rightly understood—can help the poor reduce their poverty. Unfortunately, Rauschenbusch doubted the moral merits of self-interest; in ways he doubted that economic self-interest really could be defensible, really could be rightly understood.

Victims of the Rich

If only by implication, Rauschenbusch raised questions about the morality of efforts by the poor aimed at individual self-advancement: Could a poor person justly save money that could instead be bestowed upon others among the poor? In addition, he questioned the efficacy of such efforts, by casting the poor as victims of the rich. Here Rauschenbusch went beyond saying that the poor were poor through no moral fault of their own: instead he asserted that they were poor through the moral fault of the rich.

Rauschenbusch did not deny the immorality of the paupers and criminals who populated urban slums. But he did limit their moral responsibility for their sad condition. Instead, it was the rich who deserved blame for the immorality of the poor—that is, the minority of the poor who were immoral. The rich and the poor were "two destructive and dangerous classes"; still, it was "the strong" who should be held responsible not only for themselves, but also for "the weak ones whom their climbing feet have pressed down into the mud."[175] "The wealthy class . . . contaminate[d] the morality of the working classes."[176]

In particular, while "pauper habits" were both real and deplorable, paupers themselves were ultimately not to blame for them. Instead, society was; pauper habits were "awakened and fostered by the existing inequalities."[177] Similarly, to the extent that sexual immorality was rife among the poor, again the rich were to blame: "The maximum number of marriages coincides with the minimum price of grain. Those who artificially disturb and depress the industrial prosperity of the people bear the guilt of checking marriage and driving the sexual impulse to seek illicit means of gratification."[178]

Rauschenbusch was hardly unique in depicting the wealthy of the Gilded Age as a singularly unattractive class. For that reason, one need not assert that his moral criticisms of the rich were erroneous—although they were clearly gross generalizations. Instead, the problem is quite different. By making the rich responsible for the moral failings of the poor, Rauschenbusch circumscribed the moral agency of the poor.

In depicting the poor as the victims of the rich, Rauschenbusch necessarily cast doubt on the capacity of the poor to improve either their moral or their economic status. In his estimation, society could take steps to improve the condition of the poor, as could the wealthy. But could the poor take any steps on their own to promote, say, their employability or to encourage familial responsibility? Rauschenbusch does not really address questions like these. The moral reformers may at times have wrongly exaggerated the capacity of the poor to improve their condition through moral exertion; on the whole, though, that is perhaps a more salutary error—for the poor themselves—than Rauschenbusch's abstraction from their capacity to do so.

For the reformers, the moral buck had to stop with the poor if the economic bucks were to start flowing to them: that was the basis for their belief that the poor could take steps to improve their condition by practicing the virtues. But the moral reformers' emphasis on the moral agency of the poor virtually disappears in Rauschenbusch; by depicting the poor as victims of the rich, Rauschenbusch necessarily suggested that the poor could do little, either morally or economically, to better their condition.

Economic and Moral Revolutions

Having completed this survey of Addams's and Rauschenbusch's thoughts on moral reform, let us now return to the question with which this chapter began: Did the decline of individualist economics necessitate the demise of the individualist virtues? The example of Brace and Lowell suggests not. It was possible to favor abridging laissez-faire for no other reason than to increase the effectiveness of the individualist virtues in reducing poverty.

But Brace and Lowell could maintain their allegiance to the virtues because they did not consider economic self-interest to be morally problematic. They believed that the sublimation of self-interest by the virtues—coupled with structural reforms designed to increase the rewards of virtue—would do much to reduce poverty.

By contrast, in some respects Addams and Rauschenbusch wanted not so much to reduce poverty as to lessen the power of economic self-interest. Perhaps they can more accurately be understood as moral transformers rather than reformers: unlike Brace and Lowell, they hoped less to render self-interest prudent than to overcome it by promoting altruism. In other words, Addams and Rauschenbusch could not wholeheartedly venerate virtues that aim to sublimate rather than suppress self-interest, because and to the extent that they sought a more radical moral transformation than the moral reformers envisioned—the creation of a society dedicated to collective virtue or Christian altruism. Self-interest rightly understood can have only limited appeal to those with genuine moral misgivings about economic self-interest.

To the considerable extent that Addams's and Rauschenbusch's writings had a practical impact, it was no doubt salutary: the scope of laissez-faire was diminished, and the poor were often legitimate beneficiaries of that diminution. Their moral legacy, though, was somewhat more problematic. As we have seen, Addams questioned the capacity of the poor—who were often "primitive" and "emotional," hence deficient in "the sense of prudence"[179]—to take the sorts of self-advancing actions that characterized the middle class. To expect the poor to manifest the same virtues as the middle class was to be "incorrigibly bourgeois."[180] For his part, Rauschenbusch contended that society's "existing inequalities"[181]—rather than any internal qualities that the poor themselves perhaps could alter—were the true cause of their dependency.

Central components of the demoralized (and demoralizing) conception of poverty that became a ruling paradigm in late-twentieth-century America were already present in embryonic form in the writings of Addams and Rauschenbusch early in the century: self-advancing action could be expected from the middle class, but not the poor; the responsibility for self-defeating action (or inaction) could legitimately be lodged only with society, never with the poor.

As these ideas attained dominance, the economic transformation desired by Addams and Rauschenbusch—the reduction of poverty—was ironically impeded by the moral revolution that they somewhat inconsistently espoused, in which the individualist virtues that both sublimate self-interest and lessen poverty were ignored, if not attacked.

The individualist virtues, buttressed by structural reforms, can do much to reduce poverty. But the reduction of poverty was not, finally, Addams's and Rauschenbusch's overarching goal. Instead they sought a morally transformed society, in which the scope of economic self-interest would be severely limited. And if that is the goal, the individualist virtues are not part of the solution: instead they are part of the problem.[182]

JOSEPH TUCKERMAN
National Portrait Gallery, Smithsonian Institution

WILLIAM ELLERY CHANNING
National Portrait Gallery, Smithsonian Institution

ROBERT M. HARTLEY
©Collection of The New-York Historical Society

CHARLES LORING BRACE
The Children's Aid Society

JOSEPHINE SHAW LOWELL
The Schlesinger Library, Radcliffe College

AMOS WARNER
Stanford University Archives

JACOB RIIS
Library of Congress, Prints and Photographs Division, LC-USZ62-57745

MARY RICHMOND
Courtesy of the Rockefeller Archive Center

WALTER RAUSCHENBUSCH
American Baptist Historical Society

JANE ADDAMS
Library of Congress, Prints and Photographs Division, LC-USZ62-10598

5 THE REJECTION OF MORAL REFORM

Addams and Rauschenbusch articulated—however ambivalently—a critique of moral reform that was prompted, I have argued, less by the economic revolution of industrialization than by a moral revolution questioning the relevance and desirability of individualist virtues. Now we must examine that moral revolution more closely, while bringing our story closer to the present. We can do so by examining two influential critiques of moral reform from the past generation: the rejection of moral reform as a manifestation of "blaming the victim" of poverty and as an unfair imposition of "social control" by elites over the masses.

The two works to be examined are not directly comparable to the writings of the moral reformers, which consist largely of practical advice about how the poor could most effectively be helped: one (William Ryan's *Blaming the Victim*) is a theoretical analysis of the nature of poverty, the other (Frances Fox Piven and Richard A. Cloward's *Regulating the Poor*) a theoretical analysis of responses to poverty. Nevertheless, the two books usefully illustrate the wholesale rejection of moral reform that characterized much thinking about poverty a generation ago.

Common to both volumes was a radical de-emphasis on any actions that the poor themselves might take to better their condition. Because they say little about the efforts of the poor, the works do not argue against the reformers' virtues; instead the works tacitly assume their irrelevance. The virtues that the poor should manifest, which figure so prominently in the moral reformers' analyses of poverty, play virtually no role in these influential recent discussions.

This transformation, in which the potential virtues of the poor disappear from view, points to an irony of great interest. On one hand, it can perhaps be argued that the moral reformers overrated the efficacy of the virtues as means of reducing poverty, in that multitudes of poor people faithfully practiced them but nevertheless remained poor. But on the other, those who subsequently disparaged moral reform abstracted from the virtues at a time when the virtues were more effective weapons against poverty: the efficacy of the virtues has been heightened by a vast increase in national wealth and by the implementation of numerous structural reforms that ease the lot of the poor. The virtues could do more to decrease poverty when they tended to be ignored than they could in the earlier era in which they had been widely celebrated.

In this respect American diagnoses of poverty have often been unsuited to the specific malady under consideration at any given time. Moral remedies were avidly prescribed when poverty would have been responsive to structural and environmental reforms—and moral remedies were then removed from the physician's pharmacopoeia when they were increasingly pertinent.

The Great Transformation

How should we understand the shift in the dominant understanding of poverty from the nineteenth to the twentieth century? As we saw in contrasting Brace and Lowell with Addams and Rauschenbusch, the important development was less the recognition of structural and environmental constraints upon the poor than the conscious de-emphasis of the capacity of the poor themselves to improve their situation in meaningful ways. Because that is so, the conventional view—that an earlier moral explanation of poverty, emphasizing the failings of individuals, was finally replaced by a more satisfactory environmental explanation, emphasizing the failings of society—is insufficient.

That conventional view is ably summarized by Robert H. Bremner, describing the change in attitudes at the turn of the century: "Once it was agreed that virtue and vice knew no class lines, interest in the so-called moral causes of poverty began to decline. Students of social conditions no longer deemed it profitable to exercise themselves about the precise amount of distress properly attributable to various categories of undesirable behavior." Instead, "the new school of reformers . . . insisted that social rather than individual weaknesses were the basic causes of poverty."[1]

But Bremner's formulation is insufficient. To begin with, no one ever argued that moral failings were the exclusive causes of poverty, because the importance of environmental causes was always understood. No one was harsher in his condemnation of the moral shortcomings of the poor than Hartley; yet Hartley also stated repeatedly that the moral causes of poverty and pauperism could not be eradicated without an improvement of the environment in which the poor lived. Environmental factors causing poverty never had to be discovered, because intelligent people were always aware of them.

One can assert the importance of environmental factors without necessarily denying the importance of moral factors. An emphasis on society's responsibility for poverty is in principle compatible with radically different views of what can and should be expected of the poor themselves. First, one can argue—as Hartley did—that society must act to improve the physical environment of the poor, because only then are the poor likely to exercise the prudential virtues that would help them escape poverty. Alternatively, one can restrict one's focus to society's failings, believing that there is never a need to alter the behavior of the poor: in this view, the implementation of structural and environmental reforms addressing poverty's social causes is sufficient in itself.

Structural and environmental reforms can be advocated either to facilitate moral improvement or because it is held to be irrelevant. Structural and environmental reforms can be understood to be necessary (to encourage the prudent actions of the poor) but not sufficient in themselves; alternatively, they can be understood to be both necessary and sufficient. At issue, then, is not whether the environment stood in need of improvement (which no one ever denied), but whether the behavior of the poor was also a relevant consideration, insofar as it could help them exit poverty or continue to mire them in it.

It may be that the moral reformers tended to understate the importance of structural factors as causes of poverty and pauperism, and of structural remedies as solutions. But at the same time, the moral reformers never argued for the irrelevance of structural factors altogether. In contrast, in the recent past many analysts have insisted that poverty is explicable *exclusively* in terms of structural factors: any emphasis on the occasionally self-defeating behavior of the poor, any exhortation to improve such behavior, is seen at best as a diversion, more often as an attack upon the poor. In this sense, the moral reformers were willing to consider a wider range of factors than their latter-day critics; conceivably, then, we replaced a more comprehensive perspective with a narrower one.

The real story is not that environmental causes were discovered (although their greater importance certainly did—rightly—come to be acknowledged); the real story is that the greater emphasis on structure and environment was accompanied by a conscious decision to ignore any moral issues posed by the occasionally self-defeating behavior of the poor. Logically, an increasing recognition of the importance of environmental factors does not preclude a continued recognition of the importance of moral ones. As a matter of historical fact, though, the increased emphasis on the environment was often accompanied by a reluctance to assess the behavior of the poor—both good and bad—in moral terms.

A focus on complementary moral and environmental factors was in some cases replaced by a belief that nothing but environmental factors could legitimately explain poverty. In different but overlapping ways, that belief underlies the rejection of moral reform as a form of blaming the victim or a manifestation of social control.

Blaming the Victim

William Ryan, a psychologist specializing in community planning and social problems, was an influential early critic of the Moynihan report, which in 1965 called attention to the instability of the black family as an obstacle to racial equality.[2] But his most enduring contribution to social policy—and to the English language, to which he added a useful expression—was his 1971 book, *Blaming the Victim*. In it he argued that the proper approach to social problems lay in attempts to remedy their structural causes—not the failings of those who are victimized by them:

> The crucial criterion by which to judge analyses of social problems is the extent to which they apply themselves to the *interaction* between the victim population and the surrounding environment and society, and, conversely, the extent to which they eschew exclusive attention to the victims themselves—no matter how feeling and sympathetic that attention might appear to be. Universalistic analyses will fasten on income distribution as the basic cause of poverty, on discrimination

and segregation as the basic cause of racial inequality, on social stress as the major cause of emotional disturbances. It will focus, not on problem families, but on family problems; not on motivation, but on opportunity; not on symptoms, but on causes; not on deficiencies, but on resources; not on adjustment, but on change.[3]

Ryan's argument, it should be noted, was directed not at conservatives but at liberals. He declared that "Blaming the Victim is . . . quite different from old-fashioned conservative ideologies," which "simply dismissed victims as inferior, genetically defective, or morally unfit." Instead Ryan directed his ire at liberals who believed that the poor were sometimes incapable of seizing opportunity because their environment had harmed them:

> The new ideology attributes defect and inadequacy to the malignant nature of poverty, injustice, slum life, and racial difficulties. The stigma that marks the victim and accounts for his victimization is an acquired stigma, a stigma of social, rather than genetic, origin. But the stigma, the defect, the fatal difference—though derived in the past from environmental forces—is still located *within* the victim, inside his skin.[4]

Any attempt to reduce poverty by promoting the self-advancing behavior of the poor was rejected from the outset as a manifestation of victim-blaming. To suggest that some among the poor might benefit from "better values" or "habits of thrift and foresight" was not an attempt to help the poor but an unfair attack upon them, reflecting "blind[ness] . . . to the basic causes of the problems."[5]

Ryan's unwillingness to contrast better and worse ways of responding to poverty stemmed from a misguided egalitarian conviction that solidarity with the poor precludes our making distinctions among them—praising some among them for taking steps to improve their situation while criticizing others for failing to do so. Instead, Ryan held that responsibility for the condition of all of the poor must be placed elsewhere, either with elites or society as a whole. (In this respect Rauschenbusch's depiction of pauperism as the product of "the existing inequalities"[6] can be seen as an early critique of victim-blaming.)

The title's focus on a singular "victim" aptly prefigures the book's message: it is as though the poor consist of a single undifferentiated mass, as opposed to many individuals, some of whom respond to their plight with more appropriate strategies than others. In this respect Ryan's depiction of the poor effectively prevented him from practicing what he preached: as we saw above, Ryan advocated focussing on the "*interaction* between the victim population and the surrounding environment and society," as opposed to bestowing "exclusive attention [on] the victims themselves." But in reality Ryan instead concentrated exclusive attention on the failings of "the surrounding environment and society." He gave no sense that "the victim population" can and does react in different ways—some more prudent than others—to its surrounding environment and society.

As a result, *Blaming the Victim* lurches toward one fallacious extreme while painstakingly avoiding the other. Ultimately, the poor themselves—at least as agents capable of affecting their own destiny—disappear. They are seen only as victims, who admittedly are not to be blamed, but also seem incapable of taking any actions for which they might merit praise. It is noteworthy that Ryan proclaimed categorically that "the overwhelming majority of the poor" have "no access to methods of increasing [their] income." The solution to their plight is for us (that is, the nonpoor) to "raise their income": the possibility that the poor might take steps themselves to raise their income is effectively discounted.[7]

Ryan's discussion of slum housing offers a second useful example of how the agency of the poor disappears in his analysis. He indignantly rejected the supposition that "slum dwellers play a causative role in the creation of slums," by "ruin-[ing] the property through carelessness, poor housekeeping habits, [or] neglect."[8] In his view it was inconceivable, for example, that actions taken by slum-dwellers might somehow "lure a colony of rats and cockroaches into [a] house."[9]

In fact, it is fairly apparent how slum-dwellers in many cases may bear at least partial responsibility for infestation by vermin. Slum-dwellers as well as slumlords (and municipal authorities) share responsibility for ridding their premises of garbage; and when residents fail to bag and dispose of garbage properly, they help bring on infestation. Even by Ryan's own calculations—in which evil slumlords are exclusively to blame for infestation—some one-sixth of all violations of the housing code may be attributable at least in part to tenant actions or inactions.[10] Yet he heatedly attacked the idea that one helpful response to substandard housing might be to "acculturate" the residents, so that they could take steps to prevent it from deteriorating.[11]

By contrast, in the older understanding embraced by Hartley, one could fervently argue for the construction of better and more modern housing for the poor—while also contending that some of the needed remedies were "in the power of the laboring classes to apply," such as "domiciliary and personal cleanliness" and "the prompt removal of all slops and refuse matter."[12] Hartley believed that it was in part (though only in part) up to tenement residents themselves to take actions to improve their housing. His assessment of the slum problem was broader and more comprehensive than Ryan's; it is not blaming the victim to think that Hartley's assessment was also more commonsensical and more accurate.

For psychological reasons that are fairly apparent, to suppose with Ryan that the poor are helpless victims of social forces beyond their control does them harm. As Lawrence Mead has noted, the belief that one has at least some control over one's fate is linked to happiness (for "rich and poor, successful and unsuccessful alike"), and "strongly linked to getting ahead in life."[13] Unreasonable moral demands should never be made upon the poor; but having no expectations for the poor to meet is also unreasonable.

Ryan's approach to the problems of poverty was characterized by an insistence on an absolute dichotomy: either the poor are exclusively to blame for their condition, or society is. But this dichotomy is false. There is no reason to believe that we must choose between two mutually exclusive alternatives, with the poor being either wholly responsible for their plight or wholly powerless to remedy it. There is no reason to suppose that the poor are wholly constrained by social and environmental forces or that they are moral actors who are altogether free. Instead, it is far more reasonable to suppose, as the moral reformers did, that two different sorts of factors interact: the poor are constrained by their environment, but they can still take some steps on their own to improve it.

In our time Glenn Loury is one of many analysts who have powerfully argued for the need to overcome the false dichotomies that so frequently enjoin us to choose between individual and social causes of poverty, as though one of the two sets must invariably and completely exclude the other:

> The mother of a homeless family is not simply a victim of forces acting on her; she is in part responsible for her plight and that of her children. But she is also being acted on by forces — social, economic, cultural, political — larger than herself. She is not an island; she is impacted by an environment; she does not have complete freedom to determine her future. It is callous nonsense to insist that she does, just as it is mindlessness to insist that she can do nothing for herself and her children until "society" reforms. In fact, she is responsible for her condition; but we also must help her — that is *our* responsibility.[14]

Defending Moral Judgments

Ryan's contention that moral criticism of the poor amounts to victim-blaming is marked by a certain ambivalence — if only because it is hard to obliterate the line between virtue and vice and to ignore the importance of that line. Thus, while halfheartedly minimizing the harm done to black children who are born out of wedlock ("growing up in a broken family does not unfailingly doom a child to neurosis and failure"), Ryan nonetheless was impelled to deny that "a fatherless family represents the best of all possible worlds. Two parents are almost always better than one, and the psychological task of raising a reasonably effective child . . . is a difficult one for a mother going it alone."[15] In like manner, he denied that crime was particularly prevalent among the poor, but accompanied that denial with the assertion that crime is "a malignant infection in our society."[16]

Ryan seemed — surprisingly — to acknowledge something like a universal morality that is accepted across class and racial lines. Hence he denied the existence of a culture of poverty, arguing instead "that . . . every American, beyond the first-generation immigrant, regardless of race or class, is a member of a common culture."[17] But this is precisely why illegitimacy and crime are no more defensible among ghetto blacks than among upper-class whites.

In practice, though of course not in principle, illegitimacy and crime are even less defensible among the poor. This is because the rich can at times afford to be (or can get away with being) immoral, whereas the poor seldom can. Sexual adventurism of various sorts can obviously be found in the upper class as in the underclass, but its effect upon the underclass is far more likely to be calamitous.

"Present-oriented" behavior certainly characterizes many of the rich as well as the poor, but wealth provides a cushion against the damaging effects of such behavior.

According to a nineteenth-century joke, moralistic reformers believed that "only the well-to-do have a right to have any vices."[18] While the joke is unfair to reformers, it also points to an important truth that is forgotten in the concern to avoid blaming victims. No one has a right to do wrong; in that sense, a moral double standard that demands more of the poor than the rich is obviously unfair. But to the extent that improvidence is more likely to harm the poor than the rich, as a prudential matter the poor really do have a greater stake in avoiding it. Regardless of whether immorality "causes" poverty, mundane moral virtues such as diligence, sobriety, and thrift do make it easier to escape from poverty.

Adam Smith advanced this argument powerfully, pointing to the prudential considerations that historically have promoted a strict moral code within poor communities. Smith contended that two "systems of morality" could generally be found in any society at any given time—a "strict or austere" system and a "liberal or, if you will [a] loose" one. He contended that the loose system was found more often among the wealthy, and the austere system among the poor. Although that contention may seem paradoxical, it should not. Smith argued that "wanton and even disorderly mirth, the pursuit of pleasure to some degree of intemperance, [and] the breach of chastity" did not always ruin the lives of the rich. But such behavior posed far more of a threat to the poor:

> The vices of levity are always ruinous to the common people, and a single week's thoughtlessness and dissipation is often sufficient to undo a poor workman for ever, and to drive him through despair upon committing the most enormous crimes. The wiser and better sort of the common people, therefore, have always the utmost abhorrence and detestation of such excesses, which their experience tells them are so immediately fatal to people of their condition.[19]

Smith classified the poor morally, distinguishing the "wiser and better sort" from others. He did so not to blame or punish victims but precisely to praise and reward those who avoided victimization. His perspective should teach us that the desire to avoid victim-blaming at all costs can be counterproductive, insofar as it leads us to look backward rather than forward. Our chief concern ought not to be whether the poor are to blame for having done something in the past that accounts for their current poverty; instead we should focus on what we and the poor ought to do to reduce their poverty in the future. If we emphasize how to get out of poverty (rather than who is to blame for its current existence), differentiating between the self-advancing and the self-destructive behavior of the poor becomes far more defensible.

Social Control

The critique of moral reform a generation ago went beyond an attack on the need for the poor to take action to help themselves; to some extent it also included a frontal attack on the attempt to commend virtuous behavior to the poor. That attack is most evident in the denunciation of moral reform as a manifestation of the social control exerted by punitive elites over the poor. Writing in 1978, historian David J. Rothman testified to the ubiquity of the critique of social control:

> Whereas once historians and policy analysts were prone to label some movements reforms, thereby assuming their humanitarian aspects, they are presently far more comfortable with a designation of social control, thereby assuming their coercive quality. . . . The prevailing perspective looks first to how a measure may regulate the poor, not relieve them.[20]

Moral reform began to be understood as a tool with which elites oppressed the underprivileged. The social control critique discussed by Rothman is animated by a libertarian suspicion of the authority of elites over subordinates, no matter how benevolent its purpose appears to be. The practical impact of this critique has been vast: among many other developments, the de-institutionalization of mental patients, the elimination of eligibility standards for welfare recipients, and the abandonment of in loco parentis controls by colleges and even high schools over their students can all be understood as reactions against social control.

The premise behind these alterations in policy is that the interests of more and less powerful groups necessarily clash: suspicion began to be directed against exercises of power by putative social elites, who were accused of being chiefly concerned to maximize their power by forcing others to obey them.

To be sure, radicals are not alone in finding the arbitrary exercise of power worrisome. Nevertheless, the ire of the critics of social control has often been directed less at the power of arbitrary individuals than at the binding nature of social principles that serve both to legitimate and to check power. The attempts by moral reformers to alleviate poverty came to be received with particular scorn: social policies ostensibly aimed at helping the poor were damned for actually seeking to control their behavior.

What is striking about this reaction is the unstated assumption that these two aims necessarily conflict: after all, it is at least conceivable that changing the behavior of the poor can sometimes help them in important ways. Admittedly, attempts to better others often prove ineffectual and even harmful. Nevertheless, the critique of social control errs in attacking not faulty implementation but the premise behind all implementation: the mere attempt to promote the moral welfare of others in itself suffices to draw up an indictment.

That perspective is exemplified in a series of observations by historian Raymond A. Mohl. He declared that social welfare in the past was "used for the purpose of social control," as in the attempt by the friendly visitors of charity organization societies to "shap[e] and regulat[e] behavior," for example by "cultivating such decent and proper middle-class values as thrift, honesty, work, self-reliance, sobriety, piety, respect for authority, and the like."[21] Similarly, Mohl noted that state boards of charity in the late nineteenth century "sought to make the poor industrious, religious, temperate, thrifty, and self-reliant. Above all, it was believed that if the poor worked hard they would not become dependent. This emphasis on character building clearly marks the state charity boards as agencies seeking to control the poor."[22]

No doubt that is true; still it is remarkable that the charge is not that the charity workers or the boards *failed* to inculcate these qualities, or even that they should have applied other, more effective policies. (The implicit premise of the critique, of course, is that income should have been unquestioningly transferred to the poor.) The effort to inculcate the virtues is somehow made to seem criminal, and obviously to run counter to the true interests of the poor.

The attack on social control often seems to be motivated less by a humanitarian concern for the poor than by a fancied superiority to the morality of the bourgeoisie, which is viewed as an arbitrary and unfair constraint. (An early instance of that motivation may be apparent in Addams's critique of her hypothetical charity worker's attempt to force her "incorrigibly bourgeois . . . standards" upon the poor, even though they "fail to fit the bigger, more emotional, and freer lives of working people.")[23] In this respect the critique of social control can most profitably be understood as the product of a larger rejection of moral norms. In Rothman's words:

> We are witnessing the dissolution of the Progressive version of community as a viable concept, indeed the breakdown of normality as a viable concept. To many critics, there no longer seems to be a common weal that can be defined or appealed to as a justification for action. The very notion of a harmony of interests seems deceptive and mischievous. Not only can no one agree on what is good for all of us, no one can agree on what is proper behavior for any one of us.[24]

Regulating the Poor

Of all the American works critical of social control, Frances Fox Piven and Richard A. Cloward's *Regulating the Poor: The Functions of Public Welfare* has probably had the biggest impact. Rothman alluded to it in his contrast between the regulation and the relief of the poor; Mohl's comments appeared in the course of a symposium devoted to it. In 1975 a reviewer aptly described *Regulating the Poor* as "the most influential of the recent books expounding a 'social control' interpretation of American society."[25]

Piven and Cloward argued in their widely read work that expenditures on social welfare in capitalist societies are cyclical, expanding (to ward off riots and revolution) in bad times and contracting (to promote the work ethic) as the economy improves:

> Relief arrangements are ancillary to economic arrangements. Their chief function is to regulate labor, and they do that in two general ways. First, when mass unemployment leads to outbreaks of turmoil, relief programs are ordinarily initi-

ated or expanded to absorb and control enough of the unemployed to restore order; then, as turbulence subsidies [*sic*], the relief system contracts, expelling those who are needed to populate the labor market.[26]

As their use of the word "expelling" suggests, Piven and Cloward were distinctly unsympathetic to the idea that at least the able-bodied poor might reasonably be expected to support themselves through employment. They were so far from denying that unconditional relief saps the work ethic that they openly affirmed it:

> The . . . fundamental problem with which relief reform seeks to cope is the erosion of the work role. When large numbers of people come to subsist on the dole, many of them spurning what little low-wage work may exist, those of the poor and near-poor who continue to work are inevitably affected. From their perspective, the ready availability of relief payments (often at levels only slightly below prevailing wages) undermines their chief claim to social status: namely, that although poor they nevertheless earn their livelihood. If most of them react with anger, others react by asking, "Why work?" The danger thus arises that swelling numbers of the working poor will choose to go on relief.[27]

Yet notwithstanding their recognition of the damage done by unconditional relief to the work ethic (as well as to the family),[28] Piven and Cloward wholeheartedly endorsed unconditional relief: "We *take the position that the explosion of the* [*welfare*] *rolls is the true relief reform*, that it should be defended, and expanded."[29] The moral reformers hoped to reduce both dependency and poverty, seeking to achieve two goals that to some extent are in tension with one another; but that complexity and breadth of vision disappear in Piven and Cloward's analysis, in which the dependency of the able-bodied poor is in no way problematic. As Irving Kristol has noted, in this respect their work illustrates a remarkable transvaluation of the values of social workers: "The social work profession . . . was now populated by college graduates who thought it their moral duty to help people get on welfare—instead of, as used to be the case, helping them get off welfare."[30]

Piven and Cloward were consistently hostile to any attempts to restrict welfare payments to shape the behavior of recipients. It is wrong to encourage (let alone compel) welfare recipients to work; relief arrangements are faulted for aiding the poor only "on condition that they behave in certain ways and, most important, on condition that they work."[31] Similarly, they opposed "man-in-the-house" rules, whose burden was to deny aid to welfare mothers who shared their living quarters with men (because of the expectation that the men should provide for their households). Piven and Cloward's argument on this point deserves close attention:

> These and similar measures may be justified in the language of moral virtue but their economic effect is to ensure a pool of marginal workers. The men affected must take any work at any [w]age; and if they remain with their families, the chances are that their wives and children will have to work too.[32]

This formulation once again exemplifies the problem of the false dichotomy: we are asked to believe that if something has a specific economic effect upon the poor (their acceptance of low-wage work), its moral motivation is necessarily suspect. Thus "the language of moral virtue" is hypocritical, because the measures restricting welfare "ensure a pool of marginal workers." But this conclusion does not follow from its premise. Instead, one can quite plausibly argue—as all of the moral reformers would have done—that restrictive measures are "justified in the language of moral virtue" precisely *because* they "ensure a pool of marginal workers." If diligence is indeed a virtue, and if the able-bodied poor are better off— psychologically as well as economically—as workers than as idle recipients of a dole, then the most promising alternative for the able-bodied but low-skilled poor really is to form "a pool of marginal workers." Perhaps that argument is wrong, but it is a serious one in need of a refutation that Piven and Cloward never attempted to supply; instead, their own argument adopts its supposedly self-evident falsity as a premise.

Piven and Cloward were untroubled by the decline in diligence to which they themselves pointed: "People may stop working because for one reason or another they are unable to work, or they may repudiate the obligation to work, as the young black does who remains idle on the ground that blacks are denied any but the most menial jobs."[33] The serious practical question, though, is whether idleness is preferable—both morally and economically—to taking a menial job; at the very least, the argument of *Regulating the Poor* implies that idleness is no less desirable.

In fairness, Piven and Cloward explicitly declared that their argument is "not against work."[34] In the abstract and the future, that is certainly true: Piven and Cloward endorse "fundamental economic reforms" designed to achieve "full employment at decent wages."[35] But in practice and in the present, they are unalterably "opposed to work-enforcing norms."[36]

Piven and Cloward's position is that the poor can reasonably be expected to work only in good jobs that offer decent pay. But if decent pay is defined with sufficient generosity, the demand for it can mean (and in practice often does) that the poor should work only in jobs for which they are almost never qualified to be hired.[37] Insistent on well-paying work, Piven and Cloward strongly opposed the contention that work qua work may have value for the poor, bringing discipline and regularity into lives that all too easily slip into disorder.[38]

At bottom, Piven and Cloward rejected any attempt at enforcing the work ethic as a morally objectionable double standard applied to the poor but not the rich:

> The indignities and cruelties of the dole are no deterrent to indolence among the rich; but for the poor person, the specter of ending up on "the welfare" or in "the poorhouse" makes any job at any wage a preferable alternative. And so the issue is not the relative merit of work itself; it is rather how some people are made to do the harshest work for the least reward.[39]

Piven and Cloward were hardly unique in claiming that virtue cannot fairly be expected of the poor, because it is not always manifested by the rich; instead that contention is a hallmark of much writing about welfare. For example, policy analyst Joel Handler has argued that it is unfair to ask the poor to avoid "sexual promiscuity" and "idleness," because some among the rich are guilty of them: "As the price of survival, the poor are required to engage in certain behavior not required of the rest of society or to forego amenities and pleasures enjoyed by others."[40] Similarly, Herbert Gans has objected to the fact that "promptness, dress codes, and other work rules that can no longer be enforced in many parts of the economy can be maintained in the regulations for workfare."[41]

But the conclusion to be drawn from the undoubted moral failures of some among the rich is not that the poor should therefore be given some sort of moral free pass, enabling them to act as they please—no matter how self-defeating their actions may be. Of course there are people in all social classes who are promiscuous and idle. Still, the crucial question remains whether continence and diligence are virtues that should be commended to the poor. As we saw in discussing Adam Smith, the poor have good reasons for adopting them.

Moral Imperialism and the Case for Social Control

Piven and Cloward's critique of attempts to inculcate a work ethic led them to manifest the same sort of moral imperialism toward the poor that we earlier discerned in Jane Addams. Citing a 1966 study, which found that most welfare recipients "endorsed such practices as midnight searches [to determine whether men were sharing the premises of welfare recipients, who would therefore lose eligibility] or budget counseling," they concluded that "recipients tend to identify with their oppressors."[42]

In this passage and others, Piven and Cloward depicted the poor as dupes of the rich, victims of some sort of false consciousness who fail to understand their true class interests. Welfare recipients who are themselves critical of welfare are "victims [who] are induced to collaborate as victimizers."[43] The reluctance of the working poor to accept the wage subsidies that are often available from welfare agencies is thought to offer "powerful testimony to the force with which the ideology of work and success, together with abhorrence of the dole, has been driven home to those who gain the least from their labor."[44]

An alternative explanation is, of course, possible. It is at least conceivable that many of the poor are reluctant to accept a dole because they rightly understand that avoidable dependency is morally harmful—not because they have been fooled into accepting what radical social workers regard as that obvious canard. It is at least conceivable that the poor are "induced to collaborate as victimizers" not when they criticize welfare but when they accept the assurance of elite social scientists that passive acceptance of dependency is altogether unproblematic. It is at least conceivable, as Lawrence Mead has argued, that for good reasons the poor are not "rebels against . . . society," but "more conservative than the better-off about the issues of social order," and that they therefore support the firm enforcement of "orthodox values."[45] The moral arguments against accepting relief and for the enforcement of social norms deserve a serious hearing rather than out-of-hand rejection, even—in fact especially—when these arguments are made by relief recipients themselves.

The importance of social norms is actually evident in the argument of *Regulating the Poor*, which points to the need for social control even as it criticizes social control. Piven and Cloward presented the riots in the black ghettoes of the 1960s as a sign that "old patterns of servile conformity were shattered," as "the trauma and anger of an oppressed people . . . [were] turned against the social order."[46] They point to a "transvaluation," in which "disorderly [acts came] to be defined as morally proper": idleness was defended "on the ground that blacks [were] denied any but the most menial jobs," and theft came "to be justified on the ground that whites have always stolen from and exploited blacks, so reparations [were] due."[47]

According to Piven and Cloward's own testimony, the breakdown of order in the ghettoes increased crime and worsened public education.[48] They reported that vandalism became far more common in schools. In New York City schools, for example, the number of fires tripled between 1959 and 1969 (going from 109 to 330), and the number of broken panes of glass rose 71 percent in the same years (going from 161,000 to 275,000).[49]

Piven and Cloward explained these developments as the product of the loss of social control experienced by blacks migrating from the rural South to northern cities: the black migrants were "freed" from the "near-feudal pattern of control" that they had experienced in the South, and they were also "cut loose from their own traditional institutions—especially from their churches and from the established patterns of community relations that shape and direct people's lives."[50] They particularly emphasized "the weakening of the family as an agency of social control," as "the proportion of female-centered families among the ghetto poor of the larger cities range[d] well above half."[51] As a result, there were alarming increases in juvenile delinquency, drug addiction, and serious crimes.[52]

Piven and Cloward openly acknowledged the proliferation of social disorder in the inner cities. To be sure, they did not contend that the expansion of welfare was to blame for it: "Symptoms of disorganization may . . . spread among the poor, not because of the expanded availability of relief, but as a consequence of the socioeconomic dislocations [e.g., the migrations of southern rural blacks to the urban north] which lead to the expansion of relief-giving in the first place." But at the same time, they also did not contend that the expansion of welfare in any way lessened this social disorder: "Although the poor relief that is sometimes given . . . mitigates hardship, it does not repair the ruptures in social life that result from economic dislocation."[53]

Surprisingly, on Piven and Cloward's own showing there is much to be said for social control. If the granting of unconditional relief will not repair disorder, perhaps the inculcation of a work ethic—specifically, the insistence on regular employment for the able-bodied poor—will. If the loss of social control is harmful, and if unconditional relief does nothing to reduce that harm, heated indignation is not a reasonable reaction to the attempt to recreate social control by means of the discipline of work.

The (Moral) World Turned Upside Down

Piven and Cloward aptly employed the term "transvaluation" to describe the shift in moral attitudes regarding the proper behavior to be expected of the poor. As we have seen, that transvaluation was by no means restricted to—or altogether characteristic of—the poor themselves; it also featured prominently in the thought of influential analysts of poverty like Ryan and Piven and Cloward. Their writings, which present the poor as victims of society, consistently avoid any suggestion that the poor can perhaps choose behavior likely to mitigate their poverty.[54] Perhaps the moral reformers of the past occasionally made too much of the role that, say, heavy drinking played in exacerbating poverty; still, the appropriate response to the pendulum's swinging too heavily in one direction is not to arrest its movement at the opposite extreme.[55]

A useful example of the moral transvaluation that characterized much thinking about poverty a generation ago is apparent in the changed understanding of the composition of the black community. Writing in 1970, Nathan Glazer and Daniel Patrick Moynihan captured the alteration—describing it, in fact, as "an amazing transvaluation of values"—by quoting a spokesman for black militant groups who protested the construction of a proposed state office building in Harlem. The protesters, the spokesman explained, were "the people who truly represent the community—the welfare mothers, the students, a lot of the young bloods."[56] In this understanding, the black community was not "truly" represented by "the professional men, the businessmen, the civil servants, the workers, all of whom might well have given overwhelming approval to the building of a state office building in Harlem."[57] A representative black, in other words, could apparently not be gainfully employed.

More broadly, the transvaluation was reflected in the fate of the concept of the "deserving poor." One might think that the concept simply disappeared from our vocabulary as we rejected the moral outlook of the reformers, but that is not altogether so. Instead, political scientist Thomas Halper has persuasively argued, the term was simply redefined in the 1960s. Although Halper exaggerated the contrast that he drew for effect, he nevertheless pointed to a development of great importance. In a startling revaluation, the undeserving poor (according to the lights of the moral reformers) were suddenly deemed deserving:

> The old undeserving poor who were despised as insufficiently motivated have become today's deserving poor who are denied the opportunities and experiences

from which motivation springs; the old undeserving poor who were decried as "shiftless" have become today's deserving poor who refuse to be passively shunted off to "dead end" jobs; the old undeserving poor who were scorned as criminal ne'er-do-wells have become today's deserving poor who find themselves forced to respond to unjust conditions by going outside the law.[58]

By contrast, "The poor who seem to accept and support the dominant values and institutions of the society [were] derided as ignorant, naive, unaware of their true class interest, dupes of the power structure. These formerly deserving poor [were] now looked on as suckers unworthy of compassion or significant material assistance—in short, as the new *undeserving* poor."[59] In Halper's formulation, the deserving poor as newly understood "owe[d] their title to having rejected all that yesterday's deserving poor believed."[60]

The Cultural Contradiction of Poverty

How can we account for this transvaluation, evident in the unbridgeable gulf separating, for example, Mary Richmond from Frances Fox Piven? Clearly it resulted at least in part from developments that can only be alluded to here. Thus, in thinking about the rejection of moral reform, one would surely need to consider the impact of Prohibition and the Depression. Prohibition was regarded as a failure that discredited attempts to solve social problems by improving character, "an expression of the narrow-mindedness of American farmers and villagers" (even though it did not lead to an increase in crime and did succeed "in reducing alcohol consumption in the United States by between one-third and one-half").[61] And the Depression offered convincing evidence that poverty was "the result of bad luck rather than weak character, and that the social and economic forces that created poverty were often beyond the control of individuals."[62]

Ultimately, a full account of the transvaluation would probably also necessitate an explanation of the rise of moral relativism. The discussion here will necessarily be more modest: although the widespread poverty of the 1930s did much to discredit moral explanations of poverty, it is also useful to consider the way in which mass prosperity helped call the reformers' moral message into question.

The link between increased prosperity and the rejection of a strict morality of self-control has been sketched most notably by Daniel Bell in his seminal discussion of the cultural contradictions of capitalism. But earlier explorations of this theme exist as well. For example, recall Adam Smith's explication of the two sorts of moral systems. Smith asserted that a strict moral code was most common among the poor: for Smith, people were arguably most moral when they had to be, when their survival seemingly depended upon their rigid adherence to moral precepts.

But if "the vices of levity" are more common among "people of fashion" (that is, social and intellectual trendsetters), perhaps prosperity in some cases at least provides a cushion that makes a strict moral code seem questionable. All of the well-to-do are not people of fashion, of course; still, it is chiefly the well-to-do who can afford to be people of fashion. At least to the extent that people of fashion set the tone for a prosperous society, Smith's understanding appears to reverse that of Bertolt Brecht. As prosperity is generalized, morality becomes more permissive: *Erst kommt das Fressen, dann geht die Moral.*

Smith did not suggest that prosperity somehow undercuts the very morality that originally produced it. In a previous chapter, though, we saw Walter Rauschenbusch make an argument along these lines, at least with respect to the specific virtue of thrift. Rauschenbusch in turn echoed an earlier understanding of religion's capacity first to create wealth and then to be destroyed by it. Consider, for example, the following formulation by the founder of Methodism, John Wesley:

> I fear, wherever riches have increased, the essence of religion has decreased in the same proportion. Therefore I do not see how it is possible, in the nature of things, for any revival of true religion to continue long. For religion must produce both industry and frugality, and these cannot but produce riches. But as riches increase, so will pride, anger, and love of the world in all its branches. How then is it possible that Methodism, that is, a religion of the heart, though it flourishes now as a green bay tree, should continue in this state? For the Methodists in every place grow diligent and frugal; consequently they increase in goods. Hence they proportionately increase in pride, in anger, in the desire of the flesh, the desire of the eyes, and the pride of life. So, although the form of religion remains, the spirit is swiftly vanishing away.[63]

This passage nicely prefigures the view that Bell was later to elaborate. Bell's aim was to account for the decline in standing of the virtues—which he catalogued as "work, sobriety, frugality [and] sexual restraint"—that the moral reformers preached. He concluded that "the breakup of the traditional bourgeois value system . . . was brought about by the bourgeois economic system—by the free market, to be precise."[64]

Bell contended that the old virtues were undermined by the rise of "a consumption society, . . . with its emphasis on spending and material possessions."[65] Whereas "the basic American value pattern" had once "emphasized the virtue of achievement," so that "a man displayed his character in the quality of his work," in a startling reversal American culture became "primarily hedonistic, concerned with play, fun, display, and pleasure." He captured the change from the morality that "stressed interference with impulses" to what he called "fun morality" with an arresting quote from a *Time* magazine cover story about California: "I have seen the future . . . and it plays."[66]

Arguably, then, increasingly comfortable elites grew skeptical of virtues that were no longer so necessary to them: the advent of mass prosperity called into question the need for diligence, sobriety, and thrift—the virtues that were plausibly thought to create prosperity. This shift in moral outlook has also been captured by James Q. Wilson, although Wilson does not emphasize growing prosperity as its cause; instead he argues that a nineteenth-century "ethos of self-control" (promoting "temperance, fidelity, moderation, and the acceptance of personal responsibility"—that is, the virtues extolled by the moral reformers) was rejected and replaced by a twentieth-century "ethos of self-expression," celebrating liberation from social constraints.[67] As Wilson notes, "Today, and for the last few decades, enlightened people scoff at moral uplift."[68] Whereas the moral reform efforts of the nineteenth century were led by America's social and intellectual elites, "today one can imagine the graduates of our best universities leading almost any cause save one designed to instill orthodox morality."[69]

The moral reorientation discerned by Bell and Wilson is relevant to poverty insofar as elites have been consistent in refusing to preach to the poor the merits of virtues that they are no longer so intent on practicing themselves. The rejection of moral reform as an approach to reducing poverty may be explained, at least in part, by the altered self-understanding of American elites: those who do not principally pride themselves on their diligence, sobriety, and thrift will not insistently recommend these virtues to the poor.

One can suggest that social and intellectual elites—rather than the poor and downtrodden—were primarily responsible for the denigration of the virtues. Lawrence Mead calls attention to the alteration in social views effected by those who "sought . . . to challenge conventional beliefs about personal and social discipline. They wanted a society that was . . . less insistent on the work ethic, law abidingness, and the conventional family."[70]

James Q. Wilson has provided specific illustrations of the harmful impact that elites have had upon the larger population:

> Almost every new drug—heroin, cocaine, LSD, speed—was initially endorsed by elite users, only to be abandoned by them just about the time they caught on with a less privileged mass public. Theories that single-parent families are desirable alternative lifestyles were not invented by single mothers but by intellectuals who thought that they were removing a stigma from an oppressed class.[71]

The developments sketched by Mead and Wilson were catastrophic for the following reason: if an ethos of self-control is in fact helpful to the poor, then its replacement by an ethos of self-expression traps and further impoverishes them. Myron Magnet has recently developed this theme, focusing on the harm done to the poor by the triumph of a hedonistic morality among the nonpoor.

In a sense, Magnet updates Bell and Wilson (by analyzing the impact of the ideas of the 1960s), while exploring the relevance of those ideas to the specific problem of poverty. In the 1960s, he argues, many of the prosperous preached the benefits of liberation from the traditional constraints of morality. Their liberationist ethic, he contends, had a disastrous impact on the worldview and behavior of the poor: "Poverty turned pathological . . . because the new culture that the Haves invented—their remade system of beliefs, norms, and institutions—permitted, even celebrated, behavior that, when poor people practice it, will imprison them inextricably in poverty. It's hard to persuade ghetto fifteen-year-olds not to get pregnant, for instance, when the entire culture, from rock music to upscale perfume commercials to highbrow books, is intoxicated with the joy of what before AIDS was called 'recreational' sex."

Magnet contends that the American upper classes "withdrew respect from the behavior and attitudes that have traditionally boosted people up the economic ladder—deferral of gratification, sobriety, thrift, dogged industry, and so on through the whole catalogue of antique-sounding bourgeois virtues."[72] As Magnet notes (echoing the passage from Adam Smith discussed above), this cultural revolution has harmed the poor much more than the rich: "The Haves may pay a price for experimenting with sexual liberation or drugs or dropping out (almost always temporarily), but it is usually not a catastrophic price, nothing like the price the Have-Nots pay in ruined lives."[73]

Magnet is unabashedly conservative, so it is noteworthy that variants of his argument are also made by those on the left. For example, Christopher Jencks has argued that liberalized attitudes toward sex, marriage, and parenthood, which "almost certainly improved the lives of the educated elite," have had disastrous effects on poor children: "Shotgun weddings and lifetime marriages caused adults a lot of misery, but they ensured that almost every child had a claim on some adult male's earnings unless his father died. That is no longer the case." Now that "we are rich enough that affluent couples can afford the luxury of supporting two households, . . . elite support for the two-parent norm has eroded." As a result of this cultural change, "we can hardly expect the respectable poor to carry on the struggle against illegitimacy and desertion with their old fervor."[74]

Comparable arguments can be made about the virtues of diligence and thrift: precisely the lessons that the poor did not need (and often could not afford) to learn were taught by mainstream society. If too many poor people have been reluctant to take entry-level jobs, perhaps it is in part because they "have been told by parents, welfare departments, and the ever more affluent middle class generally that the small amounts they could earn by doing them are 'peanuts'—too little for a self-respecting person to bother with."[75] Thrift is said to be less common among today's poor because of the "major historical shift [among the nonpoor] in the direction of flying now and paying later," a shift that cannot be negated because "this is no longer the nineteenth century and there is no way of isolating the ghetto from the mass media and inundating it with McGuffey's readers."[76]

James Q. Wilson has contended that in the last hundred years "the world has experienced a shift from an era in which crime chiefly responded to material circumstances to one in which it responds in large measure to cultural ones"—a shift partially explained by "the collapse in the legitimacy of what once was respectfully called middle-class morality but today is sneeringly referred to as 'middle-class values.'"[77] My argument here—akin to Magnet's—is that a comparable shift has occurred with respect to poverty (even though poverty itself is a measurement of "material circumstances"): the culture produced by prosperity undermined the attitudes and behaviors that help create prosperity among the poor. The advent of that culture—an offshoot of prosperity that restricts its further spread—has embroiled us in what can be called (with apologies to Bell) the cultural contradiction of poverty.

In what sense is there a cultural contradiction? Because the virtues commended by the moral reformers fell into disrepute just when they might have been most effective in reducing poverty—as prosperity greatly increased, in tandem with a newfound commitment to expanding opportunities for the disadvantaged.

The scarcity endemic to the American economy in the past ensured that many would be poor, even if they practiced the virtues extolled by the reformers. By contrast, the virtues ought to be more effective weapons against poverty in an era of abundance, when full-time work even at low-paying jobs often suffices to lift one out of poverty. As Lawrence Mead has noted, "too few of the poor work steadily for low wages to be the immediate cause of need in most cases" today.[78] In contrast to the past, today "poverty is very uncommon among adults who work usual hours at *any* legal wage. The 'working poor' are considerably outnumbered by the nonworking."[79] But full-time work may well be less sought after by the poor than in the past, even though full-time work is at long last a reasonably reliable conduit out of poverty. The diligence espoused by the moral reformers is perhaps less common among the poor today, just when it could be expected to be more effective in combating poverty.

To speak of a decline in diligence is not to rule out the possibility that structural transformations of the economy (such as the loss of manufacturing jobs or the movement of jobs from the inner cities to the suburbs) may have harmed the poor. But it is to say that substantial opportunities nevertheless exist (as is demonstrated by the experiences of immigrants in the labor market);[80] it is therefore plausible to argue (again with Mead) that our chief aim today should no longer be "to enlarge opportunity by changing social structure, but rather to help make the poor more able to take advantage of existing opportunities"[81]—or, at the very least, that changes in social structure should be explicitly designed to encourage the practice of virtues such as diligence and thrift that facilitate the seizing of opportunities.[82]

As we have seen, a central aim of the moral reformers was to enable and encourage the poor to take advantage of such opportunities as existed. For this reason, the moral reformers continue to have great relevance for the analysis of poverty today. But America today is obviously a much wealthier country than it was a century ago; the absence of wealth in the America that they knew may ironically point to the moral reformers' shortcomings as analysts of poverty in their own time. The arguments against moral reform may well be less persuasive now (at the close of an era in which moral reform has largely been derided) than they were in moral reform's heyday (when its merits were largely unquestioned).

The Irony of Moral Reform

As we have seen, the moral reformers were driven almost ineluctably to support structural reform as an extension of their program. Recall Lowell's logic: if it was easier to prevent dependency than to rehabilitate the dependent, and if the harshness of industrial conditions encouraged too many workers to give up their struggle and embrace dependency, then those conditions had to be improved.

Nevertheless, it must also be admitted that the most far-reaching, significant structural reforms—such as old-age pensions, workers' compensation, and unemployment insurance—cannot be regarded as prominent goals of any of the moral reformers, with the possible exception of Brace. I do not mean this as a criticism, since the moral reformers' careers largely predated the impetus to enact policies like these. It would be absurd to criticize Tuckerman in the 1830s or Hartley in the 1840s and 1850s for failing to support comprehensive reforms that were seldom advocated until the early twentieth century.

Nevertheless, structural reform has to be regarded as a tangential concern of the moral reformers, not a primary one: the primary goal was to make the poor less poor by making them more virtuous. For that reason, the moral reformers endorsed structural and environmental reforms primarily as a means to a moral end. The crucial thing was for the poor to exercise the virtues that would reduce their poverty and prevent their dependency; structural and environmental reforms were endorsed because and to the extent that they were expected to increase the likelihood of virtuous behavior.

It is at least arguable, though, that the reformers were more concerned about the need to improve the behavior of the poor than they had reason to be. I have already hypothesized that the reformers were somewhat successful because they were in a sense preaching to the converted—encouraging the virtues among people who were already predisposed to practice them. If that is so, the need for moral reform would have been comparatively small.

An unlikely source—Groucho Marx—offers a comparison that supports this contention. Groucho was famous for not wanting to become a member of any club that would admit him; by the same token, it may be said, the interest shown by many among the poor in joining the moral reform "club" (in other words, their very receptivity to the reformers' message) points to the fact that they didn't really need to be admitted. Teaching the virtues to those who are already interested in learning to practice them is far from superfluous, but it is less essential (if also far more practicable) than teaching them to skeptics.

In any event, when judged by today's standards, the overall moral condition of yesterday's poor can seem positively enviable; for the most part, moral instruction does not seem to have been all that necessary for them. Lawrence Mead has argued this case effectively. As he notes, "The poor in [Jacob] Riis's day lived mostly in two-parent families, and children worked alongside their parents. The answer to poverty was higher wages, which economic growth eventually provided. Today we see mostly female-headed families living on welfare and single men, among whom not even the adults work regularly. On the whole, the immigrant poor of old were poor *despite* work, while the current poor are needy for *lack* of it." Accordingly, "the leading domestic issue has changed from how to raise wages and benefits for working people to how to turn more poor people into workers."[83]

In Mead's view, the contrast between yesterday's poor and today's poor means that moral reform was less urgent a century ago than it is now: "The old efforts for social control were undertaken largely by local notables interested in respectability, and they were aimed largely at 'vices,' especially drunkenness and prostitution. . . . The conditions in [today's] ghetto are . . . worse in human, if not economic, terms than anything faced by earlier social controllers. The moral reformers wanted to keep men out of saloons, but at least most poor men were working in that era, and most families were intact. Today, even poor people have higher incomes than average Americans did then, but the family, crime, and drug problems are much worse than a century ago." As a result, "yesterday's poor usually could take care of themselves, even if they drank; many of today's fail to do even that."[84]

If the nineteenth-century poor for the most part were already convinced of the importance of diligence, sobriety, and thrift, then perhaps structural reforms were more important in and of themselves (rather than as means of encouraging moral behavior) than the moral reformers may have supposed. To say this is not at all to denigrate the importance of the moral and behavioral issues that Tuckerman and the others emphasized: the reformers' virtues were not and are not irrelevant to reducing poverty. In fact, structural reforms such as old-age pensions, workers' compensation, and unemployment insurance were themselves intended to reduce poverty (and did, and in many respects still do, reduce it) only for the diligent— that is, those attached to the workforce.[85] The structural reforms presupposed and required for their success a population of reasonably virtuous needy workers (and their families): one can certainly argue that the efforts of the moral reformers (more broadly, the social consensus endorsing the virtues touted by the reformers) helped ensure and increase the population's virtue.

Conceivably, though, yesterday's poor were less in need of training in the virtues than of a more prosperous economy and increased opportunities that permitted them to exercise their already existent virtues. If that was indeed the case, perhaps it was not education in the virtues but structural reforms—coupled with, and made possible by, the tremendous expansion of the economy—that were most important in lifting millions of Americans out of poverty in this century. In the words of social welfare historian Clarke Chambers: "Tested pragmatically, social-welfare-as-social-reform worked. . . . Prosperity (unevenly distributed, as many social workers were quick to point out) seemed to offer, together with reforms already won, a way to remedy the dependency that came from social poverty."[86] The structural changes that the moral reformers emphasized less were probably more important in reducing poverty than the moral virtues that they emphasized more.

But today, ironically, the situation is reversed: many structural reforms have been enacted, while the self-defeating behavior of the poor decried by the reformers is comparatively more common now than in the past. As a result, one can argue that the analysis of the moral reformers is in fact more pertinent today—more genuinely relevant to the condition of the poor—than it was at the time and in the circumstances that produced it. To quote Mead once again:

> Researchers might return to a discourse about poverty more like that of a century ago. Then the debate chiefly was about the mentality or morality of the poor and how they might be reformed. . . . Contemporary writers criticize the Victorians for neglecting structural causes of poverty in an era when destitution was commonplace and equal opportunity policies unknown. In today's environment, following decades of economic expansion and social reform, a focus on enforcement and psychology is much more defensible.[87]

Poverty Then and Now

To illustrate both the failings of the moral reform analysis in its own time and its greater applicability in ours, consider a statement made by Lowell—who was notably sympathetic to structural reform—in 1896 (that is, after her experience of the 1893 depression):

> If it could be said that there were in the United States numbers of honest, industrious, intelligent, and energetic people who were in a chronic state of distress and suffering, that would be a horrible situation; and yet it would be a situation which would make the helping of them easier and more encouraging than is the helping of the people that now have to be dealt with; for since their distress is due to inherent faults, either physical, mental, or moral, it becomes very difficult to cure it.[88]

In this passage Lowell did not attribute poverty principally to the moral failings of the poor; she correctly pointed to the existence of "physical" and "mental" defects as well. Still, she did attribute poverty principally to a broad range of "inherent faults" of the poor.

Only eight years later, though, the important Progressive Era reformer Robert Hunter effectively questioned Lowell's premise, pointing to the existence of "many, many thousand families, who [were] in no sense paupers, [but were] in poverty." The poor, "the large class in any industrial nation who [were] on the verge of distress," were "able to get a bare sustenance, but they [were] not able to obtain *those necessaries which* [would] *permit them to maintain a state of physical efficiency.*"[89] Hunter estimated that there were 10 million poor Americans in his day (out of a total population of 82 million).[90]

But who were these poor people? Hunter insisted that the poor—those "who are up before dawn, who wash, dress, and eat breakfast, kiss wives and children, and hurry away to work or to seek work"—had to be distinguished from paupers, those "who have lost all self-respect and ambition, who rarely, if ever, work, who are aimless and drifting, who like drink, who have no thought for their children, and who live more or less contentedly on rubbish and alms."[91] Paupers were poor "because of their own folly and vice"; by contrast, the far larger class of the working poor (including the poor who aspired unsuccessfully to work) were "poor as a result of social wrongs," products of "miserable and unjust social conditions, which punish the good and the pure, the faithful and industrious, the slothful and vicious, all alike."[92]

Hunter argued persuasively that there were indeed "numbers of honest, industrious, intelligent, and energetic people" who needed only to fall ill, lose work, or age to be "in a chronic state of distress and suffering." But ironically, as Lowell's own remarks suggest, Hunter's findings meant that the problem of poverty—for all that it was more widespread than Lowell may have supposed—was actually easier to solve, not harder: since most of the distress of poor people was due not to "inherent faults," structural reforms and economic expansion were able to reduce poverty dramatically.

Because of the impact of structural reforms and economic expansion, in many respects the lot of the poor today is immeasurably better than it was in the nineteenth century or during the Depression. Two sets of statistics illustrate the contrast. First, productivity increases have made work far more remunerative than it was in the past. In constant 1982 prices, an hour of work is estimated to have bought less than $2 of personal consumption in 1900, less than $3 of personal consumption in 1929—but almost $10 in personal consumption in 1990, so that an hour's work earned roughly six times as much in 1990 as in 1900.[93]

Second, data from the Department of Labor's Consumer Expenditure Interview Survey indicate that families classified as poor—according to the Census Bureau's official definition of poverty—spent 71 percent of their income in 1992–1993 on necessities (food, shelter, utilities, and apparel): a significantly larger proportion than the 46 percent that the nonpoor spent on these items, but still notably less than 100 percent.[94] Robert Chapin's 1907 budget study of working-class New York City families offers a useful contrast here. In effect Chapin placed what we would now call the poverty line at $800, arguing that an income below that was "not enough to permit the maintenance of a normal standard."[95] He found that families with incomes between $700 and $800 devoted not 71 percent but 85 percent of their funds to these necessities (defined in the Chapin study as food, rent, fuel and light, and clothing). Even the comparatively well-off families, with incomes between $1,000 and $1,100, devoted 83 percent of their funds for the necessities.[96] One can confidently assert that the quality of the food, clothing, housing, fuel, and light available in 1992 far outstripped the quality of the same items in

1907; in addition, it is also striking that almost twice as much of the income of the poor in the more recent year—29 percent as opposed to 15 percent—was available for expenditure on items other than these necessities.

In an important article demographer Nicholas Eberstadt enumerates several other striking contrasts between poverty today and poverty in the more recent past. First, unemployment has never again been nearly so severe as it was in the Depression; in the recession year of 1992, the unemployment rate for the nonfarm labor force was less than one-fourth the 1934 level, and the median spell of unemployment was less than ten weeks. The existence of unemployment insurance means that even long spells of joblessness are not nearly so catastrophic as they were in the past.

In addition, the death of a father—a prime cause of poverty in the past—has virtually disappeared: whereas 8.5 percent of children under eighteen had lost their father to death in 1920, the percentage shrank by two-thirds as of 1965 (and by still more in the 1990s). Furthermore, government expenditures on behalf of the poor have increased vastly. In 1992 cash and noncash public benefits for persons with low incomes exceeded $22,000 for a family of four—the equivalent of $2,300 in 1929, a sum greater than that earned by three-fourths of all 1929 families. Finally, today's poor consume far more than they earn, so that statistics reporting the income of the poor (as in the Census Bureau's official measurements of poverty) greatly overstate the material deprivation that they suffer.[97]

With these developments in mind, it is helpful to reconsider a central premise of Hartley's understanding of poverty: he maintained that material improvement in the life of the poor was needed to promote their moral betterment. However valid that argument may have been in the mid-nineteenth century, it is likely to be less valid today: from a material standpoint today's poor are already much better off than were the poor of the nineteenth century.

But as Eberstadt proceeds to point out, this good news about the material condition of the poor tells only half the story. A greater proportion of children lived in fatherless homes in 1993 than in 1946, despite the fatherlessness caused by World War II. Criminality has surged, with four times as many persons serving time in prison in 1992 as in the early 1960s. Finally, a greater proportion of Americans were recipients of relief—that is, means-tested assistance—during the early 1990s than during the Depression: 20 percent of the white population (and 53 percent of the black population) in 1992, compared with 16 percent of the white population (and 26 percent of the black population) in 1935.[98]

Eberstadt summarizes his findings as follows:

> Despite tremendous material advances, revolutionary improvements in knowledge and technology, and a vast augmentation of national wealth, the country's domestic problems have by no means been eliminated. Paradoxically, by the early 1990s such problems as crime, dependency, and family breakdown were far more acute than they had been during the Great Depression, when general income levels, and general levels of schooling, were so much lower.[99]

As Eberstadt's analysis makes clear, the vastly greater consumption of the poor themselves has obviously not solved the problem of poverty. Instead, our antipoverty efforts today must deal with problems that were not faced and could not have been imagined during the New Deal — "problems . . . devolv[ing] from predictably injurious patterns of individual and parental behavior," patterns that "may account for a great fraction of the domestic problems we confront." Eberstadt concludes by calling for "the reassertion of individual and familial responsibilities" — moral reform — in order to deal with "the dysfunctions that sadden and dismay us most about our national condition."[100]

The Efficacy of the Virtues

One way of making sense of Eberstadt's findings is to say that the greater wealth of the country has vastly reduced poverty for those who practice the reformers' virtues. The claim that "honest, industrious, intelligent, and energetic people" are highly unlikely to be poor — at least to be poor for anything like a lengthy spell — is considerably more plausible today than it was in Lowell's time. Susan Mayer summarizes what has happened:

> As countries get richer, they often implement policies [i.e., the structural reforms discussed above] to reduce poverty among families hit by random catastrophes such as the death of a spouse, protracted illness, or job loss. When nations do this, poverty declines, but those who remain poor also become less like everyone else. . . . As poverty rates are lowered and poverty becomes less dependent on bad luck, those who stay poor for long periods of time are increasingly likely to be those who suffer from multiple liabilities [i.e., the "physical, mental, or moral" faults of which Lowell spoke].[101]

Those who remain poor in a rich country are therefore harder to help than those who are poor in a poorer country. Recognizing this fact, we can say that Lowell was perhaps not so much wrong as prematurely right: her analysis is more applicable to conditions today than to the conditions that she herself witnessed.

Drawing again on Mayer's work, we can say that the moral reformers were also prematurely right in a second respect: their choice of pauperism (or the vices associated with dependency) as opposed to poverty (or material insufficiency) as the foremost target of their efforts. We saw in Chapter 1 that this choice was explained in part by the fact that the problem of poverty must have seemed (and indeed was) comparatively insoluble a century ago — since it was easier to reduce pauperism, it made sense to try to do so.

Today, by contrast, our welfare policies have clearly returned to the attempt to reduce pauperism, but for the opposite reason: the problem of poverty — certainly as it was understood by the standards of a century ago — is no longer insoluble, because it has instead largely been solved. In Mayer's formulation, "When extra money prevents hunger or homelessness, or when it buys medical care and other necessities, it can make a big difference. . . . But in the United States most poor families can meet these basic material needs through a combination of Food Stamps, Medicaid, housing subsidies, government income transfers, and private transfers of cash, goods, and services. Under these circumstances the question is seldom whether money for basic necessities would help, . . . but usually whether money for goods and services beyond some [already attained] minimum would significantly" improve matters.[102]

The moral reformers were concerned with character formation because they couldn't (and in any case didn't want to) redistribute income to the poor; today we are concerned with character formation because we have already redistributed a great deal of income to the poor. How much? According to the calculations of Robert Rector and William F. Lauber of the Heritage Foundation, between 1965 and 1994 welfare spending came to no less than $5.4 trillion in 1993 dollars: some 70 percent more (adjusted for inflation) than the cost of America's victory in World War II.[103]

It is far more plausible today than in Lowell's time to deny that "honest, industrious, intelligent, and energetic" people suffer protracted spells of poverty, because on the face of it poverty is now a much easier fate to avoid. A decade ago a group of welfare analysts (including liberals such as Robert Reischauer and Alice Rivlin as well as conservatives such as Charles Murray and Mead) summarized what needs to be done to climb out of poverty:

"The probabilities of remaining involuntarily in poverty are remarkably low for those who

- complete high school
- once an adult, get married and stay married (even if not on the first try)
- stay employed, even if at a wage and under conditions below their ultimate aims[.]

Those who do these three traditional things may experience periods in poverty, but are quite unlikely to stay involuntarily poor."[104] As the authors subsequently noted, "These are demanding, although not superhuman, tasks."[105] And the recommended behaviors are indeed effective tools against poverty. For example, several Berkeley sociologists critical of Richard Herrnstein and Charles Murray's The Bell Curve have reexamined the data set used by Herrnstein and Murray; upon doing so, they found that "marriage affects the risk of poverty more than does any other attribute. . . . Being married reduced the chances that a man was poor from 23 in 100 to 1 in 100. Being married reduced a woman's odds from 45 in 100 to 4 in 100."[106]

Yet despite the increased efficacy of the virtues as weapons against poverty, we have recently been too diffident about commending them to the poor (who in turn have been too diffident about exercising them); as a result, the plight of the poor has been worse than it would otherwise have been. Thus, as Mead reminds us, "work effort among the poor has dropped sharply" since the 1960s. "The working poor left poverty, and the poor became almost by definition nonworking."[107] Thrift is also thought to be less common among today's poor than yesterday's: Stephan Thernstrom contended in 1969 that the poor then had "never developed the penny-pinching facility of their predecessors. They have more possessions, certainly, but perhaps less security comes from having the possessions."[108]

The problem of alcohol has certainly not disappeared from poverty-stricken areas,[109] but today it has been supplemented by those posed by crack cocaine and heroin. And while a case could be made for the saloon as a positive social force in poor neighborhoods in the past[110] (and was occasionally made, even by temperance reformers),[111] a comparable defense of crack houses is altogether inconceivable. Finally, we have seen that the reformers were more or less able to take for granted the existence of intact families among the poor; these families, Herbert Gans observed in 1968, "enable[d] most parents to find satisfactions . . . that compensated for the bad jobs they had to take, and the hard work they had to endure." By contrast, the black poor of today enjoy "fewer of the cultural and psychological rewards of family life."[112]

Let me now summarize what we have learned from this brief impressionistic tour of poverty past and present. It was unreasonable to believe in the nineteenth century that practice of the moral virtues was a sufficient condition for exiting poverty. (For the most part, though, the moral reformers did not themselves hold this unreasonable belief.) But as we enter the twenty-first century it is also unreasonable to believe that practice of the moral virtues is not a necessary condition for exiting poverty. A single-minded focus on structural and environmental reform—consciously abstracting from the virtues proclaimed by the moral reformers, to some extent consciously disdaining those virtues—has proven to be an ineffective antipoverty policy.

As Nathan Glazer observed in an influential article, social policies that try to "deal with the breakdown of traditional ways of handling distress"—in which self-help was emphasized on the familial as well as the communal level—tend further to weaken those traditional structures, "making matters in some important respects worse. . . . Our efforts to deal with distress are themselves increasing distress."[113] Thus "the breakdown of traditional modes of behavior is the chief cause of our social problems," and "some important part of the solution . . . lies in traditional practices and traditional restraints." Successful social policy therefore lies in "the creation and building of new traditions, or new versions of old traditions"[114]—including the tradition that emphasized self-help through practice of the virtues espoused in moral reform.

There is good reason to believe that the celebration of the virtues espoused by Tuckerman, Hartley, Brace, and Lowell offers a better guide to our contemporary predicament than the conscious abstraction from the virtues more recently found in the works of figures like Ryan and Piven and Cloward. But even if the moral reformers' emphasis on the importance of the virtues is preferable to the tendency of more recent observers to ignore them, perhaps it makes a difference that the two groups of observers did not look at the same population of poor people. Ryan and Piven and Cloward were chiefly concerned with the urban poverty of blacks in the last half of the twentieth century, whereas the moral reformers (at least beginning with Hartley) were chiefly concerned with the urban poverty of European immigrants in the nineteenth century.

I have already addressed the chronological issue, arguing that a virtue-based antipoverty strategy is, if anything, more plausible today than in the past. The remaining issue, then, is whether the difference in ethnic composition of the two poverty populations matters. Can an urban antipoverty strategy that was largely designed for European immigrants in the past offer useful guidance in designing one for today's urban poverty population, which consists disproportionately—though not predominantly—of African Americans?[115] To begin to address that question, we will next examine the African American historical experience of moral reform and —for purposes of comparison—the experience of one particular group of European immigrants, the Irish Americans.

PART THREE

THE CONTEMPORARY PROSPECTS FOR MORAL REFORM

6 AFRICAN AMERICANS, IRISH AMERICANS, AND MORAL REFORM
HISTORICAL CONSIDERATIONS

For several reasons an evaluation of the virtues as antipoverty weapons for impoverished American blacks today properly begins with a study of the African American experience of moral reform. First of all, the historical experience of American blacks offers a useful test of my assertion that the moral reformers espoused virtues that they deemed "universal"—applicable to all, practicable by all. If the moral reformers truly believed that virtue was the sole criterion by which people should be judged, they should have been color blind, devoid of any racial prejudice directed against blacks. Were they? Did they think that blacks could and did manifest the virtues—either more or less than European immigrants did?

Because it provides answers to these questions, an assessment of the moral reformers' position on the race question is of considerable interest—perhaps as much for what it tells us about the reformers themselves as for what it may tell us about nineteenth-century American blacks. As we will see, the moral reformers' occasional observations about blacks reveal no prejudice directed against them, nor any suggestion that blacks were notably deficient in manifesting the virtues that the reformers extolled. In fact, the reformers saw much virtue in the northern blacks they encountered (more, apparently, than they discerned in the Irish immigrant poor). The moral reformers' example makes it abundantly clear that speaking the language of virtue was not and need not be a rhetorical cover for discriminating against blacks.

In addition, the historical experience of African Americans yields a second lesson of perhaps greater importance: the language of virtue was not only spoken to blacks from the outside by the moral reformers (a small group of white patricians) but emphatically and insistently from the inside as well. Moral reform was a crucial component of the solution to the predicament of black poverty offered by three prominent African American leaders: Booker T. Washington, W. E. B. DuBois, and Malcolm X (a contemporary of Ryan and Piven and Cloward, whose views—surprisingly—in many respects had more in common with Brace's or Lowell's views than with theirs). An examination of their views reveals the ample precedent within the canon of African American political thought for the belief that practice of the virtues is an essential component of a successful antipoverty program.

Finally, the historical experience of black Americans points to useful clues that help explain when and why moral reform does (and does not) succeed. Those clues stand out still more clearly, though, when we analyze the contrasting Irish American experience of moral reform in the nineteenth century. The nineteenth-century Irish American poor were criticized for moral deficiencies that are strikingly similar to those sometimes attributed to the African American poor today. The Irish American rise out of poverty resulted at least in part from increased practice of the virtues commended by the moral reformers. If moral reform has had less notable successes among African Americans, to some extent that is because of the far greater discrimination that they have suffered. To some extent, though, it may also be because of the lesser prestige accorded the virtues in the mid-twentieth century (when masses of blacks migrated to northern cities) than in the mid-nineteenth century (when masses of Irish immigrants did).

Color-Blind Reformers

The moral reformers of the nineteenth century generally had little to say about American blacks, simply because there were few black residents in northeastern cities until the black migration northward that began during World War I. In 1890 blacks made up just 3 percent of the total population of seventeen large cities in the north and west (including Boston, Chicago, Detroit, New York, and Philadelphia).[1] As late as 1920, 85 percent of all American blacks still lived in the south; three-quarters were still in the south when the United States entered World War II.[2]

Thus, if reformers like Hartley and Brace discussed the poverty of immigrants much more frequently than the poverty of blacks, it was because immigrants formed a much more prominent part of their respective caseloads than did blacks. One striking demographic fact about nineteenth-century America is that large numbers of immigrants and blacks never inhabited the same area: few immigrants settled where blacks lived (in the south), and few blacks inhabited the regions in which immigrants congregated (everywhere else). Between 1870 and 1920, remarkably, there was never a single state with a population that was both 10 percent black and 10 percent foreign-born. Ten percent or more of the population was black in states running from Delaware to Texas, and 10 percent or more of the population was foreign-born in states running from Maine to California; but there was absolutely no overlap between the two sets of states.[3]

But if the moral reformers encountered few blacks in the course of their work among the urban poor, their abhorrence of racism is nevertheless clear from their occasional observations about blacks. Universalist to the core, the reformers believed that virtue rather than pigment was what made the person. Blacks were thought fully capable of practicing the virtues, and—like whites—they were judged by whether or not they did so. Tuckerman argued that any prejudices regarding "these fellow beings, the colored, are altogether unworthy of us not only as Christians but as Republicans."[4] Instead he insisted that "a *man*, be his nation, complexion, condition, or capacity what it may, is an image of God."[5] It is not surprising that blacks were included among the heroes of Tuckerman's didactic tales of poor people who were exemplars of virtue.[6]

One sometimes discerns in other reformers' writings a greater respect and sympathy for blacks—who, it must be recalled, were largely Protestant—than for immigrants, specifically Irish Catholic immigrants. The basis for that preference is illustrated in one particular historical vignette: in 1842 a largely Irish mob in Philadelphia attacked a group of blacks who were marching in a temperance parade.[7] As this episode would suggest, the moral reformers tended to find more virtue in the free blacks of the north than in their Irish immigrant counterparts. Obviously not all free blacks were virtuous; one doubts, for example, that those who shared (in Hartley's words) "the most degrading employments" with Irish immigrants were notable in his estimation for their virtue.[8] Still, on balance the reformers were more respectful than critical of the black population that they encountered.

The judgment that blacks were superior in virtue to the Irish is certainly evident in Hartley's and Brace's writings; some have argued that it is also apparent in Lowell's work. All three reformers' assessments were undoubtedly swayed by a seminal episode of New York history, in which innocent blacks were assaulted by mobs of Irish immigrants: the New York City draft riots of July 1863.

The riots were spurred by immigrant working-class resentment of growing job competition with blacks, as well as the Emancipation Proclamation and the military draft. Beginning on July 13 and ending on July 17, they featured attacks by Irish American mobs on blacks (as well as abolitionists, Republicans, and those who looked wealthy enough to afford the $300 fee that procured an exemption from the draft). At least 105 people died in the riots, which were quelled only when the police were assisted by Union army troops who were called away from Gettysburg to pacify the city.[9]

Brace alluded briefly to the riots in one of his rare discussions of black New Yorkers, in which his respect for their thirst for education—as well as his rejection of racial prejudice—is evident. Speaking of one of the industrial schools that he founded to aid New York's poor children, he approvingly cited the heroism of one of his workers, who insisted that the schools serve black as well as white children. The school opened "after the July riots in 1863 against the colored people." At that time the woman in charge of the school rejected the demand voiced by a group of "hard-looking, heavy-drinking Irish women," mothers of some of the pupils, who wanted to prevent black children from attending:

> In the most amiable and Quaker-like manner, but with the firmness of the old
> Puritan stock from which she sprung, she assured them that, if every other scholar
> left, so long as that school remained it should never be closed to any child on
> account of color. They withdrew their children, but soon after returned them.[10]

The riots impinged far more directly upon Lowell than upon Brace. Not yet married, she was living with her parents—the Shaws—on Staten Island when riots broke out there, as an offshoot of the Manhattan disturbances, between July 14 and

July 20. A black man who had been a butler for the Shaw family was among those attacked by the rioters; he had become a successful caterer, and his shop was completely destroyed. When the mob exhausted its supply of black targets, it turned its attention to prominent abolitionists like the Shaws. Along with the rest of her family, Lowell took shelter with a neighbor who hid them during the worst of the rioting.[11]

Presumably because of her abolitionist background (her brother, Robert Gould Shaw, manifested his abolitionism by fighting, and dying, in Civil War combat as the colonel of the Fifty-fourth Massachusetts Regiment of black troops), Lowell was the only one of the reformers upon whom I have focused to work extensively with blacks as well as with the urban immigrant poor. She began her peacetime charitable activity by supervising Virginia schools that the National Freedmen's Relief Association of New York established for ex-slaves.[12]

As her biographer notes, Lowell's work with southern blacks was guided by a premise similar to the one that would underlie her later and better-known work with New York's urban poor: she believed that "the ex-slaves must be educated in the ways of middle-class values and exposed . . . to the discipline of free labor."[13] But if Lowell sought to achieve the same ends in her work with the poor of both races, some historians have speculated that the spirit in which she labored on behalf of the two groups differed as a result of her bitter memories of the draft riots: they contend that Lowell's work with the urban immigrant poor reflected a preference for American blacks (who patriotically fought and died for the Union under her brother's command) over urban immigrants (some of whom betrayed the war effort, most notably in the draft riots).[14]

The riots were discussed far more extensively by Hartley—in his annual reports on the city's poverty for the AICP—than they were by Brace and Lowell. One finds in Hartley's account a comparative evaluation of the black and Irish poor similar to Brace's: considerable admiration for the virtuous black poor of New York, coupled with criticism of its immigrant Irish poor.

The riots cannot have come as a total surprise to Hartley, who pointed to some of the underlying causes well beforehand, in 1860. He noted then that the Irish were "mostly rude, uninstructed laborers," who "compete[d] with the negroes, between whom and themselves there is an inveterate dislike, for the most degrading employments." While conceding that the Irish had "many good qualities and excellent traits of character," he also thought that they were "excitable and impulsive," had "little thrift, economy, or forecast," and were "often addicted to intemperance." They tended soon to "find themselves at the foot of the social ladder."[15]

Three years later Hartley discussed the riots, which he thought occurred because of the rioters' conviction "that their interests [were] most unjustly and wickedly compromised by an unnecessary war, which was begun and carried on for the freedom of the slave, whose labor coming in competition with their own, would throw them out of employment." He took note of "the cruelties practised upon the colored people, the vindictive hate exhibited against them as a class," as "the significant features of the riot."[16]

Hartley's sympathy for the black victims of the riot is thoroughly apparent. He decried the "outrages of the mob," the most "wanton, disgraceful and cruel" of which were "the murderous assaults on the colored population, . . . this least offending and most defenceless class."[17] He observed that "the actual perpetrators of lawless violence . . . were mostly Irish," while also taking pains to note that "it were unjust to include all of that nationality among the rioters," since "many . . . at their own personal risk afforded protection to the persecuted negroes."[18]

A year later, Hartley reiterated his sympathy for New York's black population, observing that the riots were responsible for blacks' uncharacteristic requests for relief from the AICP. Blacks (in this respect unlike the Irish, in Hartley's judgment) were ordinarily reluctant to accept relief, because they preferred self-reliance to pauperization:

> Another strongly marked feature in the relief of the past year, was the unusual number of *colored* applicants. As a class, they are generally an honest, humble, hard-working people, who seldom seek aid when they can subsist without it; nor desire its continuance beyond the duration of the necessity which calls for it.[19]

In Hartley's reading the New York riot of 1863 occurred when the peaceful, law-abiding, hard-working productive black minority was unfairly set upon by the violent, law-breaking, less productive Irish minority. If Hartley had been asked to designate what is now known as a "model minority," he would surely have been far more likely to nominate the blacks than the Irish of New York.

This admiration for American blacks is also evident in the writings of later moral reformers. Toward the end of the nineteenth century Amos Warner tabulated causes of poverty among 7,225 Americans of various ethnicities (including native-born white Americans, Germans, "colored" people, and the Irish, among many others). His tabulations showed that causes indicating misconduct (such as "drink," "immorality," "shiftlessness and inefficiency," "crime and dishonesty," "roving disposition," "imprisonment of breadwinner," "orphans and abandoned children," and "neglect by relatives") were responsible for far less poverty among blacks (15.7 percent) than among any other group: by contrast, 32.4 percent of Irish poverty, 29.2 percent of native white American poverty, and 17.8 percent of German poverty was attributable to misconduct.[20]

Warner observed that "those who know the colored people only casually or by hearsay may be surprised to find the misconduct causes running so low among them"; but having worked with the black poor in Washington and Baltimore, he found the division between the two sorts of causes "a natural result," which confirmed "the reliability of the statistics." Warner pointed to the penchant for both individual and communal self-reliance among blacks (as well as a great susceptibility to disease, an indication of "misfortune" rather than "misconduct") to explain the infrequency of misconduct as a cause of their poverty: he noted that "the colored people . . . have a dread of being assisted, especially when they think an institution will be recommended," and he further pointed to the presence of "many associations among them for mutual help."[21]

Admittedly, Warner depicted a population that was far from wholly virtuous when judged by the tenets of moral reform: he also spoke of "a certain apathy" that characterized blacks; criticized their "hand-to-mouth way of working at odd jobs, rather than taking steady work"; and declared that "criminal and semi-criminal" black men "have a brutal way of making their women support them."[22] Nevertheless, the fact remains that in Warner's estimation misconduct accounted for very little of the poverty among blacks, less than it accounted for in any other ethnic group. In particular, misconduct could be blamed for more than twice as much Irish poverty as black poverty. If Warner can be charged with "blaming the victim" of late-nineteenth-century poverty, blacks were clearly the victims he thought least deserving of blame.

For a literary rather than a statistical assessment of urban black poverty at the end of the nineteenth century, we can turn to Jacob Riis's 1890 exposé *How the Other Half Lives*. As Riis noted, New York's black population had already begun to be augmented by migrants from the south; it had doubled, he believed, since 1880.[23] The migration from the south may explain much of the condescension evident in Riis's depiction of New York's black poor, since the virtues prized by the reformers were arguably more likely to be found among free-born blacks (the antebellum population described by Hartley) than among ex-slaves.[24]

Still, if Riis's characterization of the blacks of New York was not devoid of condescension, on balance it was favorable. He was clearly appalled by the prejudice directed against blacks in the job market ("trades of which he had control in his Southern home are not open to him here")[25] and the housing market (although blacks proved "cleaner, better, and steadier tenants" than European immigrants, they were charged over 13 percent more in rent for the same apartments).[26]

Riis also proclaimed that the black community had made great strides since it abandoned the slums of what is now known as Greenwich Village: "With his cutting loose from the old tenements there has come a distinct and gratifying improvement in the tenant, that argues louder than theories or speeches the influence of vile surroundings in debasing the man. . . . There is no more clean and orderly community in New York than the new settlement of colored people that is growing up on the East Side from Yorkville to Harlem."[27] Riis also spoke favorably of black religiosity ("his churches are crowded to the doors on Sunday nights when the colored colony turns out to worship") and educability ("he is both willing and anxious to learn, and his intellectual status is distinctly improving").[28]

On the other side of the ledger, Riis criticized what he saw as black improvidence: "He loves fine clothes and good living a good deal more than he does a bank account." Of greater concern, there is undoubtedly an element of racism in Riis's critique of the black man's "ludicrous incongruities, his sensuality and his lack of moral accountability," which he portrayed as effects of "temperament," not just as legacies of "centuries of slavery."[29] Still, overall Riis believed that the black shortcomings to which he pointed were products of white prejudice:

> It may be well to . . . see how much of the blame is borne by the prejudice and greed that have kept [the black man] from rising under a burden of responsibility to which he could hardly be equal. And in this view he may be seen to have advanced much farther and faster [in the quarter-century since emancipation] than before suspected, and to promise, after all, with fair treatment, [to succeed] quite as well as the rest of us, his white-skinned fellow-citizens, had any right to expect.[30]

Finally, Riis's critique of the black poor of New York must be put in perspective. The hard fact is that he was equally critical, in different ways, of all of the immigrant groups that he surveyed: Jews, Italians, Bohemians, and (especially) the Chinese. Riis harshly denounced New York's Chinese residents, whom he accused of gambling, consuming opium, and rejecting governmental authority (in that they were unwilling to cooperate with police attempts to apprehend criminals).[31] This much at least it is safe to say: if an 1890 reader of *How the Other Half Lives* had judged by the evidence it presents, he would have been far more likely to predict that American blacks rather than Chinese Americans would be known a century later as members of a model minority.

Booker T. Washington and Moral Reform

As we have seen repeatedly, the urban moral reformers commended the virtues to the immigrant poor as means of reducing poverty. Significantly, the same virtues were preached to the black poor—both rural and urban—by many of the most prominent African American political thinkers and leaders. Booker T. Washington preached the same virtues that Tuckerman, Hartley, and the others extolled. His decision to do so cannot fairly be criticized as a sign of an Uncle Tom–like eagerness to accommodate the white segregationist power structure of the south, because the same virtues were also preached by black leaders who were notably less accommodating, notably more confrontational—his contemporary W. E. B. DuBois and, much more recently, Malcolm X. These examples argue strongly for the existence of a powerful consensus in favor of the virtues, one that has often transcended seemingly impassable racial barriers.

Washington's commitment to moral reform was in part the product of a direct biographical link with some of its white Protestant proponents. As historian Nathan Irving Huggins has remarked,

> Booker T. Washington's . . . teachers, those who had a shaping influence on his life such as Mrs. Viola Ruffner . . . and General Samuel Chapman Armstrong[,] . . . were strong-willed, tough . . . Yankee missionaries who were certain of the proper formula for Negro uplift. This formula reduced itself to the familiar Protestant virtues: industry, frugality, cleanliness, temperance, order, decorum, and

punctuality. With such traits men and women (even freedmen) could do what they set out to do; or, failing, could at least be of good character. The message was attractive, even compelling, to men and women like Washington because it was so reasonable, clear, and simple; and it focused on self-improvement and self-reliance rather than on conditions of inequity which one might have been powerless to change.[32]

But Washington's commitment to moral reform also reflected his experience as a slave and his understanding of why slavery was unjust: not only because slaves were deprived of their freedom, but also because slavery imperiled the virtues of diligence and thrift. He declared in his autobiography that "the whole machinery of slavery was so constructed as to cause labour, as a rule, to be looked upon as a badge of degradation, of inferiority. Hence labour was something that both races . . . sought to escape."[33] He also spoke of the black population "just out of slavery" as a "penniless" one that had "placed a premium on thriftlessness."[34]

Washington's diagnosis of the ills of slavery led to an obvious remedy: inculcating in the freedmen and their descendants the virtues that slavery generally precluded. He worried that a people that was "not taught to love labour" tended to breed "a worthless idle class, which spends a great deal of its time in trying to live by its wits."[35] Washington's pupils were offered an industrial education that aimed not only to explain how to work (e.g., how to be a carpenter or a mechanic) but also *why* they should work: because "all forms of labour, whether with the head or with the hand, [are] honourable."[36] "The great lesson which the race needs to learn in freedom," he argued, "is to work willingly, cheerfully and efficiently."[37] Washington hoped to teach that "labour is dignified and beautiful," so that his pupils would "love labour instead of trying to escape it."[38]

Washington also tirelessly expounded the gospel of thrift. "The civilization of New England and of other such prosperous regions rests more, perhaps," he argued, "upon the savings banks of the country than upon any other one thing." He called upon southern blacks to emulate New Englanders, because "we cannot get upon our feet, as a people, until we learn the saving habit; until we learn to save every nickel, every dime and every dollar that we can spare."[39]

Like urban moral reformers, Washington took practical steps to facilitate the practice of thrift. His wife organized women's meetings in the town of Tuskegee, which attempted to convey practical lessons about thrift ("economy in the house as regards food," the need to "put away thirty cents for every dollar you spend").[40] These meetings were then followed up by the rural equivalent of friendly visiting, to encourage the application of the lessons: "Find out by judicious visiting whether any advancement is made. Do not expect too much in a short time, and, above all, do not be dictatorial while visiting."[41]

At the Tuskegee campus itself Washington encouraged thrift through the establishment of a school savings bank department (akin to the Penny Provident Fund of the New York COS) that encouraged students not to "carry their available cash around in their pockets, but [to] hasten to the bank with it." As with the Penny Provident Fund, the savings were "not in dollars for the most part, but in quarters, dimes, and even pennies."[42]

Washington was also a temperance advocate. He proudly endorsed Joel Chandler Harris's contention that "a temperate race is bound to be industrious, and the Negroes are temperate when compared with the whites."[43] Washington himself may well have been a teetotaler,[44] and Tuskegee Institute prohibited its students from drinking alcoholic beverages.[45] Like many others (for example, Hartley), Washington initially opposed the legal prohibition of alcohol, but then reconsidered and endorsed it. He argued that effective prohibition statutes would reduce crime and encourage harder work and increased savings.[46]

Washington endorsed a self-help strategy for American blacks that centered on the practice of the reformers' virtues. But emphasizing the virtues did not require him to ignore the racial prejudice directed against blacks, in the north as well as the south. Just as advocates of the urban poor like Brace and Lowell could consistently endorse both structural and moral reforms, so could Washington call on his fellow blacks to practice the virtues while also decrying the discrimination that often crippled their efforts at self-advancement.

Washington called attention to the gross disparities in expenditures for the education of black and white children in the south: "Can the white child of the South who receives $4.92 per capita for education, or the black child who receives $2.21, be said to be given an equal chance in the battle of life?"[47] In a similar vein, Washington's commitment to the virtues did not in any way preclude his telling the following heartrending story, in which the potentially devastating effects of white prejudice upon black virtue are all too apparent:

> Not long ago a mother, a black mother, who lived in one of your Northern states, had heard it whispered around in her community for years that the Negro was lazy, shiftless, and would not work. So when her boy grew to sufficient size, at considerable expense and great self-sacrifice, she had her boy thoroughly taught the machinist's trade. A job was secured in a neighboring shop. With dinner bucket in hand, and spurred on by the prayers of the now happy mother, the boy entered the shop to begin his first day's work. What happened? Had any one of the twenty white Americans been so educated that he gave this stranger a welcome into their midst? No, not this. Every one of the twenty white men threw down his tools and deliberately walked out, swearing that he would not give a black man an opportunity to earn an honest living. Another shop was tried, with the same result, and still another the same. Today this promising and ambitious black man is a wreck—a confirmed drunkard, with no hope, no ambition. My friends, who blasted the life of this young man? On whose hands does his blood rest?[48]

For Washington, then, neither the attainment of the virtues by blacks nor the cessation of prejudice by whites would suffice in itself to improve the condition of blacks. Individually each was necessary, but only the combination of the two would suffice:

All the Negro race asks is that the door which rewards industry, thrift, intelligence, and character be left as wide open for him as for the foreigner who constantly comes to our country. More than this, he has no right to request. Less than this, a Republic has no right to vouchsafe.[49]

W. E. B. DuBois As Advocate of Moral Reform

With good reason, W. E. B. DuBois is generally seen as Washington's greatest critic and rival, an inveterate opponent of Washington's willingness to accommodate powerful southern whites who were committed to racial segregation. But from the standpoint of moral reform, what is striking is not how little but how much DuBois and Washington had in common. On a practical level, DuBois's prescription for black America was largely identical to Washington's: he too called for an end to white prejudice—but also, and emphatically, for a greater black commitment to the virtues espoused in moral reform.[50]

When he wrote his autobiography at age ninety, DuBois did so from a perspective altogether alien to moral reform: that of a self-professed Communist who was shortly to expatriate himself to Ghana, where he died. Nevertheless, the autobiography also makes clear how deeply DuBois was influenced in his boyhood by judgments akin to those of the moral reformers. Speaking of his upbringing in western Massachusetts, DuBois remarked that "none of the colored folk I knew were so poor, drunken and sloven as some of the lower class Americans and Irish. I did not then associate poverty or ignorance with color, but rather with lack of opportunity; or more often with lack of thrift, which was in strict accord with the philosophy of New England and of the 19th century."[51]

DuBois's early attitude toward dependency also reflected the New England philosophy. Not long after DuBois's birth, his father abandoned his mother and him. Still, she strove to be self-supporting, and he strove to help in that effort. What was evidently DuBois's lifelong pride in his youthful attempts to avoid dependency shines through the reminiscence that he offered as a ninety-year-old Communist:

> My mother's limited sources of income were helped through boarding the barber, my uncle, supplemented infrequently by her own day's work, and by some kindly unobtrusive charity. But I was keen and eager to eke out this income by various jobs; splitting kindling, mowing lawns, doing chores. I early came to understand that to be "on the town," the recipient of public charity, was the depth not only of misfortune but of a certain guilt. I presume some of my folk sank to that, but not to my knowledge. We earned our way.[52]

The impact of moral reform upon DuBois is clear as well in his discussion of his mother's injunction against drinking: "My mother laid down . . . one of her few strict commands; . . . she said firmly that I was never to go into a liquor saloon, or even near it. I never did, and indeed, so strong was the expression of her wishes that never in my life since have I felt at ease drinking at a bar."[53] His personal commitment to moral reform is also evident in a 1944 description of his attitudes and behavior while a student at Fisk University in 1887: "I drank no alcohol and knew nothing of women, physically or psychically, to the incredulous amusement of most of my more experienced fellows; I above all believed in work—systematic and tireless."[54]

What is still more important, though, is that DuBois's belief in the desirability and efficacy of moral reform is also evident in his scholarly writing—most notably in his 1899 sociological classic, *The Philadelphia Negro*. In that work DuBois attacked white prejudice while also calling for self-help and moral uplift as solutions to the problems faced by blacks.

DuBois clearly regarded racial discrimination as a principal cause of many of the difficulties faced by black Philadelphians:

> Every one knows that in a city like Philadelphia a Negro does not have the same chance to exercise his ability or secure work according to his talents as a white man. . . . [The] economic rise [of Negroes] is . . . hindered by . . . a widespread inclination to shut against them many doors of advancement open to the talented and efficient of other races.[55]

But DuBois did not believe that discrimination was the only problem faced by blacks in the quest for good employment. Instead he spoke of "the lack of training and experience among Negroes" as a second difficulty, apart from "the prejudice of whites."[56] In his judgment, "color prejudice . . . [was] not . . . responsible for all, or perhaps the greater part of the Negro problems, or of the disabilities under which the race labor[ed]"; but "on the other hand it [was] a far more powerful social force than most Philadelphians realize[d]."[57]

Discrimination was hateful in large part because of its moral impact. Its effect was to negate the rewards that should properly result from practice of the virtues:

> For thirty years and more Philadelphia has said to its black children: "Honesty, efficiency and talent have little to do with your success; if you work hard, spend little and are good you may earn your bread and butter at those sorts of work which we frankly confess we despise; if you are dishonest and lazy, the State will furnish your bread free." Thus the class of Negroes which the prejudices of the city have distinctly encouraged is that of the criminal, the lazy and the shiftless; . . . but for the educated and industrious young colored man who wants work and not platitudes, wages and not alms, just rewards and not sermons—for such colored men Philadelphia apparently has no use.[58]

Restriction of economic opportunities for blacks was wrong, because it was "bound to make [the Negro community] a burden on the public; to debauch its women, pauperize its men, and ruin its homes."[59] Whites guilty of "shutting black boys and girls out of most avenues of decent employment . . . [were] increasing pauperism and vice."[60] DuBois called for an end to racial discrimination, because it would promote black self-reliance:

> Probably a change in public opinion on this point [i.e., granting equal employment opportunities to blacks] would not make very much difference in the posi-

171

tions occupied by Negroes in the city: some few would be promoted, some few would get new places—the mass would remain as they are; but it would make one vast difference: it would inspire the young to try harder, it would stimulate the idle and discouraged and it would take away from this race the omnipresent excuse for failure: prejudice. Such a moral change would work a revolution in the criminal rate during the next ten years. Even a Negro bootblack could black boots better if he knew he was a menial not because he was a Negro but because he was best fitted for that work.[61]

In view of DuBois's moral analysis of the evils of discrimination, it is not surprising that he coupled his critique of prejudice with a fervent call for moral uplift. With respect to sexual morality, his study of black Philadelphians led him to conclude that "the lax moral habits of the slave régime still show themselves in a large amount of cohabitation without marriage."[62] (DuBois drew this conclusion from his survey of the heavily black Seventh Ward, which showed, for example, that just over 40 percent of black women aged 30–39 were without husbands.)[63]

Because the "large number of homes without husbands . . . increase[d] the burden of charity and benevolence," and also because the "poor home life [of fatherless homes] . . . increase[d] crime," DuBois saw the need for "social regeneration."[64] Like many social analysts today (most notably William Julius Wilson), DuBois recognized that the "low wages" earned by black men reduced "the chances of marriage" for black women; the small pay received by men could result in "irregular and often dissipated lives."[65] But his structural explanation of the frailty of the black family did not preclude a strict moral assessment: "The great weakness of the Negro family is still lack of respect for the marriage bond. . . . Sexual looseness is today the prevailing sin of the mass of the Negro population."[66]

As we saw earlier, DuBois firmly believed that black Philadelphians were unjustly denied numerous opportunities for employment that were rightfully theirs. He did not regard this injustice as an excuse for crime, but he did preach the gospel of diligence as a necessary antidote to crime. "Idleness and crime," he insisted, "are beneath and not above the lowest work":[67]

No doubt the amount of crime imputed to the race is exaggerated, no doubt features of the Negro's environment over which he has no control excuse much that is committed; but beyond all this the amount of crime that can without doubt rightly be laid at the door of the Philadelphia Negro is large and is a menace to a civilized people. Efforts to stop this crime must commence in the Negro homes; they must cease to be, as they often are, breeders of idleness and extravagance and complaint. Work, continuous and intensive; work, although it be menial and poorly rewarded; work, though done in travail of soul and sweat of brow, must be so impressed upon Negro children as the road to salvation, that a child would feel it a greater disgrace to be idle than to do the humblest labor. The homely virtues of honesty, truth and chastity must be instilled in the cradle, and although it is hard to teach self-respect to a people whose million fellow-citizens half-despise them, yet it must be taught as the surest road to gain the respect of others.[68]

DuBois advocated thrift as well as diligence as a remedy for black poverty. Calling attention to money that was misspent on food, clothing, furnishings, amusements and "miscellaneous ornaments and gewgaws," DuBois concluded that "probably few poor nations waste more money by thoughtless and unreasonable expenditure than the American Negro, and especially those living in large cities like Philadelphia." While conceding that "all this is a natural heritage of a slave system," he also contended that

> it is not the less a matter of serious import to a people in such economic stress as Negroes now are. The Negro has much to learn of the Jew and Italian, as to living within his means and saving every penny from excessive and wasteful expenditures.[69]

As for drinking, DuBois maintained that "the intemperate use of intoxicating liquors is not one of the Negro's special offences."[70] Still, he concluded that "the saloon is . . . an economic problem among Negroes," if not a moral one. He estimated that the black residents of one Philadelphia ward disbursed a total of somewhere between $10,000 and $20,000 each year in bars—"a large sum for a poor people to spend in liquor."[71]

DuBois did not put much stock in charity as a solution to the many problems facing black Philadelphians. Thus, with no irony whatsoever, he repeated the mantra of the Charity Organization Societies: "After all, the need of the Negro, as of so many unfortunate classes, is 'not alms but a friend.'"[72] Ultimately, it was not alms but black self-help that DuBois counted on to improve the black community's prospects:

> The bulk of the work of raising the Negro must be done by the Negro himself, and the greatest help for him will be not to hinder and curtail and discourage his efforts. Against prejudice, injustice and wrong the Negro ought to protest energetically and continuously, but he must never forget that he protests because those things hinder his own efforts, and that those efforts are the key to his future.[73]

He spoke of the "vast amount of preventive and rescue work which the Negroes themselves might do," such as "exposing the dangers of gambling . . . and inculcating respect for women."[74] Passages like these (and others quoted above) no doubt explain the remark by DuBois's biographer that *The Philadelphia Negro* is replete with "stern admonitions to black people to behave like lending-library patrons."[75] That is a fair comment—provided one adds that DuBois had good reason to believe that the habits of lending-library patrons would be useful to people seeking to exit poverty.[76]

Malcolm X and Muslim Moral Reform

Unlike Washington and DuBois, Malcolm X did not come to manhood in an atmosphere suffused with moral reform. And for most of his brief career, he also

173

espoused a venomous hatred toward whites that was altogether alien to Washington and DuBois. Nevertheless, he achieved eminence as an exemplar of moral reform in his own life, and as an exponent of the virtues as a necessary means to the elevation of his people.

In some respects, Malcolm's autobiography bears comparison with Washington's. *Up from Slavery* is a rags-to-riches story, recounting how a black man born into slavery achieves prominence by practicing and inculcating the virtues of diligence, sobriety, and thrift. So is the *Autobiography of Malcolm X*, which is the story of a black man's escape not from physical bondage but from a spiritual enslavement to a degrading and self-destructive life of crime: it could aptly have been titled *Up from Burglary*. As the political scientist Jennifer Hochschild perceptively remarks,

> Malcolm X['s] . . . *Autobiography* is the classic stuff of the ideology of the American dream. His prison conversion shows that anyone can participate in the dream. . . . By teaching himself to read and write, Malcolm shows that the route to success is through hard work and initiative. By admitting guilt about his past life, finally, Malcolm shows that worldly success must be associated with virtue to be truly successful. The elements are all here, even though Malcolm used them through most of his life to resist the blue-eyed devil, his institutions, and his racial ideology.[77]

The practical program preached by Malcolm was strikingly reminiscent of that of Washington and DuBois: in the judgment of sociologist John Sibley Butler, "The Black Muslims took the economic philosophy of Booker T. Washington and added a religious dimension."[78] That claim is certainly supported by the *Autobiography*, in which Malcolm speaks emphatically of black entrepreneurship and self-help as keys to black progress:

> The American black man should be focusing his every effort toward building his own businesses. As other ethnic groups have done, let the black people, wherever possible, however possible, patronize their own kind, hire their own kind, and start in those ways to build up the black race's ability to do for itself. That's the only way the American black man is ever going to get respect. One thing the white man never can give the black man is self-respect! The black man never can become independent and recognized as a human being who is truly equal with other human beings until he has what they have, and until he is doing for himself what others are doing for themselves.[79]

After his conversion, Malcolm espoused what has been called "black moral puritanism— . . . promot[ing] self-reliance, rigorous self-discipline, a strong work ethic, and law-abiding behavior."[80] The diligence that he called for reflected the Muslim belief that "all work is honest, and even the meanest job can be done with dignity."[81] To achieve economic success, Muslims were urged to "observe the operations of the white man. He is successful. He makes no excuses for his failures. He works hard. . . . You do the *same*."[82]

Sobriety is a second cardinal Muslim virtue. Malcolm viewed alcohol as "a curse on the so-called Negroes."[83] He took obvious pride in the "strict moral code" (which prohibited "any use of tobacco, alcohol, or narcotics" as well as "fornication")[84] of the Muslims, and in their "phenomenal record of dope-addiction cures of longtime junkies."[85]

Malcolm also presented thrift as a solution to the problem of black poverty. He claimed that blacks' propensity to bet on the numbers game resulted in immense sums being transferred to the underworld, "all taken from poor Negroes. . . . [A]nd we wonder why we stay so poor."[86] He ridiculed members of the black bourgeoisie for their improvidence, as they "rush[ed] to throw away their little money in the white man's luxury hotels, his swanky nightclubs, and big, fine, exclusive restaurants."[87] It was as an economist more than a moralist that he deplored the purported fact that "forty per cent of the expensive imported Scotch whisky consumed in America goes down the throats of the status-sick black man; but the only black-owned distilleries are in bathtubs, or in the woods somewhere."[88] Malcolm echoed Elijah Muhammad's command to "stop wasting . . . money, stop spending money for tobacco, dope, cigarettes, whiskey, fine clothes, fine automobiles, expensive rugs and carpets, idleness, sport and gambling."[89]

Muslim Puritanism is most apparent, of course, in its strict code of sexual relations. Malcolm's biographer notes that "the sexual mores of the [Black Muslim] movement were highly circumscribed. . . . Premarital sex, which was called fornication, was absolutely forbidden. As time passed and the Nation grew, its members began to demolish the myth that the majority of America's blacks were promiscuous, sports-crazy, hard-drinking, indolent lawbreakers."[90] Not surprisingly, Malcolm insisted on "the importance of the father-male image in the strong household"; he believed that "honesty, and chastity, are vital in a person, a home, a community, a nation, and a civilization."[91] It is also not surprising that the Moynihan report, the subject of almost universal condemnation elsewhere in the black community, actually "found a receptive audience among members of the Nation of Islam."[92]

Responding to the moral crisis of the black community, Malcolm called for moral as well as economic self-help:

> The black man in the ghettoes . . . has to start self-correcting his own material, moral, and spiritual defects and evils. The black man needs to start his own program to get rid of drunkenness, drug addiction, prostitution. The black man in America has to lift up his own sense of values.[93]

A great many elements in Malcolm's program were thoroughly in accord with the gospel according to Washington and DuBois—not to speak of (mutatis mutandis) Tuckerman, Hartley, Brace, and Lowell. He hoped to revive the traditional virtues of moral reform as a basis for uplifting the black community. In C. Eric Lincoln's summation,

> The rank-and-file Muslim is expected to evince general character traits that can only benefit the society as a whole. Men are expected to live soberly and with dignity, to work hard, to devote themselves to their families' welfare, and to deal honestly with all others. They are expected to obey all constituted authority — even the usurped and corrupt authority of the whites, until the Black Nation returns to power. . . . Above all, self-reliance and a sense of mutual responsibility are the hallmarks of Muslim morality.[94]

Writing in 1963, Nathan Glazer and Daniel Patrick Moynihan did not blink from calling the Muslims a "racist movement." But they also noted "how much of Horatio Alger" was found in it, in its emphasis on the "traditional virtues," so that "the Negro may make himself wealthy and successful" by "saving his money and devoting himself to his business. . . . Thus, even the most extreme of present-day Negro movements suggests the extent of the shift to middle-class patterns, and the power they now possess."[95]

The Failure of Muslim Moral Reform

With the benefit of hindsight, it is clear that the Muslims did not fulfill the hopes of Malcolm X (and many others) for them as agents of the remoralization of the black community. (In this respect, of course, we will never know whether things might have turned out differently had Malcolm X survived). Speaking of developments in Chicago (the headquarters of the Nation of Islam), journalist Nicholas Lemann captures the decline in their efforts to promote economic self-help and moral transformation:

> The Muslims, who in their day may have been the largest organization made up primarily of the ghetto poor, and who were much admired in black Chicago for their ability to turn around even prison inmates and prostitutes, are down to an active membership of several hundred people at best, and most of the old Muslim businesses — the bakeries and restaurants — are gone. Wallace Muhammad, the son of Elijah, who took over the leadership of the Nation of Islam after his father's death in 1975, . . . lost power to Farrakhan, who . . . is more a popular orator than the leader of an organization.[96]

How can one account for the inability of the Muslims to promote self-help and moral reform more effectively? Defects in the Muslim moral message explain much of it. These failings suggest in turn that Malcolm can be understood in some sense as an apostate of moral reform.

The most important defect was the Muslims' anti-white racism, which vitiated much of their insistence on the moral responsibility of blacks, their responsibility to improve their own condition. It is sobering to realize that Malcolm X's most enduring legacy (notwithstanding his frequent insistence on the importance of black self-help) may well have been to legitimize hatred of whites, who were supposedly the exclusive source of all black shortcomings. Malcolm's biographer has argued this point eloquently:

He attributed his youthful criminality entirely to white oppression. "The white man makes you a drug addict," he told one African American crowd. He even suggested that his gambling habit had been the fault of the whites who had manufactured the dice. The skill with which he substituted the outer enemy for the inner enemy called conscience gave enormous impetus to the school of thought that claims that whites are responsible for virtually all of the black community's problems. At times, Malcolm propounded that thesis himself. He suggested that whites are responsible for the disproportionate number of illegitimate, unwanted children in our black ghettos. He even asserted that whites are to blame for the fact that many blacks hate their parents.[97]

A second defect of almost equal significance can be described as Muslim moral extremism: as Malcolm proudly pointed out, the Nation of Islam forbade not only "fornication," but also "any eating of the filthy pork, . . . any use of tobacco. . . . No Muslim who followed Elijah Muhammad could dance, . . . date, attend movies, or sports."[98] That is to demand not the delay but the denial of gratification —a severe asceticism far beyond anything that any of the moral reformers would have dreamed of imposing on the poor. While severe asceticism has an obvious appeal to a few (such as Malcolm X himself),[99] it is not surprising that the prohibition of harmless popular pleasures alienates a mass of others.

The contempt often directed at women was another sign of the movement's extremism. As Malcolm X's biographer has noted, "Malcolm characterized women as 'tricky' and 'deceitful.' . . . It was not easy to reconcile Malcolm's harsh remarks about women with his insistence that black men should respect and protect their women, instead of abusing and exploiting them." The sexism that Malcolm occasionally manifested was, in fact, built into Elijah Muhammad's cosmology: "Eons ago, when the moon had separated from the earth, only men had existed. Later on, the genitals of the weaker males had involuted. The result was 'wo-men,' or weak men."[100]

Elijah Muhammad's absurd cosmology (which Malcolm discarded, along with its attendant racism, in the last years of his life)[101] points to another problem. It is one thing to believe in the virtues of diligence, sobriety, and thrift; it is quite another to believe that the creation of the "devil race" of white people was set in motion some 6,600 years ago by an evil black "big-head" scientist, Mr. Yacub, who "had learned how to breed races scientifically."[102] The reasonable aspects of Muslim morality must have fallen on many deaf ears because they were perhaps inextricably intertwined with a theology that is altogether unreasonable.

Finally, both the extremism and the absurdity of Black Muslim doctrine made it an obvious vehicle for hypocrites and charlatans. Malcolm X faithfully practiced the severe asceticism that he preached. But his departure from discipleship was provoked by his discovery that Elijah Muhammad did not. In his *Autobiography* Malcolm claimed that in 1963 he discovered that "Muslims had been betrayed by Elijah Muhammad himself"; in that year two of Elijah Muhammad's secretaries filed paternity suits against him for fathering four of their children.[103]

Nor did this incident exhaust Elijah Muhammad's hypocrisy. Donations earmarked for Black Muslim hospitals, nursing homes, and factories that went unbuilt lined his pockets: they paid for his half-million-dollar mansion in Chicago and other luxurious homes in Arizona and Mexico, and they enabled him to amass more than $3 million in personal bank deposits. One of Elijah Muhammad's sons and one of his grandsons did federal jail time for selling drugs. Nor was Muslim drug-dealing confined to the royal family: at one point the FBI estimated that a "Muslim mob controlled eighty percent of the heroin" sold in Philadelphia.[104] No doubt the Nation of Islam would have had greater success in remoralizing the black masses if more of its leaders had been able—like Malcolm X—credibly to exemplify the process of moral regeneration.

The Black Muslim legacy may ultimately be less instructive as an example of what moral reform hopes to achieve than as an explanation of why and how it can fail to achieve it. We must keep that legacy in mind as we consider other factors that have helped and hindered African American efforts to achieve moral reform.

Poverty and Virtue Among African Americans

My argument to this point about African American moral reform may seem puzzling. In brief, we have seen that the nineteenth-century black population in northern cities was (in the estimation of the moral reformers) reasonably virtuous, and that several of the most eminent black leaders of the twentieth century ardently campaigned on behalf of the virtues. But if these things are true, and if moral reform is a useful weapon for fighting poverty (as I have contended throughout) an obvious question emerges. Why was and is poverty among blacks such an enormous problem that Stephan and Abigail Thernstrom—whose assessment of the condition of American blacks has been controversial because of its overall optimism—assert that "the single most depressing fact about the state of black America today" is its high poverty rate?[105]

Several answers to this question can be suggested. First, with respect to the moral reformers' assessment of northern blacks, it must be recalled that the nineteenth-century northern black population was unrepresentative and small. There is every reason to suppose that enslavement tended to diminish diligence and thrift, whereas freedom helped bring out these virtues by providing an incentive to practice them. (To deny that slavery lessened black practice of the virtues is to say, as Washington observed in a related context, "that slavery was no disadvantage to us.")[106] It is not particularly surprising that the reformers should have found considerable virtue in the comparatively small free black population of the north; nor would it be surprising if virtue had been less characteristic of the far larger population of southern blacks—done moral damage by both slavery and its Jim Crow aftermath—that subsequently migrated north.

Second, the conditions faced by northern blacks seem to have worsened significantly in the years approaching the Civil War, as discrimination against them increased and their economic standing declined.[107] That development was of momentous importance: for reasons powerfully articulated by both Washington and DuBois, discrimination is the great enemy of virtue. A principal motive, if not the only motive, for diligence, sobriety, and thrift is the likelihood that their practice will improve the chances of achieving success: although virtue may be its own reward, the reformers' virtues were also justified in more utilitarian terms, as means to the end of prosperity (or at least lessened poverty). But when virtue goes unrewarded, as it obviously did for the mass of blacks both north and south who were confronted by discrimination, it is unsurprising when virtue becomes less common. DuBois contended that white Philadelphia effectively offered the city's blacks no premium for "work[ing] hard, spend[ing] little, and [being] good."[108] It would be astonishing if Philadelphia's failure to do so did not decrease diligence, thrift, and moral excellence among its black residents.

Finally, the timing of the great black migration from south to north badly served the cause of moral reform. To make a broad generalization, white immigrants came to northern cities in the nineteenth century, when the moral reformers' virtues held almost unquestioned sway; black migrants came to the same cities in the twentieth century, when those virtues were accorded less esteem (and were at times actively disdained). The argument is often made—not altogether convincingly—that black migrants were at a disadvantage because of their late arrival in the north, inasmuch as opportunities for unskilled labor were much greater in the nineteenth century than in the twentieth.[109] Perhaps it is true that black migrants—at least those who migrated during and in the aftermath of World War II—were harmed by their coming north after industrialization had peaked (and as de-industrialization began); but it is also possible that they were harmed by arriving after "moralization" had peaked, and as de-moralization—the attack upon the virtues—was taking effect.

Unlike the black migrants of the twentieth century, nineteenth-century European immigrants benefited, then, from their arrival in a country marked by a strong cultural consensus endorsing the virtues. The impact of that consensus becomes particularly clear if we examine perhaps the greatest triumph of nineteenth-century moral reform: the effect that it had upon Irish American immigrants.

Irish immigrants experienced great poverty in America, poverty that can in some measure be attributed to a deficiency of virtue. But most Irish Americans subsequently emerged from poverty, and that emergence can in some measure be attributed to a greater manifestation of virtue. Both the "before" and the "after" phases of the Irish American experience in the nineteenth century offer useful clues as we consider the prospects for moral reform (particularly African American moral reform) today.

The Irish-Black Comparison

Can the experience of any European immigrant group in the past fairly be compared to the experience of African Americans, either past or present? One argument—to which we shall return—for denying the comparability of the groups is that blacks undeniably faced more severe discrimination than any European immigrant group.[110] A second argument is that the voluntary character of the immigration of European groups to America renders their experience qualitatively different from that of American blacks. It is sometimes contended that European immigrants have had greater success than blacks in America precisely because they—unlike blacks—were immigrants. That is to say, people who freely chose to come to America (as opposed to those who are descendants of slaves forcibly imported hundreds of years ago) are more likely to manifest the eagerness and enthusiasm that help produce success.

In this reading, voluntary immigration in itself is a factor that leads to success. Nathan Irving Huggins asserted that West Indian black immigrants have had more success than native-born American blacks (and West Indian blacks who remain on the islands), because of the "selective and liberating force of immigration."[111] Sociologist Orlando Patterson amplifies this contention, arguing more broadly that "immigrants almost always do better than natives, and this holds equally for Euro-American natives in comparison with European and Asian immigrants."[112] And political scientist Lawrence Mead calls attention to the other side of this coin, observing that "*a large part of . . . today's poor might well be described as people, or their descendents, who did not really choose to come to America,*" such as those "native-born blacks . . . [who] descend from involuntary Americans—slaves."[113]

Jennifer Hochschild's comparison of the immigrant and black experiences develops the contrast to which Mead's remarks point:

> Most white immigrants chose to come and stay; those unwillingly brought to America were mostly persuaded by love, hope, [and] goods . . . that immigration had been the right choice. Those not so persuaded could leave, and many did. African Americans, of course, were as far from choosing to come to America as one could be, and they received neither love, hope, nor material inducements to make them change their minds about coming once they were here.[114]

The depiction of blacks as involuntary Americans seemingly differentiates them from nineteenth-century European immigrants in general. Significantly, though, nineteenth-century Irish immigrants apparently tended to resemble blacks in this respect: they too can be understood as involuntary Americans. As Mead notes, "The troubled history of the Irish in their early decades in America originated in the massive exodus from Ireland precipitated by the potato famine of the 1840s, a movement that no doubt swept along many who did not want to leave home."[115]

Kerby Miller, the leading historian of Irish immigration to America, develops this theme at great length. He argues that Irish Catholics "often regarded emigration as involuntary exile," a view which led them to "adapt to American life in ways which were often alienating and sometimes dysfunctional."[116] Miller's contention is that the Irish experience in America was problematic at least in part because the Irish perceived themselves "not as voluntary, ambitious emigrants but as involuntary nonresponsible 'exiles,' compelled to leave home by forces beyond individual control, particularly by British and landlord oppression."[117]

In many ways Irish Catholic culture was antithetical to the traits facilitating success in urban America, those espoused by the moral reformers: "In broadest terms, much evidence indicates that, in contrast to the Protestants they encountered in Ireland and North America, the Catholic Irish were more communal than individualistic, more dependent than independent, more fatalistic than optimistic, more prone to accept conditions passively than to take initiatives for change, and more sensitive to the weight of tradition than to innovative possibilities for the future."[118]

In these respects, there was a "cultural as well as [a] socioeconomic gulf between peasant Ireland and bourgeois America which at mid-century seemed almost insurmountable."[119] In the judgment of one mid-nineteenth-century Protestant notable (New York's George Templeton Strong), "Our Celtic fellow citizens are almost as remote from us in temperament and constitution as the Chinese."[120] In particular, the Irish were thought to be culturally remote because of their failure to behave in accordance with the traditional Protestant virtues, "individual effort, thrift, caution, sobriety, and a canny, tight-lipped self-reliance." Instead, they "challenged the code of the community at almost every point. . . . The Irish did not seem to practice thrift, self-denial, and other virtues desirable in the 'worthy, laboring poor.'"[121] On the whole, then, there is reason to believe that Irish Americans were initially less receptive to the message of moral reform than were other European immigrant groups.

Thus, in the words of sociologist Andrew M. Greeley,

> Practically every accusation that has been made against the American blacks was also made against the Irish: their family life was inferior, they had no ambition, they did not keep up their homes, they drank too much, they were not responsible, they had no morals, it was not safe to walk through their neighborhoods at night, . . . they were not willing to pull themselves up by their bootstraps, . . . and they would always remain social problems for the rest of the country.[122]

These critiques were not without a factual basis: as historians today have noted (relying partly on testimony from sympathetic Irish American observers), "there is abundant evidence that the majority of the Irish immigrants were ignorant and uneducated and poor managers."[123]

Irish skepticism about the utility, desirability, and practicability of the virtues could not have been unrelated to the massive social problems that beset urban Irish Americans in the nineteenth century—social problems that continue to confront us today. Crime, alcoholism, drug addiction, prostitution, family instability, and illegitimacy were all rampant. In William Stern's summary of the evidence, "New York's Irish truly formed an underclass; every variety of social pathology flourished luxuriantly among them."[124]

Like twentieth-century blacks, nineteenth-century Irish Americans migrated to cities from rural areas, and they experienced great difficulties in making that transformation. This similarity, along with others, has not gone unremarked. For example, Glazer and Moynihan assert that

> the black immigrants in New York City in the 1950's and 1960's were a displaced peasantry, not at all unlike their Irish and Italian predecessors, most, in truth, like the Irish, who arrived with all the stigmata acquired from living under rulers of a different race. (The gulf between ruler and ruled in, say, eighteenth-century Ireland was just as great as that between black and white in the American South.) The Negroes were not highly competitive; they were undercompetitive. They had been raised that way in the South, and were not instantly transformed by Bedford-Stuyvesant, which became not a ghetto but a slum.[125]

Thomas Sowell has elaborated on the historical similarities between blacks and Irish, which extend not only to "social pathologies (alcoholism, violence, broken homes)," but also include "the fields in which they advanced (sports, entertainment, religion, writing, politics), the fields they avoided (science and mathematics), the businesses in which they succeeded (life insurance, banking, publishing), the businesses in which they made little headway (manufacturing, merchandising)."[126]

Because the Irish found the adjustment to urban life so fraught with difficulties, it was by no means clear in the mid-nineteenth-century that the Irish were to enjoy greater upward mobility than blacks—at least northern blacks. (In this context, recall DuBois's judgment, presumably from the late 1870s or early 1880s, that "none of the colored folk I knew were so poor, drunken and sloven as some of the lower class Americans and Irish.")[127] Irish Bostonians in 1860 "unquestionably were lowest in the occupational hierarchy"; blacks, who "did not remain simple unskilled laborers to the same extent as the Irish, . . . clearly" stood closer to the position of native whites.[128]

Similarly, in the 1850s a Cleveland newspaper contended that blacks were "much better citizens than the hordes of Catholic Irish who are yearly floating to our shores."[129] Frederick Law Olmsted, the patrician reformer (and good friend of Brace) who created New York's Central Park, observed that blacks were deemed more valuable than the Irish in the South, so that the Irish were assigned the most unhealthy and dangerous jobs there.[130]

At the least it is safe to say that the Irish and blacks were often lumped together as social dregs, with neither group judged obviously superior to the other. The Irish were described as "niggers turned inside out," and blacks were sometimes called "smoked Irish" (a description that was neither meant nor taken as a compliment).[131]

How the Irish Became "White"—and "Protestant"

Yet despite the manifold difficulties that confronted Irish urban immigrants in the mid-nineteenth century, in the course of generations the Irish American community achieved significant upward mobility. The degree to which it has been upwardly mobile is seldom appreciated and understood. In 1981 Andrew Greeley summarized much of the relevant evidence:

> In terms of education, occupation, and income, Irish Catholics are notably above the national average for other whites. In education and occupation they are also now even with the British Protestant group and substantially ahead of that group in income. Finally, while they lag somewhat behind Jews in occupational prestige and education, their average income in the years from 1975 to 1978 is slightly ahead of both the British Protestants and the Jews.[132]

How should that ascent be understood? In part it was undoubtedly achieved because the Irish (along with all the other European immigrant groups) were the beneficiaries of the discrimination suffered by blacks. In Orlando Patterson's formulation, "Only [Afro-Americans] were systematically shut out of the emerging industrial revolution at the end of the nineteenth century, preventing them from developing those critical patterns of behavior and cultural tools necessary for keeping in phase with the nation's changing economy."[133]

In this respect, the contrast between Irish American immigrants and free northern blacks has been argued persuasively (if somewhat anecdotally) by historian Noel Ignatiev:

> Black workers, already being driven out of artisanal trades by prejudice, . . . could find no refuge in the manufacturing area, and hence were pushed down below the waged proletariat, into the ranks of the destitute self-employed: ragpickers, bootblacks, chimneysweeps, sawyers, fish and oyster mongers, washerwomen, and hucksters of various kinds. In contrast, . . . Irish immigrants . . . were being transformed into the waged labor force of industry. The distinction between those who did and those who did not have access to the most dynamic area of the economy became a principal element defining "race" in the North.[134]

In Ignatiev's reading the Irish were upwardly mobile because they "became white"—that is, they were judged suitable for employment opportunities that were unfairly denied to blacks. That indeed tells a crucial part of the story, but not all of it. The Irish also achieved upward mobility because in a sense they "became Protestant," by adopting the virtues espoused by the moral reformers. Over time they came to practice those virtues assiduously—to the point where, Greeley notes, "on various measures of the achievement syndrome called the Protestant ethic, the Irish Catholics score higher than anyone else—save the Jews."[135]

Although the Irish "became Protestant" in this sense, they did not, of course, convert from Catholicism. On the contrary, Catholic observance increased over time among Irish American immigrants. Significantly, though, the Catholicism to which they adhered in America differed from the Catholicism that had characterized Ireland by stressing self-advancement through practice of the traditionally "Protestant" virtues espoused by the moral reformers: diligence, sobriety, thrift, and familial responsibility. Patterson partially explains the Irish American ascent, which he explicitly presents as a model for contemporary blacks, in terms of "an amazing capacity for hard work, and a deep and abiding commitment to the sanctity of their families."

> Even in the face of oppressively low wages and nativist hostility, including the burning of their churches and convents, the Irish worked long, backbreaking hours for their families, the men often dying young as a result. And, contrary to present sociological dogma that it is poverty that creates familial dislocation, destitution and anti-Irish bigotry resulted in a tightening of familial bonds among the Irish who were seemingly trapped in the ghettos of nineteenth-century America.[136]

Hard work, or diligence, unquestionably had much to do with the advance of the Irish, even according to Ignatiev: "The initial turnover from black to Irish labor does not imply racial discrimination; many of the newly arrived Irish, hungry and desperate, were willing to work for less than free persons of color, and it was no more than good capitalist sense to hire them."[137] (What does imply racial discrimination is the subsequent unwillingness of white employers to hire black workers for lower pay still; in Ignatiev's view, the employers were motivated by the belief that "White men will not work with [the Negro].")[138]

To buttress his claim about Irish diligence, Ignatiev quotes an 1860 passage from a black writer who explained the initial displacement of black workers by Irish immigrants in terms of Irish willingness to work for less than native whites or blacks. The Irish were reportedly advised as follows by a Catholic priest: "If you wish to succeed, you must do everything that [native white and black laborers] do, no matter how degrading, and do it for less than they can afford to do it for." And in the black writer's mind, the Irish followed this advice:

> The Irish adopted this plan; they lived on less than the Americans could live upon, and worked for less, and the result is, that nearly all of the menial employments are monopolized by the Irish, *who now get as good prices as anybody.* There were other avenues open to American white men, and though they have suffered much, the chief support of the Irish has come from the places from which we have been crowded.[139]

Thrift and sobriety were also important factors in the Irish American rise. To begin with, the charge of Irish improvidence had always been something of a canard.[140] In Newburyport, Massachusetts, Stephan Thernstrom has shown, Irish working-class families were considerably more likely to accumulate property than their native counterparts: "The [Irish] immigrant laborer received wages no higher than those of the Yankee workman, but he had a greater determination to save and to own."[141]

Nor was the behavior of the Newburyport Irish in any way uncharacteristic; for example, more than half of the depositors in many antebellum urban savings banks (such as the New York Savings Bank, the Emigrants Savings Bank of New York, and Boston's Provident Institution for Savings) are known or estimated to have been Irish.[142] Beginning in the 1840s, impoverished Irish immigrants were remitting millions of dollars to compatriots who had remained in Ireland; according to one estimate, $65 million was sent to Ireland between 1848 and 1864, an indication of what one historian has called "an amazing record of thrift."[143]

In the course of the nineteenth century, sobriety became an increasingly common virtue among Irish Americans, in large part because of Catholic clerical insistence upon it. In the antebellum era New York's Archbishop John Hughes argued for the importance of temperance on this-worldly (as well as other-worldly) grounds, noting that in parishes with temperance associations "prosperity had been the reward of industry and as a matter of course, more of the comforts of life are enjoyed."[144]

Hughes's crusade for temperance was taken up by the Catholic Total Abstinence Union (CTAU), founded in 1872, one of the great success stories of nineteenth-century moral reform. As its historian has noted, "By the almost universal testimony of the time, intemperance in drink was *the* moral and social problem of [Irish Catholics] between 1840 and World War I. Today no one would maintain that the abuse has been eliminated, but no one would assert either, that it constitutes the chief moral problem among Irish Catholics."[145] Accepting the point of view of "respectable, Protestant America,"[146] the CTAU helped produce a substantial reduction in drinking among Irish Catholics: according to one estimate, 60 percent of Irish women and almost a third of Irish men were total abstainers by the 1880s.[147]

To be sure, it would be wrong to suggest that Irish American moral reform even came close to eradicating poverty by the start of the twentieth century. For example, in 1891 two-thirds of New York's almshouse inmates were still Irish-born (only a small drop from what the figure had been in 1870), and in 1900 Irish residents of Boston's North End and West End still received a share of public relief that far exceeded their percentage of the total population.[148]

Still, moral reform does seem to have made a difference, most obviously in drastic reductions in crime rates. By the 1880s and 1890s the Irish proportion of arrests for violent crime dropped from a staggering 60 percent to less than 10 percent, as the Irish went from being law breakers to law enforcers.[149] And if economic progress was less dramatic, nevertheless it was also far from nonexistent. As Kerby Miller summarizes developments, "Between 1870 and 1921 Irish-America emerged from the near-ubiquitous poverty . . . of the Famine decades. The process was slow, . . . but by the early twentieth century Irish-America was a relatively mature and exceptionally diverse society, enjoying some real prosperity [and] far greater security than in 1850–70."[150]

Explaining Irish American Moral Reform

What accounts for the apparent success of moral reform among nineteenth-century Irish Americans? The short—and largely correct—answer is the influence of the Catholic Church. Moral reform took hold because and insofar as Irish immigrants were re-Catholicized.

Contrary to what might be assumed, the pre-famine Irish population was not particularly religious. It is estimated that only about 40 percent of Catholics in Ireland before the famine regularly attended church. That comparatively low figure seems to have carried over into New York: about 40 percent of New York's Catholics are thought to have attended Sunday services in the 1860s.[151] Because of a lack of religious instruction, initially many Irish American Catholics were Catholic in name only. As a New York priest remarked in 1865, "Half of our Irish population here is Catholic merely because Catholicity was the religion of the land of their birth."[152]

Thus "the task of the church in the United States was not merely to preserve the faith of the newcomers, but in many cases to change nominal Catholics into practicing believers."[153] It is important to realize, though, that it was not the immigrants alone who were religiously transformed in America; in important respects, Catholicism itself was also altered. It became more hospitable to the traditional virtues of moral reform.

The Catholicism indigenous to nineteenth-century Ireland was not notably compatible with the spirit of moral reform. Instead it was a fatalistic religion, deeply skeptical of the possibility of moral self-improvement and the desirability of economic advancement. It subordinated virtues like "enterprise, initiative, and action to the exigencies of tradition, community, and conformity"; it de-emphasized "striving for material success" and "severely limited the scope for self-regeneration through reason and 'good works.'"[154]

Not surprisingly, then, the Catholicism of Irish immigrants to America was not initially very different. As Stephan Thernstrom has observed,

> The Catholicism the [Irish] immigrant brought to the New World was a fatalistic peasant religion which sharply conflicted with the optimistic, expansionist assumptions of American social thought of the age. Clerics who could write that "in more than 99 cases in a 100 we shall have reason to rejoice if the son turns out as well as the father" were challenging the essence of the ideology of mobility.[155]

Similarly, Oscar Handlin has argued that "the Irish [in Boston] were completely alien to the idea of progress. . . . Reform was [thought to be] a delusion inflating men's sense of importance, distorting the relative significance of earthly values, and obscuring the true goals of their endeavor—salvation of the eternal soul. Such movements were suspect because they exaggerated the province of reason, exalting it above faith, futile because they relied upon temporal rather than spiritual agencies, and dangerous because they undermined respect for established institutions."[156]

Significantly, though, Irish Catholicism was transformed on these shores: it was Americanized, even "Protestantized" (in the sense that a much greater appreciation of the desirability of upward mobility—and of the utility of the moral reformers' virtues as means of achieving it—emerged). In Newburyport, for example, Thernstrom has shown that Catholicism "was well on its way to being 'Americanized' within a generation of its establishment": the local parish priests, who "were dedicated to accumulating property as well as to saving souls, . . . saw clearly that a thrifty, hard-working, well-educated congregation would contribute to that end."[157] As Thernstrom summarizes the evidence, "The large Irish, Roman Catholic component of the [Newburyport] working class was securely attached to a church . . . firmly committed to the prevailing American ideology of enterprise and success."[158]

What was true in Newburyport was also true elsewhere. Kerby Miller emphasizes the Americanness of the Irish American church:

> The leaders of the Irish-*American* church were deeply sensitive to nativist charges that being Irish and Catholic was . . . incompatible with becoming American and respectable. As a result, the church assiduously promoted . . . bourgeois values and upward mobility among its adherents. . . . Church teachings, as reflected in sermons and parochial school readers, commanded emigrants and their children to industry, thrift, sobriety, and self-control—habits which would not only prevent spiritual ruin but also shape good citizens and successful businessmen. Although in 1870 most Irish Americans remained mired in the lower classes and although evidence of continued emigrant intemperance and turbulence abounded, by then newly formed, church-sponsored associations of upwardly mobile Irish-Americans were avidly seeking prosperity through piety and self-help.[159]

There was secular as well as spiritual support for the virtues espoused in moral reform. Despite intense clashes with Protestant nativists, Irish American newspapers consistently advised their readers (in the words of an editorial) to "take pattern by the Yankee . . . [and] imitate the energy, patience and prudence of his character."[160] Middle-class emigrants recommended that working-class Irish Americans "imitate Yankee models, of thrift, sobriety, industry, and individualism."[161] For example, in 1855 the woolen manufacturer John Ryan spoke of his hope to see the Irish people "in the great, numerous, industrious, intelligent, and independent class of people in the United States, who live in comfort and independence, by their labor, sobriety, industry, and frugality."[162]

This support for the traditional virtues extended into Irish American support for Irish nationalism. Some nationalists admittedly were tempted (with some reason) to blame England for all Irish failings: as one Irish American put it, "Unless I ascribed guilt to England, I could not excuse the Irish for all those failings that made the English [and Yankee employers] feel superior."[163]

But at the same time, Irish Americans also endorsed nationalism as a motive for virtuous behavior: A nationalist pamphlet argued that "true" Irishmen were "frugal, sober, and industrious," because such characteristics were conducive to political as well as personal success.[164] The same identification of Irish nationalism with the traditionally Protestant virtues is evident in the contention of a leading intellectual (newspaper editor and writer John Boyle O'Reilly) that "[w]e can do Ireland more good by our Americanism than by our Irishism."[165] Americanism was manifested, for instance, in the virtue of sobriety: hence many nationalists adopted the slogan "Ireland sober is Ireland free."[166] In one historian's summation, Irish American nationalists "wanted the Irish . . . to advance by practicing the individualistic virtues of self-reliance, thrift, pride, and hard work. . . . The Irish nationalists wanted, in other words, to make Ireland over and to make it over largely in the image of America."[167]

What accounts, then, for the success of Irish American moral reform? Irish American Catholicism endorsed it, as did Irish American secular nationalism: both forces were clearly animated by the belief that the virtues of diligence, sobriety, thrift, and familial responsibility were desirable and useful. It is hard to believe, though, that Irish American Catholicism and secular nationalism would have been nearly so supportive of the virtues promoted by moral reform in the absence of a broader American consensus favoring them. To put it baldly, the nineteenth-century Irish American poor began to act more virtuously (and to become less poor) in some measure because so many other Americans believed that it was necessary to act virtuously if one wished to avoid being poor.

By contrast, if the African American poor of the twentieth century have been less receptive to the message of virtue, that is no doubt in part because discrimination has often unjustly denied them success as the reward for virtue. In part, though, it is probably also because other Americans have been more hesitant about conveying the message of virtue. It is possible that we cannot reasonably hope for moral reformation of today's poor—regardless of race—in the absence of a broader moral consensus in favor of the virtues. What is the likelihood that such a consensus may now be emerging? That is the question to which we next turn.

7 THE CONTEMPORARY CLIMATE FOR MORAL REFORM

What are the prospects for the success of moral reform among impoverished American blacks today—and, more broadly, among all poor Americans today? An answer to that question must begin with the realization that most Americans (black or white) are not poor—and that their prosperity has much to do with practice of the virtues. If we are to understand the persistent poverty of part of the black population in particular, we need to realize that—and why—much of that population is not poor. In the words of sociologist John Sibley Butler, "If there is an economic cure for the underclass, it will not be found by studying that group alone, but rather by studying the Afro-Americans who have followed successful paths to economic stability."[1]

But the example of successful American blacks is often understudied or even ignored, to the point where it is arguably the middle-class black rather than the underclass black who could be considered today's invisible man. Orlando Patterson makes this argument forcefully, pointing to the myopia of much contemporary American social science, which focuses on black failure while saying little or nothing about black success:

> The major problem in the social sciences today with regard to Afro-Americans is not why the bottom 25 percent fails, but why the miracle of working- and middle-class successes persists among them. Social science is at a complete loss to explain the two-thirds of Afro-American people leading normal, uncursed lives, very much a part of the American mainstream.[2]

What characterizes these mainstream African Americans, in Patterson's judgment, is their commitment to the virtues of diligence and moral accountability. "Hard work, intelligence, and industriousness" account for the "very real status and power" acquired by middle-class American blacks.[3] "By the most conservative estimate," Patterson argues, some 60 percent of American blacks "want to . . . control and be responsible for themselves and their communities." This population comprises "the vast majority of that resilient core of hard-working, God-fearing men and women of the working and middle classes who have triumphed over racial and class discrimination to become models of self-determining Americans."[4] Thus "the great majority of Afro-Americans . . . are a . . . law-abiding group of people who share the same dreams as their fellow citizens, . . . and, to every dispassionate observer, are, in their values, habits, ideals, and ways of living, among the most 'American' of Americans."[5]

Statistical evidence confirms Patterson's unsurprising suggestion that virtue helps explain the triumphs over adversity of successful American blacks. Most obviously, diligence and familial responsibility correlate negatively with poverty. In 1995, 62 percent of black children in female-headed families were poor; but among black children in intact, two-parent families, just 13 percent were poor.[6] As one would expect, blacks who work full-time are also seldom poor: in 1995, only 2.5 percent of black males aged 18–64 who worked year-round and full-time were poor. While the figure for black females was notably higher (7.5 percent), it still paled in comparison to the figures for black females employed less than full-time (31.6 percent) or not at all (54.2 percent).[7]

Exercising the virtues has significantly lessened the poverty of many twentieth-century African Americans, just as it lessened the poverty of many nineteenth-century Irish Americans. In fact, a focus on comparatively prosperous blacks—that is, the majority of all blacks—properly reminds us that efforts to promote the virtues among African Americans are more notable for their successes than their failures.

What are the prospects, though, for extending that success to the significant minority of American blacks who remain poor? That question inevitably raises broader ones in turn: How receptive are poor Americans—black and white—to practicing the virtues? And how willing and able are Americans who are not poor—black and white—to promote them?

Ambivalent Resources for Moral Reform

As we saw in the previous chapter, the principal resources of Irish American moral reform were found in religion and nationalism. In assessing the current prospects for moral reform among blacks in particular, we should begin by considering whether African American religion and nationalism are conducive to efforts to promote it.

It might be tempting to assume a priori that religion—submission to God's will—tends to promote moral reform; it might also be tempting to assume that nationalism—embodying as it so often does opposition to a group that is thought to oppress one's own—tends to hinder it. Moral reform, after all, is an effort at self-improvement; and religion seems to focus one's efforts on combating the enemy within, whereas nationalism seems to direct attention away from oneself, toward the external enemy thought to be responsible for one's problems.

But Irish American historical experience calls that generalization into question. In fact, both the religion and the nationalism of Irish Americans generally favored the cause of moral reform; but neither did so invariably. It is fair to say that a comparable ambivalence affects contemporary African American efforts at moral reform.

For several reasons, African American religion is not an altogether reliable proponent of moral reform. To begin with, just as it would have been misleading to exaggerate the religiosity of Irish emigrants at the time of the famine, so it is also misleading to exaggerate the religiosity of American blacks today. To be sure, American blacks are obviously a religious people, with higher rates of church attendance than other Americans;[8] but it is also the case that religion—as measured by church attendance—seems to be weakest where it might be most useful for purposes of moral reform, among the black population of the central cities of the north.[9]

Just as the religion of Irish emigrants did not at the outset invariably and effectively support moral reform, neither does African American religion do so today. There is some evidence showing that religious faith and church-going are correlated with greater success for inner-city blacks (and others as well);[10] nevertheless, the effects of religion should not be exaggerated.[11] The decisive consideration, though, is that even if faith really does encourage good works, exactly how to promote faith remains regrettably unclear.[12]

It is also important to realize that not all faiths are created equal—at least in terms of their efficacy in promoting moral reform. It is helpful to recall that believers in the existence of a culture of poverty have often seen as one of its hallmarks not irreligion, but belief in "fundamentalist" religion. Fundamentalism—in these respects well exemplified by the Catholicism of Ireland's famine emigrants—in turn is thought to go along with "a sense of helplessness and low sense of personal efficacy," as well as "strong inclinations toward belief in magical practices . . . and low levels of aspirations for the self."[13]

There is certainly reason to believe that fundamentalism has not engendered moral reform among blacks, to the extent that it emphasizes (again, like Irish Catholicism before its Americanization) the passivity of people, who are seen as playthings of fate rather than shapers of their own destiny. Sociologist Elijah Anderson has portrayed fundamentalism as—ironically—a factor promoting rather than discouraging illegitimacy in the inner city:

> Many women in the black underclass emerge from a fundamentalist religious orientation and hold a "pro-life" philosophy. Abortion is therefore usually not an option. . . . New life is sometimes characterized as a "heavenly gift," an infant is sacred to the young woman. . . . A birth is usually met with great praise, *regardless of its circumstances*, and the child is genuinely valued. Such ready social approval works against many efforts to avoid illegitimate births.[14]

Other observers of African American religion have noted (and lamented) its failure to promote moral reform more effectively. A century ago, DuBois spoke of the timidity of the black church in "setting moral standards for the people." He contended that "the congregation does not follow the moral precepts of the preacher, but rather the preacher follows the standard of his flock." In DuBois's estimation, "The average Negro preacher . . . is a shrewd manager, a respectable man, a good talker, a pleasant companion, but neither learned nor spiritual, nor a reformer."[15]

That judgment is largely echoed today by Patterson, in a remarkably candid discussion. Patterson declares that a "major disadvantage of fundamentalist religion is that it has a limited scope as a medium of moral transformation. The transformation wrought by this religion only marginally and sporadically permeates the secular *moral* life, in sharp contrast with its impact on the secular *social* and *political* world of Afro-Americans."[16]

Patterson regrets that the black church "has had only limited impact on the secular, personal lives of lower class Afro-Americans." As he points out,

> It is hard to understand why this is so. . . . The moral dictates of Afro-American fundamentalism are forcefully and unambiguously hammered home in every service: fornication, adultery, the bearing of illegitimate children, teenage sexuality, personal violence, and drug and alcohol addiction are all relentlessly condemned in every sermon as sins incurring everlasting punishments and damnation in hell. . . . And yet, in spite of all this churching and praying [the Afro-American lower classes] continue to commit these acts (these sins) with greater frequency than all other Americans. What happens between the sermon and the bed? How could so great a divide exist between a fervently believed-in creed and the behavior of its adherents?[17]

Patterson praises the black church for promoting "an ethic of personal responsibility" (in which individuals acknowledge their wrongful acts and take full responsibility for them), but criticizes it (as well as its white fundamentalist counterpart) for failing to inculcate "personal autonomy" (in which individuals take steps to change their behavior). Noting only that "poverty and racism . . . most emphatically" do not explain the failure to inculcate it, Patterson offers no solution to the "hopeless, tragic puzzle" that he presents.[18]

Excessive optimism about the power of African American religion to promote moral reform is unwarranted; but excessive pessimism, on the other hand, is not warranted either. As we will see in Chapter 8, the evident success of individual African American religious leaders as moral reformers—those who succeed in promoting personal autonomy, hence are not fundamentalist in my use of that word— has begun to arouse great interest among policy analysts; that success should not be minimized.

Nevertheless, Roman Catholicism's nineteenth-century success in promoting moral reform cannot easily be replicated by black churches today. That is because the hierarchical structure of Catholicism gave it a great hold over individual Irish American worshipers, which enhanced its effectiveness as an agent of moral reform. By contrast, the structure of African American religion is much more amorphous, and its hold over individual worshipers is much weaker. In all likelihood, then, African American religion will be notably less successful in advancing the cause of moral reform today than Irish Catholicism was in the nineteenth century.

Ambivalence with respect to moral reform characterizes black nationalism today, just as it characterized Irish American nationalism in the past. The nationalism of an oppressed people can, of course, be directed externally—at the hated oppressors, who are blamed for all the problems of the oppressed; but it can also be directed internally—to encourage the moral and practical self-reliance of the op-pressed. In the Irish American case, we saw, nationalism led to both hatred of the English and desire to incorporate (or emulate) what were thought to be their char-acteristic virtues.

Black nationalism obviously also can and does lead in both of these directions. We have seen how the hatred for whites so often expounded by Malcolm X under-mined his insistence on black self-help and moral responsibility. Nevertheless, black nationalism, like black religion, can promote as well as undercut moral re-form. Jennifer Hochschild captures the ambivalence perfectly, pointing to nation-alism's "two opposite effects—a passion for success in order to honor one's . . . race, and a rejection . . . of white standards of success, in reaction to mistreatment of one's . . . race. Both occur."[19]

Black nationalism is by no means an inveterate opponent of moral reform; instead it can and frequently does undergird communal efforts to achieve it. In Glenn Loury's assessment, "Just about every effective strategy of which I am aware that is being carried out in poor black communities to combat the scourges of violence, low academic achievement, and family instability builds positively on . . . ethnic consciousness"—as opposed to an abstract universal commitment to hu-man virtue.[20]

Even a black nationalism that is explicitly hostile to whites can in some cir-cumstances engender moral reform. Thus, as Hochschild reminds us, "To the degree that rejection of the white-created dominant ideology moves beyond pos-turing into activities to improve housing, jobs, political accountability, and self-respect, poor blacks who reject the [American] dream may enhance their lives."[21]

The relevant question regarding moral reform is less whether blacks are na-tionalists than what their nationalism entails. On this score there are considerable grounds for encouragement. Summarizing an array of evidence from survey data, Hochschild concludes that "most African Americans abjure strong versions of black nationalism, *especially when the survey question implies rejecting mainstream val-ues* [in effect, the traditional virtues] *rather than adding a distinctive black compo-nent to them.*"[22]

The Black Bourgeoisie and the Debate over Its Virtues

In Chapter 3 we considered the likelihood that Hartley's harsh rhetoric about the Irish poor may have harmed the cause of moral reform by suggesting that the virtues were "English," so that engaging in self-advancing behavior would have been construed as craven submission to the Protestant enemy. That discussion was, of course, prompted by today's frequently voiced concern that self-advancing be-havior is sometimes derided in the inner cities as an Uncle Tom–like display, in which one "acts white." To what extent, then, is the cause of moral reform harmed by the perception that the virtues (and the success attendant upon them) are some-how "white"?

One way of answering this question is through an assessment of the contrasting evaluations of the most successful blacks—members of the black bourgeoisie. As John Sibley Butler has noted, there are "negative connotations" to being called a "black *bourgeois*, or 'Bourge,' in the Afro-American culture. . . . In an interesting kind of way, despite the struggle of Afro-Americans, economic success is suspect within the black community."[23] In a similar vein, Henry Louis Gates, Jr., deplores the extent to which "culturally speaking, the 'street' has been deemed the repository of all that is real, that is 'black.'"[24]

Ironically, as Gates observes, "the full-fledged rise of black-bourgeois-bashing preceded the full-fledged rise of the black bourgeoisie"—that is, it predated the emergence in the last generation of a sizable black middle class.[25] It is of some interest to realize, though, that the original critique of the black bourgeoisie took it to task not for "acting white," but instead for casting off virtue: its members were faulted not for embodying phony virtues that are inauthentic and somehow "white," but for failing to embody genuine virtues that are universal. The critique of the black bourgeoisie, in other words, is not inevitably an attack on the virtues of diligence and thrift—but has also been mounted in their defense.

The classic work in this vein is the eminent sociologist E. Franklin Frazier's 1957 study, *The Black Bourgeoisie*. In it Frazier lamented what he saw as the ethical decline and fall of a virtuous black bourgeoisie, which he argued was replaced by a successor group far less concerned with good behavior than with conspicuous consumption; in this respect his narrative presents a black equivalent—more than a decade beforehand—of Daniel Bell's *Cultural Contradictions of Capitalism* (discussed in Chapter 5).

In Frazier's conception, the first black bourgeoisie (the free blacks of the antebellum north, who are estimated to have amassed some $50 million in assets) embodied the virtues:

> The savings and business undertakings on the part of the free Negroes reflected the spirit and values of their environment. Through thrift and saving, white American artisans hoped to accumulate wealth and get ahead. This spirit was encouraged among the free Negroes by their leaders. . . . These free Negroes were trained in the "old style" bourgeois spirit represented by Benjamin Franklin. It was not until after Emancipation that the new bourgeois spirit would take hold among the leaders of the freedmen.[26]

The change discerned by Frazier involved a "revolt against missionary education": "Piety" was discarded, and there began to be "less talk about thrift and the dignity of labor. . . . Respectability became less a question of morals and manners and more a matter of the external marks of a high standard of living."[27] In effect, then, the decline and fall of the black bourgeoisie amounted to (and is explained by) a repudiation of the principles of Booker T. Washington, in which the virtues were understood as the only legitimate conduit to success.

Thus, whereas the old black bourgeoisie had been "frugal and abstemious in

[its] habits," striving "to attain middle-class respectability through industry and morality,"[28] its successor class rejected the need for "stable family life and conventional sex behavior," regarding "these values . . . as 'old fashioned' virtues." Money, rather than the virtues, now became "the chief requirement for social acceptance"; even money that was acquired from "gambling, prostitution, bootlegging, and the 'numbers.'"[29] The black bourgeoisie was defective, Frazier declared, largely because of its immorality—its proclivity toward "excessive drinking and sex," and "gambling," which "often involves a waste of money which many middle-class Negroes can not afford."[30]

As it happens, the empirical validity of Frazier's portrait of the black bourgeoisie is very much open to question.[31] The actual character of the bourgeoisie—black or white—matters greatly, of course; but so too does the motive for criticizing it. It is one thing to criticize those who allegedly fail to manifest the virtues; it is quite another to criticize them because they actually do manifest them.[32] What is worrisome about some contemporary criticism of the black bourgeoisie—unlike Frazier's—is that it often seeks (in Patterson's words) to "discredit the hard work, intelligence, and industriousness" of middle-class blacks.[33]

Are the Virtues (and Success) "White"?

Related to the critique of the virtues of the black (and white) bourgeoisie is a rejection of the success that often follows in their wake. Attempting to refute this attack upon success, Gates has pointed out that "we don't have to fail in order to be black. As crazy as this sounds, recent surveys of young black kids reveal a distressing pattern. Far too many say that succeeding is 'white,' education is 'white,' aspiring and dreaming are 'white,' believing that you can make it is 'white.'"[34]

The belief that self-advancing, virtuous behavior is "white" and to be shunned has undeniably arisen in the last generation:

> Since the 1960s some African Americans have come to define black identity in opposition not merely to some amorphous white identity, but specifically to white middle-class values. Working hard, saving money, acceding to authority, doing well in school, maintaining a stable two-parent family—all those mainstream, Protestant, bourgeois values . . . became for some blacks associated with illegitimate white dominance and intolerable black submission. For them, achieving the American dream means becoming white—something no self-respecting African American would choose to do. Conversely, honoring one's blackness means rejecting conventional success.[35]

This outlook is not only pernicious (complicating efforts to promote morals as it does), but also logically incoherent. Either one can strive to lessen black poverty or one can mount an ideological attack upon the virtues: one cannot consistently do both. The incoherence is evident, for example, in a passage written by Christopher Jencks, who is normally among the most perceptive analysts of black poverty:

Most whites see racial differences in crime and illegitimacy as evidence that the black community does not accept—or at least does not enforce—the same norms of behavior as the white community. Most whites also assume that differences of this kind contribute to blacks' economic troubles. . . . One inevitable result is that while many whites are prepared to treat blacks as equal if they "act white," few are prepared to treat blacks as equals if they "act black." . . . I can see no good way of resolving this kind of cultural conflict.[36]

Jencks does not explain precisely what he means by acting "black" and "white." But it is perfectly clear from the context that he does not mean, say, listening to James Brown and playing basketball (as opposed to listening to the Carpenters and—Tiger Woods notwithstanding—playing golf). Instead he evidently means that crime and illegitimacy are somehow "black," whereas obedience to the law and procreation within marriage are somehow "white." But if that is the case, the resolution to the cultural conflict that he describes is surely apparent: blacks should unhesitatingly act increasingly "white," in their own interests as well as the interests of society at large.

The purported dilemma of which Jencks writes does not pose a racial issue, but a practical one. Blacks who "act white" will (and should) advance their interests more effectively than do others; they will be far less likely to be poor. By contrast, blacks who "act black" (and, for that matter, whites who "act black") will do great damage to themselves and to others; they are far more likely to become (and remain) poor.

The virtues must trump race for anyone who is seriously concerned about improving the condition of the black poor; to act virtuously is not so much to "act white" as to act nonpoor. And those who act nonpoor radically increase their prospects of becoming nonpoor.

The best proof for my contention that acting virtuously does not amount to acting white is found, not surprisingly, in the attitudes and behaviors of the black middle class. Alan Wolfe's study of the American middle class shows that middle-class blacks move to the suburbs for exactly the same reasons that middle-class whites do: they are concerned about "the poor quality of inner-city public schools," and about "single-parent families and other urban problems that [may] contribute to bad schooling."[37] "Acting black"—to repeat Hochschild's formulation—ought to mean (and generally does mean) "adding a distinctly black component to [mainstream values]." But to the extent that "acting black" is instead thought to connote crime and illegitimacy, it is and should be unacceptable to all who wish to escape poverty, whether black or white; just as "acting Irish" (as Hartley might have defined it) was and should have been unacceptable to Irish Americans who strove to uplift their community and reduce its poverty by promoting moral reform.[38]

How Great Is the Fear of "Acting White"?

Both academic studies and anecdotal evidence confirm that self-advancing behavior is indeed rejected by some blacks because it is understood as "acting white."[39] Although that perspective has a long history, one can reasonably suppose that it is more common today than in the past.[40] On the supply side, radical black nationalists have more access to mass audiences through radio and television than they did in the past; on the demand side, one effect of the integration of schools is that bright black students (who in the segregated past would not have been separated out from other blacks) are likely to be tracked with mostly white students, so that academic success really does mean interacting with (if not acting like) whites.[41]

The rejection of behavior that involves "acting white" (that is, behavior according with mainstream moral standards) is obviously furthered by a perceived need for racial solidarity that militates against the acceptance of universal moral judgments. A generation ago, the ethnographer Ulf Hannerz discussed this phenomenon in a study of the black ghetto in Washington, D.C.: "In accepting the mainstream morality of most white Americans, the [ghetto's] 'respectables' also pass judgment on the 'undesirable' behavior of other ghetto dwellers and thus commit an infraction against the solidarity of ghetto dwellers. This, perhaps, is the most significant way in which a 'respectable' is a renegade."[42]

The belief that universal moral judgments amount to betrayal of one's particular race is deplorable: it poses a significant obstacle to moral reform. But at the same time, it would be wrong to suppose that attitudes along these lines are unique to the black ghetto. Instead, Wolfe's examination of middle-class morality suggests that the discomfort with judgment to which Hannerz alludes is an *American* phenomenon—not an African American one. In Wolfe's reading, it is middle-class Americans of all races who "are reluctant to pass judgment on how other people act and think," who have "added an Eleventh Commandment . . . : 'Thou shalt not judge.'"[43] Although white Americans are not afraid of "acting white," they too are often reluctant to criticize those (of any race) who fail to do so.

It is not enough, though, to assert that whites share culpability with blacks for often failing to enforce universal moral standards. A more important consideration is that surprisingly few blacks actually reject universal moral standards (and self-advancing behavior) on the grounds that they supposedly enjoin blacks to act white.

Suggestive evidence on this score can be found in a 1996 nationwide sample of about 2,000 high school students,[44] which found that just 19 percent of teens say that their friends (not themselves) "look down on" those who get good grades.[45] Significantly, though, no group diverged widely from that percentage: 18 percent of white students, 21 percent of black students, and 25 percent of Hispanic students affirmed that their friends looked down on successful students. Among inner-city teens, 24 percent held this view.[46] One could certainly wish that no inner-city students, rather than a fourth of them, affirmed that they had friends who thought poorly of academic success. Still, disdain for academic success was said to be voiced by the friends of only a distinct minority of black and inner-city youths: it was not a prevailing view.

In other respects as well, the survey found that black students manifested notably traditionalist views.[47] Just over half of all students—but almost two-thirds of black students—supported "kicking constant troublemakers out of class so teachers can concentrate on the kids who want to learn."[48] An overwhelming 84 percent of all students—including 84 percent of black students—endorsed holding inner-city students to the same standards applied to their middle-class counterparts.[49] Black students were also notably more likely than whites to favor greater structure and firmness in schools: for example, the regular checking of homework by teachers (who would demand that poor work be redone until it is right), or mandatory after-school classes for students receiving D's and F's.[50] Finally, black students were much more likely to emphasize the extreme importance of subjects such as world history, biology, chemistry, and advanced math.[51]

This array of impressive statistics does not, to be sure, refute the fact that large numbers of black students continue to be abysmally educated. Still, it is important (and at least in some ways reassuring) to realize that poor education comes about not because the value of education is derided, but despite the fact that it is widely esteemed.[52]

The findings cited above should engender skepticism about the extent to which self-advancing behavior is rejected by blacks as an example of "acting white." That skepticism, in turn, is reinforced by other data. For example, Hochschild cites much evidence from surveys indicating continued black adherence to the virtue of diligence. The surveys indicate that poor blacks will accept jobs at wages below those that comparably poor whites will accept; the professed willingness of blacks to accept low-wage work is almost as great as that of immigrants. Compared with young white men without jobs, unemployed young black men profess to be much more willing to accept unskilled jobs at low wages.[53]

Obviously, not all blacks (nor all poor blacks) can fairly be called diligent: Hochschild herself cites data showing that three times as many poor blacks as well-off blacks profess to find "nothing" bothersome about not working.[54] Still, her conclusion that "many [poor blacks] work now, and most would given the chance" is largely valid.[55] There is every reason to suppose that increased virtue would mitigate the problems of inner-city poverty—but there is no reason to suppose that inner-city residents en masse are devoid of virtue, or that they consciously reject the call for virtue as a stratagem of malicious white oppressors.

Receptivity to Virtue

The foregoing observations point to a larger truth that is crucial for the prospects of moral reform: for the most part the very poor are not, finally, all that different from you and me in their assessment (as opposed in many cases to their practice) of the virtues. Many among the poor fail to practice the virtues with sufficient assiduity; but few actively despise them. It is noteworthy that policy analysts from both right and left—who disagree on so many other matters—unite in rejecting the image of today's poor as principled opponents of the virtues.

As self-proclaimed defenders of the poor, it is perhaps predictable that those on the left would affirm the overall commitment of the poor to the virtues. For example, Hochschild argues that the black poor largely acknowledge the need for virtuous behavior to escape poverty; they both "believe in and try to act in accord with the precepts of the American dream."[56] She judges that at most 10 percent of all blacks can be said to be members of the "estranged poor," those who are both poor and deviant.[57]

Similarly, William Julius Wilson's surveys of the Chicago poor show that "black residents in the inner-city ghetto neighborhoods . . . verbally endorse, rather than undermine, the basic American values concerning individual initiative" as a means of escaping poverty.[58] For example, fewer than 3 percent of the respondents denied the importance of hard work as a means of getting ahead, whereas 66 percent stressed its importance.[59] Remarkably, a substantial majority also agreed "that America is a land of opportunity where anybody can get ahead, and that individuals get pretty much what they deserve."[60] The problem in Wilson's view is not that the inner-city poor have the wrong values—but that "many of those who subscribe to [the right ones] . . . find it difficult to live up to them," because of "the constraints and limited opportunities facing people in inner-city neighborhoods."[61]

It is important to realize that many conservatives also believe that the poor profess the right beliefs while too often failing to act on them. For example, Lawrence Mead is justly regarded as a conservative analyst of welfare. But a basic premise of the "new paternalism" that he advocates—in effect, a contemporary, more authoritative version of moral reform that attempts to use public policy in some ways to mandate the self-advancing behavior of the poor—is that the poor for the most part want to practice the virtues, want to adhere to conventional moral norms. As he notes, "Poor people express the same desire to work as other people. . . . Poor people also affirm other middle-class norms such as law-abidingness, maintaining stable marriages, and getting through school."[62] Thus it is wrong for critics to claim that "work requirements force new values on the poor." Instead, their "purpose is to enforce the values [the poor] already have, and for this they are usually *grateful*."[63]

To note this consensus is not to minimize—let alone deny—the serious policy disagreements that separate Wilson from Mead. In practice it matters greatly whether Wilson is right to suggest that the poor primarily need to be given new incentives or new opportunities to advance themselves—for example through a job-creation program—or whether Mead is right to suggest that instead they primarily need to be placed in a structured environment, in which they would be required to live up to the values that they themselves profess. (Note, though, that in practice the different policy recommendations are not altogether mutually exclusive: for example, poor people could be required to work in jobs created by the government. In addition, each analyst's program might be more appropriate for a different segment of the poor, with some among the poor principally needing increased opportunities, and others the enforcement of mainstream values.)

In any event, if moral reform works best when it is preached to the converted (those already affirming the importance of the virtues), its prospects are obviously better if the Mead-Wilson consensus is correct. Moral reform would have virtually no chance of success if today's poor had to be dragged kicking and screaming to practice the virtues. Fortunately, though, that is not the case. Instead, the moral reform mission today is in this respect no different than it was a century ago: it consists of convincing people that they are indeed capable of practicing virtues whose importance they themselves already acknowledge in many cases.

An Underclass Society?

There is good reason to suppose that most of the poor are more receptive to virtue than is sometimes supposed. In assessing the prospects for moral reform, though, an equally relevant consideration is that the nonpoor have hardly been spotless exemplars of virtue—or its single-minded proponents. The prospects for moral reform can conceivably be endangered by the attitudes and behaviors of the nonpoor, as well as by those of the poor. According to this hypothesis, which builds upon our earlier discussion of the cultural contradictions of poverty, the loss of virtue in the inner city reflects broader developments in the nation as a whole. The nonpoor have arguably been too permissive in responding to the occasionally self-destructive behavior of the poor; the nonpoor have arguably also set a bad example, too often acting self-destructively—or at the least not virtuously—themselves. This linkage of the defective behavior of all social classes is nicely captured in a formulation by the political scientist Mark Hughes: "We are an 'underclass' society, not a society with an 'underclass.'"[64]

Support for this melancholy assertion can be found in a series of observations made by William Julius Wilson, in which he contrasts the Mexican American and African American poor of inner-city Chicago. Wilson notes that "the Mexican immigrant neighborhoods in the inner city feature lower levels of joblessness and higher levels of social organization than comparable African-American neighborhoods."[65] He attributes this contrast in part to cultural differences, the fact that "Mexicans come to the United States with a clear conception of a traditional family unit that features men as breadwinners."[66] What is most significant for our purposes, though, is Wilson's assertion that "the intensity of the commitment to the marital bond among Mexican immigrants will very likely decline *the longer they remain in the United States and are exposed to U.S. norms, patterns of behavior, and changing opportunity structures* for men and women."[67]

It is a sad comment on American social mores that Wilson's argument—that Americanization will decrease the virtue of Mexican immigrants—is quite plausible. As we saw in Chapter 5, the commitment of Americans to the virtues has arguably waned in this century. For example, Christopher Jencks has contended that "single parenthood began its rapid spread during the 1960s, when elite attitudes toward sex, marriage, divorce, and parenthood were undergoing a dramatic change. . . . Instead of feeling morally superior to anyone who had a baby without marrying, the young began to feel morally superior to anyone who disapproved of unwed mothers."[68] The rejection of the two-parent family as a norm affected American (and, for that matter, western industrialized) society as a whole; its impact was simply most visible and most devastating among the poor.

Empirical evidence bears out Jencks's contention that the assault on the two-parent family has by no means been restricted to the poor. William Galston reminds us that problems of familial pathology in the inner city are "far from being aberrant," because they are only "intensified versions of trends clearly visible throughout our society."

> In 1960, only 5 percent of America's children were born out of wedlock; by 1995 that figure had topped 30 percent. Between 1960 and 1980, the rate of divorce more than doubled before stabilizing at the highest rate, by far, in the industrialized world. More than 40 percent (by some projections, 50 percent) of marriages undertaken today will end in divorce. Not surprisingly, the rate of children living apart from their biological fathers has risen from 17 percent to 36 percent in the past three decades; close to half of these children have not seen their fathers during the past year.[69]

The congruence of developments among and outside the poor is not restricted to the domain of sex and marriage. Has diligence declined among the poor? Clearly, if diligence can be measured by participation in the workforce: in 1959 more than two-thirds of heads of poor families worked at least part-time, but by 1989 less than half did.[70] Nevertheless, the poor are not unique in their increasing detachment from the workforce. The proportion of white men not in the civilian labor force rose sharply between 1954 and 1992, rising from 14 to 24 percent.[71] Some of this increase is explained by the ability of older male workers to take early retirement—not an altogether regrettable development. But part of it is also explained by the far more regrettable increased detachment from the labor force on the part of white men aged 16–24 who are also not in school.[72]

Nor is intemperance in any way restricted to the poor or to blacks. It is true that "most research finds the heaviest drug and alcohol use, and the worst effects therefrom, in the poorest communities."[73] But affluent people are more likely to be diagnosed as drug abusers than are the poor.[74] And with respect to the supposed racial divide concerning drug use, it is noteworthy that as of 1997 use of crack cocaine—despite its popular image as a drug used primarily by blacks—was "about three times more common among whites than among blacks."[75] To speak more broadly, "Whites engage in *more* drug use than blacks if abuse of alcohol is included in the definition of drug use. Whites drink more alcohol than blacks (or Latinos), drink more frequently, start drinking at a younger age, and (among those under age twenty-five) drink more on any given occasion. They also use illicit drugs at least as much as do blacks."[76]

Turning to another virtue, we see that failure to save is undoubtedly a serious problem among American blacks and the American poor. Remarkably, more than half of all black households had no balances in either checking or savings accounts in 1994 (compared with just one-sixth of other households).[77] Low-income households in general have a "much lower savings rate" than do others: while lack of income by itself explains a significant part of this discrepancy, it "certainly [does] not [explain] all of [the] wealth disparities that exist, especially among the poor."[78]

But these discouraging statistics—like the others that we have seen—cannot be understood in a vacuum: personal savings are also increasingly uncharacteristic even of affluent Americans. In 1998 the personal savings rate of Americans fell to 0.5 percent of disposable income, which means that they were spending 99.5 percent of their after-tax income—a rate unapproached since the era of the Depression (when the inability to save was far more comprehensible). Commenting on this development, economics columnist Robert J. Samuelson observes that "it's as if the entire country had chanted in unison, 'Hell no, we won't save.'"[79]

In fairness, it must also be noted that the personal savings rate is a statistic of dubious validity (since it does not take account of things like the appreciation in value of homes, stocks, and even individual retirement accounts).[80] Nevertheless, it is also fair to speak of "an ingrained cultural streak—call it a reckless optimism, or a willingness to take risks—that leads Americans to salt away less than, say the Japanese," to the point where some among the affluent regard "saving too much . . . as practically un-American."[81] (Americans are in fact "significantly less disposed to save" than their counterparts in other developed countries.)[82] To the extent that the decline in saving by the affluent reflects a disdain for prudence, it does not send a salutary message to the poor.

Finally, there is much plausibility to the contention that the pathologies of youthful inner-city criminals in many respects mirror and exaggerate worrisome tendencies of the broader culture. Orlando Patterson makes this case effectively:

> Far from being different, the problem of . . . inner-city youths is that they have too completely embraced and taken to their pathological extreme some of America's most cherished values: its materialism and conspicuous expenditure, its cutthroat competitiveness, its celebration of masculine bravado, its love of aggression, its Wall Street dictum that "greed is good." In the pathologies of urban underclass youth, Americans see their own materialist culture in broad billboard colors, staring back at them. What is the difference between the gaudy display of jewelry by underclass young men and the vulgar extravagance of a Donald Trump? And where did underclass youth acquire their murderous code of responding to being dissed with the violent defense of their honor? They learned it . . . from spending countless hours in front of their television sets where Euro-American stars such as Marlon Brando, John Wayne, and Clint Eastwood . . . portray the murderous honorific code of an earlier, even more violent underclass. . . . Violence is not an Afro-American pathology; it is an American pathology.[83]

The moral defects of the American mainstream can reasonably be said to bear at least some of the blame for the moral defects of the American underclass. The problem faced by inner-city residents is only in part that they are isolated from the mainstream; it is also (in the words of the sociologist Mitchell Duneier) that "they do not have the standard of living to buffer them from the destructive effects of the permissiveness, freedom, and spontaneity of American life." Because "many patho-logical social trends in the ghetto are more concentrated reflections of life in the wider society, . . . the poorest and most estranged members of society are not likely to take seriously cultural lessons . . . [from those who] are themselves caught up in those webs of conflicting value orientations that include permissive attitudes to-ward teenage sex, childbearing out of wedlock, adultery, and divorce that are preva-lent in the wider society."[84]

Retreat from the Underclass Society?

Thus, if the moral failings of the underclass in part reflect the moral failings of society as a whole,[85] the moral improvement of the underclass is likely to be facili-tated by the moral improvement of the rest of society. Reflecting that view, the journalist Nicholas Lemann speculated in 1991 that if "the national culture swung back toward more conservative mores, the underclass would begin to shrink."[86]

There is, in fact, good reason to suppose that the national culture has become more conservative of late. Karl Zinsmeister, the editor of *American Enterprise*, points to attitudinal data indicating "that many Americans have changed their minds on critical social questions, and are edging their way back toward tradition, moderation, and sanity."[87] (For example, 66 percent of respondents to a 1998 sur-vey said that they were chiefly worried by the prospect "that the country will be-come too tolerant of behaviors that are bad for society"; less than half as many respondents—28 percent—were chiefly worried by the prospect "that the country will become too intolerant of behaviors that don't do any real harm in society.")[88] Extrapolating from survey data like these, Zinsmeister contends that "a backlash against cultural decay has spread" beyond a minority of cultural conservatives and now is "'crossing over' into the broader culture."[89]

Not only have the opinions of Americans altered; still more important, their actions have changed as well. As a result, several of the social pathologies associ-ated with the underclass have become notably less severe. Welfare caseloads, for example, have declined sharply, falling by some 48 percent: 14.1 million people were on welfare in January 1993, compared with 7.3 million in August 1999.[90] The national commitment to work as opposed to dependency is also evident more broadly in increased participation in the labor force (fueled by the employment of a greater proportion of women, which more than counteracts the proportion of men who have dropped out of the labor force): 64 percent of the eligible popula-tion is currently in the work force, up from only 57 percent in 1970,[91] so that "a far higher proportion of Americans work than ever worked before."[92]

The fall in crime rates has been equally striking. Between 1992 and 1996, violent crime fell by 16.3 percent, and murder by 20.4 percent. FBI figures show that 1996 was the sixth straight year in which rates for both violent crime and property crime fell. Overall, America's crime rate was lower in 1996 than in any year since 1977.[93] The total number of violent crimes committed in 1995 was lower than the comparable figure for 1973, despite the increase in population in the intervening years.[94] The murder rate is now at its lowest level since the 1960s.[95]

The drop in crime is presumably related to a decline in the consumption of crack cocaine; according to National Development and Research Institute data, the percentage of newly arrested criminals who tested positive for crack cocaine has been falling steadily since 1987 in seven major cities, with arrestees younger than 18 registering the steepest declines.[96] Other drug indicators have shown improvement as well. Overall drug use in America has fallen by half in the past fifteen years.[97] Per capita alcohol consumption dropped by more than 10 percent between 1990 and 1996; per capita consumption in 1996—2.19 gallons ethanol—was the second-lowest it has been in thirty-four years (only the 1995 level was lower).[98] In addition, alcohol consumption among those aged 12 to17 is near its lowest point since government surveys began to measure it in 1974.[99]

Births out of wedlock are also declining. Illegitimacy among whites seems now to have reached a plateau: in 1997 the rate stood at 37.0 births out of wedlock per thousand white women, aged 15–44—down modestly from the high of 38.3 births in 1994. Black births out of wedlock have fallen by 19 percent since 1989 (when the rate stood at 90.7 births), to a 1997 rate of 73.4 births. The rate for black births out of wedlock is now lower than at any year since 1969, when the measurement was introduced. In the words of one summary of the data, "The fraction of all U.S. births coming from unmarried women is still distressingly high. But for the first time in a generation, the trend is in the right direction."[100]

How significant are the changes in American attitudes and the improvements in these assorted statistical indicators? To what extent do they presage the likelihood of a future triumph of moral reform, in which better behavior overall (including better behavior among the poor) will result in decreased poverty? Although these monumental questions do not admit of a simple, unambiguous answer, there are reasons for hope—though also for concern.

Return to Moral Reform?

One can indeed argue that we have recently entered an era of moral reform, in which social pathologies are likely to continue to decline. Zinsmeister argues this optimistic case effectively, contending that "Americans are expressing a new public temperament." As a result, "many of the social trendlines that turned ugly in the '60s and '70s have begun to level off and even retreat, in many cases to their lowest levels in two or three decades."[101] He suggests that "a new pattern of recovery and even reversal has emerged. This positive pattern is beginning to look every bit as broad and interlinked as our social collapse was when it showed up in the late '60s."[102]

Francis Fukuyama provides a historical context for this argument, observing that the current cyclical pattern (in which the moral regression that occurred a generation ago has now seemingly been followed by moral reform) has historical counterparts—including, significantly, the nineteenth-century movement for moral reform, which emerged in reaction to an earlier period of moral decay. As he notes, "There is considerable evidence that the late eighteenth and early nineteenth centuries were periods of rising social disorder and moral confusion, in which various indices of social capital declined for both Britain and the United States." In those years, surprisingly few Americans seem to have been churchgoers; there is also spotty evidence that crime and illegitimacy increased (and, as we saw in Chapter 2, good evidence that alcohol consumption was remarkably high).[103]

Nineteenth-century moral reform—embodied at its outset by Tuckerman and Channing, among others—arose, predictably enough, to counter these trends: "Victorianism was . . . a radical movement that emerged in reaction to the kinds of social disorder that seemed to be spreading everywhere in the beginning of the nineteenth century, a movement that deliberately sought to create new social rules and instill virtues in populations that were seen as wallowing in degeneracy."[104] And Victorian moral reform achieved what it set out to accomplish. U.S. church membership doubled between 1800 and 1850, alcohol consumption (as we have seen) declined swiftly and significantly, and crime decreased.[105] Fukuyama summarizes the evidence as follows:

> [The] attempts to renorm. . . American society from the 1830s . . . were a monumental success. The impact on social capital . . . was extraordinary, as masses of rude, illiterate agricultural workers and urban poor were converted into what we now understand as the working class. Under the discipline of the time clock, these workers understood they had to keep regular hours, stay sober on the job, and maintain minimal standards of decent behavior.[106]

Fukuyama then suggests that this earlier remoralization of society is perhaps now being replicated today, so that "the pattern experienced in the second half of the nineteenth century in . . . America . . . [may] repeat itself in the next generation or two."[107] To make this case he draws not only on statistical data documenting the declines in crime and illegitimacy, but also on assorted other cultural indicators, such as the growing recognition that single-parent families are harmful to children, and the interest in male responsibility manifested by both the Promise Keepers and the participants in the Million Man March.[108]

Thus we've arguably done it (that is, moral reform) before, and there's some reason to believe that we can do it again. Fukuyama is realistic enough to admit that the success of moral reform will not be achieved easily or automatically: "People will have to recognize that their communal lives have deteriorated, that they are engaging in self-destructive behaviors, and that they have to work actively to renorm their society through discussion, argument, cultural argument, and even culture wars." Nevertheless, "There is evidence that this has happened to some extent already, and earlier periods in human history give us a certain confidence that renorming or remoralization is possible."[109]

But even if remoralization is possible, how much is it likely to achieve? Unfortunately, there are reasons to doubt that the contemporary return to moral reform will be as effective as one might wish.

Causes for Concern

To begin with, the statistical good news (to this point, at least) is simply not all that good yet. The modest improvements in most statistical indicators have hardly returned us to the conditions that prevailed before conditions worsened a generation ago. Gertrude Himmelfarb's mordant commentary makes this point effectively:

> The decline or stabilization of some of the indices of social disarray does not begin to bring us back to the status quo ante—that now maligned period of the 1950s before the precipitous rise of those indices. . . . Illegitimacy has increased sixfold, and the number of children living with one parent has risen from less than one-tenth to more than one-quarter. Violent crime, although considerably lower than it was only a few years ago, is still almost four times that of the 1950s. And the much heralded reduction of the percentage of families on AFDC has brought us down from five times that of the 1950s to three and one-half times.[110]

A second reason for caution concerns the precise impact of the improvements in the statistical indicators. It is clear that what might be called underclass behavior (crime, illegitimacy, welfare dependency) is now decreasing. But surprisingly—and depressingly—it is less clear that the underclass itself has begun to shrink. Charles Murray has pointed to bits of discouraging data that should be kept in mind by optimists about the prospects for moral reform. First, the percentage of young (16- to 24-year-old) black males who are not in school (or in the armed forces or in prison) but also not in the labor force has risen from 18 percent in 1982 (in the midst of a recession, when difficulty in finding jobs might explain discouraged workers' departure from the labor force) to 23 percent in 1997—when good times had effectively created a full-employment economy.[111] Thus, "if trendlines in labor-force participation are a valid indicator of the course of the underclass, then it is unquestionably growing."[112]

Murray also points to fragmentary evidence suggesting that the declines in welfare caseloads reflect the disproportionate departure of former white recipients and of former recipients not in large cities—so that the reductions may be taking place principally among women who "are not part of the underclass."[113] Finally, Murray notes that the decline in the illegitimacy *rate* among blacks (the number of children born per thousand unmarried women—the statistic that we examined above) has not yet been accompanied by a decline in the illegitimacy *ratio* (the percentage of children born to unmarried as opposed to married women).

In other words, the decline in black births out of wedlock is not the result of a rise in black births in wedlock, or an increase in the percentage of blacks born into two-parent families.[114] That is significant, in Murray's view, because it means that the overwhelming majority of inner-city black children continue to be born into fatherless homes: the decline in the illegitimacy rate simply means that slightly fewer such children are now being born. But inner cities continue, regrettably, to be communities in which black children see few examples of men acting as bread-winners for their families, whom young boys growing up could learn to emulate.

Furthermore, a modest decline in the illegitimacy rate in 1999 does little or nothing to counteract the ill effects of illegitimacy in the previous generation: the decline in babies born to single mothers in 1997 does not affect the socialization of children born to single mothers in 1990 or 1985. "Whatever bad things go with high illegitimacy rates are still going on, and will continue to have reverberating effects well into the next century as the next generation grows up."[115] Summarizing the data, Murray concludes that "behaviorally, it is not at all clear that much has changed" in underclass neighborhoods since the 1991–1992 recession—although they are "probably somewhat more prosperous" now than they were then.[116]

Murray and Himmelfarb both point to the continuing problem of illegitimacy as a reason to doubt the likely effectiveness of current efforts at moral reform. They are right to do so; the weakening of the family sharply differentiates our condition from the one confronted by the nineteenth-century moral reformers (and greatly hampers our attempts to replicate their efforts). As we saw in Chapter 2, the moral reformers had little to say about single-parent families (though we also saw that what little they did say was often remarkably prescient); whereas the two-parent family was overwhelmingly the norm among the poor (and the nonpoor) of the nineteenth century, single parenthood is obviously far more common today.

That dramatic transformation is in turn explicable in terms of other changes that have affected American society in the twentieth century. Fukuyama explains the weakening of the family as a response to

> two very important developments [that] occurred sometime during the early post-war period. The first involved advances in medical technology—primarily the birth control pill, which permitted women to better control their own reproductive cycles. The second was the movement of women into the paid labor force in most industrialized countries and the steady rise in their incomes . . . relative to [those of] men over the next thirty years.[117]

In Fukuyama's view, the effect of the invention of the birth-control pill (and of the legalization of abortion) was to liberate men from the norms that had earlier enjoined them to look after the women whom they had impregnated, by marrying them in shotgun weddings. And the rise in female employment and income made it more thinkable for women to support themselves and to raise children on their own. Women in the labor force also tend to have fewer children, and parents with fewer children are likely to divorce more readily.[118]

But to understand the rise of the single-parent family is not to say that we know how to cope with its consequences. As Fukuyama notes, "It is not clear that there is a good substitute for reproduction outside [that is, a good alternative to reproduction within] nuclear families."[119] And for all of his optimism about the remoralization of society, Fukuyama denies that we are "likely to see dramatic changes . . . in norms regarding sex, reproduction, and family life. . . . The different technological and economic conditions of our age make it extremely unlikely that anything like a return to Victorian [sexual and familial] values will take place."[120] But in the absence of such a return, can moral reform among the poor—dependent as it is upon the examples of men who obey the law, work, and provide for their families—be expected to succeed?

A final reason for caution about the prospects for moral reform today is that the contemporary moral climate differs significantly from the climate in which the nineteenth-century reformers worked and wrote. Recall in this context Alan Wolfe's account of the congenital nonjudgmentalism of today's upholders of middle-class values. That reluctance to judge is altogether alien to the moral certainty that guided the reformers' judgments. The moral distance between today's morality and yesterday's is captured effectively in Wolfe's choice of words: at one point he speaks (correctly) of the widespread—and salutary—contemporary belief that middle-class "values" eventually translate into middle-class incomes.[121]

The moral reformers, on the other hand, believed not in "values" but in "virtues" as the means of lessening poverty. That is not a mere semantic difference. As Himmelfarb observes, the term "values" brings with it "the assumptions that all moral ideas are subjective and relative, that they are mere customs and conventions"; by contrast, "so long as morality was couched in the language of 'virtue,' it had a firm, resolute character," because "the word 'virtue' carried with it a sense of gravity and authority, as 'values' does not."[122]

All of these considerations should temper any belief that our efforts at moral reform are sure to be crowned by success; but they should by no means cause us to abandon those efforts, since success is conceivable even if it is uncertain. It is noteworthy that even Himmelfarb and Murray—skeptical as they are about the import of our accomplishments to date on the road back to moral reform—acknowledge that some recent developments give genuine cause for optimism. Both point to fragmentary evidence of moral improvement—and not only in the broader society, but among the poor as well.

Murray, for example, observes that "broad swaths of American society are becoming more civil, more responsible, and less self-indulgent. The good news is truly good, and it extends beyond the qualities measured by statistics."[123] Significantly, he has also hypothesized that improvements in the behavior of the nonpoor may ultimately also generate better behavior among the poor.

Murray has pointed to what he calls "the partial restoration of traditional society"[124]—that is, the return to traditional moral viewpoints that began to be rejected in the 1960s. He has called attention to a return to traditional sexual and marital behaviors that is most prominent among well-educated whites, but evident among others as well: more than 90 percent of the children of white college graduates live with two parents, and only 2 percent of the children born to white female college graduates are illegitimate. According to the "large, careful, nationally representative" survey conducted by the authors of *The Social Organization of Sexuality*, the median number of sex partners reported by American women in their lifetime (starting at age 18) is two.[125]

While Murray is dubious of the significance of the recent decline in the illegitimacy rate, he also speculates that the apparent strengthening of the two-parent family may soon affect the black poor as well. He agrees that "we may reasonably hope to see significant declines in the illegitimacy ratio in years to come"—since out-of-wedlock births tend to decline as women age, and since notably fewer teenagers are now becoming mothers.[126]

Murray does not contend that the various encouraging developments that he discerns (among them a rise in educational standards and the impact of a current religious revival)[127] are affecting all social classes uniformly—hence the danger that the restoration will be only "partial." On the other hand, he does suggest that aspects of the restoration are apparent not only among the best-educated and most prosperous, but also among the middle and working classes. And even if the return to traditionalism is most evident among the elites, that is still significant, because their "influence on cultural norms is vast." Their values will ultimately "become the basis for the social sanctions and rewards that control behavior so much more effectively than laws." For all of these reasons he remarks—most pertinently for our purposes—that "as these norms of the larger society change, one may plausibly hope that they will change behavior everywhere, including behavior in the underclass."[128] According to Murray, it is not clear that the moral regeneration of the underclass has begun to occur; but he evidently agrees that there is reason to hope for its occurrence in the future.

For her part, Himmelfarb agrees that a reaction is taking place against what she regards as the "dominant ethos" of moral permissiveness. The reaction—the return toward more traditional, less permissive morality—is taking place "among young people who will shape the culture of the future."[129] She points to survey data indicating that young people are becoming more religious and less permissive sexually. One particularly telling piece of data suggests that the latter reaction is also affecting inner-city youth: "83 percent of inner-city high-school juniors and seniors, asked about the ideal age to have sex, gave an age older than that when they themselves had had sex."[130]

Even those who are skeptical of the import of the improvements in various statistical indicators also acknowledge that there are genuine causes for hope— hope for the moral improvement of the poor, and of the rest of society as well. But in any event, regardless of its prospects for success, moral reform must still be attempted. Nothing else is as likely to improve the condition of the contemporary urban poor as a return to the virtues—both on their part and on ours.

But if that is the case, how are we attempting (and how might we attempt) to promote the virtues, both in charitable work on behalf of the poor and in public policy aimed at reducing poverty? And how do our contemporary efforts compare with those of our nineteenth-century forebears? These are the questions to which I turn in the concluding chapter.

8 THE CONTEMPORARY PRACTICE OF MORAL REFORM

URBAN MINISTRIES, PUBLIC POLICY, AND THE PROMOTION OF VIRTUE

On balance the moral climate today—while less favorable to reform in some respects than it was in the nineteenth century—is decidedly better than it was a generation ago. Not surprisingly, that change has made itself felt in both public and private attempts to reduce poverty. In the private sphere, efforts to improve the condition of the poor by religiously motivated appeals to virtue—analogous to the past efforts of Tuckerman and Brace—seemed laughably anachronistic a generation ago. In contrast, today they are viewed by many as the last best hope of regeneration in the more distressed parts of the inner city. Thus a White House aide to President Clinton remarked in 1997 that "the hot social-policy topic these days" is the power of religious institutions to deal with the problems of the poor, a reflection of the fact that "everything else has failed."[1] Similarly, "the hottest new topic in crime fighting" now is said to be "the power of religion":

> The only way to rescue kids from the seductions of the drug and gang cultures is with another, more powerful set of values: a substitute family for young people who almost never have two parents, and may not even have one, at home. And the only institution with the spiritual message and the physical presence to offer those traditional values . . . is the church.[2]

The shift in public policy is equally clear. We have rejected a policy approach that attempted to solve the problems of the poor chiefly—if not exclusively—by transferring money to them. As Nicholas Lemann points out, so great was the belief in the power of income transfers in the not-too-distant past that a Republican presidency—Richard Nixon's—was the one that can most fairly be charged with "[throwing] money at our [social] problems": among other pieces of antipoverty legislation, Nixon "signed into law . . . a subsidized housing program, . . . increases in welfare payments, a major expansion of the food stamps program, and a new program under Social Security that made payments to disabled people."[3]

In contrast, welfare policy today (in the words of a 1987 manifesto that accurately forecasted its evolution) is guided increasingly by the premise that "low income is in a sense the least of [the] problems" of many among the poor, for whom "a failure to take responsibility for themselves and for their actions is at the core."[4] And problems of personal irresponsibility are harder to solve than those of low income. Thus, while it is easy to transfer money, "to overcome behavioral dependency requires a much more human, complex, and difficult engagement."[5] But that is the goal that public policy increasingly sets for itself today: to improve behavior by encouraging self-reliance.

The following examinations of charitable practice and public policy are intended to explore the premises of some contemporary efforts to fight poverty with virtue. I focus particularly on the ways in which current efforts compare to and contrast with those undertaken in the nineteenth century.

Urban Ministries and Moral Reform, Yesterday and Today

The practice of charitable moral reform today shares the goals of the nineteenth-century moral reformers: promoting self-reliance and discouraging dependency. But in crucial respects, today's means differ from those adopted in the past. These changes in the practice of moral reform in some respects make success more likely than it was in the nineteenth century. Moral reform today, compared with its nineteenth-century counterpart, has been both democratized and (to coin an ugly word for a lovely thing) ecumenicized.

These generalizations about contemporary efforts at moral reform are necessarily tentative. In particular, we know much less about the workings of today's faith-based charities and their impact than we should. In the words of the political scientist John DiIulio:

> The "faith factor" literature remains in its infancy, and, even with the recent surge of interest in the topic among leading social scientists and policy analysts, it will be some time before we can identify the conditions, if any, under which given types of church-centered programs work, or specify how, if at all, faith-based efforts can be taken to scale in ways that cut crime, reduce poverty, banish illiteracy, or yield other positive, predictable, and desirable social consequences.[6]

But despite the gaps in current knowledge, we can glean some insights into the workings of moral reform today through a contrast with its workings in the past. One decisive consideration is that nineteenth-century moral reform was primarily a movement led by elites striving to inculcate virtue among the masses. To be sure, not all nineteenth-century moral reform was elitist in origin; another book could surely be written, for example, about religious, immigrant, and ethnic mutual aid societies that strove to reduce poverty by promoting virtue.[7] Nevertheless, the great theorists and practitioners of moral reform—from Tuckerman through Lowell— were undeniably products of the American social elite.

To succeed, then, moral reformers in the past generally had to cross an enormous social divide, which can only have complicated their work. For example, the utter inability of Hartley to address the Irish American poor in ways that promoted rather than frustrated his efforts to reform them was clearly a product of that divide. In fairness, other reformers were more aware of the problem posed by the gulf between rich and poor; but their greater awareness did not afford them an easy solution to it. Channing feared that the urban poor's "connection with the affluent, *though not close enough for spiritual communication,* [was] near enough to inflame appetites, desires, wants, which cannot be satisfied."[8]

One need not dismiss moral reform as an illegitimate attempt at social control to acknowledge that privileged reformers would have found it hard to address the urban poor persuasively. Paul Boyer, the preeminent historian of moral reform, largely rejects the view that the movement was motivated by the desire of elites for social control of the masses.[9] Nevertheless, he succinctly formulates the difficulties that elite reformers had to confront:

> Here are "we," striving valiantly to uphold the moral order; over there the sinister, faceless "they" gnaw away at its foundations. . . . The missionary society visitor who vanished to another part of the city after a fleeting encounter in the slums was patently not a neighbor motivated by personal interest in a specific family but an emissary from a different social class impelled by more abstract concerns.[10]

Inevitably, then, even with the best will in the world, questions like the following must have arisen in the minds of poor people interacting with moral reformers: Since their lives are so different from ours, and their understanding of our lives is limited, how valid can their moral prescriptions for us be?

Perceiving the realities of the gulf separating them from the poor, socially privileged moral reformers understood that it would have been false to claim a close kinship with the poor. Lowell, for instance, was praised after her death by a radical Episcopalian clergyman (Father James O. S. Huntington) for what she did *not* do in relating to the poor: "She did not attempt to lay aside the advantages of the position that belonged to her; she did not try to transport herself into their conditions; there was nothing unreal or unnatural in her or her work."[11]

In principle, of course, it is reasonable to suppose that the cause of moral reform would have been better served by leaders who did not require transportation into the conditions of the poor, because they themselves shared those conditions: leaders whose relations with the poor would have been more "real" and "natural." Not surprisingly, some nineteenth-century observers were aware of the benefits derived from sharing the background of those whom moral reform might assist. Consider, for instance, this 1886 statement by a Hartford minister named John S. Kimball: if God "wants to reach down amid the muck and filth and coarseness and brutality of the lowest strata of society[,] . . . he does not send an Emerson or a Channing, but a redeemed rum-seller or a converted pugilist to do it."[12] Kimball's statement not only pointed to the solution but in a way (with its reference to "muck and filth and coarseness and brutality") exemplified the problem as well.

Democratized Moral Reform

In contrast with moral reform in the past, what is striking about contemporary efforts is how often they are led precisely by redeemed drug-dealers (if not rum-sellers) or converted criminals. It is no longer elites who attempt to uplift the downtrodden; for the most part it is now the formerly downtrodden, having reformed themselves, who now attempt to reform others. Keeping in mind Adam Smith's contention that "strict or austere" morality characterized the common people, whereas "people of fashion" adopted a "loose" morality,[13] perhaps we can say that moral reform is now returning to the class to which it properly belongs. Moral reform has been democratized.

Its democratization is evident in Robert L. Woodson Sr.'s discussion of faith-based efforts at reviving inner cities. In his summation, "Many . . . community healers have come out of our prisons. They have experienced what it is to live in drug-infested, crime-ridden neighborhoods. Many have themselves fallen but have been able to recover through their faith in God."[14] Unlike the elite moral reformers of the nineteenth century, then, they have the advantage of sharing "the same 'zip code' as the people they serve. They have a firsthand knowledge of the problems they live with, and they have a personal stake in the success of their solutions."[15]

Woodson's generalization is certainly borne out in many individual cases. Thus one of the most prominent moral reformers today is the Reverend Eugene Rivers, a black Pentecostal who ministers to at-risk youth in the impoverished Boston neighborhood of Dorchester. Rivers's Philadelphia upbringing was hardly typical of ghetto youths: his parents were black nationalists and intellectuals. But his father left his mother when Rivers was three. Rivers joined a street gang at age twelve, he fathered a child out of wedlock, and at one point he created three identities for himself so that he simultaneously collected welfare checks in Philadelphia, New York, and New Haven.[16]

Rivers's background thus gives him a certain "street edge" that presumably makes it somewhat easier for him to relate to at-risk youth today than it was for, say, Charles Loring Brace in the 1850s.[17] This democratic capacity to interact easily and comfortably with those who are to be uplifted is also evident in the advice of a second prominent contemporary reformer, Freddie Garcia: in his view, would-be reformers must have warm personalities, because those who seem to have been "baptized in lemon juice" (Hartley may come to mind here) are sure to fail.[18]

Another reformed reformer is Juan Rivera, whom Garcia converted. Rivera now works to rehabilitate drug addicts and alcoholics at Victory Fellowship in San Antonio, Texas. But in his prior life he was an addict and burglar; in addition, two of his siblings have died violent deaths.[19] Again, one suspects that his interactions with substance abusers are more natural, more likely to be effective, than were Tuckerman's in the 1830s, because Tuckerman was an aristocratic reformer.[20]

The Reverend Floyd Flake—pastor of a prominent African American church in Queens, New York, and a former member of Congress—offers a final example of the democratization of moral reform. Flake has recently written a book describing his pastoral work, and it is striking how often his advice recapitulates that given by the nineteenth-century moral reformers. Like them, he advocates "the assumption of personal responsibility[, which] will provide you with the necessary power to accomplish your life goals."[21]

Flake commends the virtue of diligence: "If you're unemployed and aren't even looking for work, you're lazy."[22] (Flake's father "worked two or three jobs at a time," and Flake himself began working when he was eight; in his own estimation, his "work ethic" has "contributed enormously" to his success.)[23]

He also stresses the importance of thrift and sobriety:

> Don't depend on the lottery—you can use those dollars more wisely by investing them or putting them into your bank account. You may not save a million dollars, but you will be surprised at how much you can accumulate over time. If you . . . drink, for instance, imagine how much money you would have today if you had saved the cost of . . . the alcoholic beverages that you drink regularly. If you spend your money this way, you might as well set your dollar bills on fire or flush them down the toilet.[24]

Finally, he argues that familial responsibility lessens economic hardship: "Poverty is a reality for many individuals because they have not gotten their family relationships in order. When animosity occurs between husband and wife and they break up, money is drained from the family coffers. Money starts leaking everywhere. . . . A centralized pool of money provides great leverage to build wealth. Financial fragmentation may not provide enough to pay the bills, let alone provide extra income for investments." Thus "it is our responsibility to reclaim the sanctity of marriage and the family. We have a duty to ourselves and especially to our children."[25]

But what sets Flake apart from the patrician reformers of the nineteenth century is that he has more standing to give that advice to the less fortunate. Flake grew up in Houston as one of thirteen children born to impoverished parents. He was raised in a "tiny two-bedroom house" that lacked running water, he "wore second-hand clothes, and . . . [he] ate plenty of meatless meals." Neither of his parents had more than a sixth-grade education.[26] Thus, when Flake commends the virtues that promote upward mobility, he speaks from experience that must often grant him a respectful hearing; he has risen from poverty himself by exercising those virtues.

The Ecumenicism of Contemporary Moral Reform

Moral reform today seems to be more ecumenical as well as more democratic than it was in the past. Its ecumenicism probably increases its effectiveness in various ways. Most notably, it is now easier to preach moral reform across denominational lines than it was a century ago. For all that racial divides complicate efforts at moral reform today, we should not gloss over the ways in which these efforts have also been simplified: in particular, it is significant that the Protestant-Catholic divide—so problematic a century ago—has now dwindled into insignificance. Unlike in the nineteenth century, Americans seldom believe any longer that being a Catholic (or a Protestant, or a Jew) precludes the practice of the virtues; they are more open to argument on behalf of the virtues coming from people of faiths different from theirs.

In short, in the words of sociologist James Davison Hunter, "The distinctions that long divided Americans—those between Protestants, Catholics, and Jews—[are now] virtually irrelevant."[27] In Hunter's arresting formulation, "The practical effects of the birth of Christianity and the Reformation have, at least in the U.S. context, become both politically and culturally defunct."[28] Because the religious divide loomed so large in the past, Catholics then could be reformed chiefly by other Catholics (and seldom by Protestants); by contrast, Catholics today are more likely to be open to Protestant messages (and vice versa). The surge of religious tolerance increases the number of moral reform agencies that can improve people's lives.

The evidence here is necessarily anecdotal, but it is nonetheless suggestive. Rivers himself is the offspring of an interfaith union, between a Pentecostal woman and her Black Muslim mate. (A friend describes Rivers as "a perfect Muslim Pentecostal.")[29] Of greater importance is that his work (like that of many other inner-city Protestant preachers) is based on interfaith alliances. As a *Newsweek* reporter explains, "In urban areas like Boston, Newark and Philadelphia clergy are learning to reach across denominational lines and tap each other's strengths."[30] Thus Rivers works closely with Boston's Roman Catholic Bernard Cardinal Law, whom Rivers describes as his "*patrone.*"[31]

The cooperation between the black Pentecostal preacher and the Cardinal is possible because of the moral consensus that unites them. Thus Law contends that Rivers espouses "a pro-poor, pro-family, pro-life platform that I can enthusiastically support."[32] For his part, Rivers and other black Protestant clergy have been influenced by Catholic social teachings, which offer "a body of thought that fits the problems of the inner city into a coherent Christian perspective." Social Catholicism is appealing to them because it offers an alternative to the individualism of America's secular left and right: society is understood not as a social contract between isolated individuals, but as an interdependent organism, in which the rights of individuals must be balanced against their duties to civil society and state.[33]

Thus the religion preached by Rivers is eclectic and ecumenical in important respects. Significantly, he also preaches it pragmatically, in the sense that for Rivers it is clearly as much a means to a moral end as an end in itself. His attitude in this respect is reminiscent of Brace's: Brace de-emphasized doctrinal preaching when its limited capacity to effect the moral conversion of many youths became clear to him.[34] Rivers's work has evolved in a similar direction: "In the early days, [he] pushed religion harder on the kids, but found that it intimidated—and turned off—many of them. So now he keeps preaching to a minimum."[35]

The role of religious doctrine in Flake's work should also not be overstated. A reporter has summarized Flake's views as follows: to "believe that his larger agenda is religious . . . [is to] misunderstand his leadership and the role of many black churches in New York City and across America." In fact that role is "building community, saving lives and giving children hope for the future as much as propounding any religious creed." In Flake's own words: "It is easy to diminish me. . . . Why reduce me to just a preacher?"[36]

The decreased relevance of particular religious denominations sharply differentiates the terrain on which moral reform is preached today from the terrain of the nineteenth century. The specific characteristics of different denominations are far less important now than they were then. In practice, reformers have a wider potential audience than they did in the past. Thus Woodson notes that today's reformers "do not target their services exclusively to individuals of any particular race or background," so that their offerings "are open to all comers."[37] In short, the message of moral reform is potentially more transparent today than it was in the past, less subject to refraction through different denominational lenses: today's reformers, unlike those of the past, can reasonably hope to be able to reach people of many different denominations (or of no denomination at all).

Government Help and Self-Help

In another respect today's reformers are perhaps more similar to their counterparts from the past. We have seen that the commitment of yesterday's reformers to preaching virtue to the poor did not lead them invariably to oppose more material aid to the poor (and in particular governmental action on behalf of the poor). In similar fashion, many of today's reformers do not believe that moral reform is inconsistent with antipoverty efforts that offer material support.

Rivers, for example, argues explicitly that efforts of faith-based organizations in the inner cities will be insufficient by themselves to reduce poverty in inner cities: "Without public support and back-up, financial and logistical, there's no way churches or other community folk can turn the tide. But if we learn how to work together, then there's no limit to what can be accomplished before it's too late."[38] His belief that faith-based charities are unable to solve urban problems without the assistance of other forces is amply seconded by DiIulio, a great supporter of the work of such charities:

> Not even an army of well-led, well-supported churches and faith-based programs could save the nation's most severely at-risk children, revitalize blighted neighborhoods, and resurrect the civil society of inner-city America without the active human and financial support of suburban churches, secular civil institutions, profit-making corporations, and, last but not least, government at all levels.[39]

Flake is also not a doctrinaire opponent of governmental action to assist the poor. He notes that "the government has been a partner in providing assistance to many Americans who have found success." Thus there is nothing wrong with accepting "government help," provided that one "refuse[s] to become totally dependent on it." Rightly understood, government assistance is "a leveraging tool," a means that enables people to accomplish their ends. Flake's own church unapologetically accepts "government assistance through housing subsidies and contracts for various services," while also "leverag[ing] its own church resources from tithes and offerings to create public-private partnerships."[40]

Nevertheless, Flake clearly believes that the private (meaning nongovernmental) half of these partnerships is the more important one. That priority is evident in his own career trajectory: he gave up a safe congressional seat in order to devote himself full-time to his pastoral work, declaring that "there is more important work to be done in the church" than in Congress.[41]

The important work that Flake does consists largely of enabling people to help themselves. He and his church do so in part by establishing institutions and programs that facilitate self-help; for example, his church maintains twelve different investment clubs for its members.[42] But he also attempts to make self-help possible through psychological motivation, convincing people to believe in themselves, to believe that employing the virtues can lead to success. "Bootstrappers [that is, those who practice self-help and pull themselves up by their own bootstraps] do not see themselves as victims but have confidence in their ability to rise beyond the limited expectations that others may have imposed on them."[43]

Since "there is no shame in being poor, only in complaining about it and not doing anything about it,"[44] the poor must therefore take steps—must practice the virtues—to ease and hopefully to end their poverty. But to do so, they must have faith in themselves: "You must believe in yourself, your ability to get the work done, and your ability to achieve. If you don't believe it, no one will."[45] For Flake religion—in this respect exactly unlike the fundamentalism that some have associated with a culture of poverty—should give people faith that they can indeed take the necessary steps: "God does have a plan for our lives, . . . [but] we also have the authority, power, and responsibility to chart our own course as much as we are able. . . . That's what is meant by the oft-used phrase 'The Lord helps those who help themselves.'"[46] Flake's "role" is to "help facilitate this holy transaction within people," in which they learn to help themselves (and thus to be helped by God).[47]

Promoting Virtue through Public Policy

Flake and today's other urban moral reformers undeniably seek to encourage virtuous behavior among the poor, to promote the self-help of the poor; but they also agree that public policy has a role to play in reducing poverty. But public policy today also seeks to reduce poverty by promoting virtue; increasingly public policy is guided by the realization that poverty cannot be substantially reduced unless virtuous behavior is somehow fostered. On a theoretical level James Q. Wilson has made this argument most forcefully and persuasively, calling attention to "the growing awareness that a variety of public problems can only be understood—and perhaps addressed—if they are seen as arising out of a defect in character formation."[48] In Wilson's view "large improvements" can be made in areas like welfare or crime only if "virtue"—by which Wilson means "acting with due restraint on one's impulses, due regard for the rights of others, and reasonable concern for distant consequences"—can somehow be inculcated.[49]

The difficulty, needless to say, lies in figuring out precisely how to encourage virtue. In a few cases virtue can in some sense be mandated. Most obviously, welfare recipients are generally expected to work now as a condition of receiving benefits. Virtue is arguably also mandated in some publicly funded homeless shelters, whose residents must agree to forswear violence, substance abuse, and sexual activity; to bathe daily; to keep a neat appearance; and to submit to drug testing at the request of shelter staff.[50] Policies like these exemplify the "new paternalism" advocated by Lawrence Mead, which attempts to improve the behavior of the dependent (to reduce their dependency). In effect, the dependent sign a social contract, agreeing to behave in certain ways in exchange for receiving assistance.

But because government cannot and should not direct the behavior of most people, the new paternalism is likely to be applied only to the long-term poor and dependent.[51] In seeking to affect the broader population of working-age individuals with low incomes, public policy can generally promote the virtues chiefly by offering incentives to practice them (and disincentives for neglecting them). As Francis Fukuyama notes, "In many cases, people make different moral choices in the context of different economic incentives, and no amount of preaching and cultural argument will be sufficient to shift the overall direction of change more than marginally, unless those incentives are changed."[52] Thus public policy can "shape social choices around the margin in ways that are both helpful and unhelpful, by ensuring public safety, on the one hand, or by creating perverse incentives for single-parent families on the other."[53]

The crux of the argument over public policy is no longer whether the virtues should be promoted; virtually everyone would like to encourage diligence and familial responsibility, and virtually everyone agrees that simply subsidizing the poor (without seeking to promote their diligence and familial responsibility) is insufficient. What continues to be controversial, though, is the extent to which the virtues can successfully be promoted by incentives as opposed to mandates. As noted in Chapter 7, that is the heart of the dispute between Mead and William Julius Wilson: Do the poor primarily need greater incentives to be encouraged to do the right thing, or do they primarily need to be placed in a more structured environment in which they will be told to do the right thing?

A likely answer is that some among the poor—those with few if any behavioral difficulties—might respond positively to greater incentives. By contrast, others—those with greater behavioral difficulties—would probably respond only to greater structure (if to anything). Unfortunately, no one is really sure how many of the poor would fit into each group.

A case can be made—and with some qualifications will be made below—for programs designed to increase the incentives of the poor to be diligent and thrifty.

But that case must come with an important caveat: the effectiveness of attempts to encourage the virtues by means of incentives is very much in doubt, at least with respect to the likely response of the hard-core poor. Thus Mead calls into question one such policy, which aimed to foster individual responsibility for inner-city youth by offering them substantial sums of money ($20,000) "to use for further education and training, provided that they finish high school and avoid pregnancy and crime." That policy might seem unobjectionable. But as Mead observes, "It is implausible that merely improving the returns to virtue will accomplish much. The incentives for youth to get through school and avoid trouble are already great. If poor youth misbehave, the main reason is not that their rewards are limited but that they are not in control of their lives. If they were, they would seldom be poor for long in the first place."[54]

Space does not permit an assessment of the proper mix of mandates and incentives—or, more broadly, an extensive analysis of public policy. But I will offer at least an impressionistic survey of several recent policy developments that can—and sometimes can only—be understood as attempts to promote virtue.[55] As we will see, the ideas and intuitions of the moral reformers continue to live on in various policies and policy proposals of the moment, all of them aimed at promoting the four virtues—familial responsibility, sobriety, thrift, and diligence—that the reformers emphasized.

Promoting Familial Responsibility

The restoration of the two-parent family is undoubtedly the greatest challenge confronting contemporary efforts at remoralizing the poor. Those efforts are undoubtedly aided by the emergence of a broad consensus acknowledging the superiority of the two-parent family.[56] But that consensus also incorporates, however ruefully, a recognition that public policy can do relatively little to promote the formation of two-parent families. Thus it is significant that the 1996 welfare reform law, which has as one of its goals the formation and maintenance of two-parent families, nevertheless "includes no specific strategies for encouraging" them.[57] That omission may reflect an implicit realization of the limits of public policy.[58] In the words of David Popenoe, a strenuous advocate of the need to increase the number of two-parent families, "the causes for the decline of marriage and fatherhood lie mainly in the moral, behavioral, and even spiritual realms," so that

> the decline is mostly resistant to public-policy and government cures. The fact is that, regardless of governmental system and political persuasion, marriage decline and fatherlessness have occurred in all industrialized societies in the West as these societies have become more affluent. Marriage decline is almost as great in Sweden, the West's most accomplished welfare state, as it is in the United States, the most laissez-faire of the industrialized nations.[59]

One thing that the law could do, though, is to reward rather than penalize poor people who marry. Some benefits for the poor—for example, benefits that provide food and health care—must be universally available. But families with two parents who are married could nevertheless be given priority as recipients of what are by contrast known as "limited-supply" benefits: examples include "enrollment slots in Head Start, public-housing units, financial aid for education, and job training." Whereas in the past the rule has been that such benefits are distributed either on a first-come, first-served basis, or to those most in need, limited-supply benefits could instead be made available "first to married, two-parent families."[60] Similar policies have been applied in the past: until the late 1960s, "many public-housing projects . . . gave preference to low-income married couples over single heads of households. And the disappearance of marriage in low-income families corresponds with the dismantling of this preference for the married poor."[61]

How can public policy address the plight of single parents? Two policies merit discussion in this context, relating to fathers and mothers respectively. First, the increase in efforts over the past few decades to secure child-support payments from fathers living apart from their children deserves comment. The Family Support Act of 1988, for example, enables states to impose legal child-support obligations on a greater number of absent fathers and to increase the number who actually meet their obligations. The legislation encourages the use of techniques like genetic testing to augment the percentage of unwed fathers whose paternity is legally identified.[62]

In part the increased emphasis on child support reflects a greater moralism—a heightened desire to compel people who have acted irresponsibly to pay for the consequences of their irresponsibility. In that respect it marks a return to the perspective of the social worker Lilian Brandt, whose moral critique of deserting fathers we examined in Chapter 2. Thus Nathan Glazer has discussed the emphasis on child support as an example of a "regulation based on traditional morality and demands." His analysis of the policy's successful moralism is illuminating:

> Strangely enough, in some respects . . . [moral traditionalism] worked. . . . Even in the early days of welfare reform, in the early 1960s, many congressmen asked, why shouldn't fathers pay for their children? The social workers responded that the fathers were poor, they had started new families, they couldn't be found, efforts to find them would harm their relations with their former female partners and their children, and the whole effort couldn't possibly pay. Nevertheless, Congress insisted that stronger efforts be made to find fathers and make them pay. . . . Fathers had responsibilities: they should be made to fulfill them. And that was one welfare reform that seemed to be working.[63]

But if the demand for child support illustrates the appeal of moral traditionalism, it arguably also illustrates its insufficiency. In fact, few single mothers on welfare receive child support from the fathers of their children: in 1996, only about 13 percent of the nation's 7.4 million AFDC child-support cases received at least one payment.[64] The figure was that low because many of the objections raised by Glazer's social workers have much merit: even with the best will in the world, welfare fathers seldom earn enough to pay child support to welfare mothers. For this reason, moral exhortation by itself can do little good. It is not enough for impoverished welfare fathers to recognize that they should pay child support; they must also earn enough to be able to make the payments.

In light of this recognition, policy experiments are now underway in which welfare fathers receive services—employment training, support groups, and mediation services (to resolve conflicts with custodial parents)—that they do not ordinarily receive now.[65] Such policies are not without risks: "Providing employment opportunities primarily to low-income, unwed fathers could encourage men to father children out of wedlock, in much the same way that the current system provides perverse incentives for women to bear children out of wedlock."[66]

Nevertheless, the appeal of these policies is that they might make welfare fathers both better able to pay child support and more willing to pay it. Recognition of the need to offer carrots as well as sticks to poor unwed fathers is also evident in legislation proposed by a number of congressional Republicans, such as Representative E. Clay Shaw Jr. of Florida, to create a $2-billion federal program in which community organizations would give poor fathers job training and parenting advice, and would encourage them to marry.[67]

The emphasis on parenting advice as well as job training in these policy experiments is of particular interest. At bottom, it can be understood as a tacit acknowledgment that job training is unlikely to make many welfare fathers employable at very good wages—at least in the short term. As a practical matter, then, these destitute fathers will likely be able to begin paying child support only if they are willing to accept the low-wage jobs that are available to them, and to work steadily at them. Only then will they develop a work history that could subsequently enable them to be hired for better jobs.

It is here that the focus on parenting advice and encouragement to marry comes into play: the argument is that the emotional rewards of family and marriage are most likely to induce the fathers to take low-wage jobs.[68] As Channing suggested long ago, the familial ties of the poor can motivate virtuous behavior: fundamentally, the movement to enhance the services available to fathers who owe child support rests on this realization.[69]

In the absence of stable families with two parents, a second policy innovation that has won favor is the creation of what are known as "second-chance" homes for unwed teenage mothers. As one of its proponents, William Galston, has noted, these homes represent the revival of "an old institution—the maternity home—in a new form." The homes aim to provide the young mothers with "the support and structure that a functioning family provides—needs typically not met in the homes in which they were raised."[70] In these homes teenage single mothers who are on welfare are supervised by experienced mothers who seek to teach the teenage mothers how to care for their children effectively.[71]

Galston indicates that prototypes for these homes exist in Washington, D.C., and other cities.[72] He also mentions that the 1996 welfare reform law supports their creation, by requiring unmarried teenage mothers to live in adult-supervised settings as a condition for receiving assistance; when a mother's family is abusive or neglectful, the law indicates that she should be placed in a second-chance home.

The premise of the second-chance homes is that the young mothers must learn responsibility, in part by abiding by the sorts of rules (and imbibing the sorts of lessons) that friendly visitors once espoused:

> The mothers who live in these homes must stay in school or job training. They must stay drug free and abide by curfews. They learn to cook and clean, to manage money, to get along with one another, and resolve conflicts. In return, they get help with day care and health care and schoolwork. Most important, they learn how to nurture their children.[73]

The second-chance homes are in certain respects reminiscent of the female reformatories that Lowell advocated and helped institute (with the significant difference that illegitimate children did not live in the reformatories). Lowell's biographer assesses the impact of the reformatories, noting that "perhaps a majority of [their residents] were from severely disorganized homes"; in her judgment, the residents "benefited from a strict regimen of discipline, domesticity, and moral uplift."[74] A century later, we seem again to be turning to discipline, domesticity, and moral uplift for help in coping with the manifold problems associated with out-of-wedlock births.

Temperance Efforts Today

If familial responsibility is the most salient of the reformers' virtues today, sobriety would seem at first glance to be the least relevant. Numerous efforts are nevertheless afoot today to reduce alcohol consumption because of its impact on social disorder in poor neighborhoods.[75] These efforts differ from the efforts of moral reformers, in that today's temperance campaign emphasizes alcohol's role in fostering crime more heavily than its role in worsening poverty.

There are ample grounds for today's focus on crime. For example, a 1998 Department of Justice publication notes that more than one-third of the nation's violent crimes each year involve offenders who seem (to the victims) to have been drinking at the time of the assault.[76] Similarly, more than one-third of convicted offenders report that they were drinking at the time of the offense.[77]

It is, of course, true that "most alcohol consumption does not result in crime: the vast majority of those who consume alcohol do not engage in criminal behavior."[78] Nevertheless, as William Bennett (writing with DiIulio and John Walters) has noted, it is also true that "alcohol, like drugs, acts as a 'multiplier' of crime" — and that it figures prominently in disorder and crime, "especially in poor, minority, inner-city neighborhoods, where liquor outlets cast their shadows everywhere."[79]

The upshot of Bennett's argument is a call to restrict the availability of alcohol by imposing stricter zoning ordinances for liquor stores (to reduce the number of outlets). He also advocates limiting advertisements for alcoholic beverages.[80] As many of the moral reformers understood, it is possible to limit consumption without banning it; the ravages imposed upon the inner city by alcohol have renewed enthusiasm for doing so in many quarters—even among conservatives not normally sympathetic to governmental regulation.[81]

Policies that are still more restrictionist are also being implemented today, for example in Chicago, where "Mayor Richard M. Daley has been promoting a 'vote dry' campaign, with City Hall lawyers teaching citizens['] groups how to outlaw the sale of alcohol in a precinct, typically a few blocks of 400 to 500 people." Nearly fifty precincts or parts of precincts have gone dry in the last ten years; it is estimated that the number could rise sharply because of the Daley administration's advocacy. In a more moderate (but also more widespread) effort to limit consumption, thirty-eight of Chicago's fifty wards have placed a moratorium on the issuance of new liquor licenses.[82]

Chicago's temperance campaign is motivated by precisely the disorders to which Bennett calls attention: neighborhoods "crowded cheek by jowl with bars and liquor stores," where "alcohol so dominates the landscape that little else seems able to thrive." Among the leaders of the temperance campaign is a Roman Catholic priest, the Reverend Michael Pfleger, who circulated a petition designed to put certain liquor stores out of business. Pfleger has protested for many years against the vast number of billboards advertising alcoholic beverages in poor, black neighborhoods. He argues that the disorderly atmosphere promoted by extensive trafficking in alcohol has done serious economic damage to Chicago's black neighborhoods, causing other shopkeepers to flee (and thereby depriving residents of job opportunities as well as outlets for needed merchandise).[83]

Whatever practical impact the Chicago temperance movement turns out to have, the symbolism of Daley's support for it is worthy of mention. Daley is the scion of the Chicago Democratic political machine, and political machines were the principal political target of the moral reform movement in the late nineteenth century—in some measure because the machines were so closely tied to urban saloons. Many of the most prominent ward bosses were saloonkeepers.

In New York, for example, Jacob Riis fought alongside Theodore Roosevelt against Tammany Hall, in part because it offered protection to organized vice: under Tammany control, the police "collect[ed] blackmail from saloon keepers, gambling hells, policy shops, and houses of ill fame," at the instigation of "the politician who controlled all and took the profits."[84] In Chicago, Jane Addams (who in this respect was a moral reformer) attempted unsuccessfully to unseat Johnny Powers, the alderman for the ward in which Hull House was located: Powers, who "managed several saloons,"[85] flouted the law by offering protection to gambling houses and saloons that remained open after the legal closing hour.[86]

Because of the historical connection between political machines and urban saloons, it is of some interest that Daley's personal attitudes have more in common with those of the moral reformers of the past—the machine's bitter opponents—than with those of the machine politicians of the past. Daley's strict moral code has a sabbatarian component: he does not conduct business on Sundays. Daley has also called on the police to curtail the public drunkenness and rowdiness that characterized Chicago's celebration of St. Patrick's Day in the past.[87] Thus his support for temperance and propriety points in a sense to the unlikely triumph of the "reform" mentality of the past over the "machine" mentality of the past—or at least to a synthesis of the two. If even the Chicago political machine (such as it now is) endorses temperance legislation, there is reason to believe that we may indeed be achieving some sort of consensus in support of moral reform.[88]

It is possible to employ less forcible measures than Daley's in the effort to reduce alcohol consumption: raising taxes on alcoholic beverages is one obvious alternative. It is worth noting that tax increases won much support in a 1981 panel of alcohol policy experts assembled by the federal government's National Research Council (NRC). The panel concluded that "the demand for alcoholic beverages, like other commodities, is responsive to price."[89] Since the real prices for alcoholic beverages had dropped sharply in the recent past (when taxes were not indexed for inflation), the panel concluded that the "large reductions in the real cost of alcohol to consumers in recent years [had probably] . . . exacerbated drinking problems." It expressed support for reversing the downward trend in alcohol prices by raising taxes.[90]

Federal alcohol taxes have in fact subsequently been raised. In 1985 the tax rate on distilled spirits was increased by about 19 percent. And in 1991 the tax on beer doubled, the tax on wine was hiked almost sevenfold, and the tax on distilled spirits was raised by an additional 8 percent. As a result of these changes, the tax on a six-pack of beer is currently 32 cents, the tax on a 750-milliliter bottle of wine stands at about 21 cents, and the tax on a 750 milliliter bottle of 80 proof distilled spirits amounts to $2.14. Nevertheless, because of inflation, "the distilled spirits tax rate would have [had] to be 75 percent higher and the beer tax rate would have had to be 162 percent higher to maintain their real values as of 1951," when the taxes were last raised.[91] State excise taxes have also declined in real terms (falling by over 50 percent between 1966 and 1989).[92] Thus, notwithstanding the tax hikes, it is still the case that the real price of alcohol has "declined significantly" in the last generation.[93]

How does cheap alcohol interact with the problem of poverty? The NRC panel concluded that heightened taxes on alcohol might well benefit "poor households that are burdened by the heavy drinking habit of a member." It argued that consumption would likely decline because of the price increase: "To the extent that the heavy-drinking member reduces his (in most cases) or her alcohol consumption in response to higher prices, earnings may increase and health care expenditures may be reduced, thus tending to improve the net economic position of the household."[94] That reasoning was supported in a paper commissioned by the panel which contended that higher taxes would reduce expenditures on alcoholic beverages "for a high but unknown percentage of poor households."[95]

In fairness, it is far from clear that intemperance has much impact upon the problem of poverty today. A 1993 review of the literature on alcohol and the labor market concluded that "the literature has not attained consensus" regarding the impact of drinking on performance in the workplace.[96] Nevertheless, the review also spoke of "the current wisdom . . . that detrimental effects of drinking on performance in the labor market may be the single most important component of alcohol-related 'economic costs.'"[97]

The empirical economics literature of today professes uncertainty about one of the specific claims of the moral reformers. But in a broader sense, researchers today express judgments about intemperance that accord very well with the perspective of the moral reformers. It is noteworthy that the NRC panel affirmed an approach that is very similar to that of the reformers. The panel report concluded that the real lesson to be drawn from the failure of Prohibition is not that "it is futile and mischievous to legislate drinking morals"; the proper conclusion instead is that "the quantity of alcohol consumption and the rates of problems varying with consumption can . . . be markedly reduced by substantial increases in real price and reductions in the ease of availability."[98] As the panel concluded, "It is clear that a *laissez faire* approach has not prevailed, and there are sound reasons why it has not."[99] That is what the mayor of Chicago contends today; it is also what the moral reformers contended a century ago and more.

Self-Reliance Reconsidered

Public policy today is obviously also attempting to encourage the virtues of diligence and thrift. It is interesting to note, though, that a key premise of many policies and policy proposals in these areas is seemingly somewhat self-contradictory: in effect, the policies reflect the belief that people can reasonably be assisted and supported in their efforts to become self-reliant. For example, if a welfare mother anxious to work is given a subsidy to help pay for transportation to the job site (or for child care), is she self-reliant (because she is working) or dependent (because her work-related expenses are subsidized)?

The obvious answer is both. Some policies designed to promote thrift and diligence embody the realization that self-reliance and dependence are not all-or-nothing propositions: it may be impossible to be slightly pregnant, but it is arguably possible to be somewhat self-reliant. Subsidies for transportation and child care in effect aim to wean the welfare poor from absolute and prolonged dependency; they offer an incentive (or at least reduce or eliminate a disincentive) in the hope of promoting virtuous behavior.

The goal of these subsidies is to replace absolute dependency with a partial dependency that facilitates employment (thereby providing the means to at least some measure of self-reliance). The hope is that the welfare poor will gradually become (more and more) self-reliant, and the expectation is that some measure of properly targeted subsidization will assist them on their way.

Should self-reliance be understood as an all-or-nothing proposition? That question points to an interesting tension (if not contradiction) in the thought of the nineteenth-century moral reformers. We can see the tension most clearly in Lowell, who argued for an absolutist conception of self-reliance while also insisting on the need to aid the working poor.

On one hand, Lowell was quite dogmatic about the evils of dependency: "Human nature is so constituted that no man can receive as a gift what he should earn by his own labor without a moral deterioration."[100] If that statement is meant as an absolute truth, it takes in a lot of territory: even parental gifts—of whatever magnitude—to grown children, meant to ease their start in adult life, are impermissible.[101] What is more relevant to our concerns is Lowell's declaration here that any help given to the poor, apart from what they earn themselves, leads to their moral deterioration.

But as we have seen, there was also another side to Lowell, one that argued in favor of "mak[ing] the life of wage-earners less hard."[102] In this second statement Lowell does not suggest that the wage-earners themselves should make their life less hard, presumably because she did not believe that it was altogether in their power to do so. Instead, it is implicitly others—employers, and perhaps also the government—who are to take action to improve their lives. Here workers' earnings—at least if those earnings are defined in terms of the market wage that their labor could command—are in need of some sort of subsidy if social justice is to prevail.[103] Lowell's conception of self-reliance is notably less absolute here than in the previous quotation.

The structural reforms advocated by Lowell and the other moral reformers can be understood in terms of the tension between these two statements. Pauperization —absolute, avoidable, vice-ridden dependency—was condemned in the strongest possible moral terms. But at the same time, assistance to poor people aspiring toward self-reliance was defended. In a useful formulation of historian Hace Sorel Tishler, the moral reformers contended that "helping the poor to help themselves presented no contradiction."[104]

Encouraging Thrift

A number of recent policies and proposals aimed at encouraging thrift can be understood as efforts to help the poor help themselves. To begin with, some welfare policies have been altered because it is now understood that not long ago the welfare system actively discouraged thrift among the poor: recipients who managed to accumulate assets were penalized for doing so.

The way in which asset limits formerly penalized thrift is well illustrated in this 1990 news story about the misfortune of a Milwaukee welfare mother:

A penny saved is a penny earned. Usually.

Take the case of Grace Capitello, a 36-year-old single mother with a true talent for parsimony. To save on clothing, Ms. Capitello dresses herself plainly in thrift-store finds. To cut her grocery bill, she stocks up on 67-cent boxes of saltines and 39-cent cans of chicken soup. . . .

Ms. Capitello's stingy strategies helped her build a savings account of more than $3,000 in the last four years. Her goal was to put away enough to buy a new washing machine and maybe one day send [her daughter] . . . to college. To some this might make her an example of virtue in her . . . neighborhood, known more for boarded-up houses than high aspirations. But there was just one catch: Ms. Capitello is on welfare . . . and saving that much money on public aid is against the law. . . .

Last month, the Milwaukee County Department of Social Services took her to court, charged her with fraud and demanded that she return the savings.[105]

The asset limit of which Capitello ran afoul limited AFDC recipients to no more than $1,000 in savings. Thus recipients who prudently attempted to amass even modest savings as a precaution against future emergencies were rewarded for their prudence by the threat of forfeiting their eligibility for welfare payments.[106] Stunned by the consequences of the asset limitation, the judge who tried Capitello's case had this reaction: "I don't know how much more powerfully we could say it to the poor in our society: Don't try to save." He concluded that only the rich in America were given an incentive to save.[107]

There is evidence supporting the contention that asset limits discouraged savings by the welfare poor: a 1997 survey of credit union members with low incomes found that 49 percent of the recipients of public assistance among them agreed that "I would save more, but the government would cut my benefits if I did."[108] Acknowledging and responding to the problems posed by strict asset limitations in the past, one of the less-remarked-upon features of the 1996 welfare reform legislation permitted states to raise such limitations, in order to reduce welfare recipients' incentive not to save. As of October 1997, some 39 states had increased their limit on the assets that recipients can legally accrue.[109]

But the movement to encourage thrift among the poor goes beyond the reduction of disincentives to save; it also incorporates efforts to provide positive incentives for saving. While it is certainly the case that the poor save less than the non-poor,[110] the movement's adherents do not explain that disparity in terms of the willful improvidence of the poor, or (altogether) by their simple inability to reduce consumption.[111]

Instead, the assumption—derived from empirical studies—is that poor families often act thriftily (for example, by using coupons, buying in bulk, and conserving energy), manifesting the behaviors that could be expected to result in savings.[112] It is also argued that many welfare mothers are "careful financial managers—with so little income, they have to be."[113] The thrift displayed by many poor people leads to the conclusion that more of the poor would save more money—if they were offered incentives to save comparable to those for the nonpoor (who benefit from the deductibility of interest on their home mortgages and the tax deferment of income invested in corporate retirement plans).[114] Michael Sherraden, the leading advocate of policies designed to increase the savings of poor Americans, makes the case for altered policy in these words:

> Typically, the poor have been told that they should work hard and save more, but historically, there have been few programs or incentives to encourage them to do so. The United States in particular is characterized by strong exhortations for the poor to become more thrifty, but saving by the poor has not often been facilitated by public policy.[115]

Sherraden's contention is that what appear to be income-related differences in saving (the nonpoor save more) can be explained at least in part by the workings of different opportunities and constraints, rather than by individual preferences: if the poor save little, it is not because few among them want to save, but because they are offered few incentives to save.[116]

How might the poor be encouraged to save? Sherraden advocates the creation of what are known as Individual Development Accounts (IDAs). Contending that the poor will become more future-oriented to the degree that they are habituated to save, Sherraden views IDAs as a means of encouraging that habituation.[117]

IDAs are modeled on Individual Retirement Accounts (IRAs). As with IRAs, deposited funds (and earnings accrued) are tax-benefited—in some cases tax-exempt, in others tax-deferred. The funds cannot be withdrawn to pay for immediate consumption, but instead can be used only for specific purposes that require long-term saving—for example, purchasing a first home, paying for education or job training, or opening a small business.[118] The accounts aim to encourage the home ownership, employability, and entrepreneurship of the poor: in short, to encourage their adoption of "middle-class" goals.

As conceived by Sherraden, IDAs would not be restricted to the poor, but would instead be open to all Americans. Only the poor, though, would benefit from subsidized contributions. Those subsidies would always be in the form of matching funds: at the extreme, a poor person's contribution of $1 might be matched by as much as $9 from the government or from a nonprofit.[119] (Where IDAs have actually been implemented, though, the match tends to be less generous: more often one-to-one or two-to-one.)[120] Both in Sherraden's conception and as actually implemented, in all cases IDAs extend help only to those who save at least some money on their own, thereby manifesting the willingness to help themselves.

It is also significant that in practice IDAs do more than match dollars with dollars. Because the poor are thought to be in need of knowledge as well as dollars, participants in many IDAs attend mandatory financial counseling sessions, in which they learn how to manage money.[121] IDAs clearly hope to make the poor more like the middle class; but since being middle class is not only a matter of having money but also knowing what to do with it, IDAs strive to teach the poor how to handle money in addition to providing them with more of it. The proponents of IDAs understand that knowledge is virtue: they seek to promote the virtue of thrift among the poor by striving to teach them what they need to know to be successfully thrifty.[122]

The IDA idea has moved off the drawing board of its academic proponent and is now being implemented in various forms all across the land. Another little-remarked-upon feature of the 1996 welfare reform legislation permits states "to allow recipients to establish individual development accounts to accumulate assets for further education, purchasing a home, or starting a business and not have these assets count in determining their eligibility for assistance." As of October 1997, some 22 states had instituted IDA programs.[123]

Interest in promoting and experimenting with the IDA idea also extends to the foundation world. The Downpayments on the American Dream Policy Demonstration, a six-year project launched in 1997 with $8 million in funds from the Ford, Joyce, and Charles Stewart Mott foundations (added to $4 million raised by local partners such as churches, corporations, and banks) will set up over 2,000 IDAs in thirteen different sites, to "test the extent to which low-income people will save when provided with the right incentives."[124]

IDAs will not be a panacea, just as earlier efforts to promote the savings of the poor were not: all of the poor are not objectively able to save (because some simply lack available funds), and some of the poor—without the requisite capacity for self-denial—are subjectively unable to do so. As one analyst puts it, "By requiring participants to make a very real (if short-term) sacrifice, and by insisting upon the financial education component, IDAs can, by design, sort out the people that they *can* help from those that they can't. . . . Some people simply aren't ready—or aren't willing—to accept the discipline required by IDAs."[125]

Still, if IDAs cannot help everyone, they can certainly help some among the poor. Recognizing their capacity, public policy may well be taking increasingly active steps to encourage thrift among the poor by subsidizing it as well as teaching it. We are seeking to encourage the poor to help themselves by saving, even to the point of helping them to help themselves by matching their savings.

Promoting Diligence through Welfare Reform

Public policy's attempt to encourage diligence is, of course, most obvious in the welfare reform enacted in 1996: recipients are no longer entitled to a lifetime of support but are expected to work in order to receive support. In this respect the promotion of diligence is arguably the central premise of the new welfare system, as *New York Times* reporter Jason DeParle indicated in a 1997 article:

> If the emerging programs share a unifying theme, it can be summarized in a word: work. States are demanding that recipients find it faster, keep it longer and

perform it as a condition of aid. Most states regard even a low-paying, dead-end job as preferable to the education and training programs they offered in the past.[126]

The emphasis on work has been accompanied by a notable drop in the rolls of welfare recipients, as noted in Chapter 7. Much of the decline, though, predated the passage—not to speak of the implementation—of the 1996 legislation: welfare rolls actually peaked in 1994, not 1996 or 1997.[127]

How should we react to this unprecedented decline? On one hand, it is true that we still know too little to celebrate welfare reform as an unequivocal triumph. For example, although a 1998 General Accounting Office (GAO) assessment of welfare reform is generally quite favorable, it also makes clear how many all-important questions remain unanswered. We don't yet know the extent to which families who have left welfare return to it; we don't yet know how economically stable families are after leaving welfare; we don't yet know what happens to children who lose assistance because their families fail to comply with the new requirements of welfare programs.[128] We don't yet know how reformed welfare programs will function in a weak economy in which unemployment rises.[129]

But on the other hand, one particular pessimistic reading of the evidence is misguided. This reading effectively discounts the significance of the decline in the number of welfare recipients: the decline has occurred, it is argued, only because the "cream" of the welfare population, those who are most easily employable, have found jobs. The real test, it is argued, will come only later, when attempts are made to find employment for the "hard-core recipients" (such as "the homeless, the addicted, the battered, the disturbed, the illiterate and the criminal"), who are thought to make up perhaps one-third of the original caseload. These efforts, it is predicted, are likely to founder.[130]

On one level, this view is absolutely correct: common sense would suggest that those who have left the welfare rolls already are those who are comparatively employable, and that those remaining on the rolls are less so. But on another level, it is seriously wrongheaded: it implies that what was in fact a scandal of the old system (the dependency, in some cases the prolonged dependency, of the employable) actually points to a failing of the new system. In other words, one can concede that the welfare rolls currently include a great many people who may well be unemployable; nevertheless, one should also trumpet the current employment of many past recipients who were employable as a *triumph* of welfare reform in the present—not an indication of its likely failure in the future.

In short, much if not all of the "cream" of the welfare population should not have formed part of the welfare population in the first place. Although there may be occasional exceptions to this rule, in general the employment of employable dependents deserves celebration. And this rise in employment among the previously dependent must be explained at least in part in terms of an altered moral understanding that has returned us closer to the perspective of the moral reformers: to the belated recognition that diligence and self-reliance are morally superior to avoidable dependency.

The employment of employable former recipients has obviously been made possible by the great economic prosperity that has created so many millions of jobs recently. But prosperity cannot have reduced the rolls all by itself; as many observers have noted, the rolls surged in the 1960s, an earlier period of economic expansion and job creation.[131] Instead the decline in the number of recipients must also be attributed to an increased acknowledgment of the moral dangers of prolonged dependency.

One further explanation also comes to mind. In discussing nineteenth-century efforts to promote diligence, we saw that efforts to find employment for job-seekers seem seldom to have been very effective. By contrast, it is at least conceivable that advances in technology and communication make job-finding efforts more successful today. I base this suggestion on a 1998 Manpower Demonstration Research Corporation (MDRC) study of welfare reform in Los Angeles, a study that has been hailed as "the first solid evidence that welfare reform is beginning to work in the nation's largest cities."[132]

The study compared two different groups of Los Angeles welfare recipients, one of which was placed in a program stressing rapid job placement, while the other remained in the county's traditional welfare program, which emphasized remedial education more than job placement: 43 percent of those in the work program found jobs, compared with just 32 percent in the traditional program.[133] The researchers attributed this difference in part to the work program's provision of "high quality job search assistance." The staff who trained recipients for the job search inculcated attitudes that facilitate employment, "help[ing] enrollees identify their skills and strengths and present themselves with confidence to prospective employers," and requiring them to attend job club meetings "consistently and punctually in professional dress."[134]

But the study also mentioned a second factor. Staff members seem to have been knowledgeable about the local job market and effective in placing their clients and following up on their progress. They "aggressively develop[ed] linkages to local employers, match[ed] enrollees to specific job openings, and maintain[ed] periodic contact with both enrollees and their employers to monitor their work performance."[135]

Since one case does not a generalization make, I will gladly concede that there must have been many effective job-hunting programs in the nineteenth century (and that there must be many ineffective ones today). Nevertheless, could nineteenth-century charity workers—before the existence of telephones and computers—have developed linkages and maintained contact as effectively as their counterparts today can? One can plausibly suggest that contemporary efforts to help the poor find jobs are likely to be more systematic and hence on balance more effective than the necessarily haphazard attempts of Tuckerman and the legion of nine-teenth-century friendly visitors.

Facilitating and Rewarding Work

A constant theme throughout this book has been that the virtues are effectively promoted not just through mortal exhortation, but also through concrete policies. That is obviously the case with diligence today. As with thrift, in part today's poli-cies attempt to remove disincentives that had previously discouraged diligence. In the past families were often

> better off on welfare than working at a low-wage job, and families already on welfare had few incentives to work. . . . For working families with incomes low enough to still qualify for assistance, after 12 months the AFDC grant would be reduced dollar for dollar for earnings, except for a $90 monthly allowance for work expenses.[136]

But under welfare reform, "earnings-disregard" policies (like asset limits) have been liberalized, to permit families to keep more of their grants while working, or to keep them longer.[137] If work did not pay in the past, the aim now is to make sure that it does pay.

As this example suggests, the goal of welfare reform rightly understood is ulti-mately less economic (to cut welfare costs) than moral (to encourage self-reliance, even if it is only partial, subsidized self-reliance).[138] In fact, the effort to make work pay in many cases increases the costs of welfare, as former recipients are given subsidies—for child care and transportation expenses—that make it easier for them to get and hold jobs.

The focus on recipients' finding employment (and even their success in doing so) does not necessarily diminish states' social work costs, because welfare officials understand that helping former recipients retain employment can be more diffi-cult—and perhaps even ultimately more important—than helping them find it initially. Some thirty-five states continue to offer advice and counseling ("case man-agement," in the jargon) to former recipients who have found work, to facilitate job retention, reemployment, and "advancement assistance."[139]

That practice, it is worth noting, accords well with the understanding of social work articulated by Mary Richmond a century ago: she contended that the friendly visiting of a poor family should not cease "as soon as acute distress is past," because "improved material conditions" tended to increase the family's receptivity to ad-vice.[140] Richmond believed that friendly visiting was apt to be more successful once the need for it was—to the superficial eye—less urgent.

In this respect, as in others, the contemporary practice of social work seems now to be drawing somewhat closer to its nineteenth-century roots. As the GAO report on welfare reform explains, those who work with welfare recipients now have "a range of new responsibilities," such as "communicating to recipients their responsibility to become employed, motivating recipients to seek work, . . . and collecting more information about applicants and recipients to determine what services would facilitate their becoming more self-sufficient."[141] But as would be understood by anyone acquainted with the work of the moral reformers, those are actually not "new responsibilities": instead they are the oldest responsibilities in the social work book.

The subsidization of work points to a similarity between many contemporary efforts to promote diligence and IDAs as a mechanism to promote thrift: both are "liberal" policies (examples of government activism) in the service of a "conservative" moral goal (individual and familial self-sufficiency). Wisconsin's Governor Tommy Thompson, who is arguably America's leading proponent of welfare reform, makes it clear that welfare reform is a sort of liberal-conservative fusion:

> I have debated conservatives who think that welfare reform is going to save money. And I have told them that changing a system from dependence to independence is going to cost more, because you have to put money into child care and into job training and medical care and transportation. The liberals have complimented me on that.[142]

The case for welfare reform as a liberal-conservative synthesis can also be argued more broadly. Reform was made possible by the willingness of both liberals and conservatives to concede the partial validity of one another's position. On one hand, "many conservatives have begun to agree that, while some welfare recipients need an attitude adjustment, others simply need more practical assistance — child care and transportation subsidies, for example — in order to get and keep a job." On the other hand (in the words of Donna Franklin, a one-time critic of the concept of the culture of poverty), "most liberals will [now] concede there is a culture of poverty. There is no socialization around work."[143]

We have achieved widespread agreement on two propositions: first, that it is morally incumbent upon the poor to work, to strive for self-sufficiency; and second, that it is acceptable to subsidize the efforts of the poor to achieve self-sufficiency. We insist that the poor work, but, like Lowell, we are also willing to take steps (to implement policies and pay taxes to finance them) that are designed to make the life of the working poor "less hard."[144]

To some extent, then, the problem of the welfare poor (more precisely, the formerly welfare poor) has been and is being transformed into the problem of the working poor. The GAO report provides a thoughtful description of this evolution:

> To the extent that these families' earnings do not increase over time [after they leave welfare] and their employment-based fringe benefits are limited, their ability to maintain employment and support themselves may depend to a great extent on the availability of income supports, such as subsidized medical and child care and the earned income tax credit. Federal and state policies and programs for

assisting low-income working families are likely to play a critical role in the future success of welfare reform.[145]

Perhaps the most radical proposal aimed at assisting the working poor is found in a policy recently championed by Columbia University economist Edmund Phelps: he proposes to subsidize the wages of the working poor as an alternative to welfare.

Phelps writes as an unabashed partisan of the virtue of diligence: "Work is at the center of a normal life," in part because it satisfies the "need to contribute," hence the need "to be depended on (instead of always depending on)."[146] He is harshly critical of proposals dating from the 1960s (advanced both by economists on the right like Milton Friedman and those on the left like James Tobin) for a negative income tax, because they failed to appreciate "what a defect it was that . . . a substantial universal payment was not to be conditional on working." Such a policy would only have encouraged those "lack[ing] the vision and the will to resist yet another year of avoiding life's challenges and risks."[147] Views like these suggest that Phelps can fairly be described as a conservative moralizer.

Because of his great regard for the virtue of diligence, Phelps is also deeply worried by the "declines in men's labor force participation," which are "far steeper than is generally realized."[148] But he explains this decline largely in terms of the declining rewards for low-wage labor, an explanation that liberals put forth more often than conservatives. He argues that "the past quarter-century has brought an end to an era of good wages at the low end."[149] Work became less common among the poor, because wages began to rise much more slowly and less equally in the 1970s and 1980s (and then to cease rising and even to decline); at the same time, of course, the welfare state was expanding, which provided more income to those who did not work. In Phelps's view, then, the reward from work went down, even as the need to work went down as well: these two factors account for the increasing detachment of the poor from the labor force.[150]

Phelps's proposed solution to this problem is the subsidization of low wages, which he describes as "a pro-employment policy that draws upon and builds up the low-wage workers' capacity for self-help," which "would cause welfare to wither away."[151] The subsidies would apply only to full-time workers in the private sector,[152] and they would be graduated: in his illustration, those earning $4 an hour would receive a $3 subsidy per hour (for a $7 gross hourly wage), whereas those earning $12 an hour would receive only a $.06 subsidy per hour (for a $12.06 gross hourly wage).[153]

Phelps does not, it should be noted, believe that low-wage workers are unfairly paid—at least if pay is a measure of productivity.[154] They are, on the other hand, paid too little to be firmly attached to the labor force—and it is in our collective social interest that they be firmly attached to it, because steady work promotes virtue and discourages vice. Thus the goal of the subsidy proposal is "to enable low-productivity workers to support themselves through their own labor, . . . because earning one's way is valuable to people, *and* to encourage self-help and participation through employment in the legitimate business of the economy."[155]

Subsidies for low-wage workers are intended to solve the following problem: "From a social [as opposed to an economic] standpoint, work is now seriously undervalued by the marketplace, especially at the low end where the private reward to employment has fallen to a dangerous level."[156] Phelps contends that the subsidies' encouragement of work that would otherwise command low wages would therefore benefit not only the poor, but all of society:

> By empowering those with relatively low earning power to be self-supporting and exercise the usual responsibilities, and by drawing into the capitalist mainstream millions of less productive persons who are now depending on welfare, workfare, begging, hustling, and crime, the employment subsidy plan would improve the quality of life for everyone else.[157]

To achieve this desired end, Phelps would target the proposed subsidies, we saw above, so that those earning the least would be subsidized most heavily: in other words, the strongest incentive to work would be given to those most in need of it. Thus employment would be made more attractive chiefly to those at greatest risk of "the hazards of welfare, unemployment, acute alcoholism, and crime. If there is more joy in heaven at the conversion of a sinner, then it makes sense to target the government's money where resulting conversions are a good bet."[158]

The goal, then, is to provide incentives that will encourage the poor to act more like the nonpoor: as Phelps puts it, "Once the bourgeois repast is sweetened and made more widely available, more people will respond with bourgeois behavior."[159] As should be clear by now, Phelps unhesitatingly agrees that it is vital to insist on bourgeois behavior. He denies, though, that a policy restricted to moral exhortations to the poor will achieve the desired effect:

> As long as [the] productivity [of the bottom third of workers] does not lift off to levels far above what has so far been seen in this country, they will not be able to afford the mainstream way of life, with its bourgeois values. Low-wage subsidies and those venerable values go together. Without the appreciation of those values there is no likelihood that we will see the enactment of low-wage employment subsidies. But without those subsidies a large minority of the population will not be able to live according to those values.[160]

Practical objections to Phelps's proposal can obviously be raised. Conceivably, for example, employers would react to a program to subsidize wages by lowering the wages that they themselves offered, so that the net benefit to workers would be lowered if not eliminated. Perhaps a more telling objection, though, is that Phelps may be unduly optimistic about the impact of wage subsidies. Are the "conversions," in which the poor would abjure "the hazards of welfare, unemployment, acute alcoholism, and crime" in the name of better-paying, full-time work the "good bet" that Phelps thinks they are?

For some among the poor, the desired conversions undoubtedly would occur. It is likely, though, that Phelps attributes too much economic rationality—too much responsiveness to incentives—to others whom his plan also targets. Glenn Loury worries that the sort of economic carrots that Phelps would bestow will not automatically increase attachment to the labor force in many cases. He suggests that "even well-supported" job opportunities for ghetto youth will not always achieve this end, because "too many young ghetto dwellers are unfit for work. They lack the traits of temperament, character, and intellect to function effectively in the workplace. They have not been socialized within families from the earliest ages to delay gratification, to exercise self-control, to communicate effectively, to embrace their responsibilities."[161]

Loury points to a difficulty that must be taken seriously: some small but not trivial portion of the population is unlikely ever to respond to moral reform, no matter how wisely it is administered. But recognizing this limitation, we must nevertheless attempt to promote the virtues as effectively as we can. To this end, we should certainly continue to experiment with economic incentives designed to encourage virtue, as both Sherraden and Phelps would have us do. In many cases, however, the mandates that Mead advocates will promote virtue more effectively. Finally, the private sector work done by Flake and his many counterparts will also play a crucial role: by imbuing self-confidence, in effect it seeks to give people the needed capacity to respond effectively to incentives (and mandates) to practice the virtues, to believe that their efforts can increase their prosperity and self-reliance.

In different and in some respects even contradictory ways, public policy and charitable practice are already doing much to encourage the poor to fight poverty with virtue. They can and should do more, and in the future it is likely that they will. Nevertheless, it is well to conclude this brief discussion of the contemporary practice of moral reform with this realization: the promotion of virtue is not exclusively—perhaps not even primarily—a matter for public policy. In some ways it may be easier to encourage diligence, sobriety, thrift, and familial responsibility by means of personal example than governmental edict. Cultural change as well as policy change is needed if we are to be most effective in encouraging the poor to attain self-reliance through practice of the virtues.

And in this context it is pertinent to recall an observation of Tocqueville's about attempts of liberal democracies to promote religion: although "it is ever the duty of lawgivers" in democratic times to further belief in the immortality of the soul, "it is far from easy to say what those who govern democratic peoples should do to make [spiritual conceptions] prevail"; Tocqueville's sole suggestion is that governments "daily . . . act as if they believed [in the immortality of the soul] themselves."[162] By the same token, if we want to encourage diligence, sobriety, thrift, and familial responsibility among the poor (as we should and must), it would be no small thing for us to act as if we believed in those virtues by practicing them ourselves.

BIOGRAPHICAL APPENDIX

This biographical appendix is not meant to be read straight through, but to serve as a reference. Throughout the volume I refer to individuals who are little known today; as an aid to the reader (who understandably might have trouble differentiating among the various reformers) I provide essential biographical information here.[1] Thus, when I speak (for example) of Tuckerman's opposition to prohibition, readers who seek a biographical context for that piece of information can find it here.

The individual biographies are followed by a section that discusses the various historical connections that link many of the reformers. I include this section because I have argued for the existence of a moral reform tradition uniting the various individual reformers; readers may wonder about the extent of the individual reformers' knowledge of and acquaintance with one another.

A. THE FOUR PRINCIPAL MORAL REFORMERS

Joseph Tuckerman was born in 1778 to a family headed by a successful Boston merchant. After receiving bachelor's and master's degrees at Harvard University, he became pastor of a Congregationalist church in Chelsea, Massachusetts in 1801. Prompted by his close friend William Ellery Channing (the subject of a separate biography below), Tuckerman relinquished his Chelsea pulpit in 1826 to become "minister to Boston's poor" under the auspices of the American Unitarian Association. (I discuss the emergence of Unitarianism out of Congregationalism in the Channing biography that follows.) As minister to the poor, Tuckerman visited Boston's jails and prisons, preached to the poor, and paid calls upon them in their homes. Considered America's first prominent social worker, Tuckerman found jobs for newly released prisoners, helped alcoholics reduce their drinking, and advocated an expanded public school system. Tuckerman held various public welfare posts (serving for a time as overseer of the Boston poor); he was also active in numerous private social welfare agencies in Boston, including the Boston Society for the Prevention of Pauperism. A victim of poor health for many years, he died in 1840.

Robert Milham Hartley was born into a prominent family in England in 1796. His father was a manufacturer who emigrated with his family to America when Hartley was three years old. Hartley was a deeply religious young man who initially prepared for a career in the ministry. Illness subsequently led him to alter his career path, and he became a dry goods merchant in New York City. In New York Hartley took an active part in local Bible and tract societies. He helped organize the New York City Temperance Society in 1829, subsequently becoming that organization's secretary. His work as a temperance advocate led him to a broader concern with poverty—an interest prompted by his discovery that milk produced by cows fed from the refuse of local distilleries was spreading disease among infant consumers living in New York's tenements. Along with many prominent Christian merchants in New York, Hartley helped found the New York Association for Improving the Condition of the Poor (AICP) in 1843; Hartley became its first general agent, filling that post for more than thirty years. The AICP attempted to improve the character of the poor through regular visits (by wealthy volunteers who were churchgoers) to their homes. It also sought to improve the material conditions in which the poor lived, for example by establishing medical dispensaries for the poor and creating a model tenement house for them. Hartley gave up his AICP post in 1876 when he turned eighty; he died in 1881.

Charles Loring Brace was born into an old New England family in 1826. He studied at Yale College, Yale Divinity School, and Union Theological Seminary in New York City. After a European sojourn in 1850–1851 (accompanied by his friend Frederick Olmsted, who was later to create New York's Central Park), Brace returned to New York, where he worked in a Methodist mission in the Five Points district, among the poorest sections of the city. Brace began to take a special interest in New York's population of vagrant youths, many of whom were orphans or stepchildren. Along with several other clergymen, he established special religious meetings for vagrant boys. When the meetings proved to have little success in effecting moral reformation, Brace founded the Children's Aid Society in 1853. The society attempted to aid urban youths by providing them with moral and industrial education in its schools, and shelter (for which payment was required) in its lodging houses. The capstone of Brace's efforts to assist the impoverished youths of New York City was his program of placing them out with families in rural areas in the Midwest and upstate New York. By 1862 Brace had sent some 60,000 New York children west. The outplacement system proved controversial: westerners claimed that many of the transplanted youths became criminals, and Catholics objected to the placement of their youthful co-religionists in Protestant homes. Although Brace defended outplacement, he began to emphasize more heavily his society's efforts to assist young boys and girls who remained in the city. He died in 1890; his son then succeeded him as head of the Children's Aid Society.[2]

Josephine Shaw Lowell was born in 1843 in a Boston suburb, daughter to wealthy parents supportive of social reform. Lowell's parents were prominent Unitarians, well acquainted with such members of Boston's liberal intelligentsia as Margaret Fuller, Emerson, and Thoreau. When she was three her family moved to Staten Island (now part of New York City), so that her mother could receive treatment from a specialist for her failing vision. Josephine Shaw married Charles Russell Lowell (nephew of the poet James Russell Lowell) in 1863: he died in Civil War combat the next year, and Lowell gave birth to a daughter just weeks after his death. (Lowell's brother, Robert Gould Shaw, also died in the war, in which he served as colonel of the Union's first black regiment.) Lowell became involved in charitable work during the war as part of the Women's Central Association of Relief (which aided Union soldiers); after the war she worked for the National Freedmen's Relief Association to promote the education of newly emancipated southern blacks. Lowell then began to take an interest in urban poverty, first by chairing Richmond County's (i.e., Staten Island's) committee of the State Charities Aid Association in 1872. In 1876 she became the first woman Commissioner of the State Board of Charities. Lowell helped found the Charity Organization Society (COS) of New York in 1882, with the aim of promoting the self-reliance of the city's poor. She continued to work tirelessly for New York's COS until her death while also taking a steadily greater interest in economic reforms to advance the cause of workers. Lowell founded a group that became the Consumers' League in 1890: it sponsored consumer boycotts against stores thought to mistreat and underpay their employees. She supported collective bargaining for workers (with industrial arbitration to resolve disputes between employers and unions); during the depression of 1893–1894 she organized a relief committee that offered emergency employment to some of those who had been thrown out of work. Lowell died in 1905.

B. FOUR IMPORTANT ALLIES OF THE MORAL REFORMERS

William Ellery Channing, who aided Tuckerman in establishing Boston's ministry to the poor, was the founder of American Unitarianism. He was born in Rhode Island in 1780. Channing graduated from Harvard College in 1798, and he became minister of the Federal Street Church in Boston in 1803 (retaining this position until his death in 1842). Despite the poor health that plagued him all his life, Channing won wide recognition as a powerful orator. His rejection of Calvinist or Congregationalist orthodoxy was closely linked to ideas that animated the moral reform movement: in particular, he and other Unitarians emphasized the human potential for virtue and perfectibility and the freedom of the human will. Channing organized a group of liberal ministers that evolved in 1825 into the American Unitarian Association. In addition to promoting the rise of the moral reform movement, Channing deeply influenced the course of American literature: writers like Emerson, Bryant, Longfellow, Lowell, and Holmes all acknowledged their indebtedness to Channing's ideas.

Jacob Riis was born in Denmark in 1849, the son of a schoolmaster. He did not enjoy formal schooling and so became a carpenter. Finding no employment in his trade, Riis immigrated to America in 1870. From 1870 to 1877 he wandered through several northeastern and midwestern states in search of work, often experiencing severe poverty. In 1877 Riis became a reporter and photographer for the *New York Tribune*; he covered the "beat" of criminal activity in New York's tenement districts, and in doing so became interested in the lives of the immigrant poor more generally. He summarized his discoveries about New York poverty in his landmark 1890 work, *How the Other Half Lives: Studies Among the Tenements of New York*. A tireless supporter of social reform, Riis crusaded against slum housing and for city playgrounds and "fresh air" camps for children residing in tenements. He was a great admirer and close ally of Theodore Roosevelt, whom he came to know during Roosevelt's tenure as New York City police commissioner. Riis died in 1914.

Mary Richmond was born in Illinois in 1861 to working-class parents; her father was a carriage blacksmith. She grew up in Baltimore; her mother died when Richmond was only three, and she was brought up by a widowed grandmother and two maiden aunts. After graduating from high school Richmond supported herself through clerical work in New York and bookkeeping jobs in Baltimore. In 1889 she was hired as assistant treasurer of the Baltimore Charity Organization Society; in 1891 she became the agency's executive (a post typically held by those with graduate training). Richmond took an active role in training the agency's volunteer friendly visitors. Contending that social work (as it came to be called) should evolve into a profession, in 1898 Richmond taught some of the initial offerings of the New York Summer School of Philanthropy, the first institution to offer academic social work training. In 1900 she moved to Philadelphia to head its Society for Organizing Charity; in 1909 Richmond's career reached its zenith, when she became director of the Charity Organization Department of the Russell Sage Foundation in New York. Richmond wrote extensively about the practice of social work. In the text I have emphasized her early work, *Friendly Visiting Among the Poor* (1899). In her later, more canonical works—*Social Diagnosis* (1917), and *What is Social Work?* (1922)—she laid the groundwork for the discipline of American social work. Richmond died in 1928.

Amos Warner was born in Iowa in 1861, shortly after the death of his physician father. His mother moved the family to Nebraska. Warner studied at the University of Nebraska and then did graduate work in economics at Johns Hopkins University. He became secretary of the Baltimore Charity Organization Society in 1887, subsequently returning to the University of Nebraska to head its economics department in 1889. In 1891 Warner was named by President Benjamin Harrison to become the first superintendent of charities for the District of Columbia. His 1894 book *American Charities* was the first scientific attempt to explain the problems of poverty and the effectiveness or ineffectiveness of various charitable responses to them. Warner taught briefly at Stanford University, but ill health forced him to give up his academic position. He died while still a young man in 1900.

C. TWO PROMINENT CRITICS OF MORAL REFORM

Jane Addams was born into a wealthy Illinois family in 1861. She studied at Rockford Seminary in Illinois. Abandoning a proposed medical career because of her own ill health, she traveled extensively in Europe in the 1880s. While in England in 1887 she visited Toynbee Hall, the pioneer settlement house, whose residents lived among the urban poor in London's East End, working to aid them. On her return to America, Addams created a Chicago settlement house with her friend Ellen Gates Starr in 1889. The house, located in a depressed area on South Halsted Street, had formerly been owned by Charles J. Hull; thus the settlement came to be known as Hull House. Hull House expanded greatly over the years, at one point encompassing thirteen buildings and a staff of 65. It offered cultural and recreational opportunities to the immigrant poor in the neighborhood. Hull House also became a training ground for social workers; along with Addams herself, many other residents became prominent social reformers. Addams wrote extensively, offering advice on improving cities and lessening poverty that grew out of her experiences at Hull House; her 1910 autobiographical work, *Twenty Years at Hull-House*, is her best-known book. Addams became the first woman to head the National Conference of Charities and Correction (later renamed the National Conference of Social Work) in 1910. In 1912 she campaigned actively for Theodore Roosevelt, the Progressive Party's candidate for president. Widely admired before World War I, Addams became controversial because of her pacifism after America's entry into the war. She died in Chicago in 1935.

Walter Rauschenbusch, the son of a Baptist minister, was the seventh in a direct line of Rauschenbusches who served as ministers. His parents had migrated from Germany after the abortive revolution of 1848. Rauschenbusch was born in 1861 in Rochester, New York, where his father taught at the Rochester Theological Seminary. He was educated in Germany before receiving his B.A. from the University of Rochester; he graduated in 1886 from Rochester Theological Seminary. For the next ten years Rauschenbusch ministered to a congregation of impoverished German Baptists in the Hell's Kitchen neighborhood on Manhattan's West Side. Eager to understand and improve social conditions, he read widely in the literature of social reform; he was particularly influenced by the writings of Henry George and Beatrice and Sidney Webb. Rauschenbusch lost most of his hearing while visiting with parishioners who were ill; his deafness led him to give up his pastoral work in 1897,[3] when he succeeded his father at Rochester Theological Seminary. In 1907 he published *Christianity and the Social Crisis*, a critique of organized religion's complacency in the face of social injustice. The book had a wide impact, and Rauschenbusch emerged as the leader of the Social Gospel movement in the United States—and as a forthright advocate of socialism. Disheartened by the conflict between his two homelands — Germany and the United States — in World War I, Rauschenbusch died in 1918.

D. LINKS BETWEEN THE REFORMERS

Because Tuckerman worked in Boston, whereas Hartley, Brace, and Lowell were all New Yorkers, connections between him and them might seem unlikely; nonetheless, they exist. Although Hartley's son and biographer asserted that his father created the instructions guiding AICP visitors "out of his own mind," uninfluenced by prior experiments with visitation of the poor, instead it is likely that Hartley profited from Tuckerman's English-language edition of Baron De Gerando's *The Visitor of the Poor:* De Gerando's rules for visitors correspond almost exactly with Hartley's.[4] Hartley was obviously familiar with Tuckerman's writings; he referred to Tuckerman's *The Principles and Results of the Ministry at Large in Boston* at least once in writing the AICP's annual reports.[5]

Tuckerman also had a connection with Brace's work: the first president of the Boston children's mission, which was founded in 1849 as an outgrowth of Tuckerman's efforts, subsequently became the first treasurer of New York's Children's Aid Society under Brace.[6] Finally, Lowell's parents (Frank and Sarah Shaw) lived in Boston until they moved to Staten Island in 1847: their Unitarian dedication to social reform had initially been inspired by Tuckerman.[7]

Because Hartley and Brace were both leading New York philanthropists from the mid-1850s through the mid-1870s, I think it probable that they knew one another. Neither man is mentioned in the other's biography, though. But in an 1868 summary of the first quarter-century of the AICP's history, Hartley noted that the Children's Aid Society was founded "not by this association, but by the demands of an enlightened public sentiment which it had largely contributed to create."[8] He went on to express his admiration for the Children's Aid Society, asserting that "too much can scarcely be said in praise of this wise, efficient and economical charity."[9]

Lowell and Brace were both prominent New York philanthropists in the fifteen years preceding his death in 1890. Thus I think it likely that they too were acquainted; again, though, neither of them is mentioned as an acquaintance in the other's biography. (Lowell's biographer does note that Lowell was absent from the 1877 annual meeting of the State Charities Aid Association, attended by Brace, at which her work was discussed.)[10] Brace certainly was aware of the activities of the Charity Organization Society that Lowell helped found. He authored what we would today call a blurb in its praise, included in the second annual report of the COS in 1884: "The information received from your Society has certainly been a help to our Agents in making inquiries regarding the worthiness of applicants for charitable aid."[11]

Lowell also shared important ties with two younger reformers, Jacob Riis and Mary Richmond. Lowell and Riis were good friends as well as frequent collaborators in reform efforts; he was one of the eulogists at her 1905 memorial service.[12] Richmond acknowledged her debt to Lowell (one of the "workers in New York, who, against such odds, are making advances in the reform of municipal abuses") in her 1899 preface to *Friendly Visiting Among the Poor*.[13] In 1924 Richmond elaborated on her acquaintance with Lowell in a brief biographical essay, in which she mentioned meeting Lowell at a conference in Baltimore in 1890 and discussed the intellectual influence that Lowell had exerted upon her.[14]

Finally, Addams and Richmond were rivals, but for the most part—at least if we judge from Richmond's statements—reasonably friendly rivals.[15] *Friendly Visiting Among the Poor* acknowledges Addams for her "leadership" of the "group . . . who . . . have given us, at Hull House in Chicago, so admirable an object lesson in the power of neighborliness."[16] At Addams's invitation Richmond attended the Conference of American Settlements at Hull House in 1899. In a private letter Richmond observed that "Miss Addams . . . showed the most delightful tact and good feeling throughout all the meetings." Richmond added that she would "always feel more sympathetic toward the settlements for having attended these meetings." She declared that the "political economy" of the settlement movement was "rather crude"—but then pointed out that it was "as much a 'pseudo science' as our organized charity is."[17]

One final connection links Rauschenbusch to the contemporary American left: the deeply religious Rauschenbusch is the maternal grandfather of a prominent academic spokesman for the American left, the avowedly atheistic Richard Rorty.[18]

NOTES

Abbreviations Used in the Notes

AICP New York Association for Improving the Condition of the Poor
BJS United States Bureau of Justice Statistics
COS Charity Organization Society of the City of New York
GAO United States General Accounting Office
NCHS National Center for Health Statistics
NIAAA National Institute on Alcohol Abuse and Alcoholism
PNCCC *Proceedings of the National Conference of Charities and Correction*

Introduction

1. Susan E. Mayer, *What Money Can't Buy: Family Income and Children's Life Chances* (Cambridge, Mass.: Harvard University Press, 1997), pp. 5–6.

2. Lawrence M. Mead, *The New Politics of Poverty: The Nonworking Poor in America* (New York: Basic Books, 1992), p. 220.

3. Mead, *New Politics of Poverty*, pp. 160, 181. For a more extensive discussion, see Mead, ed., *The New Paternalism: Supervisory Approaches to Poverty* (Washington, D.C.: Brookings, 1997), a collection of essays that includes analyses of paternalistic policies in areas such as teen-pregnancy prevention, child support, homelessness, drug policy, and education, as well as welfare reform.

4. Oscar Handlin, "Poverty from the Civil War to World War II," in Leo Fishman, ed., *Poverty amid Affluence* (New Haven, Conn.: Yale University Press, 1966), p. 3.

5. Herbert J. Gans, "Culture and Class in the Study of Poverty: An Approach to Antipoverty Research," reprinted in *People, Plans, and Policies: Essays on Poverty, Racism, and Other National Urban Problems* (New York: Columbia University Press and Russell Sage Foundation, 1991), p. 303.

6. None of these individuals is particularly well known today. For that reason the book includes an appendix that provides brief biographies for these four reformers—and also for four of their associates, and two of their prominent critics, who figure prominently in this narrative. The biographical appendix is not meant to be read straight through, but to be used as a reference source. For example, in the narrative I refer repeatedly to "Brace." As they come across such a reference, readers who wish to remember exactly which reformer "Brace" was can then refer to the appendix for the essential information.

7. The final section of the biographical appendix explores the unity of the moral reform tradition, examining the historical evidence of the links that tie many of the reformers together.

8. *Joseph Tuckerman on the Elevation of the Poor: A Selection from His Reports as Minister at Large in Boston*, edited by E. E. Hale (New York: Arno Press and The New York Times, 1971 [rpt. 1874]), p. 36. This volume is a posthumous collection of extracts from Tuckerman's writings; the original dates of publication for the individual selections are unfortunately not provided.

9. AICP, Fourth Annual Report (1847), p. 13. The first nine AICP annual reports are reprinted in *Annual Reports of the New York Association for Improving the Condition of the Poor, Nos. 1–10, 1845–1853* (New York: Arno Press and The New York Times, 1971). There was no second annual report; the third report for 1846 follows immediately upon the first report for 1845.

10. Charles Loring Brace, *The Dangerous Classes of New York and Twenty Years' Work among Them*, 3rd ed., with addenda (Montclair, N.J.: Patterson Smith, 1967 [rpt. 1880]), pp. 22–23.

11. Josephine Shaw Lowell, *Public Relief and Private Charity* (New York: Arno Press and The New York Times, 1971 [rpt. 1884]), p. 94.

12. Jane Addams, *Democracy and Social Ethics*, edited by Anne Firor Scott (Cambridge, Mass.: Harvard University Press, 1964 [rpt. 1907]), p. 212. *Democracy and Social Ethics* was originally published in 1902.

13. Addams, *Democracy*, pp. 38–39.

14. Daniel P. Moynihan, *The Politics of a Guaranteed Income: The Nixon Administration and the Family Assistance Plan* (New York: Random House, 1973), p. 24.

15. Tom Wolfe, *A Man in Full* (New York: Farrar Straus Giroux, 1998), p. 171.

16. Wolfe alludes to this generational contrast by contrasting the sardonic attitude of Conrad's teacher—a contemporary of Conrad's parents—with Conrad's own admiration for bourgeois virtue.

17. In another sense, though, failing to practice the cardinal virtues was itself a manifestation of familial irresponsibility: providers who did not work regularly, who drank, and who spent extravagantly could not care adequately for family members who depended on them.

1. Principles and Intentions

1. Michael B. Katz, "Reframing the 'Underclass' Debate," in Katz, ed., *The "Underclass" Debate: Views from History* (Princeton, N.J.: Princeton University Press, 1993), pp. 463–464.

2. Thomas Sowell, *Ethnic America: A History* (New York: Basic Books, 1981), pp. 282–283. The emphases are mine.

3. Sowell's emphasis on the differing cultural values of immigrant groups as a source of their differing economic performance has come in for harsh criticism. See, for example, Stephen Steinberg, *The Ethnic Myth: Race, Ethnicity, and Class in America*, 2nd ed. (Boston: Beacon Press, 1989): Steinberg accuses Sowell of "writing a morality tale whereby groups—notably Jews and Asians—who have 'the right stuff' overcome every impediment of race and class to reach the economic pinnacle," whereas "other groups—especially blacks —suffer from historically conditioned cultural defects that condemn them to lag behind in the economic competition." At bottom, Steinberg faults writers like Sowell for assuming (p. xiv) that ethnic groups are "endowed with a given set of cultural values," and for failing to "understand these values in terms of their material sources." Steinberg's discussion of these material sources is often illuminating. It is interesting, for example, that the middle-class values of Jewish immigrants are explicable partly in terms of their class origins: immigrant Jews were better prepared for life in urban America than immigrants from other groups from peasant backgrounds, because Jews were more urbanized and more frequently skilled workers (pp. 91–98). But Steinberg's critique proves only that "Jewish values" were not altogether an uncaused cause; he does not prove that the values were unrelated to success after immigration. In fact (p. 86) he even concedes that having the proper values tended to produce economic success: "The climb up the economic ladder unquestionably required

fortitude, self-sacrifice, ingenuity, and all the other virtues" pointed to by writers who explain immigrant success in terms of cultural value systems. For his part, Sowell (*Ethnic America*, p. 274) denies that ethnic success is somehow a reward to the morally deserving; he explicitly declares that "it is not personal merit but simply good fortune to be born into a group whose values and skills make life easier to cope with."

In short, to explain the source of good or bad values is not to discount their importance in furthering or hindering the climb out of poverty. Robert M. Hartley, for example, would have agreed with much of Steinberg's analysis. Thus he understood well that New York's Irish immigrants were not themselves to blame for behavior that in his view helped keep them in poverty. See AICP, Fourteenth Annual Report (1857), p. 15: "Their habits in their own country having been formed under circumstances which gave no proper stimulus to thriftiness, frugality, and industry, they have become so thoroughly pauperized in spirit, that to rise by their own exertions to a self-supporting condition, is an idea which seems to surpass their comprehension." Nevertheless, even if the absence of "thriftiness, frugality, and industry" can be explained, Hartley realized that it still has to be lamented; furthermore, "thriftiness, frugality, and industry" still have to be promoted.

4. See Sowell, *Ethnic America*, p. 284: "History shows new skills being rather readily acquired in a few years, as compared to the generations—or centuries—required for *attitude* changes. Groups today plagued by absenteeism, tardiness, and a need for constant supervision at work or in school are typically descendants of people with the same habits a century or more ago." The emphasis is Sowell's.

5. Reverend Robert Adair, quoted in Bruce Laurie, *Working People of Philadelphia, 1800–1850* (Philadelphia: Temple University Press, 1980), p. 46.

6. Laurie, *Working People*, p. 46.

7. Laurie, *Working People*, p. 48.

8. Laurie, *Working People*, p. 51.

9. Jill Siegel Dodd, "The Working Classes and the Temperance Movement in Ante-Bellum Boston," *Labor History* 19 (1978): 521.

10. Dodd, "Working Classes," p. 523.

11. Dodd, "Working Classes," p. 526.

12. Dodd, "Working Classes," p. 529.

13. The study was conducted by Edward M. Glaser and Harvey L. Ross. It is described in Edward C. Banfield, *The Unheavenly City Revisited* (Boston: Little, Brown, 1974), pp. 249–250. According to Glaser and Ross, the successful men—but not the unsuccessful ones—were influenced early in life by an effective parent.

14. Katz, *Improving Poor People: The Welfare State, the "Underclass," and Urban Schools as History* (Princeton, N.J.: Princeton University Press, 1995), pp. 68–69.

15. Katz, *In the Shadow of the Poorhouse: A Social History of Welfare in America* (New York: Basic Books, 1986), p. 18.

16. Robert H. Bremner, "The Rediscovery of Pauperism," in *Current Issues in Social Work Seen in Historical Perspective* (New York: Council on Social Work Education, 1962), p. 11.

17. Katz, *The Undeserving Poor: From the War on Poverty to the War on Welfare* (New York: Pantheon Books, 1989), p. 11.

18. Oscar Handlin, "Poverty from the Civil War to World War II," in Leo Fishman, ed., *Poverty amid Affluence* (New Haven, Conn.: Yale University Press, 1966), p. 15.

19. Handlin, "Poverty from the Civil War to World War II," pp. 9–10.

20. See *Joseph Tuckerman on the Elevation of the Poor: A Selection from His Reports as*

Minister at Large in Boston, edited by E. E. Hale (New York: Arno Press and The New York Times, 1971 [rpt. 1874]), p. 63: "Any one who depends on charity for the means of subsistence during the time of this dependence, and in the degree of it, is poor. No one, in the strict sense of the term, is poor who is not thus dependent."

21. Quoted in Daniel McColgan, *Joseph Tuckerman: Pioneer in American Social Work* (Washington, D.C.: Catholic University of America Press, 1940), p. 424. The emphasis appears in the text.

22. See, for example, Tuckerman's "Essay on the Wages Paid to Females for Their Labour, in the Form of a Letter, from a Gentleman in Boston to His Friend in Philadelphia," in David J. Rothman and Sheila M. Rothman, eds., *Low Wages and Great Sins: Two Antebellum American Views on Prostitution and the Working Girl* (New York: Garland Publishing, 1987 [rpt. 1830]), pp. 25–26: "I would ask any one to go into the families of forty, or fifty . . . [women], who depend upon their daily labour for their daily bread; and to hear there . . . of the wants, and sufferings which are felt, even when, by the unremitted toil of a week, they have earned a dollar, or at most, a dollar and a half. They owe a few dollars of rent, which they cannot pay. Their clothing is hardly sufficient for warmth in the cold of autumn, and how much less in that of winter? And they know not how, or where, to obtain more. Their food is often scanty, as well as of the coarsest kind." Tuckerman's essay won a prize after he submitted it to a competition organized by Matthew Carey, a Philadelphia journalist and pamphleteer who argued consistently that low wages rather than moral depravity were the principal source of poverty. We may conclude that Tuckerman was clearly familiar with and sympathetic to "economic" explanations of poverty as well as "moral" ones. On Carey, see Katz, *In the Shadow,* pp. 7–9; and Benjamin J. Klebaner, "Poverty and Its Relief in American Thought, 1815–61," in Frank R. Breul and Steven J. Diner, eds., *Compassion and Responsibility: Readings in the History of Social Welfare Policy in the United States* (Chicago: University of Chicago Press, 1980), pp. 117–118.

23. See Tuckerman, "An Essay on the Wages," p. 35: "May any means be devised of raising the wages of the poor, and thus of improving their condition, by enabling them more entirely to provide for their own support? To this question, I think, every political economist would unhesitatingly say, no." Tuckerman understood low wages as a product of the law of supply and demand. His only solution (p. 39) was to hope that employers would be willing, "when their [workers'] wages [we]re generally reduced in inverse proportion to the demand for their work," to pay as much as they could in wages, "consistently with any fair profits to themselves."

24. Hale, *Joseph Tuckerman,* pp. 71–72.

25. Hale, *Joseph Tuckerman,* p. 73.

26. Hale, *Joseph Tuckerman,* p. 74.

27. William Ellery Channing, "Ministry for the Poor," in *The Works of William E. Channing, D.D.* (Boston: American Unitarian Association, 1903), p. 73. "Ministry for the Poor" was an address delivered by Channing in 1835. Note that the sufferings of the poor caused by material hardship are described as "inevitable."

28. Charles Murray, *In Pursuit: Of Happiness and Good Government* (New York: Simon and Schuster, 1988), pp. 80–81.

29. Hale, *Joseph Tuckerman,* p. 81.

30. Charles Loring Brace, *The Dangerous Classes of New York and Twenty Years' Work among Them,* 3rd ed., with addenda (Montclair, N.J.: Patterson Smith, 1967 [rpt. 1880]), p. 45.

31. Quoted in Josephine Shaw Lowell, "Felix Qui Causam Rerum Cognovit," *Charities*

Review 2 (1893): 422. See also William Rhinelander Stewart, *The Philanthropic Work of Josephine Shaw Lowell Containing a Biographical Sketch of Her Life Together with a Selection of Her Public Papers and Private Letters* (Montclair, N.J.: Patterson Smith, 1974 [rpt. 1911]), p. 129, where Lowell describes "the various poor people who are being brought to our notice by our Charity Organization Society": "They all want work, work, work; many are widows with young children; many are men who have had accidents; so far, we have not really found many 'unworthy,' or at least those are not the ones that make an impression." The statement appears in a letter dated February 18, 1883.

32. Stewart, *Philanthropic Work*, p. 222. The statement appears in an 1899 essay, "The Uses and Dangers of Investigation in Public and Private Charities."

33. Stewart, *Philanthropic Work*, pp. 163–164. The statement appears in an 1890 essay, "The Economic and Moral Effects of Public Outdoor Relief."

34. Lowell, *Public Relief and Private Charity* (New York: Arno Press and The New York Times, 1971 [rpt. 1884]), pp. 75–76.

35. Lowell, "Houses of Refuge for Women; Their Purposes, Management, and Possibilities," *Proceedings of the New York State Conference of Charities and Correction* 1 (1900): 255.

36. Amos G. Warner, *American Charities: A Study in Philanthropy and Economics* (New York: Arno Press and The New York Times, 1971 [rpt. 1894]), p. 296.

37. Katz, *In the Shadow*, pp. 41–42. See also Frances Fox Piven and Richard A. Cloward, "The Historical Sources of the Contemporary Relief Debate," in Fred Block, Richard A. Cloward, Barbara Ehrenreich, and Frances Fox Piven, *The Mean Season: The Attack on the Welfare State* (New York: Pantheon, 1987), pp. 11–12: "From the start enormous energy and inventiveness were invested in devising relief programs that carefully scrutinized and categorized supplicants (the impotent versus the able-bodied, the resident versus the vagrant), hedged in the giving of aid with elaborate conditions, subjected recipients to strict disciplinary regimens and close surveillance, and exposed them to public rituals of degradation as 'paupers.' Otherwise, it was feared that social provision would encourage the poor to shun work, or rather, to shun the kinds of work and the terms of work for which they were deemed fit."

38. See, for example, Katz, *In the Shadow*, p. 51: the abolition of outdoor relief in Brooklyn in the late 1870s is said to have resulted in family breakups (as parents "sent their children to agencies and asylums, with the hope of retrieving them when their fortunes improved") and an increase in tramping (as men in search of work went on the road in hopes of finding it). I do not at all wish to make light of the tragedy of family dissolution; still, it is noteworthy that Katz focuses on family dissolution—as opposed, say, to mass starvation—to show the folly and cruelty of the abolition of outdoor relief. We may conclude that nothing remotely like mass starvation occurred in the wake of its abolition; if it had, Katz would surely proclaim the fact.

39. Hale, *Joseph Tuckerman*, p. 25.

40. Quoted in Mary E. Richmond, *Friendly Visiting among the Poor: A Handbook for Charity Workers* (Montclair, N.J.: Patterson Smith, 1969 [rpt. 1899]), p. 125.

41. Tuckerman, "Introduction" to the Baron De Gerando, *The Visitor of the Poor*, trans. "A Lady of Boston" (Boston: Hilliard, Gray, Little, and Wilkins, 1832), p. ix. As the title suggests, *The Visitor of the Poor* was a European work that offered advice on how to counsel and assist the poor. The anonymous translator was Elizabeth Palmer Peabody, sister of Mrs. Horace Mann and Mrs. Nathaniel Hawthorne, who had served as secretary to Tuckerman's friend and colleague Channing. Information about the translator is reported in Dorothy G.

Becker, "The Visitor to the New York City Poor, 1843–1920," *Social Service Review* 35 (1961): 383n.

42. AICP, Eleventh Annual Report (1854), p. 33.

43. Brace, *Dangerous Classes*, p. 440.

44. Lowell, *Public Relief*, p. 96.

2. The Virtues Taught by the Moral Reformers

1. AICP, Tenth Annual Report (1853), p. 34.

2. AICP, Seventeenth Annual Report (1860), p. 55.

3. "On the Elevation of the Laboring Classes," in *The Works of William E. Channing, D.D.* (Boston: American Unitarian Association, 1903), p. 39. Channing delivered this address in 1840. For Smith's critique of the potentially dehumanizing impact of the division of labor, see Edwin Cannan, ed., *An Inquiry into the Nature and Causes of the Wealth of Nations* (New York: Modern Library, 1937), pp. 734–735.

4. Daniel T. Rodgers, *The Work Ethic in Industrial America 1850–1920* (Chicago: University of Chicago Press, 1978), p. 19. On p. 10 Rodgers quotes Channing extolling the moral benefits of work.

5. William Rhinelander Stewart, *The Philanthropic Work of Josephine Shaw Lowell Containing a Biographical Sketch of Her Life Together with a Selection of Her Public Papers and Private Letters* (Montclair, N.J.: Patterson Smith, 1974 [rpt. 1911]), p. 215. The statement appears in an 1898 essay, "The Evils of Investigation and Relief."

6. Stewart, *Philanthropic Work*, p. 414. The statement appears in "The Living Wage," an 1898 address.

7. "Charity and Homemaking," in Mary E. Richmond, *The Long View: Papers and Addresses*, edited by Joanna C. Colcord and Ruth Z. S. Mann (New York: Russell Sage Foundation, 1930), p. 80. Richmond's essay was originally published in 1897.

8. Rodgers, *Work Ethic*, p. 28.

9. Eugene Bardach, "Implementing a Paternalist Welfare-to-Work Program," in Lawrence M. Mead, ed., *The New Paternalism: Supervisory Approaches to Poverty* (Washington, D.C.: Brookings, 1997), pp. 257, 259.

10. William Julius Wilson, *When Work Disappears: The World of the New Urban Poor* (New York: Alfred A. Knopf, 1996), p. 73.

11. Jacob A. Riis, "Special Needs of the Poor in New York," *Forum* 14 (1892): 498.

12. Richmond, *Friendly Visiting among the Poor: A Handbook for Charity Workers* (Montclair, N.J.: Patterson Smith, 1969 [rpt. 1899]), p. 33.

13. Joseph Tuckerman, "An Essay on the Wages Paid to Females for Their Labour, in the Form of a Letter, from a Gentleman in Boston to His Friend in Philadelphia," in David J. Rothman and Sheila M. Rothman, eds., *Low Wages and Great Sins: Two Antebellum American Views on Prostitution and the Working Girl* (New York: Garland Publishing, 1987 [rpt. 1830]), p. 35.

14. AICP, Ninth Annual Report (1852), p. 16.

15. AICP, Ninth Annual Report (1852), pp. 26–27.

16. AICP, Twelfth Annual Report (1855), p. 18.

17. AICP, Ninth Annual Report (1852), p. 22. In the judgment of American economic historians today, immigration did less to lower wages (at least later in the nineteenth century) than Hartley suggested here. See Jeremy Atack and Peter Passell, *A New Economic View of American History from Colonial Times to 1940*, 2nd ed. (New York: W.W. Norton, 1994). Summarizing work done by Jeffrey Williamson, they conclude that "the impact of

. . . immigration upon American wages was minimal [between 1870 and 1910]. Real eastern wages might have been only about 1 percent lower if immigration had been 20 percent greater" (p. 236).

18. In boom years, of course, when the demand for labor increased, workers had less reason to fear losing their jobs and could afford to be choosier. Thus data from the prosperous years 1912 and 1913 show tremendous labor turnover among factory workers. For example, between October 1912 and October 1913, the Ford Motor Company needed to hire some 54,000 men to maintain an average work force of 13,000: "By far the greatest cause of separations was resignation, rather than discharge or layoff; and, understandably, the number of workers quitting spiraled upward in prosperous times." See David Montgomery, *Workers' Control in America: Studies in the History of Work, Technology, and Labor Struggles* (New York: Cambridge University Press, 1979), p. 41.

19. There were six severe economic downturns in the nineteenth century, spanning the years 1819–1822, 1837–1843, 1857–1859, 1873–1878, 1882–1886, and 1892–1897. Thus about one-third of the years between 1819 and 1897 consisted of hard times. See Samuel Rezneck, *Business Depressions and Financial Panics: Essays in American Business and Economic History* (New York: Greenwood Publishing, 1971), p. 9.

20. Rezneck, *Business Depressions*, p. 12.

21. Unemployment was pervasive, it has been suggested, in part because wages tended not to fall very much in bad times. See Atack and Passell, *New Economic View*, p. 543: "Labor market adjustments overwhelmingly took place through quantity, not price, adjustments. Nominal wages were sticky, resistant to downward pressure even during business recessions and periods of falling prices. One implication is that unemployment rates must have been quite volatile, and unemployment quite common."

22. Alexander Keyssar, *Out of Work: The First Century of Unemployment in Massachusetts* (New York: Cambridge University Press, 1986), p. 75. My emphasis on the plight of urban immigrant workers in particular may seem questionable, since Keyssar notes (p. 112) that "unemployment levels were below average (often well below average)" in Boston—as compared with the rest of the state—in the late nineteenth and early twentieth centuries. But this was largely because Boston's economy differed in offering a greater percentage of white-collar jobs, which tended to be more secure—and for which immigrant workers were generally unqualified. In other words, according to Keyssar even in Boston job loss was common in the positions generally held by the immigrant poor. See pp. 54, 80, and 119.

23. Keyssar, *Out of Work*, p. 50. As Keyssar explains, these figures refer to the unemployment frequency (the percentage of members of the labor force unemployed at some point during the year) rather than the unemployment rate (the percentage idled at any given time). For the distinction between frequencies and rates, see also p. 59.

24. Keyssar, *Out of Work*, p. 58.

25. Amos G. Warner, *American Charities: A Study in Philanthropy and Economics* (New York: Arno Press and The New York Times, 1971 [rpt. 1894]), pp. 178–179. Warner does not provide a percentage for the unemployment frequency, but the raw data that he offers (816,470 workers, 241,589 of whom were unemployed at some point) yield a frequency of 29.6 percent.

26. *Joseph Tuckerman on the Elevation of the Poor: A Selection from his Reports as Minister at Large in Boston*, edited by E. E. Hale (New York: Arno Press and The New York Times, 1971 [rpt. 1874]), p. 85.

27. AICP, Seventh Annual Report (1850), p. 25. The emphasis appears in the text. Note that the phenomenon feared by Tuckerman and Hartley has reportedly come to pass in

response to more recent attempts to relieve poverty. Consider, for example, the following 1968 story from the *Wall Street Journal:* "A massive industry effort to help avert future riots in Detroit appears to be backfiring as hundreds—possibly thousands—of unemployed persons from out of state come to the city seeking work. The result: Some out-of-staters have failed to get a job, swelling the unemployment that many believe contributed to last July's riot. Others have snapped up jobs that might have gone to the city's own so-called hard-core unemployed." The story is quoted in Edward C. Banfield, *The Unheavenly City Revisited* (Boston: Little, Brown, 1974), p. 265.

28. AICP, Seventh Annual Report (1850), p. 25.

29. Hale, *Joseph Tuckerman,* p. 89.

30. AICP, "The Mistake" (1850), p. 4. This advice was also proffered in many AICP annual reports.

31. Robert H. Bremner, *From the Depths: The Discovery of Poverty in the United States* (New York: New York University Press, 1956), p. 38.

32. See Edward K. Spann, *The New Metropolis: New York City, 1840–1857* (New York: Columbia University Press, 1981), p. 78; and Rezneck, *Business Depressions,* p. 79. See also Rezneck, p. 123: "Ever since the depression of 1837, perhaps no American had been more acutely conscious of the problem of urban employment and poverty than Horace Greeley."

33. See Iver Bernstein, *The New York City Draft Riots: Their Significance for American Society and Politics in the Age of the Civil War* (New York: Oxford University Press, 1990), p. 180.

34. Quoted in Rezneck, *Business Depressions,* p. 78. Greeley is most famous today, of course, for supposedly offering the related piece of advice, "Go West, young man." Although Greeley obviously applauded the underlying sentiment, the words were actually not his: they were produced by an Indiana writer, and were only reprinted (and appropriately credited) in Greeley's *New York Tribune.* See Paul F. Boller, Jr., and John George, *They Never Said It: A Book of Fake Quotes, Misquotes, and Misleading Attributions* (New York: Oxford University Press, 1989), p. 43.

35. See Robert Ernst, *Immigrant Life in New York City 1825–1863* (Syracuse, N.Y.: Syracuse University Press, 1994 [rpt. 1949]), p. 34.

36. AICP, Sixteenth Annual Report (1859), p. 14.

37. Smith, *Wealth of Nations,* p. 140.

38. Ernst, p. 62. For a more general statement, see Stephan Thernstrom, *Poverty and Progress: Social Mobility in a Nineteenth Century City* (Cambridge, Mass.: Harvard University Press, 1964), pp. 87–88: "The telling objection which has been advanced against the famous 'safety valve' theory of the frontier applies here. Migrant laborers from the city rarely had the capital or the knowledge necessary to reap the benefits of the supply of 'free land' at the frontier."

39. "Emergency Relief in Times of Unemployment," in Richmond, *Long View,* p. 511.

40. Richmond, "Emergency Relief," p. 512.

41. Keyssar, *Out of Work,* p. 153.

42. Keyssar, *Out of Work,* pp. 156–166.

43. See, for example, Josephine Shaw Lowell, *Public Relief and Private Charity* (New York: Arno Press and The New York Times, 1971 [rpt. 1884]), p. 66: "Human nature is so constituted that no man can receive as a gift what he should earn by his own labor without a moral deterioration. . . . When [outdoor relief] has once been accepted, the barrier is broken down, and rarely, or never, thereafter, is the effort made to do without it."

44. Charles Loring Brace, "The Best Method of Founding Children's Charities in Towns and Villages," *PNCCC* 7 (1880): 231–232.

45. Brace, *The Dangerous Classes of New York and Twenty Years' Work among Them*, 3rd ed., with addenda (Montclair, N.J.: Patterson Smith, 1967 [rpt. 1880]), p. 96.

46. Brace, *Short Sermons to News Boys: With a History of the Formation of the News Boys' Lodging-House* (New York: Charles Scribner, 1866), p. 135.

47. AICP, "The Mistake" (1850), p. 3.

48. Hale, *Joseph Tuckerman*, p. 54.

49. "A Discourse on the Life and Character of the Rev. Joseph Tuckerman, D.D.," in *Works of William E. Channing*, p. 589. The eulogy was delivered in 1841. For other instances of Tuckerman's efforts to find jobs for the poor, see Daniel T. McColgan, *Joseph Tuckerman: Pioneer in American Social Work* (Washington, D.C.: Catholic University of America Press, 1940), pp. 97, 129, 155, and 170.

50. AICP, First Annual Report (1845), p. 29. The Visitor's Manual is printed as Appendix A to the First Annual Report, pp. 25–32.

51. AICP, Fourth Annual Report (1847), pp. 00–00. Hartley's biographer, his son, also speaks of the AICP's efforts "to assist [the poor] when practicable in obtaining employment." See Isaac Smithson Hartley, ed., *Memorial of Robert Milham Hartley* (New York: Arno Press, 1976 [rpt. 1882]), p. 186.

52. AICP, Twenty-fifth Annual Report (1868), p. 52. On pp. 59–60, Hartley discusses a labor exchange established by New York's Commissioner of Emigration, which found employment for almost 13,000 immigrants between January and June of 1868.

53. See, for example, AICP, Fourth Annual Report (1847), p. 13: "If able-bodied and idle, they should be compelled to work"; Sixth Annual Report (1849), p. 16: "The results to many, by coercing them to industry and self-reliance, have been beneficial."

54. For a discussion of employment agencies in mid-nineteenth century New York, see Ernst, *Immigrant Life*, pp. 64–65.

55. Quoted in Lilian Brandt, *Growth and Development of AICP and COS (A Preliminary and Exploratory Review)* (New York: Community Service Society of New York, 1942), p. 105.

56. Stewart, *Philanthropic Work*, p. 145. The statement appears in an 1883 essay, "Duties of Friendly Visitors."

57. Stewart, *Philanthropic Work*, p. 147. The statement appears in "Duties of Friendly Visitors."

58. Warner, *American Charities*, p. 388.

59. Warner, *American Charities*, pp. 39, 41.

60. Warner, *American Charities*, pp. 96–97. See also p. 41.

61. Keyssar, *Out of Work*, p. 154.

62. "Study of Methods Employed by the A.I.C.P. to Secure Work for Unemployed Applicants," p. 2. This unpublished memorandum is undated, but it appears to have been written in 1908. It is found in the folder "Unemployment Problems, 1908–1929, 1930–1933," in Box 16, Community Service Society Archives, Rare Book and Manuscript Library, Columbia University. The Community Service Society is the successor agency to New York's AICP and COS.

63. Keyssar, *Out of Work*, p. 154. See also Frances A. Kellor, *Out of Work: A Study of Unemployment* (New York: Arno Press and The New York Times, 1971 [rpt. 1915]), p. 298.

64. COS, Second Annual Report (1884), pp. 46–47.

65. For the failings of commercial employment agencies, see Edward T. Devine, *Report on the Desirability of Establishing an Employment Bureau in the City of New York* (New York: Charities Publication Committee, 1909), p. 12: "Their standards of integrity and efficiency are low, . . . their real service to employers and employees, except in a few occupations, and in the case of a few well conducted agencies, is exceedingly slight. Operated primarily for profit, they have a constant temptation to over-charge, to misrepresent, and to encourage frequent changes for the sake of the fee." On pp. 19–20 Devine went on to argue that want ads in the newspapers were equally misleading and unhelpful.

66. Devine, *Report on the Desirability*, p. 23. Devine's report culminated in the opening of the National Employment Exchange (a private, for-profit enterprise) in April 1909.

67. For a discussion of the limits of employment bureaus in general, see Paul T. Ringenbach, *Tramps and Reformers, 1873–1916: The Discovery of Unemployment in New York* (New York: Greenwood Press, 1973), pp. 135–160. For the failure of the National Employment Exchange in particular, see pp. 145–148.

68. See Riis, "Special Needs," p. 498: Unemployed workers "need to know where to look [to find jobs]. . . . Some agency is needed to bring the work and those who want it together under auspices that would inspire confidence on both sides."

69. See Dorothy G. Becker, "Exit Lady Bountiful: The Volunteer and the Professional Social Worker," *Social Service Review* 38 (1964): 62n.

70. On Addams's support for Hoover, see James Weber Linn, *Jane Addams: A Biography* (New York: Greenwood Press, 1968 [rpt. 1935]), pp. 282–283. Addams admired Hoover's work as a food administrator during World War I and supported Prohibition. See pp. 335, 364–368.

71. See Lowell, "Five Months' Work for the Unemployed in New York City," *Charities Review* 3 (1894): 323–342. For the total number of workers employed, see pp. 335–336.

72. Lowell, "Five Months' Work," pp. 325, 333.

73. Lowell, "Five Months' Work," pp. 325, 327, 331–332.

74. Lowell, "Five Months' Work" pp. 334–335.

75. Lowell, "Five Months' Work," p. 324.

76. Lowell, "Five Months' Work," p. 334.

77. Lowell, "Five Months' Work," p. 335.

78. Lowell, "Methods of Relief for the Unemployed," *Forum* 16 (1894): 659.

79. Quoted in Lowell, "Five Months' Work," p. 336, from an April 13, 1894, declaration by the East Side Relief-Work Committee.

80. Keyssar, *Out of Work*, p. 255. See also Leah Hannah Feder, *Unemployment Relief in Periods of Depression: A Study of Measures Adopted in Certain American Cities, 1857 through 1922* (New York: Russell Sage, 1936), pp. 336–337.

81. Michael B. Katz, *In the Shadow of the Poorhouse: A Social History of Welfare* (New York: Basic Books, 1986), pp. 68–69.

82. Lowell, "Labor Organization as Affected by Law," *Charities Review* 1 (1891): 6.

83. Lowell, "Methods of Relief," p. 658.

84. Stewart, *Philanthropic Work*, pp. 358–359. The statement appears in an 1889 letter.

85. Stewart, *Philanthropic Work*, p. 413. The statement appears in "The Living Wage," an 1898 address.

86. Quoted in Joan Waugh, *Unsentimental Reformer: The Life of Josephine Shaw Lowell* (Cambridge, Mass.: Harvard University Press, 1997), p. 200. Lowell's statement appeared in the *New York Times*, March 22, 1895.

87. Rodgers, *Work Ethic*, p. 106.

88. Roy Rosenzweig, *Eight Hours for What We Will: Workers and Leisure in an Industrial City, 1870–1920* (New York: Cambridge University Press, 1983), p. 46. The estimate is taken from a 1960 work, Clarence Long's *Wages and Earnings in the United States, 1860–1890.* See also the summary of the evidence in Atack and Passell, *New Economic View,* pp. 536–537: "Wages grew somewhat more rapidly after 1860 than before. For example, between 1860 and 1890 the annual rate of growth of money wages in manufacturing was between 1.3 and 1.4 percent per year. . . . The rate of growth of money wages accelerated further thereafter: between 1890 and 1926 wages approximately tripled—a growth rate of a little over 3 percent per year."

89. Stewart, *Philanthropic Work,* pp. 373–374. The statement appears in Lowell's "Paper Read at the First Public Meeting of the Working Women's Society," in 1888.

90. Quoted in Isaac Smithson Hartley, *Memorial of Robert Milham Hartley,* p. 343, from AICP, Twenty-Ninth Annual Report (1872). For Hartley's attack on New York labor unions that advocated shortening the work day to eight hours, see Bernstein, *New York City Draft Riots,* p. 255.

91. Lowell, "Houses of Refuge for Women: Their Purposes, Management and Possibilities," *Proceedings of the New York State Conference of Charities and Correction* 1 (1900): 255.

92. Michael B. Katz, *Improving Poor People: The Welfare State, the "Underclass," and Urban Schools as History* (Princeton, N.J.: Princeton University Press, 1995), pp. 3–4.

93. See, for example, Harry Gene Levine, "Temperance and Prohibition in America," in Griffith Edwards, Awni Arif, and Jerome Jaffe, eds., *Drug Use and Misuse: Cultural Perspectives* (London and New York: Croom Helm and St. Martin's Press, 1983), p. 187: "From the beginning, temperance ideology contained a powerful strand of fantasy. Temperance thought offered an almost complete explanation for all social problems, . . . offer[ing] a total cause: the demonic substance—and a total solution: abstinence—for very real social and economic problems."

94. Thus the political scientist Thomas Halper has noted that charity reformers' moral critique of drinking "is bound to offend the modern reader, who has rechristened the drinking problem 'alcoholism' and discussed methods of treating the illness at innumerable cocktail parties." See Halper, "The Poor as Pawns: The New 'Deserving Poor' and the Old," *Polity* 6 (1973): 73.

95. *Joseph Tuckerman on the Elevation of the Poor: A Selection from His Reports as Minister at Large in Boston,* edited by E. E. Hale (New York: Arno Press and The New York Times, 1971 [rpt. 1874]), pp. 119–120.

96. Joseph Tuckerman, *The Principles and Results of the Ministry at Large in Boston* (Boston: James Munroe and Co., 1838), p. 166.

97. John Koren, *Economic Aspects of the Liquor Problem: An Investigation Made for the Committee of Fifty under the Direction of Henry W. Farnam* (Boston: Houghton Mifflin, 1899), pp. 43–44.

98. Koren, *Economic Aspects,* p. 15. See also pp. 45–46: the investigators were enjoined "to give a case the benefit of reasonable doubt; . . . to give intemperance as the cause of distress [only] when, aside from other contributing causes, it appears sufficient to have produced want; not to regard the expenditure of a portion of the daily wage for liquor, if unaccompanied by habitual drunkenness or incapacity for work, as the cause of distress, unless such expenditure produce[d] want for the family while a daily wage [was] being earned."

99. Koren, *Economic Aspects,* pp. 13–14. For a discussion of the discrepancy with earlier, higher estimates, see pp. 11–13. The precise figure of 25.06 percent appears on p. 96.

100. Amos G. Warner, *American Charities: A Study in Philanthropy and Economics* (New York: Arno Press and The New York Times, 1971 [rpt. 1894]), p. 60. On the other hand, focussing on paupers tended to understate the harm done to the poor by drinking; Warner believed that it did more harm among the working poor. See p. 61: "The ravages of intemperance are most plainly to be traced in classes distinctly above the pauper class. It is among artisans and those capable of earning good wages that the most money is spent for alcohol, and the most vitality burnt out by it. The man that has become a pauper does not find it easy, for one thing, to get liquor; and his vitality is apt to be so low that the exhilaration to be had from alcohol is not as much craved as by one with greater remaining strength." On the discrepancy between Warner's findings and those of the Committee of Fifty, see Koren, *Economic Aspects*, p. 47.

101. Lilian Brandt, "Alcoholism and Social Problems," *Survey* 25 (October 1, 1910), p. 18. The *Survey* was an influential journal devoted to social problems and their solutions; it evolved out of the New York COS publication *Charities Review*.

102. Koren, *Economic Aspects*, p. 23. Cf. p. 80: "The representatives of the hardest-drinking foreign nationalities, Irish, Scotch, Canadian, etc., are the first to acquire citizenship. A large part of the aliens, on the contrary, is made up of the more temperate nationalities, Russian Hebrews, Italians, Austrians, Poles."

103. The figures are taken from Table A1.1 in W. J. Rorabaugh, *The Alcoholic Republic: An American Tradition* (New York: Oxford University Press, 1979), p. 224.

104. Rorabaugh, *Alcoholic Republic*, pp. 95–97.

105. Rorabaugh, *Alcoholic Republic*, pp. 98–100.

106. Rorabaugh, *Alcoholic Republic*, pp. 77–80.

107. Ian R. Tyrrell, *Sobering Up: From Temperance to Prohibition in Antebellum America, 1800–1860* (New York: Greenwood Press, 1979), pp. 8, 107.

108. Rorabaugh, *Alcoholic Republic*, pp. 84–85, 90.

109. Tyrrell, "Temperance and Economic Change in the Antebellum North," in Jack S. Blocker, Jr., ed., *Alcohol, Reform and Society: The Liquor Issue in Social Context* (New York: Greenwood Press, 1979), pp. 51, 53.

110. Rorabaugh, *Alcoholic Republic*, p. 151.

111. Rorabaugh, *Alcoholic Republic*, pp. 200–201.

112. Rorabaugh, *Alcoholic Republic*, p. 15.

113. Rorabaugh, *Alcoholic Republic*, p. 89.

114. Rorabaugh, *Alcoholic Republic*, Table A1.1, p. 224.

115. Rorabaugh, *Alcoholic Republic*, Table A1.1, p. 224.

116. Joseph R. Gusfield, *Symbolic Crusade: Status Politics and the American Temperance Movement*, 2nd ed. (Urbana: University of Illinois Press, 1986), p. 132.

117. James Q. Wilson, "Crime and American Culture," *The Public Interest* 70 (Winter 1983), p. 30.

118. Katz, *In the Shadow of the Poorhouse: A Social History of Welfare in America* (New York: Basic Books, 1986), p. 59.

119. See Wilson, "Crime and American Culture," p. 24: "About the time Andrew Jackson was assuming the presidency, crime rates went up and stayed up through the 1830s and 1840s.... But then a striking thing happened, something totally at odds with conventional theories that urbanization or urban problems automatically produce crime.... So far as we can tell, the level of crime and public disorder in America began to decrease (or at least to level off) beginning about the middle of the nineteenth century and continuing, with some minor ups and downs, into the twentieth century. The great waves of foreign immigration,

the onset of rapid industrialization, the emergence of an urban working class—all the features of postbellum America that might have contributed to rising crime rates did not, in most of the cities that have been studied, have the predicted effect." Wilson (p. 27) ascribes the decline in crime to the efforts of moral reformers to "alter and strengthen human character."

120. "On the Elevation of the Laboring Classes," in *The Works of William E. Channing, D.D.* (Boston: American Unitarian Association, 1903), pp. 58–59. Channing delivered this address in 1840.

121. AICP, "The Mistake" (1850), p. 1.

122. Wilson, *The Moral Sense* (New York: Free Press, 1993), p. 94.

123. "Address on Temperance," in *Works of William E. Channing*, pp. 100–101. The address dates from 1837. The emphasis appears in the text.

124. AICP, Ninth Annual Report (1852), p. 28.

125. Norman H. Clark, *Deliver Us from Evil: An Interpretation of American Prohibition* (New York: W.W. Norton, 1976), p. 216.

126. Joseph Tuckerman, "An Essay on the Wages Paid to Females for Their Labour, in the Form of a Letter, from a Gentleman in Boston to His Friend in Philadelphia," in David J. Rothman and Sheila M. Rothman, eds., *Low Wages and Great Sins: Two Antebellum American Views on Prostitution and the Working Girl* (New York: Garland Publishing, 1987 [rpt. 1830]), p. 20.

127. AICP, Fourteenth Annual Report (1857), p. 17.

128. AICP, "First Report of a Committee on the Sanitary Condition of the Laboring Classes in the City of New-York, with Remedial Suggestions" (1853), p. 21.

129. Children's Aid Society, Third Annual Report (1856), p. 5.

130. Charles Loring Brace, *The Dangerous Classes of New York and Twenty Years' Work among Them*, 3rd ed., with addenda (Montclair, N.J.: Patterson Smith, 1967 [rpt. 1880)], pp. 68–69.

131. Daniel McColgan, *Joseph Tuckerman: Pioneer in American Social Work* (Washington, D.C.: Catholic University of America Press, 1940), p. 180.

132. Levine, "Temperance and Prohibition," p. 189.

133. Quoted in Hace Sorel Tishler, *Self-Reliance and Social Security, 1870–1917* (Port Washington, N.Y.: Kennikat, 1971), p. 50. Cf. Clark, *Deliver Us from Evil*, p. 11: "Among almost any representative group of social activists who worked for child labor laws, for the regulation of industrial working conditions, . . . most worked also for . . . the prohibition of the liquor traffic and the saloon."

134. Quoted in George G. Wittet, "Concerned Citizens: The Prohibitionists of 1883 Ohio," in *Alcohol, Reform and Society*, p. 125. For a comparable statement by the great Victorian analyst of poverty Charles Booth, see Koren, *Economic Aspects*, p. 125: "Drink . . . does not stand as apparent chief cause in as many cases [of pauperism] as sickness and old age; but if it were not for the drink, sickness and old age could be better met. Drink must therefore be accounted the most prolific of all causes; and it is the least necessary."

135. "Address to the Washington Temperance Society of Springfield, Illinois," in *Abraham Lincoln: Speeches and Writings, 1832–1858* (New York: Library of America, 1989), p. 81. The capitalization and the emphasis appear in the text. Lincoln delivered this address on Washington's birthday in 1842.

136. Bruce Laurie, *Working People of Philadelphia, 1800–1850* (Philadelphia: Temple University Press, 1980), pp. 40–41.

137. Laurie, *Working People*, p. 42.

138. Paul Boyer, *Urban Masses and Moral Order in America, 1820–1920* (Cambridge, Mass.: Harvard University Press, 1978), pp. 59–60.

139. Tyrrell, *Sobering Up*, p. 162.

140. Laurie, "'Nothing on Compulsion': Life Styles of Philadelphia Artisans, 1820–1850," *Labor History* 15 (1974): 364. See p. 345: in 1835 one group of mill hands declared that they had formed a temperance society "without the aid or countenance of the influential or talented members of the community." They claimed that work conditions, not the machinations of their employers, accounted for their decision: drink "confuse[d] the brain, cloud[ed] the mind, and warp[ed] the judgment," so that a drinker came to be "totally unfit to superintend the movements of complicated machinery." For evidence that temperance also appealed to workers in Boston and New York in the 1830s and 1840s, see Jill Siegel Dodd, "The Working Classes and the Temperance Movement in Ante-Bellum Boston," *Labor History* 19 (1978): 529; and Sean Wilentz, *Chants Democratic: New York City and the Rise of the American Working Class, 1788–1850* (New York: Oxford University Press, 1984), p. 324.

141. Laurie, *Working People*, p. 119.

142. Jack S. Blocker, Jr., *American Temperance Movements: Cycles of Reform* (Boston: Twayne Publishers, 1989), pp. 36–37.

143. Wilentz, *Chants Democratic*, p. 307.

144. Tyrrell, *Sobering Up*, pp. 169, 175.

145. Tyrrell, *Sobering Up*, p. 177. The efforts of Progressive reformers to decrease drinking by providing diversions ranging from social clubs and coffee houses to gymnasiums and night-school classes are summarized in Raymond Calkins, *Substitutes for the Saloon: An Investigation Originally Made for the Committee of Fifty*, 2nd ed. (New York: Arno Press, 1971 [rpt. 1919]).

146. Wilentz, *Chants Democratic*, p. 312.

147. Wilentz, *Chants Democratic*, pp. 311–312.

148. Tyrrell, *Sobering Up*, p. 206.

149. Tyrrell, *Sobering Up*, p. 201.

150. For an analysis of Hartley's evolution along these lines, see William H. Allen, *Efficient Democracy* (New York: Dodd, Mead and Co., 1907), pp. 148–149: "Behind drunkenness and irreligion Hartley found squalor, disease and ignorance that the community could prevent, but before which the immigrant mother and father were helpless even when religious and temperate. . . . Determined to get behind and beneath the causes that engendered alcoholism and other social evils, he organized in 1843 an association [the AICP] to go to the poor prepared to give . . . help fitted to their need." Allen was one of Hartley's successors as chief administrator of the AICP.

151. Wilentz, *Chants Democratic*, p. 308; Tyrrell, *Sobering Up*, p. 170.

152. Paul Faler, "Cultural Aspects of the Industrial Revolution: Lynn, Massachusetts, Shoemakers and Industrial Morality, 1826–1860," *Labor History* 15 (1974): 392–393. On the prevalence of temperance among radical workers, see also Tyrrell, *Sobering Up*, p. 209; Wilentz, *Chants Democratic*, p. 155; and Laurie, *Working People*, pp. 71–72, 175.

153. Quoted in Blocker, *American Temperance Movements*, p. 69.

154. James H. Timberlake, *Prohibition and the Progressive Movement, 1900–1920* (Cambridge, Mass.: Harvard University Press, 1963), p. 82.

155. Timberlake, *Prohibition*, pp. 83–84.

156. Timberlake, *Prohibition*, p. 89.

157. Timberlake, *Prohibition*, p. 92.

158. Hale, *Joseph Tuckerman*, p. 155. The emphasis appears in the text.

159. Quoted in Isaac Smithson Hartley, ed., *Memorial of Robert Milham Hartley* (New York: Arno Press, 1976 [rpt. 1882]), p. 126.

160. Isaac Hartley, *Memorial*, p. 125.

161. Tyrrell, *Sobering Up*, p. 275.

162. My interpretation of prohibition as a progressive reform is indebted to Timberlake, *Prohibition*. See especially p. 2: "If the Progressive Movement was nourished on a belief in the moral law, so was prohibition, which sought to remove from commerce an article that was believed to despoil man's reason and undermine the foundation of religion and representative government. . . . If progressivism represented a quickening of the humanitarian impulse, manifested in redoubled efforts of philanthropists and social workers to banish crime, poverty, and disease from the environment, prohibition was an effort to eliminate one factor that caused them. And, finally, if progressivism sought to improve the status of the lower classes by direct legislation, prohibition sought to uplift them by the same means."

163. J. C. Burnham, "New Perspectives on the Prohibition 'Experiment' of the 1920's," *Journal of Social History* 2 (1968): 64. The estimate that working-class drinking was cut in half derives from Clark Warburton's 1933 study (commissioned by Prohibition opponents), *The Economic Results of Prohibition*.

164. Brace, *Dangerous Classes*, p. 67.

165. Brace, *Dangerous Classes*, pp. 71–72.

166. Josephine Shaw Lowell, *Public Relief and Private Charity* (New York: Arno Press and The New York Times, 1971 [rpt. 1884]), p. 78.

167. See Joan Waugh, *Unsentimental Reformer: The Life of Josephine Shaw Lowell* (Cambridge, Mass.: Harvard University Press, 1997), pp. 223, 228.

168. Mary E. Richmond, *Friendly Visiting among the Poor: A Handbook for Charity Workers* (Montclair, N.J.: Patterson Smith, 1969 [rpt. 1899]), p. 61.

169. Richmond, *Friendly Visiting*, pp. 57–58.

170. Katz, *Improving Poor People*, p. 168.

171. See Robert Coit Chapin, *The Standard of Living among Workingmen's Families in New York City* (New York: Charities Publication Committee, 1909). For the total number of families and the number in each ethnic group, see pp. 38–39. For the results concerning expenditures for alcohol, see pp. 134, 147.

172. On the potential for unreliability, see Chapin, *Standard of Living*, pp. 18, 30–31, 133–134, and 221. On the whole, Chapin believed that the figures for drinking at home (as opposed to drinking away from home) were reasonably reliable. For a discussion of the unreliability of information about expenditures for alcohol in an 1875 budget study by the Massachusetts Bureau of Statistics of Labor (MBSL), see Daniel Horowitz, *The Morality of Spending: Attitudes toward the Consumer Society in America, 1875–1940* (Baltimore: Johns Hopkins University Press, 1985), p. 17.

173. For a similar judgment drawing on other budget studies, see Blocker, *American Temperance Movements*, p. 69: "Liquor was neither an omnipresent nor a dominant part of working-class life." An 1889 U.S. Bureau of Labor survey of 1600 working-class families in the northeast found that only two-fifths of Irish-headed families (and one-third of families headed by American-born fathers) reported expenditures on alcoholic beverages. An 1891 USBL survey of 1200 families found that 57 percent reported such expenditures, which averaged slightly over 3 percent of annual income.

174. Chapin, *Standard of Living*, p. 221.

175. Chapin, *Standard of Living*, Table 72, p. 148.

176. Chapin, *Standard of Living*, p. 131.

177. Chapin, *Standard of Living*, p. 249. For comparable results from the MBSL 1875 survey of 397 families (some with foreign-born and some with American-born fathers), see Horowitz, *Morality of Spending*, pp. 14 ("the MBSL report concluded that 'expenses on account of bad habits or its twin evil of extravagance were kept at a very modest and creditable minimum'") and 24 ("in no case was self-indulgence, laziness, or drunkenness given as the cause of unemployment or difficulty").

178. Chapin, *Standard of Living*, p. 135.

179. Roy Rosenzweig, *Eight Hours for What We Will: Workers and Leisure in an Industrial City, 1870–1920* (New York: Cambridge University Press, 1983), p. 46. The survey showed that "the best paid workers were 50 percent more likely to purchase 'indulgences' like alcohol and tobacco than those at the bottom of the income scale." For another argument correlating increased expenditures on alcohol with increased prosperity (drawing on a comparison of the 1889 survey with one from 1901), see John Modell, "Patterns of Consumption, Acculturation, and Family Income Strategies in Late Nineteenth-Century America," in Tamara K. Hareven and Maris A. Vinovskis, eds., *Family and Population in Nineteenth-Century America* (Princeton, N.J.: Princeton University Press, 1978), p. 214.

180. Blocker, *American Temperance Movements*, pp. 109–110. For an intriguing argument that the experience of immigration itself often tended to promote temperance (because of the need for restraints in newly formed communities), see Marcus Lee Hansen, *The Immigrant in American History* (Cambridge, Mass.: Harvard University Press, 1940), pp. 97–128.

181. Jane Addams, *Democracy and Social Ethics* (Cambridge, Mass.: Harvard University Press, 1964 [rpt. 1907]), pp. 31, 40. *Democracy and Social Ethics* was originally published in 1902. I return to Addams's critique of thrift in Chapter 4 below.

182. Mary Willcox Brown, *The Development of Thrift* (New York: Macmillan, 1899), p. 2.

183. Brown, *Development of Thrift*, p. 4.

184. Mary E. Richmond, *Friendly Visiting among the Poor: A Handbook for Charity Workers* (Montclair, N.J.: Patterson Smith, 1969 [rpt. 1899]), pp. 108–110.

185. Brown, *Development of Thrift*, p. 5.

186. See Michael Sherraden, *Assets and the Poor: A New American Welfare Policy* (Armonk, N.Y.: M. E. Sharpe, 1991), pp. 297–300. I discuss his policy proposal—and the experiments in implementing it—in Chapter 8 below.

187. Sherraden, *Assets and the Poor*, pp. 147–161.

188. Sherraden, *Assets and the Poor*, pp. 167–168.

189. Sherraden, *Assets and the Poor*, p. 213.

190. Sherraden, *Assets and the Poor*, p. 149.

191. Brown, *Development of Thrift*, p. 7.

192. Richmond, *Friendly Visiting*, pp. 109–110.

193. Brown, *Development of Thrift*, p. 5. The emphasis appears in the text.

194. Richmond, *Friendly Visiting*, p. 119.

195. I discuss the moral reformers' advice on how to spend wisely below, in Section E of this chapter.

196. Brown, *Development of Thrift*, p. 17.

197. Brown, *Development of Thrift*, p. 30.

198. Richmond, *Friendly Visiting*, p. 111.

199. AICP, Seventh Annual Report (1850), p. 20.

200. William Rhinelander Stewart, *The Philanthropic Work of Josephine Shaw Lowell*

Containing a Biographical Sketch of Her Life Together with a Selection of Her Public Papers and Private Letters (Montclair, N.J.: Patterson Smith, 1974 [rpt 1911]), pp. 147–148. The quotation appears in an 1883 essay, "Duties of Friendly Visitors." The emphasis is mine.

201. *Joseph Tuckerman on the Elevation of the Poor: A Selection from His Reports as Minister at Large in Boston,* edited by E. E. Hale (New York: Arno Press and The New York Times, 1971 [rpt. 1874]), p. 105.

202. Josephine Shaw Lowell, *Public Relief and Private Charity* (New York: Arno Press and The New York Times, 1971 [rpt. 1884]), pp. 109–110.

203. Quoted in David M. Tucker, *The Decline of Thrift in America: Our Cultural Shift from Saving to Spending* (New York: Praeger, 1991), p. 163.

204. Brown, *Development of Thrift,* pp. 33, 35.

205. See, for example, COS, Thirteenth Annual Report (1894), p. 47: "Property owners are not found among mobs seeking violence and disorder, nor do the provident classes favor intemperance and crime." The context for this remark is the COS attempt to encourage the small savings of the poor through its Penny Provident Fund (discussed below).

206. Quoted in Tucker, *Decline of Thrift,* p. 39.

207. "Address of the Philadelphia Saving Fund Society to the Public," quoted in George Alter, Claudia Goldin, and Elyce Rotella, "The Savings of Ordinary Americans: The Philadelphia Saving Fund Society in the Mid-Nineteenth Century," *Journal of Economic History* 54 (1994): 735–736. The capitalization and the emphases appear in the text.

208. Quoted in Alan L. Olmstead, *New York City Mutual Savings Banks, 1819–1861* (Chapel Hill: University of North Carolina Press, 1976), p. 14.

209. W. J. Rorabaugh, *The Alcoholic Republic: An American Tradition* (New York: Oxford University Press, 1979), p. 204.

210. Charles Loring Brace, *The Dangerous Classes of New York and Twenty Years' Work among Them,* 3rd ed., with addenda (Montclair, N.J.: Patterson Smith, 1967 [rpt. 1880]), p. 388.

211. Brace, *Dangerous Classes,* p. 394.

212. The savings bank is discussed in Brace, *Short Sermons to News Boys: With a History of the Formation of the News Boys' Lodging-House* (New York: Charles Scribner, 1866), pp. 26–28.

213. Quoted in Lilian Brandt, *The Charity Organization Society of the City of New York, 1882–1907* (New York: United Charities Building, 1907), p. 15.

214. Brandt, *Charity Organization Society,* p. 29.

215. Brown, *Development of Thrift,* p. 45.

216. COS, Eleventh Annual Report (1892), p. 20.

217. COS, Seventh Annual Report, (1888), p. 49.

218. Brown, *Development of Thrift,* pp. 46, 52, 67.

219. Stewart, *Philanthropic Work,* p. 137.

220. COS, Eleventh Annual Report (1882), p. 21.

221. "On Preaching the Gospel to the Poor: Charge at the Ordination of Charles F. Barnard and Frederick T. Gray, as Ministers at Large, in Boston," in *The Works of William E. Channing D.D.* (Boston: American Unitarian Association, 1903), p. 91. No date is given for this address.

222. James P. Smith, *Unequal Wealth and Incentives to Save* (Santa Monica, Calif.: RAND, 1995), pp. 17–18. The median household wealth for married couples was $132,200, compared with $7,600 for those who were separated, $33,670 for those who were divorced, $42,275 for those who were widowed, and $35,000 for those who had never married. These

findings derive from a 1993 National Institute on Aging survey of 7,600 households with heads aged 51–61.

223. AICP, Twelfth Annual Report (1855), p. 18.

224. AICP, Eighteenth Annual Report (1861), pp. 15–16.

225. AICP, Twenty-Ninth Annual Report (1872), p. 70.

226. See, for example, Olmstead, *New York City Mutual Savings Banks*, p. 64; Tucker, *Decline of Thrift*, p. 42; and Alter, Goldin, and Rotella, "Savings of Ordinary Americans," p. 739.

227. See Stephan Thernstrom, *Poverty and Progress: Social Mobility in a Nineteenth Century City* (Cambridge, Mass.: Harvard University Press, 1964), p. 127.

228. See Robert Coit Chapin, *The Standard of Living among Workingmen's Families in New York City* (New York: Charities Publication Committee, 1909), pp. 30–31, 266; and Tucker, *Decline of Thrift*, p. 51.

229. Thernstrom, *Poverty and Progress*, pp. 126–127.

230. Thernstrom, *Poverty and Progress*, pp. 128–129.

231. Thernstrom, *Poverty and Progress*, p. 204. Thernstrom discusses "the question of representativeness" on pp. 192–206.

232. Olmstead, *New York City Mutual Savings Banks*, p. 71; see also pp. 51–53.

233. Alter, Goldin, and Rotella, "Savings of Ordinary Americans," pp. 738, 742, 765.

234. Alexander Keyssar, *Out of Work: The First Century of Unemployment in Massachusetts* (New York: Cambridge University Press, 1986), p. 157.

235. Brown, *Development of Thrift*, p. 36.

236. Brown, *Development of Thrift*, pp. 74, 89–90.

237. Brown, *Development of Thrift*, p. 174.

238. Tucker, *Decline of Thrift*, p. 51.

239. Brown, *Development of Thrift*, pp. 155–156.

240. I. M. Rubinow, *Social Insurance: With Special Reference to American Conditions* (New York: Arno Press and The New York Times, 1969 [rpt. 1913]), p. 419.

241. Rubinow, *Social Insurance*, pp. 419, 424.

242. Brown, *Development of Thrift*, p. 37.

243. Olmstead, *New York City Mutual Savings Banks*, p. 196.

244. Alter, Goldin, and Rotella, "Savings of Ordinary Americans," p. 736. See also p. 766.

245. Brown, *Development of Thrift*, p. 36. This discrepancy is reduced but not eliminated when one factors in the existence of some 311 "stock savings banks" in the southern, western, and Pacific states.

246. Quoted in Tucker, *Decline of Thrift*, p. 52.

247. Since I am arguing that institutional arrangements facilitated saving by the poor in the past, it is worth noting that Sherraden implicitly blames the collapse of those institutional arrangements for the historical decline in thrifty behavior by the poor. See *Assets and the Poor*, p. 130: "Institutions for saving, by and large, no longer serve the poor. During the early part of this century, the poor often had savings accounts. For example, we can recall the Penny Savings Bank of New York, and its successor, the Dime Savings Bank, which still exists, but no longer seeks deposits of dimes. Today, most banks and savings and loans have left poor neighborhoods. The ones that remain are not very interested in small depositors." He concludes (pp. 299–300) that "the United States would do well to re-create savings mechanisms for the poor in the form of . . . poor people's banks, postal savings, or other institutional arrangements that offer both convenient access and strong incentives to save."

248. Quoted in Tucker, *Decline of Thrift*, p. 49.

249. COS, Fifteenth Annual Report (1897), p. 25.

250. Rubinow, *Social Insurance*, p. 39.

251. Rubinow, *Social Insurance*, p. 41.

252. Brown, *Development of Thrift*, p. 180.

253. Brown, *Development of Thrift*, p. 153.

254. Brace's support for social insurance goes unmentioned in the extant biography, compiled by his daughter Emma Brace: *The Life of Charles Loring Brace Chiefly Told in His Own Letters*. In all likelihood his support has subsequently been ignored because he manifested it in a book ostensibly devoted to religion rather than social welfare: *Gesta Christi: Or a History of Humane Progress under Christianity*. Hence Brace's advocacy of social insurance may well be unknown to historians of social welfare, who understandably would focus primarily on writings of his that are apparently more relevant to their concerns.

255. See Roy Lubove, *The Struggle for Social Security, 1900–1935* (Cambridge, Mass.: Harvard University Press, 1968), p. 25: "Before the establishment of the American Association for Labor Legislation in 1906, social insurance was not a serious subject of debate in the United States."

256. See Lubove, *Struggle for Social Security*, p. 28.

257. Brace, *Gesta Christi: Or a History of Humane Progress under Christianity*, 4th ed. (New York: A. C. Armstrong and Son, 1884), pp. 416–417. The identical passage can be found in the second edition, published in 1883. I have not seen the first edition, but Brace's introduction to the later editions gives every reason to suppose that the discussion of social insurance also appeared in the 1882 original edition.

258. On these points, see Hace Sorel Tishler, *Self-Reliance and Social Security, 1870–1917* (Port Washington, N.Y.: Kennikat, 1971), pp. 192–193, 199. See in particular p. 193: "To ask the individual to pay his fair share [for insurance] did no violence to his self-reliance. To have asked him to pay more [by ignoring the social as opposed to individual causes of, say, industrial accidents, hence society's responsibility to pay for part of the costs resulting from them] would have pauperized society."

259. Thernstrom, *Poverty and Progress*, p. 136.

260. Thernstrom, *Poverty and Progress*, pp. 136–137.

261. Brown, *Development of Thrift*, pp. 28–29.

262. Chapin, *Standard of Living*, pp. 129, 131. For critiques in other budget studies of the underconsumption that facilitated saving by the poor, see Daniel Horowitz, *The Morality of Spending: Attitudes toward the Consumer Society in America, 1875–1940* (Baltimore: Johns Hopkins University Press, 1985), pp. 22, 65.

263. Jacob A. Riis, *How the Other Half Lives: Studies among the Tenements of New York* (New York: Dover Publications, 1971), p. 86. *How the Other Half Lives* was originally published in 1890.

264. For a discussion of the extent to which Riis can fairly be charged with anti-Semitism, see Richard Tuerk, "Jacob Riis and the Jews," *New-York Historical Society Quarterly* 63 (1979): 179–201. In Tuerk's view, Riis's treatment of the Jews was indeed anti-Semitic in *How the Other Half Lives*, but came to be fairer and more favorable in his later writings. See also Lewis Fried, "Jacob Riis and the Jews: The Ambivalent Quest for Community," *American Studies* 20 (1979): 5–25. For a more general discussion of Riis's ethnocentrism that provides a qualified defense of his attitudes toward immigrants, see Joel Schwartz, "The Moral Environment of the Poor," *The Public Interest* 103 (Spring, 1991), pp. 24–26.

265. Riis, *How the Other Half Lives*, pp. 156–158.

266. See, for example, Tishler, *Self-Reliance and Social Security*, p. 96; and Tucker, *Decline of Thrift*, pp. 101, 108–109, 112.

267. Riis, *How the Other Half Lives*, p. 88.

268. Thernstrom, *Poverty and Progress*, p. 125.

269. Thernstrom, *Poverty and Progress*, p. 131.

270. Thernstrom, *Poverty and Progress*, pp. 163–164.

271. Charles Loring Brace, *The Dangerous Classes of New York and Twenty Years' Work among Them*, 3rd ed., with addenda (Montclair, N.J.: Patterson Smith, 1967 [rpt. 1880]), pp. 39, 41.

272. Brace, *Dangerous Classes*, p. 39.

273. Brace, *Dangerous Classes*, pp. 41–42.

274. The intellectual kinship between Brace and Moynihan is touched on in Francesco Cordasco, "Charles Loring Brace and the Dangerous Classes: Historical Analogues of the Urban Black Poor," *Journal of Human Relations* 20 (1972): 379–386. Cordasco does not, however, examine their common concern about family instability, which is my focus here.

275. Daniel Patrick Moynihan, "A Family Policy for the Nation," in Lee Rainwater and William L. Yancey, eds., *The Moynihan Report and the Politics of Controversy* (Cambridge, Mass.: MIT Press, 1967), pp. 392–393. This article was originally published in the September 18, 1965, issue of *America*; it is reprinted in the book in its entirety, pp. 385–394.

276. Brace, *Dangerous Classes*, p. 405.

277. See Daniel Patrick Moynihan, "The Negro Family: The Case for National Action" (that is, the Moynihan report), reprinted in Yancey, *Moynihan Report*, p. 54. The Moynihan report was originally released in March 1965; it is reprinted in the book in its entirety, pp. 41–124.

278. See *Vital Statistics of the United States 1992*. Vol. I: *Natality* (Washington, D.C.: U.S. Department of Health and Human Services, 1996), Table 1.85, p. 219. In 1992, 672.7 of every 1,000 live births to black women in New York City were to unmarried mothers.

279. See *Vital Statistics of the united States 1992*. Vol. I: *Natality*, Tables 1.25, p. 56, and 1.85, p. 219. In 1992 there were 131,742 births in New York, of which 60,798—46 percent—were to unmarried mothers. Brace's New York, of course, consisted of what is now Manhattan (although portions of the Bronx were incorporated into the city in 1874). But restricting the comparison to Manhattan only sharpens the contrast between his time and ours: in 1992, 48 percent of Manhattan births (10,374 out of 21,682) were to unmarried mothers.

280. "Ministry for the Poor," in *The Works of William E. Channing, D.D.* (Boston: American Unitarian Association, 1903), p. 74. This address was delivered in 1835.

281. Herbert J. Gans, "Escaping from Poverty: A Comparison of the Immigrant and Black Experience," in *People, Plans, and Policies: Essays on Poverty, Racism, and Other National Urban Problems* (New York: Columbia University Press and Russell Sage Foundation, 1991), p. 282. This essay was originally written in 1968.

282. Herbert G. Gutman, *Power and Culture: Essays on the American Working Class* (New York: New Press, 1987), pp. 256–258.

283. Josephine Shaw Lowell, *Public Relief and Private Charity* (New York: Arno Press and The New York Times, 1971 [rpt. 1884]), p. 73.

284. Quoted in Mary E. Richmond, *The Good Neighbor in the Modern City* (Philadelphia: J. B. Lippincott Co., 1908), p. 87.

285. Stephan Thernstrom, "Poverty in Historical Perspective," in Moynihan, ed., *On*

Understanding Poverty: Perspectives from the Social Sciences (New York: Basic Books, 1969), pp. 179–180.

286. Michael B. Katz, *Poverty and Policy in American History* (New York: Academic Press, 1983), p. 198.

287. AICP, Twenty-Ninth Annual Report (1872), p. 40.

288. Lilian Brandt, *Five Hundred and Seventy-Four Deserters and Their Families: A Descriptive Study of Their Characteristics and Circumstances* (New York: Arno Press and The New York Times, 1972 [rpt. 1905]), pp. 9–10.

289. Brandt, *Five Hundred and Seventy-Four Deserters*, p. 15.

290. Brandt, *Five Hundred and Seventy-Four Deserters*, p. 25.

291. Brandt, *Five Hundred and Seventy-Four Deserters*, p. 36.

292. Brandt, *Five Hundred and Seventy-Four Deserters*, p. 45.

293. Brandt, *Five Hundred and Seventy-Four Deserters*, p. 28.

294. Brandt, *Five Hundred and Seventy-Four Deserters*, p. 29.

295. Brandt, *Five Hundred and Seventy-Four Deserters*, p. 45.

296. Brandt, *Five Hundred and Seventy-Four Deserters*, p. 29.

297. Brandt, *Five Hundred and Seventy-Four Deserters*, pp. 54–55, 63.

298. Brandt, *Five Hundred and Seventy-Four Deserters*, p. 54.

299. Brandt, *Five Hundred and Seventy-Four Deserters*, p. 64.

300. See Richmond, "Married Vagabonds," in *The Long View: Papers and Addresses*, edited by Joanna C. Colcord and Ruth Z. S. Mann (New York: Russell Sage Foundation, 1930), pp. 69–76. The paper was originally published in 1895.

301. Richmond, *Friendly Visiting among the Poor: A Handbook for Charity Workers* (Montclair, N.J.: Patterson Smith, 1969 [rpt. 1899]), p. 45.

302. Richmond, "Charity and Homemaking," in *The Long View*, p. 79. "Charity and Homemaking" was a sequel to "Married Vagabonds"; it was originally published in 1897.

303. Richmond, *Friendly Visiting*, pp. 46–47. The emphasis appears in the text.

304. Richmond, "Married Vagabonds," p. 75. The emphasis appears in the text.

305. Richmond, "Charity and Homemaking," pp. 80–81.

306. Richmond, "Married Vagabonds," p. 72.

307. Richmond, "Charity and Homemaking," pp. 83–84. For other examples of the success of moral suasion, see "Married Vagabonds," p. 73.

308. Richmond, *Friendly Visiting*, p. 47.

309. Richmond, "Charity and Homemaking," p. 84.

310. Kathryn M. Neckerman, "The Emergence of 'Underclass' Family Patterns, 1900–1940," in Michael B. Katz, ed., *The "Underclass" Debate: Views from History* (Princeton, N.J.: Princeton University Press, 1993), pp. 204–205.

311. Neckerman, "Emergence of 'Underclass' Family Patterns," pp. 210–212.

312. Neckerman, "Emergence of 'Underclass' Family Patterns," pp. 213–214.

313. Neckerman, "Emergence of 'Underclass' Family Patterns," pp. 214–215. Cf. David Montgomery, *The Fall of the House of Labor: The Workplace, the State, and American Labor Activism, 1865–1925* (New York: Cambridge University Press, 1987): "Family ties among immigrants need not necessarily have involved much affection, but they did create social obligations that were violated only at the risk of provoking sharp community censure" (p. 89).

314. Brandt, *Five Hundred and Seventy-Four Deserters*, p. 54.

315. For a comparable argument, see Christopher Jencks, *Rethinking Social Policy:*

Race, Poverty, and the Underclass (New York: HarperPerennial, 1993): "According to [Charles] Murray, a woman who depends on the government suffers from latent poverty [that is, she would be below the poverty line in the absence of government transfer programs], while a woman who depends on a man does not. But unless a woman can support herself and her children from her own earnings, she is always dependent on someone ('one man away from welfare'). Murray assumes that AFDC has a worse effect on family life than Harold [the man in a hypothetical couple discussed by Murray in *Losing Ground*]. But that depends on Harold" (p. 86).

316. Neckerman, "Emergence of 'Underclass' Family Patterns," p. 215. On p. 211 Neckerman presents a table, drawn from Census data, charting the growth in employment by wives of manual workers between 1910 and 1940: in 1910, 17.5 percent of the wives of manual workers with no children were employed; by 1940 the figure had risen to 31.3 percent.

317. Quoted in Isaac Smithson Hartley, ed., *Memorial of Robert Milham Hartley* (New York: Arno Press, 1976 [rpt. 1882]), p. 331. Pages 327–339 contain an essay of Hartley's, "Female Labor: Its Defects, Difficulties, and Wants," which first appeared as part of the AICP's twenty-third annual report, for the year 1866.

318. Isaac Hartley, *Memorial of Robert Milham Hartley*, pp. 334–335.

319. Isaac Hartley, *Memorial of Robert Milham Hartley*, p. 336.

320. Isaac Hartley, *Memorial of Robert Milham Hartley*, p. 338. Ironically, one (unremunerated) occupation that was "exclusively monopolized by males" in Hartley's time, but which proved to be "peculiarly appropriate to females," was that of the volunteer friendly visitor to the poor. See Dorothy G. Becker, "The Visitor to the New York City Poor, 1843–1920," *Social Service Review* 35 (1961): "Each AICP district was led by an advisory committee of local residents who were expected to direct a corps of male volunteer visitors" (p. 384). Cf. Becker, "Exit Lady Bountiful: The Volunteer and the Professional Social Worker," *Social Service Review* 38 (1964): "Visiting was . . . commonly regarded [after the Civil War] as the appropriate avocation for a woman of wealth and leisure. . . . The socially acceptable 'career women' of the period were the widows and unmarried women trying to escape genteel poverty through the few avenues available—either the profession of teaching or white-collar jobs as saleswomen or clerks. These clerical workers became the charity agents of the new societies" (p. 60). As it happens, Hartley himself urged upper-class women to become friendly visitors. See AICP, Twenty-Second Annual Report (1865): "Will not the philanthropic women of New York emulate the example of their trans-Atlantic sisters in so noble a charity [i.e., friendly visiting]? . . . . This work . . . looks toward the social improvement of the masses in all that pertains to domestic life" (p. 61).

321. AICP, Twenty-Ninth Annual Report (1872), p. 40.

322. Lowell, *Public Relief*, p. 106; the quotation about widows appears on p. 102. For Richmond's fear of encouraging desertion, see *Friendly Visiting*, pp. 49–50.

323. Lowell, *Public Relief*, p. 104.

324. *On Character: Essays by James Q. Wilson* (Washington, D.C.: AEI Press, 1991), p. 22.

325. Lawrence M. Mead, *The New Politics of Poverty* (New York: Basic Books, 1992), p. 156.

326. In Chapters 7 and 8 I address the extent to which the defeatism of some among the contemporary poor creates difficulties for contemporary efforts to remoralize them.

327. *Joseph Tuckerman on the Elevation of the Poor: A Selection from His Reports as Minister at Large in Boston*, edited by E. E. Hale (New York: Arno Press and The New York Times, 1971 [rpt. 1874]), p. 25.

328. "A Discourse on the Life and Character of the Rev. Joseph Tuckerman, D.D.," in *The Works of William E. Channing, D.D.* (Boston: American Unitarian Association, 1903), p. 589. The eulogy was delivered in 1841.

329. Children's Aid Society, Third Annual Report (1856), p. 7. Note Brace's insistence on the secular character of his charity: the visitor is "not . . . a Missionary or Minister, but . . . a helper." As we will see in Chapter 3, the moral reformers were deeply religious individuals. Nevertheless, their efforts to assist the poor were in crucial respects secular.

330. AICP, Third Annual Report (1846), p. 17. The emphasis is mine.

331. AICP, Twenty-Seventh Annual Report (1870), p. 49.

332. AICP, Fourth Annual Report (1847), p. 25, Fifth Annual Report (1848), p. 19. In the second reference Hartley claims that its influence enabled many families to "exercise a wise forecast, improve their domestic habits, and become industrious and respectable." One visitor to the poor reported that forty-five families benefited from its counsel, and a second spoke of twenty-nine.

333. AICP, "The Economist" (1847), pp. 1, 3, 5, 6, 8, 9, 10, 11, 12.

334. Whatever the situation may have been in the 1840s, breadmaking was quite uncommon among New York's poor two generations later. See Robert Coit Chapin, *The Standard of Living among Workingmen's Families in New York City* (New York: Charities Publication Committee, 1909): "New York families such as those under consideration universally buy bread. Only 26 families out of [the] 318 [surveyed] reported making bread at home for the whole or a part of the year" (p. 132).

335. AICP, "The Economist," p. 8.

336. Stephan Thernstrom, *Poverty and Progress: Social Mobility in a Nineteenth Century City* (Cambridge, Mass.: Harvard University Press, 1964), pp. 67–68.

337. Dorothy G. Becker, "The Visitor to the New York City Poor, 1843–1920," *Social Service Review* 35 (1961): 394.

338. Kathleen Woodroofe, *From Charity to Social Work in England and the United States*, 2nd ed. (Toronto: University of Toronto Press, 1974), p. 97.

339. Woodroofe, *From Charity to Social Work*, p. 119.

340. Mary E. Richmond, *Friendly Visiting among the Poor: A Handbook for Charity Workers* (Montclair, N.J.: Patterson Smith, 1969 [rpt. 1899]), p. 42.

341. Richmond, *Friendly Visiting*, p. 97.

342. Dorothy G. Becker, "Exit Lady Bountiful: The Volunteer and the Professional Social Worker," *Social Service Review* 38 (1964): 59.

343. Becker, "Exit Lady Bountiful," p. 64n.

344. Evaluating friendly visitors would obviously have been an extremely subjective enterprise. The only evaluation that I know of was done by Zilpha D. Smith, an important charity worker in Boston, which had one of the most successful visitation programs of any charity organization society. Smith evaluated 201 visitors, rating 12 percent as excellent, 34 percent as good, 32 percent as fair, 5 percent as unproved, and 16 percent as poor. The visitors worked with an average of one and three-quarters families each. See "How to Do Personal Work and How to Get Others to Do It," the unpublished manuscript of a speech given by Smith to the New York Class in Practical Philanthropy, June 22, 1899, in the folder "Casework—'Friendly Visiting'—Zilpha D. Smith," Box 99, Community Service Society Archives, Rare Book and Manuscript Library, Columbia University. The Community Service Society was and is the successor agency to New York's AICP and COS.

345. See Frank Dekker Watson, *The Charity Organization Movement in the United States: A Study in American Philanthropy* (New York: Macmillan, 1922): "Friendly visiting

... was ... admitted to be the 'weak point of the charity organization society' in most places. ... By 1895, in one city with a population of nearly 300,000, a society thirteen years old had [no friendly visitors], while in another city with a population of over 200,000 a society eleven years old had given up this form of volunteer work after five years' trial" (pp. 271–272). The two prominent exceptions to this rule were Baltimore and Boston.

346. COS, Fifth Annual Report (1887), p. 38.

347. COS, Eighth Annual Report (1890), p. 44.

348. Richmond, *Friendly Visiting*, pp. 65–66.

349. Richmond, *Friendly Visiting*, pp. 124–125.

350. Richmond, *Friendly Visiting*, p. 65.

351. Paul Boyer, *Urban Masses and Moral Order in America, 1820–1920* (Cambridge, Mass.: Harvard University Press, 1978), p. 159.

352. Marian C. Putnam, "Friendly Visiting," *PNCCC* 14 (1887): 155.

353. S. O. Preston, in "Discussion on 'Personal Service,'" *Charities Review* 4 (1895): 483.

354. Becker, "Exit Lady Bountiful," p. 63. Becker notes that Lowell was among the advocates of using laborers and their wives as friendly visitors.

355. Quoted in Roy Lubove, *The Professional Altruist: The Emergence of Social Work as a Career, 1880–1930* (Cambridge, Mass.: Harvard University Press, 1965), p. 17.

356. Quoted in Alexander Keyssar, *Out of Work: The First Century of Unemployment in Massachusetts* (New York: Cambridge University Press, 1986), p. 157.

357. John Koren, *Economic Aspects of the Liquor Problem: An Investigation Made for the Committee of Fifty under the Direction of Henry W. Farnam* (New York: Houghton Mifflin, 1899), p. 227.

358. Thomas Sowell, *Ethnic America: A History* (New York: Basic Books, 1981), pp. 107, 113, 116.

359. Sowell, *Ethnic America*, p. 116.

360. Compare Aristotle, *Nicomachean Ethics*, Martin Ostwald, trans. (Indianapolis: Bobbs-Merrill, 1962), Book I, 1095b: "To be a competent student of what is right and just, . . . one must first have received a proper upbringing in moral conduct." For Aristotle as well, moral training provides answers to "how" questions, not "why" questions.

361. Compare Aristotle, *Nicomachean Ethics*, Book II, 1103b: "We are not conducting this inquiry in order to know what virtue is, but in order to become good, else there would be no advantage in studying it."

362. Quoted in Glenn C. Loury, "Uneconomical," *The New Republic*, June 29, 1998, p. 15. Loury describes the success of a home visitation program for expectant mothers in Elmira, New York: in the four years after they gave birth to a first child, the 400 mostly low-income participants in the program had a pregnancy rate that was 42 percent lower than the rate for a randomly selected control group of similar women. In Loury's assessment (p. 15), "The success of home visitation seems to be due to the fact that the nurses got the message across that becoming pregnant again is not desirable."

363. William Rhinelander Stewart, *The Philanthropic Work of Josephine Shaw Lowell Containing a Biographical Sketch of Her Life Together with a Selection of Her Public Papers and Private Letters* (Montclair, N.J.: Patterson Smith, 1974 [rpt. 1911]), pp. 215–216. The passage is taken from an 1898 paper, "The Evils of Investigation and Relief."

364. Amos G. Warner, *American Charities: A Study in Philanthropy and Economics* (New York: Arno Press and The New York Times, 1971 [rpt. 1894]), p. 302.

365. Quoted in Hace Sorel Tishler, *Self-Reliance and Social Security, 1870–1917* (Port Washington, N.Y.: Kennikat, 1971), p. 154.

366. Robert H. Bremner, *American Philanthropy*, 2nd ed. (Chicago: University of Chicago Press, 1988), p. 57.

3. Why Moral Reform Was Hard to Achieve

1. Gustave de Beaumont and Alexis de Tocqueville, *On the Penitentiary System in the United States and Its Application in France*, trans. Francis Lieber (Carbondale: Southern Illinois University Press, 1964 [rpt. 1833], p. 207. We know that Tocqueville and not Beaumont was responsible for the description of Tuckerman, because it appears in the authors' notes, which were written by Tocqueville. On the division of labor between Beaumont and Tocqueville in their co-authored work, see Seymour Drescher, *Dilemmas of Democracy: Tocqueville and Modernization* (Pittsburgh: University of Pittsburgh Press, 1968), pp. 130–131.

2. Eric C. Schneider, *In the Web of Class: Delinquents and Reformers in Boston, 1810s–1930s* (New York: New York University Press, 1992), pp. 19–20. For Schneider's critique of moral reform, see p. 191: "We continue to locate the urban crisis in the absence of moral fiber among the poor, and that means we will fail to address the [structural] source of that crisis as certainly as the reformers studied here did."

3. *Joseph Tuckerman on the Elevation of the Poor: A Selection from His Reports as Minister at Large in Boston*, edited by E. E. Hale (New York: Arno Press and The New York Times, 1971 [rpt. 1874]), p. 39.

4. Tuckerman, *The Principles and Results of the Ministry at Large in Boston* (James Munroe and Co., 1838), pp. 107–109.

5. Tuckerman, *Principles*, pp. 105–106. In all likelihood Tuckerman believed that the contrast in the rhetoric employed by successful and unsuccessful reformers reflected differing religious convictions. Tuckerman was a Unitarian who believed in human perfectibility; he probably doubted the capacity of Calvinists, who denied that all human beings could be regenerated, to promote moral reform with equal success. (Note that Hartley, whom I compare unfavorably to Tuckerman in the text immediately below, was not Unitarian but Presbyterian.) I briefly examine the split between Calvinists and Unitarians—and its impact on moral reform—in the biographical appendix at the end of the book, in the paragraph devoted to Tuckerman's friend and colleague William Ellery Channing.

6. See the manual for the AICP's visitors to the poor, which appears as Appendix A to the AICP's First Annual Report (1845), pp. 25–32. The quotation is taken from Article III, p. 26.

7. In fact, we do not have testimony—from Hartley or anyone else—about how he personally dealt with the poor: Hartley was a professional charity worker whose job was to run the AICP, not a volunteer visitor to the poor. But we do know what he said about the poor, if not to them—and it is reasonable to suppose that the volunteers who did the actual visiting would have taken their cue from Hartley's writings and sayings.

8. AICP, Ninth Annual Report (1852), p. 25.

9. Allen F. Davis, *Spearheads for Reform: The Social Settlements and the Progressive Movement, 1890–1914* (New York: Oxford University Press, 1967), p. 8. In the quotation Davis paraphrases Woods.

10. AICP, Eighth Annual Report (1851), p. 18.

11. In fairness to Hartley I should note that the Catholic clergy joined him in criticizing

the festive nature of Irish wakes. See Jay P. Dolan, *The Immigrant Church: New York's Irish and German Catholics, 1815–1865* (Baltimore: Johns Hopkins University Press, 1975): in 1827 New York's Bishop John Dubois complained that wakes were characterized by "frequent drinking instead of holy water, distasteful conversation instead of prayers"; and in 1861 the New York Provincial Council of Bishops attacked funeral celebrations that were "degraded into an exhibition of ostentatious and unseemly display, sometimes even into an occasion of revelry and rioting" (p. 61). Still, it is one thing for Catholic priests to criticize the practice of fellow Catholics; it is another thing for Protestant outsiders to do so.

12. AICP, "The Mistake" (1850), pp. 2–3. The emphasis appears in the text.

13. For a useful overview, see Thomas Sowell, *Ethnic America: A History* (New York: Basic Books, 1981), pp. 18–29. Sowell notes that "the 'laziness' or 'improvidence' of the Irish became a familiar refrain among contemporaries in Ireland—and later in America—and among sympathizers as well as critics, both scholarly and popular" (p. 18). He also mentions that "drunkenness was common," (p. 18) that "patterns of alcoholism and fighting brought over from Ireland persisted in the United States," (p. 26) and that "the poverty and improvidence of the Irish immigrants in America often reduced them to living on charity when hard times came" (p. 27). I treat this issue more extensively in Chapter 6.

14. Walter I. Trattner, *From Poor Law to Welfare State: A History of Social Welfare in America*, 5th ed. (New York: Free Press, 1994), p. 71.

15. For an illuminating discussion of Archbishop Hughes's work—beginning in the 1840s—aimed at moral reformation of the Irish Catholic poor of New York, see William J. Stern, "How Dagger John Saved New York's Irish," *City Journal* (Spring 1997): 84–105. See p. 95: Hughes "wanted to bring about an inner, moral transformation in [the Irish Catholic community], which he believed would solve their social problems in the end." The result of his labors was a drastic decline in the social pathologies of New York's Irish by the 1880s (p. 104). I discuss the increase in the religiosity of the Irish immigrant poor—who became better Catholics, thereby ironically increasing their commitment to the virtues that have historically been deemed "Protestant"—in Chapter 6.

16. See, for example, Jacqueline Jones, *The Dispossessed: America's Underclasses from the Civil War to the Present* (New York: Basic Books, 1992): "A junior high school counselor in Washington Highlands, a poor neighborhood in the District of Columbia, summed up the prevailing philosophy: 'It's not cool to be an A student. It's not cool to be a virgin. It's not cool to say you're a virgin. You shouldn't be on birth control'" (p. 280). Jones herself, it should be noted, strongly rejects the view that cultural pathologies are responsible for poverty. See p. 271: "The claim that ghetto life represented a bizarre subculture of pathology and social deviance not only objectified the black poor as 'others' but also missed larger [structural] issues." In Chapter 7 I examine the extent to which the fear of "acting white" complicates efforts to remoralize the black poor today.

17. David Matza, "The Disreputable Poor," in Reinhard Bendix and Seymour Martin Lipset, eds., *Class, Status, and Power: Social Stratification in Comparative Perspective*, 2nd ed. (New York: Free Press, 1966), p. 297.

18. Marvin Olasky, *The Tragedy of American Compassion* (Washington, D.C.: Regnery Publishing, 1992), pp. 8–9, 28.

19. Olasky, *Tragedy*, p. 124.

20. See Davis, *American Heroine: The Life and Legend of Jane Addams* (New York: Oxford University Press, 1973): "In the beginning [Addams] thought of Hull House as a religious institution. . . . Time eroded the religious atmosphere at Hull House and altered Jane Addams's personal faith until she became an agnostic, but the early years at Hull

House were dominated by the conviction that she was engaged in furthering Christ's mission on earth" (p. 74).

21. Quoted in John C. Farrell, *Beloved Lady: A History of Jane Addams' Ideas on Reform and Peace* (Baltimore: Johns Hopkins University Press, 1967), p. 61. The statement appears in a letter (dated March 13, 1889) to her sister Alice Addams Haldeman.

22. See Davis, *Spearheads*: "Settlement workers like . . . Jane Addams realized that in predominantly immigrant Catholic or Jewish neighborhoods the settlement sacrificed its chance to become an instrument for reform if it had a religious label" (p. 15).

23. Paul Boyer, *Urban Masses and Moral Order in America, 1820–1920* (Cambridge, Mass.: Harvard University Press, 1978), pp. 85–86.

24. Boyer, *Urban Masses*, p. 142.

25. Quoted in Lilian Brandt, *Growth and Development of AICP and COS (A Preliminary and Exploratory Review)* (New York: Community Service Society of New York, 1942), p. 106. On p. 107 Brandt adds that the second fundamental principle was amended in 1887: the words "or spiritual instruction" were dropped, because they had originally been included only to forestall charges of proselytism.

26. Tuckerman, *Principles*, p. 79.

27. Tuckerman, *Principles*, pp. 79–80. Tuckerman was evidently disappointed, though, by the Catholic response to his initiative. See p. 79: "Several years [ago] I sought and obtained an interview with the catholic [*sic*] Bishop upon this question; and proposed to him the appointment of a special ministry for visiting the families of the catholic poor. The Bishop agreed with me fully in respect to the desirableness of the object, and said he would appoint such a ministry when he could find the priests who could be spared for it. I suppose such priests have not yet been found; or at least, but a very insufficient number for the service." Nevertheless, Tuckerman's ecumenical initiative has won high praise from an unimpeachable Catholic source: his biographer, who was a Catholic priest. See Daniel McColgan, *Joseph Tuckerman: Pioneer in American Social Work* (Washington, D.C.: Catholic University of America Press, 1940), pp. 125–130.

28. AICP, Twentieth Annual Report (1863), pp. 31–32.

29. Carroll Smith-Rosenberg, *Religion and the Rise of the American City: The New York City Mission Movement, 1812–1870* (Ithaca, N.Y.: Cornell University Press, 1971), p. 258.

30. "An Abstract of the Secretary's Remarks at a Special Meeting of the Advisory Committees and Visitors of the Association for Improving the Condition of the Poor, Convened in the Hall of the Public School Edifice, New-York, March 3, 1847," p. 9.

31. Michael B. Katz, *Poverty and Policy in American History* (New York: Academic Press, 1983), p. 197.

32. Charles Loring Brace, *The Dangerous Classes of New York and Twenty Years' Work among Them*, 3rd ed., with addenda (Montclair, N.J.: Patterson Smith, 1967), pp. 44–45.

33. See Emma Brace, ed., *The Life of Charles Loring Brace Chiefly Told in His Own Letters* (New York: Arno Press, 1976 [rpt. 1894]), p. 171.

34. Of the more than 6,000 children placed by the Children's Aid Society in two years for which I have seen data (1873 and 1879), just over half were orphans; but almost a fourth reported both parents living, and an additional 15 percent reported one living parent. See Miriam Z. Langsam, *Children West: A History of the Placing-Out System of the New York Children's Aid Society, 1853–1890* (Madison: Wisconsin State Historical Society, 1964), Table 1, p. 26. Langsam provides data on the ethnic origins but not the religious affiliations of children placed in 1860, 1870, 1880, and 1890. If we assume that all of the Irish children and half of the German children who were placed were Catholic, more than one-fifth of

the placed children would have been Catholic in the first three years and 17 percent in 1890. See *Children West*, Table 3, p. 28. The percentage of Catholics assisted by the Children's Aid Society in New York (through its industrial schools and lodging houses) must certainly have been considerably higher. In Brace's fourth ward industrial school, for example, four-fifths of the pupils were Catholic. See Children's Aid Society, Second Annual Report (1855), pp. 11n–12n.

35. Brace, *Dangerous Classes*, p. 265. Brace disliked the Catholic Protectory not simply (or, in fact, primarily) because it was Catholic but because it was an institution. Brace firmly believed that children received better training (because they became more self-reliant) when brought up in a family rather than an institution. For Brace's critique of the effects of institutional raising on children, see *Dangerous Classes*, pp. 236–237.

36. Daniel Patrick Moynihan, "The Professors and the Poor," in Moynihan, ed., *On Understanding Poverty: Perspectives from the Social Sciences* (New York: Basic Books, 1969), p. 26.

37. Boyer, *Urban Masses*, p. 102.

38. Brace, *Dangerous Classes*, pp. 154–155.

39. Brace, *Dangerous Classes*, p. 137.

40. See Brace, *Dangerous Classes*, p. 156: Brace speaks there of "individual cases in our city, where a priest has exercised a marked influence in keeping his charge from intoxication," and he imagines the "blessings" that "a noble-minded and humane Priest . . . might confer, by elevating this degraded population."

41. Brace, *Dangerous Classes*, p. 137.

42. Jacob A. Riis, *The Children of the Poor* (New York: Charles Scribner's Sons, 1892), p. 251n. The emphasis appears in the text.

43. Olasky, *Tragedy*, pp. 21, 97; see also pp. 30, 31, and 77.

44. Beaumont and Tocqueville, *On the Penitentiary System*, p. 207.

45. Hale, *Joseph Tuckerman*, p. 46. The emphasis is mine.

46. Hale, *Joseph Tuckerman*, p. 45. The emphases are mine.

47. AICP, Thirteenth Annual Report, 1856, p. 39.

48. AICP, Eighth Annual Report, 1851, p. 19

49. AICP, Thirteenth Annual Report, 1856, p. 39.

50. Brace, *Short Sermons to News Boys: With a History of the Formation of the News Boys' Lodging-House* (New York: Charles Scribner, 1866), pp. 12–13.

51. Quoted in William Rhinelander Stewart, *The Philanthropic Work of Josephine Shaw Lowell Containing a Biographical Sketch of Her Life Together with a Selection of Her Public Papers and Private Letters* (Montclair, N.J.: Patterson Smith, 1974 [rpt. 1911]), p. 267. The quotation is taken from an 1898 address, "Children." The emphasis is mine.

52. Stephan Thernstrom, "Poverty in Historical Perspective," in Moynihan, ed., *On Understanding Poverty*, p. 168.

53. Josephine Shaw Lowell, "Houses of Refuge for Women; Their Purposes, Management and Possibilities," *Proceedings of the New York State Conference of Charities and Correction* 1 (1900): 250. The paper is credited to "Mrs. C. R. Lowell": Lowell was known by her late husband's name (Charles Russell) as well as her own.

In view of my comments above about the secular character of moral reform, I must acknowledge that Lowell concluded the passage quoted in the text by declaring that the women to be reformed needed, "in a word," to be given "religion." It is clear, though, that Lowell's understanding of religion in this context was vague, amorphous, and nondoctrinal: by religion she meant only that the women were to be taught to "develop their *souls*," to value "spiritual good and ill" above "physical good and ill" [p. 250; the emphasis appears in the text]. Lowell's paper was written to advocate the creation of state-run institutions that would have been nonsectarian: she mentions God nowhere in the paper and even says nothing about employing chaplains to minister to the institution's inmates.

54. Lowell, "Houses of Refuge," p. 255.

55. Lowell, "How to Adapt 'Charity Organization' Methods to Small Communities," *PNCCC* 14 (1887), pp. 136, 139. The emphasis appears in the text.

56. On this point see Hace Sorel Tishler, *Self-Reliance and Social Security, 1870–1917* (Port Washington, N.Y.: Kennikat, 1971), p. 60: in the 1880s and 1890s charity workers exhibited "a strong undercurrent of pessimism about the efficacy of all charitable services. The reformist faith in prevention, particularly as it was manifested in the rush to 'save the children,' was in itself a deflection from the notion that adults were probably beyond the pale of reform."

57. Amos G. Warner, *American Charities: A Study in Philanthropy and Economics* (New York: Arno Press and The New York Times, 1971 [rpt. 1894]), p. 296.

58. Brace, *Dangerous Classes*, p. 289. Gardner was for a time an employee of the Children's Aid Society; he oversaw a coffee and reading room established by the society (to offer the poor an alternative to saloons). Brace recounts his history on pp. 288–295 of *Dangerous Classes*.

59. Olasky, *Tragedy*, p. 138.

60. Olasky, *Tragedy*, p. 137.

61. Hale, *Joseph Tuckerman*, p. 25.

62. Hale, *Joseph Tuckerman*, p. 25.

63. McColgan, *Joseph Tuckerman*, p. 217. The quotation is taken from Tuckerman's diary entry for December 8, 1833; the emphasis appears in the text. In this passage Tuckerman also argued as follows: "To make [the poor] just, they must be treated with justice; to obtain their respect for their employers they must themselves be respected."

64. AICP, Fourth Annual Report (1847), p. 23. The emphasis is mine.

65. AICP, "First Report of a Committee on the Sanitary Condition of the Laboring Classes in the City of New York, with Remedial Suggestions," pp. 19–20.

66. AICP, "First Report," p. 20.

67. AICP, "First Report," p. 21. The emphasis appears in the text. Hartley's viewpoint on the link between housing and morality is nicely replicated in the classic Frank Capra Christmas movie, *It's a Wonderful Life*. When the character played by Jimmy Stewart (George Bailey) is forced to envision what life would have been like in Bedford Falls had he never lived, he discovers that the nonexistence of the Bailey Savings and Loan would completely have transformed the quality of the town's housing stock and hence its moral tone: all of Bedford Falls would have been bought up by the evil rich man, Mr. Potter (who would have renamed it Pottersville); workers would have been housed in slums (rather than being able to buy their own homes); a vice district composed of gaudy, neon-lit bars would have been created to service the discontented male slum residents (places "serv[ing] hard drinks . . . for men who want to get drunk fast," as a bartender puts it); family life would have been discouraged; and prostitution as well as drunkenness would have flourished. For the quotation from the film script, see Jeanine A. Basinger, *The It's a Wonderful Life Book* (New York: Alfred A. Knopf, 1997), p. 286.

68. AICP, "First Report," p. 24.

69. AICP, "First Report," p. 26.

70. AICP, "First Report," pp. 26–27.

71. AICP, "First Report," p. 32.

72. On these points, see David Ward, *Poverty, Ethnicity, and the American City, 1840–1925: Changing Conceptions of the Slum and the Ghetto* (New York: Cambridge University Press, 1989), pp. 38, 64, and 67. See in particular p. 67: "In New York by the end of the century the model tenement movement was responsible for the construction of 2,000 dwelling units that housed no more than 10,000 people." See also Roy Lubove, *The Progressives and the Slums: Tenement House Reform in New York City, 1890–1917* (New York: Greenwood Press, 1975 [rpt. 1962]), pp. 38–39.

73. See Howard Husock, "We Don't Need Subsidized Housing," *City Journal* (Winter 1997): 50–53.

74. See Lubove, *Progressives*, pp. 47–48; and Husock, "We Don't Need," p. 56.

75. See Lubove, *Progressives*, p. 9; and Husock, "We Don't Need," pp. 53–54.

76. For a discussion of the failure of the AICP's model tenement, see Robert H. Bremner, "The Big Flat: History of a New York Tenement House," *American Historical Review* 64 (1958): 54–62. The quotations appear on pp. 59–60. The contemporary observer was Alfred T. White, who successfully built and operated model tenements himself. Brace also concluded (perhaps as a result of the failure of the AICP's venture) that model tenements had to be "under moral supervision (so that tenants of notoriously bad character are excluded)." See Brace, *Dangerous Classes*, p. 62.

77. AICP, "First Report," p. 9.

78. AICP, "First Report," p. 12.

79. See Edward K. Spann, *The New Metropolis: New York City, 1840–1857* (New York: Columbia University Press, 1981), p. 146.

80. Quoted in Lubove, *Progressives*, p. 254.

81. Mary E. Richmond, *The Long View: Papers and Addresses*, edited by Joanna C. Colcord and Ruth Z. S. Mann (New York: Russell Sage Foundation, 1930), p. 568. The passage is taken from a 1924 biographical sketch, "Sir Charles Stewart Loch."

For a comparable argument relating to happiness rather than the exercise of moral virtue, see Charles Murray, *In Pursuit: Of Happiness and Good Government* (New York: Simon and Schuster, 1988): "Has anyone been happy while starving? Only, one may assume, under the most extraordinary circumstances. Has anyone been happy while having only a Spartan diet, with little variety but adequate nutrition? Of course, it happens all the time. There is a *threshold* before which it is nearly impossible to pursue happiness, after which the pursuit of happiness becomes readily possible" (p. 55). The emphasis appears in the text.

82. Katz, *In the Shadow of the Poorhouse: A Social History of Welfare* (New York: Basic Books, 1986), p. 68.

4. The Decline of Laissez-Faire and the Critique of Moral Reform

1. Quoted in Emma Brace, *The Life of Charles Loring Brace Chiefly Told in His Own Letters* (New York: Arno Press, 1976 [rpt. 1894]), p. 355. The statements appear in a letter written by Brace in the summer of 1877.

2. Quoted in Emma Brace, *Life*, pp. 355–356. The statements appear in a paper on profit-sharing also thought to date from 1877.

3. Quoted in William Rhinelander Stewart, *The Philanthropic Work of Josephine Shaw Lowell Containing a Biographical Sketch of Her Life Together with a Selection of Her Public Papers and Private Letters* (Montclair, N.J.: Patterson Smith, 1974 [rpt. 1911]), pp. 358–359. The statements appear in a letter written by Lowell, dated May 19, 1889.

4. For a good recent statement of this view, see David Frum, *Dead Right* (New York: Basic Books, 1994): "The bourgeois virtues developed into an almost national cultural norm because they were essential to survival in a country that was, until the 1930s, simultaneously rich in opportunities and full of terrible dangers from which there was no protection except one's own resources and the help of friends and family. The opportunities remain, but the dangers have dwindled. Why be thrifty any longer when your old age and health care are provided for, no matter how profligately you act in your youth? . . . Why be diligent when half your earnings are taken from you and given to the idle? Why be sober when the taxpayers run clinics to cure you of your drug habit as soon as it no longer amuses you?" (pp. 196–197).

5. Dores Robinson Sharpe, *Walter Rauschenbusch* (New York: Macmillan, 1942), p. 195.

6. "Beneath the Glitter," quoted in Sharpe, *Walter Rauschenbusch*, p. 82. "Beneath the Glitter" was originally published in 1887.

7. For an influential critique of the means by which men like Cornelius Vanderbilt, Jay Gould, and J. Pierpont Morgan attained their wealth, see Gustavus Myers, *History of the Great American Fortunes* (New York: The Modern Library, 1936). Myers was a contemporary of Rauschenbusch's; the first edition of his work appeared in 1909. See p. 19, where Myers declares that he was impelled to write the work because his research had "shattered the inculcated conception that . . . the great private fortunes were unquestionably the result of thrift and sagacious ability." The subdivisions of almost any chapter give a good sense of Myers's alternative understanding of how the fortunes came into being. Chapter I of Part III, for example, includes sections on "vast tracts secured by bribery," "great extent of the land frauds," "a welter of corruption," and "fraudulent oil land leases."

8. Walter Rauschenbusch, *The Righteousness of the Kingdom*, edited by Max L. Stackhouse (Nashville, Tenn.: Abingdon Press, 1968), p. 212. The emphasis appears in the text. *The Righteousness of the Kingdom* is an unpublished manuscript by Rauschenbusch that probably dates from the early 1890s (Rauschenbusch's New York period); in effect it is an early draft of the ideas that Rauschenbusch would explore in the 1907 work that brought him fame, *Christianity and the Social Crisis*. The manuscript was discovered in the archives of the American Baptist Historical Society long after Rauschenbusch's death; it was published only in 1968.

9. See Rauschenbusch, *Christianizing the Social Order* (New York: Macmillan, 1912): wealth tended to place "a man on the road to perdition by putting it in his power to quit work" (p. 295).

10. See Rauschenbusch, *Christianity and the Social Crisis*, edited by Robert D. Cross (New York: Harper Torchbooks, 1964 [rpt. 1907]), p. 376: "The custom which barred alcoholic drinks from respectable and educated homes" was "being undermined," because "the idle upper class . . . need[ed] stimulants and copie[d] their use from foreign society."

11. See Rauschenbusch, *Christianizing*, pp. 300–301: Thrift was impossible for the wealthy, since excessive wealth "unlocks the house of pleasure," making self-denial unnecessary and in fact impossible.

12. See Rauschenbusch, *Christianizing*: "Family life breaks down among the idle rich" (p. 302).

13. Jane Addams, "The Objective Value of a Social Settlement," in Jane Addams, Robert A. Woods, J. O. S. Huntington, Franklin H. Giddings, and Bernard Bosanquet, *Philanthropy and Social Progress: Seven Essays* (Freeport, N.Y.: Books for Libraries Press, 1969 [rpt. 1893]), p. 55.

14. Addams, "Objective Value," p. 55. Cf. Addams, *The Second Twenty Years at Hull-House, September 1909 to September 1929: With a Record of a Growing World Consciousness* (New York: Macmillan, 1930): "In the very first years of the American settlements, we had been afraid to be identified with the word charity, partly because the word itself was obnoxious to many of our neighbors, and partly because we wished to be of service to self-respecting working people as well as to the very poor" (p. 24).

15. Addams, "Social Settlements," in *PNCCC* 24 (1897): 345.

16. Florence Kelley, "The Sweating-System," in Residents of Hull-House, *Hull-House Maps and Papers: A Presentation of Nationalities and Wages in a Congested District of Chicago, Together with Comments and Essays on Problems Growing Out of the Social Conditions* (New York: Arno Press and The New York Times, 1970 [rpt. 1895]), p. 41.

17. Brace, *The Dangerous Classes of New York and Twenty Years' Work among Them,* 3rd ed., with addenda (Montclair, N.J.: Patterson Smith, 1967 [rpt. 1880]), p. 130.

18. Quoted in Stewart, *Philanthropic Work,* pp. 187–188. The quotation is taken from an 1895 address, "Poverty and Its Relief: The Methods Possible in the City of New York."

19. See Amos G. Warner, *American Charities: A Study in Philanthropy and Economics* (New York: Arno Press and The New York Times, 1971 [rpt. 1894]): "Any one of the causes might have been inadequate to produce pauperism had not others co-operated with it. A man is drunk and breaks his leg; is the cause [of his poverty] 'accident' or 'drink'? When this question was submitted to a group of charity organization workers, it was very promptly answered by two of them; but their answers were different. A man has been shiftless all his life, and is now old; is the cause of poverty shiftlessness or old age? A man is out of work because he is lazy and inefficient. One has to know him quite well before they can be sure that laziness is the cause. Perhaps there is hardly a case . . . where destitution has resulted from a single cause" (pp. 34–35). On p. 37 Warner adds that "this particular classification [between misfortune and misconduct] is made in deference to popular inquiry only. In the writer's opinion its chief value consists in showing how little it is worth."

20. Warner, *American Charities,* p. 38. Here Warner summarizes the results of his Table IV, which follows p. 372 in the text.

21. Warner, *American Charities,* pp. 46–47. Here Warner summarizes the results of his Table VIII, which follows p. 34 in the text. I expand on Warner's assessment of the virtue of the black poor in Chapter 6.

22. Hace Sorel Tishler, *Self-Reliance and Social Security, 1870–1917* (Port Washington, N.Y.: Kennikat, 1971), p. 57. See also pp. 44–45 and 55.

23. Addams, *The Spirit of Youth and the City Streets* (New York: Macmillan, 1918 [1st ed., 1909]), p. 107.

24. Addams, *A New Conscience and an Ancient Evil* (New York: Macmillan, 1912), p. 78.

25. Addams, *New Conscience,* p. 93.

26. Addams, "The Settlement as a Factor in the Labor Movement," in *Hull-House Maps,* p. 195.

27. Rauschenbusch, *Christianity,* p. 238.

28. Rauschenbusch, *Christianity,* p. 308.

29. Janet Forsythe Fishburn, *The Fatherhood of God and the Victorian Family: The Social Gospel in America* (Philadelphia: Fortress Press, 1981), p. 79.

30. Marvin Olasky, *The Tragedy of American Compassion* (Washington, D.C.: Regnery Publishing, 1992), p. 121. One of the books that Olasky cites to indicate the Social Gospel's supposed "willingness to do more, as long as the 'more' could be universalistic and unconditional" (that is, its reluctance in any way to condition aid to the poor on their behavior) is

the economist Richard T. Ely's *Social Aspects of Christianity*. But in a chapter of the book that Olasky cites in an endnote (see p. 261), Ely makes the following observations, all of which accord exactly with Olasky's own understanding of how charity should operate: "An unwise administration of charity tends to pauperize the masses. . . . The test of all true help is this: Does it help people to help themselves? Does it put them on their feet? . . . With respect to gifts of food and clothing, it is the exception when [the answer] is not in the negative. . . . The danger in gifts and clothing is that people will cease to try to exert themselves and will become miserable dependents on the bounty of others, losing their self-respect and manhood. . . . The office of relief of pauperism is . . . chiefly, cure of that contagious and disgusting malady. . . . All help should include effort on the part of those aided." See Richard T. Ely, *Social Aspects of Christianity and Other Essays* (New York: Thomas Y. Crowell and Co., 1889), pp. 85, 105, 106, 108.

31. Olasky, *Tragedy*, p. 125.

32. Rauschenbusch, *Righteousness*, p. 228.

33. Rauschenbusch, *Christianity*, p. 238.

34. Rauschenbusch, *Christianizing*, p. 299.

35. Addams, *Democracy and Social Ethics*, edited by Anne Firor Scott (Cambridge, Mass.: Harvard University Press, 1964 [rpt. 1907]), p. 70. *Democracy and Social Ethics* was originally published in 1902.

36. Addams, *Twenty Years at Hull-House with Autobiographical Notes* (Urbana: University of Illinois Press, 1990), p. 147. *Twenty Years at Hull-House* was originally published in 1910.

37. Addams, *Spirit of Youth*, pp. 27–28.

38. Addams, *New Conscience*, pp. 104–105.

39. Addams, *New Conscience*, p. 124.

40. Addams, *New Conscience*, p. 206.

41. Addams, *Spirit of Youth*, p. 77.

42. Addams, *Spirit of Youth*, pp. 78–80.

43. Addams, *Spirit of Youth*, p. 93. As an example, Addams recounted the tale of three boys (aged nine, eleven, and thirteen), who had seen a Wild West show featuring "the holding up of a stage coach and the lassoing of the driver," who then planned to "lasso, murder, and rob a neighborhood milk man." They bought a gun and shot at him, but since his horse shied when they attempted to lasso it, the milkman's life was saved.

44. Addams, *Spirit of Youth*, p. 19. Note the remarkable kinship between Addams's views and those of another Chicagoan, Allan Bloom. Cf. Bloom's *The Closing of the American Mind: How Higher Education has Failed Democracy and Impoverished the Souls of Today's Students* (New York: Simon and Schuster, 1987), pp. 70–71, 73: "Students today . . . know exactly why Plato takes music so seriously. They know it affects life very profoundly. . . . Plato's teaching about music is, put simply, that rhythm and melody . . . are the barbarous expression of the soul. . . . Civilization . . . is the taming or domestication of the soul's raw passions—not suppressing or excising them, which would deprive the soul of its energy—but forming and reforming them as art. . . . Rock music has one appeal only, a barbaric appeal, to sexual desire—not love . . . but sexual desire undeveloped and untutored. It acknowledges the first emanations of children's emerging sensuality and addresses them seriously, eliciting them and legitimating them, not as little sprouts that must be carefully tended in order to grow into gorgeous flowers, but as the real thing." Unlike Addams, to be sure, Bloom was "concern[ed] . . . not with the moral effects of . . . music—whether it leads to sex, violence, or drugs," but with "its effect on education" (p. 79).

45. Addams, *Democracy*, p. 17.

46. Addams and Ellen G. Starr, "Hull-House: A Social Settlement," in *Hull-House Maps*, p. 227. The essay does not include a byline, but it begins with the statement that it is published by "the two original residents of Hull-House," who were Addams and Starr (p. 207).

47. Addams, in "Discussion of Social Settlements," in *PNCCC* 24 (1897): 475.

48. Addams, *Twenty Years*, p. 78.

49. Addams, *Twenty Years*, p. 79.

50. Addams, *New Conscience*, p. 165.

51. Addams, *Second Twenty Years*, pp. 228–229.

52. See the judgment of her nephew and first biographer, James Weber Linn, *Jane Addams: A Biography* (New York: Greenwood Press, 1968 [rpt. 1935]): Prohibition decreased vice, "enormously improv[ing] the condition of the dance-halls," and lessened poverty. On the other hand, while "there was less disorder, . . . there was more murder. . . . She concluded, though no doubt by processes of reasoning somewhat different from Mr. Hoover's, that it was 'a noble experiment.' . . . She ultimately voted against repeal" (pp. 366–368).

53. Addams, *Second Twenty Years*, p. 230.

54. Quoted in Sharpe, *Walter Rauschenbusch*, pp. 164–165. The passage is taken from Rauschenbusch's collection of prayers, *Prayers of the Social Awakening*.

55. Rauschenbusch, *Christianity*, p. 242.

56. Rauschenbusch, *Christianity*, p. 376.

57. Rauschenbusch, *Righteousness*, p. 188.

58. Paul M. Minus, *Walter Rauschenbusch, American Reformer* (New York: Macmillan, 1988), p. 125.

59. Rauschenbusch, *A Theology for the Social Gospel* (Louisville, Ky.: Westminster John Knox Press, 1997 [rpt. 1917]), p. 64.

60. Cushing Strout, *The New Heavens and New Earth: Political Religion in America* (New York: Harper and Row, 1974), p. 247. In this context it may be useful to consider the testimony of Sharpe, who was Rauschenbusch's personal secretary as well as his first biographer. Writing about post-Prohibition America in 1942, Sharpe says the following: "How this stout warrior would inveigh against this traffic today if he were with us, and how he would rebuke the Church for its apathy in the face of the seriousness of the crisis which confronts the American nation in this regard. Since the angel with his sword of fire stood at the gates of Eden, never have right and wrong, virtue and vice, love and hate, decency and filth, honor and betrayal, altruism and mammonism met more squarely face to face than when this legalized liquor traffic stands before the bar [a nice, though presumably unintentional, pun—JS] of the nation's life and demands a right to live. This monster has grown in our midst, even as Rauschenbusch predicted, until today men and women, lads and lasses, frequent the cocktail lounge by day and by night. The American nation is on a spree, and the Christian Church is asleep" (*Walter Rauschenbusch*, p. 165).

61. Of the three women who figure prominently in this narrative, Addams and Richmond never married. Lowell was briefly married but lived her adult life as a single mother of great means. The Civil War death of her husband made Lowell a widow before she turned twenty-one, after only nine months of marriage; her daughter was born five weeks after his death. Lowell never remarried and dressed in black every day for the rest of her life. See Joan Waugh, *Unsentimental Reformer: The Life of Josephine Shaw Lowell* (Cambridge, Mass.: Harvard University Press, 1997), pp. 13, 79–80, 84–86.

62. Addams, *Spirit of Youth*, p. 34. Addams quotes the second of these descriptions from an unnamed source.

63. See Addams, *Democracy*, pp. 38–39. As we will see, Addams argued that charity workers were wrong to judge the poor by the standards of the middle class. She believed that early marriages were in fact imprudent for middle-class men, who tended to earn more as they grew older; but they were appropriate for manual laborers, whose income was tied to their physical strength, and who accordingly tended to earn the most between ages twenty and thirty. Furthermore, a workingman who became accustomed to spending all of his wages on himself would find it harder later in life to divide them with his family.

64. For Addams's disapproval of nonmarital sexual relations, see her review of *Modern Woman and Sex*, a book by Rachelle S. Yarros (a doctor and one-time Hull House resident), in *Survey* 70 (February 1934): 59. Addams applauded Yarros's "rejection of loose, fleeting and experimental sex relations," concurring with Yarros's judgment that "I have seen no happiness resulting from illicit relations," and with her praise of "self-discipline and sublimation of passions and appetites."

65. Addams, *Democracy*, p. 76.

66. For Rauschenbusch's socialism, see "Ideals of Social Reformers," in Robert T. Handy, ed., *The Social Gospel in America: Gladden, Ely, Rauschenbusch* (New York: Oxford University Press, 1966), p. 282: "For working purposes I am myself a socialist." "Ideals of Social Reformers" was originally published in 1897. See also *Christianity*: "Socialism . . . would be a permanent solution of the labor question. It would end the present insecurity, the constant antagonism, the social inferiority, the physical exploitation, the intellectual poverty to which the working class is now exposed even when its condition is most favorable" (pp. 407–408). For a useful brief discussion, see Sharpe, *Walter Rauschenbusch*, pp. 199–220. See especially pp. 199–200: "Rauschenbusch was not a member of the Socialist Party; he did not believe in the Marxian cataclysmic approach; he was not for the socialization of everything; he did not accept the materialism or the atheism of Marxianism; nor did he believe in their autocratic discipline. He was a believer in governmental control and ownership, more affected by the populism of the west than by Marx."

67. Fishburn, *The Fatherhood of God*, p. 122.

68. Addams and Starr, "Hull-House," p. 228.

69. Addams and Starr, "Hull-House," p. 223. Although the Penny Provident Fund operated primarily in New York, branches existed not only in Illinois, but also in five other states and Canada. See Mary Willcox Brown, *The Development of Thrift* (New York: Macmillan, 1899), p. 46.

70. Addams, *Twenty Years*, p. 175.

71. Rauschenbusch, *Christianizing*, p. 235. Cf. Karl Marx and Friedrich Engels, "Manifesto of the Communist Party," in Robert C. Tucker, ed., *The Marx-Engels Reader*, 2nd ed. (New York: W.W. Norton, 1978): "The bourgeoisie . . . draws all, even the most barbarian nations into civilisation. . . . It compels all nations, on pain of extinction, to adopt the bourgeois mode of production. . . . The bourgeoisie has subjected the country to the rule of the towns. It has created enormous cities, has greatly increased the urban population as compared with the rural, and has thus rescued a considerable part of the population from the idiocy of rural life. . . . It has made barbarian and semi-barbarian countries dependent on the civilised ones, nations [of] peasants on nations of bourgeois. . . . The bourgeoisie . . . has created more massive and more colossal productive forces than have all preceding generations together. Subjection of Nature's forces to man, machinery . . . —what earlier

century had even a presentiment that such productive forces slumbered in the lap of social labour?" (p. 477).

72. See Daniel Bell, *The Cultural Contradictions of Capitalism* (New York: Basic Books, 1976).

73. Rauschenbusch, *Christianizing*, pp. 211–212.

74. Addams, *Democracy*, p. 17.

75. Addams, *Democracy*, p. 70.

76. Addams, *Democracy*, p. 63.

77. In general, Rauschenbusch's published works are less confrontational, less insistently radical, than *Righteousness*. Presumably this change reflects at least in part Rauschenbusch's conviction that a less radical presentation of his views would be more effective rhetorically; conceivably it also reflects a genuine moderation of those views as he matured.

78. Rauschenbusch, *Righteousness*, p. 210.

79. Rauschenbusch, *Righteousness*, p. 207.

80. Jane Addams, "Social Settlements," in *PNCCC* 24 (1897): 339.

81. Addams, *Democracy and Social Ethics*, edited by Anne Firor Scott (Cambridge, Mass.: Harvard University Press, 1964 [rpt. 1907]), p. 15. *Democracy and Social Ethics* was originally published in 1902.

82. Addams, *Democracy*, pp. 15–17.

83. Quoted in William Rhinelander Stewart, *The Philanthropic Work of Josephine Shaw Lowell Containing a Biographical Sketch of Her Life Together with a Selection of Her Public Papers and Private Letters* (Montclair, N.J.: Patterson Smith, 1974 [rpt. 1911]), p. 157. The statement appears in an 1888 "Sunday School Talk to Children."

84. Walter Rauschenbusch, *Christianizing the Social Order* (New York: Macmillan, 1912), pp. 295–296. For a second critique of the double standard, see a passage quoted in Dores Robinson Sharpe, *Walter Rauschenbusch* (New York: Macmillan, 1942): "We have been told that in one of the [penal] institutions on Blackwell's Island this sign has been put up: 'It is a bad day for a young man when he gets the idea that he can get a dollar without doing a dollar's worth of work for it.' Amen! It is a good motto in the proper place. Now will not some lover of men have a few hundred mottoes painted with these words: 'It is a bad day for a young man when he first gets the idea that he can get a million dollars without doing a million dollars' worth of work for it.' Then let him distribute the signs downtown [i.e., on Wall Street] where they will do the most good" (p. 83). The statement appears in an 1890 article in *For the Right*, a journal of religion and social reform that Rauschenbusch edited for a few years.

85. See Charles Krauthammer, "Defining Deviancy Up," in Mark Gerson, ed., *The Essential Neoconservative Reader* (Reading, Mass.: Addison Wesley, 1996), pp. 372–382.

86. See Daniel Patrick Moynihan, "Defining Deviancy Down," in Gerson, ed., *Essential Neoconservative*, pp. 356–371.

87. Addams, *Democracy*, p. 17.

88. Addams, *Twenty Years at Hull-House with Autobiographical Notes* (Urbana: University of Illinois Press, 1990), p. 152. *Twenty Years at Hull-House* was originally published in 1910.

89. Addams, *Democracy*, p. 38.

90. Addams, *Democracy*, p. 66.

91. Addams, *Democracy*, p. 212.

92. Virginia Woolf, *The Captain's Death Bed and Other Essays* (New York: Harcourt, Brace, 1950), p. 96. She advanced this claim in a 1924 essay, "Mr. Bennett and Mrs. Brown."

93. See, for example, Woolf, *Captain's Death Bed*: "The Victorian cook lived like a leviathan in the lower depths, formidable, silent, obscure, inscrutable; the Georgian cook [i.e., the cook circa 1924] is a creature of sunshine and fresh air, in and out of the drawing-room, now to borrow the *Daily Herald,* now to ask advice about a hat" (p. 96). The democratizing changes discussed by Woolf are nicely evident in the British television series *Upstairs, Downstairs.*

94. See the essays on "Filial Relations" and "Household Adjustment" in Addams, *Democracy.*

95. Addams, *Democracy*, pp. 2–3.

96. Quoted in Kathleen D. McCarthy, *Noblesse Oblige: Charity and Cultural Philanthropy in Chicago, 1849–1929* (Chicago: University of Chicago Press, 1982), p. 102. The statement appeared in a 1903 article in the journal *Charities.*

97. Addams, *Democracy*, p. 31.

98. Addams, *Democracy*, p. 255.

99. Thomas Lee Philpott, *The Slum and the Ghetto: Neighborhood Deterioration and Middle-Class Reform, Chicago, 1880–1930* (New York: Oxford University Press, 1978), p. 46.

100. Philpott, *Slum and the Ghetto*, p. 50.

101. Addams, *Democracy*, p. 137.

102. Addams, *Democracy*, pp. 140–142.

103. Addams, *Democracy*, p. 146.

104. Addams, *Democracy*, pp. 147–148.

105. Addams, *Democracy*, p. 149.

106. In an 1885 article in *Harper's Monthly*, Richard T. Ely (then at the start of his career as an economist and proponent of the Social Gospel) charged that Pullmanism was "benevolent, well-meaning feudalism," because the resident had "everything done for him, nothing by him." The quotations from his article appear in Philpott, *Slum and the Ghetto*, pp. 58–59. See also p. 60, for an assessment by a resident of the model town: "We are born in a Pullman house, fed from the Pullman shop, taught in the Pullman school, catechized in the Pullman church, and when we die we shall be buried in the Pullman cemetery and go to the Pullman hell."

107. Addams, *Democracy*, p. 154.

108. Addams, *Democracy*, pp. 148–149.

109. Addams, *Democracy*, p. 176.

110. Mary E. Richmond, *Friendly Visiting among the Poor: A Handbook for Charity Workers* (Montclair, N.J.: Patterson Smith, 1969 [rpt. 1899]), p. 108.

111. Richmond, *Friendly Visiting*, p. 109.

112. Richmond, *Friendly Visiting*, pp. 109–110.

113. Addams, *Democracy*, p. 149.

114. Rauschenbusch, *Christianity and the Social Crisis*, edited by Robert D. Cross (New York: Harper Torchbooks, 1964 [rpt. 1907]), pp. 215–216.

115. Rauschenbusch, *Christianizing*, p. 161. See also p. 342: "Under the normal conditions of American life in the past, it was possible for the average man to support his family, raise his children, and still save something for a rainy day." In this context, note also that the two empirical studies (discussed in Chapter 1) that suggest the efficacy of the reformers' virtues in promoting upward mobility—drawn from Bruce Laurie's research on Philadelphia workers and Jill Siegel Dodd's research on Boston workers—discuss conditions in the antebellum era rather than the late nineteenth century.

116. For the inapplicability of the rags-to-riches model, see Stephan Thernstrom, *Poverty and Progress: Social Mobility in a Nineteenth Century City* (Cambridge, Mass.: Harvard University Press, 1964), p. 161: the belief that property ownership transformed American workers into capitalists was "sheer fantasy," since "a mere handful of the property-owning laborers of Newburyport [the Massachusetts city examined by Thernstrom] ventured into business for themselves." For the popular recognition that the rags-to-riches model was inapplicable, see p. 164: "One ingredient of the appeal of mobility literature and oratory was that pleasant fantasies of sudden wealth and a vicarious sharing in the spectacular successes of other ordinary men provided a means of escaping the tedious realities of daily existence. Fantasies of this sort are not likely to flourish among men who have no hope at all of individual economic or social betterment."

117. Richard T. Ely, *Social Aspects of Christianity and Other Essays* (New York: Thomas Y. Crowell and Co., 1889), pp. 97–98.

118. Ely, *Social Aspects*, p. 98.

119. Thernstrom, *Poverty and Progress*, p. 212.

120. James T. Kloppenberg, *Uncertain Victory: Social Democracy and Progressivism in European and American Thought, 1870–1920* (New York: Oxford University Press, 1986), p. 155.

121. Kloppenberg, *Uncertain Victory*, p. 155. The emphases are mine.

122. Rauschenbusch, *Christianizing*, p. 342.

123. Thernstrom, *Poverty and Progress*, pp. 164–165. The emphasis appears in the text.

124. See Thernstrom, *Poverty and Progress*, p. 205.

125. Thernstrom, "Working-Class Social Mobility in Industrial America," in Melvin Richter, ed., *Essays in Theory and History: An Approach to the Social Sciences* (Cambridge, Mass.: Harvard University Press, 1970), p. 230.

126. Thernstrom, "Working-Class Social Mobility," pp. 230–231. Thernstrom elaborated on these findings in *The Other Bostonians: Poverty and Progress in the American Metropolis, 1880–1970* (Cambridge, Mass.: Harvard University Press, 1973), pp. 45–110.

127. Thernstrom, "Working-Class Social Mobility," p. 230.

128. Thernstrom, "Working-Class Social Mobility," p. 230.

129. See Addams, "Social Settlements": "Last Sunday I took dinner with a workingman who makes twenty-five dollars a month. Upon that he supports his father and mother, his wife and his three children, and does it with a certain degree of success. He does not want to save. He does not consider it righteous that he should do anything with his money but take care of his family. He says: 'I have no idea of saving money for my children. I leave that for the *bourgeoisie*. We workingmen invest our money in our children. Just as my father and mother took care of me, I am now taking care of them, and my children will take care of me.' Nothing could so induce them to be thrifty as the presence of half a dozen little mouths clamoring for food. They need that form of savings-bank, if I may use the expression" (p. 343). This worker is presumably the socialist tailor, whose story is also told in *Democracy and Social Ethics*; Addams's other account of him is mentioned in the section on thrift in Chapter 2.

130. Addams, *Democracy*, pp. 27–28.

131. Addams, *Democracy*, p. 38.

132. Addams, *Democracy*, p. 39. Similarly unflattering descriptions of the poor can also be found in Rauschenbusch's writings. See, for example, *The Righteousness of the Kingdom*, edited by Max L. Stackhouse (Nashville, Tenn.: Abingdon Press, 1968), p. 230, where the poor are said to live in "a world . . . in which brute pleasure is the aim and brute force

and selfishness are the means." See also *Christianity*, p. 274, a passage in which Rausch-enbusch worried that "the reproduction of the race is left to the poor and ignorant," as "the shiftless, and all those with whom natural passion is least restrained, will breed most freely."

133. See Jim Sleeper, *Liberal Racism* (New York: Viking, 1997): "Sometimes, prompted by misdirected and self-congratulatory compassion, liberal racism patronizes nonwhites by expecting (and getting) less of them than they are fully capable of achieving. Intending to turn the tables on racist double standards that set the bar much higher for nonwhites, lib-eral racism ends up perpetuating double standards by setting the bar so much lower for its intended beneficiaries that it denies them the satisfaction of equal accomplishment and opportunity" (p. 4). One of Sleeper's chief—and deserving—targets is Andrew Hacker's *Two Nations: Black and White, Separate, Hostile, Unequal* (New York: Charles Scribner's Sons, 1992). On pp. 171–172, for example, Hacker expresses his sympathy for the view that "black and white children have different 'learning styles.'" Unlike whites, blacks are said to care more about the "style"—as opposed to the "substance"—of speech, to be less able to deal with abstractions, to be less exact about "time" and "measurement," to be less able to construct an orderly argument, to be "more attuned to their bodies and physical needs." It is remarkable that Hacker means these assertions to be supportive of blacks; believers in the inferiority of blacks have quite comfortably mouthed all of them.

134. Addams, *Democracy*, p. 59.

135. Addams, *Democracy*, pp. 66–67.

136. Addams, "Social Settlements," p. 345.

137. See, for example, Charles Loring Brace, *The Dangerous Classes of New York and Twenty Years' Work among Them*, 3rd ed., with addenda (Montclair, N.J.: Patterson Smith, 1967 [rpt. 1880]): "The effort for Total Abstinence [from alcohol] . . . has addressed the working-man—as, in fact, he often is—as a child, and saved him from his own habits" (pp. 66–67).

138. Addams, *Democracy*, pp. 47–48.

139. See also Addams, *Democracy*, pp. 59–62, for the story of an elderly woman, injured in a fire, who was diligent (she made and sold quilts) but not sober (she was also an opium addict).

140. Addams, *Democracy*, p. 49.

141. Addams, *Democracy*, p. 154.

142. For an instance of Addams's own moral imperialism, see *Twenty Years*, p. 198: a group of debaters severed their connection to Hull House after the settlement had failed to expel from its Men's Club some "toughs" who had fought with the debaters. (During the fight a shot was fired by one of the toughs, although no one was hurt.) Addams's account of her meeting with the debaters is illuminating: "In response to my position that a desire to avoid all that was 'tough' meant to walk only in the paths of smug self-seeking and personal improvement and was exactly what the Settlement did not stand for, they contended with much justice that ambitious young people were obliged for their own reputation, if not for their own morals, to avoid all connection with that which bordered on the tough, and that it was quite another matter for the Hull-House residents who could afford a more generous judgment." In contrast to Addams, then, the debaters suggest that the upwardly mobile poor need a moral code that is stricter—not one that is more lax—than that of the middle class. In fairness to Addams, she concludes the anecdote with the concession that the debat-ers' "wholesome bourgeois position . . . was most reasonable."

143. Adam Smith, *The Theory of Moral Sentiments* (Indianapolis: Liberty Classics, 1976), p. 276.

144. Smith, *Theory*, pp. 277–278.

145. Smith, *Theory*, p. 353.

146. *Joseph Tuckerman on the Elevation of the Poor: A Selection from His Reports as Minister at Large in Boston*, edited by E. E. Hale (New York: Arno Press and The New York Times, 1971 [rpt. 1874]), pp. 84–87.

147. Hale, *Joseph Tuckerman*, p. 88.

148. Hale, *Joseph Tuckerman*, pp. 88–89.

149. Walter Rauschenbusch, *The Righteousness of the Kingdom*, edited by Max L. Stackhouse (Nashville, Tenn.: Abingdon Press, 1968), p. 210.

150. Rauschenbusch, *A Theology for the Social Gospel* (Louisville, Ky.: Westminster John Knox Press, 1997 [rpt. 1917]), p. 158.

151. Rauschenbusch, *Righteousness*, p. 209.

152. Rauschenbusch, *Righteousness*, p. 219. The emphasis appears in the text.

153. Rauschenbusch, *Righteousness*, p. 212.

154. Rauschenbusch, *Righteousness*, p. 218.

155. Rauschenbusch, *Righteousness*, p. 210. The emphasis appears in the text.

156. Rauschenbusch, *Righteousness*, p. 208.

157. Rauschenbusch, *Christianity and the Social Crisis*, edited by Robert D. Cross (New York: Harper Torchbooks, 1964 [rpt. 1907]), p. 147.

158. Rauschenbusch, *Christianity*, p. 149.

159. Rauschenbusch, *Christianity*, p. 349. For similar reasons Rauschenbusch also criticized the working-class tendency to be satisfied by the practical gains won by trade unions in raising wages and improving working conditions. See pp. 406–408: "As long as the working class simply attempts to better its condition somewhat and to secure a recognized standing for its class organization, it stands on the basis of the present capitalistic organization of industry." Instead, "socialism is the ultimate and logical outcome of the labor movement."

160. See, for example, the following 1893 statement by Robert Treat Paine, Jr., the president of the Boston Associated Charities, quoted in Frank Dekker Watson, *The Charity Organization Movement in the United States: A Study in American Philanthropy* (New York: Macmillan, 1922): "Has not the new charity organization movement too long been content to aim at a system to relieve or even uplift judiciously single cases without asking if there are not prolific causes permanently at work to create want, vice, crime, disease and death; and whether these causes may not be wholly or in a large degree eradicated? If such causes of pauperism exist, how vain to waste our energies on single cases of relief, when society should rather aim at removing the prolific sources of all the woe. . . . The diseases of society are more aggravated, the dangers are graver, the need of radical remedies is more absolute than the new charity has yet fully and fairly faced" (p. 278).

161. Rauschenbusch, "The New Evangelism," in Robert T. Handy, ed., *The Social Gospel in America: Gladden, Ely, Rauschenbusch* (New York: Oxford University Press, 1966), p. 327. "The New Evangelism" was originally published in 1904.

162. Reinhold Niebuhr, "Walter Rauschenbusch in Historical Perspective," in Ronald H. Stone, ed., *Faith and Politics: A Commentary on Religious, Social and Political Thought in a Technological Age* (New York: George Braziller, 1968), pp. 35–36.

163. Donald B. Meyer, *The Protestant Search for Political Realism, 1919–1941* (New York: Greenwood Press, 1960), p. 74.

164. Rauschenbusch, *Christianizing the Social Order* (New York: Macmillan, 1912), p. 206.

165. Rauschenbusch, *Righteousness*, p. 234.

166. Jane Addams, *Democracy and Social Ethics*, edited by Anne Firor Scott (Cambridge, Mass.: Harvard University Press, 1964 [rpt. 1907]), p. 31. *Democracy and Social Ethics* was originally published in 1902.

167. Rauschenbusch, *Righteousness*, p. 235.

168. For a comparable intimation that familial love should somehow be extended to all members of society, see Addams, *Democracy*: "Just when our affection becomes large enough to care for the unworthy among the poor as we would care for the unworthy among our own kin, is certainly a perplexing question. To say that it should never be so, is a comment upon our democratic relations to them which few of us would be willing to make" (p. 63).

169. Rauschenbusch, *Righteousness*, p. 277.

170. Rauschenbusch, *Righteousness*, pp. 277–278.

171. Rauschenbusch, *Righteousness*, p. 278.

172. Since this critique is embodied in an early manuscript that Rauschenbusch himself never published, it might be argued that I am making too much of it. If my aim here were to assess Rauschenbusch's historical influence, it would certainly be misleading to place any weight at all on opinions that went undiscovered until 1968. But my concern is quite different: I am trying to explicate Rauschenbusch's moral misgivings about the individualistic virtues espoused in moral reform. It is undoubtedly significant that these moral misgivings are less evident in Rauschenbusch's later published writings, which adopt more conventional moral positions. Still, the more radical early exposition stands, and one can legitimately analyze its argument. In exactly the same way, students of Marx make much of early writings of his that remained unpublished for fifty years after his death, even though they sometimes advance positions that Marx later abandoned.

173. Rauschenbusch, *Righteousness*, p. 275.

174. In this context see James T. Kloppenberg, *Uncertain Victory: Social Democracy and Progressivism in European and American Thought, 1870–1920* (New York: Oxford University Press, 1986): "Rauschenbusch had little impact on the working class [he] aimed to assist. [His] influence extended primarily to those reform-minded members of the urban middle class who formed one of the several muddy currents of progressive sentiment in the pre-World War I period" (p. 210).

175. Rauschenbusch, *Righteousness*, p. 224. See also Rauschenbusch's brief discussion of social work, *"Unto Me"* (Boston: Pilgrim Press, 1912): "The causes of misery are never only in the people who are miserable. They are chiefly in those who profit by their misery. The lower tenth of society is submerged because the upper tenth is riding on the other nine tenths and putting the heads of some under water" (p. 26).

176. Rauschenbusch, *Righteousness*, p. 229.

177. Rauschenbusch, *Righteousness*, p. 226.

178. Rauschenbusch, *Righteousness*, p. 244.

179. Addams, *Democracy*, p. 39.

180. Addams, *Democracy*, p. 38.

181. Rauschenbusch, *Righteousness*, p. 226.

182. For a variant of this argument, see Irving Kristol, *Two Cheers for Capitalism* (New York: New American Library, 1979): "The essence of [the anti-capitalist] spirit is to be found, not in *The Communist Manifesto*, but in the young Marx who wrote: '*The enemy of being is having*.' This sums up neatly the animus which intellectuals from the beginning

... have felt toward the system of liberal capitalism. This system is in truth 'an acquisitive society,' by traditional standards. . . . Those who benefit most from capitalism . . . cease to think of acquiring money and begin to think of acquiring power so as to improve the 'quality of life,' and to give *being* priority over *having*. That is the meaning of the well-known statement by a student radical of the 1960s: 'You don't know what hell is like unless you were raised in [the wealthy New York suburb] Scarsdale.' Since it is the ambition of capitalism to enable everyone to live in Scarsdale or its equivalent, this challenge is far more fundamental than the orthodox Marxist one, which says—against all the evidence—that capitalism will fail because it *cannot* get everyone to live in Scarsdale" (pp. 16–17). The emphases appear in the text. In effect I am suggesting that Addams and Rauschenbusch made both of these contradictory arguments: they not unreasonably resented the fact that only the rich could live in Scarsdale; but they also hoped to transform people so that no one would want to live there.

5. The Rejection of Moral Reform

1. Robert H. Bremner, *From the Depths: The Discovery of Poverty in the United States* (New York: New York University Press, 1956), p. 134. Note that in this passage Bremner reports the discovery of the irrelevance of the "so-called" moral causes of poverty. By implication, genuine moral causes of poverty do not exist.

2. For a summary of and commentary on Ryan's critique, see Lee Rainwater and William L. Yancey, *The Moynihan Report and the Politics of Controversy* (Cambridge, Mass.: MIT Press, 1967), pp. 220–232. The critique itself, "Savage Discovery: The Moynihan Report," is reprinted on pp. 457–466; it originally appeared in the November 22, 1965, issue of *The Nation*.

3. William Ryan, *Blaming the Victim* (New York: Pantheon Books, 1971), p. 248. The emphasis appears in the text.

4. Ryan, *Blaming the Victim*, p. 7. The emphasis appears in the text.

5. Ryan, *Blaming the Victim*, p. 28.

6. Walter Rauschenbusch, *The Righteousness of the Kingdom*, edited by Max L. Stackhouse (Nashville, Tenn.: Abingdon Press, 1968), p. 226.

7. Ryan, *Blaming the Victim*, pp. 134–135.

8. Ryan, *Blaming the Victim*, pp. 164–165.

9. Ryan, *Blaming the Victim*, p. 171.

10. Ryan, *Blaming the Victim*, pp. 171–172.

11. Ryan, *Blaming the Victim*, p. 167.

12. AICP, Eleventh Annual Report (1854), p. 33.

13. Lawrence M. Mead, *The New Politics of Poverty: The Nonworking Poor in America* (New York: Basic Books, 1992), pp. 64, 145.

14. Glenn C. Loury, *One by One from the Inside Out: Essays and Reviews on Race and Responsibility in America* (New York: Free Press, 1995), p. 29. The emphasis appears in the text.

15. Ryan, *Blaming the Victim*, p. 75.

16. Ryan, *Blaming the Victim*, pp. 189, 197.

17. Ryan, *Blaming the Victim*, p. 119.

18. Quoted in Marvin E. Gettleman, "Charity and Social Classes in the United States, 1874–1900, II," *American Journal of Economics and Sociology* 22 (1963), pp. 417–418. The joke appeared in 1895 in *The Philistine*, a humorous publication, as part of a spoof of Charity Organization Society doctrine.

19. Adam Smith, *An Inquiry into the Nature and Causes of the Wealth of Nations* (New York: Modern Library, 1937), p. 746.

20. David J. Rothman, "The State as Parent," in Willard Gaylin, Ira Glasser, Steven Marcus, and Rothman, *Doing Good: The Limits of Benevolence* (New York: Pantheon Books, 1978), p. 83.

21. Raymond A. Mohl, "The Abolition of Public Outdoor Relief, 1870–1900: A Critique of the Piven and Cloward Thesis," in Walter I. Trattner, ed., *Social Welfare or Social Control? Some Historical Reflections on* Regulating the Poor (Knoxville: University of Tennessee Press, 1983), pp. 42–43.

22. Mohl, "Abolition of Public Outdoor Relief," p. 47.

23. Jane Addams, *Democracy and Social Ethics*, edited by Anne Firor Scott (Cambridge, Mass.: Harvard University Press, 1964 [rpt. 1907]), p. 38. *Democracy and Social Ethics* was originally published in 1902.

24. Rothman, "State as Parent," p. 87.

25. William A. Muraskin, "Review of *Regulating the Poor*," *Contemporary Sociology: A Journal of Reviews* 4 (1975): 607. See also James T. Patterson, *America's Struggle against Poverty 1900–1994* (Cambridge, Mass.: Harvard University Press, 1994), pp. 31 and 250–251 (note 31): Patterson cites "especially . . . *Regulating the Poor*" to exemplify the "argument stress[ing] the pernicious role of the elite classes" in denying material aid to the poor.

26. Frances Fox Piven and Richard A. Cloward, *Regulating the Poor: The Functions of Public Welfare*, updated ed. (New York: Vintage Books, 1993), p. 3. Almost all of Piven and Cloward's evidence comes from America beginning with the New Deal, but they apparently saw the existence of this cycle as a sort of universal law applicable to all capitalist societies. Thus the cycle was already apparent in "the Western relief systems originat[ing] in the mass disturbances that erupted during the long transition from feudalism to capitalism beginning in the sixteenth century" (p. 8).

27. Piven and Cloward, *Regulating the Poor: The Functions of Public Welfare* (New York: Pantheon Books, 1971), p. 343. This statement appears in the epilogue to the 1971 edition, the only portion of the original work that is not reproduced in the updated 1993 edition. Note that pp. 1–340 are identical in both editions.

28. See Piven and Cloward, *Regulating the Poor*, 1971 edition: "When attachments to the work role deteriorate, so do attachments to the family, especially the attachment of men to their families. For all practical purposes, the relief check becomes a surrogate for the male breadwinner. The resulting family breakdown and loss of control over the young is usually signified by the spread of certain forms of disorder—for example, school failure, crime, and addiction. In other words, the mere giving of relief . . . does little to stem the fragmentation of lower-class life, even while it further undermines the patterns of work by which the lower class is ordinarily regulated" (pp. 343–344). One can easily imagine Charles Murray penning this passage to illustrate the evils of unconditional relief; remarkably, Piven and Cloward blandly included it in the context of an argument favoring unconditional relief.

29. Piven and Cloward, *Regulating the Poor*, 1971 ed., p. 348. The emphasis appears in the text. Piven and Cloward concluded the 1993 updated edition by reaffirming this belief. They quoted the language from the 1971 edition about the expansion of the rolls as the true welfare reform, then added that "We still think so" (p. 399).

30. Irving Kristol, "Welfare: The Best of Intentions, the Worst of Results," in Paul S. Weinberger, ed., *Perspectives on Social Welfare: An Introductory Anthology*, 2nd ed. (New York: Macmillan, 1974), p. 241. In this essay, which is chiefly devoted to *Regulating the*

Poor, Kristol argues that "the 'welfare explosion' was the work, not of 'capitalism' or of any other 'ism,' but of men and women like Miss Piven and Mr. Cloward" (p. 241).

31. Piven and Cloward, *Regulating the Poor*, 1993 ed., p. 22.

32. Piven and Cloward, *Regulating the Poor*, 1993 ed., pp. 127–128.

33. Piven and Cloward, *Regulating the Poor*, 1993 ed., p. 228.

34. Piven and Cloward, *Regulating the Poor*, 1993 ed., p. xix. This passage appears on p. xvii in the 1971 edition.

35. Piven and Cloward, *Regulating the Poor*, 1971 ed., pp. 345, 348.

36. Piven and Cloward, *Regulating the Poor*, 1971 ed., p. 347.

37. See Mead, *New Politics of Poverty*: "Liberal analysts tend to qualify 'job' with terms like 'good,' 'decent,' 'suitable,' or 'meaningful'; for them, typically a job is not really a job unless it pays enough to support an average family on one income, offers promotion prospects, health and pension benefits, and is interesting and affirming to do." Mead rejects this view, arguing that "if [the nonworking poor] can be expected to behave like the nonpoor, there is no reason why they should not get ahead in the current economy just as immigrants are doing. But if one thinks they have special, personal disadvantages for which society is responsible, then virtually no job market will seem to provide enough, or good enough, jobs for them" (pp. 108–109). On p. 97 Mead notes that "the main reason youth, women, and minorities are usually paid less than prime-aged white males is that, on average, they are younger, less experienced, and less educated."

38. See Piven and Cloward, *Regulating the Poor*, 1993 ed., pp. 392–397, where they reject the claim that "work would transform family structure, community life, and the so-called 'culture of poverty.'"

39. Piven and Cloward, *Regulating the Poor*, 1993 ed., p. xix. This passage appears on p. xvii in the 1971 edition.

40. Joel F. Handler, *Reforming the Poor: Welfare Policy, Federalism, and Morality* (New York: Basic Books, 1972), p. 139.

41. Herbert J. Gans, *The War against the Poor: The Underclass and Antipoverty Policy* (New York: Basic Books, 1995), p. 96.

42. Piven and Cloward, *Regulating the Poor*, 1993 ed., p. 172.

43. Piven and Cloward, *Regulating the Poor*, 1993 ed., p. 173.

44. Piven and Cloward, *Regulating the Poor*, 1993 ed., p. 175.

45. Mead, *New Politics of Poverty*, p. 156.

46. Piven and Cloward, *Regulating the Poor*, 1993 ed., p. 227.

47. Piven and Cloward, *Regulating the Poor*, 1993 ed., pp. 228–229.

48. Piven and Cloward, *Regulating the Poor*, 1993 ed., pp. 227, 231.

49. Piven and Cloward, *Regulating the Poor*, 1993 ed., p. 235.

50. Piven and Cloward, *Regulating the Poor*, 1993 ed., p. 223.

51. Piven and Cloward, *Regulating the Poor*, 1993 ed., p. 225.

52. Piven and Cloward, *Regulating the Poor*, 1993 ed., p. 226.

53. Piven and Cloward, *Regulating the Poor*, 1993 ed., p. 369.

54. For an important elaboration of this argument, see Mead, *Beyond Entitlement: The Social Obligations of Citizenship* (New York: Free Press, 1986), pp. 55–61. See especially p. 55: "Starting in the early 1960s the poor and disadvantaged were understood to be so conditioned by their environment that to expect better functioning from them, such as work, became almost inconceivable. The responsibility for their difficulties, even behavioral ones, was transferred entirely to government or society." See also p. 58: "Virtue could not be expected from people living in ghetto environments 'where honesty can become a luxury

and ambition a myth.'" The internal quotation is taken from the 1964 annual report of the Council of Economic Advisers to the President.

55. In this context consider also what was probably the single most influential work about poverty written in the 1960s: Michael Harrington's *The Other America: Poverty in the United States* (New York: Penguin, 1963). See p. 22: "One might define the contemporary poor in the United States as those who, for reasons beyond their control, cannot help themselves. All the most decisive factors making for opportunity and advance are against them. They are born going downward, and most of them stay down. They are victims whose lives are endlessly blown round and round the other America." See also pp. 158–159: Harrington spoke openly of "the drunkenness, the unstable marriages, [and] the violence of the other America," but he also insisted that "the other Americans are those who live at a level of life beneath moral choice."

56. Nathan Glazer and Daniel Patrick Moynihan, *Beyond the Melting Pot: The Negroes, Puerto Ricans, Jews, Italians, and Irish of New York City*, 2nd ed. (Cambridge, Mass.: MIT Press, 1970), p. xlv. As Glazer and Moynihan added, "Presumably, even in referring to 'students,' the spokesman did not have in mind those who were studying but those who were demonstrating" (pp. xlv–xlvi).

57. Glazer and Moynihan, *Beyond the Melting Pot*, p. xlvi.

58. Thomas Halper, "The Poor as Pawns: The New 'Deserving Poor' and the Old," *Polity* 6 (1973): 79.

59. Halper, "Poor as Pawns," p. 80. The emphasis appears in the text.

60. Halper, "Poor as Pawns," p. 86.

61. James Q. Wilson, "Crime and American Culture," *The Public Interest* 70 (Winter 1983), p. 33.

62. Susan E. Mayer, *What Money Can't Buy: Family Income and Children's Life Chances* (Cambridge, Mass.: Harvard University Press, 1997), p. 24.

63. Quoted in David M. Tucker, *The Decline of Thrift in America: Our Cultural Shift from Saving to Spending* (New York: Praeger, 1991), p. 20. Note that similar arguments were also made by writers with a more secular orientation, as in this remarkable letter sent by John Adams to Thomas Jefferson: "Will you tell me how to prevent riches from becoming the effects of temperance and industry? Will you tell me how to prevent riches from producing luxury? Will you tell me how to prevent luxury from producing effeminacy intoxication extravagance Vice and folly?" The letter is quoted in Daniel T. Rodgers, *The Work Ethic in Industrial America 1850–1920* (Chicago: University of Chicago Press, 1978), p. 103. The capitalization and punctuation replicate the passage in Rodgers's text.

64. Daniel Bell, *The Cultural Contradictions of Capitalism* (New York: Basic Books, 1976), p. 55. Bell did not speak of "work, sobriety, frugality, [and] sexual restraint" as virtues, but as qualities emphasized by "the Protestant ethic and the Puritan temper." To these qualities he added "a forbidding attitude toward life." But insofar as the reformers preached the joys of domesticity to the poor, their attitude was more sentimental—and life-affirming—than forbidding.

65. Bell, *Cultural Contradictions*, pp. 64–65.

66. Bell, *Cultural Contradictions*, pp. 70–71.

67. *On Character: Essays by James Q. Wilson* (Washington, D.C.: AEI Press, 1991), p. 28.

68. Wilson, "Crime and American Culture," pp. 44–45.

69. Wilson, *On Character*, p. 37.

70. Mead, *New Politics of Poverty*, p. 35.

71. Wilson, "Liberalism, Modernism, and the Good Life," in Mary Ann Glendon and David Blankenhorn, eds., *Seedbeds of Virtue: Sources of Competence, Character, and Citizenship in American Society* (Lanham, Md.: Madison Books, 1995), p. 30.

72. Myron Magnet, *The Dream and the Nightmare: The Sixties' Legacy to the Underclass* (New York: William Morrow and Co., 1993), p. 19.

73. Magnet, *Dream and the Nightmare*, p. 31.

74. Christopher Jencks, *Rethinking Social Policy: Race, Poverty, and the Underclass* (New York: HarperPerennial, 1993), pp. 134–136. See also the formulation of Paul E. Peterson, "The Urban Underclass and the Poverty Paradox," in Jencks and Peterson, eds., *The Urban Underclass* (Washington, D.C.: Brookings Institution, 1991): "The most powerful force contributing to the formation of the urban underclass, perversely enough, may be the changing values of mainstream American society, in which the virtues of family stability, mutual support, and religiously based commitment to the marriage vow no longer command the deference they once did" (p. 19).

75. Edward Banfield, *The Unheavenly City Revisited* (Boston: Little, Brown, and Co., 1974), p. 114. For a more recent discussion, see Peter D. Salins, *Assimilation, American Style* (New York: Basic Books, 1997): "Many unskilled American-born workers, regardless of race or ethnicity, have been conditioned by unions, the specifications of governmental job programs or contracts, an awareness of the higher standards that prevail in many occupations, and perhaps by the alternatives of welfare or crime to disdain 'dead-end' jobs, hard work, extended workdays, and low pay" (p. 138).

76. Stephan Thernstrom, "Poverty in Historical Perspective," in Daniel Patrick Moynihan, ed., *On Understanding Poverty: Perspectives from the Social Sciences* (New York: Basic Books, 1969), pp. 170, 181. On the demise of thrift among the well-to-do, see Bell's discussion of installment buying and consumer debt in *Cultural Contradictions*, pp. 69–70. Bell noted that "for years, such was the grim specter of middle-class morality that people were afraid to be overdrawn at the bank, lest a check bounce. By the end of the 1960s, the banks were strenuously advertising the services of cash reserves that would allow a depositor to overdraw up to several thousand dollars (to be paid back in monthly installments). No one need be deterred from gratifying his impulse at an auction or a sale. The seduction of the consumer had become total" (p. 70).

77. Wilson, *The Moral Sense* (New York: Free Press, 1993), p. 10.

78. Mead, "Poverty: How Little We Know," *Social Service Review* 68 (1994): 328.

79. Mead, *New Politics of Poverty*, p. 6. The emphasis appears in the text. See also p. 69: in 1987, among adults working more than half the year, "only 4 percent were poor."

80. See Salins, *Assimilation, American Style*: "In places where generations of experts on urban affairs and advocates of the poor have said there are no jobs for the unskilled and poorly educated, immigrants seem to be working, challenging the conventional wisdom that the economy of the modern American metropolis has no room at the bottom" (p. 136).

81. Mead, *New Politics of Poverty*, p. 23.

82. See Chapter 8, in which I discuss structural reforms—Individual Development Accounts and subsidies for low-wage jobs—that are specifically intended to facilitate the thrift and diligence of the poor.

83. Mead, *New Politics of Poverty*, p. 6. The emphases appear in the text.

84. Mead, *New Politics of Poverty*, p. 221.

85. On this point see Roy Lubove, *The Struggle for Social Security, 1900–1935* (Cambridge, Mass.: Harvard University Press, 1968): "The purpose of the Social Security Act was summed up in this way [in a 1962 assessment]: 'Only to a very minor degree does it modify

the distribution of wealth and it does not alter at all the fundamentals of our capitalistic and individualistic economy. Nor does it relieve the individual of primary responsibility for his own support and that of his dependents. . . . Social security does not dampen initiative or render thrift outmoded.' [Lubove himself then adds:] Eligibility and benefits in the contributory old-age and unemployment insurance titles were closely work-related" (p. 175). Note that Lubove saw the connection between benefits and participants' work history as a sign of social security's inadequacy. See p. 180: "Must economic security remain so closely tied to stable, long-term labor force participation?"

86. Clarke A. Chambers, "An Historical Perspective on Political Action vs. Individualized Treatment," in Weinberger, ed., *Perspectives on Social Welfare*, pp. 82–83.

87. Mead, "Poverty: How Little We Know," pp. 339–340.

88. Quoted in William Rhinelander Stewart, *The Philanthropic Work of Josephine Shaw Lowell Containing a Biographical Sketch of Her Life Together with a Selection of Her Public Papers and Private Letters* (Montclair, N.J.: Patterson Smith, 1974 [rpt. 1911]), pp. 197–198. The quotation is taken from an 1896 magazine article, "The True Aim of Charity Organization Societies."

89. Robert Hunter, *Poverty: Social Conscience in the Progressive Era*, edited by Peter d'A. Jones (New York: Harper and Row, 1965 [rpt. 1904]), p. 5. The emphasis appears in the text.

90. Hunter, *Poverty*, pp. 60–61. For the total population figure in 1904, see Jones's "Introduction to the Torchbook Edition," p. xv.

91. Hunter, *Poverty*, pp. 3–4.

92. Hunter, *Poverty*, pp. 62–63.

93. See Stanley Lebergott, *Pursuing Happiness: American Consumers in the Twentieth Century* (Princeton, N.J.: Princeton University Press, 1993), pp. 61–62, 67.

94. See Maya Federman, Thesia I. Garner, Kathleen Short, W. Boman Cutter IV, John Kiely, David Levine, Duane McGough, and Marilyn McMillen, "What Does It Mean to Be Poor in America?," *Monthly Labor Review* 119, no. 5 (May 1996), p. 7.

95. Robert Coit Chapin, *The Standard of Living among Workingmen's Families in New York City* (New York: Charities Publication Committee, 1909), p. 245.

96. Chapin, *Standard of Living*, Table 15: Expenditures for Given Objects. Averages and Percentages—By Income, p. 70.

97. Nicholas Eberstadt, "Prosperous Paupers and Affluent Savages," *Society* (January/February 1998), pp. 393–394, 397. Eberstadt points to the 1991 Consumer Expenditure Survey of the Department of Labor to support his claim that the consumption of the poor significantly exceeds their income: the survey showed (p. 397) that the bottom fifth of households "reported an average pretax income of only $6,000 but average total expenditures of nearly $13,500." Eberstadt attributes this discrepancy not to participation in the underground economy but to people's capacity to maintain their level of consumption even when income drops, by "draw[ing] down savings, sell[ing] assets, tak[ing] out loans, get[ting] help from friends and family." Eberstadt's article first appeared in *Society* in 1996; it was reprinted in 1998 as part of a commemoration of the journal's thirty-fifth anniversary.

98. Eberstadt, "Prosperous Paupers," pp. 394–395.

99. Eberstadt, "Prosperous Paupers," p. 396.

100. Eberstadt, "Prosperous Paupers," p. 401.

101. Mayer, *What Money Can't Buy*, p. 13. See also p. 149.

102. Mayer, *What Money Can't Buy*, p. 3.

103. Robert Rector and William F. Lauber, *America's Failed $5.4 Trillion War on Poverty*

(Washington, D.C.: Heritage Foundation, 1995), p. 2. Rector and Lauber understand failure as the inability to curb dependency and to discourage behaviors such as low work effort and illegitimacy. In fairness, some unspecified portion of the astounding sum that their calculations yield obviously went and now goes to support people who were and are unavoidably dependent, incapable of supporting themselves because of mental and physical defects. Lawrence Mead cites estimates that a fifth or a quarter of welfare recipients lack the capacity to work; see his "Welfare Employment," in Mead, ed., *New Paternalism*, p. 75. If these estimates are roughly accurate, somewhere between $1 trillion and $1.5 trillion would have been spent even in a welfare system that discouraged avoidable dependency. Still, that is a fairly small fraction of Rector and Lauber's $5.4 trillion total.

104. Michael Novak, John Cogan, Blanche Bernstein, Douglas J. Besharov, Barbara Blum, Allan Carlson, Michael Horowitz, S. Anna Kondratas, Leslie Lenkowsky, Glenn C. Loury, Lawrence Mead, Donald Moran, Charles Murray, Richard P. Nathan, Richard J. Neuhaus, Franklin D. Raines, Robert D. Reischauer, Alice M. Rivlin, Stanford Ross, and Michael Stern, *The New Consensus on Family and Welfare: A Community of Self-Reliance* (Washington, D.C., and Milwaukee: American Enterprise Institute and Marquette University, 1987), p. 5.

105. Novak et al., *New Consensus*, p. 29.

106. Claude S. Fischer, Michael Hout, Martín Sánchez Jankowski, Samuel R. Lucas, Ann Swidler, and Kim Voss, *Inequality by Design: Cracking the Bell Curve Myth* (Princeton, N.J.: Princeton University Press, 1996), pp. 89–90.

107. Mead, *New Politics of Poverty*, pp. 7–8.

108. Thernstrom, "Poverty in Historical Perspective," p. 171.

109. For a discussion of the impact of drinking on crime and social disorder in the contemporary inner city, see William J. Bennett, John J. DiIulio, Jr., and John P. Walters, *Body Count: Moral Poverty . . . and How to Win America's War against Crime and Drugs* (New York: Simon and Schuster, 1996), pp. 64–76.

110. See Jon M. Kingsdale, "The 'Poor Man's Club': Social Functions of the Urban Working-Class Saloon," *American Quarterly* 25 (1973): 472–489. Kingsdale observed that "the workingman's saloon was a leisure-time institution playing a large part in the social, political, even the economic aspects of his life. It performed a variety of functions, major and minor: Furnishing the cities' only public toilets, providing teamsters with watering troughs, cashing checks and lending money to customers, in addition to serving as the political and recreational focus of the workingman" (p. 476).

111. See Raymond Calkins, *Substitutes for the Saloon*, 2nd ed. (New York: Arno Press, 1971 [rpt. 1919]). Calkins noted that "the American liquor saloon has furnished the people immense opportunities for social fellowship, relaxation, and amusement"; he also lamented the failure of the community to provide "other agencies to perform the same function without the meretricious aid of whiskey and of beer" (p. iii). To cite just one example of a social benefit offered by the saloon, Calkins pointed out that "a man out of employment does not go to the charity organization society but to [the] club saloon" for men in his trade. "The saloons become, in fact, labor bureaus" (p. 9).

112. Gans, "Escaping from Poverty: A Comparison of the Immigrant and Black Experience," in *People, Plans, and Policies: Essays on Poverty, Racism, and Other National Urban Problems* (New York: Columbia University Press and Russell Sage Foundation, 1991), p. 282. This essay was originally written in 1968.

113. Nathan Glazer, *The Limits of Social Policy* (Cambridge, Mass.: Harvard University Press, 1988), p. 3. "The Limits of Social Policy" is the first in a series of essays collected in

the book of that title. It was originally published as an article in *Commentary* in September 1971.

114. Glazer, *Limits of Social Policy*, p. 8.

115. For a brief look at the racial composition of the poverty population, see Mead, "The Rise of Paternalism," in Mead, ed., *The New Paternalism*: "In 1995, blacks comprised 13 percent of the public but 27 percent of the poor, and 29 percent of blacks were poor." Mead then adds a still more remarkable but less familiar statistic that concerns the racial composition of the long-term poor: "Among people poor for at least eight years out of ten, a majority are black" (p. 37, note 36). With specific respect to urban poverty, see U.S. Bureau of the Census, *Poverty in the United States: 1995*: in 1995 only 30 percent of all Americans but 45 percent of all poor Americans lived in central cities (p. viii). See also Table 5, Percent of Persons in Poverty by Definition of Income and Selected Characteristics: 1995: blacks living in central cities were more than twice as likely to be poor as central-city whites (pp. 24 and 26). Exactly a third of the black central-city population was poor in 1995, compared with 16.2 percent of central-city whites. Finally, see Edmund S. Phelps, *Rewarding Work: How to Restore Participation and Self-Support to Free Enterprise* (Cambridge, Mass.: Harvard University Press, 1997): "Of the Standard Metropolitan Areas in which the majority are classified as poor, not one is predominantly white" (p. 56).

6. African Americans, Irish Americans, and Moral Reform

1. Stanley Lieberson, *A Piece of the Pie: Blacks and White Immigrants since 1880* (Berkeley and Los Angeles: University of California Press, 1980), p. 258. The seventeen cities are listed in the table on p. 266.

2. Lieberson, *Piece of the Pie*, p. 9.

3. Lieberson, *Piece of the Pie*, p. 38.

4. Quoted in Daniel Walker Howe, *The Unitarian Conscience: Harvard Moral Philosophy, 1805–1861* (Cambridge, Mass.: Harvard University Press, 1970), p. 242.

5. Quoted in Howe, *Unitarian Conscience*, p. 243. The emphasis appears in the text.

6. Howe, *Unitarian Conscience*, p. 243. On p. 281 Howe notes that Tuckerman, who "believed in racial equality and privately encouraged others in opposition to slavery, . . . felt that he could not afford to make his own views public." Tuckerman could not speak out because his work with the poor, specifically including poor blacks, was dependent on the continued financial support of wealthy Unitarians hostile to abolitionism. It is noteworthy that Tuckerman's work with Boston's black poor nevertheless won the praise of the abolitionist William Lloyd Garrison.

7. See Noel Ignatiev, *How the Irish Became White* (New York: Routledge, 1995), p. 23.

8. AICP, Seventeenth Annual Report (1860), p. 51.

9. Joan Waugh, *Unsentimental Reformer: The Life of Josephine Shaw Lowell* (Cambridge, Mass.: Harvard University Press, 1997), p. 74. For an extensive treatment of the riots, see Iver Bernstein, *The New York City Draft Riots: Their Significance for American Society and Politics in the Age of the Civil War* (New York: Oxford University Press, 1990).

10. Charles Loring Brace, *The Dangerous Classes of New York and Twenty Years' Work among Them*, 3rd ed., with addenda (Montclair, N.J.: Patterson Smith, 1967 [rpt. 1880]), p. 214.

11. Waugh, *Unsentimental Reformer*, pp. 74–75.

12. Waugh, *Unsentimental Reformer*, pp. 89–90.

13. Waugh, *Unsentimental Reformer*, p. 93.

14. See, for example, Paul Boyer, *Urban Masses and Moral Order in America, 1820–*

1920 (Cambridge, Mass.: Harvard University Press, 1976), pp. 147–148; and George M. Fredrickson, *The Inner Civil War: Northern Intellectuals and the Crisis of the Union* (New York: Harper and Row, 1965), p. 212. See also Waugh, *Unsentimental Reformer*, p. 94, for a partial critique of these interpretations. Waugh agrees that Lowell attempted to instill "worthy values" in both the ex-slaves and the urban poor; but she rejects the assumption that Lowell's work with the urban poor was "oppressive," in effect a punishment for their disloyalty during the war.

15. AICP, Seventeenth Annual Report (1860), pp. 50–51.

16. AICP, Twentieth Annual Report (1863), p. 26.

17. AICP, Twentieth Annual Report (1863), p. 35.

18. AICP, Twentieth Annual Report (1863), p. 44.

19. AICP, Twenty-first Annual Report (1864), p. 34. The emphasis appears in the text.

20. Amos G. Warner, *American Charities: A Study in Philanthropy and Economics* (New York: Arno Press and The New York Times, 1971 [rpt. 1894]), pp. 46–47. Here Warner summarizes his Table VIII, which is found after p. 34 in the text. I have rounded Warner's figures to tenths of a percent from the hundredths of a percent that he provided.

21. Warner, *American Charities*, p. 47.

22. Warner, *American Charities*, pp. 47–48.

23. Jacob A. Riis, *How the Other Half Lives: Studies among the Tenements of New York* (New York: Dover Publications, 1971), p. 115.

24. See Thomas Sowell, *Ethnic America: A History* (New York: Basic Books, 1981): "'Free persons of color' . . . were years—or even generations—ahead of the slaves in their acculturation to American society. Most 'free persons of color' could read and write in 1850, although only 1 or 2 percent of the slaves could do so" (p. 195). See also pp. 199–200 for Sowell's account of slavery's legacy in destroying the virtues of thrift, diligence, and personal responsibility: blacks "lack[ed] . . . experience in budgeting or in managing their own daily lives under slavery and [acquired] . . . habits of carelessness, little foresight, and dependence on whites [that were] engendered by that system. . . . As workers, blacks had acquired little sense of personal responsibility under slavery. Lack of initiative, evasion of work, half-done work, unpredictable absenteeism, and abuse of tools and equipment were pervasive under slavery, and these patterns did not suddenly disappear with emancipation." On the other hand, it has also been argued (based on a survey of migrants' letters) that southern blacks who moved to northern cities a generation after Riis published his book— during World War I—were animated by "the values so long and so uncritically labeled 'white Anglo-Saxon Protestant'": they sought "the freedom and affluence of middle-class life," and they believed that "the way to get them was to work hard, spend thriftily, build associations with other aspiring Negroes, and attend carefully to their children's education." See Timothy L. Smith, "Native Blacks and Foreign Whites: Varying Responses to Educational Opportunity in America, 1880–1950," *Perspectives in American History* 6 (1972): 326.

25. Riis, *How the Other Half Lives*, p. 115.

26. Riis, *How the Other Half Lives*, pp. 116–117.

27. Riis, *How the Other Half Lives*, p. 116.

28. Riis, *How the Other Half Lives*, p. 118.

29. Riis, *How the Other Half Lives*, p. 118.

30. Riis, *How the Other Half Lives*, p. 119.

31. Riis, *How the Other Half Lives*, pp. 77–83. Although Riis should obviously not have blamed the Chinese collectively for these failings, it should be noted that there was a genu-

ine basis for his concerns. Cf. Sowell, *Ethnic America*: "Chinatowns in the last quarter of the nineteenth century were centers of vice, not only for the Chinese but for whites seeking prostitution, drugs, and gambling. The Chinese introduced opium into the United States. The white clientele of Chinatown vice districts were often ruffians and hoodlums, who added to the dangerousness of an area where tong violence might break out at any time" (p. 141).

32. Nathan Irving Huggins, *Revelations: American History, American Myths*, edited by Brenda Smith Huggins (New York: Oxford University Press, 1995), pp. 214–215. Mrs. Ruffner was the wife of the owner of a coal mine in Malden, West Virginia; Washington was her servant for more than a year. General Armstrong headed the Hampton Institute, at which Washington received his formal education.

33. Booker T. Washington, *Up from Slavery*, in *Three Negro Classics*, with an introduction by John Hope Franklin (New York: Avon Books, 1965), p. 38. *Up from Slavery* was originally published in 1901.

34. Washington, "Progress of the American Negro," in Howard Brotz, ed., *Negro Social and Political Thought, 1850–1920: Representative Texts* (New York: Basic Books, 1966), p. 398. "Progress of the American Negro" is a chapter of *The Negro in Business*, a book that Washington published in 1907.

35. Washington, *Working with the Hands* (New York: Arno Press and The New York Times, 1969 [rpt. 1904]), p. 21.

36. Washington, *Working with the Hands*, p. 20.

37. Washington, *Working with the Hands*, p. 64.

38. Washington, *Up from Slavery*, p. 200.

39. Washington, *Character Building: Being Addresses on Sunday Evenings to the Students of Tuskegee Institute* (New York: Haskell House Publishers, 1972 [rpt. 1902]), p. 276. Both in format and in contents, *Character Building* is strikingly reminiscent of Brace's 1866 collection of his *Short Sermons to News Boys*. The latter volume consists of hortatory addresses on the virtues facilitating upward mobility that Brace addressed to the residents of a Children's Aid Society lodging house. I see the similarity between the two works as a sign of the reformers' belief in the universality of the virtues, which were thought to be of equal relevance to youths, regardless of whether they were southern rural blacks or northern urban immigrants. Brace and Washington also shared a common preference for rural over urban America: Brace urged his urban charges to migrate to the country, and Washington advised his rural students against migrating to the cities.

40. Washington, *Working with the Hands*, pp. 119, 126–127.

41. Washington, *Working with the Hands*, p. 124. On p. 129 Washington described his broader educational undertaking (that is, his teaching directed to neighborhood people who were not enrolled as students at Tuskegee) as "settlement work."

42. Washington, *Working with the Hands*, pp. 185–186.

43. Washington, *Working with the Hands*, pp. 238–239.

44. See Louis R. Harlan, *Booker T. Washington: The Wizard of Tuskegee, 1901–1915* (New York: Oxford University Press, 1983): "There is no direct evident that Washington himself ever drank, and much hearsay evidence from his friends that he did not. His daughter Portia said that he drank, particularly in his later years, as ill health brought him pain" (p. 400).

45. Harlan, *Booker T. Washington*, p. 231.

46. Harlan, *Booker T. Washington*, pp. 231–232.

47. Washington, *Working with the Hands*, p. 243. Washington went on to note that

"each Negro child of school age in [Louisiana] . . . had spent on him for education last year but $1.89, while each child of school age in the State of New York had spent on him $20.53"—figures that do much to explain the gap in learning (and the gap in income) between white immigrants who settled in the North and blacks who were concentrated in the South.

48. Washington, "Democracy and Education," in Brotz, ed., *Negro Social and Political Thought,* p. 369. "Democracy and Education" was an address delivered in 1896.

49. Washington, *Working with the Hands,* p. 246.

50. On the kinship between Washington and DuBois, see Antonio McDaniel, "The 'Philadelphia Negro' Then and Now: Implications for Empirical Research," in Michael B. Katz and Thomas J. Sugrue, eds., *W. E. B. DuBois, Race, and the City:* The Philadelphia Negro *and Its Legacy* (Philadelphia: University of Pennsylvania Press, 1998): "Surprisingly, like Booker T. Washington, DuBois . . . offered a solution to the race problem that suggested that African Americans accept the behavioral norms and necessities of the status quo. DuBois called on African Americans to change themselves into an acceptable group within the confines of the normative structures that dominated American elite bourgeois culture" (p. 188).

51. W. E. B. DuBois, *The Autobiography of W. E. B. DuBois: A Soliloquy on Viewing My Life from the Last Decade of Its First Century* (New York: International Publishers, 1968), p. 75. The autobiography was published posthumously; DuBois died in 1963.

52. DuBois, *Autobiography,* p. 95.

53. DuBois, *Autobiography,* p. 81.

54. Quoted in Smith, "Native Blacks and Foreign Whites," p. 326. The passage is taken from a 1944 essay, "My Evolving Program for Negro Freedom," in Rayford W. Logan, ed., *What the Negro Wants.*

55. W. E. B. DuBois, *The Philadelphia Negro: A Social Study, Together with a Special Report on Domestic Service by Isabel Eaton* (New York: Schocken Books, 1967 [rpt. 1899]), p. 98.

56. DuBois, *Philadelphia Negro,* p. 111.

57. DuBois, *Philadelphia Negro,* p. 322.

58. DuBois, *Philadelphia Negro,* pp. 351–352.

59. DuBois, *Philadelphia Negro,* p. 140.

60. DuBois, *Philadelphia Negro,* p. 394.

61. DuBois, *Philadelphia Negro,* p. 395.

62. DuBois, *Philadelphia Negro,* p. 67.

63. DuBois, *Philadelphia Negro,* p. 70. But see also p. 71, where DuBois took comfort from the fact that "the conjugal condition of the Negroes approache[d] so nearly that of the whites, when the economic and social history of the two groups [had] been so strikingly different." According to 1890 census data for the whole city, presented on p. 70, 51.3 percent of all black males over 15, and 42.5 percent of all black females over 15, were married; the comparable figures for white men and women (given on p. 71) were 52.0 percent and 49.0 percent, respectively. On p. 72 DuBois concluded that "the thoroughly independent Negro family . . . is a more successful institution than we had a right to expect," in view of the attacks visited upon monogamy under slavery.

64. DuBois, *Philadelphia Negro,* p. 68.

65. DuBois, *Philadelphia Negro,* p. 110.

66. DuBois, *Philadelphia Negro,* p. 72.

67. DuBois, *Philadelphia Negro,* p. 391.

68. DuBois, *Philadelphia Negro*, p. 390.

69. DuBois, *Philadelphia Negro*, p. 178.

70. DuBois, *Philadelphia Negro*, p. 277. His judgment on this score was anticipated by Amos Warner. In his survey of causes of poverty among various ethnic groups, Warner found that 15.28 percent of all poverty could be blamed on "drink." But alcohol was responsible for only 6.23 percent of "colored" poverty. Of the ten groups for which he provided data, only the one described as "Russian and Polish" (which presumably consisted largely of Jews) had a lower figure, at 3.24 percent. See Warner, *American Charities*, p. 46 and Table VIII (which appears after p. 34).

71. DuBois, *Philadelphia Negro*, p. 282.

72. DuBois, *Philadelphia Negro*, p. 358. Cf. Frank Dekker Watson, *The Charity Organization Movement in the United States: A Study in American Philanthropy* (New York: Macmillan, 1922), p. 151: "The friendly visitor is the personal embodiment of the slogan of many [charity organization] societies, 'Not alms, but a friend.'"

73. DuBois, *Philadelphia Negro*, p. 390.

74. DuBois, *Philadelphia Negro*, p. 391.

75. David Levering Lewis, *W. E. B. DuBois: Biography of a Race, 1868–1919* (New York: Henry Holt and Co., 1993), p. 190.

76. The unreasonableness of DuBois's moral standard is suggested in McDaniel, "Philadelphia Negro": "The moralistic tone of *The Philadelphia Negro*, especially toward the behavior of working-class and lower-class African Americans, served to legitimate European American moral criteria" (p. 184). McDaniel's observation is correct, but contrary to his supposition it is not particularly damning. DuBois apparently believed that his moral criteria were not essentially European American, but universal; he also believed, quite plausibly, that African Americans could aspire to live by those criteria, and that African Americans who did live by them would be more likely to emerge from poverty.

77. Jennifer L. Hochschild, *Facing Up to the American Dream: Race, Class, and the Soul of the Nation* (Princeton, N.J.: Princeton University Press, 1995), p. 169.

78. John Sibley Butler, *Entrepreneurship and Self-Help among Black Americans: A Reconsideration of Race and Economics* (Albany: State University of New York Press, 1991), p. 282.

79. Malcolm X, *The Autobiography of Malcolm X*, with the assistance of Alex Haley (New York: Grove Press, 1966), p. 275.

80. Michael Eric Dyson, *Making Malcolm: The Myth and Meaning of Malcolm X* (New York: Oxford University Press, 1995), p. 170.

81. C. Eric Lincoln, *The Black Muslims in America*, 3rd ed. (Grand Rapids, Mich.: William B. Eerdmans Publishing Co., 1994), p. 86.

82. Quoted in Lincoln, *Black Muslims*, p. 87. The passage is taken from a 1960 Muslim enumeration of the five "keys to black economic security." The emphasis appears in the text.

83. Quoted in Lincoln, *Black Muslims*, p. 77. The quotation is taken from a 1960 talk at Boston University.

84. Malcolm X, *Autobiography*, p. 221. The strict moral code also enjoined diligence, in its prohibition of "tak[ing] long vacations from work."

85. Malcolm X, *Autobiography*, p. 259. The Muslim program to combat addiction is discussed on pp. 259–263.

86. Malcolm X, *Autobiography*, p. 216.

87. Malcolm X, *Autobiography*, p. 276.

88. Malcolm X, *Autobiography*, p. 313.

89. Quoted in Lincoln, *Black Muslims*, p. 86. The quotation is taken from a 1958 address.

90. Bruce Perry, *Malcolm: The Life of a Man Who Changed Black America* (New York: Station Hill, 1991), p. 148.

91. Malcolm X, *Autobiography*, p. 227.

92. Daryl Michael Scott, *Contempt and Pity: Social Policy and the Image of the Damaged Black Psyche, 1880–1996* (Chapel Hill: University of North Carolina Press, 1997), p. 190. Cf. Lee Rainwater and William L. Yancey, *The Moynihan Report and the Politics of Controversy* (Cambridge, Mass.: MIT Press, 1967): "The spring of 1966 . . . produced defenses of the [Moynihan] report. The most notable of these appeared in *Muhammad Speaks* (April 8, 1966). There it was noted that . . . the Moynihan Report gives 'substance to some of the Honorable Elijah Muhammad's contentions and claims'" (p. 267).

93. Malcolm X, *Autobiography*, p. 276.

94. Lincoln, *Black Muslims*, p. 78.

95. Nathan Glazer and Daniel Patrick Moynihan, *Beyond the Melting Pot: The Negroes, Puerto Ricans, Jews, Italians, and Irish of New York City*, 2nd ed. (Cambridge, Mass.: MIT Press, 1970), pp. 82–83.

96. Nicholas Lemann, *The Promised Land: The Great Black Migration and How It Changed America* (New York: Alfred A. Knopf, 1991), p. 302. It is arguable, though, that Wallace Muhammad is currently a more important leader than Farrakhan. On this point, see Lisa Miller, "Black Muslims Flock to a Moderate Cleric of Radical Pedigree," *Wall Street Journal*, July 9, 1999: "For all his fire-in-the-belly rhetoric, his high-media profile and his ability to polarize Americans, Mr. Farrakhan isn't the dominant voice in the African-American Muslim community today. That distinction belongs to . . . [the] son of Mr. Farrakhan's mentor, Elijah Muhammad"—Wallace Muhammad (p. A1). Muhammad's Muslim American Society includes 200,000 adherents, up from 80,000 in 1975.

97. Perry, *Malcolm*, p. 198.

98. Malcolm X, *Autobiography*, p. 221.

99. See Perry, *Malcolm*: "The former fast-living drug addict who had tried to solve the problem of gratification by continual indulgence had become an ascetic who mastered the need for gratification by denying it. . . . While the wayward, teen-age Malcolm had 'pleasured' himself at the cost of the guilty conscience he had tried so hard to deny, the ascetic Malcolm purchased self-respect at the terrible price of an almost completely joyless existence" (pp. 149–150).

100. Perry, *Malcolm*, p. 168.

101. See Malcolm X, *Autobiography*, p. 362, for Malcolm's 1964 statement: "The true Islam has shown me that a blanket indictment of all white people is as wrong as when whites make blanket indictments against blacks." See also his 1965 statement: "The Islam I believed in now was the Islam which was taught in Mecca—that there was no God but Allah, and that Muhammad ibn Abdullah who lived in the Holy City of Mecca fourteen hundred years ago was the Last Messenger of Allah" (p. 372). Cf. M. S. Handler's "Introduction" to the *Autobiography*: "Malcolm's attitude toward the white man underwent a marked change in 1964—a change that contributed to his break with Elijah Muhammad and his racist doctrines. Malcolm's meteoric eruption on the national scene brought him into wider contact with white men who were not the 'devils' he had thought they were. . . . A second factor that contributed to his conversion to wider horizons was a growing doubt about the authenticity of Elijah Muhammad's version of the Muslim religion—a doubt that

grew into a certainty with more knowledge and more experience" (p. xiii). For evidence that Malcolm had already rejected any global condemnation of whites as early as 1959, see Perry, *Malcolm*, pp. 205–206.

102. Malcolm X, *Autobiography*, p. 165. Malcolm's wholly unskeptical account of this "key lesson of Mr. Elijah Muhammad's teachings" begins on p. 164 and ends on p. 167. No doubt because of Malcolm's assassination, the *Autobiography* is a disjointed book: the first fifteen chapters, written from the perspective of an ardent disciple of Elijah Muhammad, were not revised to be made compatible with the last four chapters, in which Malcolm's disillusionment with and departure from Elijah Muhammad is made clear. For indications that Malcolm had in fact long been skeptical of many of the more outlandish tenets of Elijah Muhammad's doctrine, see Perry, *Malcolm*, pp. 122, 204–207.

103. Malcolm X, *Autobiography*, pp. 294–295. There is evidence, though, suggesting that Malcolm had been aware of Elijah Muhammad's sexual profligacy many years earlier, but chose to keep silent about it. See Perry, *Malcolm*, pp. 230–232.

104. Perry, *Malcolm*, pp. 224–225.

105. Stephan Thernstrom and Abigail Thernstrom, *America in Black and White: One Nation, Indivisible* (New York: Simon and Schuster, 1997), p. 234.

106. Washington, *Character Building*, p. 119. Washington contended that "our condition and capacity are not equal to those of the majority of the white people with whom we come in daily contact." To deny the factual superiority of whites, he maintained, "is to say that slavery was no disadvantage to us" (p. 119).

107. See Ignatiev, *How the Irish Became White*, p. 100, for a summary of the judgments of several historians of the black experience in the antebellum North.

108. DuBois, *Philadelphia Negro*, pp. 351–352.

109. See, for example, Herbert J. Gans, *People, Plans, and Policies: Essays on Poverty, Racism, and Other National Urban Problems* (New York: Columbia University Press and Russell Sage Foundation, 1991), pp. 279–280. For a critique of this argument, see Nathan Glazer, *Ethnic Dilemmas 1964–1982* (Cambridge, Mass.: Harvard University Press, 1983): "Admittedly there is less need for unskilled labor now than in the periods of peak European migration. But this cannot be translated into the conclusion that there are fewer *jobs* available. For while the number of unskilled jobs has declined, the number of those who are capable of filling only unskilled jobs has also declined. Black migrants have a higher level of education than European immigrants of the beginning of the century and are consequently not as restricted in the kinds of jobs they can fill. The fact that many jobs for the unskilled are not filled shows that there has not been a substantial decline in the ratio of jobs to applicants" (pp. 88–89). The emphasis appears in the text. See also Lawrence M. Mead, *The New Politics of Poverty: The Nonworking Poor in America* (New York: Basic Books, 1992): "Unless we regard literacy as an advanced skill, the labor market is not much more demanding today than it ever was" (p. 104). To substantiate this claim, Mead notes that the number of blue-collar jobs in New York City actually increased by 140,000 in the late 1980s. Furthermore, between 1972 and 1981 the proportion of all New York City jobs that demanded low skills held virtually steady, going from 58 to 57 percent.

110. See, for example, the conclusion of Lieberson, *Piece of the Pie*: "The early living conditions of the new Europeans after their migration to the United States were extremely harsh and their point of entry into the socioeconomic system was quite low. However, it is a non sequitur to assume that new Europeans had it as bad as did blacks or that the failure of blacks to move upward as rapidly reflected some ethnic deficiencies. The situation for new Europeans in the United States, bad as it may have been, was not as bad as that experienced

by blacks at the same time" (p. 383). Lieberson points, for example, to the higher mortality rates suffered by northern blacks and to their exclusion from labor unions at the turn of the century. Note, though, that Lieberson's argument concerns the immigrants from southern, central, and eastern Europe who came to America after 1880, rather than the Irish immigrants who began their mass arrival in America before the Civil War.

111. Huggins, *Revelations*, p. 151.

112. Orlando Patterson, *The Ordeal of Integration: Progress and Resentment in America's "Racial" Crisis* (Washington, D.C.: Civitas Counterpoint, 1997), p. 181.

113. Mead, *New Politics of Poverty*, pp. 154–155. The emphasis appears in the text.

114. Hochschild, *Facing Up to the American Dream*, p. 245.

115. Mead, *New Politics of Poverty*, p. 154.

116. Kerby A. Miller, *Emigrants and Exiles: Ireland and the Irish Exodus to North America* (New York: Oxford University Press, 1985), pp. 3–4.

117. Miller, *Emigrants and Exiles*, p. 556.

118. Miller, *Emigrants and Exiles*, p. 107.

119. Miller, *Emigrants and Exiles*, p. 328.

120. Quoted in Carl Wittke, *The Irish in America* (Baton Rouge: Louisiana State University Press, 1956), p. 40.

121. William V. Shannon, *The American Irish* (New York: Macmillan, 1963), p. 39.

122. Andrew M. Greeley, *That Most Distressful Nation: The Taming of the American Irish* (Chicago: Quadrangle Books, 1972), pp. 119–120.

123. Wittke, *Irish in America*, p. 41. Wittke quotes the judgment of the Irish American journalist Thomas D'Arcy McGee, who acknowledged that his compatriots had not been taught "fundamental cleanliness, sobriety, caution, perseverance, or the other minor details." For comparable nineteenth-century observations, see Miller, *Emigrants and Exiles*, pp. 268–272.

124. William J. Stern, "How Dagger John Saved New York's Irish," *City Journal* (Spring 1997), p. 92.

125. Glazer and Moynihan, *Beyond the Melting Pot*, p. lxiv.

126. Sowell, *Ethnic America*, p. 290. Two more similarities can be mentioned. A generation ago, Glazer and Moynihan noted (*Beyond the Melting Pot*, p. 38) that "the problem of the Negro in America is the problem of the Negro men more than the Negro women." According to Kerby Miller (*Emigrants and Exiles*, p. 494), the same pattern held among the nineteenth-century Irish: "Irish-American females enjoyed markedly greater upward mobility and more successful adjustment to American society than their male peers." Furthermore, among both groups the more successful members ironically experienced the greatest frustrations in dealings with the dominant majority group. Orlando Patterson observes (*Ordeal of Integration*, pp. 50–51) that "the greatest expressions of rage" against whites are voiced today not by the black poor but by "the Afro-American middle class." But as he points out (p. 51), that is a predictable consequence of integration (and the consequent improvement in prospects for middle-class blacks): "As individuals in both groups meet more and more, the possibility for conflict is bound to increase." Miller (*Emigrants and Exiles*, p. 497) discerns the same phenomenon among the nineteenth-century Irish: "Constantly in contact with native Protestant employers and peers, . . . middle-class Irish-Americans still endured irritating, if not economically damaging, slights and prejudices" that were encountered less often by the less successful and less integrated members of the Irish American working class. See also p. 531: "In the face of persistent bigotry, middle-class

Irish-Americans' efforts to embrace bourgeois America often led to harsh rebuffs and heightened ethno-religious consciousness." For a third similarity between Irish immigrants in the past and blacks today, see note 140 below.

127. DuBois, *Autobiography*, p. 75.

128. Oscar Handlin, *Boston's Immigrants: A Study in Acculturation*, revised and enlarged ed. (Cambridge, Mass.: Harvard University Press, 1959), p. 70. Note, though, Handlin's observation that "Negroes were better off [in Boston] than elsewhere in the United States."

129. Quoted in Wittke, *Irish in America*, p. 116.

130. Wittke, *Irish in America*, p. 125.

131. Ignatiev, *How the Irish Became White*, p. 41.

132. Greeley, *The Irish Americans: Their Rise to Money and Power* (New York: Harper and Row, 1981), p. 111. For more recent evidence, see Patterson, *Ordeal of Integration*, p. 168. Patterson cites 1989 data showing that Irish Americans then were the second most prosperous ethnic group of European descent (trailing only the Jews), with a household income 18 percent above the American average. By contrast, Americans of British Protestant ancestry had an income that was far lower and ranked fifth among these groups.

133. Patterson, *Ordeal of Integration*, p. 121.

134. Ignatiev, *How the Irish Became White*, pp. 115–116. Ignatiev relies almost exclusively on evidence from the Philadelphia area. For an extensive discussion of the discrimination faced by blacks (as compared not with Irish immigrants but with those from southern, central, and eastern Europe) in securing crafts occupations, see Lieberson, *Piece of the Pie*, pp. 339–354.

135. Greeley, *That Most Distressful Nation*, p. 266.

136. Patterson, *Ordeal of Integration*, p. 167. Other factors to which Patterson points in explaining Irish Americans' ascent from poverty include political patronage and preferential hiring for public employment (which he sees as the nineteenth-century equivalent of affirmative action), and a willingness to advance their interests by changing rules in ways that worked to their advantage (for example, by protesting against religious discrimination in public schools). In this context he says that the Irish "did not turn themselves into good little Celtic models of the Protestant ethic, meekly playing by the rules they found." But this remark reflects a misunderstanding of the Protestant ethic. There is nothing in the Protestant ethic counseling meekness; the moral reformers' virtues are means of achieving self-advancement, not self-abnegation. Thus Lowell was second to none in supporting the Protestant ethic; but her commitment to it did not preclude her praise for those workers—many of them Irish American—who sought to advance their interests by changing the rules through the institution of collective bargaining.

137. Ignatiev, *How the Irish Became White*, p. 110.

138. Ignatiev, *How the Irish Became White*, p. 111. The claim that "White men will not work with [the Negro]" is quoted from an 1851 edition of the *African Repository*, a newspaper for blacks.

139. Quoted in Ignatiev, *How the Irish Became White*, pp. 110–111. The quotations are taken from *The Liberator*. The emphasis is mine.

140. A more valid critique would be that the Irish were not entrepreneurial, despite their thrift. See Handlin, *The Newcomers: Negroes and Puerto Ricans in a Changing Metropolis* (Cambridge, Mass.: Harvard University Press, 1965): "Irish surplus earnings were either unprofitably hoarded or expended on higher living standards and on houses which

produced no income" (p. 26). Here the charge is less that the Irish were unthrifty than that the product of their thrift was not profitably invested. Interestingly, the same observation has been made about blacks today. Cf. Hochschild, *Facing Up to the American Dream*: "Blacks with capital to spare invest less than do comparable whites and Latinos in dividend-bearing stocks or interest-bearing bonds, and more in apparently safe and solid things like houses and cars" (p. 177).

141. Stephan Thernstrom, *Poverty and Progress: Social Mobility in a Nineteenth Century City* (Cambridge, Mass.: Harvard University Press, 1964), pp. 155–156.

142. George Potter, *To the Golden Door: The Story of the Irish in Ireland and America* (Boston: Little, Brown and Co., 1960), pp. 512–513.

143. Wittke, *Irish in America*, p. 51. See also Shannon, *American Irish*, p. 39.

144. Quoted in Jay P. Dolan, *The Immigrant Church: New York's Irish and German Catholics, 1815–1865* (Baltimore: Johns Hopkins University Press, 1975), p. 129.

145. Sister Joan Bland, *Hibernian Crusade: The Story of the Catholic Total Abstinence Union of America* (Washington, D.C.: Catholic University of America Press, 1951), p. 275. The emphasis appears in the text.

146. Bland, *Hibernian Crusade*, p. 267. See, for instance, a 1901 statement by Archbishop John Ireland: "Total abstinence . . . is but one virtue, but it is a fertile virtue that begets of itself many others, particularly some virtues that we need very much to be successful. . . . If our people had saved up for the last fifty years the money that went into saloons, . . . how different socially would they not be, how much more influence they would have" (quoted on p. 226).

147. Stern, "How Dagger John Saved New York's Irish," p. 104.

148. Miller, *Emigrants and Exiles*, p. 506.

149. Stern, "How Dagger John Saved New York's Irish," p. 104.

150. Miller, *Emigrants and Exiles*, p. 492.

151. Dolan, *Immigrant Church*, p. 56.

152. Dolan, *Immigrant Church*, p. 57.

153. Dolan, *Immigrant Church*, p. 8.

154. Miller, *Emigrants and Exiles*, pp. 116–117.

155. Thernstrom, *Poverty and Progress*, p. 174.

156. Handlin, *Boston's Immigrants*, p. 131.

157. Thernstrom, *Poverty and Progress*, p. 175.

158. Thernstrom, *Poverty and Progress*, p. 179.

159. Miller, *Emigrants and Exiles*, pp. 332–333. The emphasis appears in the text.

160. Quoted in Miller, *Emigrants and Exiles*, p. 268.

161. Miller, *Emigrants and Exiles*, p. 325.

162. Quoted in Potter, *To the Golden Door*, p. 531.

163. Quoted in Miller, *Emigrants and Exiles*, p. 551.

164. Quoted in Miller, *Emigrants and Exiles*, p. 337.

165. Quoted in Shannon, *American Irish*, p. 135.

166. Shannon, *American Irish*, p. 135.

167. Shannon, *American Irish*, p. 133.

7. The Contemporary Climate for Moral Reform

1. John Sibley Butler, *Entrepreneurship and Self-Help among Black Americans: A Reconsideration of Race and Economics* (Albany: State University of New York Press, 1991), pp. 323–324.

2. Orlando Patterson, *The Ordeal of Integration: Progress and Resentment in America's "Racial" Crisis* (Washington, D.C.: Civitas Counterpoint, 1997), p. 85. Patterson's use of the word "miracle," it should be clear, is ironic. As is apparent from the next paragraph in the text, Patterson understands the success of most American blacks as a predictable consequence of the exercise of what I am calling the virtues.

3. Patterson, *Ordeal of Integration*, p. 24.

4. Patterson, *Ordeal of Integration*, p. 83. Patterson believes that the goal of moral autonomy is, on the other hand, generally questioned by "the top 15 percent and the misled bottom quarter of the Afro-American social hierarchy," which tend to maintain that black efforts at self-advancement necessarily fail.

5. Patterson, *Ordeal of Integration*, p. 171.

6. Stephan Thernstrom and Abigail Thernstrom, *America in Black and White: One Nation, Indivisible* (New York: Simon and Schuster, 1997), p. 236, Table 2.

7. Thernstrom and Thernstrom, *America in Black and White*, p. 242, Table 7.

8. See John J. DiIulio, Jr., "The Coming of the Super-Preachers," *The Weekly Standard*, June 23, 1997, p. 24: 82 percent of blacks are church members, and 82 percent "say that religion is very important in their everyday lives." (By contrast, only 58 percent of all Americans claim that religion is very important in their everyday lives.) DiIulio quotes a judgment by the Gallup polling organization, that American blacks "of all faiths are in many ways the most religious people in America."

9. See Glenn C. Loury and Linda Datcher Loury, "Not by Bread Alone: The Role of the African-American Church in Inner-City Development," *The Brookings Review* (Winter 1997), p. 12. In this context, consider the implications of a remark by one of today's most prominent religiously oriented black moral reformers, Boston's Reverend Eugene Rivers: he speaks of "the forgotten 40 percent of the inner-city blacks who *are* working, support families and go to church." (Quoted in Kenneth L. Woodward, "The New Holy War," *Newsweek*, June 1, 1998, p. 27; the emphasis appears in the text.) Forty percent is not an insignificant figure, but it is far below the national figure of 82 percent mentioned in note 8 above.

10. See DiIulio, "Coming of the Super-Preachers," where he cites (among other studies) research by David Larson and Byron Johnson showing that "churchgoing cuts by 50 percent many of the major crime and other life risks associated with growing up male in predominantly poor, black inner-city neighborhoods" (p. 25). The pioneer study in this field is Richard B. Freeman, "Who Escapes? The Relation of Churchgoing and Other Background Factors to the Socioeconomic Performance of Black Male Youths from Inner-City Tracts," in Freeman and Harry J. Holzer, eds., *The Black Youth Employment Crisis* (Chicago: University of Chicago Press, 1986), pp. 353–376.

11. See Loury and Loury, "Not by Bread Alone": "A sober review of the evidence does not support the view that inner-city churches are now having a substantial impact on the quality of life in low-income communities by altering the socioeconomic status of individual church members. (We say this despite the many examples of outstanding urban ministries doing excellent work in particular communities.) . . . Studies of the effects of religiosity on income and schooling invariably find only small positive effects" (p. 12). On the other hand, small positive effects are obviously better than negative effects or no effects at all.

12. In this context, see Freeman, "Who Escapes?" for what Freeman presents as one possible reading of its findings: "Those regressions tell us nothing about what to do. All they show is that there are good families and good kids and bad families and bad kids in the inner

city. The good ones go to church. The bad ones live on welfare. The good ones will be good no matter what; the bad ones will be bad no matter what. Put a bad kid in church and he'll disrupt everything. There's nothing in the analysis that says what to do" (p. 371).

13. See Peter H. Rossi and Zahava D. Blum, "Class, Status, and Poverty," in Daniel P. Moynihan, ed., *On Understanding Poverty: Perspectives from the Social Sciences* (New York: Basic Books, 1969), p. 39. In the essay Rossi and Blum summarized the findings of the post–World War II empirical social science literature on the respects in which the poor supposedly differ from the nonpoor. They reported that one of the characteristics frequently ascribed to the poor in this literature is "fundamentalist religious views" (one of the "value orientations" of the poor). It should be noted that Rossi and Blum themselves questioned the reality of a culture of poverty (see pp. 56–57); their goal in the essay was simply to specify the attributes generally ascribed to the poor by those who believe that such a culture exists.

14. Elijah Anderson, *Streetwise: Race, Class, and Change in an Urban Community* (Chicago: University of Chicago Press, 1990), p. 136. The emphasis is mine.

15. W. E. B. DuBois, *The Philadelphia Negro: A Social Study, Together with a Special Report on Domestic Service by Isabel Eaton* (New York: Schocken Books, 1967 [rpt. 1899]), pp. 205–206.

16. Patterson, *Ordeal of Integration*, p. 106. The emphases appear in the text.

17. Patterson, *Ordeal of Integration*, p. 107.

18. Patterson, *Ordeal of Integration*, p. 108.

19. Jennifer L. Hochschild, *Facing Up to the American Dream: Race, Class, and the Soul of the Nation* (Princeton, N.J.: Princeton University Press, 1995), p. 123.

20. Glenn C. Loury, "The Conservative Line on Race," *The Atlantic Monthly*, November 1997, p. 153. "The Conservative Line on Race" is an extensive review of Stephan and Abigail Thernstrom's *America in Black and White*.

21. Hochschild, *Facing Up to the American Dream*, pp. 212–213.

22. Hochschild, *Facing Up to the American Dream*, pp. 139–140. The emphasis is mine.

23. Butler, *Entrepreneurship and Self-Help*, p. 251.

24. Henry Louis Gates, Jr., "Parable of the Talents," in Gates and Cornel West, *The Future of the Race* (New York: Alfred A. Knopf, 1996), p. 21.

25. Gates, "Parable of the Talents," p. 10.

26. E. Franklin Frazier, *Black Bourgeoisie* (New York: Free Press, 1957), p. 34.

27. Frazier, *Black Bourgeoisie*, pp. 80–81.

28. Frazier, *Black Bourgeoisie*, p. 125.

29. Frazier, *Black Bourgeoisie*, p. 127.

30. Frazier, *Black Bourgeoisie*, pp. 231–232.

31. In effect, Butler's *Entrepreneurship and Self-Help* is meant to serve as an empirical refutation of Frazier. Its claim is that the black bourgeoisie has continued to manifest the virtues that Frazier ascribed exclusively to the old black bourgeoisie. See especially pp. 234–235, where Butler argues that the black bourgeoisie has "(1) adjusted to hostility by turning inward and developing economic and community institutions; (2) developed a strong tradition of family stability and excellent quality of life through housing, health care, and other means, and, perhaps . . . most important . . . (3) beg[u]n a very strong emphasis on the importance of higher education."

32. Cf. Nathan Glazer, *Ethnic Dilemmas 1964–1982* (Cambridge, Mass.: Harvard University Press, 1983): "There is a substantial difference between the perspective of Frazier and contemporary radical critics of middle-class objectives. Frazier was attacking the Negro

middle class for . . . aping a life it did not have the political or economic strength actually to achieve. He found nothing wrong with a life that emphasized work, stable family relationships, achievement. He objected to the fact that too many in the Negro middle classes were willing to settle for the shadow of that life, rather than the substance. Radical Negro writers today attack its substance" (pp. 51–52).

33. Patterson, *Ordeal of Integration*, p. 24.

34. Gates, "Two Nations . . . Both Black," *Forbes*, September 14, 1992, p. 138.

35. Hochschild, *Facing Up to the American Dream*, p. 132.

36. Christopher Jencks, *Rethinking Social Policy: Race, Poverty, and the Underclass* (New York: HarperPerennial, 1993), p. 18.

37. Alan Wolfe, *One Nation, After All: What Middle-Class Americans Really Think About: God, Country, Family, Racism, Welfare, Immigration, Homosexuality, Work, the Right, the Left, and Each Other* (New York: Viking, 1998), p. 184. On pp. 184–185 Wolfe quotes the judgments of a number of suburbanites critical of urban life—all of whom are black. See also Thernstrom and Thernstrom, *America in Black and White*, p. 202, for a comparable discussion of black suburbanites who worried about the threat of crime in their community; in their view the danger increased when the opening of a new basketball court in the suburb lured inner-city black youngsters who wished to play on it.

38. Consider in this context Thomas Sowell, *Ethnic America: A History* (New York: Basic Books, 1981): "If the Irish were pariahs in the nineteenth century and fully accepted in the twentieth century, the moralistic approach sees only society's belated change to doing the right thing. It ignores the very possibility that the Irish who are accepted today may be very different from the nineteenth-century emigrants from Ireland whose personal behavior would still be wholly unacceptable to others today, including today's Irish Americans" (p. 296).

39. For a selection of the studies and anecdotes, see Hochschild, *Facing Up to the American Dream*, pp. 132–133, and the relevant citations on p. 303.

40. See Hochschild, *Facing Up to the American Dream*, p. 134.

41. Hochschild, *Facing Up to the American Dream*, p. 133.

42. Ulf Hannerz, *Soulside: Inquiries into Ghetto Culture and Community* (New York: Columbia University Press, 1969), p. 35.

43. Wolfe, *One Nation, After All*, p. 54.

44. See Jean Johnson and Steve Farkas with Ali Bers, *Getting By: What American Teenagers Really Think about Their Schools* (New York: Public Agenda, 1997), pp. 50–51, for a discussion of the survey's methodology

45. Johnson et al., *Getting By*, p. 12.

46. Johnson et al., *Getting By*, p. 52, note 2.

47. For a summary of further evidence confirming the strong commitment to education manifested by blacks overall, see Hochschild, *Facing Up to the American Dream*, pp. 159–160.

48. Johnson et al., *Getting By*, Table 5, p. 43.

49. Johnson et al., *Getting By*, p. 20; for the percentage among African American students, see Table 8, p. 46.

50. Johnson et al., *Getting By*, p. 32. See Table 5, p. 43: 74 percent of black students and 58 percent of white students think that class work should be checked and redone until it is right. See Table 7, p. 45: 84 percent of black students and 68 percent of white students would require after-school classes for kids who get D's and F's in major subjects.

51. Johnson et al., *Getting By*, p. 32. See Table 6, p. 44: among black students, 62

percent affirmed the extreme importance of learning biology, chemistry, and physics; 57 percent the extreme importance of learning advanced math such as calculus; and 43 percent the history and geography of such places as Europe or Asia. The comparable figures for white students were 39 percent, 34 percent, and 27 percent, respectively.

52. For a comparable argument, see Glazer and Daniel Patrick Moynihan, *Beyond the Melting Pot: The Negroes, Puerto Ricans, Jews, Italians, and Irish of New York City*, 2nd ed. (Cambridge, Mass.: MIT Press, 1970): "Negroes do place a high value on education. . . . Parents continually emphasize to children the theme of the importance of education as a means of getting ahead; and this is true among the uneducated as well as the educated, the failures as well as the successful. And yet the outcome is a poor one" (p. 45). On p. 49 they explain this anomaly in terms of "home and family and community—not in [their] overt values, which as we have seen are positive in relation to education, but in [their] conditions and circumstances"—specifically, the large number of broken homes. Cf. the comment of Rubin Harris (a black parent in the wealthy Ohio suburb of Shaker Heights): "It's not that black parents aren't involved in their children's education. . . . They just need to be more effectively involved." Harris is quoted in Lynette Clemetson, "Trying to Close the Achievement Gap," *Newsweek*, June 7, 1999, p. 37.

53. Hochschild, *Facing Up to the American Dream*, p. 160. For further evidence along these lines (drawn from blacks' actions as well as their responses to surveys), see pp. 161–162.

54. Hochschild, *Facing Up to the American Dream*, p. 208.

55. Hochschild, *Facing Up to the American Dream*, p. 162.

56. Hochschild, *Facing Up to the American Dream*, p. 185.

57. Hochschild, *Facing Up to the American Dream*, p. 200. For Hochschild's definition of the "estranged poor" (in effect her synonym for the underclass), see p. 185, and particularly note 3 on pp. 321–322.

58. William Julius Wilson, *When Work Disappears: The World of the New Urban Poor* (New York: Alfred A. Knopf, 1996), p. 179.

59. Wilson, *When Work Disappears*, p. 67.

60. Wilson, *When Work Disappears*, p. 180.

61. Wilson, *When Work Disappears*, p. 67.

62. Lawrence M. Mead, *The New Politics of Poverty: The Nonworking Poor in America* (New York: Basic Books, 1992), p. 140.

63. Mead, *New Politics of Poverty*, p. 174. The emphasis appears in the text. For a second useful formulation, see Mead, "Welfare Employment," in Mead, ed., *The New Paternalism: Supervisory Approaches to Poverty* (Washington, D.C.: Brookings Institution Press, 1997): "When asked, . . . most welfare recipients and other poor people say that they want to work. If they do not actually work, the reason is that the practical difficulties seem overwhelming, not that they reject the idea. Not working, in fact, causes them shame and discouragement, since they are not living by their own values. This gap between intention and behavior is what makes work enforcement necessary. But acceptance of the work ethic also makes it possible. Mandatory work programs do not ask most people to do something alien to them" (p. 64).

64. Quoted in Hochschild, *Facing Up to the American Dream*, p. 186.

65. Wilson, *When Work Disappears*, pp. 51–52.

66. Wilson, *When Work Disappears*, p. 98.

67. Wilson, *When Work Disappears*, p. 106. The emphasis is mine.

68. Jencks, *Rethinking Social Policy*, p. 134.

69. William A. Galston, "A Progressive Family Policy for the Twenty-First Century," in

Will Marshall, ed., *Building the Bridge: 10 Big Ideas to Transform America* (Lanham, Md.: Rowman and Littlefield, 1997), p. 153.

70. See Mead, *New Politics of Poverty*, p. 7. Nor can this change be explained as an artifact of the increased numbers of single female family heads, for whom work outside the home presents obvious (though not usually insurmountable) difficulties. If single female family heads are excluded, almost three-quarters of other heads worked at least part-time in 1959, but less than 57 percent did so in 1989. The statistics about nonwork are equally illuminating: more than half of all heads of poor families did not work at all in 1989, compared with less than 31 percent in 1959.

71. Hochschild, *Facing Up to the American Dream*, p. 186.

72. See Charles Murray, *The Underclass Revisited* (Washington, D.C.: AEI Press, 1999): "White labor-force dropout [among those aged 16–24] is up 25 percent from 1990 to 1997. This is concentrated among white teenage males aged sixteen to nineteen, who showed a 33 percent increase. . . . As of . . . 1997 . . . almost 9 percent of the [white] sixteen-to-twenty-four-year-old group were out of the labor force" (p. 13).

73. Hochschild, *Facing Up to the American Dream*, p. 323, note 18.

74. Hochschild, *Facing Up to the American Dream*, p. 187.

75. Murray, *Underclass Revisited*, p. 24

76. Hochschild, *Facing Up to the American Dream*, p. 187. The emphasis appears in the text.

77. Glenn C. Loury, "Why More Blacks Don't Invest," *New York Times Magazine*, June 7, 1998, p. 70.

78. James P. Smith, *Unequal Wealth and Incentives to Save* (Santa Monica, Calif.: RAND, 1995), p. 13.

79. Robert J. Samuelson, "'Hell No, We Won't Save,'" *Washington Post*, February 17, 1999, p. A17.

80. On this point see Mickey D. Levy, "The Economy Is Safe from a 'Savings Crisis,'" *Wall Street Journal*, February 4, 1999, p. A22.

81. Jacob M. Schlesinger, "Few Americans Heed Washington's Urging for Bigger Nest Eggs," *Wall Street Journal*, June 29, 1999, p. A6.

82. Seymour Martin Lipset, *American Exceptionalism: A Double-Edged Sword* (New York: W.W. Norton and Co., 1996), p. 289.

83. Patterson, *Ordeal of Integration*, pp. 182–183.

84. Mitchell Duneier, *Slim's Table: Race, Respectability, and Masculinity* (Chicago: University of Chicago Press, 1992), p. 127.

85. It is noteworthy that Tuckerman made a comparable argument, blaming the moral failings of the wealthy for the moral failings of the poor. See, for example, *Joseph Tuckerman on the Elevation of the Poor: A Selection from His Reports as Minister at Large in Boston*, edited by E. E. Hale (New York: Arno Press and The New York Times, 1971), p. 124. There Tuckerman harshly criticized the "vanity, extravagance, and sensual indulgence" of the rich, specifically because of "the example which is continually wending its way from the high grounds to the very lowest depths of social life." Because they set such a bad moral example, he thought that "the rich are in truth accountable for much of the abject poverty of the world."

86. Nicholas Lemann, *The Promised Land: The Great Black Migration and How It Changed America* (New York: Alfred A. Knopf, 1991), p. 286.

87. Karl Zinsmeister, "Chin Up: Some Ugly Trends Grow Lovelier," *American Enterprise*, January/February 1999, p. 5.

88. Zinsmeister, Stephen Moore, and Karlyn Bowman, "Is America Turning a Corner?," *American Enterprise*, January/February 1999, p. 37. For additional survey data showing a national trend against permissiveness with regard to welfare and crime, see pp. 42 and 45. For evidence of Americans' increasing religiosity and increasing interest in "preserving traditional family values," see pp. 49–50.

89. Zinsmeister, "Chin Up," p. 5.

90. Hanna Rosin and John F. Harris, "Welfare Reform Is on a Roll," *Washington Post*, August 3, 1999, p. A1.

91. Zinsmeister et al., "Is America Turning a Corner?," p. 48.

92. Jeff Madrick, "The Worker's Just Reward," *New York Times*, August 1, 1999, section 4, p. 15.

93. Richard Nadler, "Glum and Glummer," *National Review*, September 28, 1998, p. 28.

94. Lawrence Kudlow, *American Abundance: The New Economic and Moral Prosperity* (New York: American Heritage Custom Publishing, 1997), p.176.

95. Zinsmeister et al., "Is America Turning a Corner?," p. 44.

96. Kudlow, *American Abundance*, p. 171.

97. Kudlow, *American Abundance*, p. 176.

98. NIAAA, Surveillance Report #47, *Apparent Per Capita Alcohol Consumption: National, State and Regional Trends, 1977–96*, December 1998, pp. 1, 4.

99. Kudlow, *American Abundance*, p. 176.

100. Data are taken from NCHS, *Births: Final Data for 1997*, National Vital Statistics Reports, volume 47, number 18 (document downloaded from the NCHS web site http://www.cdc.gov.nchswww/, on August 25, 1999), pp. 8, 43–44. The birth rate for black unmarried mothers in 1997 is compared with the 1969 rate in the April 29, 1999, press release accompanying the report, "Teen Birth Rate Down in All States," downloaded from the NCHS web site on August 25, 1999. The summary of the data is taken from Zinsmeister et al., "Is America Turning a Corner?," p. 38.

101. Zinsmeister, "Chin Up," p. 5.

102. Zinsmeister at al., "Is America Turning a Corner?," p. 36.

103. Francis Fukuyama, *The Great Disruption: Human Nature and the Reconstitution of Social Order* (New York: Free Press, 1999), pp. 264–266.

104. Fukuyama, *Great Disruption*, p. 267.

105. Fukuyama, *Great Disruption*, pp. 267–268.

106. Fukuyama, *Great Disruption*, p. 268.

107. Fukuyama, *Great Disruption*, p. 271.

108. Fukuyama, *Great Disruption*, pp. 272–273.

109. Fukuyama, *Great Disruption*, p. 250.

110. Gertrude Himmelfarb, "Democratic Remedies for Democratic Disorders," *The Public Interest* 131 (Spring 1998), pp. 4–5.

111. Murray, *Underclass Revisited*, pp. 11–12. It should be noted, though, that Murray's data mask some news that is genuinely good: the number of black males aged 16–24 who are enrolled in school has surged impressively. According to unpublished data from the Bureau of Labor Statistics, on one hand the number of black males aged 16–24 not in school and not in the labor force increased by 18 percent between October 1982 and October 1987, rising from 236,000 to 279,000. That is the bad news to which Murray rightly points. But on the other hand, in those years the number of black males aged 16–24 who were not in school declined by 16 percent (even as the total population of black males in that age group—excluding those in prison and the armed forces—rose by 1 percent). It is

good news that many more young black males are remaining longer in school; between 1982 and 1997 the number of black males aged 16–24 who were enrolled in school increased by an impressive 24 percent.

112. Murray, *Underclass Revisited*, p. 14.

113. Murray, *Underclass Revisited*, p. 21. Further evidence in support of Murray's hypothesis can be found in a recent Brookings Institution study. In a reporter's summary, the study found that "urban counties containing the 30 largest American cities have 20 percent of the nation's population, but 39 percent of the welfare recipients—up from 33 percent in 1994." The report also found that "whites are leaving the welfare rolls much faster than black and Hispanic families, and the minority share of the caseload has, as a result, risen to the highest level on record. Black and Hispanic welfare recipients together outnumber whites by about 2 to 1." See Robert Pear, "As Welfare Rolls Shrink, Cities Shoulder Bigger Load," *New York Times*, June 6, 1999, p. 22.

114. Murray, *Underclass Revisited*, pp. 17–18.

115. Murray, *Underclass Revisited*, p. 22.

116. Murray, *Underclass Revisited*, p. 25. To discount the significance of behavioral change in underclass neighborhoods, Murray also argues—less persuasively, in my view—that we should not make too much of the precipitous decline in crime. He attributes the decline, reasonably enough, to the great increases in incarceration that have characterized the past generation. What this means is that the reduction in crime has been achieved "not by socializing the underclass but by putting large numbers of its members behind bars" (p. 8). That may be true; but an inner-city grandmother who is less fearful of muggers than she was twenty years ago is nonetheless benefited by the reduction in crime.

117. Fukuyama, *Great Disruption*, pp. 101–102.

118. Fukuyama, *Great Disruption*, pp. 102–103.

119. Fukuyama, *Great Disruption*, p. 38. For an important elaboration of this argument, see James Q. Wilson, "Human Remedies for Social Disorders," *The Public Interest* 131 (Spring 1998), p. 27. There Wilson argues that "the family problem lies at the heart of the emergence of" an underclass. Although "we are vastly richer" than we were a century ago, "the money has not purchased public safety, racial comity, or educational achievement." That is because "it is not money but the family that is the foundation of public life. . . . The evidence concerning the powerful effect of this familial foundation is now so strong that even some sociologists believe it": even when one controls for income, children in one-parent families are much more likely to drop out of school, to be both out of work and out of school, to become single parents themselves—in short, to become part of the underclass.

120. Fukuyama, *Great Disruption*, p. 275.

121. See Wolfe, *One Nation, After All*: "From a middle-class point of view, the ideal society would be one in which everyone—immigrants, minorities, the poor—would uphold middle-class values so that someday they might obtain middle-class incomes" (p. 321).

122. Himmelfarb, *The De-Moralization of Society: From Victorian Virtues to Modern Values* (New York: Alfred A. Knopf, 1995), p. 11.

123. Murray, *Underclass Revisited*, p. 36.

124. Murray, "The Partial Restoration of Traditional Society," *The Public Interest* 121 (Fall 1995): 122.

125. Murray, "Partial Restoration," pp. 124–125.

126. Murray, *Underclass Revisited*, p. 18. On the decline in births to teenagers, see NCHS, *Births: Final Data for 1997*: "From 1991 to 1997, the [birth] rates for non-Hispanic black and Puerto Rican teenagers dropped 24 to 27 percent" (p. 2).

127. Murray, "Partial Restoration," pp. 129–132. Economic historian Robert W. Fogel also argues for the existence of a religious revival that is promoting more traditional moral behavior among many (obviously not all) Americans. He speaks of the revival as a Fourth Great Awakening, which began about 1960. "Fueled by a revulsion with the corruptions of contemporary society," the revival has heightened its adherents' desire to live virtuously. Thus it constitutes "a rebellion against preoccupation with material acquisition and sexual debauchery; against indulgence in alcohol, tobacco, gambling, and drugs; against gluttony; against financial greed; and against all other forms of self-indulgence that titillate the senses and destroy the soul. The leaders of the revival are attempting to win their hearers to piety and to an ethic which extols individual responsibility, hard work, a simple life, and dedication to the family." The quotation is taken from "The Fourth Great Awakening and the Political Realignment of the 1990s," the unpublished manuscript of a lecture delivered at the American Enterprise Institute for Public Policy Research, September 11, 1995. The passage is cited by permission of the University of Chicago Press, the publisher of Fogel's *The Fourth Great Awakening and the Future of Egalitarianism*, which appeared in May 2000.

128. Murray, "Partial Restoration," p. 133.

129. Himmelfarb, "Democratic Remedies," p. 19.

130. Himmelfarb, "Democratic Remedies," pp. 00–00. In this context see also Gregg Easterbrook, "America the O.K.," *The New Republic*, January 4 and 11, 1999, p. 20. Easterbrook speaks there of what he calls the "'younger brother effect.' The '90s generation of inner-city kids, having seen the medically destructive effects of crack and the self-genocide it produced in minority communities, wants little to do with the opiate of the '80s." This explanation helps account for the fact—discussed above—that crack cocaine use is now far more common among whites than among blacks.

8. The Contemporary Practice of Moral Reform

1. Quoted in Joe Klein, "In God They Trust," *The New Yorker*, June 16, 1997, p. 40. Klein does not identify the aide.

2. John Leland, "Savior of the Streets," *Newsweek*, June 1, 1998, p. 22.

3. Nicholas Lemann, *The Promised Land: The Great Black Migration and How It Changed America* (New York: Alfred A. Knopf, 1991), pp. 207–208. For a very different understanding of Nixon administration social policy (put forth by an influential advisor who helped formulate the policy), see Daniel P. Moynihan, *The Politics of a Guaranteed Income: The Nixon Administration and the Family Assistance Plan* (New York: Random House, 1973). Speaking of the Family Assistance Plan, the unenacted capstone of the administration's social policy, Moynihan argues that "the president's proposal was *not a guaranteed income in the meaning the public had come to attach to that term*" (pp. 10–11). In Moynihan's view the term "guaranteed income" connotes "that people ought not to have to work for a living." In contrast, "the heart of the [Nixon] proposal was to supplement the income of persons already working, and it sincerely looked to the prospect of finding work for others who were not working." (The emphasis appears in the text.) In short, Moynihan rejects Lemann's claim that the Nixon administration threw money at our social problems; instead it sought (unsuccessfully) to promote virtue by assisting the working poor. See also p. 156, though, for a statement that tallies more closely with Lemann's view: "In a steady succession of legislative messages [Nixon] proposed to spend more money for the direct provision of the needs of low-income groups than any president in history."

4. Michael Novak, John Cogan, Blanche Bernstein, Douglas J. Besharov, Barbara Blum, Allan Carlson, Michael Horowitz, S. Anna Kondratas, Leslie Lenkowsky, Glenn C. Loury, Lawrence Mead, Donald Moran, Charles Murray, Richard P. Nathan, Richard J. Neuhaus, Franklin D. Raines, Robert D. Reischauer, Alice M. Rivlin, Stanford Ross, Michael Stern, *The New Consensus on Family and Welfare: A Community of Self-Reliance* (Washington, D.C., and Milwaukee: American Enterprise Institute and Marquette University, 1987), p. 99.

5. Novak et al., *New Consensus*, p. 5.

6. John J. DiIulio, Jr., "The Lord's Work: The Church and the 'Civil Society Sector,'" *The Brookings Review* (Fall 1997): 30.

7. For a useful account of such organizations in the early twentieth century, see David T. Beito, "Mutual Aid, State Welfare, and Organized Charity: Fraternal Societies and the 'Deserving' and 'Undeserving' Poor, 1900–1930," *Journal of Policy History* 5 (1993): 419–434.

8. "Ministry for the Poor," in *The Works of William E. Channing, D.D.* (Boston: American Unitarian Association, 1903), p. 77. The emphasis is mine. "Ministry for the Poor" was an address delivered by Channing in 1835. Channing hoped, of course, that the ministry for the poor would strengthen the bond between Boston's rich and poor; still, his description of the bond's weakness testifies to his recognition of the great difficulties that had to be overcome so that the ministry might succeed.

9. See Paul Boyer, *Urban Masses and Moral Order in America, 1820–1920* (Cambridge, Mass.: Harvard University Press, 1978), pp. 57–60. See especially pp. 59–60: "To the poor of the Jacksonian city ... prostitution, drunkenness, and family disintegration were not abstract symptoms of urban disruption but the stuff of day-to-day existence. It should hardly surprise us that they sometimes gave at least cautious support to organized efforts to erect a shield against these threatening features of city life."

10. Boyer, *Urban Masses*, p. 56.

11. Quoted in Joan Waugh, *Unsentimental Reformer: The Life of Josephine Shaw Lowell* (Cambridge, Mass.: Harvard University Press, 1997), p. 171.

12. Quoted in Paul T. Ringenbach, *Tramps and Reformers, 1873–1916: The Discovery of Unemployment in New York* (New York: Greenwood Press, 1973), p. 90.

13. Adam Smith, *An Inquiry into the Nature and Causes of the Wealth of Nations* (New York: The Modern Library, 1937), p. 746.

14. Robert L. Woodson Sr., *The Triumphs of Joseph: How Today's Community Healers Are Reviving Our Streets and Neighborhoods* (New York: Free Press, 1998), p. 8.

15. Woodson, *Triumphs of Joseph*, p. 92.

16. Biographical information about Rivers is drawn from Leland, "Savior of the Streets," pp. 24–25.

17. Leland, "Savior of the Streets," p. 24.

18. Woodson, *Triumphs of Joseph*, p. 91.

19. Woodson, *Triumphs of Joseph*, pp. 82–89.

20. Many others who work with the poor today have backgrounds akin to those of Rivers and Rivera. David Sykes, a Boston instructor for STRIVE, a program that tries to inculcate attitudes and behaviors likely to make the inner-city poor more employable, is an ex-convict who served six years for assault before reforming himself at STRIVE. (See Hanna Rosin, "About Face," *The New Republic*, August 4, 1997, p. 19.) Similarly, Joseph T. Jones, who heads Healthy Start Men's Services in Baltimore, was a drug addict, prison inmate, and an

unwed father by age 22. (See Jason DeParle, "Welfare Overhaul Initiatives Focus on Fathers," *New York Times*, September 3, 1998, p. A20. In DeParle's words, Jones is "like many other men involved in this work," because "he has a personal connection to the streets.")

21. Floyd Flake and Donna Marie Williams, *The Way of the Bootstrapper: Nine Action Steps for Achieving Your Dreams* (San Francisco: HarperSanFrancisco, 1999), p. 13.

22. Flake and Williams, *Way of the Bootstrapper*, p. 130.

23. Flake and Williams, *Way of the Bootstrapper*, pp. 7, 131–132.

24. Flake and Williams, *Way of the Bootstrapper*, p. 79.

25. Flake and Williams, *Way of the Bootstrapper*, p. 152.

26. Flake and Williams, *Way of the Bootstrapper*, pp. 3–8.

27. James Davison Hunter, *Culture Wars: The Struggle to Define America* (New York: Basic Books, 1991), p. 43.

28. Hunter, *Culture Wars*, p. 132.

29. Klein, "In God They Trust," p. 41.

30. Kenneth L. Woodward, "The New Holy War," *Newsweek*, June 1, 1998, pp. 26–27.

31. Woodward, "New Holy War," p. 27.

32. Quoted in Woodward, "New Holy War," p. 27.

33. Woodward, "New Holy War," p. 27.

34. See Charles Loring Brace, *The Dangerous Classes of New York and Twenty Years' Work among Them*, 3rd ed., with addenda (Montclair, N.J.: Patterson Smith, 1967 [rpt. 1880]), p. 80, for Brace's discussion of the failure of an early reformatory attempt of his, which preceded his creation of the Children's Aid Society. Initially he had hoped to effect the moral reformation of New York's street urchins by means of a series of "boys' meetings," in which the youths were addressed by preachers. The effort, however, was unsuccessful: "Sometimes the salutatory exercises from the street were showers of stones; sometimes a general scrimmage occurred over the benches; again, the visitors or missionaries were pelted by some opposition-gang, or bitter enemies of the lads who attended the meeting. . . . One pungent criticism we remember—on a pious and somewhat sentimental Sunday-school brother, who, in one of our meetings, had been putting forth vague and declamatory religious exhortation—in the words 'Gas! Gas!' whispered with infinite contempt from one hard-faced young disciple to another." The emphasis appears in the text. See also Brace, *Short Sermons to News Boys: With a History of the Formation of the News Boys' Lodging-House* (New York: Charles Scribner, 1866), pp. 9–10. Brace there describes the opposition that he had to overcome from various devout critics who believed that his work betrayed "a 'humanitarian' tendency, and . . . belong[ed] to European 'socialism' and 'infidelity,'" because Brace "urge[d] the entire change of circumstances and the emigration to country homes, as *of far more importance to a certain class of vagrant children than any possible influence of Sunday-schools or Chapels.*" The emphasis is mine.

35. Leland, "Savior of the Streets," p. 25.

36. Anemona Hartocollis, "A Church's Seeds for a Charter School: At Allen Christian in Queens, Values Transcend Creed, Founder Says," *New York Times*, February 14, 1999, p. 33.

37. Woodson, *Triumphs of Joseph*, p. 92.

38. Quoted in DiIulio, "The Lord's Work," p. 31. See also a comment by Mark Scott, an associate of Rivers, quoted in Woodward, "New Holy War": "The churches can't do it alone. We're the glue of civic life, addressing values and spiritual issues that the government can't address. But just saying 'let the churches do it,' without the government, won't work" (p. 28).

39. DiIulio, "Lord's Work," p. 29.

40. Flake and Williams, *Way of the Bootstrapper*, p. 22. Elsewhere Flake has declared that "the best role for government . . . is to be partner in the process [in which the church] takes a blighted urban community and turns it around." He is quoted to that effect in Nile Harper, *Urban Churches, Vital Signs: Beyond Charity Toward Justice* (Grand Rapids, Mich.: William B. Eerdmans, 1999), p. 30.

41. Quoted in Harper, *Urban Churches*, p. 30.

42. Flake and Williams, *Way of the Bootstrapper*, p. 43.

43. Flake and Williams, *Way of the Bootstrapper*, p. 3.

44. Flake and Williams, *Way of the Bootstrapper*, p. 69.

45. Flake and Williams, *Way of the Bootstrapper*, p. 178.

46. Flake and Williams, *Way of the Bootstrapper*, p. 110.

47. Flake and Williams, *Way of the Bootstrapper*, p. 186. Note also that Flake responds in effect to Walter Rauschenbusch's charge that self-help is somehow un-Christian. See pp. 78–79: "Many people feel that to be a Christian you have to be poor, . . . but for me, ministry, wealth, and joy were never in conflict. . . . Many of my biblical heroes, like Abraham and Solomon, were wealthy, so I knew I'd be in good company. Fortunately, the strong work ethic, character, and values that my parents bequeathed to me made my quest for the good life a balanced and moral one. . . . For me, the acquisition of money has been nothing more than a way to enjoy the good things in life and to help others." Tuckerman, Hartley, and Brace presumably had a similar understanding of the compatibility of Christianity with the pursuit of material success. On the other hand, Rauschenbusch would probably have thought it significant that Flake's "biblical heroes" in this context are Abraham and Solomon rather than Jesus.

48. *On Character: Essays by James Q. Wilson* (Washington, D.C.: AEI Press, 1991), p. 11.

49. Wilson, *On Character*, p. 22.

50. See Thomas J. Main, "Homeless Men in New York City: Toward Paternalism through Privatization," in Lawrence M. Mead, ed., *The New Paternalism: Supervisory Approaches to Poverty* (Washington, D.C.: Brookings Institution Press, 1997), p. 163. As Main notes (p. 166), this paternalist approach amounts to a rejection of the structuralist view that "changing lifestyles could not be a solution to homelessness." The structuralist view denies that "the attempt to enforce work, sobriety, and stability" can reduce homelessness, which is instead understood to result primarily from a shortage of housing for those with low incomes.

51. On this point see Mead, "The Rise of Paternalism," in *New Paternalism*, p. 26: "Paternalistic programs are still the exception. Paternalism has appeared only in contexts in which the clients are self-selected. People who end up on means-tested aid for long periods, in homeless shelters, or in drug rehabilitation very likely do have problems organizing their lives, and demands that they work or otherwise function are likely to be constructive. The same argument could not be made for the beneficiaries of social insurance programs, who typically have a work history." See also p. 2.

52. Francis Fukuyama, *The Great Disruption: Human Nature and the Reconstitution of Social Order* (New York: Free Press, 1999), p. 128.

53. Fukuyama, *Great Disruption*, p. 244.

54. Mead, *The New Politics of Poverty: The Nonworking Poor in America* (New York: Basic Books, 1992), p. 161.

55. The assessment will not, however, consider such mundane (though all-important)

matters as the ways in which various proposed policies would be administered and their likely costs. Such questions are, of course, addressed in the more technical policy literature from which I draw. The two major proposed policy innovations to be examined are Individual Development Accounts to promote thrift and wage subsidies to promote diligence. For detailed discussions of how the programs would be administered and what their likely costs would be, see, respectively, Michael Sherraden, *Assets and the Poor: A New American Welfare Policy* (Armonk, N.Y.: M. E. Sharpe, 1991), pp. 234–279; and Edmund S. Phelps, *Rewarding Work: How to Restore Participation and Self-Support to Free Enterprise* (Cambridge, Mass.: Harvard University Press, 1997), pp. 103–173.

56. See Fukuyama, *Great Disruption*: "When the Moynihan report was issued thirty years ago at the beginning of the Great Disruption [Fukuyama's term for the rise in crime, welfare dependency, and illegitimacy that began in the 1960s], it was almost universally condemned by respectable opinion for 'blaming the victim' and being ethnocentric. Today the weight of scholarly opinion has shifted 180 degrees: family structure and values are widely recognized as playing an important role in determining social outcomes. Academic treatises do not directly influence individual behavior, of course, but . . . abstract ideas have a way of filtering down to the level of popular consciousness in a generation or two" (p. 272). See also p. 274: "Empirical social science evidence on the deleterious effects of disrupted families continued to accumulate, to the point that it could not be ignored. By the late 1990s, many more people were prepared to accept Barbara Dafoe Whitehead's judgment that 'Dan Quayle was right' about the importance of families than even five years earlier."

57. Ronald B. Mincy and Hillard Pouncy, "Paternalism, Child Support Enforcement, and Fragile Families," in *New Paternalism*, p. 152.

58. On this point see Wade F. Horn and Andrew Bush, "Fathers and Welfare Reform," *The Public Interest* 129 (Fall 1997): "We know much more about promoting work than we do about making families form or keeping them together. . . . [Thus] most efforts at welfare reform have proceeded with what many proponents concede is ultimately a secondary, but at least attainable, strategy: improving the way we help single-parents confront their struggle for self-sufficiency" (p. 40).

59. David Popenoe, *Life Without Father: Compelling New Evidence that Fatherhood and Marriage Are Indispensable for the Good of Children and Society* (New York: Free Press, 1996), p. 218. Cf. the formulation in Barbara Dafoe Whitehead, *The Divorce Culture: Rethinking Our Commitments to Marriage and Family* (New York: Vintage Books, 1998): "The breakdown of marriage was not caused by changes in the tax code or divorce laws, and it is unlikely to be resolved by the legislative actions of Congress and the states" (p. 192).

60. Horn and Bush, "Fathers and Welfare Reform," p. 43.

61. Horn and Bush, "Fathers and Welfare Reform," p. 43.

62. Whitehead, "Dan Quayle Was Right," *The Atlantic Monthly*, April 1993, p. 70. This legislation is discussed in a sidebar, "The Family and Public Policy," appearing on the bottom of pp. 70–71.

63. Nathan Glazer, *The Limits of Social Policy* (Cambridge, Mass.: Harvard University Press, 1988), p. 35.

64. GAO, *Welfare Reform: States Are Restructuring Programs to Reduce Welfare Dependence* (HEHS-98-109), June 1998, p. 64.

65. See Mincy and Pouncy, "Paternalism," pp. 143–149, for discussions of Wisconsin's Children First and Young Unwed Fathers programs, and the Manpower Demonstration Research Corporation's Parent's Fair Share demonstration project. Unfortunately, the

MDRC experiment seems to have increased noncustodial fathers' child support payments only modestly. See DeParle, "Report on Effort to Aid Poor Fathers Offers Discouraging News," *New York Times*, September 29, 1998, p. A16.

66. Horn and Bush, "Fathers and Welfare Reform," p. 45.

67. DeParle, "Welfare Overhaul Initiatives," p. A1.

68. Mincy and Pouncy, "Paternalism," p. 150.

69. See Channing, "Ministry for the Poor," for the argument that the "narrow condition" of the poor "obliges them to do more for one another than is done among the rich" and thereby imparts "a vigor and tenderness to the love of parents and children . . . not always found in the luxurious classes" (p. 74).

70. William A. Galston, "A Progressive Family Policy for the Twenty-First Century," in Will Marshall, ed., *Building the Bridge: 10 Big Ideas to Transform America* (Lanham, Md.: Rowman and Littlefield, 1997), p. 159.

71. James Q. Wilson, "Human Remedies for Social Disorders," *The Public Interest* 131 (Spring 1998): 30–31.

72. See also the discussion of comparable homes (operated in Massachusetts under the Teen Living Program) in Wilson, "Human Remedies for Social Disorders," p. 31. In Wilson's formulation, the homes "aim at teaching not self-esteem but self-respect. . . . The homes teach girls how to be mothers, how to deal effectively with other people, why it is important to get an education, and how to cope with the temptation of drugs" (p. 31).

73. Galston, "Progressive Family Policy," p. 159.

74. Waugh, *Unsentimental Reformer*, p. 139.

75. The focus here is limited to alcohol—as opposed to illegal drugs—because alcohol was the substance that chiefly concerned the moral reformers, and it could legally be consumed when the reformers did their work. Because that was so, efforts today to reduce the consumption of illegal substances like cocaine and heroin differ fundamentally from yesterday's efforts to reduce alcohol consumption. For this reason, the moral reformers' experiences and observations do not offer particularly helpful advice for the contemporary campaign to curb the consumption of illegal drugs.

76. BJS, *Alcohol and Crime: An Analysis of National Data on the Prevalence of Alcohol Involvement in Crime* (1998), p. v.

77. BJS, *Alcohol and Crime*, pp. iii, vi.

78. BJS, *Alcohol and Crime*, p. 1.

79. William J. Bennett, DiIulio, and John P. Walters, *Body Count: Moral Poverty . . . and How to Win America's War against Crime and Drugs* (New York: Simon and Schuster, 1996), p. 66.

80. Bennett, DiIulio, and Walters, *Body Count*, pp. 74–75.

81. In this context, consider the implicit threat of governmental regulation in the following remark by Bennett, in "Face the Facts about Alcohol and Crime," *New York Times*, July 29, 1997: "I have a reputation for being a conservative. And I am. But conservatives need to go where the facts, not ideology, lead. And the facts tell us that there is a very strong link between alcohol availability, consumption and crime. . . . If the liquor industry does not start acting in a more socially responsible way, it may soon find itself held in the same kind of esteem in which the tobacco companies are now held. The alcohol industry can act now. Or it can deny reality and pay later" (p. A23).

82. Dirk Johnson, "Temperance Movement Grows in Chicago, a Precinct at a Time," *New York Times*, April 19, 1998, p. 14.

83. Johnson, "Temperance Movement," p. 14.

84. Jacob A. Riis, *The Battle with the Slum* (New York: Macmillan, 1902), pp. 68–69.

85. Jane Addams, *Democracy and Social Ethics*, edited by Anne Firor Scott (Cambridge, Mass.: Harvard University Press, 1964 [rpt. 1907]), p. 243. *Democracy and Social Ethics* was originally published in 1902. Addams does not mention Powers's name in her discussion. He is named in the biographies of Addams; see, for example, Daniel Levine, *Jane Addams and the Liberal Tradition* (Madison: State Historical Society of Wisconsin, 1971), pp. 73–79.

86. Addams, *Democracy*, p. 262. Addams's opposition to Powers was not, however, primarily motivated by his collusion with organized vice; instead it reflected his reluctance to build an additional public school in the ward and to improve the cleaning of its streets. See Levine, *Jane Addams*, p. 76.

87. Johnson, "Temperance Movement," p. 14.

88. It should be mentioned that Mayor Daley's personal abstemiousness is very much in the tradition established by his father, Mayor Richard J. Daley. See Lemann, *Promised Land*: "Daley . . . led a modest existence. He lived in a workingman's house in Bridgeport, went to mass every morning, didn't run around with women, and did not participate in the glossy social life of the rich. . . . His one conspicuous luxury, custom-made suits, was more a tribute to the grandeur of his office than an example of his own taste for the finer things in life, which was otherwise undetectable" (p. 90).

89. Mark H. Moore and Dean R. Gerstein, eds., *Alcohol and Public Policy: Beyond the Shadow of Prohibition* (Washington, D.C.: National Academy Press, 1981), p. 69. Pages 1–124 in this volume consist of the report to the National Research Council of the Panel on Alternative Policies Affecting the Prevention of Alcohol Abuse and Alcoholism. The rest of the volume contains seven scholarly papers commissioned by the panel as an aid to its research.

90. Moore and Gerstein, *Alcohol and Public Policy*, p. 73. See also p. 69: according to the panel's calculations, "Between 1960 and 1980, the 'real' cost to the consumer of a bottle of liquor declined by 48 percent, of beer by 27 percent, and of wine by 19 percent."

91. Michael Grossman, Jody L. Sinclair, John Mullahy, and Richard Anderson, "Alcohol and Cigarette Taxes," *Journal of Economic Perspectives* 7, no. 4 (Fall 1993): 212.

92. Philip J. Cook and Michael J. Moore, "This Tax's for You: The Case for Higher Beer Taxes," *National Tax Journal* 47 (1994): 560.

93. Grossman et al., "Alcohol and Cigarette Taxes," p. 212.

94. Moore and Gerstein, *Alcohol and Public Policy*, p. 73.

95. Cook, "The Effect of Liquor Taxes on Drinking, Cirrhosis, and Auto Accidents," in *Alcohol and Public Policy*, p. 281.

96. Mullahy, "Alcohol and the Labor Market," in Michael E. Hilton and Gregory Blass, eds., *Economics and the Prevention of Alcohol-Related Problems* (Washington, D.C.: U.S. Department of Health and Human Services, 1993), p. 157. Mullahy adds that the body of relevant literature is "still quite small." The lack of consensus is explained, he contends, by the fact that "researchers have actually been exploring somewhat different hypotheses using different sets of data."

97. Mullahy, "Alcohol and the Labor Market," p. 142.

98. Moore and Gerstein, *Alcohol and Public Policy*, p. 64.

99. Moore and Gerstein, *Alcohol and Public Policy*, p. 112.

100. Josephine Shaw Lowell, *Public Relief and Private Charity* (New York: Arno Press and The New York Times, 1971 [rpt. 1884]), p. 66.

101. In this context it is worth mentioning that Josephine Shaw's parents were far wealth-

ier than the parents of the young man she married, Charles Russell Lowell. See Waugh, *Unsentimental Reformer*, p. 78: Colonel Lowell was "young and penniless" when he married his bride, but he refused to accept any money from his wealthy in-laws. On the other hand, after his death his widow Josephine Shaw Lowell received a comfortable income from her parents during their lifetime (and a large inheritance thereafter). The biographical evidence provided by Waugh suggests that Lowell's insistence on the need to earn what one has may well reflect in part her admiration for her late husband's principled stance (and perhaps her guilt for not abiding by it herself).

102. Lowell, "Houses of Refuge for Women: Their Purposes, Management and Possibilities," *Proceedings of the New York State Conference of Charities and Correction* 1 (1901): 255.

103. Consider in this context a statement of Lowell's that appears in an 1889 letter: "If the working people had all they ought to have, we should not have the paupers and criminals." The statement is quoted in William Rhinelander Stewart, *The Philanthropic Work of Josephine Shaw Lowell Containing a Biographical Sketch of Her Life Together with a Selection of Her Public Papers and Private Letters* (Montclair, N.J.: Patterson Smith, 1974 [rpt. 1911]), pp. 358–359.

104. Hace Sorel Tishler, *Self-Reliance and Social Security, 1870–1917* (Port Washington, N.Y.: Kennikat, 1971), p. 193.

105. Quoted in Sherraden, *Assets and the Poor*, pp. 129–130. The story first appeared on the front page of the February 6, 1990, *Wall Street Journal*. A comparable 1992 Connecticut case is briefly recounted in R. Glenn Hubbard, Jonathan Skinner, and Stephen P. Zeldes, "Precautionary Saving and Social Insurance," *Journal of Political Economy* 103 (1995): 361, note 1.

106. James P. Smith, *Unequal Wealth and Incentives to Save* (Santa Monica, Calif.: RAND, 1995), pp. 22–23.

107. Sherraden, *Assets and the Poor*, p. 130.

108. Sondra Beverly, "How Can the Poor Save? Theory and Evidence on Saving in Low-Income Households," Working Paper 97-3, Center for Social Development, Washington University, 1997, p. 37.

109. GAO, *Welfare Reform*, p. 45.

110. See, for example, Smith, *Unequal Wealth*: There is "very little evidence of any savings behavior by poorer households" (p. 11). See also Beverly, "How Can the Poor Save?" for this not particularly surprising observation: "Empirical evidence generally indicates that low-income households have lower-than-average saving rates" (p. 2).

111. See Beverly, "How Can the Poor Save?": "The inability to reduce consumption, or to reduce consumption very much, may *partly* explain why low-income households have lower saving rates" (p. 14). The emphasis is mine. Cf. p. 17: "Instead of assuming that low-income individuals are unable to save, we should identify variables which help to explain saving . . . and identify ways to facilitate low-income saving."

112. Beverly, "How Can the Poor Save?," pp. 16–17. Beverly does not describe any of the empirical studies, and her source for them is not particularly reassuring; she cites an unpublished 1993 manuscript produced by the Center for Urban Poverty and Social Change at Case Western Reserve University.

113. Sherraden, *Assets and the Poor*, p. 210.

114. Sherraden, *Assets and the Poor*, pp. 192, 207.

115. Sherraden, *Assets and the Poor*, p. 195.

116. Cf. Beverly, "How Can the Poor Save?," pp. 40–41.

117. See Sherraden, *Assets and the Poor*: "If there is a culture of poverty, . . . it is fundamentally asset-based" (p. 138). In other words, poor people who accumulate assets will emerge from a culture of poverty by doing so. See also p. 152: "Orientation toward the future begins in part with assets, which in turn shape opportunity structures, which in turn are quickly internalized."

118. For Sherraden's description of IDAs, see *Assets and the Poor*, pp. 220–233.

119. Sherraden, *Assets and the Poor*, pp. 201–202, 221–222. Tom Riley, a thoughtful and sympathetic analyst of IDAs, rightly questions the message sent when the savings of the poor are matched at high ratios: "A nine-to-one return for every dollar you save doesn't really teach anything about savings—it's more a handout than an incentive." See Riley, "Individual Development Accounts," *Philanthropy*, January/February 1999, p. 13.

120. See, for example, the match rates for thirteen IDAs being launched as part of the Downpayments on the American Dream Policy Demonstration, in the Corporation for Enterprise Development, "Downpayments on the American Dream Policy Demonstration Partners," *Assets*, Fall 1997, p. 3. The Corporation for Enterprise Development is a nonprofit institution that actively promotes the creation of IDAs. *Assets* is its quarterly newsletter.

121. See, for example, the discussion of the IDA administered by Indianapolis's Eastside Community Investments in Dana Canedy, "Down Payments on a Dream," *Ford Foundation Report*, Winter 1998, p. 5. See also "How IDAs Work," document downloaded from the Corporation for Enterprise Development web site (http://www.cfedonline.org), August 17, 1998: IDA participation is conditional on developing an asset acquisition plan, in which the income and consumption patterns of participants are studied—and on attending mandatory economic literacy sessions, in which money management is taught.

122. Consider in this context a remark by Riley, "Individual Development Accounts": "It might be argued that the real utility of a successful IDA is the inverse of their popular impression," according to which—contrary to Riley's view—"the *financial education classes* are the medicine and the *cash* is the sugar" (p. 12). The emphases appear in the text. As evidence for the greater importance of IDAs' educational component he cites the Ford Foundation's description of the impact that an IDA had on one participant, who "benefited even more from the financial counseling" than from the savings: "The classes changed the way she thought about money—and her life" (p. 12).

123. GAO, *Welfare Reform*, p. 47.

124. Canedy, "Down Payments on a Dream," p. 5. See also Roy Boshara and Robert E. Friedman, "20 Promising Ideas for Savings Facilitation and Mobilization in Low-Income Communities in the US," Corporation for Enterprise Development, 1997, p. 26.

125. Riley, "Individual Development Accounts," p. 12. The emphasis appears in the text.

126. DeParle, "U.S. Welfare System Dies as State Programs Emerge," *New York Times*, June 30, 1997, p. A1.

127. See GAO, *Welfare Reform*, p. 95.

128. GAO, *Welfare Reform*, p. 105.

129. GAO, *Welfare Reform*, p. 111.

130. Dana Milbank, "Under the Underclass," *The New Republic*, August 4, 1997, pp. 20–21.

131. See, for example, Michael Barone, "The Good News Is the Good News Is Right," *The Weekly Standard*, September 8, 1997, p. 24.

132. Judith Havemann, "Welfare Reform Success Cited in L.A.," *Washington Post*, August 20, 1998, p. A1.

133. See Havemann, "Welfare Reform," for a summary of the findings.

134. Stephen Freedman, Marisa Mitchell, and David Navarro, "The Los Angeles Jobs-First GAIN Evaluation: Preliminary Findings on Participation Patterns and First-Year Impacts," Manpower Demonstration Research Corporation, August 1998, downloaded from the MDRC web site (http://www.mdrc.org), September 1, 1998, section V ("Background"), part A ("Program Overview"). See also GAO, *Employment Training: Successful Projects Share Common Strategy* (HEHS-96-108), May 1996, p. 3. The GAO studied six successful employment-training programs. It found that one feature common to all six projects was "improving participants' employability skills as part of their training curriculum. . . . Employers want workers who exhibit attributes such as dependability, promptness, ability to work effectively in groups, and ability to resolve conflicts appropriately."

135. Freedman, Mitchell, and Navarro, "Los Angeles Jobs," section V, part A. See also GAO, *Employment Training*, p. 3: another feature common to all six programs was that they "link[ed] occupational skills training with the local labor market and made adjustments in course offerings to meet employer demand."

136. GAO, *Welfare Reform*, p. 44.

137. GAO, *Welfare Reform*, pp. 44–45.

138. For an argument along these lines, see Daniel Casse, "Why Welfare Reform Is Working," *Commentary*, September 1997: "It is a mistake to believe that the welfare debate was ever about the amount of money the country was spending. If, over the last 30 years, billions of dollars had gone into a poverty assistance program that had actually helped to foster stable families, safe and clean public housing, higher achievement in education, and a reduction in illegitimate births, no one would ever have complained about a welfare 'crisis' in the first place. Money alone was never the problem. Instead, what distinguishes the current reform is that it has forced both federal and state governments to take seriously the idea that welfare policy can deter, or encourage, behavior" (p. 42).

139. GAO, *Welfare Reform*, pp. 82–83.

140. Mary E. Richmond, *Friendly Visiting among the Poor: A Handbook for Charity Workers* (Montclair, N.J.: Patterson Smith, 1969, [rpt. 1899]), p. 111.

141. GAO, *Welfare Reform*, p. 73. On p. 73 the shift in welfare workers' responsibilities is nicely explained in these terms: "Staff interactions with recipients have shifted away from a pattern of 'Ms. Jones, has anything changed? No? Okay, see you in 6 months,' to a much greater focus on helping recipients obtain work." Note also that the passage quoted in the text speaks of recipients becoming "more" self-sufficient. Here self-sufficiency is understood to be situated on a continuum: it is a more-or-less proposition, not an all-or-nothing proposition.

142. Quoted in DeParle, "Getting Opal Caples to Work," *New York Times Magazine*, August 24, 1997, p. 54. See also DeParle's comment on p. 33: welfare reform in Wisconsin "is tougher than anything that has come before: virtually no one is exempt [from work requirements]. It is also more generous than anything that has come before: the state is offering child care and health care not just to welfare recipients but to all low-income working families, and it is creating thousands of community-service jobs." See, finally, E. J. Dionne, Jr., "Welfare Reform: The Clues Are in Wisconsin," *Washington Post*, September 23, 1997, p. A17: Dionne claims that Thompson "is trying to reconcile his own conservatism with his state's progressive tradition." As an example of the governor's commitment to progressivism, Dionne notes that the state government of Wisconsin spent only $12 million a year on child care when Thompson took office in 1987; by contrast, it was expected to spend $180 million in 1998.

143. Havemann and Barbara Vobejda, "A Job Program Tries to Tackle the Intangibles," *Washington Post*, June 16, 1997, p. A13.

144. Cf. the formulation by the economist Robert M. Solow, "Guess Who Likes Work-fare," in Amy Gutmann, ed., *Work and Welfare* (Princeton, N.J.: Princeton University Press, 1998): in an "idealized work requirement, . . . every capable person works, but welfare benefits (or a beefed-up Earned Income Tax Credit) top up the lowest earnings to allow a 'decent' standard of living. Work is 'packaged' with welfare" (p. 22). Edmund Phelps's pro-posed wage subsidies, discussed immediately below in the text, exemplify the sort of policy that Solow recommends.

145. GAO, *Welfare Reform*, p. 110.

146. Phelps, *Rewarding Work*, pp. 11-12.

147. Phelps, *Rewarding Work*, pp. 111 and 189 note 7.

148. Phelps, *Rewarding Work*, p. 32.

149. Phelps, *Rewarding Work*, p. 28.

150. Phelps, *Rewarding Work*, p. 54.

151. Phelps, *Rewarding Work*, p. 94.

152. Phelps, *Rewarding Work*, p. 108.

153. Phelps, *Rewarding Work*, p. 113.

154. See Phelps, *Rewarding Work*: "The relatively low wage rate of a great many workers in this country is, after all, an indication of their low productivity—the ineffectiveness of their labor input in generating revenues for businesses" (p. 44).

155. Phelps, *Rewarding Work*, p. 133. The emphasis appears in the text. Phelps is, of course, aware that programs already in existence—such as the Earned Income Tax Credit and the minimum wage—seek to increase the pay of low-wage workers. He argues, though, that these means poorly serve their desired end. See pp. 132–134 for his critique of the Earned Income Tax Credit: too many of its benefits go to comparatively well-off workers, whereas (p. 134) "it encourages *least* the employment of those whose job attachment and capacity for self-help are weakest." (The emphasis appears in the text.) For his critique of the minimum wage, see pp. 145–147: like many other economists, Phelps contends that the minimum wage discourages employers from hiring low-productivity workers.

156. Phelps, *Rewarding Work*, p. 155.

157. Phelps, *Rewarding Work*, p. 171.

158. Phelps, *Rewarding Work*, p. 114. An obvious alternative to the carrot of employ-ment subsidies would be the stick of the removal of the safety net. For Phelps's response to this argument, see p. 105: eliminating welfare would not do much by itself to increase employment, and would be too risky a policy in any case.

159. Phelps, *Rewarding Work*, p. 163.

160. Phelps, *Rewarding Work*, p. 154.

161. Glenn C. Loury, "Comment," in *Work and Welfare*, p. 52.

162. Alexis de Tocqueville, *Democracy in America*, translated by George Lawrence, ed-ited by J. P. Mayer (New York: Doubleday Anchor, 1969), pp. 543, 545–546.

Biographical Appendix

1. Except where otherwise indicated, the biographies are drawn from entries in Walter I. Trattner, editor in chief, *Biographical Dictionary of Social Welfare in America* (New York: Greenwood Press, 1986); and Allen Johnson and Dumas Malone, eds., *Dictionary of Amer-ican Biography* (New York: Scribner's, 1958–1964). Information about Addams, Brace, Hart-ley, Lowell, Richmond, Riis, Tuckerman, and Warner draws upon the discussions in Tratt-

ner's *Biographical Dictionary;* information about Channing and Rauschenbusch draws upon the discussions in Johnson and Malone's *Dictionary of American Biography.*

2. See Paul Boyer, *Urban Masses and Moral Order in America, 1820–1920* (Cambridge, Mass.: Harvard University Press, 1978), p. 107.

3. See Paul M. Minus, *Walter Rauschenbusch, American Reformer* (New York: Macmillan, 1988), pp. 99–100.

4. See Dorothy G. Becker, "The Visitor to the New York City Poor, 1843–1920," *Social Service Review* 35 (1961): 383.

5. See AICP, Twentieth Annual Report (1863), p. 28.

6. See Jeffrey Richardson Brackett, *Supervision and Education in Charity* (New York: Macmillan, 1903), p. 17.

7. See Joan Waugh, *Unsentimental Reformer: The Life of Josephine Shaw Lowell* (Cambridge, Mass.: Harvard University Press, 1997), p. 27.

8. Quoted in Lilian Brandt, *Growth and Development of AICP and COS (A Preliminary and Exploratory Review)* (New York: Community Service Society of New York, 1942), p. 61.

9. AICP, Twenty-fifth Annual Report (1868), p. 34.

10. See Waugh, *Unsentimental Reformer,* pp. 121–122.

11. See COS, Second Annual Report (1884), Appendix L, p. 62.

12. See Louise Ware, *Jacob A. Riis: Police Reporter, Reformer, Useful Citizen* (New York: D. Appleton-Century, 1938), p. 244. See also pp. 85, 241.

13. Mary E. Richmond, *Friendly Visiting among the Poor: A Handbook for Charity Workers* (Montclair, N.J.: Patterson Smith, 1969 [rpt. 1899]), p. xxxiii.

14. See Richmond, "A Background for the Art of Helping," in Richmond, *The Long View: Papers and Addresses,* edited by Joanna C. Colcord and Ruth Z. S. Mann (New York: Russell Sage Foundation, 1930), pp. 579–583.

15. For an alternate view, stressing the "mutual antagonism" between Addams and Richmond, see Donna L. Franklin, "Mary Richmond and Jane Addams: From Moral Certainty to Rational Inquiry in Social Work Practice," *Social Service Review* 60 (1986): 504–525. The "mutual antagonism" quotation appears on p. 511. Franklin's essay makes no mention of the evidence—discussed immediately below in the text—that points toward Richmond's admiration for Addams. On pp. 510–512 Franklin discusses Richmond's suspicion of the theorization that characterized Hull House's approach to social problems; on p. 518 she alludes to Richmond's successful opposition to a campaign to elect Addams president of the National Conference of Social Work in 1922, to mark the organization's fiftieth anniversary. If one imputes a healthy dose of personal ambition to Richmond, I doubt that she could reasonably have been expected to support Addams's candidacy: Addams had already served as the organization's president in 1910; but Richmond herself—clearly a major figure among American social workers—never presided over it.

16. Richmond, *Friendly Visiting,* p. xxxiii.

17. Richmond's 1899 letter is included in Ralph E. Pumphrey and Muriel W. Pumphrey, eds., *The Heritage of American Social Work: Readings in Its Philosophical and Institutional Development* (New York: Columbia University Press, 1961), pp. 259–267. Information on Richmond's attendance at the settlement conference appears on p. 259, note 2. The quotations are taken from pp. 266–267.

18. See Peter Steinfels, "Beliefs," *New York Times,* July 11, 1998, p. A11. Rorty's emphatic dismissal of religion as an appropriate support for the contemporary American left is the subject of Steinfels's essay. I am grateful to John Barry for calling the Rauschenbusch-Rorty connection to my attention.

BIBLIOGRAPHY

Addams, Jane. *Democracy and Social Ethics*. Edited by Anne Firor Scott. 1907. Reprint, Cambridge, Mass.: Harvard University Press, 1964.
———. *A New Conscience and an Ancient Evil*. New York: Macmillan, 1912.
———. "The Objective Value of a Social Settlement." In Jane Addams, Robert A. Woods, J. O. S. Huntington, Franklin H. Giddings, and Bernard Bosanquet. *Philanthropy and Social Progress: Seven Essays*, pp. 27–56. 1893. Reprint, Freeport, N.Y.: Books for Libraries Press, 1969.
———. "Review of *Modern Woman and Sex*, by Rachelle S. Yarros." *Survey* 70 (February 1934): 59.
———. *The Second Twenty Years at Hull-House, September 1909 to September 1929: With a Record of a Growing World Consciousness*. New York: Macmillan, 1930.
———. "The Settlement as a Factor in the Labor Movement." In Residents of Hull-House, *Hull-House Maps and Papers: A Presentation of Nationalities and Wages in a Congested District of Chicago, Together with Comments and Essays on Problems Growing Out of the Social Conditions*, pp. 183–204. 1895. Reprint, New York: Arno Press and The New York Times, 1970.
———. "Social Settlements." *Proceedings of the National Conference of Charities and Correction* 24 (1897): 338–346.
———. *The Spirit of Youth and the City Streets*. 1909. Reprint, New York: Macmillan, 1918.
———. *Twenty Years at Hull-House with Autobiographical Notes*. Urbana: University of Illinois Press, 1990.
———, and Ellen G. Starr. "Hull-House: A Social Settlement." In Residents of Hull-House, *Hull-House Maps and Papers*, pp. 207–230.
Allen, William H. *Efficient Democracy*. New York: Dodd, Mead and Company, 1907.
Alter, George, Claudia Goldin, and Elyce Rotella. "The Savings of Ordinary Americans: The Philadelphia Saving Fund Society in the Mid-Nineteenth Century." *Journal of Economic History* 54 (1994): 735–767.
Anderson, Elijah. *Streetwise: Race, Class, and Change in an Urban Community*. Chicago: University of Chicago Press, 1990.
Aristotle. *Nicomachean Ethics*. Translated by Martin Ostwald. Indianapolis: Bobbs-Merrill, 1962.
Atack, Jeremy, and Peter Passell. *A New Economic View of American History from Colonial Times to 1940*. 2nd ed. New York: W.W. Norton, 1994.
Banfield, Edward. *The Unheavenly City Revisited*. Boston: Little, Brown, and Company, 1974.
Bardach, Eugene. "Implementing a Paternalist Welfare-to-Work Program." In Lawrence M. Mead, ed., *The New Paternalism: Supervisory Approaches to Poverty*, pp. 248–278. Washington, D.C.: Brookings Institution Press, 1997.
Barone, Michael. "The Good News Is the Good News Is Right." *The Weekly Standard*, September 8, 1997, pp. 23–25.
Basinger, Jeanine A. *The It's a Wonderful Life Book*. New York: Alfred A. Knopf, 1997.
de Beaumont, Gustave, and Alexis de Tocqueville. *On the Penitentiary System in the United*

States and Its Application in France. Translated by Francis Lieber 1833. Reprint, Carbondale: Southern Illinois University Press, 1964 (rpt. 1833).

Becker, Dorothy G. "Exit Lady Bountiful: The Volunteer and the Professional Social Worker." *Social Service Review* 38 (1964): 57–72.

——. "The Visitor to the New York City Poor, 1843–1920." *Social Service Review* 35 (1961): 382–396.

Beito, David T. "Mutual Aid, State Welfare, and Organized Charity: Fraternal Societies and the 'Deserving' and 'Undeserving' Poor, 1900–1930." *Journal of Policy History* 5 (1993): 419–434.

Bell, Daniel. *The Cultural Contradictions of Capitalism*. New York: Basic Books, 1976.

Bennett, William J. "Face the Facts about Alcohol and Crime." *New York Times*, July 29, 1997, p. A23.

——, John J. DiIulio, Jr., and John P. Walters. *Body Count: Moral Poverty . . . and How to Win America's War against Crime and Drugs*. New York: Simon and Schuster, 1996.

Bernstein, Iver. *The New York City Draft Riots: Their Significance for American Society and Politics in the Age of the Civil War*. New York: Oxford University Press, 1990.

Beverly, Sondra. "How Can the Poor Save? Theory and Evidence on Saving in Low-Income Households." Working Paper 97-3, Center for Social Development, Washington University, 1997.

Bland, Sister Joan. *Hibernian Crusade: The Story of the Catholic Total Abstinence Union of America*. Washington, D.C.: Catholic University of America Press, 1951.

Blocker, Jack S., Jr. *American Temperance Movements: Cycles of Reform*. Boston: Twayne Publishers, 1989.

Bloom, Allan. *The Closing of the American Mind: How Higher Education Has Failed Democracy and Impoverished the Souls of Today's Students*. New York: Simon and Schuster, 1987.

Boller, Paul F., Jr., and John George. *They Never Said It: A Book of Fake Quotes, Misquotes, and Misleading Attributions*. New York: Oxford University Press, 1989.

Boshara, Roy, and Robert E. Friedman. "20 Promising Ideas for Savings Facilitation and Mobilization in Low-Income Communities in the US." Washington, D.C.: Corporation for Enterprise Development, 1997.

Boyer, Paul. *Urban Masses and Moral Order in America, 1820–1920*. Cambridge, Mass.: Harvard University Press, 1978.

Brace, Charles Loring. "The Best Method of Founding Children's Charities in Towns and Villages." *Proceedings of the National Conference of Charities and Corrections* 7 (1880): 227–237.

——. *The Dangerous Classes of New York and Twenty Years' Work among Them*. 3rd ed., with addenda. 1880. Reprint, Montclair, N.J.: Patterson Smith, 1967.

——. *Gesta Christi: Or a History of Humane Progress under Christianity*. 4th ed. New York: A. C. Armstrong and Son, 1884.

——. *Short Sermons to News Boys: With a History of the Formation of the News Boys' Lodging-House*. New York: Charles Scribner, 1866.

Brace, Emma, ed. *The Life of Charles Loring Brace Chiefly Told in His Own Letters*. 1894. Reprint, New York: Arno Press, 1976.

Brackett, Jeffrey Richardson. *Supervision and Education in Charity*. New York: Macmillan, 1903.

Brandt, Lilian. "Alcoholism and Social Problems." *Survey* 25 (October 1, 1910): 17–21.

——. *The Charity Organization Society of the City of New York, 1882–1907*. New York: United Charities Building, 1907.

——. *Five Hundred and Seventy-Four Deserters and Their Families: A Descriptive Study of Their Characteristics and Circumstances*. 1905. Reprint, New York: Arno Press and The New York Times, 1972.

——. *Growth and Development of AICP and COS (A Preliminary and Exploratory Review)*. New York: Community Service Society of New York, 1942.

Bremner, Robert H. "The Big Flat: History of a New York Tenement House." *American Historical Review* 64 (1958): 54–62.

——. *From the Depths: The Discovery of Poverty in the United States*. New York: New York University Press, 1956.

——. "The Rediscovery of Pauperism." In *Current Issues in Social Work Seen in Historical Perspective*, pp. 10–19. New York: Council on Social Work Education, 1962.

Brotz, Howard, ed. *Negro Social and Political Thought, 1850–1920: Representative Texts*. New York: Basic Books, 1966.

Brown, Mary Willcox. *The Development of Thrift*. New York: Macmillan, 1899.

Burnham, J. C. "New Perspectives on the Prohibition 'Experiment' of the 1920's." *Journal of Social History* 2 (1968): 51–68.

Butler, John Sibley. *Entrepreneurship and Self-Help among Black Americans: A Reconsideration of Race and Economics*. Albany: State University of New York Press, 1991.

Calkins, Raymond. *Substitutes for the Saloon: An Investigation Originally Made for the Committee of Fifty*. 2nd ed. 1919. Reprint, New York: Arno Press, 1971.

Canedy, Dana. "Down Payments on a Dream." *Ford Foundation Report*, Winter 1998, pp. 4–7.

Casse, Daniel. "Why Welfare Reform Is Working." *Commentary*, September 1997, pp. 36–42.

Chambers, Clarke A. "An Historical Perspective on Political Action vs. Individualized Treatment." In Paul S. Weinberger, ed., *Perspectives on Social Welfare: An Introductory Anthology*, 2nd ed., pp. 77–94. New York: Macmillan, 1974.

Channing, William Ellery. "Address on Temperance." In *The Works of William E. Channing, D.D.*, pp. 99–116. Boston: American Unitarian Association, 1903.

——. "A Discourse on the Life and Character of the Rev. Joseph Tuckerman, D.D." In *Works of William E. Channing*, pp. 578–599.

——. "Ministry for the Poor." In *Works of William E. Channing*, pp. 73–87.

——. "On Preaching the Gospel to the Poor: Charge at the Ordination of Charles F. Barnard and Frederick T. Gray, as Ministers at Large, in Boston." In *Works of William E. Channing*, pp. 88–92.

——. "On the Elevation of the Laboring Classes." In *Works of William E. Channing*, pp. 36–66.

Chapin, Robert Coit. *The Standard of Living among Workingmen's Families in New York City*. New York: Charities Publication Committee, 1909.

Charity Organization Society of the City of New York. Annual Reports, 1–25 (1883–1907).

Children's Aid Society. *Annual Reports of the Children's Aid Society*, Nos. 1–10, Feb. 1854–Feb. 1863. Reprint, New York: Arno Press and The New York Times, 1971.

Clark, Norman H. *Deliver Us from Evil: An Interpretation of American Prohibition*. New York: W.W. Norton, 1976.

Clemetson, Lynette. "Trying to Close the Achievement Gap." *Newsweek*, June 7, 1999, pp. 36–37.

Cook, Philip J. "The Effect of Liquor Taxes on Drinking, Cirrhosis, and Auto Accidents." In Mark H. Moore and Dean R. Gerstein, eds., *Alcohol and Public Policy: Beyond the Shadow of Prohibition*, pp. 255–285. Washington, D.C.: National Academy Press, 1981.

——, and Michael J. Moore. "This Tax's for You: The Case for Higher Beer Taxes." *National Tax Journal* 47 (1994): 559–573.

Cordasco, Francesco. "Charles Loring Brace and the Dangerous Classes: Historical Analogues of the Urban Black Poor." *Journal of Human Relations* 20 (1972): 379–386.

Corporation for Enterprise Development. "Downpayments on the American Dream Policy Demonstration Partners." *Assets*, Fall 1997, p. 3.

——. "How IDAs Work." Document downloaded from the Corporation for Enterprise Development web site (http://www.cfedonline.org), August 17, 1998.

Davis, Allen F. *American Heroine: The Life and Legend of Jane Addams*. New York: Oxford University Press, 1973.

——. *Spearheads for Reform: The Social Settlements and the Progressive Movement, 1890–1914*. New York: Oxford University Press, 1967.

DeParle, Jason. "Getting Opal Caples to Work." *New York Times Magazine*, August 24, 1997, pp. 32–61.

——. "Report on Effort to Aid Poor Fathers Offers Discouraging News." *New York Times*, September 29, 1998, p. A16.

——. "U.S. Welfare System Dies as State Programs Emerge." *New York Times*, June 30, 1997, pp. A1, A11.

——. "Welfare Overhaul Initiatives Focus on Fathers." *New York Times*, September 3, 1998, pp. A1, A20.

Devine, Edward T. *Report on the Desirability of Establishing an Employment Bureau in the City of New York*. New York: Charities Publication Committee, 1909.

DiIulio, John J., Jr. "The Coming of the Super-Preachers." *The Weekly Standard*, June 23, 1997, pp. 23–26.

——. "The Lord's Work: The Church and the 'Civil Society Sector.'" *The Brookings Review*, Fall 1997, pp. 27–31.

Dionne, E. J., Jr. "Welfare Reform: The Clues Are in Wisconsin." *Washington Post*, September 23, 1997, p. A17.

"Discussion on 'Personal Service.'" *Charities Review* 4 (1895): 477–492.

Dodd, Jill Siegel. "The Working Classes and the Temperance Movement in Ante-Bellum Boston." *Labor History* 19 (1978): 510–531.

Dolan, Jay P. *The Immigrant Church: New York's Irish and German Catholics, 1815–1865*. Baltimore: Johns Hopkins University Press, 1975.

Drescher, Seymour. *Dilemmas of Democracy: Tocqueville and Modernization*. Pittsburgh: University of Pittsburgh Press, 1968.

DuBois, W. E. B. *The Autobiography of W. E. B. DuBois: A Soliloquy on Viewing My Life from the Last Decade of Its First Century*. New York: International Publishers, 1968.

——. *The Philadelphia Negro: A Social Study, Together with a Special Report on Domestic Service by Isabel Eaton*. 1899. Reprint, New York: Schocken Books, 1967.

Duneier, Mitchell. *Slim's Table: Race, Respectability, and Masculinity*. Chicago: University of Chicago Press, 1992.

Dyson, Michael Eric. *Making Malcolm: The Myth and Meaning of Malcolm X*. New York: Oxford University Press, 1995.

Eberstadt, Nicholas. "Prosperous Paupers and Affluent Savages." *Society*, January/February 1998, pp. 393–401.

Ely, Richard T. *Social Aspects of Christianity and Other Essays.* New York: Thomas Y. Crowell and Company, 1889.

Ernst, Robert. *Immigrant Life in New York City 1825–1863.* 1949. Reprint, Syracuse, N.Y.: Syracuse University Press, 1994.

Faler, Paul. "Cultural Aspects of the Industrial Revolution: Lynn, Massachusetts, Shoemakers and Industrial Morality, 1826–1860." *Labor History* 15 (1974): 367–394.

Farrell, John C. *Beloved Lady: A History of Jane Addams' Ideas on Reform and Peace.* Baltimore: Johns Hopkins University Press, 1967.

Feder, Leah Hannah. *Unemployment Relief in Periods of Depression: A Study of Measures Adopted in Certain American Cities, 1857 through 1922.* New York: Russell Sage, 1936.

Federman, Maya, Thesia I. Garner, Kathleen Short, W. Boman Cutter IV, John Kiely, David Levine, Duane McGough, and Marilyn McMillen. "What Does It Mean to Be Poor in America?" *Monthly Labor Review* 119, no. 5 (May 1996): 3–17.

Fischer, Claude S., Michael Hout, Martín Sánchez Jankowski, Samuel R. Lucas, Ann Swidler, and Kim Voss. *Inequality by Design: Cracking the Bell Curve Myth.* Princeton, N.J.: Princeton University Press, 1996.

Fishburn, Janet Forsythe. *The Fatherhood of God and the Victorian Family: The Social Gospel in America.* Philadelphia: Fortress Press, 1981.

Flake, Floyd, and Donna Marie Williams. *The Way of the Bootstrapper: Nine Action Steps for Achieving Your Dreams.* San Francisco: HarperSanFrancisco, 1999.

Fogel, Robert W. "The Fourth Great Awakening and the Political Realignment of the 1990s." Unpublished manuscript of a lecture delivered at the American Enterprise Institute for Public Policy Research, September 11, 1995.

Franklin, Donna L. "Mary Richmond and Jane Addams: From Moral Certainty to Rational Inquiry in Social Work Practice." *Social Service Review* 60 (1986): 504–525.

Frazier, E. Franklin. *Black Bourgeoisie.* New York: Free Press, 1957.

Fredrickson, George M. *The Inner Civil War: Northern Intellectuals and the Crisis of the Union.* New York: Harper and Row, 1965.

Freedman, Stephen, Marisa Mitchell, and David Navarro. "The Los Angeles Jobs-First GAIN Evaluation: Preliminary Findings on Participation Patterns and First-Year Impacts." Manpower Demonstration Research Corporation, August 1998, document downloaded from the MDRC web site (http://www.mdrc.org), September 1, 1998.

Freeman, Richard B. "Who Escapes? The Relation of Churchgoing and Other Background Factors to the Socioeconomic Performance of Black Male Youths from Inner-City Tracts." In Freeman and Harry J. Holzer, eds., *The Black Youth Employment Crisis,* pp. 353–376. Chicago: University of Chicago Press, 1986.

Fried, Lewis. "Jacob Riis and the Jews: The Ambivalent Quest for Community." *American Studies* 20 (1979): 5–25.

Frum, David. *Dead Right.* New York: Basic Books, 1994.

Fukuyama, Francis. *The Great Disruption: Human Nature and the Reconstitution of Social Order.* New York: Free Press, 1999.

Galston, William A. "A Progressive Family Policy for the Twenty-First Century." In Will Marshall, ed., *Building the Bridge: 10 Big Ideas to Transform America,* pp. 149–162. Lanham, Md.: Rowman and Littlefield, 1997.

Gans, Herbert J. "Culture and Class in the Study of Poverty: An Approach to Antipoverty Research." In Gans, *People, Plans, and Policies: Essays on Poverty, Racism, and Other National Urban Problems,* pp. 299–327. New York: Columbia University Press and Russell Sage Foundation, 1991.

——. "Escaping from Poverty: A Comparison of the Immigrant and Black Experience." In Gans, *People, Plans, and Policies*, pp. 279–284.

——. *The War against the Poor: The Underclass and Antipoverty Policy.* New York: Basic Books, 1995.

Gates, Henry Louis, Jr. "Parable of the Talents." In Gates and Cornel West, *The Future of the Race*, pp. 1–52. New York: Alfred A. Knopf, 1996.

——. "Two Nations . . . Both Black." *Forbes*, September 14, 1992, pp. 132–138.

Gettleman, Marvin E. "Charity and Social Classes in the United States, 1874–1900, II." *American Journal of Economics and Sociology* 22 (1963): 417–426.

Glazer, Nathan. *Ethnic Dilemmas, 1964–1982.* Cambridge, Mass.: Harvard University Press, 1983.

——. *The Limits of Social Policy.* Cambridge, Mass.: Harvard University Press, 1988.

——, and Daniel Patrick Moynihan. *Beyond the Melting Pot: The Negroes, Puerto Ricans, Jews, Italians, and Irish of New York City.* 2nd ed. Cambridge, Mass.: MIT Press, 1970.

Greeley, Andrew M. *The Irish Americans: Their Rise to Money and Power.* New York: Harper and Row, 1981.

——. *That Most Distressful Nation: The Taming of the American Irish.* Chicago: Quadrangle Books, 1972.

Grossman, Michael, Jody L. Sinclair, John Mullahy, and Richard Anderson. "Alcohol and Cigarette Taxes." *Journal of Economic Perspectives* 7, no. 4 (Fall 1993): 211–222.

Gusfield, Joseph R. *Symbolic Crusade: Status Politics and the American Temperance Movement.* 2nd ed. Urbana: University of Illinois Press, 1986.

Gutman, Herbert G. *Power and Culture: Essays on the American Working Class.* New York: New Press, 1987.

Hacker, Andrew. *Two Nations: Black and White, Separate, Hostile, Unequal.* New York: Charles Scribner's Sons, 1992.

Hale, E. E., ed. *Joseph Tuckerman on the Elevation of the Poor: A Selection from His Reports as Minister at Large in Boston.* 1874. Reprint, New York: Arno Press and The New York Times, 1971.

Halper, Thomas. "The Poor as Pawns: The New 'Deserving Poor' & the Old." *Polity* 6 (1973): 71–86.

Handler, Joel F. *Reforming the Poor: Welfare Policy, Federalism, and Morality.* New York: Basic Books, 1972.

Handler, M. S. "Introduction." In Malcolm X, *The Autobiography of Malcolm X*, with the assistance of Alex Haley, pp. ix–xiv. New York: Grove Press, 1966.

Handlin, Oscar. *Boston's Immigrants: A Study in Acculturation.* Revised and enlarged edition. Cambridge, Mass.: Harvard University Press, 1959.

——. *The Newcomers: Negroes and Puerto Ricans in a Changing Metropolis.* Cambridge, Mass.: Harvard University Press, 1965.

——. "Poverty from the Civil War to World War II." In Leo Fishman, ed., *Poverty amid Affluence*, pp. 3–17. New Haven, Conn.: Yale University Press, 1966.

Handy, Robert T., ed. *The Social Gospel in America: Gladden, Ely, Rauschenbusch.* New York: Oxford University Press, 1966.

Hannerz, Ulf. *Soulside: Inquiries into Ghetto Culture and Community.* New York: Columbia University Press, 1969.

Hansen, Marcus Lee. *The Immigrant in American History.* Cambridge, Mass.: Harvard University Press, 1940.

Harlan, Louis R. *Booker T. Washington: The Wizard of Tuskegee, 1901–1915*. New York: Oxford University Press, 1983.

Harper, Nile. *Urban Churches, Vital Signs: Beyond Charity toward Justice*. Grand Rapids, Mich.: William B. Eerdmans, 1999.

Harrington, Michael. *The Other America: Poverty in the United States*. New York: Penguin, 1963.

Hartley, Isaac Smithson, ed. *Memorial of Robert Milham Hartley*. 1882. Reprint, New York: Arno Press, 1976.

Hartocollis, Anemona. "A Church's Seeds for a Charter School: At Allen Christian in Queens, Values Transcend Creed, Founder Says." *New York Times*, February 14, 1999, pp. 33–34.

Havemann, Judith. "Welfare Reform Success Cited in L.A." *Washington Post*, August 20, 1998, pp. A1, A8.

——, and Barbara Vobejda. "A Job Program Tries to Tackle the Intangibles." *Washington Post*, June 16, 1997, pp. A1, A12–13.

Himmelfarb, Gertrude. "Democratic Remedies for Democratic Disorders." *The Public Interest* 131 (Spring 1998): 3–24.

——. *The De-Moralization of Society: From Victorian Virtues to Modern Values*. New York: Alfred A. Knopf, 1995.

Hochschild, Jennifer L. *Facing Up to the American Dream: Race, Class, and the Soul of the Nation*. Princeton, N.J.: Princeton University Press, 1995.

Horn, Wade F., and Andrew Bush. "Fathers and Welfare Reform." *The Public Interest* 129 (Fall 1997): 38–49.

Horowitz, Daniel. *The Morality of Spending: Attitudes toward the Consumer Society in America, 1875–1940*. Baltimore: Johns Hopkins University Press, 1985.

Howe, Daniel Walker. *The Unitarian Conscience: Harvard Moral Philosophy, 1805–1861*. Cambridge, Mass.: Harvard University Press, 1970.

Hubbard, R. Glenn, Jonathan Skinner, and Stephen P. Zeldes. "Precautionary Saving and Social Insurance." *Journal of Political Economy* 103 (1995): 360–399.

Huggins, Nathan Irving. *Revelations: American History, American Myths*. Edited by Brenda Smith Huggins. New York: Oxford University Press, 1995.

Hunter, James Davison. *Culture Wars: The Struggle to Define America*. New York: Basic Books, 1991.

Hunter, Robert. *Poverty: Social Conscience in the Progressive Era*. Edited by Peter d'A. Jones. 1904. Reprint, New York: Harper and Row, 1965.

Husock, Howard. "We Don't Need Subsidized Housing." *City Journal*, Winter 1997, pp. 50–58.

Ignatiev, Noel. *How the Irish Became White*. New York: Routledge, 1995.

Jencks, Christopher. *Rethinking Social Policy: Race, Poverty, and the Underclass*. New York: HarperPerennial, 1993.

Johnson, Allen, and Dumas Malone, eds. *Dictionary of American Biography*. New York: Scribner's, 1958–1964.

Johnson, Dirk. "Temperance Movement Grows in Chicago, a Precinct at a Time." *New York Times*, April 19, 1998, p. 14.

Johnson, Jean, and Steve Farkas with Ali Bers. *Getting By: What American Teenagers Really Think about Their Schools*. New York: Public Agenda, 1997.

Jones, Jacqueline. *The Dispossessed: America's Underclasses from the Civil War to the Present*. New York: Basic Books, 1992.

Jones, Peter d'A. "Introduction to the Torchbook Edition." In Robert Hunter, *Poverty: Social Conscience in the Progressive Era*, pp. vi–xxiv. New York: Harper and Row, 1965.

Katz, Michael B. *Improving Poor People: The Welfare State, the "Underclass," and Urban Schools as History*. Princeton, N.J.: Princeton University Press, 1995.

——. *In the Shadow of the Poorhouse: A Social History of Welfare in America*. New York: Basic Books, 1986.

——. *Poverty and Policy in American History*. New York: Academic Press, 1983.

——. "Reframing the 'Underclass' Debate." In Katz, ed., *The "Underclass" Debate: Views from History*, pp. 440–477. Princeton, N.J.: Princeton University Press, 1993.

——. *The Undeserving Poor: From the War on Poverty to the War on Welfare*. New York: Pantheon Books, 1989.

Kelley, Florence. "The Sweating-System." In Residents of Hull-House, *Hull-House Maps and Papers: A Presentation of Nationalities and Wages in a Congested District of Chicago, Together with Comments and Essays on Problems Growing Out of the Social Conditions*, pp. 27–41. 1895. Reprint, New York: Arno Press and The New York Times, 1970.

Kellor, Frances A. *Out of Work: A Study of Unemployment*. 1915. Reprint, New York: Arno Press and The New York Times, 1971.

Keyssar, Alexander. *Out of Work: The First Century of Unemployment in Massachusetts*. New York: Cambridge University Press, 1986.

Kingsdale, Jon M. "The 'Poor Man's Club': Social Functions of the Urban Working-Class Saloon." *American Quarterly* 25 (1973): 472–489.

Klebaner, Benjamin J. "Poverty and Its Relief in American Thought, 1815–61." In Frank R. Breul and Steven J. Diner, eds., *Compassion and Responsibility: Readings in the History of Social Welfare Policy in the United States*, pp. 114–131. Chicago: University of Chicago Press, 1980.

Klein, Joe. "In God They Trust." *The New Yorker*, June 16, 1997, pp. 40–48.

Kloppenberg, James T. *Uncertain Victory: Social Democracy and Progressivism in European and American Thought, 1870–1920*. New York: Oxford University Press, 1986.

Koren, John. *Economic Aspects of the Liquor Problem: An Investigation Made for the Committee of Fifty under the Direction of Henry W. Farnam*. Boston: Houghton Mifflin, 1899.

Krauthammer, Charles. "Defining Deviancy Up." In Mark Gerson, ed., *The Essential Neoconservative Reader*, pp. 372–382. Reading, Mass.: Addison Wesley, 1996.

Kristol, Irving. *Two Cheers for Capitalism*. New York: New American Library, 1979.

——. "Welfare: The Best of Intentions, the Worst of Results." In Paul S. Weinberger, ed., *Perspectives on Social Welfare: An Introductory Anthology*, 2nd ed., pp. 237–242. New York: Macmillan, 1974.

Kudlow, Lawrence. *American Abundance: The New Economic and Moral Prosperity*. New York: American Heritage Custom Publishing, 1997.

Langsam, Miriam Z. *Children West: A History of the Placing-Out System of the New York Children's Aid Society, 1853–1890*. Madison: Wisconsin State Historical Society, 1964.

Laurie, Bruce. "'Nothing on Compulsion': Life Styles of Philadelphia Artisans, 1820–1850." *Labor History* 15 (1974): 337–366.

——. *Working People of Philadelphia, 1800–1850*. Philadelphia: Temple University Press, 1980.

Lebergott, Stanley. *Pursuing Happiness: American Consumers in the Twentieth Century*. Princeton, N.J.: Princeton University Press, 1993.

Leland, John. "Savior of the Streets." *Newsweek*, June 1, 1998, pp. 20–25.

Lemann, Nicholas. *The Promised Land: The Great Black Migration and How It Changed America*. New York: Alfred A. Knopf, 1991.

Levine, Harry Gene. "Temperance and Prohibition in America." In Griffith Edwards, Awni Arif, and Jerome Jaffe, eds., *Drug Use and Misuse: Cultural Perspectives*, pp. 187–200. London and New York: Croom Helm and St. Martin's Press, 1983.

Levy, Mickey D. "The Economy Is Safe from a 'Savings Crisis.'" *Wall Street Journal*, February 4, 1999, p. A22.

Lewis, David Levering. *W. E. B. DuBois: Biography of a Race, 1868–1919*. New York: Henry Holt and Company, 1993.

Lieberson, Stanley. *A Piece of the Pie: Blacks and White Immigrants since 1880*. Berkeley and Los Angeles: University of California Press, 1980.

Lincoln, Abraham. "Address to the Washington Temperance Society of Springfield, Illinois." In *Abraham Lincoln: Speeches and Writings, 1832–1858*, pp. 81–90. New York: Library of America, 1989.

Lincoln, C. Eric. *The Black Muslims in America*. 3rd ed. Grand Rapids, Mich.: William B. Eerdmans Publishing Company, 1994.

Linn, James Weber. *Jane Addams: A Biography*. 1935. Reprint, New York: Greenwood Press, 1968.

Lipset, Seymour Martin. *American Exceptionalism: A Double-Edged Sword*. New York: W.W. Norton and Company, 1996.

Loury, Glenn C. "Comment." In Amy Gutmann, ed., *Work and Welfare*, pp. 45–54. Princeton, N.J.: Princeton University Press, 1998.

———. "The Conservative Line on Race." *The Atlantic Monthly*, November 1997, pp. 144–154.

———. *One by One from the Inside Out: Essays and Reviews on Race and Responsibility in America*. New York: Free Press, 1995.

———. "Uneconomical." *The New Republic*, June 29, 1998, pp. 14–15.

———. "Why More Blacks Don't Invest." *New York Times Magazine*, June 7, 1998, pp. 70–71.

———, and Linda Datcher Loury. "Not by Bread Alone: The Role of the African-American Church in Inner-City Development." *The Brookings Review*, Winter 1997, pp. 10–13.

Lowell, Josephine Shaw. "Children." In William Rhinelander Stewart, *The Philanthropic Work of Josephine Shaw Lowell Containing a Biographical Sketch of Her Life Together with a Selection of Her Public Papers and Private Letters*, pp. 267–276. 1911. Reprint, Montclair, N.J.: Patterson Smith, 1974.

———. "Duties of Friendly Visitors." In Stewart, *Philanthropic Work of Josephine Shaw Lowell*, pp. 142–150.

———. "The Economic and Moral Effects of Public Outdoor Relief." In Stewart, *Philanthropic Work of Josephine Shaw Lowell*, pp. 158–174.

———. "The Evils of Investigation and Relief." In Stewart, *Philanthropic Work of Josephine Shaw Lowell*, pp. 207–217.

———. "Felix Qui Causam Rerum Cognovit." *Charities Review* 2 (1893): 420–426.

———. "Five Months' Work for the Unemployed in New York City." *Charities Review* 3 (1894): 323–342.

———. "Houses of Refuge for Women; Their Purposes, Management, and Possibilities." *Proceedings of the New York State Conference of Charities and Correction* 1 (1900): 245–256.

———. "How to Adapt 'Charity Organization' Methods to Small Communities." *Proceedings of the National Conference of Charities and Corrections* 14 (1887): 135–143.

———. "Labor Organization as Affected by Law." *Charities Review* 1 (1891): 6–11.

———. "The Living Wage." In Stewart, *Philanthropic Work of Josephine Shaw Lowell*, pp. 409–415.

———. "Methods of Relief for the Unemployed." *Forum* 16 (1894): 655–660.

———. "Paper Read at the First Public Meeting of the Working Women's Society." In Stewart, *Philanthropic Work of Josephine Shaw Lowell*, pp. 372–380.

———. "Poverty and Its Relief: The Methods Possible in the City of New York." In Stewart, *Philanthropic Work of Josephine Shaw Lowell*, pp. 175–189.

———. *Public Relief and Private Charity.* 1884. Reprint, New York: Arno Press and The New York Times, 1971.

———. "Sunday School Talk to Children." In Stewart, *Philanthropic Work of Josephine Shaw Lowell*, pp. 150–158.

———. "The True Aim of Charity Organization Societies." In Stewart, *Philanthropic Work of Josephine Shaw Lowell*, pp. 196–207.

———. "The Uses and Dangers of Investigation in Public and Private Charities." In Stewart, *Philanthropic Work of Josephine Shaw Lowell*, pp. 217–223.

Lubove, Roy. *The Professional Altruist: The Emergence of Social Work as a Career, 1880–1930.* Cambridge, Mass.: Harvard University Press, 1965.

———. *The Progressives and the Slums: Tenement House Reform in New York City, 1890–1917.* 1962. Reprint, New York: Greenwood Press, 1975.

———. *The Struggle for Social Security, 1900–1935.* Cambridge, Mass.: Harvard University Press, 1968.

Madrick, Jeff. "The Worker's Just Reward." *New York Times*, August 1, 1999, section 4, p. 15.

Magnet, Myron. *The Dream and the Nightmare: The Sixties' Legacy to the Underclass.* New York: William Morrow and Company, 1993.

Malcolm X. *The Autobiography of Malcolm X*, with the assistance of Alex Haley. New York: Grove Press, 1966.

Marx, Karl, and Friedrich Engels. "Manifesto of the Communist Party." In Robert C. Tucker, ed., *The Marx-Engels Reader*, 2nd ed., pp. 469–500. New York: W.W. Norton, 1978.

Matza, David. "The Disreputable Poor." In Reinhard Bendix and Seymour Martin Lipset, eds., *Class, Status, and Power: Social Stratification in Comparative Perspective*, 2nd ed., pp. 289–302. New York: Free Press, 1966.

Mayer, Susan E. *What Money Can't Buy: Family Income and Children's Life Chances.* Cambridge, Mass.: Harvard University Press, 1997.

McCarthy, Kathleen D. *Noblesse Oblige: Charity and Cultural Philanthropy in Chicago, 1849–1929.* Chicago: University of Chicago Press, 1982.

McColgan, Daniel. *Joseph Tuckerman: Pioneer in American Social Work.* Washington, D.C.: Catholic University of America Press, 1940.

McDaniel, Antonio. "The 'Philadelphia Negro' Then and Now: Implications for Empirical Research." In Michael B. Katz and Thomas J. Sugrue, eds., *W.E.B. DuBois, Race, and the City: The Philadelphia Negro and Its Legacy*, pp. 155–194. Philadelphia: University of Pennsylvania Press, 1998.

Mead, Lawrence M. *Beyond Entitlement: The Social Obligations of Citizenship.* New York: Free Press, 1986.

———, ed. *The New Paternalism: Supervisory Approaches to Poverty.* Washington, D.C.: Brookings Institution Press, 1997.

——. *The New Politics of Poverty: The Nonworking Poor in America*. New York: Basic Books, 1992.

——. "Poverty: How Little We Know." *Social Service Review* 68 (1994): 322–350.

——. "The Rise of Paternalism." In Lawrence M. Mead, ed., *The New Paternalism: Supervisory Approaches to Poverty*, pp. 1–38. Washington, D.C.: Brookings Institution Press, 1997.

——. "Welfare Employment." In Lawrence M. Mead, ed., *The New Paternalism: Supervisory Approaches to Poverty*, pp. 39–88. Washington, D.C.: Brookings Institution Press, 1997.

Meyer, Donald B. *The Protestant Search for Political Realism, 1919–1941*. New York: Greenwood Press, 1960.

Milbank, Dana. "Under the Underclass." *The New Republic*, August 4, 1997, pp. 20–24.

Miller, Kerby A. *Emigrants and Exiles: Ireland and the Irish Exodus to North America*. New York: Oxford University Press, 1985.

Miller, Lisa. "Black Muslims Flock to a Moderate Cleric of Radical Pedigree." *Wall Street Journal*, July 9, 1999, pp. A1, A7.

Mincy, Ronald B., and Hillard Pouncy. "Paternalism, Child Support Enforcement, and Fragile Families." In Lawrence M. Mead, ed., *The New Paternalism: Supervisory Approaches to Poverty*, pp. 130–160. Washington, D.C.: Brookings Institution Press, 1997.

Minus, Paul M. *Walter Rauschenbusch, American Reformer*. New York: Macmillan, 1988.

Modell, John. "Patterns of Consumption, Acculturation, and Family Income Strategies in Late Nineteenth-Century America." In Tamara K. Hareven and Maris A. Vinovskis, eds., *Family and Population in Nineteenth-Century America*, pp. 206–240. Princeton, N.J.: Princeton University Press, 1978.

Mohl, Raymond A. "The Abolition of Public Outdoor Relief, 1870–1900: A Critique of the Piven and Cloward Thesis." In Walter I. Trattner, ed., *Social Welfare or Social Control? Some Historical Reflections on Regulating the Poor*, pp. 35–50. Knoxville: University of Tennessee Press, 1983.

Montgomery, David. *The Fall of the House of Labor: The Workplace, the State, and American Labor Activism, 1865–1925*. New York: Cambridge University Press, 1987.

——. *Workers' Control in America: Studies in the History of Work, Technology, and Labor Struggles*. New York: Cambridge University Press, 1979.

Moore, Mark H., and Dean R. Gerstein, eds. *Alcohol and Public Policy: Beyond the Shadow of Prohibition*. Washington, D.C.: National Academy Press, 1981.

Moynihan, Daniel Patrick. "A Family Policy for the Nation." In Lee Rainwater and William L. Yancey, eds., *The Moynihan Report and the Politics of Controversy*, pp. 385–394. Cambridge, Mass.: MIT Press, 1967.

——. "Defining Deviancy Down." In Mark Gerson, ed., *The Essential Neoconservative Reader*, pp. 356–371. Reading, Mass.: Addison Wesley, 1996.

——. "The Negro Family: The Case for National Action" (i.e., the Moynihan report), reprinted in Rainwater and Yancey, eds., *Moynihan Report*, pp. 41–124.

——. *The Politics of a Guaranteed Income: The Nixon Administration and the Family Assistance Plan*. New York: Random House, 1973.

——. "The Professors and the Poor." In Moynihan, ed., *On Understanding Poverty: Perspectives from the Social Sciences*, pp. 3–35. New York: Basic Books, 1969.

Mullahy, John. "Alcohol and the Labor Market." In Michael E. Hilton and Gregory Blass, eds., *Economics and the Prevention of Alcohol-Related Problems*, pp. 141–174. Washington, D.C.: U.S. Department of Health and Human Services, 1993.

Muraskin, William A. "Review of *Regulating the Poor.*" *Contemporary Sociology: A Journal of Reviews* 4 (1975): 607–613.

Murray, Charles. *In Pursuit: Of Happiness and Good Government.* New York: Simon and Schuster, 1988.

———. "The Partial Restoration of Traditional Society." *The Public Interest* 121 (Fall 1995): 122–134.

———. *The Underclass Revisited.* Washington, D.C.: AEI Press, 1999.

Myers, Gustavus. *History of the Great American Fortunes.* New York: Modern Library, 1936.

Nadler, Richard. "Glum and Glummer." *National Review,* September 28, 1998, pp. 26–30.

National Center for Health Statistics. National Vital Statistics Reports, vol. 47, no. 18, *Births: Final Data for 1997.* Document downloaded from the National Center for Health Statistics web site (http://www.cdc.gov/nchswww/), August 25, 1999.

———. "Teen Birth Rate Down in All States." April 29, 1999. Document downloaded from the National Center for Health Statistics web site (http://www.cdc.gov/nchswww/), August 25, 1999.

National Institute on Alcohol Abuse and Alcoholism. Surveillance Report #47, *Apparent Per Capita Alcohol Consumption: National, State and Regional Trends, 1977–96,* December 1998.

Neckerman, Kathryn M. "The Emergence of 'Underclass' Family Patterns, 1900–1940." In Michael B. Katz, ed., *The "Underclass" Debate: Views from History,* pp. 194–219. Princeton, N.J.: Princeton University Press, 1993.

New York Association for Improving the Condition of the Poor. "An Abstract of the Secretary's Remarks at a Special Meeting of the Advisory Committees and Visitors of the Association for Improving the Condition of the Poor, Convened in the Hall of the Public School Edifice, New-York, March 3, 1847," included in the New York Public Library's microfilm edition of the AICP Annual Reports, Reel 1 (1845–1865).

———. *Annual Reports of the New York Association for Improving the Condition of the Poor,* Nos. 1–10, 1845–1853. Reprint, New York: Arno Press and The New York Times, 1971.

———. Annual Reports, 11–29 (1854–1872).

———. "The Economist" (1847), included in the New York Public Library's microfilm edition of the AICP Annual Reports, Reel 1 (1845–1865).

———. "First Report of a Committee on the Sanitary Condition of the Laboring Classes in the City of New-York, with Remedial Suggestions" (1853), included in the New York Public Library's microfilm edition of the AICP Annual Reports, Reel 1 (1845–1865).

———. "The Mistake" (1850), included in the New York Public Library's microfilm edition of the AICP Annual Reports, Reel 1 (1845–1865).

———. "Study of Methods Employed by the A.I.C.P. to Secure Work for Unemployed Applicants." Unpublished and undated memorandum, in folder "Unemployment Problems, 1908–1929, 1930–1933," Box 16, Community Service Society Archives, Rare Book and Manuscript Library, Columbia University.

Niebuhr, Reinhold. "Walter Rauschenbusch in Historical Perspective." In Ronald H. Stone, ed., *Faith and Politics: A Commentary on Religious, Social and Political Thought in a Technological Age,* pp. 33–45. New York: George Braziller, 1968.

Novak, Michael, John Cogan, Blanche Bernstein, Douglas J. Besharov, Barbara Blum, Allan Carlson, Michael Horowitz, S. Anna Kondratas, Leslie Lenkowsky, Glenn C. Loury, Lawrence Mead, Donald Moran, Charles Murray, Richard P. Nathan, Richard J. Neuhaus, Franklin D. Raines, Robert D. Reischauer, Alice M. Rivlin, Stanford Ross, and Michael Stern. *The New Consensus on Family and Welfare: A Community of Self-*

Reliance. Washington, D.C., and Milwaukee: American Enterprise Institute and Marquette University, 1987.

Olasky, Marvin. *The Tragedy of American Compassion*. Washington, D.C.: Regnery Publishing, 1992.

Olmstead, Alan L. *New York City Mutual Savings Banks, 1819–1861*. Chapel Hill: University of North Carolina Press, 1976.

Patterson, James T. *America's Struggle against Poverty, 1900–1994*. Cambridge, Mass.: Harvard University Press, 1994.

Patterson, Orlando. *The Ordeal of Integration: Progress and Resentment in America's "Racial" Crisis*. Washington, D.C.: Civitas Counterpoint, 1997.

Pear, Robert. "As Welfare Rolls Shrink, Cities Shoulder Bigger Load." *New York Times*, June 6, 1999, p. 22.

Perry, Bruce. *Malcolm: The Life of a Man Who Changed Black America*. New York: Station Hill, 1991.

Peterson, Paul E. "The Urban Underclass and the Poverty Paradox." In Christopher Jencks and Paul E. Peterson, eds., *The Urban Underclass*, pp. 3–27. Washington, D.C.: Brookings Institution Press, 1991.

Phelps, Edmund S. *Rewarding Work: How to Restore Participation and Self-Support to Free Enterprise*. Cambridge, Mass.: Harvard University Press, 1997.

Philpott, Thomas Lee. *The Slum and the Ghetto: Neighborhood Deterioration and Middle-Class Reform, Chicago, 1880–1930*. New York: Oxford University Press, 1978.

Piven, Frances Fox, and Richard A. Cloward. "The Historical Sources of the Contemporary Relief Debate." In Fred Block, Richard A. Cloward, Barbara Ehrenreich, and Frances Fox Piven, *The Mean Season: The Attack on the Welfare State*, pp. 3–43. New York: Pantheon, 1987.

———. *Regulating the Poor: The Functions of Public Welfare*. New York: Pantheon Books, 1971.

———. *Regulating the Poor: The Functions of Public Welfare*. Updated ed. New York: Vintage Books, 1993.

Popenoe, David. *Life without Father: Compelling New Evidence That Fatherhood and Marriage Are Indispensable for the Good of Children and Society*. New York: Free Press, 1996.

Potter, George. *To the Golden Door: The Story of the Irish in Ireland and America*. Boston: Little, Brown and Company, 1960.

Pumphrey, Ralph E., and Muriel W. Pumphrey, eds. *The Heritage of American Social Work: Readings in Its Philosophical and Institutional Development*. New York: Columbia University Press, 1961.

Putnam, Marian C. "Friendly Visiting." *Proceedings of the National Conference of Charities and Correction* 14 (1887): 149–155.

Rainwater, Lee, and William L. Yancey, eds. *The Moynihan Report and the Politics of Controversy*. Cambridge, Mass.: MIT Press, 1967.

Rauschenbusch, Walter. "Beneath the Glitter." In Dores Robinson Sharpe, *Walter Rauschenbusch*, pp. 81–82. New York: Macmillan, 1942.

———. *Christianity and the Social Crisis*. Edited by Robert D. Cross. 1907. Reprint, New York: Harper Torchbooks, 1964.

———. *Christianizing the Social Order*. New York: Macmillan, 1912.

———. "Ideals of Social Reformers." In Robert T. Handy, ed., *The Social Gospel in America: Gladden, Ely, Rauschenbusch*, pp. 274–289. New York: Oxford University Press, 1966.

——. "The New Evangelism." In Handy, ed., *Social Gospel in America*, pp. 323–330.

——. *The Righteousness of the Kingdom.* Edited by Max L. Stackhouse. Nashville, Tenn.: Abingdon Press, 1968.

——. *A Theology for the Social Gospel.* 1917. Reprint, Louisville, Ky.: Westminster John Knox Press, 1997.

——. *"Unto Me."* Boston: Pilgrim Press, 1912.

Rector, Robert, and William F. Lauber. *America's Failed $5.4 Trillion War on Poverty.* Washington, D.C.: Heritage Foundation, 1995.

Residents of Hull-House. *Hull-House Maps and Papers: A Presentation of Nationalities and Wages in a Congested District of Chicago, Together with Comments and Essays on Problems Growing Out of the Social Conditions.* 1895. Reprint, New York: Arno Press and The New York Times, 1970.

Rezneck, Samuel. *Business Depressions and Financial Panics: Essays in American Business and Economic History.* New York: Greenwood Publishing, 1971.

Richmond, Mary E. "A Background for the Art of Helping." In Richmond, *The Long View: Papers and Addresses,* edited by Joanna C. Colcord and Ruth Z. S. Mann, pp. 574–583. New York: Russell Sage Foundation, 1930.

——. "Charity and Homemaking." In Richmond, *Long View,* pp. 77–85.

——. "Emergency Relief in Times of Unemployment." In Richmond, *Long View,* pp. 510–525.

——. *Friendly Visiting among the Poor: A Handbook for Charity Workers.* 1899. Reprint, Montclair, N.J.: Patterson Smith, 1969.

——. *The Good Neighbor in the Modern City.* Philadelphia: J. B. Lippincott Company, 1908.

——. "Married Vagabonds." In Richmond, *Long View,* pp. 69–76.

——. "Sir Charles Stewart Loch." In Richmond, *Long View,* pp. 557–573.

Riis, Jacob A. *The Children of the Poor.* New York: Charles Scribner's Sons, 1892.

——. *How the Other Half Lives: Studies among the Tenements of New York.* New York: Dover Publications, 1971.

——. "Special Needs of the Poor in New York." *Forum* 14 (1892): 492–502.

Riley, Tom. "Individual Development Accounts." *Philanthropy,* January/February 1999, pp. 11–13.

Ringenbach, Paul T. *Tramps and Reformers 1873–1916: The Discovery of Unemployment in New York.* New York: Greenwood Press, 1973.

Rodgers, Daniel T. *The Work Ethic in Industrial America 1850–1920.* Chicago: University of Chicago Press, 1978.

Rorabaugh, W. J. *The Alcoholic Republic: An American Tradition.* New York: Oxford University Press, 1979.

Rosenzweig, Roy. *Eight Hours for What We Will: Workers and Leisure in an Industrial City, 1870–1920.* New York: Cambridge University Press, 1983.

Rosin, Hanna. "About Face." *The New Republic,* August 4, 1997, pp. 16–19.

——, and John F. Harris. "Welfare Reform Is on a Roll." *Washington Post,* August 3, 1999, pp. A1, A6.

Rossi, Peter H., and Zahava D. Blum. "Class, Status, and Poverty." In Daniel P. Moynihan, ed., *On Understanding Poverty: Perspectives from the Social Sciences,* pp. 36–63. New York: Basic Books, 1969.

Rothman, David J. "The State as Parent." In Willard Gaylin, Ira Glasser, Steven Marcus, and David J. Rothman, *Doing Good: The Limits of Benevolence*, pp. 67–96. New York: Pantheon Books, 1978.

Rubinow, I. M. *Social Insurance: With Special Reference to American Conditions.* 1913. Reprint, New York: Arno Press and The New York Times, 1969.

Ryan, William. *Blaming the Victim.* New York: Pantheon Books, 1971.

Salins, Peter D. *Assimilation, American Style.* New York: Basic Books, 1997.

Samuelson, Robert J. "'Hell No, We Won't Save.'" *Washington Post*, February 17, 1999, p. A17.

Schlesinger, Jacob M. "Few Americans Heed Washington's Urging for Bigger Nest Eggs." *Wall Street Journal*, June 29, 1999, pp. A1, A6.

Schneider, Eric C. *In the Web of Class: Delinquents and Reformers in Boston, 1810s–1930s.* New York: New York University Press, 1992.

Schwartz, Joel. "The Moral Environment of the Poor." *The Public Interest* 103 (Spring 1991): 21–37.

Scott, Daryl Michael. *Contempt and Pity: Social Policy and the Image of the Damaged Black Psyche, 1880–1996.* Chapel Hill: University of North Carolina Press, 1997.

Shannon, William V. *The American Irish.* New York: Macmillan, 1963.

Sharpe, Dores Robinson. *Walter Rauschenbusch.* New York: Macmillan, 1942.

Sherraden, Michael. *Assets and the Poor: A New American Welfare Policy.* Armonk, N.Y.: M. E. Sharpe, 1991.

Sleeper, Jim. *Liberal Racism.* New York: Viking, 1997.

Smith, Adam. *An Inquiry into the Nature and Causes of the Wealth of Nations.* Edited by Edwin Cannan. New York: Modern Library, 1937.

Smith, James P. *Unequal Wealth and Incentives to Save.* Santa Monica, Calif.: RAND, 1995.

Smith, Timothy L. "Native Blacks and Foreign Whites: Varying Responses to Educational Opportunity in America, 1880–1950." *Perspectives in American History* 6 (1972): 309–335.

Smith, Zilpha D. "How to Do Personal Work and How to Get Others to Do It." Unpublished manuscript of a speech given to the New York Class in Practical Philanthropy, June 22, 1899, in folder "Casework—'Friendly Visiting'—Zilpha D. Smith," Box 99, Community Service Society Archives, Rare Book and Manuscript Library, Columbia University.

Smith-Rosenberg, Carroll. *Religion and the Rise of the American City: The New York City Mission Movement, 1812–1870.* Ithaca, N.Y.: Cornell University Press, 1971.

Solow, Robert M. "Guess Who Likes Workfare." In Amy Gutmann, ed., *Work and Welfare*, pp. 3–22. Princeton, N.J.: Princeton University Press, 1998.

Sowell, Thomas. *Ethnic America: A History.* New York: Basic Books, 1981.

Spann, Edward K. *The New Metropolis: New York City, 1840–1857.* New York: Columbia University Press, 1981.

Steinberg, Stephen. *The Ethnic Myth: Race, Ethnicity, and Class in America.* 2nd ed. Boston: Beacon Press, 1989.

Steinfels, Peter. "Beliefs." *New York Times*, July 11, 1998, p. A11.

Stern, William J. "How Dagger John Saved New York's Irish." *City Journal*, Spring 1997, pp. 84–105.

Stewart, William Rhinelander. *The Philanthropic Work of Josephine Shaw Lowell Containing a Biographical Sketch of Her Life Together with a Selection of Her Public Papers and Private Letters.* 1911. Reprint, Montclair, N.J.: Patterson Smith, 1974.

Strout, Cushing. *The New Heavens and New Earth: Political Religion in America.* New York: Harper and Row, 1974.

Thernstrom, Stephan. *The Other Bostonians: Poverty and Progress in the American Metropolis, 1880–1970.* Cambridge, Mass.: Harvard University Press, 1973.

——. *Poverty and Progress: Social Mobility in a Nineteenth Century City.* Cambridge, Mass.: Harvard University Press, 1964.

——. "Poverty in Historical Perspective." In Daniel Patrick Moynihan, ed., *On Understanding Poverty: Perspectives from the Social Sciences,* pp. 160–186. New York: Basic Books, 1969.

——. "Working-Class Social Mobility in Industrial America." In Melvin Richter, ed., *Essays in Theory and History: An Approach to the Social Sciences,* pp. 221–238. Cambridge, Mass.: Harvard University Press, 1970.

——, and Abigail Thernstrom. *America in Black and White: One Nation, Indivisible.* New York: Simon and Schuster, 1997.

Timberlake, James H. *Prohibition and the Progressive Movement, 1900–1920.* Cambridge, Mass.: Harvard University Press, 1963.

Tishler, Hace Sorel. *Self-Reliance and Social Security, 1870–1917.* Port Washington, N.Y.: Kennikat, 1971.

de Tocqueville, Alexis. *Democracy in America.* Translated by George Lawrence, edited by J. P. Mayer. New York: Doubleday Anchor, 1969.

Trattner, Walter I., editor in chief. *Biographical Dictionary of Social Welfare in America.* New York: Greenwood Press, 1986.

——. *From Poor Law to Welfare State: A History of Social Welfare in America.* 5th ed. New York: Free Press, 1994.

Tucker, David M. *The Decline of Thrift in America: Our Cultural Shift from Saving to Spending.* New York: Praeger, 1991.

Tuckerman, Joseph. "Essay on the Wages Paid to Females for their Labour, in the Form of a Letter, from a Gentleman in Boston to His Friend in Philadelphia." In David J. Rothman and Sheila M. Rothman, eds., *Low Wages and Great Sins: Two Antebellum American Views on Prostitution and the Working Girl.* 1830. Reprint, New York: Garland Publishing, 1987.

——. "Introduction" to the Baron De Gerando, *The Visitor of the Poor* (trans. "A Lady of Boston"), pp. iii–xxx. Boston: Hilliard, Gray, Little, and Wilkins, 1832.

——. *The Principles and Results of the Ministry at Large in Boston.* Boston: James Munroe and Co., 1838.

Tuerk, Richard. "Jacob Riis and the Jews." *New-York Historical Society Quarterly* 63 (1979): 179–201.

Tyrrell, Ian R. *Sobering Up: From Temperance to Prohibition in Antebellum America, 1800–1860.* New York: Greenwood Press, 1979.

——. "Temperance and Economic Change in the Antebellum North." In Jack S. Blocker, Jr., ed., *Alcohol, Reform and Society: The Liquor Issue in Social Context,* pp. 45–67. New York: Greenwood Press, 1979.

United States Bureau of Justice Statistics. *Alcohol and Crime: An Analysis of National Data on the Prevalence of Alcohol Involvement in Crime* (1998).

United States Bureau of Labor Statistics. Unpublished data on employment status for blacks by school enrollment, sex, and age, October 1982 and October 1997.

United States Bureau of the Census. *Poverty in the United States: 1995.*

United States Department of Health and Human Services. *Vital Statistics of the United States 1992.* Vol. I: *Natality.* Washington, D.C.: United States Department of Health and Human Services, 1996.

United States General Accounting Office. *Employment Training: Successful Projects Share Common Strategy.* HEHS-96-108, May 1996.

——. *Welfare Reform: States Are Restructuring Programs to Reduce Welfare Dependence.* HEHS-98-109, June 1998.

Ward, David. *Poverty, Ethnicity, and the American City, 1840–1925: Changing Conceptions of the Slum and the Ghetto.* New York: Cambridge University Press, 1989.

Ware, Louise. *Jacob A. Riis: Police Reporter, Reformer, Useful Citizen.* New York: D. Appleton-Century, 1938.

Warner, Amos G. *American Charities: A Study in Philanthropy and Economics.* 1894. Reprint, New York: Arno Press and The New York Times, 1971.

Washington, Booker T. *Character Building: Being Addresses on Sunday Evenings to the Students of Tuskegee Institute.* 1902. Reprint, New York: Haskell House Publishers, 1972.

——. "Democracy and Education." In Howard Brotz, ed., *Negro Social and Political Thought, 1850–1920: Representative Texts,* pp. 362–371. New York: Basic Books, 1966.

——. "Progress of the American Negro." In Brotz, ed., *Negro Social and Political Thought,* pp. 396–401.

——. *Up from Slavery.* In *Three Negro Classics,* with an introduction by John Hope Franklin, pp. 23–205. New York: Avon Books, 1965.

——. *Working with the Hands.* 1904. Reprint, New York: Arno Press and The New York Times, 1969.

Watson, Frank Dekker. *The Charity Organization Movement in the United States: A Study in American Philanthropy.* New York: Macmillan, 1922.

Waugh, Joan. *Unsentimental Reformer: The Life of Josephine Shaw Lowell.* Cambridge, Mass.: Harvard University Press, 1997.

Whitehead, Barbara Dafoe. "Dan Quayle Was Right," *The Atlantic Monthly,* April 1993, pp. 47–84.

——. *The Divorce Culture: Rethinking Our Commitments to Marriage and Family.* New York: Vintage Books, 1998.

Wilentz, Sean. *Chants Democratic: New York City and the Rise of the American Working Class, 1788–1850.* New York: Oxford University Press, 1984.

Wilson, James Q. "Crime and American Culture." *The Public Interest* 70 (Winter 1983): 22–48.

——. "Human Remedies for Social Disorders." *The Public Interest* 131 (Spring 1998): 25–35.

——. "Liberalism, Modernism, and the Good Life." In Mary Ann Glendon and David Blankenhorn, eds., *Seedbeds of Virtue: Sources of Competence, Character, and Citizenship in American Society,* pp. 17–34. Lanham, Md.: Madison Books, 1995.

——. *The Moral Sense.* New York: Free Press, 1993.

——. *On Character: Essays by James Q. Wilson.* Washington, D.C.: AEI Press, 1991.

Wilson, William Julius. *When Work Disappears: The World of the New Urban Poor.* New York: Alfred A. Knopf, 1996.

Wittet, George G. "Concerned Citizens: The Prohibitionists of 1883 Ohio." In Jack S. Blocker, Jr., ed., *Alcohol, Reform and Society: The Liquor Issue in Social Context,* pp. 111–147. New York: Greenwood Press, 1979.

Wittke, Carl. *The Irish in America*. Baton Rouge: Louisiana State University Press, 1956.

Wolfe, Alan. *One Nation, After All: What Middle-Class Americans Really Think About: God, Country, Family, Racism, Welfare, Immigration, Homosexuality, Work, the Right, the Left, and Each Other*. New York: Viking, 1998.

Wolfe, Tom. *A Man in Full*. New York: Farrar Straus Giroux, 1998.

Woodroofe, Kathleen. *From Charity to Social Work in England and the United States*. 2nd ed. Toronto: University of Toronto Press, 1974.

Woodson, Robert L., Sr. *The Triumphs of Joseph: How Today's Community Healers Are Reviving our Streets and Neighborhoods*. New York: Free Press, 1998.

Woodward, Kenneth L. "The New Holy War." *Newsweek*, June 1, 1998, pp. 26–29.

Woolf, Virginia. *The Captain's Death Bed and Other Essays*. New York: Harcourt, Brace, 1950.

Zinsmeister, Karl. "Chin Up: Some Ugly Trends Grow Lovelier." *American Enterprise*, January/February 1999, pp. 4–7.

——, Stephen Moore, and Karlyn Bowman. "Is America Turning a Corner?" *American Enterprise*, January/February 1999, pp. 36–51.

INDEX

Adams, John, 291n63
Addams, Jane, xx, 93, 109–121, 243; condescension to the poor, 118–119; criticizing the middle class, xxi; critiquing moral reform, 108–109; on the economic virtues, 107–108; impact of the industrial revolution, 112–115, 115–118; against individualist virtues, 98–101, 129–130; on love toward the poor, 287n168; on moral double standards, 110–111; moral imperialism of, 285n142; moral traditionalism of, 103–105; on noneconomic virtues, 105–107; on popular culture, 105, 279n44; and Prohibition, 40, 280n52; on reforming society rather than individuals, 102–103; religion of, 272–273n20; rivalry with Mary Richmond, 245, 323n15; on saving money, 43, 284n129; settlement houses, 81; story of the *Luftmensch*, 119–120; supporting Hoover for president, 26, 256n70; supporting opposition candidate for alderman, 224; view of popular culture compared with that of Allan Bloom, 279n44; virtues and rewards, 120–121
African Americans, xxi–xxii, 161–182; black bourgeoisie, 306–307nn31, 32; Booker T. Washington, 167–170, 297n39; compared to European immigrants, 158; compared to Irish Americans, 180–182; education among, 272n16, 308n52, 310n111; experience of moral reform, 161–162; failure of Black Muslim moral reform, 176–178; fear of acting "white," 196–198; free persons compared to slaves, 296n24; Malcolm X, 173–176; males enrolled in school, 310–311n111; men compared to women, 302n126; migration from the south, 166, 179; moral reformers encountering, 162–167; and nationalism, 192–193; and the need for virtuous behavior, 199; negative connotations of being middle class, 193–195; prejudice against, 169–171, 179, 183; religion among, 190–192, 305nn8, 9, 10, 11, 12; representation of, 144; riots against, 163–

165; saving money, 304n146; slavery affecting, 178; and social control, 143; statistics of poverty, 295n115; successes of, 189–190; taking on "white" values, 193–198; Tuckerman's work with, 295n6; unmarried mothers, 310n100; W. E. B. DuBois, 170–173, 298nn50, 63
AICP. *See* Association for Improving the Condition of the Poor (AICP)
Alcohol consumption, 28–43, 317n75; Addams and Rauschenbusch against, 106; among Irish Americans, 185; Association for Improving the Condition of the Poor on legislation prohibiting, 40; of better-paid workers, 272n179; Booker T. Washington on, 169; causing family breakups, 65; causing poverty, 257–258nn98, 100; class distinctions in, 5, 36–38; compared to consumption of drugs, 157; consumption patterns, 30–32; criticisms of the moral reformers, 32–34; Dores Robinson Sharpe on, 280n60; drinking at home, 261n172; function of saloons, 294nn110, 111; of immigrants, 41–43; of Irish Americans, 272n13; John Ireland on, 304n146; Malcolm X on, 175; in the present day, 204, 223–226; Prohibition, 39–41 (*see also* Prohibition of alcohol); relationship to poverty, 29–30, 34–35; Temperance movement, 30–32; temperance societies formed by workers, 260n140; and unions, 38–39; W. E. B. DuBois on, 170, 173, 299n70
Alger, Horatio, 115, 176
American Charities (Warner), 242
American Enterprise, 203
American Federation of Labor (AFL), 39
Anderson, Elijah, 191
Aristotle, 270nn359, 360
Artificial creation of jobs, 19, 25–27
Asset limits, 227–228
Association for Improving the Condition of the Poor (AICP), xvi, 38, 240; attitude toward serving the poor, 78; and finding jobs for the poor, 19, 22–23, 24–25; housing for

343

the poor, 89, 90; pamphlet distributed to the poor, 69; precursor to, 47; and the prohibition of alcohol, 40; and religion, 82; report on riots against blacks, 164; saving patterns of the poor, 50
Attitudes toward rehabilitation of the poor, 84–87, 131–133
Autobiography of Malcolm X, 174, 177

Banks, 46–47, 50–53
Bardach, Eugene, 16
Beer, 32. *See also* Alcohol consumption
Bell, Daniel, xxi, 145, 146, 194
The Bell Curve (Herrnstein and Murray), 156
Bennett, William, 223–224, 317n81
The Black Bourgeoisie (Frazier), 194
Black Muslim movement, 174–178
Blacks, 143, 144, 158. *See also* African Americans
Blaming the Victim (Ryan), 131, 133–135
Bloom, Allan, 279n44
Bootblacking, 22
Booth, Charles, 54, 60–61, 100, 259n134
Boston Associated Charities, 72–73, 286n160
Bourgeois morality, xx–xxi, 112, 236, 277n4; and civilization, 281–282n71. *See also* Class distinctions
Boyer, Paul, 36; on class distinctions and moral reform, 213; on the religion of the moral reformers, 81
Brace, Charles Loring, xvi, 240; about the inclination of the poor toward virtue, 10; accepting capitalism, 124; aid to poor in finding jobs, 21–22; on alcohol and poverty, 34, 35; attitudes toward rehabilitation, 85, 87; "boys' meetings," 314n34; on broken homes, 58–59; and the Catholic protectory, 274n35; compared to Booker T. Washington, 297n39; contrasted with Eugene Rivers, 214; encouraging the saving of money, 47–48; and individualist virtues, 129; influence of Tuckerman on, 244; intellectual kinship to Moynihan, 266n274; making contact with vagrant children, 69; pioneering support for social insurance, 54–55, 97, 126, 265n254; on the poor in New York, 101; preference for blacks over the Irish, 163; on the prohibition of alcohol, 40–41; and religion, 82–83, 216, 314n34; on self-reliance, 13–14; support for workers' compensation, xviii; views of, xvii; Walter Rauschenbusch about, 123

Brandt, Lilian, 30, 221; on the desertion of families by husbands, 61–62; on supporting fatherless families, 66
Brecht, Bertolt, 87, 146
Bremner, Robert H., 7, 19; criticizing the moral reformers, 75; shift of focus away from moral causes of poverty, 132
Brown, Mary Willcox, 43–44; on child labor, 56, 57; on the need for thrift, 45; on savings banks, 52; on social insurance, 54
Bryan, William Jennings, 26
Burial costs, 51–52
Butler, John Sibley, 174, 189, 194

Capitalism, 108, 124, 145, 146; cycles in relieving the poor under, 289n26; Marx about, 287–288n182
Capitello, Grace, 228
Catholic Total Abstinence Union, 185
Catholicism, 81–84; Brace against the Catholic Protectory, 274n35; in comparison to the black church, 192; contemporary social, 216; in the Irish American community, 186–187; Tuckerman's proposed ministry to be led by the priests of, 273n27. *See also* Religion
Chambers, Clarke, 151
Channing, William Ellery, 9, 241; against alcohol consumption, 33; countering lax morality, 205; encouraging the saving of money, 49; on family ties, 60; and Joseph Tuckerman, 22, 69, 239; love in poorer families, 317n69; on the positive and negative effects of labor, 15; on serving the urban poor, 212–213
Chapin, Robert, 42; on expenditures of the poor, 153–154; on saving by not eating, 56
Charity Organisation Review, 10
Charity Organization Society (COS), xvi, 12; acting as an employment agency, 25; on desertion of families by husbands, 62; and finding jobs for the poor, 23–24; founding of by Josephine Shaw Lowell, 241; praised by Charles Loring Brace, 244; and the prohibition of alcohol, 41; and religion, 81; on saving money, 48, 53; and temperance research, 30
Charity organizations. *See under* names of individual organizations
Chicago, 224–225
Child care, 321n142
Children, 69; affected by a broken home, 59; as an economic asset, 61; child support from

fathers, 221–222; finding work for, 21–22; illegitimate, 206–207, 209; in the labor market, 56; outplacement of, 240, 273–274n34, 314n34; rehabilitation of, 85–86; religion of 273–274n34

Children First (Wisconsin), 316n65

Children's Aid Society, xvi, 314n34; aid to poor in finding jobs, 21; encouraging the saving of money, 47–48; founding by Charles Loring Brace, 240; outplacement of children, 273–274n34; and religion, 83; Robert Hartley about, 244

Chinatowns, 297n31

Chinese immigrants, 4, 167, 296–297n31. *See also* Immigrants

Christianity and the Social Crisis (Rauschenbusch), 243

Civil war, 296n24

Clark, Norman, 33

Class distinctions, 72; among African Americans, 193–195; bourgeois values, xx–xxi, 112, 236, 277n4; democratization of moral reform, 213–215; example of the middle class to the poor, 200–203; growing underclass, 206–207; and marriage, 281n63; middle-class values, xx, 112, 236; and morality, 136–137; origins of nineteenth-century moral reform, 212; poor as victims of the rich, 128–129; shift in values, 147–148; wealthy class, 128–129, 309n85

Clinton, Bill, 211

Cloward, Richard A., 131, 139–144

Committee of Fifty, 29, 30

Communism, 170

Communist Manifesto, 108

Conservative politics, xvii–xviii, 234, 317n81

Consumer debt, 292n76

Consumer Expenditure Interview Survey (Department of Labor), 153

Consumer's League, 241

Consumption of goods, 146, 293n97, 319n111

Contemporary practice of moral reform, 211–245; class distinctions, 212–213; democratization of, 213–215; encouraging savings, 227–229; government help in, 217–218; promoting familial responsibility, 220–223; promoting self-reliance, 226–227; public policy, 218–220; reform of welfare, 230–233; rewarding employment, 233–237; role of religion in, 215–217

Corporation for Enterprise Development, 320n120

Crime, 203–204; and alcohol consumption, 35, 223; decline in postbellum America, 258–259n119; among Irish Americans, 185; and property owners, 263n205; reduction of, 311n116; and religion, 305n10; in suburbia, 307n37

Criticism of moral reform, 3–4

Cultural contradiction of poverty, 145–149

The Cultural Contradictions of Capitalism (Bell), xxi, 194

Culture: immigrant, 248–249nn3, 4; mainstream, 105, 203–204, 292n74; popular, 104–105

Daley, Richard J., 318n88

Daley, Richard M., 224, 318n88

De Gerando, Baron, 244

Democracy and Social Ethics (Addams), 109, 110, 112–113

Democratization of moral reform, 213–215

DeParle, Jason, 230–231, 313n20

Department of Labor's Consumer Expenditure Interview Survey, 153

Dependency, 7–12, 293n103. *See also* Self-reliance

The Depression, 145, 154

Desertion of families by husbands, 61–66. *See also* Family

Deserving poor, 144–145

Devine, Edward T., 25

Difficulties of moral reform. *See* Obstacles to moral reform

DiIulio, John, 212; on alcohol consumption, 223; on government support, 217

Diligence, 15–28; aid to poor in finding jobs, 21–25; among the poor of today, 201; Booker T. Washington espousing, 168; decline of, 149; and immigration to the West, 19–20; influence of work on family, 289n28; moral argument for work, 15–17; rewarding employment, 233–237; stressed by Floyd Flake, 215; unemployment, 17–21 (*see also* Unemployment); W. E. B. DuBois on, 172; and welfare reform, 230–233

Disabilities, 8

Discrimination. *See* Prejudice against blacks

Dodd, Jill Siegel, 5–6, 283n115

Dow, Neal, 37

Downpayments on the American Dream Policy Demonstration, 230, 320n120

Dress and grooming, 22

Drug use, 157, 201, 204, 312nn127, 130, 317n75

Dubois, John, 271n11
DuBois, W. E. B., xxii, 167, 170–173; on
alcohol consumption, 299n70; on the
black church, 191; charged with accepting
the status quo, 298n50; compared to
Malcolm X, 175; on Irish Americans, 182;
and moral reform, 161; moral standard of,
299n76
Duneier, Mitchell, 203

Earned Income Tax Credit, 322nn144, 155
Easterbrook, Gregg, 312n130
Eberstadt, Nicholas, 154–155
Economic downturns, 253n19
Economic incentives, 219, 220
Economic Opportunity Act of 1964, xiv
Economics, 97–98
"The Economist," 69
Education, 197–198; among African Americans,
308n52, 310–311nn111, 113; and the
black bourgeoisie, 306n31
Ely, Richard T., 115, 278n30
Emancipation Proclamation, 163
Employment, 21–25; charitable organizations
acting as employment agencies, 23–25;
during boom years, 253n18; dead-end
jobs, 292n75; failings of commercial
agencies, 256n65; Lawrence Mead on,
290nn37, 54; rewarding, 233–237; training
programs, 321nn134, 135; unemployment,
17–21, 154; unskilled labor, 24; and
welfare reform, 230–233; of workers'
wives, 268n316. See also Diligence
Environmental causes of poverty, 132–133,
290n54
Ernst, Robert, 20
Ethnic America (Sowell), 4
Ethnicity, xxi–xxii, 78, 101–102, 201. See also
under individual ethnicity
Expenditures of the poor, 153–154

False dichotomies of poverty, xviii–xix, 24, 57,
70, 135–136, 140–141
Familial responsibility, xxii, 58–67, 220–223
Family, 58–67, 157; Addams and
Rauschenbusch supporting, 107; breakups
due to abolition of outdoor relief, 251n38;
desertion of families by husbands, 61–66;
effect of broken homes, 58–60; Floyd
Flake stressing, 215; influence of work
upon, 289n28; irresponsibility toward,
248n17; patterns and poverty, 65–66;
responsibilities, xxii, 220–223; and saving

money, 49; single-parent, xxii, 200–201,
206–208, 309n70; ties within immigrant,
267n313; women's self-reliance, 66, 67
(see also Women)
Family decomposition, xxii, 207–208, 251n38,
311n119, 316n56
Family Support Act of 1988, 221
Farrakhan, Louis, 176, 300n96
Fishburn, Janet Forsythe, 107
Fisk University, 171
Flake, Floyd, 214–215, 216–217, 217–218, 237;
on self-help, 315n47
Fogel, Robert W., 312n127
Food preparation, 69–70
Forced migration, 180–181
Franklin, Donna, 234
Frazier, E. Franklin, 194–195
Freeman, Richard B., 305n12
Friedman, Milton, 235
Friendly Visiting Among the Poor (Richmond),
242, 245
Friendly visitors. See Visiting the poor
Fukuyama, Francis, 205–206; on economic
incentives, 219; on the Great Disruption,
316n56; on women, 207
Fundamentalist religion, 191–192, 306n13. See
also Religion

Galston, William, 222–223
Gans, Herbert, xvi, 60; on family life, 157; on
prescribing behavior to the poor, 142
Garcia, Freddie, 214
Gardner, Orville, 87
Garrison, William Lloyd, 295n6
Gates, Henry Louis, Jr., 194, 195
General Accounting Office (GAO), 231, 233,
234–235, 321n134
George, Henry, 243
Ghettoes, 143, 197. See also Tenement housing
Glazer, Nathan, 144, 157; on African American
men, 302n126; on the Black Muslim
movement, 176; on child support, 221;
comparing the Irish to blacks, 182; on
unskilled labor, 301n109
Gould, Jay, 277n7
Government help, 217–218, 314n38. See also
Welfare system
The Great Disruption, 316n56
Greeley, Andrew M., 181, 183
Greeley, Horace, 20
Gusfield, Joseph, 32

Hacker, Andrew, 285n133

Hale, Edward Everett, 35
Halper, Thomas, 144
Handler, Joel, 142
Handlin, Oscar, xv, 12; on Irish immigrants, 186; on the scarcity of resources, 7
Hannerz, Ulf, 197
Happiness, 276n81
Harrington, Michael, 291n55
Harris, Joel Chandler, 169
Harris, Rubin, 308n52
Harrison, Benjamin, 242
Hartley, Robert M., xvi, 239–240; against alcohol consumption, 32, 33, 34, 35; on the artificial creation of jobs, 19; attitude toward the poor, 78–80, 271n7; attitude toward rehabilitation, 85; on becoming more presentable, 22; on buying food in bulk, 70; criticizing the Washingtonians, 37–38; on the desertion of families by husbands, 61; and finding jobs for the poor, 17–18, 22–23; and housing for the poor, xviii, 88–91, 135; on the ignorance of the poor, 69; on immigrating westward, 19–20; influence of Tuckerman on, 244; and Irish Americans, 73, 163, 193, 212, 248n3; on labor, 15; on material improvement in the life of the poor, 154; on the need for thrift, 45; on the prohibition of alcohol, 39–40; and religion, 82; on riots against blacks, 164–165; on the saving patterns of the poor, 50; on self-reliance, 13; on the shortcomings of the poor, 132; on shorter hours for workers, 28; views of, xvii; on women supporting themselves, 66–67
Healthy Start Men's Services, 313n20
Heritage Foundation, 156
Herrnstein, Richard, 156
Himmelfarb, Gertrude, 206; on the difference between "virtues" and "values," 208; on illegitimacy, 207; on the reaction to moral permissiveness, 209
Hochschild, Jennifer, 174; on African American values, 196, 198, 199; on forced migration, 180; on nationalism, 193
Housing for the poor: It's a Wonderful Life (film), 275n67; tenement housing, 276nn72, 76
Housing reform, 88–92
How the Other Half Lives (Riis), 56, 166, 242
Huggins, Nathan Irving, 167–168, 180
Hughes, John, 73, 80, 185, 272n15
Hull House, 81, 272n20; as an alternative to saloons, 105–106; debate at, 285n142;

encouraging diligence and thrift, 107–108; founding by Jane Addams, 99, 243; Mary Richmond on, 245, 323n15
Hunter, James Davison, 216
Hunter, Robert, 152–153
Huntington, James O. S., 213

Ignatiev, Noel, 183, 184
Illegitimate children, 206–207, 209; born to African American mothers, 310n100; and comparison between past and present, 266n279
Immigrants: alcohol consumption among, 41–43; Catholicism of Irish immigrants, 186; compared to blacks in present day, 158; cultural values of, 248n3–249n4; and the decline of crime, 258n119; effect on unemployment, 18; family ties among immigrants, 60; and finding work, 18; ignorance among immigrants, 68; Irish, 180–188 (see also Irish Americans); Italian, 72–73; Japanese, 4; living conditions of, 301–302n110; living in same area as blacks, 162; migrating to the West, 19–20; Riis's opinion of, 167; saving money, 56; served by Hartley, 78–79; and temperance, 262n180; timing of arrival, 179; unemployment levels, 253n21; and wages, 252–253n17
Income, 28, 42
Individual Development Accounts (IDAs), 44, 229–230, 234, 315n55, 320nn119, 120, 121, 122
Individualist virtues, 97–130, 131–158; Addams on, 109–121 (see also under Addams, Jane); and alcohol, 226; blaming the victim, 133–136; critique of moral reform, 108–109; the economic virtues, 107–108; environmental causes of poverty, 132–133; and individualist economics, 129; laissez-faire economics, 97–98; morality and class distinctions, 135–136; the nineteenth-century poor adhering to, 150–152; noneconomic virtues, 105–107; Piven and Cloward's argument against, 139–144; restricting laissez-faire to promote, 102–103; Ryan's argument against, 133–136; shift in attitude toward, 145–149; as social control, 137–139; transvaluation of attitudes, 144–145; Tuckerman's opinion of, 122; and the virtues of the poor, 99–102
Industrial insurance, 51–52

Industrial Revolution, 16, 112–118
Ireland, John, 304n146
Irish Americans, xxii, 20, 179–188; achieving
    upward mobility, 183–185; assimilation of,
    302n126, 303nn132, 136; characteristics
    of, 181; compared to African Americans,
    163, 180–182; cultural values of, 248n3;
    difference between contemporary and
    past, 307n38; explanation of the success of
    moral reform among, 186–189; Hartley's
    attitude toward, 80; prosperity of, 303n132;
    religion compared to the black church,
    192; wakes of, 271n11
Irony of moral reform, 131, 150–152
Italian immigrants, 72–73. See also Immigrants
It's a Wonderful Life (film), 275n67

Jackson, Andrew, 258n119
Japanese immigrants, 4. See also Immigrants
Jefferson, Thomas, 291n63
Jencks, Christopher, 148; on the poverty of
    African Americans, 195–196; on single
    parenthood, 200–201
Job retention, 233. See also Employment
Jones, Jacqueline, 272n16
Jones, Joseph T., 313n20

Katz, Michael B., 3; on the deserving poor, 6;
    on family ties, 61; on Josephine Shaw
    Lowell, 27; on moral reformers' failure to
    pursue the elimination of poverty, 7; on
    temperance legislation, 28
Kelley, Florence, 100–101
Kennedy, John F., 12
Keyes, Emerson, 53
Keyssar, Alexander, 18, 21
Kimball, John S., 213
Kloppenberg, James T., 116
Knowledge, 67–75; imparting across class lines,
    71–72; imparting across ethnic barriers,
    72–73; practical advice, 69–71; teaching of
    virtues, 73–75
Krauthammer, Charles, 111
Kristol, Irving, 140, 289n30

Labor. See Diligence
Labor market, 19. See also Employment
Laissez-faire economics, 97–98
Lauber, William F., 156
Laurie, Bruce, 5, 283n115
Law, Bernard, 216
Leary, Timothy, 43
Lemann, Nicholas, 176, 203, 211, 312n3

Levine, Harry Gene, 35
Liberal politics, xviii, 234
Lincoln, Abraham, 36
Lincoln, C. Eric, 175–176
Loch, Charles Stewart, 12–13
Loury, Glenn, 136, 237
Lowell, Charles Russell, 240–241, 318n101
Lowell, Josephine Shaw, xvi, 240–241; analysis
    of the poor, 155; attitudes toward
    rehabilitation, 85, 86, 295n14; and class
    distinction, 213; connections to Brace,
    Riis, and Richmond, 244–245; creating
    artificial employment for the poor, 25–27;
    on dependency vs. self-reliance, 227;
    economic radicalism of, 25; efforts to
    organize labor, 27–28; on encouraging
    dependency, 10–11; encouraging the
    saving of money, 48; on encouraging
    women's self-reliance, 67; on family ties,
    60; on the faults of the poor, 152; female
    reformatories, 223; and finding jobs for the
    poor, 23; and individualist virtues, 129; on
    labor, 16; on the need for thrift, 46;
    parents of, 318n101; on physical needs,
    88; on preventing dependency, 150; on the
    prohibition of alcohol, 41; and religion,
    81, 274n53; on riots against blacks, 163–
    164; on savings banks, 46; on self-reliance,
    14; teaching the poor, 74–75; unionization
    of labor, xviii, 97–98; views of, xvii; on the
    virtues of the poor, 101
Lubove, Roy, 292n85
Luftmensch story, 119–120

Magnet, Myron, 147–148
Mainstream culture. See Culture
Malcolm X, xxii, 167, 173–177; attitudes toward
    whites, 300n101; hatred for whites, 193;
    lifestyle of, 300n99; and moral reform, 161
Manpower Demonstration Research Corpora-
    tion (MDRC), 232, 316n65
Marriage, 222–223; affecting children, 59; class
    distinctions and the timing of, 281n63;
    and poverty, 58; and saving money, 49;
    statistics on wealth, 263n222; of women
    moral reformers, 280n61. See also Family
Marx, Groucho, 150
Massachusetts Bureau of Statistics of Labor
    (MBSL), 18, 50, 55, 261n172, 262n177
Matza, David, 80
Mayer, Susan, xv, 155–156
Mead, Lawrence, xv, 237; on climbing out of
    poverty, 156; contrasting past and present

poverty conditions, 150–151; on control over one's life, 135; on desire of welfare recipients to work, 308n63; dispute with William Julius Wilson, 219; on economic incentives, 220; on employment, 290n37; on forced migration, 180; moral attitudes of the poor, 142–143; and the "new paternalism," 68, 199, 219, 315n50; on the relevance of moral questions to contemporary poverty, 152; on self-control, 147; statistics on African American poverty, 295n115; on welfare recipients, 293n103; on working for low wages, 149

Mexican Americans, 200

Middle-class values, xx, 112, 236, 281n63, 311n121

Migration of blacks from the south, 166, 179

Miller, Kerby, 180–181, 185, 187

Million Man March, 205

Mobility of labor, 20

Mohl, Raymond A., 138–139

Moral reform: contemporary practice of, 211–245 (see also under Contemporary practice of moral reform); irony of, 131, 150–152; principles of, 3; rejection of, 92–93, 131

Morality, 179; and class distinctions, 135–136; double standards for, 110–111, 137, 145–146, 282n84

Moynihan, Daniel Patrick, xxi, 83; on African American men, 302n126; on the black family, 133; on the Black Muslim movement, 176; on the breakup of the family, 59; comparing the Irish to blacks, 182; on moral standards, 111; on Nixon's social policy, 312n3; on transvaluation of attitudes, 144

Muhammad, Elijah, 175, 177–178; 300nn96, 101, 301n102

Muhammad, Wallace, 176, 300n96

Murray, Charles, 9, 156; on African Americans not in the labor force, 310n111; on American society, 208–209; on the continued growth of the underclass, 206–207; on decline in crime, 311n116; on happiness, 276n81

Muslim movement, 174–178

Nation of Islam, 174–178

National Conference of Charities and Correction, 243

National Conference of Social Work, 323n15

National Development and Research Institute, 204

National Freedmen's Relief Association, 164, 241

National Research Council (NRC), 225, 226

Nationalism, 187–188, 192–193

Neckerman, Kathryn, 65–66

The New Deal, 155, 289n26

"New paternalism," xv, 68, 199, 219, 315n50

New York City draft riots, 163–165

New York Times, 230

New York Tribune, 242

Nixon, Richard, 211, 312n3

Obstacles to moral reform, 76–93; attitudes of some moral reformers, 76–80; difficulty in rehabilitating the poor, 84–87; material needs of the poor, 13, 20, 57, 69–70, 87–88, 254n38; need for housing reform, 88–92; religious pluralism, 80–84

Olasky, Marvin, 80, 84, 278n30

Olmstead, Frederick Law, 182

O'Reilly, John Boyle, 188

Outdoor relief, 12, 251n38, 254n43

Outplacement of children, 240, 273n34, 314n34

Paine, Robert Treat, Jr., 286n160

Paternalism. See "New paternalism"

Patterson, Orlando, 180, 183; on the black church, 191–192; on middle-class blacks, 195, 302n126; on the poor following broader cultural mores, 202; on the prosperity of Irish Americans, 303n132; on the successes of African Americans, 189, 305n2; on work ethic among Irish Americans, 184

Pauperism, 7–12

Peabody, Elizabeth Palmer, 251n41

Penny Provident Fund, 48; branch opened at Hull House, 108; compared to savings at Tuskegee, 168–169; locations of operations, 281n69

Personal responsibility, xiv–xv, 211–212

Personal Responsibility and Work Opportunity Reconciliation Act of 1996, xiv

Pfleger, Michael, 224

Phelps, Edmund, 235–237, 322nn144, 155, 158

The Philadelphia Negro (DuBois), 171, 173, 299n76

Philadelphia Saving Fund Society, 46–47, 51, 52

Philips, Willard, 46

Physical wants of the poor, 87–92

Pintard, John, 47

Piven, Frances Fox, 131, 139–144
Plato, 68
Political machines, 224–225
Popenoe, David, 220
Popular culture. *See* Culture
Postal savings system, 52–53
Potato famine, 180
Poverty in the past, compared with poverty today, xv, xxii, 7, 58, 148–149, 152–158, 264n247
Powers, Johnny, 224
Prejudice against blacks, 179, 183; Booker T. Washington on, 169–170; W. E. B. DuBois on, 170–171. *See also* African Americans
The Principles and Results of the Ministry at Large in Boston (Tuckerman), 244
Progressive party, 243
Progressive reform, 260n145, 261n162
Prohibition of alcohol, 39–41, 105, 261n162; Addams's assessment of, 106, 280n52; failure of, 145, 226. *See also* Alcohol consumption
Promise Keepers, 205
Protestantism, 81. *See also* Religion
Prudence, 125–128. *See also* Virtues
Public policy, 218–220; encouraging self-reliance, 226–227; on saving money, 227–229
Public works programs, 19
Pullman, George M., 113–114, 283n106

Rauschenbusch, Walter, xx, 93, 121–130, 243, 277n8; criticizing the rich, 128–129; critique of moral reform, 108–109; critique of the individualist virtues, 98–101, 124–128, 129–130; depiction of pauperism, 134; early writings of, 287n172; on the economic virtues, 107–108; on moral standards, 103–105, 110–111, 282n84; on noneconomic virtues, 105–107; on prosperity and morality, 146; on reforming society rather than individuals, 102–103; and religion, 122–123; on self-help and Christianity, 315n47; on upward mobility, 115–118
Rector, Robert, 156
Regulating the Poor: The Functions of Public Welfare (Piven and Cloward), 131, 139
Rehabilitation of the poor, 84–87, 131–133
Reischauer, Robert, 156
Relief programs, 251n38
Religion, 78, 80–84; among African Americans,

190–192, 305nn8, 9, 10; Black Muslim movement, 174–178; Catholic church in the Irish American community, 183–184, 186–187; of children, 273n34; and contemporary moral reform, 215–217; Floyd Flake on, 218; of Jane Addams, 272n20; and Josephine Shaw Lowell, 274n53; in motivating the poor, 211; and thrift, 126; Unitarianism, 241; Walter Rauschenbusch's, 122–123
Resources, scarcity of, 7
Richmond, Mary, 16, 242; contrast to Frances Fox Piven, 145; on coping methods of the unemployed, 21; countering Jane Addams's critique of the economic virtues, 114; on the desertion of families by husbands, 63–65; on encouraging women's self-reliance, 67; on family ties, 60–61; on finding work, 17; on friendly visitors, 71–72; on helping the poor, 71; influence of Josephine Shaw Lowell on, 244–245; on the need for thrift, 45; on the prohibition of alcohol, 41; rivalry with Jane Addams, 323n15; on saving money, 44; on visitation of the poor, 233
Riis, Jacob, 17; anti-Semitism of, 265n264; characterization of blacks in New York, 166–167; on the Children's Aid Society, 83; fighting Tammany Hall, 224; friendship with Josephine Shaw Lowell, 244; on immigrant thrift, 56–57; Mead on the poor of Riis's day, 150; prejudice against Chinese-Americans, 296n3
Riley, Tom, 320nn119, 122
Rivera, Juan, 214
Rivers, Eugene, 214, 216, 217
Rivlin, Alice, 156
Rodgers, Daniel, 15–16
Roosevelt, Theodore, 224, 242, 243
Rorabaugh, W. J., 47
Rorty, Richard, 245, 323n18
Rothman, David J., 138, 139
Rubinow, I. M., 53
Russell Sage Foundation, 242
Ryan, John, 187
Ryan, William, 131, 133–136

Saloons, 294nn110, 111
Samuelson, Robert J., 202
Saving money, 43–58, 319n116; Booker T. Washington espousing, 168; institutional arrangements for the poor, 264n247; Irish

Americans, 184–185, 303n140; Jane Addams on, 284n129; limits of, 53–55; Malcolm X on, 175; means of encouraging, 47–49; practicalities of, 44–46; present-day patterns, 201–202; public policy on, 227–229; Rauschenbusch on, 283n115; saving patterns of the poor, 49–53; savings banks, 46–47; stressed by Floyd Flake, 215; underconsumption and, 55–58; W. E. B. DuBois on, 173; welfare system's former discouragement of, 227–228

Savings banks, 46–47, 50–53
Savings stamps, 48
Schneider, Eric C., 271n2
Scott, Mark, 314n38
"Second chance" homes, 222–223
Self-help, 217–218. *See also* Self-reliance
Self-reliance, 3–14; contemporary practice of, 226–227; effectiveness in ending poverty, 4–6; importance of, 12–14; reduction of dependency, 7–12; women and, 267n315. *See also* Diligence
Seligman, Daniel, 91
Settlement houses, 81, 109–110, 243
Sex outside of marriage, 209; illegitimate children, 206–207, 209, 266n279; Jane Addams's disapproval of, 281n64; Malcolm X on, 175
Sharpe, Dores Robinson, 280n60
Shaw, E. Clay, Jr., 222
Shaw, Robert Gould, 164, 241
Sherraden, Michael, 44, 229, 237
Single-parent families, xxii, 200–201, 206–208; problems of, 311n119; and work, 309n70. *See also* Family
Slavery, 178, 295n24
Sleeper, Jim, 285n133
Slums, 135. *See also* Tenement housing
Smith, Adam, 20, 120–121; on the two systems of morality, 137, 145; morality among the poor and upper classes, 214
Smith, James P., 49
Sobriety, 28–43, 223–226; measures to encourage, 34–35; prohibition of alcohol as a means to achieve, 39–41; workers' support for, 35–39
Social control of the poor, 137–139, 143–144
Social Diagnosis (Richmond), 242
Social Gospel movement, 93, 124, 125, 243, 278n30. *See also* Rauschenbusch, Walter
Social insurance, 53–55, 126, 265n257

The Social Organization of Sexuality, 209
Social Security, 292n85
Social work, 242
Socialism, 281n66
Society for Organizing Charity (Philadelphia), 242
Society for the Prevention of Pauperism (New York), 47
Solow, Robert M., 322n144
Sowell, Thomas, 4, 5, 182; on difference between Irish Americans of past and present, 307n38; on the improvidence of the Irish, 272n13
Starr, Ellen Gates, 243
State Charities Aid Association, 241
Steinberg, Steven, 248n3
Stern, William, 182
Street trades, 22
STRIVE program, 313n20
Strong, George Templeton, 181
Subsidies for work, 235–236
Suburbia, 307n37
Sulzberger, C. L., 75
Sweden, social democrats in, 33–34
Sykes, David, 313n20

Tammany Hall, 224
Teaching of virtues. *See* Knowledge
Temperance movement, 30–32; and immigration, 262n180; societies formed by workers, 260n140. *See also* Alcohol consumption; Sobriety
Tenement housing, 90–91, 135, 276nn72, 76. *See also* Ghettoes
The Theory of Moral Sentiments (Smith), 120
Thernstrom, Abigail, 178
Thernstrom, Stephan, 51, 55–56; on the Catholicism of Irish immigrants, 186, 187; on children as economic assets in the past, 61; on judging present against the past, 116; on limits of savings banks, 57; on the need to rehabilitate children, 86; on poverty among blacks, 178; on practical advice for the poor, 70; on savings banks, 58; on thrift among Irish Americans, 184; on thrift among the poor, 157; on upward mobility, 117, 284n116
"Third way," xviii
Thompson, Tommy, 234, 321n142
Thrift, 43–58, 168, 173, 175, 227–230, 292n76; argument against, 43; dangers of, 53–57; defense of, 44–45; measures to encourage,

47–48; as a situational virtue, 45–46. *See also* Saving money
Tobin, James, 235
Tocqueville, Alexis de, 77, 237, 271n1
Tough love attitude, 76–77
Toynbee Hall, 243
Transvaluation of attitudes, 144–145
Trattner, Walter I., 79
Tuckerman, Joseph, xvi, 239; accepting capitalism, 124; on aiding the poor in finding jobs, 22; on alcohol and poverty, 29, 34, 35; on the artificial creation of jobs, 19; attitude toward rehabilitation, 84–85; and Christian principles in economics, 122; contrasted with Juan Rivera, 214; countering lax morality, 205; criticizing the rich, 309n85; on dependency, 8–10; on finding work, 17; on housing for the poor, 88; on the ignorance of the poor, 68–69; influence on Robert Hartley, 244; and laissez-faire economics, 122; moral reason for self-reliance, 13; on physical needs, 88; practical reason for self-reliance, 12; practicing tough love, 77–78; on prejudice against blacks, 162–163; on the prohibition of alcohol, 39; and proposed ministry by Catholic priests to the Catholic poor, 273n27; and religion, 81–82, 271n5; and slavery, 295n6; on treatment of the poor, 275n63; views of, xvii; on wages for women, 250n22
Tuskegee Institute, 168–169
Twenty Years at Hull House (Addams), 243
Tyrrell, Ian, 36

Undeserving poor, 144–145
Unemployment, 17–21, 24, 154, 253n21. *See also* Employment
Unions, xviii, 11, 27–28, 38–39; criticized by Rauschenbusch, 286n159
United Hebrew Charities, 75
Unskilled labor, 17–18; number of jobs available for, 301n109; saving patterns of, 49–53; unemployment of, 24
Up from Slavery (Washington), 174
Upward mobility, 115–118
Urban poverty, xx

Values, compared to virtues, 208
Victimization of the poor, 133–136
Victorianism, 205
Victory Fellowship, 214

Virtues, 15–75; Addams on, 102; argument against individualist, 131–158 (*see also* Individualist virtues); collective versus individualist, 114, 125–127; compared to values, 208; comparing, 120–121; criticized by Addams and Rauschenbusch, 99–100; critique of Walter Rauschenbusch, 124–128; diligence, 15–28 (*see also* Diligence); and the economy, 98; example of the middle class to the poor, 200–203; family values, 58–67 (*see also* Familial responsibility; Family); *Luftmensch* story, 119–120; noneconomic, 105–107; prudence, 125–128; public policies encouraging, 218–220; receptivity of the poor to, 198–200; saving money, 43–58 (*see also* Saving money; Thrift); sobriety, 28–43 (*see also* Alcohol consumption; Sobriety); teaching of, 67–75 (*see also* Knowledge); traditional morals, 103–105
Visiting the poor, 69, 71–72, 74, 233; advice on, 251n41; for expectant mothers, 270n362; friendly visitors, 269n345, 270n354; women volunteers, 268n320
The Visitor of the Poor (De Gerando), 244

Wages, 28, 42; earned by women, 250n22; growth of, 257n88; and immigrants, 252n17; subsidies for, 322n144
Walters, John, 223
War on Poverty, xiv–xv
Warner, Amos, 11, 18, 242; assessment of the likelihood of rehabilitation, 86; on the Brooklyn Charity Organization Society, 23–24; on the causes of poverty, 278n19; classification of the poor, 101–102; on intemperance, 29; opinion of blacks, 165–166; on teaching the poor, 74
Washington, Booker T., xxii, 167–170; compared to Brace, 297n39; compared to Malcolm X, 174, 175; and moral reform, 161; repudiation of values of, 194
Washington Post, 74
Washington Temperance Society, 37–38
Washingtonians, 37–38
Wealth, compared to virtue, 9–10
Wealthy class, 128–129. *See also* Class distinctions
Webb, Beatrice, 243
Webb, Sidney, 243
Welfare system, 139–140, 142; and child

support, 221–222; debate over, 321n138; discouragement of saving money in the past, 227–228; Lawrence Mead on, 295n115; percentage of people in, 203; policies hindering the poor, 155–156; present-day, 211–212, 230–233; recipients' desire to work, 308n52; reform of, 230–233; statistics on, 311n113

Wesley, John, 146

What Is Social Work? (Richmond), 242

Whiskey, 32. *See also* Alcohol consumption

White, Alfred T., 276n76

Wilson, James Q., 67; on public programs and the promotion of virtue, 218–219; on the shift of values, 146–147, 148; on single-parent families, 311n119; on the temperance movement, 32–33

Wilson, William Julius, 16–17; compared to W. E. B. DuBois, 172; contrasting Mexican Americans to African Americans, 200; dispute with Lawrence Mead, 219; surveys of the Chicago poor, 199

Wolfe, Alan, 196, 197, 208

Wolfe, Tom, xxi

Women, 66; and birth control, 207; as heads of families, 309n70; Malcolm X's attitudes toward, 177; rule against living with men while on welfare, 140, 142; and self-reliance, 67, 267n315; wages earned by, 250n22

Woodroofe, Kathleen, 70

Woods, Robert, 78

Woodson, Robert L., 214, 217

Woolf, Virginia, 112

Work. *See* Diligence

Work relief, 26–27. *See also* Artificial creation of jobs

Workers, 49–54; and temperance societies, 260n140. *See also* Unskilled labor

Workfare, 322n144

Yarros, Rachelle S., 281n64

Young Unwed Fathers (Wisconsin), 316n65

Zinsmeister, Karl, 203, 204

Zottoli, Joseph T., 35

JOEL SCHWARTZ has published widely in political philosophy and public policy. He has taught political science at the University of Michigan, the University of Toronto, and the University of Virginia; served as executive editor of *The Public Interest*; and conducted research at the Statistical Assessment Service and the Hudson Institute in Washington, D.C. He is currently a contributing editor of *Philanthropy*, as well as a program officer in the Division of Research Programs at the National Endowment for the Humanities. The opinions expressed in this work are his own; they do not necessarily reflect the views of the National Endowment for the Humanities, or of the United States federal government.